American Government: Brief Edition

Second Edition

For my family.

Sara Miller McCune founded SAGE Publishing in 1965 to support the dissemination of usable knowledge and educate a global community. SAGE publishes more than 1000 journals and over 600 new books each year, spanning a wide range of subject areas. Our growing selection of library products includes archives, data, case studies and video. SAGE remains majority owned by our founder and after her lifetime will become owned by a charitable trust that secures the company's continued independence.

Los Angeles | London | New Delhi | Singapore | Washington DC | Melbourne

American Government: Brief Edition

Stories of a Nation

Second Edition

Scott F. Abernathy
University of Minnesota

FOR INFORMATION:

CQ Press

An imprint of SAGE Publications, Inc.

2455 Teller Road

Thousand Oaks, California 91320

E-mail: order@sagepub.com

SAGE Publications Ltd.

1 Oliver's Yard

55 City Road

London EC1Y 1SP

United Kingdom

SAGE Publications India Pvt. Ltd.

B 1/I 1 Mohan Cooperative Industrial Area

Mathura Road, New Delhi 110 044

India

SAGE Publications Asia-Pacific Pte. Ltd.

18 Cross Street #10-10/11/12

China Square Central

Singapore 048423

Acquisitions Editor: Scott Greenan

Content Development Editors: Jennifer Jovin-Bernstein and Sarah Calabi

Editorial Assistant: Tiara Beatty

Production Editor: Bennie Clark Allen

Copy Editor: Megan Markanich

Typesetter: C&M Digitals (P) Ltd.

Proofreader: Larry Baker

Indexer: Integra

Cover Designer: Candice Harman

Marketing Manager: Jennifer Jones

Printed in Canada

Library of Congress Cataloging-in-Publication Data

Names: Abernathy, Scott Franklin, 1966- author.

Title: American government : stories of a nation / Scott F. Abernathy, University of Minnesota.

Description: Brief edition, Second edition. | Thousand Oaks : CQ Press, A Division of Sage [2022] | Includes index.

Identifiers: LCCN 2020036367 | ISBN 9781071816899 (paperback) | ISBN 9781071816912 (epub) | ISBN 9781071816943 (epub) | ISBN 9781071816929 (pdf)

Subjects: LCSH: United States—Politics and government—Textbooks.

Classification: LCC JK31 .A23 2022 | DDC 320.473—dc23

LC record available at https://lccn.loc.gov/2020036367

21 22 23 24 25 10 9 8 7 6 5 4 3 2 1

BRIEF CONTENTS

Preface   xxviii

Acknowledgments   xxxix

About the Author   xlv

PART I: FOUNDATIONS   1

Chapter 1.   American Political Stories: Claiming Rights, Demanding
             to Be Heard   2

Chapter 2.   The Constitution of the United States: A New Vision of
             Representative Government   30

Chapter 3.   Federalism: The Changing Boundaries between the Nation
             and the States   64

Chapter 4.   Civil Liberties: Building and Defending Fences   96

Chapter 5.   Civil Rights: How Equal is Equal?   128

PART II: POLITICAL BEHAVIOR AND MASS POLITICS   161

Chapter 6.   Public Opinion: How Are Americans' Voices Measured, and
             Do They Matter?   162

Chapter 7.   The Media: Truth, Trust, and Power   192

Chapter 8.   Parties, Elections, and Participation:
             Making Representative Democracy Happen   220

Chapter 9.   Interest Groups and Social Movements: Collective Action,
             Power, and Representation   256

PART III: INSTITUTIONS   283

Chapter 10. Congress: Representation, Organization, and Legislation   284

Chapter 11. The American Presidency: Individuals, Institutions, and Power 316

Chapter 12. The Federal Bureaucracy: Putting The Nation's Laws
Into Effect   346
Chapter 13. The Federal Judiciary: Politics, Power, And
The "Least Dangerous" Branch   376

PART IV: POLICY   409

Chapter 14. Public Policy: Promoting The General Welfare and
Advancing Americans' Interests   410

Appendices   449
Glossary   493
Notes   506
Index   535

Melanie Stetson Freeman/*The Christian Science Monitor* via Getty Images

DETAILED CONTENTS

Preface   xxviii

Acknowledgments   xxxix

About the Author   xlv

PART I: FOUNDATIONS   1

Chapter 1. American Political Stories: Claiming Rights, Demanding to Be Heard   2

Standing Rock: Water Protectors Claim Their Rights and Freedoms in North Dakota   4

Interaction of the Protesters with Law Enforcement Officials Shows How Fundamental Rights and Freedoms Are Connected   6

American Political Culture Is Built on a Set of Shared Ideas   8

Equality Is about Having the Same Rights or Status   9

Inalienable Rights Exist above Any Government Powers   9

Liberty Involves Both Freedom from Interference and to Pursue One's Dreams   10

The Pursuit of Happiness Is at the Core of the American Dream   10

American Political Culture Has Many Roots   10

Practicing Political Science: Millennials and the American Dream   11

American Exceptionalism Flows from the Nation's Historical Development   12

Politics and Political Action Set the Stage for Revolution   12

Colonial Settlements Establish a Precedent for Independence   12

A Global War Forces Change in Colonial Policy   13

The Idea of Independence Is Given Voice in Political Propaganda   14

Revolutionaries Take Action, Their Eyes on Increasing the Powers of Colonial Legislatures   15

The Sons of Liberty Attempt to Mobilize Colonists around British Tax Policies   15

The Crisis Accelerates as Protests Intensify   16

The Boston Tea Party Adds Fuel to the Revolutionary Fire   16

The Institution of Slavery Denies the Natural Rights of African Americans   17

Revolutionary Women, Though Excluded, Build Institutions of Their Own   18

Indigenous Peoples in North America Challenge Colonization   19

Independence Becomes Institutionalized   20

The American Revolution Is Still under Construction   22

The Structure of Institutions Affects How Citizens Participate   **22**

**Conclusion: The American Experiment Continues, and
You Are Part of It**   **26**

Chapter 2. The Constitution of the United States: A New Vision of Representative Government   30

James Madison Plans for a Republic That Will Last   **32**

**The Confederal System Makes Coordination between
the States Difficult**   **34**

The Articles of Confederation Attempt to Unite the States While
Preserving Their Authority   34

Under the Confederal System, States Have Sovereignty and Equal
Representation   35

The Confederal Government Is Designed to Be Weak   35

The Prospect of Changes to the Systems of Slavery and Representation
Sow Unrest   36

Fears of Unrest and Rebellion Worry State Governments   37

Rebellion Begins   37

From Shays' Rebellion Comes New Opportunity   38

Delegates Reach a Compromise at the Constitutional Convention   **39**

Delegates Debate Forms of Representation and the Powers of the National
Government   41

The Virginia Plan Outlines a System of Proportional Representation for the States   42

The New Jersey Plan Maintains Equal Votes in the Legislature   43

The Great Compromise Calls for a Bicameral Legislature with Different
Methods of Representation in Each Chamber   44

Chip Somodevilla/Getty Images

Delegates Work Out Details of the New Government   **45**

The Legislative Branch Is Made the Most Powerful   46

The Executive Branch Puts the Laws into Effect   46

The Judiciary Is Designed to Interpret Constitutional Conflicts   47

Separation of Powers Allows for Checks and Balances on Government   48

Delegates Address the "Unfinished Parts" but Leave the Problem of Slavery Behind   48

The Founders Reach a Fateful Compromise on Slavery   50

Practicing Political Science: Slavery, Population, and the Balance of Power between Southern and Northern States   **51**

James Madison Holds Contradictory Views on Slavery   54

The Constitution Is Finished but Not Yet Made the Law of the Land   54

Federalists and Anti-Federalists Argue over Ratification   **55**

Will This Experiment Work? Federalists and Anti-Federalists Debate the Dangers of Power in a Large Republic   56

A Republic Must Be Able to Handle the Problem of Faction   57

Federalists and Anti-Federalists Fear Different Forms of Tyranny   58

Federalists and Anti-Federalists Debate Where Power Should Be Concentrated   59

Federalists Argue for a Strong National Government   59

Anti-Federalists Fear Losing Representation at the National Level   60

A Bill of Rights Is a Key Issue in the Ratification Debates   60

Conclusion: The Motives of the Framers and the Effects of the Constitution Are Still Being Debated   **62**

Chapter 3. Federalism: The Changing Boundaries between the Nation and the States   **64**

Marijuana Policy Today Reveals Tensions between State and Federal Law   **65**

Two Californians Sue for Access to Medical Marijuana   67

In *Gonzales v. Raich*, the Supreme Court Sides with Federal Law   68

Conflict between State and Federal Policy on Marijuana Continues   69

The Constitution Divides Power between the Nation and the States   **70**

There Is More Than One Way to Divide Power between Levels of Government   70

AP Photo/Ben Margot

The Supremacy, Necessary and Proper, and Commerce Clauses Are the Keys to American Federalism ... 71

The Constitution Describes the Powers Belonging to the Nation and the States ... 72

Most Powers of the National Government Are Explicit ... 72

The Powers of State Governments Are Less Explicit ... 73

Members of Indigenous Nations Have a Relationship with the Federal Government That Is Different from American Federalism ... 73

Practicing Political Science: Does Marijuana Legalization Affect Crime Rates? ... **75**

For Much of American History, the Boundaries between the Nation and the States Were Sharper Than They Are Today ... **76**

Early Supreme Court Decisions Shape the Division between State and National Power ... 76

McCulloch v. Maryland Relies on the Necessary and Proper Clause to Assert the Power of Congress ... 77

Gibbons v. Ogden Uses the Commerce Clause to Affirm the Power of Congress to Regulate Trade ... 77

Barron v. Baltimore Rules That the Due Process Clause Applies Only to the National Government ... 77

The Era of Dual Federalism Separates the Powers of the Nation and the States ... 78

States' Rights Grow during the Civil War and Reconstruction ... 78

Under Dual Federalism, the Supreme Court Restricts African Americans' Rights after the Civil War ... 79

In the Age of Industry and National Expansion, Cooperative Federalism Emerges ... 80

President Franklin Roosevelt's Response to the Great Depression Reshapes American Federalism ... **81**

President Roosevelt Greatly Expands the Role of the National Government ... 82

The Supreme Court Pushes Back against President Roosevelt's New Deal Expansions ... 83

President Roosevelt Strikes Back with a Court-Packing Plan ... 84

In the New Deal, Cooperative Federalism Replaces Dual Federalism ... 85

Modern American Federalism Remains Cooperative but Faces Challenges ... **86**

President Lyndon Johnson's Great Society Expands Cooperative Federalism ... 88

With New Federalism Comes Devolution and Attempts to Roll Back National Power ... 88

Alex Wong/Getty Images

State Governments Have Several Tools to Preserve Their Interests 89

Challenges to Cooperation 90

Conclusion: The Evolution of Federalism Continues 93

Chapter 4. Civil Liberties: Building and Defending Fences 96

Cell Phone Tracking Capability Challenges the Boundary between Public and Private 98

The Supreme Court Places Restrictions on the Use of Cell Phone Tracking Data 98

The Court Continues to Wrestle with the Challenges to Civil Liberties Posed by Technological Change 99

The Bill of Rights Establishes Protections for Americans' Civil Liberties 101

The Bill of Rights Takes Center Stage in the Ratification Debates 101

The Bill of Rights Establishes Civil Liberties Protections, and Selective Incorporation Applies Them to the States 102

The Relationship between Members of Indigenous Nations and the Bill of Rights Has Evolved over Time 105

The First Amendment's First Two Protections Both Involve Religion 105

The Establishment and Free Exercise Clauses Ensure Separation of Church and State 105

Courts Have Tested the Establishment Clause over Funding for Religious Schools 106

Courts Have Also Tested the Establishment Clause over Prayer in School 106

Courts Have Addressed the Boundaries of the Establishment of Religion 107

Courts Have Addressed the Boundaries of the Freedom of Religious Expression 107

The First Amendment Also Protects Expression: Speech, Press, Assembly, and Petitioning the Government 109

Free Expression Was Challenged in the Early Years of the Republic 109

Courts Have Attempted to Balance Political Expression against the Needs of National Security 109

Courts Have Weighed Press Freedoms against National Security 111

Symbolic Speech Is Protected as a Form of Political Expression 111

Other Forms of Expression Have More Limited Protection 112

Freedom of Assembly Is Broadly Protected 113

Neville Elder/Corbis via Getty Images

Practicing Political Science: Interpreting the Second Amendment in
the Twenty-First Century   **114**

**The Constitution Also Protects Individuals Involved with
the Criminal Justice System**   **115**

The Fourth Amendment Protects against Unlawful Search, Seizure,
Warrants, and Evidence   116

The Fifth Amendment Guarantees the Accused Certain Procedures
for Their Defense   118

The Sixth Amendment Guarantees the Accused Certain Rights to
Trials and Representation   118

The Eighth Amendment Guards against Cruel and Unusual Punishment   119

**The Ninth and Tenth Amendments Help Shape Freedoms in
the Nation and Across the States**   **119**

The Defense of Marriage Act Restricts the Rights of Same-Sex
Couples to Marry   120

The Ninth Amendment and Privacy, a Right Not Enumerated   121

Early Affirmation of Rights to Privacy Involved the Use of
Contraceptives   122

Expansions of Privacy Rights Involved Sexual Conduct between
Consenting Adults   122

Privacy Rights Also Include a Woman's Decision to Terminate
a Pregnancy   122

The Tenth Amendment Is Intended to Protect State Powers   123

The Final Blow to DOMA   123

Conclusion: Civil Liberties Involve Fences Still under Construction   **124**

Chapter 5. Civil Rights: How Equal Is Equal?   128

Protesters Act to Secure Rights for Americans with Disabilities   **130**

The Americans with Disabilities Act Expands Protections for People
with Disabilities   133

**Civil Rights Amendments Emerge from the Civil War—but
Provide Limited Protection in Practice**   **134**

The Supreme Court Denies Citizenship Rights to African Americans,
Helping to Spark a War That Splits the Nation   134

Secession Ensues, and Then Civil War   135

Constitutional Amendments Abolish Slavery and Affirm Voting and
Citizenship Rights for African Americans during Reconstruction 136

Racial Oppression Continues despite New Protections 138

Opponents of Jim Crow Attempt to Use the Judiciary to Challenge It, but Fail 138

**Challenges to Legal Segregation Achieve Successes But
Face Resistance** **139**

Thurgood Marshall and the NAACP Devise a Strategy to End
School Segregation 140

The Supreme Court Rules That "'Separate but Equal' Has No Place" 142

The South Resists Desegregation 144

Citizens Engage in New Forms of Civil Disobedience and Protest 145

Practicing Political Science: Can the Supreme Court Effect Social Change? **146**

The Court Delivers New Decisions Aimed at Strengthening Civil Rights 148

The Court Limits Itself in Addressing Segregation in Practice Rather
Than by Law 148

American Women Work to Secure Their Civil Rights **150**

Women's Early Civil Rights Efforts Focus on Enfranchisement 150

The Second Wave Focuses on Ongoing Inequalities 152

The Supreme Court Uses Different Standards of Scrutiny on Gender
Discrimination and Sexual Harassment 154

Americans Confront Overlapping Forms of Discrimination **155**

Civil Rights Challenges Persist for Other Groups as Well 156

Conclusion: Have Americans' Civil Rights Been Secured? **158**

PART II: POLITICAL BEHAVIOR AND MASS POLITICS

161

Chapter 6. Public Opinion: How Are Americans' Voices Measured, and Do They Matter?

162

Public Opinion May Be Moved by Important Events Like Ferguson **163**

Public Opinion Reflects Different Fergusons 165

**Practicing Political Science: Looking for a "Break in Trend" in Data and
Drawing Conclusions over Time** **167**

Public Opinion Is The Sum Total of Individual Beliefs and Attitudes **169**

There Are Competing Views about the Meaning of Public Opinion 169

The Minimalist Paradigm Holds That Most People's Opinions
Consist of Stereotypes and Nonattitudes 169

Another Perspective Says That People Can Overcome Information Gaps 171

Public Opinion Is Transmitted and Measured in Several Ways **172**

Citizens' Opinions Are Transmitted to Public Officials through Direct
and Indirect Channels 172

Scientific Polling Is Based on Efforts to Accurately Sample
Representative Populations 173

Public Opinion Survey Validity Varies by Type 174

How Public Opinion Surveys Are Constructed Affects Their Validity 175

Individual Opinions Vary According to Direction, Intensity, Stability,
and Salience 176

Polls Are Used for Commercial, Academic, and Political Purposes 177

Political Socialization and Political Ideology Shape Public Opinion **177**

Political Socialization Shapes Individual Attitudes 178

Families, Schools, and Peers Are Early Shapers of Information
and Opinion 178

Personal Experience and Focusing Events Affect Individual
Attitudes over Time 178

Partisan Identification, Individual and Group Identities, and Elite Attitudes
Inform Our Views 179

Political Ideology 179

Gender 180

Racial and Ethnic Identity 181

Government and Media Influence Public Opinion 181

**Ferguson and the Effects of Public Opinion on Democratic
Representation** **182**

National Anthem Protests in the NFL Draw on #BlackLivesMatter 184

A Tragedy in Charlottesville Focuses the Nation's Attention on Deep
Divisions in American Society 186

Protests, Unrest, and Anger Spread across the Nation after the Killing
of George Floyd by a Minneapolis Police Officer 187

Conclusion: How Meaningful Is Public Opinion? **188**

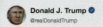

The Photo Works/Alamy Stock Photo

Chapter 7. The Media: Truth, Trust, and Power — 192

Can a Foreign Government Use the American Media to Influence a Presidential Election? — 194

While a Special Counsel Investigates, the Cable News Media Go All in on Russia — 195

"Fake News" Highlights the Power of Both the Media and Consumers — 196

The Evolution of American Media Shows That Issues of Power and Trustworthiness Are Not New — 198

Early Newspapers and Pamphlets Shape a New Nation — 198

Freedom of the Press Becomes Enshrined in the Constitution through the Bill of Rights — 199

The Media Go "Mass" with the Penny Presses in the Eighteenth and Nineteenth Centuries — 199

Journalists Become Investigators and Activists in the Nineteenth Century — 200

The Twentieth Century Brings Radio and TV News Directly into Americans' Homes — 201

New Media Have Reinvented the Media Landscape — 203

Questions of Bias Challenge Americans' Trust in the Media's Objectivity — 204

Bias and the Perception of Bias Is a Problem in Media Coverage — 205

The News Can Function as Entertainment — 207

Contemporary Pressures Affect How the Media Cover Campaigns and Elections — 208

Media Ownership and Content Are Subject to Regulation — 208

Regulation Affects Who Owns the Media and How We Consume It — 208

Regulation Affects Media Technologies and Ownership — 209

Regulation Also Affects Content — 210

The Power of the Media to Affect the Public Is Tested — 211

Scholars Have Differed on the Media's Effects — 213

Practicing Political Science: Do the Media Make Us Smart (or Not So Smart)? Or Do We Make Them Look Good (or Not So Good)? — 215

Americans May Be Separated by a Digital Divide — 216

Conclusion: Debates about the Power of the Media Continue — 217

Chapter 8. Parties, Elections, and Participation: Making Representative Democracy Happen — 220

Bernie Sanders Challenges the Democratic Party to Become More Progressive, Twice — **222**

In 2016, Bernie Sanders Pushes the Democratic Party, and the Party Pushes Back — 223

In 2020, Bernie Sanders Runs against the Establishment Again and Finds the Party Has Moved Closer to Him — 225

Parties Act to Identify, Support, and Nominate Candidates for Elected Office — **226**

Parties Unite People as Organizations — 227

Political Parties Are Decentralized — 227

Party Leaders Are Advisers, Not Rulers — 228

Parties Shape Elections by Recruiting and Supporting Candidates — 228

Parties Select Candidates through the Nomination Process — 228

Political Scientists Debate the Power of Parties to Choose the Nominees — 229

Political Polarization, Gridlock, and Two-Party Dominance Are the Defining Features of Parties in Government Today — 230

Polarization Leads to Gridlock in American Governance — 230

While the Landscape of Parties in Government Has Changed, It Has Historically Been Dominated by Two Major Parties — 231

America's Early Party Systems Introduce Two-Party Competition and National Campaigns — 231

Slavery and the Civil War Shape the Democratic and Republican Parties — 231

Democratic Party Dominance Emerges from the Great Depression — 231

The Current Party System Is Marked by Partisanship and Gridlock — 232

America's Electoral System Leads to Two-Party Dominance — 232

Minor Parties May Challenge the Two Major Parties — 233

The Rules Governing National Elections Shape the Transmission of Americans' Preferences Into Laws and Policies — **233**

In Congressional Elections, Constituency Is Key — 233

Senators Represent Their Entire States — 234

Members of the House Represent Their Districts — 234

Redistricting and Gerrymandering Shape Constituencies and Elections in House Races	234
Partisan Gerrymandering Involves Strategic Calculations	234
Racial and Ethnic Gerrymandering Aims to Increase Minority Representation	235
The Supreme Court Continues to Weigh in on Gerrymandering	236
Practicing Political Science: What Are We Really Hoping to Achieve in Drawing District Boundaries?	**237**
Congressional Incumbents Have Significant Institutional Advantages	239
Presidential Elections Have Many Stages and Moving Parts	240
Candidates Lay the Foundations for Their Campaigns Long before Formal Nomination	240
Candidates Try to Secure Their Party's Nomination	240
Nominees Compete in the General Election	240
The Rules of the Electoral College Decide the Presidency	241
Regulating Campaign Spending Has Proved Tricky	242
Political Participation Can Take Many Forms	**242**
Americans' Civic Engagement Can Be Fluid	244
Parties Strive to Get Voters to Identify with Them	244
The Decision to Vote or Not Vote Involves Many Factors	246
Individual Factors Shape Electoral Participation	247
Socioeconomic Status and Educational Attainment	247
Age	247
Racial and Ethnic Identities	247
Gender	248
Partisan Attachment	249
Legal and Institutional Factors Enable and Constrain Voter Turnout	249
#MeToo Highlights the Possibilities and Challenges of Digital Political Participation	250
Scholars Debate the Differences between Digital and Traditional Political Participation	251
Immediacy and Interactivity Bring Conversations into Politics, and Politics into Conversations	251
Conclusion: The 2020 Elections	**253**

Chapter 9. Interest Groups and Social Movements: Collective Action, Power, and Representation   256

A Housing Bubble Bursts, and Interest Groups Pop Up   **258**
    Financial Engineering Sows the Seeds for a Major Crisis   258
    The Lobbyists' Pressure Play Begins   259
    Counterpressure Arises from Outside Groups   260
    The Bailout Begins   261

Americans Face Challenges in Acting Collectively in a Representative Democracy   **262**
    Theories of Interest Group Formation Focus on the Challenges of Faction   263
    Theories of Interest Group Formation Also Explore the Challenges of Collective Action   264

Interest Groups Vary By Type and Tactic   **266**
    "Inside" Interest Groups Lobby to Influence Policymaking   267
      Today's Lobbyists Are Professionals   267
      Lobbyists Influence Legislation in Congress   268
      Lobbyists Influence Executive Branch Implementation   269
      Lobbyists Influence Judicial Actions   269
      Lobbying Activities Are Regulated   270
      Interest Groups Exert Influence through Webs and Networks   270
      Interest Groups Are Involved in Election-Related Activities   271
    Grassroots Lobbying and Political Protesters Act from "Outside" to Influence Policy   272
    Interest Groups Face Challenges in Representation   273

Occupy Wall Street Illustrates the Struggles, Successes, and Failures of Social Movements   **273**
Practicing Political Science: Depicting Income Inequality in the United States   **275**

Social Movements Employ Different Tactics from Interest Groups to Make Change and Educate   **278**
    The Success of Social Movements Is Difficult to Measure   278

Conclusion: Organizing in American Political Life   **280**

Alex Wroblewski/Getty Images

PART III: INSTITUTIONS 283

Chapter 10. Congress: Representation, Organization, and Legislation 284

Two "Years of the Women" Highlight the Promise and Challenge of More Inclusive Representation in Congress 285

The Election of 1992 Brings New Voices to Congress 286

A Singular Event Galvanizes a New Field of Candidates 286

Practicing Political Science: Gender and Metaphors of Power in Image 287

The Departure of Congressional Incumbents Presents an Opportunity for Women in 1992 288

The Class of 1992 Mobilize Significant Resources in Their Electoral Bids 288

In 2018, Women Again Ran in Historic Numbers and, Again, Changed the Composition of Congress 289

The Diversity of Women's Voices in 2018 Had Grown Since 1992 289

The Women of 2018 Join a Congress Populated by Many Members of the Class of 1992 290

The Constitution Defines Congress's Shape and Powers 291

The House and Senate Serve Different Roles 291

The House of Representatives Is Designed for Greater Accountability 291

The Senate Is Designed for Greater Stability 292

Congress Has Three Key Powers: Lawmaking, Budgeting, and Oversight 293

Legislative Authority Is Key to Congressional Power 293

The Budgeting Process Is Another Key Power of Congress 293

Congress Also Has the Power of Oversight 293

Other Congressional Powers Involve Advice and Consent and Senatorial Courtesy 295

Congress Possesses the Power of Impeachment 295

Congress Is Organized Around Formal and Informal Rules 296

Political Parties Shape How Congress Is Structured 297

Party Leaders Play an Important Role in the House of Representatives 297

Party Leaders Also Shape Action in the Senate 298

Steve Kagan/The LIFE Images Collection/Getty Images

The Work of Congress Is Done through the Committee System 298

    Party Leaders and Seniority Shape Committee Membership and Leadership 298

    Different Types of Committees Perform Different Roles 298

Congressional Staff and the Congressional Bureaucracy Help Members Represent Their Constituents 299

Norms Are Informal Contributors to Congressional Organization 299

The Legislative Process is Complex by Design **300**

The First Step Is Bill Introduction 300

Referral to Committee Involves Political Strategy 302

Bills Are Altered—and Die—Due to Committee and Subcommittee Action 302

    Rules and Institutions Shape Consideration in the House 302

    Individual Senators Play a Stronger Role in Senate Consideration 303

The House and Senate Resolve Differences between Their Bills 304

Bills Go Back to the Floor for Reconsideration 305

The President Takes Action 305

Members Represent Constituents in How They Act and Who They Are **305**

Acting in Congress Involves Visible and Invisible Legislative Work 306

    Legislators' Voting Decisions Are Affected by Constituents' Interests and Political Parties 306

    Representatives' Actions Are Shaped by Level of Constituent Knowledge 307

    Key Aspects of Lawmaking Happen outside the Public Eye 307

    Partisan Polarization Strongly Affects Voting and Cooperation 308

Descriptive Representation Is about Who Members Are 308

    Racial and Ethnic Gerrymandering Increases Descriptive Representation 310

    Essentialism Problematizes a Focus on Identity 311

Substantive Representation Connects How Members Act and Who They Are 311

    Deliberation May Be Improved by Substantive Representation 312

    Members May Choose to Represent Those outside of Their Constituencies 312

Conclusion: The Complexity of Representation **313**

Alex Wong/Getty Images

Chapter 11. The American Presidency: Individuals, Institutions, and Power 316

In This Corner . . . Donald J. Trump: The President as Prizefighter-In-Chief 318

Conflict Has Been at the Center of President Trump's Presidency at Home 318

Conflict on the World Stage Has Also Defined the Trump Presidency 319

Turnover in the President's Administration Raises Concerns 320

Conflict with His Defense Department over Syria Foreshadows More Confrontation down the Road 321

President Trump Challenges China and the World Health Organization during the Global Pandemic 322

Presidential Character Has Been Emphasized by Trump's Supporters and His Opponents 322

Practicing Political Science: The Problem of Small Numbers in the Study of the Presidency 324

The Constitution Outlines the Powers of the American Presidency and Places Limits on Those Powers 325

Delegates Settle Questions of Selection, Qualifications for Office, and Length of Terms 325

The President Is Granted Considerable Powers 326

As Chief Executive, the President Carries Out the Nation's Laws 327

As Chief Diplomat, the President Guides Foreign Policy 327

As Commander in Chief, the President Is Responsible for the Nation's Security 328

Presidents Use the State of the Union Address to Advance Their Goals 329

The President Has Important but Proscribed Powers in the Legislative Process 330

Presidents Have the Power to Issue Pardons 330

The Powers of the Presidency Are Constitutionally Limited 330

Institutions and Other Informal Sources of Power Shape the Modern Executive Branch 331

The Vice Presidency Plays a Limited but Important Role 332

The Cabinet and the Executive Branch Bureaucracy Help Advise the President 333

Handout/Getty Images

The Executive Office of the President Assists the President with Policy	333
The First Spouse Can Help the President Connect	334
Political Parties Influence the Power of the Executive	334
The President Tries to Use the Media to Shape Public Opinion	335
Americans' Evaluations of Presidential Performance Can Affect the President's Policy Agenda	336

Presidents Have Pushed the Limits of Their Power to Preserve National Security — **337**

President Obama Orders the Killing of an American Citizen Abroad in the Fight against Terrorism	338
Anwar al-Awlaki Attributes His Radicalization to American Foreign Policy	338
The Process Involved in President Obama's Decision Raises Concerns	338
Abraham Lincoln Pushes the Boundaries of Executive Power during the American Civil War	340
President Lincoln Defies the Federal Judiciary	340
President Lincoln Defends His Emergency Powers	341

The President Has Several Tools for Unilateral Action — **342**

Conclusion: The Paradoxes of Power Continue — **344**

Chapter 12. The Federal Bureaucracy: Putting the Nation's Laws into Effect — 346

Federal Bureaucratic Action Consists of Many Actors and Evolves Over Time — **348**

Hurricanes Harvey, Irma, and Maria Test the Federal Response	348
Katrina Provides Uncomfortable Lessons about the Federal Response	350
Did the Bureaucracy Learn from Katrina?	352

Theories of Bureaucratic Organization Focus on Rules, People, and Tasks — **353**

Weber's Theory Focuses on Rules	354
Barnard's Theory Focuses on People	355
Wilson's Theory Focuses on Tasks	355

Pedro Portal/El Nuevo Herald/Getty Images

The Bureaucracy Has Developed in Response to Demands and Crises — 356

The Founders Are Skeptical of, and Unclear about, the Role of the Bureaucracy — 356

Delegates Aim to Avoid Tyranny but Preserve Efficiency — 356

How Officers Would Be Removed Remains Unsettled — 357

Washington Forms the First Administration and the First Cabinet Departments — 357

The Jacksonian Era Sees the Rise of Political Patronage — 359

Post–Civil War, the Bureaucracy Grows along with the Nation's Territories — 360

Bureaucratic Expansion in the Progressive Era Focuses on Labor and Eliminating Patronage — 361

Twentieth-Century Crises Expand Clientele Agencies and the Military Bureaucracy — 362

In the Mid-Twentieth Century, the Social Safety Net Grows — 362

The Late Twentieth Century Brings Reform and Scaling Back — 362

A Functioning Bureaucracy Depends upon Effective Organization — 363

The Federal Bureaucracy Is a Web of Organizations — 363

Bureaucratic Authority Is Hierarchical — 364

Implementation Is Only One of the Bureaucracy's Core Goals — 365

Rulemaking Fills in the Blanks — 366

Adjudication Settles Disputes — 366

Bureaucrats Can Act as Representatives, But They Are Shielded from Politics — 366

The Bureaucracy Is Constrained by Oversight and Reform — 367

Separation of Powers Makes Overseeing the Bureaucracy Difficult — 368

The President Is at the Top of the Federal Bureaucracy — 368

Congress Creates and Funds the Federal Bureaucracy — 369

The Judiciary, the Media, and Public Opinion Also Influence the Bureaucracy — 369

Current Reform Efforts Involve Deregulation and Privatization — 370

Following Katrina, the Private Sector Comes under Scrutiny — 371

The Private Sector's Role Is Again Examined after Harvey, Irma, and Maria — 372

Conclusion: What Does a "Good" Bureaucracy Look Like? — 372

Practicing Political Science: Analyzing Congressional Testimony — 373

Chip Somodevilla/Getty Images

Chapter 13. The Federal Judiciary: Politics, Power, and the "Least Dangerous" Branch — 376

The Politics of Supreme Court Confirmations Place Nominees on "Trial" — 378

Sonia Sotomayor's Confirmation Highlights the Role of Lived Experience in Judicial Decision Making — 379

Robert Bork's Unsuccessful Nomination Highlights the Role of Politics in Confirmations — 380

One Nominee Gets His Opportunity, the Other Does Not: Merrick Garland and Neil Gorsuch — 382

Justice Brett Kavanaugh's Confirmation Involves an Investigation and a Potentially Major Shift in the Court — 382

The Constitution Casts the Judiciary as a Unique but Weaker Branch — 383

The Constitution Grants the Federal Judiciary Supremacy over Lower State Courts — 384

During Ratification, Concerns about Judicial Abuse of Power Are Addressed — 384

Congress Fills in the Blanks with the Judiciary Act of 1789 — 385

Appointment to the Federal Judiciary Is Often Political — 385

Presidents Balance Legal and Political Considerations in Making Supreme Court Nominations — 386

A Key Part of President Trump's Legacy Will Be Federal Judicial Appointments — 387

The Supreme Court's Role in National Policymaking Is Defined but Limited — 387

There Are Limitations on the Power of the Supreme Court — 387

The Supreme Court Has the Power of Agenda-Setting — 388

The "Trial" of John Marshall Establishes the Principle of Judicial Review — 388

The Election of 1800 Gives Rise to a Federalist Judicial Strategy — 389

Chief Justice John Marshall Confronts Politics and the Power of the Supreme Court — 390

Marbury v. Madison Leads to the Establishment of Judicial Review — 391

The American Legal System Is Defined by Federalism — 393

Cases Are Divided into Criminal and Civil Types — 393

State Courts Handle the Majority of Cases in the United States — 394

Kevork Djansezian/Getty Images

Most of the Impactful Cases Are Handled by the Federal Judiciary ... 394

The Federal District Courts Serve as the Bottom Level of
the Federal Judiciary ... 394

The Appellate Courts Sit in the Middle ... 395

The Supreme Court Sits at the Top ... 395

Cases Involving Federal Questions Proceed through the Federal Judiciary ... 396

The Supreme Court Decides Whether to Take Cases on Appeal ... 398

Once Cases Are Taken Up, the Supreme Court Considers and
Decides Them ... 400

**Judicial Review Raises Questions of Constitutional
Interpretation and Judicial Decision Making** ... **401**

Justices Take Several Approaches to Constitutional Interpretation ... 401

The Legal Model Emphasizes Facts and Previous Decisions ... 402

The Attitudinal Model Emphasizes Policy Preferences ... 402

The Strategic Model Emphasizes Strategic Calculation ... 403

Justices Exercise Degrees of Judicial Restraint and Judicial Activism ... 403

**Practicing Political Science: Examining the Relationship between
Judicial Review and Justices' Ideologies** ... **404**

Conclusion: The Trial of the Supreme Court Continues ... **407**

PART IV: POLICY 409

Chapter 14. Public Policy: Promoting the General
Welfare and Advancing Americans' Interests 410

**American Dreamers' Futures Depend upon Whether
a Public Policy Will Continue** ... **412**

Changes in Demographics Will Continue to Shape American
Public Policy ... 412

President Trump Acts to End DACA, but the Supreme Court Stays His Hand ... 414

The Domestic Policy Process Is Dynamic ... 414

Step 1: Problem Definition ... 416

Step 2: Agenda-Setting ... 416

Step 3: Policy Formation and Adoption ... 416

Step 4: The Budgeting Process ... 416

Drew Angerer/Getty Images

Step 5: Implementation   417

Step 6: Evaluation   417

Step 7 (Maybe): Termination   417

American Health Care Policy Has Evolved Significantly since the Great Society   **417**

President Obama Takes on Health Care Reform with the Patient Protection and Affordable Care Act   418

Efforts to Repeal and Replace the ACA Are Ongoing   419

Health Care Is Only One of Many Policies Designed to Protect Americans' Basic Needs   420

Need-Based Public Assistance Programs Are Tied to Incomes   421

Housing Policy Focuses on Affordability and Access   422

Environmental Policy Has Long Focused on Cleaning and Protecting the Country's Natural Resources   422

Fiscal Policy Guides the Economy and Responds to Crises   **423**

The Government Monitors the Health of the Economy   424

The Federal Government Sets the National Budget   424

Step 1: The President Proposes a Budget   424

Step 2: Congress Acts   425

Uncharted Waters: American Economic Policy in Response to COVID-19   426

Congress Passes Coronavirus Relief and Puts It on the National Tab   427

Taxation, Deficits, and Debts Are All Part of the National Checkbook   430

Practicing Political Science: Did the Federal Reserve Just Call in the Helicopters?   **431**

U.s. Foreign Policy Has Changed with the Nation's Place in Global Affairs   **433**

America Was Isolationist for Much of Its History   433

American Influence in the Western Hemisphere Grew in the Nineteenth Century   434

The Twentieth and Twenty-First Centuries Have Been Defined by Four Global Wars   434

World War I Established America as a Major Global Player   435

World War II Established America as a Superpower   435

The Cold War Involved America and the Soviet Union in Many Regional Conflicts   436

Chip Somodevilla/Getty Images

The United States Adopts a Policy of Containment toward
Soviet Expansion ... 437

The Collapse of the Soviet Union Leaves the United States as
the World's Only Superpower ... 438

The War on Terror Reshapes the Middle East ... 438

Immigration Connects Foreign Policy to Domestic Policy ... **440**

The Arab Spring Begins as a Regional Political Movement ... 441

A Civil War in Syria Draws in Global Powers ... 442

American Foreign Policy Contributes to the Displacement of Syrians ... 443

In Spite of Restrictions under American Domestic Policy, Some Displaced
Syrians Arrive to Make Their Claims on the American Dream ... 443

Conclusion: The Story of American Politics Continues ... **446**

Appendices

Appendix 1: Declaration of Independence ... 449

Appendix 2: Articles of Confederation ... 453

Appendix 3: Constitution of the United States ... 459

Appendix 4: *Federalist* No. 10 ... 474

Appendix 5: *Federalist* No. 51 ... 479

Appendix 6: Political Party Affiliations in Congress and the Presidency,
1789–2017 ... 483

Appendix 7: Summary of Presidential Elections, 1789–2016 ... 488

Glossary ... **493**

Notes ... **506**

Index ... **535**

PREFACE

Real People, Real Politics, Real Stories
Engaging Students for Political Participation

The story of American politics is at its heart a story about people: the ways they engage the political system, the strategies they form to shape political outcomes, and their collective efforts to build and change institutions over time. It is also about how individuals' experiences and choices are molded by the political system, how the contingencies surrounding their actions have altered the political outcomes, and how they have responded to the struggles they have faced. When people *act* to confront injustices, advocate for policies they care about, and rally support for their causes, the political world around them can be *transformed*.

This book, *American Government: Stories of a Nation, Brief Edition*, focuses on the many ways individuals have participated in the political life of the United States. By sharing real narratives about real people across each chapter, students learn precisely *how* others have used the tools of political engagement to bring about change. Rather than merely exhorting students to become involved, the extended profiles shine a spotlight on the steps others have taken, providing a richer foundation for students' own political engagement. In that sense, the book is very much a guidebook for students as they wrestle to define their place in the American political landscape, to make their own voices heard, and to add their own threads to the quilt of American representative democracy. The narratives told in this book can help students better grasp the core ideas, political dynamics, and institutions that underlie American government—and they will also engage and inspire students to take action themselves.

Stronger Connections with the Political World. The first benefit of the approach is that the stories are interesting to students. Class-testing has shown that they actually read and relate to the chapters. Your students will be able to step into the shoes of the people about whom they are learning, and in doing so they will be doing much more than skimming for key terms or IDs. By combining the deep dives into one or a few key stories in each chapter with solid research-backed core content, *American Government: Stories of a Nation, Brief Edition*, will guide your students to a genuine engagement with the material, the theories that try to explain political outcomes, and the enduring questions of American representative democracy. And they will connect the dots between those elements.

The first chapter of the book, for example, clearly identifies and explains the founding ideals of American democracy—liberty, equality, natural rights, the American dream, American exceptionalism. But those ideas are each situated within a set of vivid stories about people and groups coming from different times, places, and experiences who claimed their rights as citizens.

Starting on page 1, students engage with the oil pipeline protests by members of the Standing Rock Sioux Nation and their supporters in 2016 and 2017, making claims on their fundamental rights. By engaging in depth with these protests and law enforcement's responses to them, students not only explore the exercise of fundamental rights and freedoms but also come to understand how they do not exist apart from those who would claim them or from the political landscape in which they are exercised.

Later in the chapter, they pick up the narrative thread again to hear how Thomas Jefferson went about arguing for natural rights in drafting the Declaration of Independence and the revolution of ideas that followed. As important, they learn what he and others left out. They hear the voices of people like Esther de Berdt Reed, who spoke on behalf of women in colonial America. Together, these stories help students understand so-called key terms in ways no ordinary descriptive text can.

A Richer Understanding of Political Dynamics. Anyone who has taught American politics knows that there is a chasm between how basic political dynamics can be described on paper and how they exist in the real world. The approach in this book is designed to show students how others have wrestled with questions of power, action, and change, whether in very different times and circumstances or in situations ripped from today's headlines. They witness how some have succeeded, others failed, but, more importantly, how many have operated in the space between success and failure, adjusting their strategies along the way. With this approach, students will better understand that political outcomes are not predetermined but are instead the results of strategic choices made by political actors, usually undertaken in an uncertain environment, often amid unequal relationships of power.

For example, an exploration of political campaigns and elections becomes more immediate through a thoughtful examination of the ways in which political parties are struggling to attract the Latino or Latina vote (and questioning the existence of such a monolithic entity), and efforts by Latino or Latina candidates themselves, in an era of profound demographic change. The chapter on Congress focuses on two election years that have been called the "Year of the Woman": 2018 and 1992. Not only does a focus on women running for, joining, and navigating Congress allow for a deeper analysis of congressional representation than more formulaic approaches, but it also reinforces and makes relatable traditional coverage of constituency, congressional rules and institutions, and the legislative process.

Greater Instructional Flexibility. Third, *American Government: Stories of a Nation, Brief Edition,* is adaptable to the approach you want to use. This is not a book that pushes a specific perspective or one that envisions a teacher as a repository of fact. These narratives allow for an emphasis on institutions, behavior, or a combination of both. In Chapter 9, for example, two stories are used to present the core concepts underlying a study of interest groups and social movements: one of the efforts of lobbyists in the wake of the financial crisis of 2008, the other of Occupy Wall Street (OWS) and its efforts to call attention to economic inequality in the years following. They can be used to highlight the ways in which institutions structure political action, the ways in which individuals make strategic choices in their efforts to solve problems of collective action, or both. In addition to allowing for analytical flexibility, the book also consciously strives to avoid weighing in on one side or another of heated debates but instead guides students to use their own engagement with them to more deeply understand American politics.

The chapter on the media (Chapter 7), for example, begins with an in-depth exploration of a topic very much on students' minds as well as on those of the nation as a whole: fake news. By exploring what former secretary of state Hillary Clinton called "weaponized information"—referring to allegations of Russian use of media, especially social media, to sway the outcome in Donald Trump's favor—students gain a deeper understanding of citizens' roles as receivers and shapers of the media. Rather than focusing on whether or not the Russian government successfully "hacked" the presidential election of 2016, we ask what the *potential that they did* means for conclusions about the power of the media and Americans' abilities to critically receive their products.

By concluding with a case study of a fake Martian invasion broadcast over the radio in 1938, students come to understand that these questions—though different in the era of social media—are not new. Evaluating Americans' competencies to sift through the bombardment of media aimed at drawing them in, entertaining them, and shaping their knowledge and attitudes—all at the same time—is as old and relevant as the media themselves. As active participants in the American political process, students need and demand these key skills.

Greater Inclusiveness

The fourth reason you and your students will find this book useful is just as important and closely connected to the politically engaged approach in this book, and the tools used to achieve it. This book embraces inclusivity throughout, both so that all students will find their identities and voices validated and because an inclusive approach also reinforces core concepts and skills. In this book, diversity is not a list of boxes to check off. Americans' diverse identities have powerfully shaped political processes and outcomes even when not successful in any given struggle.

We hear from individuals such as Lemuel Haynes, who, in 1776, observed the conflict between the ideals of the American revolutionaries and the practice of denying individuals their fundamental rights and freedoms, and called them out on it. And Judith Heumann, who, as a leading disability rights advocate, called upon the ideals expressed during the civil rights movement for African Americans in reshaping

Americans' conceptions of people with disabilities and the nation's public policies. We end the book (and the chapter on foreign policy; Chapter 14) with a narrative of a Syrian refugee and his family arriving in North Texas, staking their own claims on the American dream.

Through the power of narrative, my goal is that all students reading and using this book will find that they are also a part of the American experience, whether or not their voices have been heard. They will also be assisted in understanding the complexities of American government in ways that will endure once the semester is long over.

Organization of the Book

Tools for Real-World Engagement

By now you've noticed that *American Government: Stories of a Nation, Brief Edition,* approaches American politics a little bit differently than other introductory textbooks. Still, if you look at the table of contents, you'll see that the text covers everything you'd expect and require in a book that primes your students for future engagement in the political world, or, perhaps, future study in the field. You'll also notice that this book covers topics having to do with political participation and behavior before it covers institutions, which is a natural outgrowth of the fact that we highlight the role that real people have played in the development of our government—although the chapters could certainly be assigned out of order to suit your preferences.

Part I, Foundations, begins with an introduction to the central themes in American politics (Chapter 1), then covers the Constitution (Chapter 2), federalism (Chapter 3), civil liberties (Chapter 4), and civil rights (Chapter 5). Part II, Political Behavior and Mass Politics, explores public opinion (Chapter 6), the media (Chapter 7), parties, elections, and participation (Chapter 8), and interest groups and social movements (Chapter 9). Part III, Institutions, covers Congress (Chapter 10), the presidency (Chapter 11), bureaucracy (Chapter 12), and the judiciary (Chapter 13). Part IV, Policy, explores domestic, economic, and foreign policy (Chapter 14).

The Case Studies: Deep Dives into Real Politics
Help Students Grapple with Challenging Current Issues

As you'll soon discover, this textbook harnesses the power of stories, both in the service of engaging students with the core concepts and skills and in showing them how others—in times present and past—have charted their own courses to shape and reshape American government.

One of the key tools in this goal is the use of case studies, extended narrative sections focusing on real-world action in American politics, in each chapter, each with clearly defined learning objectives to guide students in their reading. These narratives are not used as marginal introductory elements that serve only as gateways into the main material, nor just as examples that extend the lessons, but as key elements of the text itself. As a teacher of undergraduates for many years at the University of Minnesota, my experience has been that students often read right past the chapter-opening vignettes in their textbooks. I'll bet you have had that same frustrating experience. It's not because those brief intros are poorly written or boring, either; it's that students know these supplemental narratives are, by design, peripheral and might be skipped to get to the real, testable content. That is a real missed opportunity for them to learn and remember core concepts but also to understand how individual choices shape outcomes.

Narratives are powerful things. They help shape the political world in which we each live. They help define who we are as individuals and as a people. And stories are also excellent teaching tools, making the material relatable, memorable, and real. This book harnesses the full power of narrative to draw students into the study of American politics, highlighting the unpredictable outcomes of people's actions and strategies—both of individuals and of groups of individuals acting together.

How does this approach work in practice?

In the chapter on public opinion (Chapter 6), I begin with the aftermath of the fatal police shooting of Michael Brown in Ferguson, Missouri, in 2014. The basic questions are these: Has public opinion about the way African Americans are treated by police changed since that event and others related to it? And, if so, does public opinion, or changes in public opinion, matter to American public policy?

The chapter begins by setting up the story, focusing on the one-year anniversary of the tragic event. Learning objectives guide students to a full set of issues that political scientists consider when presenting the topic of American public opinion—assessing the components and formation of opinions, ways of measuring it, patterns of change in people's attitudes, and the larger meaning and impact of public opinion in American democracy. No political science content gets lost at the expense of the case studies—and with plenty of built-in guidance, no student gets lost in the narrative.

The nuts-and-bolts sections of the chapter—each, like the case study, with attached learning objectives (see below)—explore debates over the stability, coherence, and meaning of public opinion; the ways in which public opinion is measured, its importance to representative democracy, and the challenges inherent in scientific polling; and political socialization. Like every chapter, Chapter 6 also has a comprehensive guide for review that connects the learning objectives, take-home points of the stories, major political science themes, and key terms to help students confirm that they have fully comprehended the chapter.

The exploration of public opinion continues by bringing the discussion of Ferguson and its effects into the present with an examination of public opinion on the tragic events of Charlottesville, Virginia, in 2017 as well as the national anthem protests by Colin Kaepernick and other players in the NFL. In these sections, students examine how the lens of the events of Ferguson may or may not have changed how Americans viewed police and community relations.

Finally, the chapter concludes with the protests and unrest that followed the death of George Floyd while in the custody of Minneapolis police officers in 2020. These events are new, and the nation is still processing what they mean and what will emerge from the discussions and policy processes that follow. Presented thoughtfully and respectfully—but without avoiding the difficult questions and issues—*American Government: Stories of a Nation, Brief Edition,* provides students with the proper context and analytical tools to assist them in formulating their own opinions and responses to challenging and critical events like these in American politics today.

Practicing Political Science Feature Boxes: Critically Considering Data, Image, and Text in Political Persuasion

This book acknowledges the challenges of dealing with the political world that students will inevitably have to confront in their own lives. To that end, it also provides students with specific skills with which to bring the deeper understandings they will develop to bear on their own political realities. Each chapter includes one Practicing Political Science box designed to assist students in becoming more capable and critical readers of arguments made through data, image, and text. While students will engage with all three types of features, we will spend the most time considering the use of data, especially their use in presenting arguments and conveying narratives.

In an increasingly data-driven world, the ability to act as a critical interpreter of data, and perhaps most importantly of the stories told based on the sometimes-competing interpretations of those data, is a fundamental skill. Data, and their interpretation, constitute an exercise of power. Students will critically reflect on how the data were obtained, how they were interpreted and displayed, and how political narratives were constructed around them. In doing so, students will engage with the use of data to advance a particular political objective and become more thoughtful and critical readers of the stories constructed around numbers and statistics.

In the data-based Practicing Political Science feature in the chapter on public opinion (Chapter 6), for example, I present data from the Pew Research Center on perceptions of how important it is for the nation to make changes to secure equal rights. The data are broken down by respondents' racial identities. Between 2014 and 2015, immediately following Ferguson and related protests, both African American and white public opinion appeared to shift toward increasing support for needed changes. The What Do You Think? section asks students to reflect upon what other kinds of evidence might be useful to confirm that the events of 2014–2015 caused the apparent shift in opinion. In doing so, students are guided to reflect on possible "breaks in trend" in longitudinal survey data.

Image literacy is as crucial to the pedagogical objectives of this book as textual literacy. Instead of offering images solely as illustrative enhancements to the text, the book also examines the ways in which images themselves have played and continue to play a role in the development of American government and politics. Political stories are told not only through text, especially in a political space increasingly driven by social media. Through a critical presentation of the use of images, students will gain skills in interpreting images as they gain a deeper understanding of the political world of which they are part and which they will help to shape.

Finally, students are guided in critical analyses of text and text-based arguments. For example, in the chapter on the bureaucracy (Chapter 12), which focuses on the federal response to twenty-first-century hurricanes, students hear and respond to the congressional testimony of residents of New Orleans in the aftermath of Katrina wherein they leveled accusations that the government's response was inequitable and biased especially against poor, Black residents.

Other Features That Reinforce the Fundamentals

Several other features of the book also serve to reinforce the core content materials and also help students understand why the chosen narratives will help them gain a deeper and more memorable understanding of this material.

- Learning Objectives sections at the beginning of each chapter guide students' reading of and engagement with the material, signposting the goals and setting clear expectations for what they will master. Each main section of the chapter is attached to a specific learning objective. While the nuts-and-bolts sections are accompanied by learning objectives designed to reinforce key terms and concepts, those associated with the case studies link to the deeper concepts associated with the material.

- Chapter Review sections conclude each chapter by offering students additional opportunities to review core concepts, connect them to the stories, think critically about the issues, and master key terms—all helpfully framed around the chapter's learning objectives.

An Approach That Works for Teachers and Students

I have had the privilege of teaching incarcerated youths, homeless adolescents, fourth graders, seventh graders, undergraduates, and graduate students. Across all of these experiences, I have learned that narrative is a powerful educational tool. People are born to be storytellers and story hearers; it seems to be in our makeup. We are wired to respond to narrative and its ability to convey the contingency, complexity, and uncertainty of collective human action and the hopes of what might be accomplished if it succeeds. Our students care about these stories. They are also already talking about them—all the time. My goal, in this book, is to give students both a framework and a set of tools with which to discuss the complexities and contradictions of American government and politics. The stories told within this book will resonate with and engage your students. They are not sugarcoated. This book does not shy away from the difficult issues with which your students are already dealing.

Over the past few years, we have taken the time to ask hundreds of college students to respond to a set of survey questions after conducting a class test of several draft chapters of the book and receiving feedback from adopters of the first and second editions of the full version of the text, on which this brief edition is based. Here is what just a handful of students have said about how well they thought the book's approach works. Note that these are unedited—real students' own words:

I want to keep reading.

I LOVED how I could relate more to the examples or there were more recent issues on public opinion that I saw firsthand like the news, such as the Ferguson incident. I would say the biggest strengths of this book are keeping the readers engaged. It does not feel like an ordinary American Government textbook . . . which is very important if you want your students to actually read.

It was very easy for me to connect the stories to the overall concepts of the chapter which is critical in a textbook. Student are usually not thrilled about being forced to read chapter after chapter of information on American Government but this approach lightens that burden. Bravo.

I was very engaged with this approach. I thought it was extremely helpful and interesting. I agree 100 percent with the stories and this method because it got my attention.

This textbook excites me as it speaks of issues that have happened recently that I have actually lived to experience.

The stories (specially as a woman and a minority) most definitely helped me connect the concept to the story. I like the stories that were used because they were interesting and I haven't heard of them before.

[I] enjoyed this approach. It made this book more pleasurable to read. I could put myself in the shoes of these women [in Congress] at the time and get a better understanding of the mindset of the time. It's encouraging to read the stories and see that though the odds were against them, they didn't give up. They're not made up stories but real women with real issues and had the drive to push forward despite the obstacles.

Stories that are devoid of people, their actions, aspirations, and mistakes are not very interesting. Fortunately, as teachers of American government, we rarely encounter stories like that. The political world that we teach our students about is vibrant, fascinating, and charged. The description of the chapter content that was just given and a glance at the table of contents of the book show that this book takes up stories that emerge directly from that political world, stories that will draw your students into a real understanding of their political world, and their place in it.

That is why stories are such powerful things.

Teaching Resources

This text includes an array of instructor teaching materials designed to save you time and to help you keep students engaged. To learn more, visit sagepub.com or contact your SAGE representative at **sagepub.com/findmyrep**.

MEASURE RESULTS, TRACK SUCCESS

SAGE Course Outcomes

The journey to retaining and applying course content differs for every student. To successfully navigate this journey, course goals should remain clear, consistent, and constructive. For instructors, the ability to track and measure individual progress is vital to ensuring student success.

SAGE | CQ Press is invested in mapping measurable course outcomes to chapter-level learning objectives for all of our introductory textbook offerings through **SAGE course outcomes**. Each of our titles is crafted with specific course outcomes in mind, vetted by leading advisers in the field, and adapted from renowned syllabi from across the country.

AMERICAN GOVERNMENT

COURSE OUTCOMES
for **AMERICAN GOVERNMENT**

Upon successful completion of this course, students will be able to

Outcome 1
ARTICULATE the foundations of American government, including its history, critical concepts, and important documents and achievements.

Outcome 2
EXPLAIN the main institutions of American government, including their roles and interrelationships.

Outcome 3
DESCRIBE the roles and relative importance of major entities and influences in American political life.

Outcome 4
ANALYZE the development and impact of important governmental policies.

FOR STUDENTS, understanding the objectives for each chapter and the goals for the course is essential for getting the grade you deserve!

FOR INSTRUCTORS, being able to track your students' progress allows you to more easily pinpoint areas of improvement and report out on success.

Tracking student progress can be challenging—promoting success should never be.

Want to see how these outcomes tie in with this book's chapter-level objectives? Visit us at **https://edge.sagepub.com/abernathybrief2e** for complete outcome-to-objective mapping.

ACKNOWLEDGMENTS

There are many, many people who have helped to make this book a reality, some of whom probably have, or had, no idea that they did so. I am grateful to all of them. Just as the Ninth Amendment makes it clear that Americans' fundamental rights and freedoms can never be fully enumerated, this will be a necessarily incomplete statement of my gratitude.

First, I would like to thank some of my teachers over the years. I owe a great debt to William S. Kilborne Jr. for teaching me how to write and to William Voss and Sharon Foster for inspiring a group of middle school students to explore the natural and social worlds and to embrace the wonderful uncertainly of being outside of our comfort zones.

I would like to also thank David Schaafsma for teaching me why stories matter, as well as Sisters Luke and Priscilla from the Missionaries of Charity in Calcutta and Ellen Maling of Bridge Over Troubled Waters in Boston, who taught me what it means to do service, what it means to be a professional, and what it means to change the world, one very small step at a time. I would also like to thank R. Douglas Arnold, my dissertation adviser, as well as Jennifer Hochschild and Larry Bartels for their mentorship. John J. DiIulio Jr., in a small conference room for an independent study at Princeton, taught me American bureaucratic politics. I owe each of these professors much more than I can repay.

Colleagues at the University of Minnesota, past and present, have offered their knowledge, feedback, and support over the years: Teri Caraway, John Freeman, Paul Goren, Timothy Johnson, Andrew Karch, Daniel Kelliher, Howard Lavine, Nancy Luxon, Joanne Miller, Michael Minta, C. Daniel Myers, Robert Nichols, August Nimtz, Kathryn Pearson, Wendy Rahn, Martin Sampson, Peter Seim, Paul Soper, Joe Soss, Dara Strolovitch, John Sullivan, and Joan Tronto, among many. I owe special thanks to W. Phillips Shively for not trying to talk me out of writing an American government textbook and supporting me throughout the process.

Thanks to the many students over the years who inspired and motivated me to write the book. Graduate student teaching assistants offered their own insights and suggestions on the project: in particular, Emily Baer, Adam Dahl, Ashley English, John Greenwood, Daniel Habchi, Serena Laws, Eli Meyerhoff, Zein Murib, Adam Olson, and Paul Snell. Members of the staff in the Department of Political Science have been invaluable over the years, especially Alexis Cuttance, Jessie Eastman, Kyle Edwards, Rose Miskowiec, and Becky Mooney.

To the many talented, warm, and professional people at SAGE/CQ Press, I owe much. The book began with an idea floated to Earl Pingel, who then passed it along to Charisse Kiino. Though Charisse has moved on from the role of acquisitions editor to other responsibilities, her stamp is very much on this book, and I am grateful for it.

In addition, many thanks go to Gail Bushman, Matthew Byrnie, Kerstin Christiansen, Christina Fohl, Eric Garner, Jade Henderson, Michele Rhoades, Michele Sordi, and Rose Storey. All have made me feel like part of the SAGE/CQ Press family in addition to doing their jobs superbly. Though he is not technically part of the SAGE/CQ Press group, I am indebted to Chuck McCutcheon for collaborating on the parties chapter in the first edition.

I would like to thank the many colleagues who very helpfully offered their time, praise, criticisms, and support throughout the process of writing this book. To Sylvia Peregrino, Amber Archuleta-Lucero, Claudia Chacon, Jerardo Navarro, and many others at El Paso Community College, I am especially thankful. Other colleagues have offered feedback in reviews, surveys, focus groups, and class testing. In addition to several who wish to remain anonymous, they include the following:

Milan Andrejevich, Ivy Tech Community College, South Bend

Stephen Anthony, Georgia State University

Juan Arzola, College of the Sequoias

Yan Bai, Grand Rapids Community College

Thomas J. Baldino, Wilkes University

Kathleen Barrett, University of West Georgia

Patricia Bodelson, St. Cloud State University

Seth Bordner, Kent State University

Christopher Borick, Muhlenberg College

Madelyn Bowman, Tarrant County College South

Todd Bradley, Indiana University Kokomo

Mark Brewer, University of Maine

Jeffrey Brown, Wayne County Community College

Susan Burgess, Ohio University

James D. Buthman, Hartwick College

Timothy Campbell, Labette Community College

Mary Carver, Longwood University

Kimberly Casey, Northwest Missouri State University

LaTasha Chaffin, College of Charleston

Ben Christ, Harrisburg Area Community College

Dewey Clayton, University of Louisville

Diana Cohen, Central Connecticut State University

Kathleen Cole, Metropolitan State University

Todd Collins, Western Carolina University

Michael Coulter, Grove City College

Kevin Davis, North Central Texas College

Chris Deis, Depaul University, Lincoln Campus

Joseph S. Devaney, East Georgia State College

Richardson Dilworth, Drexel University

Agber Dimah, Chicago State University

Cristina Dragomir, SUNY Oswego

Lauren Elliott-Dorans, Ohio State University

Bond Faulwell, Johnson County Community College

Bonnie Ford, Collin College

Daniel Franklin, Georgia State University

John Frendreis, Loyola University Chicago

Frank Fuller, Chestnut Hill College

Melissa Gaeke, Marist College

Maria Garcia-Acevedo, California State University, Northridge

Sarah Gershon, Georgia State University

Tobias Gibson, Westminster College

Patrick Gilbert, Lone Star College

Andra Gillespie, Emory University

Frederick Gordon, Columbus State University

George Gordon, Illinois Wesleyan University

Andrea Graff, Lincoln Land Community College

Greg Granger, Northwestern State University

Matthew Green, The Catholic University of America

Matthew Gritter, Angelo State University

Gloria Guevara, California State University, Northridge

Homer Guevara, Northwest Vista College

Paul-Henri Gurian, University of Georgia

Mel Hailey, Abilene Christian University

Therese M. Hammond, Penn State Lehigh Valley

Tesa Rigel Hines, Purdue University Northwest

Jeneen Hobby, Cleveland State University

Tom Hoffman, Spring Hill College

Michael Hoover, Seminole State College

Jennifer Hopper, Washington College

JoyAnna Hopper, University of Missouri

Tony Horton, Arkansas State University

William Housel, Louisiana Scholars' College

Robert Housner, Everett Community College

Mark Jendrysik, University of North Dakota

Caitlin Jewitt, Virginia Tech

April Johnson, University of Illinois at Chicago

Gabe Jolivet, Ashford University

Mily Kao, Mesa Community College

Kimberly Keenan, City College of San Francisco

Christopher Kelley, Miami University

Athena King, Eastern Michigan University

John Klemanski, Oakland University

Lisa Krasner, Truckee Meadows Community College

Andrew Levin, Harper College

La Della Levy, College of Southern Nevada Henderson Campus

Eric Lomazoff, Villanova University

Benjamin Lundgren, Santa Clara University

James Malone, Hillsborough Community College

Mack Mariani, Xavier University

Alyx Mark, North Central College

Shane Martin, Fitchburg State University

Wendy Martinek, Binghamton University

Valerie Martinez-Ebers, University of North Texas

Michael McConachie, Collin College

Karen McCurdy, Georgia Southern University

Mary McHugh, Merrimack College

Stephen Meinhold, University of North Carolina Wilmington

Melissa Merry, University of Louisville

Keesha Middlemass, Trinity University

Mark Miller, Clark University

Patrick Moore, Richland College

Samantha Mosier, Missouri State University

Brian Naples, Panola College

Sharon A. Navarro, University of Texas at San Antonio

Brian Newman, Pepperdine University

Timothy Nokken, Texas Tech University

Hyung Park, El Paso Community College

Sara Parker, Chabot College

Scott Parker, Sierra College

Lisa Perez-Nichols, Austin Community College

Robert Peters, Western Michigan University

Clarissa Peterson, DePauw University

William Pierros, Concordia University Chicago

Blayne Primozich, El Paso Community College

Elizabeth Prough, Madonna University

Nicholas Pyeatt, Penn State Altoona

Andrée Reeves, University of Alabama in Huntsville

Ted Ritter, John Tyler Community College

Joseph Robbins, Shepherd University

Jason Robles, Colorado State University

Michelle Rodriguez, San Diego Mesa College

James Ronan, Rowan University

Jon Ross, City Colleges of Chicago

Paul Rozycki, Mott Community College

Mikhail Rybalko, Texas Tech University

Ray Sandoval, Richland College

Erich Saphir, Pima Community College

Scot Schraufnagel, Northern Illinois University

Deron Schreck, Moraine Valley Community College

Eric Schwartz, Hagerstown Community College

Allen Settle, California Polytechnic State University

John Seymour, El Paso Community College

Brett Sharp, University of Central Oklahoma

Maurice C. Sheppard, Madison Area Technical College

Amy Shriver Dreussi, University of Akron

Abha Singh, University of Texas at El Paso

Sue Ann Skipworth, University of Mississippi

Nate Steffen, Bismarck State College

Gwyn Sutherland, Elizabethtown Community and Technical College

Bob Switky, Sonoma State University

John Szmer, University of North Carolina at Charlotte

Barry Tadlock, Ohio University

Chris Thuot, Onondaga Community College

Anip Uppal, Central New Mexico Community College

Troy Vidal, Columbus State University

Danny Vyain, Ivy Tech Community College

Kimball Waites, Big Bend Community College

Adam Warber, Clemson University

Jessica Webb, Kalamazoo Valley Community College

Zach Wilhide, Tidewater Community College

Mark Williams, St. Charles Community College

Claire Wofford, College of Charleston

Tony Wohlers, Cameron University

Patrick Wohlfarth, University of Maryland

Laura Wood, Tarrant County College

Tyler Young, Collin College

Kimberly Zagorski, University of Wisconsin–Stout

Penultimately, I am deeply grateful to the other members of our little band of political troubadours: Sarah Calabi, Scott Greenan, and Jennifer Jovin-Bernstein. This book is the result of their efforts as much as mine. Also helping to shape and create this project: Naomi Kornhauser and Tiara Beatty on photo editing; Rachel Keith and Megan Markanich on copyediting; Bennie Clark Allen on production; and Erica DeLuca, Jennifer Jones, and Jackie Palm on marketing.

Finally, I would like to thank friends and family: Mark Dailey, Erik Ness, and other buttheads. Also, the members of the Knox Block ring. They are my friends; their kids are like cousins to mine, and firepits rule. Also, Molly, an itinerant and very intelligent dog who crashes on our couch from time to time. My family, Mom, Julie, and Jeannette, to whom I am deeply thankful, and at times apologetic for randomly timed phone calls seeking support and discussing the history of Central Asia and/or the Dallas Cowboys. Russell and Sadie, who have grown—too quickly—into wonderful and wonderfully different people. And lastly to my wife, Sara, and to all of us "keepin' on keepin' on."

—Scott F. Abernathy
Minneapolis, Minnesota
June 2020

ABOUT THE AUTHOR

 **Scott F. Abernathy** was born and raised in Fort Worth, Texas. While an undergraduate at Dartmouth College, he volunteered for three months with Mother Teresa's Missionaries of Charity in Calcutta, India. After graduation, hoping to do service work closer to home, Scott worked as an on-street counselor with homeless adolescents in Boston, Massachusetts.

Scott then received a master of curriculum and instruction and taught fourth and seventh grades in Wisconsin public schools. Hoping to learn more about the underlying systems that drove the educational outcomes he was trying to change, Scott completed an MPA in domestic policy and then a PhD in politics from Princeton University. Scott is now an associate professor of political science and a University Distinguished Teaching Professor at the University of Minnesota. He is also the author of *School Choice and the Future of American Democracy* and *No Child Left Behind and the Public Schools*, both from the University of Michigan Press.

His current research explores the ways in which members of interest groups and social movements use narrative in text, speech, and image to reframe and socially reconstruct their populations in the service of agenda-setting and policy implementation. The work focuses on disability rights policy in the United States.

While Scott says that being a street outreach worker was the most transforming job he ever had, he admits that the chance to teach students, not in a subway stop or a squat, but through the writing of this textbook, is pretty neat as well.

FOUNDATIONS

CHAPTER 1

AMERICAN POLITICAL STORIES

Claiming Rights, Demanding to Be Heard

More than 300 new citizens were sworn in at a naturalization ceremony in June 2018 in Boston, Massachusetts. Their stories of immigration are part of the American political story: people claiming their constitutional rights and asking to be counted.

Melanie Stetson Freeman/*The Christian Science Monitor* via Getty Images

By connecting to those stories about the foundations of American government, you will be able to do the following:

1.1 Explain how diverse Americans have used the political process to make claims on their fundamental rights and freedoms.

1.2 Define the key elements of American political culture.

1.3 Identify the political, social, and economic events and institutions that gave rise to the American Revolution.

1.4 Describe the core features of American political institutions.

In my undergraduate Introduction to American Government course here at the University of Minnesota, on the first day of class, I tell my students, "I don't care *what* you think," which does tend to generate some uncomfortable silence. But I mean it. Before things get too out of hand, though, I quickly follow up with "However, I care very much about *how* you think. That is what this course is about."

This book is no different. My hope is that it will help you question what everyone tells you that you *should* know or think, to become more confident in making your own ideas known, and to sharpen your ability to interpret for yourself the political world around you. This book uses stories to help accomplish those goals. These stories are a central part of the book's structure and objectives. Each chapter's stories illustrate important concepts in the study of American politics. They

are meant to make those ideas come to life—to help you understand that American government is not something that exists apart from you. And because they are *real* stories, in all their messy, complicated glory, they will also encourage you and your classmates to think in ways that are not either/or and to walk in the shoes of people who may be very different from you.

Some of these stories may be familiar to you, some of them won't be. Even when we go back to events and people in history that you may have read about and studied, we will usually be doing so using a different lens. We will be trying to assess the political landscape as *they* perceived it, the choices as they saw them, the opportunities that they hoped to take advantage of, the lack of rights and freedoms that they observed and that they wanted to change.

In this chapter, and in the book generally, we raise fundamental questions when we try to define what we mean by a "good government" or a bad one. Whose rights get protected? Whose get restricted? How do these questions get resolved? Who gets to decide? The stories told in this book illustrate how big questions like these are resolved, revisited, and re-resolved through **politics**, the process of influencing the actions and policies of a **government**. Politics and government are closely connected, but they are not the same thing. Politics describes processes; government describes the rules and institutions that arise from political action and conflict and that structure future political action. Throughout the book, we'll hear from people who have engaged with those institutions and who have taken part in those processes.

Read the stories; absorb the nuts-and-bolts facts and concepts that emerge along the way in these chapters. Most importantly, however, connect the two. Use the stories to more deeply understand the complexity of American politics, then and now. Use them to understand the diversity of the voices that are a part of the national conversation. Use the stories to make your own voices stronger, better informed, more politically savvy, and more effective.

We start with members of the Standing Rock Sioux Nation claiming their rights not only to protest against an oil pipeline but also over the land and the water and the future on which it depends. We will then go back in time to the American Revolution and Thomas Jefferson's drafting of the Declaration of Independence.

What could these stories possibly have in common? In them we will witness the efforts of vastly different people who have wrestled with what fundamental rights and freedoms mean in American democracy and see how they as individuals and groups have tried to answer that question, staking their own claims upon their rights.

Standing Rock: Water Protectors Claim Their Rights and Freedoms in North Dakota

1.1 Explain how diverse Americans have used the political process to make claims on their fundamental rights and freedoms.

Shekóli. A single arrow may be snapped over one's knees with ease, but a bundle of arrows may not. This old adage is exemplified by the strength and fortitude shown by the gathering of water protectors in Hunkpapa territory north of the Standing Rock Sioux nation.[1]

In the letter just quoted, Ray Halbritter, chair of the Oneida Nation of New York and publisher of *Indian Country Today*, was referring to protests aimed at stopping a $3.7 billion pipeline project designed to transport oil from the rich Bakken fields of North Dakota to Illinois, where it could then be sent along to major refineries and oil markets. Energy Transfer Partners (ETP; now called Energy Transfer Operating LP), one of the largest owners and operators of oil and natural gas pipelines in the United States, was the parent company to the developers.[2]

Though the pipeline would run mostly through private land, whose owners had largely already ceded access, it would also be running under bodies of water. This brought federal agencies into the mix, especially the U.S. Army Corps of Engineers, who were tasked with studying the pipeline's potential environmental and cultural impacts and risks.[3] By early 2016, the Army Corps had issued all necessary permits. Other federal agencies, however, including the Environmental Protection Agency (EPA) and the U.S. Department of the Interior, urged the Army Corps to undertake a more thorough environmental impact assessment. The Dakota Access Pipeline's path would take it just north of the Standing Rock Reservation and under Lake Oahe.

In April a small group of people from the Standing Rock Reservation began gathering and camping near the banks of the Cannonball River on Army Corps land in protest and education. Each day they would walk about a mile to a construction site. Through their exercise of their civil liberties of free speech, freedom of the press, and assembly, the protesters aired their grievances with the federal government. They demanded tribal sovereignty, the preservation of sacred places, and water.

They worried about a potential oil leak into the waterways upon which they and other Americans downstream depended: "'We say "mni wiconi": Water is life,' said David Archambault II, the chairman of the Standing Rock Sioux . . . 'We can't put it at risk, not for just us, but for everybody downstream. . . .

Members of the Colorado River Tribes hold a banner in September 2016 to show their support for Native Americans of the Standing Rock Reservation who oppose the construction of the Dakota Access Pipeline. Although the protests started small, indigenous and nonindigenous supporters from around the country joined in to support the Standing Rock Sioux Nation as they claimed their rights.
Carl Juste/Miami Herald/TNS via Getty Images

We're looking out for our future, the children who are not even born yet. What is it they will need? It's water. When we start talking about water, we're talking about the future generations.'"[4]

The Standing Rock protesters were few in number and off the national radar when they started. In the summer and early fall of 2016, that began to change. Members of 280 indigenous nations joined the protests "in what activists [called] the largest, most diverse tribal action in at least a century."[5] They were later joined by nonindigenous supporters from across the country, #NoDAPL on Twitter, and Facebook campaigns to show solidarity. A group of military veterans announced in November that up to two thousand of their members would join Standing Rock to act as "human shields" and stand against, in their words, the "assault and intimidation at the hands of the militarized police force."[6]

Like others who had claimed their rights before them, residents of Standing Rock and their supporters used tools other than protest. They also pursued legal action to stop construction until a thorough study of the pipeline's impact on sacred sites and potential environmental impacts was undertaken. In July 2016, the Standing Rock Sioux Nation sued the U.S. Army Corps of Engineers to halt the issuance of permits and order a stop to construction near the Standing Rock Reservation. They formed organizations, such as the Water Protector Legal Collective, to "provide legal advocacy, jail and court support, criminal defense, and civil and human rights to the Native peoples and their allies who gathered there."[7]

Interaction of the Protesters with Law Enforcement Officials Shows How Fundamental Rights and Freedoms Are Connected

As the Standing Rock protests grew in the summer and fall of 2016, tensions between the protesters and state, local, and federal law enforcement officers grew. In August, construction began on the disputed portion of the pipeline. Less than two weeks later, North Dakota governor Jack Dalrymple declared a state of emergency, citing public safety risks associated with the protests. In September, he mobilized about thirty National Guard members to a security checkpoint up the road.

Many local landowners and residents became nervous, viewing, according to an article in the *New York Times*, "the demonstrations with a mix of frustration and fear, reflecting the deep cultural divides and racial attitudes."[8] There were charges of violence on both sides. In July, a protester's hand was badly injured in an explosion; its source was disputed. Protesters condemned private security contractors' use of dogs, claiming several of their number had been bitten.

Morton County sheriff Kyle Kirchmeier asserted that some protesters were believed to be readying pipe bombs. "Officers said that protesters had attacked them with firebombs, logs, feces and debris. . . . One woman who was being arrested, the authorities said, had pulled a gun out and fired at a police line."[9] Members of Standing Rock insisted that their protests were peaceful: "Weapons, drugs and alcohol are prohibited from the protest camp. Children march in daily demonstrations. The leaders believed the reports of pipe bombs were a misinterpretation of their calls for demonstrators to get out their wooden chanupa pipes—which have deep spiritual importance—and pass them through the crowd."[10] In November, law enforcement officials used water cannons on protesters in subzero weather, citing aggressive behavior by members of a crowd numbering in the hundreds. Sixteen protesters were arrested.

Arrested protesters claimed that their constitutional protections had been violated and that they were arrested only to later—sometimes weeks later—have the charges dropped, because, "although the protesters were on private property, no authority figure specifically requested that they leave.[11]

In the first weeks of his presidency, Donald J. Trump moved to speed up the pipeline's completion, with the Army Corps formally approving construction of the last mile in February 2017. In a video broadcast in the Standing Rock camp, Linda Black Elk, a member of the protesters' "healer council," urged them to carry on: "Pray for the water. Pray for the people. Pray for the water protectors. Pray for the tribe."[12]

In February 2017, Standing Rock protesters set fire to their camp just before they were removed under an order signed by North Dakota's governor. Efforts to stop the pipeline continued in the courts, however.

First Liberty Institute

The last group of protesters to hold out was forcibly removed under the evacuation order of North Dakota's new governor, Doug Burgum, two weeks later. Forty-six were arrested. In all, more than six hundred protesters had been arrested since the protests began. The governor and the North Dakota state legislature took further steps: "About an hour after the protest camp was cleared, Mr. Burgum signed into law four bills that had been passed largely as a result of the protests. They expand the scope of criminal trespassing laws, make it illegal to cover your face with a mask or hood while committing a crime, and increase the penalties for riot offenses."[13] By early 2017, the Standing Rock protest camps had been cleared. Construction continued, as did legal efforts by members of the Standing Rock Sioux Nation. But the underlying questions—about the policies themselves and law enforcement's responses to them—remained.

By 2020—in response to the Standing Rock protests—ten states had passed legislation designed to restrict protests against oil pipelines and similar facilities. In January, the Ohio state legislature was debating one of these bills. If passed, it would make it "a first-degree misdemeanor to 'knowingly enter or remain on pipeline rights of way, even when they're on public land or when protesters have property owners' permission to be there.'"[14] The hearing ended in protest, with one opponent shouting, "You aren't the people's government. You're the oil and gas industry's government!"[15]

Fundamental rights and freedoms do not exist in a vacuum. As we can see, these actions can draw in many other actors in the American political space, including the media, politicians, governmental agencies, law enforcement, the courts, and powerful interest groups. The protesters at Standing Rock were claiming their access to sacred places and to clean water. They used tools protected by the very first amendment to the U.S. Constitution: the freedom to speak, publish, and assemble in order to air their grievances with the government of the United States. However, law enforcement's response to the actions of the protesters raised questions about the degree to which the freedoms of Americans are truly protected today when being investigated, arrested, and tried for crimes. We will explore these tensions when we examine civil liberties in Chapter 4.

As members of both their tribal nations and the United States, indigenous Americans have a different political relationship to the national government than other Americans, who are members of both the nation and the individual states.[16] We will explore these differences in Chapter 3. For now, however, we note that the protection of fundamental rights and freedoms for all Americans has required action and participation, has often had to overcome tremendous resistance along the way, and will never be settled once and for all.

In the next section, we turn back to the American Revolution and the drafting of the Declaration of Independence when a group of individuals set out to enumerate, and then defend, Americans' fundamental rights and freedoms. Their efforts, like those of the Standing Rock protesters, involved protest, conflict, and strategic political action.

American Political Culture Is Built on a Set of Shared Ideas

When they asserted their rights, members of the Standing Rock Sioux Nation did so on the basis of a handful of ideas that form the foundation of the American Republic itself. Indeed, these ideas were affirmed in the Declaration of Independence in 1776, making them part of the country's basic DNA: "We hold these truths to be self-evident, that all men are created equal, that they are endowed by their Creator with certain unalienable Rights, that among these are Life, Liberty, and the pursuit of Happiness." These were revolutionary ideas, but they were not original ones. They weren't supposed to be. In drafting the Declaration of Independence, Thomas Jefferson and his coauthors drew upon a set of ideas about liberty and government that were widely known in the colonies and Great Britain—ideas Jefferson knew needed to be persuasive and compelling enough to successfully launch a revolution. From the histories and philosophical works of ancient Greece and Rome, they borrowed the idea of **democracy** (from the Greek *demos*, meaning "people," and *kratos*, or "power"), whereby power is held by the people.

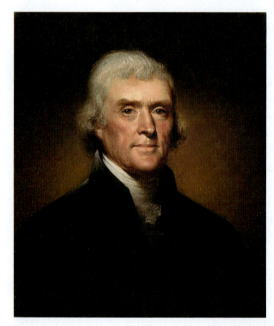

Thomas Jefferson in an 1800 painting by Rembrandt Peale.
GraphicaArtis/Getty Images

They also borrowed from English Enlightenment philosopher John Locke, who had argued against the divine, or God-given, right of kings to rule with absolute power. Locke claimed that people are born with **natural rights** that kings cannot give or take away. A legitimate government, to Locke, is one that involves a **social contract** in which people give to their governments the power to rule over them to ensure an orderly and functioning society. If a government breaks that social contract by violating people's natural rights, then the people have the right to replace that unjust government with a just one.

From the French Enlightenment, Jefferson and his colleagues drew on the works of Baron de Montesquieu, who gave an institutional form to the ideas of natural rights and the social contract in proposing that power in government should be divided between different branches so that no one branch could become too powerful.

Jefferson also drew upon Scottish Enlightenment thinkers such as David Hume. Given the historical tendency of leaders to abuse political power, Hume believed a just government should be carefully designed and the lessons of science and history carefully applied to its structure to keep the greedy and ambitious from using political power to their own advantage.

Later in the chapter we will see how the ideas underpinning the Declaration of Independence gave rise to a revolution and helped form the basis for the institutions of modern government. Those ideas—liberty, equality, rights, happiness, and others—also endure in other ways. Today they shape the shared set of beliefs, customs, traditions, and values that define the relationship of Americans to their government and to other American citizens. We call those shared beliefs **American political culture**.

Equality Is about Having the Same Rights or Status

Central to all of this—and the first key idea expressed in the Declaration of Independence—is a commitment to equality, to all people having the same rights and status. This might involve **social equality**, which means no individuals have an inherently higher social status than others. Unlike Europe, with its nobility and royalty, America was founded on the idea that all individuals could reach the social status that they sought based on their own efforts. **Political equality** exists when members of a society possess the same rights under the laws of the nation. Gains in political equality for many groups of Americans—such as indigenous Americans whose efforts we began the chapter with—have been made over decades or centuries of political struggle, and many question whether political equality for all has been fully achieved.

Finally, **economic equality** refers to a situation in which wealth is relatively evenly distributed across society. America does not have economic equality. In fact, differences in wealth and incomes are as stark today as they have ever been in the nation's history. Rather than emphasizing equality of economic *outcomes*, American political ideas tend to focus on ensuring equality of economic *opportunity*.

These are two very different concepts. For example, think about American public education in high schools. Equality of opportunity would mean that every student had a right to attend equally good public high schools. Equality of outcomes, however, might mean they have the right to achieve the same graduation rates or test scores. Americans weigh the differences between opportunity and outcomes all the time when they seek to resolve many important civil rights issues and make choices about domestic public policy options.

Inalienable Rights Exist above Any Government Powers

The thinking behind the Declaration of Independence and the government that was eventually based upon it is that some truths and some rights are *self-evident*. These are called **inalienable rights** in the sense that they exist before and above any government or its powers. Thomas Jefferson names "life, liberty, and the pursuit of happiness" as among those inherent, self-evident rights. Since they—unlike *privileges* that a government might grant—may not rightly be taken away by a government, a just system of political rule must be constructed in such a way as to protect rights and their expression. While specific rights for an individual may be taken away—such as when a person is incarcerated—the *process* through which that happens must itself protect these fundamental rights. To many of the Standing Rock protesters, the actions of law enforcement in restricting or suppressing their protests violated their procedural rights.

Liberty Involves Both Freedom from Interference and to Pursue One's Dreams

Another foundational American ideal expressed in the Declaration is a commitment to **liberty**, to social, political, and economic freedoms. That liberty might involve freedom *from* interference by a government or a freedom *to* pursue one's dreams. The degree to which the government should focus on freedom *from* or freedom *to* remains a hotly debated topic in American politics. There is often also a tension between these two visions of liberty. Consider the question of religious faith in a public high school if a student wants to start a faith-based student club at their school. A student may claim his freedom *to* explore his faith in this club. By allowing the group to meet, however, public school officials might risk violating other students' freedoms *from* having a government endorse a particular religious faith or endorse religious over nonreligious beliefs.

The Pursuit of Happiness Is at the Core of the American Dream

When Thomas Jefferson wrote about "the pursuit of happiness," he was tapping into another core American political value: the belief that individuals should be able to achieve prosperity through hard work, sacrifice, and their own talents. The idea of the **American dream** has drawn immigrants to the nation's shores and borders since its founding, and it continues to do so today. Some observers, however, question whether the American dream remains alive and well in an era of such profound economic inequality.

American Political Culture Has Many Roots

America's religious traditions have also helped shape American political culture in ways more significant than in many modern democratic governments. Some of the very first British colonies were founded by groups of individuals fleeing persecution for their religious beliefs and hoping to practice their faiths without interference. While the diversity of religious faiths represented in American society continues to expand, America was, and is, a nation partly defined by religious faith and expression. In this book, we will continue to explore the theme of how a nation founded upon liberty, especially religious liberty, wrestles with decisions about if—or how—to place boundaries on religious expression.

MILLENNIALS AND THE AMERICAN DREAM

The state of the American dream in the twenty-first century is something that we can study empirically. Words are not the only ways to tell stories, nor are images and videos. Data can tell political stories as well. In this book, we will investigate data—numbers, statistics, and survey results—as well as the stories that political actors and reporters construct around the numbers. Make no mistake, data stories can be and are used for political purposes. In investigating data stories in this book, the goal is twofold: to help you become more capable and confident interpreters of data and to help you gain the skills to critically examine the narratives constructed around data.

▼ FIGURE 1.1

Is the American Dream Alive or Dead for You?

Most people say they have achieved the American dream - or are on their way to achieving it

Do you believe your family has achieved the American dream? (%)

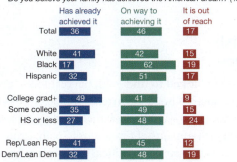

Source: Harvard Kennedy School Institute of Politics, "Harvard IOP Fall 2015 Poll: Trump, Carson Lead Republican Primary; Sanders Edging Clinton among Democrats, Harvard IOP Poll Finds," December 10, 2015, http://iop.harvard.edu/survey/details/harvard-iop-fall-2015-poll.

We start with what at first glance seems like a very simple data story—one taken from the results of a Harvard University survey of eighteen- to twenty-nine-year-olds conducted in December of 2015.[17] See Figure 1.1.

In the 2015 Harvard survey, Americans between the ages of eighteen and twenty-nine were just about equally split between those who believed that the American dream was still alive (49 percent) and those who did not (48 percent).

WHaT Do You Think?

The authors of the survey report placed these results in context and went into much more detail about other factors. But let's imagine that they did not. What conclusions might you draw from this figure alone? Does it reflect your experience? What other data from this survey would you want to know? If you could break out groups of young adult Americans based upon identities and characteristics, what would you examine?

As it turns out, in the Harvard survey, college graduates (58 percent) were more likely than those who had not graduated or ever enrolled (42 percent) to say the American dream was still alive. Young adult Americans in the survey who said that they were supporters of Democratic presidential candidate Bernie Sanders (56 percent) or Republican Party candidate Donald Trump (61 percent) reported that they felt the American dream was dead. What might these results mean for your understanding of the political attitudes of young adult Americans today?

Today, questions about the proper role of religion in the nation endure. What kinds of holiday displays are acceptable for a community to officially sponsor? Would a ban on immigration by members of specific religious faiths be constitutional?

American Exceptionalism Flows from the Nation's Historical Development

Finally, when Americans tell stories about themselves, their politics, and their histories, they often refer to the ways in which the nation is different because of the historical patterns of the nation's development. **American exceptionalism** refers to these historical and cultural differences, shaped in many ways by the voices of those who have contributed to the national chorus but also by the fact that America was an experiment, starting anew, without the legacy of the European monarchies to constrain its promise.[18]

Politics and Political Action Set the Stage for Revolution

> 1.3 Identify the political, social, and economic events and institutions that gave rise to the American Revolution.

In April 1607, three British ships made their way up what would later become known as the James River in Virginia. After deciding on a spot far enough up the river to avoid Spanish warships, they established Jamestown, the first permanent British settlement in the modern-day United States of America.[19] Over the course of the next 170 years, the turbulent political, social, and economic experiences they faced would shape the conditions that led to their eventual separation from Great Britain and establish the foundations of a set of institutions that continue to influence American politics today.

Colonial Settlements Establish a Precedent for Independence

The colonists who established Jamestown hoped to find gold, harvest forest products, and maybe find a valuable trade route.[20] Though chartered by the Crown, the British colonists at Jamestown—and those who would follow them—were subject to less oversight than those sent out by the governments of France and Spain. From the beginning, British colonists began to develop their own political institutions. In 1619 the Virginia colony developed its own legislative assembly, the House of Burgesses, which was the first elected assembly in colonial America.[21] Each of the other thirteen colonies eventually did the same. These assemblies instilled in their colonies a tradition of self-governance and a resistance to being told what to do by Great Britain, especially by the British legislature, Parliament.

In terms of the subsequent development of the thirteen British colonies and the American states that later grew out of them, the initial political and economic structure of the colonies proved to be as important as any other factor. The colonists' history and sense of autonomy would increasingly come into conflict with the policies of a British empire bent on increasing control.

A Global War Forces Change in Colonial Policy

The Treaty of Paris in 1763 ended the fourth major military conflict between two global powers, France and Great Britain, in less than seventy-five years. In Europe, this conflict was known as the **Seven Years' War**.[22] In the American colonies, it was known as the French and Indian War. Fighting took place across the globe and involved most of the European powers of the time.

Hoping to coordinate alliances with indigenous peoples—and to keep them from allying with the French—Great Britain requested that its colonies meet at a conference in Albany, New York, in the summer of 1754.[23] The so-called Albany Congress accomplished very little. However, one of its delegates, Benjamin Franklin, who later became America's first international celebrity, presented to the Congress a plan for closer coordination between the colonies. The **Albany Plan** called for a "Plan of Union" in which colonial legislatures would choose delegates to form an assembly under the leadership of a chief executive appointed by Great Britain.[24] This governing body would have power over dealings with Native American peoples and collective self-defense.

Benjamin Franklin's proposal for a unified legislative body was not adopted by the colonial governments. It was not an idea whose time had come. Great Britain preferred to deal with its North American colonies individually rather than as a potentially powerful unified colonial legislature. For their part, many colonies did not want to give up their own sovereignty, especially when it involved land claims that might allow a lucky few colonies (especially Virginia) to grow even larger and more powerful at the expense of the small coastal colonies, such as Rhode Island and Delaware, whose boundaries were constricted by the ocean and those of neighboring colonies.

Benjamin Franklin may not have expected his plan to be adopted. He was a very savvy politician. But his plan did help plant the seeds for an American union.

After the Seven Years' War, Great Britain was the unquestioned European power in Canada and in the modern United States east of the Mississippi River. With victory, however, came problems: Great Britain had to now confront increasingly assertive colonies. It had acquired a vast new territory that now had to be administered, defended, and paid for. But money was scarce. War had left Great Britain with a significant amount of debt, and the British government fully expected its thirteen colonies to pay the British Crown to cover their costs and not make the debt problem even worse.[25]

Beginning in 1763, Parliament passed a series of acts and proclamations that enlarged the scope of Great Britain's involvement in colonial affairs, producing a backlash from colonists who felt that Great Britain was going too far. To make matters worse, these acts were instituted during an economic depression in the colonies. Colonial legislatures became increasingly resistant to Parliament's interference in areas of economic life that the colonies had been in charge of for decades.

The Idea of Independence Is Given Voice in Political Propaganda

In this uncertain political environment, there were a few colonists who advocated resistance to Great Britain, some who remained loyal to Great Britain, and many more who were undecided and afraid of actions that might lead to a hopeless war against the greatest military power in the world. It was this last group, the undecided, who found themselves in the crosshairs of a radical few. Those few had a powerful, cheap, and flexible technology on their side. It was called the printing press, and the American radicals used it very well. From the printing presses came inexpensive and easy-to-produce papers called pamphlets; the printers came to be called pamphleteers. Enough people had access to and the ability to read their products to make the pamphlet a revolutionary technological innovation.[26] The pamphleteers were engaged in **political propaganda**; their goal was to change public opinion and thus influence people's actions.[27] American pamphleteers were not trying to show their intelligence or literary skill. They were trying to mobilize people in support of their cause. Words and ideas, as the pamphleteers knew well, could also constitute strategic political action.

Of all the American pamphlets, the most widely read was Thomas Paine's 1776 pamphlet *Common Sense*, which was a massive best seller in its day. *Common Sense* ultimately "had more influence in focusing the spirit of revolt than the writings of all the intellectuals taken together."[28]

Calling King George III the "royal brute of England," Paine challenged the legitimacy of the British monarchy, refuted arguments in favor of reconciling differences with Great Britain, and announced that "the period of debate is closed."[29] He used the dreaded *I* word, *independence*, writing that independence from Great Britain was not only possible but sure to come to pass.[30] Drawing on the idea that the American colonists had a unique destiny in the world and in history, Paine called the colonists into action at just the time when many were ready to receive his message.

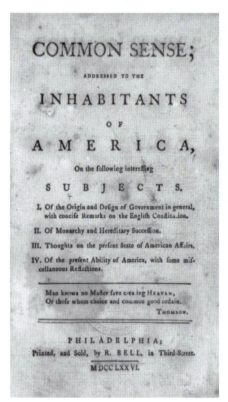

The cover of Thomas Paine's pamphlet *Common Sense* (1776).
Library of Congress

Revolutionaries Take Action, Their Eyes on Increasing the Powers of Colonial Legislatures

Words alone, however powerful, were not enough to mobilize the colonists to make a final break from Great Britain. Colonial radicals began a planned strategy of resistance—one that involved propaganda; organization; and, occasionally, violence. A phrase we commonly associate with resistance to British tax policy is "No taxation without representation!" While it was used at the time, the phrase did not fully capture the struggle between colonists and Great Britain.

It might seem logical to assume that a protester declaring "No taxation without representation" wanted to gain representation—in this case by electing a member of Parliament who could promote the interests of the colonists. American radicals, however, generally did not want to be represented in Parliament. Representatives would have been out of communication with the colonies during debates, given the vast distances involved, and would have been consistently outvoted in Parliament even if some arrangement for their representation could be worked out. Instead, the colonists argued that the power of taxation should be held by colonial legislatures, not British Parliament. In many ways, colonial opposition to British policies was conservative rather than revolutionary. Its adherents wanted to go back to the way things had been prior to the Seven Years' War when British colonial policy was more hands-off. Economic and political realities, however, made this an unrealistic goal.

The Sons of Liberty Attempt to Mobilize Colonists around British Tax Policies. In 1765, in response to Great Britain's tax policies, a group of merchants and workingmen, including Sam Adams, formed the **Sons of Liberty**. It was a working-class organization, with a potentially much larger appeal to the general public than the revolutionary elites had. That potential made the Sons of Liberty both attractive and scary to the wealthy elites in the revolutionary movement. They feared that they might not be able to control the actions of the Sons of Liberty. Through rallies, sermons, protests, and heavy use of the newspapers, the Sons of Liberty tried to mobilize public opinion in support of resistance to Great Britain and its tax policies. They also resorted to mob violence, including rioting and looting.[31]

The group's violent actions backfired as a political strategy, sparking fear among uncommitted colonists. In response, radicals changed their strategy. They planned and organized boycotts of British goods, pressuring fellow colonists to comply.

In October 1765, at the invitation of Massachusetts's colonial legislatures, nine of thirteen colonies sent representatives to New York to prepare a colonial response to Britain's policies.[32] This so-called Stamp Act Congress (named after the Stamp Act, another British tax) issued a Declaration of Rights and Grievances, which was, in many ways, quite mild. While it protested the imposition of taxes without colonial consent, it also affirmed colonial loyalty to the British Crown. Most importantly, however, the Stamp Act Congress was an assembly of representatives from different colonies, an early example of the colonies working together.

The Crisis Accelerates as Protests Intensify.

Despite continuing tensions, the next few years were relatively quiet politically, with radicals losing power and influence. Beginning in 1770, however, that began to shift.

The exact sequence of events leading up to the Boston Massacre in 1770 is not entirely clear, nor is the exact role of radicals in escalating the situation. It involved a confrontation between a mob of Bostonians and a small group of British soldiers, beginning with taunts and snowballs and ending in the deaths of five American colonists. Sam Adams and other radicals quickly mobilized to use the press to rally support for their cause, describing "the blood of our fellow citizens running like water through King Street."[33]

The Boston Tea Party Adds Fuel to the Revolutionary Fire.

In 1773 the Boston Sons of Liberty seized upon another crisis to create further divisions between the colonists and Great Britain. It began over a bailout of the East India Company by the government of Great Britain. Though corrupt and poorly managed, the East India Company was no ordinary company. It ruled much of India with its own private army. It could count among its investors some of the wealthiest and most powerful men in Great Britain. It was—in modern terms—too big to fail. But the company was nearly bankrupt, and it had large stocks of unsold tea.

It needed a bailout, and it got one with the Tea Act, passed by Great Britain in 1773. The act gave the East India Company a tax-free monopoly on the tea trade to the colonies. New England merchants were not pleased and saw "ruin staring them in the face."[34]

It was the fear of what Great Britain might do next as much as what it actually *had* done that drove many merchants into the radical camp. In late 1773, three ships entered Boston Harbor loaded with tea. With the merchants increasingly on their side, the Sons of Liberty provoked a crisis, dumping the tea from the ships into the harbor, an event known as the Boston Tea Party.

Not everyone in the American colonies cheered the actions of the radicals. Their lawlessness worried many. The violence that accompanied the protest seemed to some completely unjustifiable. Despite the limited support for the radicals, their strategic actions placed the British government in a very difficult situation. It could not ignore the attack on British property and commerce. Asserting control, however, risked driving moderate colonists into the radical camp.

Parliament, with the support of King George III, clamped down. Hard. In a series of actions in 1774, known in the colonies as the **Intolerable Acts**, Britain sought to make an example of Massachusetts and its radicals. If Parliament and the Crown thought that this show of resolve—backed, if necessary, by force—would quiet the colonies, they were wrong. Instead of driving a wedge between the colonies, the Intolerable Acts brought them together. Writing many years after the Revolution, John Adams observed this:

The colonies had grown up under constitutions of government so different, there was so great a variety of their religions, they were composed of so many different nations . . . that to unite them in the same principles in theory and the same system of action, was certainly a very difficult enterprise. . . . Thirteen clocks were made to strike together—a perfection of mechanism which no artist had ever before effected.[35]

The actions of the British government and the Boston radicals had both helped to synchronize these thirteen clocks.

The Institution of Slavery Denies the Natural Rights of African Americans

The first group of twenty Africans arrived in Jamestown, Virginia, in 1619 aboard a Dutch ship. Like the native peoples whose lands had been occupied by British settlers, the African peoples who followed this small group came from diverse cultures, nations, and kinship groups. Initially, some were given the status of indentured servants—people who still possessed the ability to pay off their "debts" through labor and achieve their freedom. Throughout the seventeenth and eighteenth centuries, whites who arrived from Europe also carried the status of indentured servitude. As the plantation economies of colonial America developed, however, enslaved Africans and their descendants confronted legal systems designed more and more to strip them of any legal or political rights or any hope of freedom under that legal order.

By the time Virginia's government fully codified the status of enslaved people in the eighteenth century, "no black, free or slave, could own arms, strike a white man, or employ a white servant. Any white person could apprehend any black to demand a certificate of freedom or a pass from the owner giving permission to be off the plantation."[36] Like the indigenous peoples, enslaved Africans and their descendants strove to maintain their ways of life and acted to protect their spiritual and cultural traditions, kinship networks, and families over the coming centuries.

As colonial America moved toward a revolution based on individual liberty, it was far from an equal society. To many whites, the prospect of individual advancement made America more equal than the class-stratified societies in Europe, with the exception of the almost feudal southern plantation societies.[37]

The willingness of white colonial Americans to attack Great Britain for assaults on their liberty while allowing the enslavement of Africans did not go unnoticed by British officials and some white colonists. Thomas Hutchinson, governor of Massachusetts before the war, questioned how the American revolutionaries could "justify the depriving of more than a hundred thousand Africans of their rights to liberty, and the same *pursuit of happiness*, and in some degree to their lives, if these rights are so absolutely inalienable."[38] Thomas Paine was one of only a relatively small

Lemuel Haynes, a Massachusetts minister, challenged slavery based on its violation of natural rights.

number of white pamphleteers to point out the contradiction of calling for liberty in a society that allowed slavery. In a 1775 newspaper article, he wondered how the colonists could "complain so loudly of attempts to enslave them, while they hold so many hundred thousand in slavery."[39]

This hypocrisy did not go unnoticed by enslaved people and free peoples of African descent either. In April 1773, a group of African Americans in Massachusetts petitioned the government for a redress of their grievances, drawing "a straight line between their own condition as chattel slaves and the conditions colonists were then objecting to as virtual slavery."[40] They asked that the same principles be applied to their own condition in colonial America.

In 1776 Lemuel Haynes, a Massachusetts minister, wrote an unpublished pamphlet titled *Liberty Further Extended*. The son of an African father and a white mother, Haynes became a servant to a religious white farming family in the backcountry of Massachusetts. Haynes educated himself in Puritan theology and on the pamphlets of colonial America. He volunteered as a minuteman (a volunteer reserve) in Boston in 1774 and for the Continental Army in 1776. In his pamphlet, Haynes anchored his arguments about the injustice of slavery in the principle of natural rights and the Christian theology with which colonists were very familiar:

> Liberty is a Jewel which was handed Down to man from the cabinet of heaven, and is Coaeval with his Existence. And as it proceed from the Supreme Legislature of the univers, so it is he which hath a sole right to take away; therefore, he that would take away a mans Liberty assumes a prerogative that Belongs to another, and acts out of his own domain.[41]

Revolutionary Women, Though Excluded, Build Institutions of Their Own

In many ways, women in revolutionary America were legally and politically invisible. In spite of commonalities in their legal standing, however, *colonial women* as an all-encompassing term fails to capture significant differences in the status, economic class, and religious orientation of the women in question.[42] Women who were enslaved, of African descent, or of Native American ancestry struggled against multiple forms of oppression. While sexual and physical abuse was a danger for all colonial women, those who were enslaved or indentured servants faced a higher risk.[43] War only heightened these risks; during the conflict, sexual assault was some-times practiced systematically. In 1776 in Staten Island, New York, and New Jersey, British troops repeatedly raped women in the area.[44]

White women, unless they had acquired property through widowhood, generally had no legal identity or ability to secure their personal and economic rights in a court of law. They did not have to struggle against the destruction of their families, tradi-tions, and ways of life, as women of African or Native American descent did. Theirs was a "protective oppression," designed to keep them out of involvement in govern-ment and public life. Because of more restricted educational opportunities and, there-fore, lower literacy rates than men, fewer women's voices were expressed in print. In spite of these challenges, however, many women did speak, write, and act against the restrictions on their own rights and liberties in colonial America.

Because of their general exclusion from public life, white women had fewer oppor-tunities to adopt leadership roles in revolutionary America. Religious organizations proved an important exception as women could act as leaders in them without the same risk of social approbation as they would face if acting in the male-dominated political space. Maintaining the boycotts of British goods in the years before revo-lution also "politicized women and the domestic arena"—especially in the pro-duction of substitutes for those goods.[45] The replacement of British textiles, in particular, brought many colonial women together as **Daughters of Liberty** in spinning events. While these meetings remained in the "acceptable" realm of home production in the eyes of the male-dominated White colonial society, they did provide an experience in collective organization—an act of public "joining" that was itself a departure from and challenge to traditional gendered roles.[46]

Efforts to support the Revolutionary War effort led Esther de Berdt Reed, Sarah Franklin Bache (daughter of Benjamin Franklin), and other colonial women to work to create a women's organization across, not just within, the United States. The Ladies Association of Philadelphia was "the biggest domestic fundraising campaign of the war"[47] in part because women and girls who were not wealthy could still partici-pate by donating small amounts of money.[48]

The collection, accounting, and delivery of these donations required the devel-opment of an organizational and administrative structure. Though the members focused on activities considered acceptable for White women in colonial America, the act of organizing and institution building was itself revolutionary. These fund-raising efforts were extremely successful, and this was perhaps the first truly national American women's organization.

Indigenous Peoples in North America Challenge Colonization

The social, cultural, and linguistic diversity of the indigenous peoples in North America at the time of British colonization was staggering. At the time of first contact with the European invaders, perhaps a quarter of "all human languages in the world were North American Indian."[49] Initially, British colonists depended on the adaptive technologies and agricultural advances of the indigenous peoples for their own survival. As the British colonies grew in size and confidence, however, they began to assert their ideas about land ownership more aggressively, provoking resistance by indigenous peoples who had not agreed to such terms. The violence that resulted was often horrific, including massacres of entire indigenous local communities and reprisals against individual British colonists.

By the time Thomas Jefferson sat down to draft the Declaration of Independence, the population of the indigenous peoples in the thirteen British colonies had been reduced to a fraction of its level before first contact with the Europeans. Diseases, against which indigenous peoples had little or no immunity, were the largest factor. Death from armed conflict also played a role. However, the disruption in the traditional ways of life of native peoples caused by European settlement, including the cascading effects of losing their land—which upset agreements and boundaries between them and other indigenous peoples—also had an effect. The impact of British colonization on traditional indigenous ways of life was total. The habitats upon which the indigenous peoples depended were altered and depleted. The traditional social and economic systems that had been developed before the British colonists arrived often broke down.

Indigenous peoples, however, did not sit idly by and allow this to happen. They resisted—at times militarily, and often quite successfully. Many indigenous peoples also practiced diplomacy among and between European powers and other native peoples. Sometimes this approach bore fruit, but sometimes it had disastrous outcomes, especially as the European powers were often quite willing to abandon their promises to their "allies" among the native peoples once European objectives had been met. For most indigenous peoples, resistance probably took personal, nonviolent, and largely unrecorded forms as they tried to maintain the survival of their families and kinship networks, their spiritual traditions, and their economic and social structures in the presence of powerfully destabilizing forces.[50]

Independence Becomes Institutionalized

By the time the delegates to the Second Continental Congress convened in Philadelphia in May 1775, the "war of pamphlets and protests was giving way to the war of rifles and cannon."[51] In April British general Thomas Gage ordered troops to move on Lexington, Massachusetts—to arrest radical leaders, including Sam Adams—and on Concord, Massachusetts, to seize weapons. He failed to do both, and the battles of Lexington and Concord, though small, handed the radical pamphleteers the best ammunition they could hope for. They immediately published exaggerated reports of British atrocities against colonial citizens, especially women and children. Individual colonies began to organize or expand colonial militias and organize their manufacturers for war.

Though few could probably have imagined it that May, the **Second Continental Congress** remained the government of the United States until 1781, when a new American government, one designed by the Congress, took its place.[52] The Second Continental Congress was perpetually in crisis, trying to fight a war in the face of what seemed like unending military defeats as well as inadequate supplies, troops, and hard money. Its capital even had to be moved in the face of advancing British troops.

When the Second Continental Congress first assembled, the colonies were not yet united in the cause of war. A group of wealthy elites with personal, political, or financial ties to Great Britain opposed independence. A second group, the radicals, set their sights on armed conflict with Great Britain. A third group, the moderates, agreed that a show of force might be necessary but only to serve the ultimate end of a negotiated solution. There were other divisions between slave and nonslaveholding states, large and small colonies, and urban and rural colonists. These divisions would become more important once independence had actually been achieved.

In the early months of 1776, events began to accelerate toward independence. *Common Sense* had given a clear voice to the cause, and British actions had given ammunition to the radicals. Individual colonies began to pass resolutions authorizing their delegates in Congress (often at the request of those delegates) to move for independence from Great Britain. On June 7, Richard Henry Lee of Virginia offered a motion in Congress declaring "that these united colonies are, and of right ought to be, free and independent states, that they are absolved from all allegiance to the British Crown, and that all political connection between them and the state of Great Britain is, and ought to be, totally dissolved."[53]

Congress was not quite ready to act on the Lee Resolution. The vote was postponed for three weeks in order to allow for more instructions to arrive from some of the colonies and to convince reluctant colonies and their delegates to get on board. In the meantime, a committee was appointed to draft a basic structure for a government in the event of independence. A second committee was charged with trying to secure foreign aid. Another committee, which included Jefferson, was charged with writing a declaration of, and justification for, American independence. On July 2, 1776, the Second Continental Congress approved the Lee Resolution. Two days later, on July 4, Congress approved Thomas Jefferson's revised Declaration of Independence, which announced, and defended, American independence to the world.

Congress had not accepted Jefferson's original draft of the Declaration, however. Of all of the changes that members of the Second Continental Congress made, none were more significant than the deletion of his charges against the king on the issue of slavery. The first section of the deleted charges accused the king of violating natural rights by allowing the slave trade to continue. Yet Jefferson was a slave owner, one of the largest in Virginia. His lifestyle depended on the capture, sale, and oppression of other human beings. Today, there is considerable debate about how best to acknowledge and present the complicated and uncomfortable legacies of individuals like Jefferson. Discussion over the placement of statues and other public monuments to commemorate these individuals is a current, and contentious, example.

The second deleted section, in which Jefferson charged the king with trying to incite slave rebellions in the colonies, spoke directly to the fears of many southern plantation owners. British officials had recently made offers of freedom to enslaved colonials in exchange for their joining the British against the American revolutionaries. Many eventually did.

In the end, Jefferson's charges against the king on the issue of slavery were deleted, partly due to opposition from southern state delegates. The contradiction—of a new nation announcing its birth on the foundation of freedom while holding hundreds of thousands of people in slavery—remained.

The American Revolution Is Still under Construction

From the start, the Revolutionary War went poorly for the Americans. Successive defeats, disease, and logistical problems all plagued the colonists and their general, George Washington. By adapting their tactics to suit their strengths—knowledge of the terrain and support among many of the locals—the colonists managed to use hit-and-run tactics to harass Britain and attack its long supply lines. With the help of Britain's rivals, especially France and its powerful navy, the Americans finally defeated Great Britain in 1781. The Treaty of Paris, signed in 1783 and ratified by Congress in 1784, secured the independence of the United States of America.

Militarily and politically, the American Revolution wasn't technically a revolution. King George III was not overthrown; the British Empire remained intact. The conflict in America is more properly called a secession, wherein a group of citizens break off from the larger government to form one of their own. In the backcountry, it was frequently a civil war, with members of the same communities fighting each other, often brutally.

It was, however, very much a revolution of ideas. Though imperfectly and incompletely, the idea of a government based upon natural rights and individual liberty had been given political and institutional form. Later American revolutionaries would undertake their own wars of ideas and political strategies to try to make the government live up to its promises. As part of their efforts, they would build, rebuild, and reshape the political institutions that protect and express Americans' natural rights in a representative democracy.

The Structure of Institutions Affects How Citizens Participate

1.4   Describe the core features of American political institutions.

As we have seen in the stories that have already been mentioned, while the actions of people and their ideas matter to American government, the **political institutions** that structure how citizens may be involved matter as well. To a great extent, institutions determine how conflicts over political power are resolved, and they can also shape the ideas of people acting within them. The term *political institution* often conjures images of *organizations*, like Congress or the Supreme Court. The number of political institutions in America today is almost too long to list, composed of bodies at the local, state, and national levels. However, the *rules* that structure how these organizations are formed and how they operate are equally essential to consider, including the most important American political institution, the Constitution of the United States. The Constitution, as we will explore in the next chapter, is itself largely a set of rules about how things are supposed to work. This document forms the basis of the nation's government and, in turn, creates a host of political institutions through which conflicts over political power are resolved. It places textual limits on the power of the national government in order to protect Americans' fundamental rights. It also constitutes, or creates, a people with its first seven words: "We the People of the United States."

In devising a system of government, two basic questions need to be resolved: How much power will that government claim? How will political power be distributed or withheld? Different forms of governments distribute power in very different ways. Totalitarian governments admit no limitations on their own power or competing centers of political power. Similarly, authoritarian governments suppress the voices of their citizens to maintain a grip on power; however, unlike totalitarian systems, authoritarian systems may have some economic or social institutions not under governmental control that may serve to moderate the government's power. Governments that admit no external challenge to their claims on power might be monarchies, ruled by royal figures; theocracies, ruled by religious elites; or oligarchies, ruled by a small group of powerful elites. At the other end of the spectrum of power is a **direct democracy** wherein citizens vote directly on public policies. (See Figure 1.2.)

The United States is none of these extremes. While the nation does have elements of direct democracy—in, for example, local votes to approve or reject public school budgets or property tax increases—the vast majority of conflicts over power in America are handled through a system of **representative democracy** whereby voters select representatives who then vote on matters of public policy. In doing so, voters in a representative democracy are confronted with a serious challenge: How can they be sure that their representatives are carrying out their wishes? This is a question that we will examine in some detail in this book.

By ceding some of the expression of their natural rights to a government, Americans have tried to create institutions that ensure an orderly and prosperous society. They have thus entered a social contract as described by various Enlightenment thinkers. In doing so, however, they run the risk of creating institutions that oppress instead of uplift.

The challenge is that representative democracy does not, by itself, protect against all forms of tyranny. By allowing citizens to select their representatives or vote them out of office, the nation does gain protections against abuse of power by those selected. But what if a *majority* of Americans are in favor of suppressing the rights of

Types of Governments

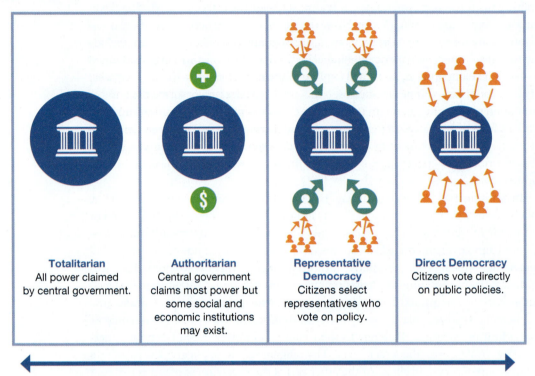

Totalitarian
All power claimed by central government.

Authoritarian
Central government claims most power but some social and economic institutions may exist.

Representative Democracy
Citizens select representatives who vote on policy.

Direct Democracy
Citizens vote directly on public policies.

Power concentrated in central government　　　　　Power concentrated in citizenry

others, as was the case in many states with laws allowing, or even requiring, racial segregation until the middle of the twentieth century?

To further protect against infringements upon individuals' rights and freedoms, whether that be from officials, a majority of the population, or others, the United States of America also has a **constitutional government**. In this type of system, limits are placed on the power of government to infringe upon people's rights in a constituting document that is recognized as the highest and most supreme law of the nation.

The institutions and rules of a government not only structure the politics of a nation but also may serve to structure its **economy** or the ways in which goods and services are produced and distributed within a society.

When comparing different economic systems, the key thing to focus on is how much power a government has to regulate the production and distribution of goods and services. In a **communist system**, a government acting on behalf of all workers in a society controls the means of production and distribution—all the factories and stores, railroads, and trucks. In a **socialist system**, private firms are allowed to operate but with significant intervention by the government, which may include governmental control of sectors of the economy, such as energy or mining, in the service of ensuring economic equality. In a **capitalist system**, private ownership of the means of production and distribution of a society's resources is emphasized and protected under the laws of that society. Capitalism emphasizes the efficiency of the marketplace in optimally allocating a society's resources. A completely unregulated capitalist system is called *laissez-faire* (from the French "let go," or "let be") and allows individuals and private firms to operate without regulation or oversight. No representative democracies currently practice laissez-faire capitalism. Instead, even nations like the United States that emphasize private economic action practice regulated capitalism whereby firms are allowed to control much of their own decision making but are also subject to governmental rules and regulations (see Figure 1.3).

▼ FIGURE 1.3

Types of Economic Systems

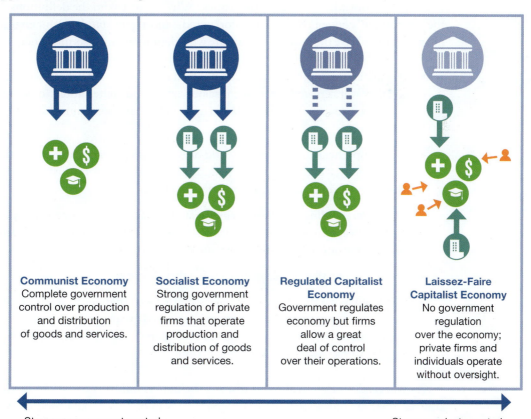

Communist Economy
Complete government control over production and distribution of goods and services.

Socialist Economy
Strong government regulation of private firms that operate production and distribution of goods and services.

Regulated Capitalist Economy
Government regulates economy but firms allow a great deal of control over their operations.

Laissez-Faire Capitalist Economy
No government regulation over the economy; private firms and individuals operate without oversight.

Stronger government control ← → Stronger private control

Conclusion: The American Experiment Continues, and You Are Part of It

A study of American government requires understanding the ideas upon which it is based. It requires an understanding of the ways in which political institutions promote, shape, or hinder the fulfillment of these fundamental ideas. It requires a study of the past and the present. However, and most importantly, a deep study of American government requires that you think, and perhaps act, as a strategic player in the political space, which is rarely, if ever, neat and clean.

Should you choose to act in American politics—should you choose to stake your own claims for your rights—you will want to be well informed, about both your own positions on critical issues and the positions of those with whom you disagree. You will want to have developed your skills in analyzing the words, images, and data that will serve as your tools along the way. And you will need to question. What is American political culture? Is there such a thing? How do the institutions of American government make "good government" more or less likely?

At the beginning of the chapter, I stated that this book would be centered on stories, and it is. But why? Why read the stories? Why not just skim the definitions for the "important" content? Because the stories and—most importantly—your engagement with them have the potential to capture what definitions and lists might not:

- The understanding that American political institutions did not fall out of the sky; they were created through conscious action and contestation, sometimes based upon success, sometimes based upon failure, and sometimes based upon pure chance

- The comprehension that in the world of American government and politics, there is rarely, if ever, an either/or solution to major problems but instead a complex interplay among ideals, actions, time, and place

- The understanding that the development of American government and politics has always involved the experiences of individuals and groups whose lives were written out of conventional narratives

- The realization that people matter, even if they do not succeed

- The knowledge that your own voices matter and that your own opinions, thoughtfully constructed and respectfully offered, matter—even if these ideas and opinions may seem to be outside some perception of what you are supposed to think or what others tell you to think

As you read, engage with, and discuss the material in this book and in your courses, there are only two things of which I will try to convince you: People like you matter. And your stories matter as well, even if nobody ever retells them in a book.

The American experiment always was a complicated and incomplete thing. It still is. At its heart, it poses one difficult and basic question: Can a people design and maintain a government that uplifts and energizes its citizens rather than oppresses them? The answer to that question is not up to other people. It is up to you.

CHAPTER REVIEW

This chapter's main ideas are reflected in the Learning Objectives. By reviewing them here, you should be able to *remember* the key points and *know* these terms that are central to the topic.

1.1   Explain how diverse Americans have used the political process to make claims on their fundamental rights and freedoms.

Remember . . .
- The American political system is designed so that different individuals and groups of people, regardless of their points of view and backgrounds, are able to make claims upon the same rights and freedoms that all share.

Know . . .
- *government* (p. 3)
- *politics* (p. 3)

1.2   Define the key elements of American political culture.

Remember . . .
- Jefferson drew on ideas of democracy, natural rights, the social contract, separation of powers, and institutional design in drafting the Declaration of Independence—ideas that shape American political culture today.

Know . . .
- *American dream* (p. 10)
- *American exceptionalism* (p. 12)
- *American political culture* (p. 9)
- *democracy* (p. 8)
- *economic equality* (p. 9)
- *inalienable rights* (p. 9)
- *liberty* (p. 10)
- *natural rights* (p. 8)
- *political equality* (p. 9)
- *social contract* (p. 8)
- *social equality* (p. 9)

1.3   Identify the political, social, and economic events and institutions that gave rise to the American Revolution.

Remember . . .
- Colonists established forms of government, political institutions, and social practices that allowed them to increasingly assert their autonomy from Great Britain.
- Economic factors also played a part in shaping the movement toward independence.
- Enslaved people, the descendants of enslaved people, and native peoples were not extended rights under the Declaration of Independence.
- Women played a role in the economy and affairs of the colonies but were not extended full rights.

Know . . .
- *Albany Plan* (p. 13)
- *Daughters of Liberty* (p. 19)
- *Intolerable Acts* (p. 16)
- *political propaganda* (p. 14)
- *Second Continental Congress* (p. 20)
- *Seven Years' War* (p. 13)
- *Sons of Liberty* (p. 15)

1.4 Describe the core features of American political institutions.

Remember . . .

- In the American model of representative democracy, the forms our political institutions take affect how people are represented.

- The institutional structure of the United States is that of a constitutional republic wherein the people elect representatives to make the most of the laws and policies in the nation rather than vote on them directly.

- Institutions can both protect and restrict rights, and people may use and change them to protect their own rights or those of others.

- America's political institutions also structure the country's economy.

Know . . .

- *capitalist system* (p. 25)
- *communist system* (p. 24)
- *constitutional government* (p. 24)
- *direct democracy* (p. 23)
- *economy* (p. 24)
- *political institutions* (p. 22)
- *representative democracy* (p. 23)
- *socialist system* (p. 24)

CHAPTER 2

THE CONSTITUTION OF THE UNITED STATES

A New Vision of Representative Government

Paulina Perez signs a giant banner printed with the preamble to the U.S. Constitution during a demonstration against a ruling by the Supreme Court in 2010 that allowed unlimited, though uncoordinated, campaign contributions by associations of individuals and corporations.

Chip Somodevilla/Getty Images

After reading this chapter, you will be able to do the following:

2.1 Describe the ideas and historical context that shaped James Madison's thinking about republics.

2.2 Explain the challenges faced by the nation following the American Revolution in trying to form a government strong enough to rule effectively but not so strong as to oppress the rights of Americans.

2.3 Describe the role that compromise over states' interests played in shaping the government during the Constitutional Convention.

2.4 Identify the institutions of government established by the Constitution and the distribution of political power among them.

2.5 Compare and contrast the arguments put forth by the Federalists and Anti-Federalists during the ratification debates.

"**W**e the People of the United States . . . " Perhaps no seven words are as important in American political history as these. Penned by Gouverneur Morris in Philadelphia, Pennsylvania, during the fateful summer of 1787, these words did more than begin a document. They sought to *constitute*, to create, a new nation. In the Declaration of Independence, Thomas Jefferson and the other members of the Second Continental Congress had announced to the colonies and to the world why they felt that separation from Great Britain was justified and necessary. Following the American Revolution, that goal was achieved . . . but then what?

In the years following the Revolution, the American states and the government that they had collectively agreed to form struggled against the realities of financial crises, the possibility of foreign invasion, and the threat of internal discord and even revolution. Against this backdrop, a group of delegates convened in Philadelphia in 1787 to create a new government—a new *kind* of government.

The delegates to the Constitutional Convention drafted and then tried to sell to skeptical individuals in the thirteen American states a blueprint for a new government, though the delegates themselves were often divided about what this government should be, how it should be structured, and how much power it should have. In spite of all of these divisions and challenges, they produced a **constitution**, a document that simultaneously creates a people, sets out fundamental principles by which these people agree to be governed, and establishes the rules and institutions through which this governing will take place.

In this chapter, we will explore the stories of the events leading up to the Constitutional Convention, the political debates within the convention, and the debates surrounding the ratification process. We will focus primarily on one person: James Madison of Virginia. Though he was hardly the most powerful political figure of the time, Madison's efforts were instrumental in shaping the Constitution of the United States.

James Madison Plans
for a Republic That Will Last

In the spring of 1786 James Madison Jr. settled into his home in Montpelier, Virginia, with two trunks full of books. As one of America's first political scientists, Madison's goal was to apply science to the study of government. The subject of his studies that spring was the unspringlike topic of death, specifically the death of governments. Kingdoms and empires had endured, sometimes for centuries, under the rule of monarchs and emperors. But **republics**, governments ruled by representatives of the people, without exception had eventually died. Madison wanted to know how a people could create a republic that lasted—one that could avoid being taken over by a small group of men or descending into civil war or anarchy, one that was strong enough to govern effectively but would not trample the rights of its citizens.

In 1786, America was in a precarious position. In the tumultuous years that followed independence, the young nation had been plagued by economic disruption, European military and economic powers, and the dangers of rebellion within the thirteen states. The country needed a clear path forward if it were to survive. To Madison, that meant a plan for a new kind of government. It needed someone who could sell such a plan to a skeptical public, too.[1] Madison poured himself into these projects systematically, scientifically, and with a great deal of energy.

Though he was shy, often sick, and a quiet public speaker, Madison was well educated, and he did his homework. In 1786, as the American government of the time came under increasingly harsh criticism and calls to fix or replace it grew louder, Madison's years of preparation allowed him to help shape the agenda of the debates taking place in his newly independent country and to get others to talk about his ideas, whether they agreed with him or not. In the spring of 1787, Madison, true to form, showed up in Philadelphia having done his homework. Together with a group of similarly practical men, he attempted to create a republic that would last, one that would be strong enough to govern but not so strong as to trample on the rights and liberties of its citizens. Madison and others sought practical, institutional solutions for the seemingly timeless tendency of political leaders to pursue power, prestige, and riches even when this meant the downfall of their own republics. That Madison and his colleagues were pragmatic politicians was no surprise; most of them had already been involved in the real-world politics of their own colonies and, later, states. Writing in 1923, Robert Livingston Schuyler captured this essential fact about those who shaped the new American Republic better than anyone since. "The Fathers," he declared, "were practical men."[2] Ideas and ideals are certainly part of America's constitutional heritage but so are politics.

Madison's immediate concern in 1786 was to prepare for a conference set to take place in Annapolis, Maryland, in the fall. Officially, the Annapolis convention had

been called to address trade and navigation disputes between states. Unofficially,
at least in the minds of Madison and those
who shared his views, the hope was that
the outcome of the convention might lead
to significant changes in the fundamental
structure of the government of the United
States. Though Madison wanted to see
major reforms, he was not optimistic about
the prospect for real change. His lack of optimism turned out to be well founded. Only
five of the thirteen states sent representatives
to the convention; the other states either did
not appoint anyone or did not do so in time
to make it to the meeting. Despite the poor
attendance, however, delegates to the convention kept the dialogue of reform moving
by calling for a convention in Philadelphia
the following spring to discuss how to make
the American government more effective
in dealing with issues of trade and other
pressing needs of the nation. Madison's
research, preparation, intellect, and understated political skill were important factors
in the creation of the Constitution of the
United States. The American Republic

An engraving of James Madison, American statesman and
political theorist, is shown here. His study of republics led him to
investigate how to create a form of people-led government that
was capable of enduring.
Ipsumpix/Corbis via Getty Images

that he helped shape was based on the premise that liberty is something with which
people are born, something that cannot be given or taken away by governments. This
concept was expressed powerfully in the Declaration of Independence in its timeless
affirmation: "We hold these truths to be self-evident, that all men are created equal."
As we have explored in Chapter 1, however, this American liberty was not originally
meant for all.

Like Jefferson and George Washington—the most respected person in America
during this period—Madison owned enslaved people. Though his own writings show
that Madison struggled personally against the institution of slavery and that he realized how the practice had corrupted past republics, Madison's Virginia plantation had
more than one hundred enslaved people. Under Virginia's laws of the time, Madison,
or any other owner, could "correct" an enslaved person for any offense. If that person
died under such a correction, the enslaver would likely not be punished at all. He could
take a child from their family and sell the child into an unknown future for profit.[3] As
the delegates convened in Philadelphia, they had to struggle with these contradictions.

The Confederal System Makes Coordination between the States Difficult

> **2.2** Explain the challenges faced by the nation following the American Revolution in trying to form a government strong enough to rule effectively but not so strong as to oppress the rights of Americans.

The government that Madison and his like-minded colleagues hoped to change was the first government of the United States. It was a confederation: a union of thirteen sovereign states in which the states, not the union, were supreme. It had been created by the **Articles of Confederation and Perpetual Union**, which had been adopted by the Second Continental Congress in 1777 and formally ratified in 1781. While they had successfully guided the country through war and the accompanying economic and material devastation, the Articles had few carrots or sticks to make member states work together to make and carry out national policy. By 1786 the American confederation was showing its limitations—at least in the minds of those who wanted a stronger union.

The Articles of Confederation Attempt to Unite the States While Preserving Their Authority

When they created the Articles of Confederation, the delegates to the Second Continental Congress had debated two related issues. Both involved mistrust. Colonists in one state did not always trust the motives of the governments of the other states. They also did not trust any government that would rule over them from far away, whether it be that of Great Britain before the war or of the new American nation after victory had been achieved.

Though it may be difficult now to imagine a United States in which states were strong and the nation was weak, the idea that the states were the real centers of power was not at all unnatural for Americans at the time. Long after the Constitution was ratified, many Americans still referred to "these United States" instead of "the United States." Since their inception as business enterprises, plantations, or religious communities, the British colonies had been self-sufficient and left alone to govern themselves. Colonists often viewed members of other colonies with distrust. They also reacted strongly against Britain's tardy attempt to create a more centralized colonial policy in the decades before the American Revolution.[4]

During the debates over the Articles of Confederation, mistrust of other colonies crystallized in conflicts over land, representation, and sovereignty. Some colonies had land claims on parts of other colonies. Small coastal colonies, such as Delaware and Rhode Island, whose size was fixed by their location, viewed the western states' claims on Native American land with worry and suspicion. How big would Virginia, whose charter had land claims extending to the "South Sea," eventually become?[5] "The most acrimonious disagreements," according to one historian, "were over control of western lands."[6] The views of the indigenous peoples on questions of ownership did not factor into these calculations.

Under the Confederal System, States Have Sovereignty and Equal Representation

Leading up to the Revolutionary War, the relationship between the colonies and Great Britain was one of mutual lack of understanding and lack of trust. The colonies failed to see how they played a part in Britain's role in global politics and struggles against other empires. For its part, Great Britain failed to understand that what had been plantations, business enterprises, and religious outposts "had grown up and become states in the making."[7] This did not, however, mean naturally united colonies or, later, naturally united states. Each state had its own interests, and each worried that it might lose control over its future to other states or to a national government with its own agendas and desires.

In the face of the prospect of large, populous, and ever-growing neighbors, smaller states demanded, and received, equal representation in the new government. (See Figure 2.1.) Each state had one vote in the new Congress. This Confederation Congress was unicameral, meaning it had only one chamber. States selected their representatives to the legislature and could choose the number of representatives that they sent, though each state's delegation had to agree on these decisions, and each state received only one vote. Finally, states—not the new union—would be sovereign, possessing ultimate political authority in almost all areas of policy, a right that was firmly established in the document.[8]

The Confederal Government Is Designed to Be Weak

The confederal government under the Articles of Confederation was intentionally made to be weak. With the Revolutionary War ongoing, colonists were still experiencing the tyranny of British rule, and they did not want to re-create it in a new American version. The confederal government could not tax its citizens, and it could not force states to carry out its policies. States could recall their representatives at will, and limits were placed on how long a representative could serve.[9] There was no independent judicial branch; a national court existed primarily to resolve differences between states but had no real way of enforcing these decisions. The president of the Confederation Congress was even less powerful than the delegates and was there mostly to keep order and count votes.

The confederal government did have certain powers. Only it could declare war and conduct foreign policy, though it had to rely on states to pay for these activities. In practice, the confederal government continually faced the challenge of getting states to contribute to the national effort. Lack of money was a constant problem, and the Continental Army was continually without adequate supplies and occasionally faced starvation.

FIGURE 2.1

The Original Thirteen Colonies and the Western Territories

These two maps show the original thirteen British colonies in 1775 and the American states and territories in 1790. Note the vast areas of land bordered by powerful states such as Virginia. Smaller coastal states feared the growth in size and power of these larger states.

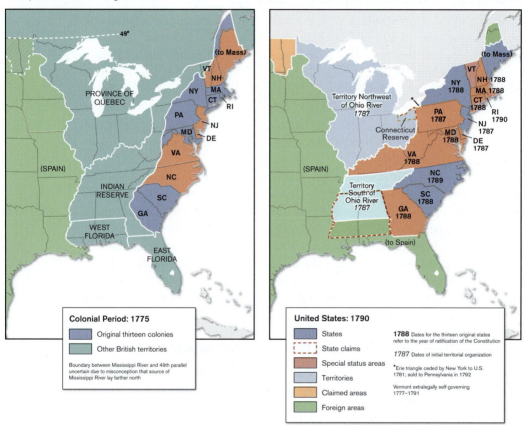

The Prospect of Changes to the Systems of Slavery and Representation Sow Unrest

To ensure that the agreements made during their creation would hold, the Articles of Confederation placed a tall hurdle in the path of potential reformers: changing or amending the articles required the approval of all thirteen of the states. In spite of what many saw as problems with the Articles, many Americans did not want to amend, much less replace, them.

Some in the southern states feared that slavery, which was allowed and unregulated under the confederal government, might be restricted or outlawed. Citizens of smaller states feared losing their equal representation in Congress and seeing it replaced by representation based on population, a change that would drastically weaken their position. And many worried that something worse than the problems with the Articles might come out of a process of revising them. When a small group of people takes it upon themselves to overturn a political order, there is no guarantee that what they create will not be worse—maybe much worse—than what came before.

Politicians in many states were still mistrustful of the actions and motives of their counterparts in other states. Many were also still nervous about the idea of a strong national government. But in the years since the American Revolution, the political landscape had altered, and the balance of political power had shifted.[10] State legislative elections in 1786 and 1787 handed strong victories to nationalist candidates, who were in favor of a stronger national government. These nationalist-controlled legislatures would be selecting the delegates to the Philadelphia convention.

Fears of Unrest and Rebellion Worry State Governments

Shays' Rebellion, named after Daniel Shays, one of its military leaders, was a grass-roots popular uprising against the Massachusetts state government—one that, in the minds of many of its citizens, had grown too powerful, too distant, too much like that of Great Britain. Though the rebellion took place in Massachusetts, the conditions that caused it and the popular anger that fueled it were also present in other states. This crisis added to the sense of urgency in the American confederation, and it provided ammunition to those who wanted to replace the structure of government under the Articles.

The roots of Shays' Rebellion were both economic and political. In the difficult economic times that followed the Revolutionary War, there was a shortage of "hard money," of gold and silver and money backed by gold and silver. What there was no shortage of was debt. Citizens and governments throughout the confederation found themselves unable to pay debts that had been incurred during the war or during the tough economic times that followed. Shopkeepers and cash-strapped state governments alike demanded that their customers and citizens pay debts and taxes in hard currency. Foreclosures—the taking of property to pay outstanding debts backed by that property—were widespread.

The first responses of citizens in Massachusetts and other states were political. Towns asked state governments to issue paper money to help citizens settle their debts. The government of Massachusetts held the line, siding with the banking interests. Many of the state's citizens began to feel that they had successfully broken with an oppressive government in London only to replace it with one nearly as bad in Boston. When their attempts at political solutions failed, citizens—especially in the western part of the state—began to take the kind of action they had against King George III and the British Parliament. They rebelled.

Rebellion Begins

To each other, the members of Shays' Rebellion were *Regulators*, a label used by the American rebels in the struggle against Great Britain.[11] Many were Revolutionary

War veterans with sufficient military skills and popular support to provide a genuine challenge to the Massachusetts government. The Regulators organized themselves by town and family, and they made a point of trying not to antagonize the local population. Instead, they focused on the courts, as had been done before the Revolution, closing them down in the hopes of stalling the foreclosure process until a solution to the debt crisis could be achieved in the state legislature. Although many closures were committed by rebels carrying weapons, some of them "were peaceful, even jocular."[12]

The rebellion and Massachusetts's response to it began to follow a script similar to that of the American Revolution. Citizens took action. The government (this time of Massachusetts, not Great Britain) clamped down, which only made the population more radical. In October 1786, the Massachusetts legislature passed the Riot Act, which granted sheriffs and other officials immunity from prosecution for killing rioters. With fears of standing armies fresh in the minds of its members, the resistance grew and became more radical, though never as radical as it was portrayed in the Boston newspapers, which accused the Regulators of wanting to redistribute private property[13] or hoping to reunite with Great Britain.[14] Both claims were untrue but served to increase the level of fear and concern within and beyond the state's borders.

The Massachusetts state militia was unable to put down the rebellion. Many militia members, themselves Revolutionary War veterans, sided with the rebels. The government of the United States, the Confederation Congress, could not raise an army; its requests to the states for money were refused by every state except Virginia. The wealthy elites in Boston ultimately paid for an army on their own, loaning money to Massachusetts for the purposes of suppressing the rebellion.

Daniel Shays, a former captain in the Revolutionary War, joined the Regulators later than many but became a commander of its largest regiment, partly due to his notable service in the war. In January 1787, Shays' regiment and two others moved on the state armory at Springfield. Major General William Shepard, commanding the newly raised state militia and in possession of artillery that the Regulators lacked, defeated Shays and the rebels, who were forced to withdraw. Two rebel leaders were hanged, and most of the other rebels eventually returned to their farms and towns. Shays escaped to Vermont and was later pardoned, though he never returned to Massachusetts. With the help of the Boston newspapers, Daniel Shays became the personification of anarchy in the United States. In reality, most of the Regulators wanted only to keep their farms and keep their family and friends out of foreclosure or debtors' jail.

From Shays' Rebellion Comes New Opportunity

After the Revolutionary War, George Washington had, as promised, stayed away from public life and retired to his slaveholding plantation in Mount Vernon. But upon receiving what turned out to be exaggerated reports of the strength of Shays' militia

An engraving depicts the British colonial governor of North Carolina (center) suppressing a Regulators' revolt in 1771. Daniel Shays and other members of the rebellion in Massachusetts patterned their protests against the state government on the actions of the Revolutionary War Regulators.

The Granger Collection, New York

from one of his most trusted former generals, Washington grew fearful of what would become of the country. In a letter to James Madison in November 1786, Washington identified precisely what was needed to "check . . . these disorders": a strong and "energetic Constitution."[15]

Madison may have sensed that Shays' Rebellion would be enough to lure Washington out of retirement and place his unequaled status among Americans behind the effort to create a new political order. Though initially reluctant to attend the Philadelphia conference, Washington eventually agreed; the Philadelphia convention would have the most famous and respected American there to give it legitimacy.[16]

Delegates Reach a Compromise at the Constitutional Convention

2.3   Describe the role that compromise over states' interests played in shaping the government during the Constitutional Convention.

In May 1787, fifty-five delegates from twelve of the thirteen states began to arrive in Philadelphia. Rhode Island had refused to participate. Though it was by some reports a hot, humid summer, the windows of the Pennsylvania State House where delegates met were shut to ensure secrecy. This secrecy was partly to allow the delegates to say what they wanted, partly because none were sure how citizens in the various states would react to their deliberations. At the time, the meeting was called the Grand Convention or the Federal Convention, not the **Constitutional Convention** as it is called today. The delegates had not been sent to Philadelphia to write a new constitution—only to fix the Articles of Confederation as necessary. Writing a new constitution might have been thought of as a revolutionary act, which it was.

James Madison arrived eleven days early with his research in hand. Though he would become perhaps the most influential person at the convention, Madison was not the only delegate who shaped the final document. Other delegates also guided and shaped the debates and outcomes. Alexander Hamilton, who had served as Washington's aide in the war, emerged as one of the leading proponents of a strong national government. James Wilson of Pennsylvania made important, often unheralded, intellectual contributions to the convention. Wilson served as an intellectual ally of Madison's during and after the convention.

Many important leaders from the Revolution could not or would not attend. Thomas Jefferson and John Adams, both future presidents and supporters of the Constitution, were out of the country in service of the American government. Others, like Samuel Adams and Patrick Henry, both vocal revolutionaries and opponents of a national constitution, were not selected as delegates or refused to go, sensing that the delegates planned to do much more than merely revise the Articles of Confederation. Their suspicions were correct. Patrick Henry became one of the most effective opponents to the document once it had been submitted to the states. "Here is a revolution as radical as that which separated us from Great Britain," he wrote.[17]

The delegates who assembled in Philadelphia certainly did not represent a snapshot of the people living in the thirteen states. All were men. Most were well educated. None were enslaved people, former enslaved people, or Native Americans. Roughly one-third were enslavers. Not all were wealthy, but they were all elites. Unlike the revolutionaries who would soon lead France into chaos in the name of democracy, however, most of the Founders of the American Republic had previous practical political experience to guide them and temper their revolutionary ideals—Madison included. Many looked to the various state constitutions for lessons on how, or how not, to balance the need for stable effective constitutional government against the dangers of creating a constitutional tyranny.

Pennsylvania's state constitution was the most democratic. All real power rested in a unicameral legislature whose legislators served one-year terms. To many elites, the Pennsylvania constitution represented nothing more than institutionalized mob rule,[18] sometimes at the expense of religious minorities. Massachusetts's constitution was much less democratic, with a much more powerful governor and property requirements to serve in the government. To the Regulators and those who sympathized with them, Massachusetts had replaced Great Britain's royal aristocracy with Boston's constitutional aristocracy. The solutions that the delegates came up with were pragmatic, political, and strategic, for better and for worse.

Delegates Debate Forms of Representation and the Powers of the National Government

By Friday, May 25, 1787, enough delegates had made it over the muddy Pennsylvania roads to begin the deliberations. Their first order of business was to unanimously select Washington as president of the convention. Madison, though not selected as the official reporter for the convention, took a seat up front and assumed the role informally. The other delegates were agreeable to this and made sure he got copies of their speeches to be entered into this unofficial record.[19] Much of what we know about what happened in Philadelphia comes from his notes.

The delegates adopted a set of rules to guide themselves, calling for absolute secrecy about their deliberations.[20] They knew that the enormous task of coming to an agreement would be made more difficult if the details of their discussions were leaked. It was said that a member of the convention was assigned to attend dinners with Franklin, who was fond of alcoholic beverages, to change the conversation if Franklin began to talk too loosely.[21] The delegates agreed not to record their individual votes so that they would not feel bound by previous votes if the same issues came up again, giving themselves the ability to compromise and change their positions as needed.

As the proceedings began, the Delaware delegation put the issue of how states were to be represented in the new government on the table—the most contentious issue of the convention and the one that determined so many other outcomes. No other question so dominated the convention during the early weeks and months of deliberations or threatened to tear it apart. How would states be represented

George Washington presiding at the Constitutional Convention at Philadelphia in 1787. Considerable measures were taken to ensure the secrecy of the proceedings at the convention.

The Granger Collection, New York

in a new government? Would it be the same one state, one vote formula as under the Articles of Confederation? Or would states be represented on the basis of their population or wealth?

The Virginia Plan Outlines a System of Proportional Representation for the States

On the third day of the convention, the delegation from Virginia presented a set of proposals for the rest of the members to consider. The ideas behind what came to be known as the **Virginia Plan** were James Madison's. Madison had been building their foundations for more than a year and had coached the rest of the Virginia delegation in the days before their presentation. The Virginia Plan was much more than a modification of the Articles of Confederation. Its proposals described a new, national form of government, although Madison and his allies used the less controversial word *federal* when presenting and defending it.

The Virginia Plan laid out the failures of the American confederation—weakness in national defense and the conduct of foreign policy, conflicts between states, and the failure to suppress internal rebellion—and presented an answer to those defects: The national government would be strong. Its constitution would be "paramount to the state constitutions."[22] It would consist of three branches: a legislative branch to make laws, an executive branch to carry out the laws, and a judicial branch to resolve disputes between the states and between the national government and the states. The national legislature would be bicameral, consisting of two houses. Members of the lower house would be elected directly by the people. The upper house would consist of representatives nominated by state legislatures and chosen by members of the lower house. The executive and some members of the judiciary would have the power to veto—or overturn—acts of the legislature, which could, in turn, override that veto. The supremacy of the national government would be unmistakable. It could make laws as needed to govern the country as a whole and use military force against states if necessary.

Many details were vague or literally left blank, such as the length of terms of members of Congress, the frequency of elections, and the number of votes needed to override a veto. The change in representation of states, however, was clear. The Virginia Plan proposed to overturn the one state, one vote structure of the Articles of Confederation. Instead there would be a system of proportional representation in which more populous states would have more members in both houses of the legislature. The answer to the question "Proportional to what?" was left somewhat vague, however: Would population counts include slaves? The Virginia Plan was not clear.

Delegates from smaller states reacted immediately and strongly to the Virginia Plan's suggestion of proportional representation. They had successfully fought it off in the Second Continental Congress, when the Articles were drafted, and they continued to fight against it. If state representation were to be based on population totals, a delegate from New Jersey warned, Virginia would have sixteen votes to South

Carolina's one, plus all there knew that Virginia's boundaries were far from settled.[23] They seemed limitless. New Jersey's William Paterson vowed never to approve the plan, saying that New Jersey "would be swallowed up."[24]

For the next two weeks, however, the convention discussed the Virginia Plan and little else. Within days of its introduction, several provisions of the plan—a government of three branches and a bicameral legislature—had already been approved. Madison and his fellow nationalists had won the first victory in the strategic political struggle over the Constitution. They had set the agenda. They had forced the opposition to respond to their ideas.

The New Jersey Plan Maintains Equal Votes in the Legislature

Two weeks later, Paterson presented the small states' response to the Virginia Plan. Known as the **New Jersey Plan**, it proposed to strengthen the power of the confederal government but make relatively few changes to the Articles of Confederation. There would be only one house in the legislature, just as under the Articles. Each state delegation (chosen by state legislatures) would still get one equal vote in that legislature. That legislature would get new powers, mostly over taxation and the economy, though it would still depend on the states for some revenue. The executive and judicial branches were much less well envisioned than under the Virginia Plan. Paterson correctly argued that his state's plan was consistent with the purpose of the meeting in Philadelphia; the original mandate of the convention had included only making some changes to the Articles. However, delegates had already been debating almost nothing except the Virginia Plan, the framework of which centered on a strong national government and provisions that would essentially replace the current form of government.

After Paterson had presented his plan, Madison proceeded to "tear the New Jersey plan to pieces."[25] Madison argued that the New Jersey Plan would leave the nation with all the problems that had motivated the convention in the first place: Tax collection across state borders would remain a disaster. Rebellions such as the one Massachusetts had just barely put down would continue to plague the Republic.[26]

Madison and James Wilson grew frustrated over the less populous states' objections to the Virginia Plan. To these two men, neither the states nor the national government were or should be supreme; the people were supreme to both. How their numbers were apportioned was beside the point. To allow equal representation in Congress for states would allow the political divisions between and within states to infect national politics. Delegates from smaller states did not see it this way. To them, equal representation was not open for negotiation; it was essential to their sovereignty. At one point, Gunning Bedford from Delaware threatened that the small states might have to break off, form their own union, and possibly even ally with a foreign power.[27] This was, in modern political terms, the "nuclear option" for the small states. There would be no going back if it were used. All knew it was a possibility, even if unlikely, but to have the idea raised so boldly and so publicly shocked the convention and high-lighted for all present the stakes with which they were playing and the possible consequences should they fail to reach an agreement.

The Great Compromise Calls for a Bicameral Legislature with Different Methods of Representation in Each Chamber

With the issue of how states would be represented threatening to break apart the convention, the question was sent to a committee. While the young nation celebrated the Fourth of July, delegates to the convention were unsure if their work would succeed, or even continue. The stakes were very high. Elbridge Gerry of Massachusetts warned, "If we do nothing, it appears we must have war and confusion."[28] On July 5, the committee responded with a proposal to give something to each side. The new national legislature would be bicameral; it would have two chambers. Representation in the lower house would follow the Virginia Plan, and representation in the upper house would follow the New Jersey Plan. Compromise having been put on the table, the mood of the convention began to shift. Bedford of Delaware—who had threatened that small states might seek an alliance with a foreign power—insisted that he had been misunderstood.[29]

On July 16, by a 5–4 vote, the delegates agreed to what would be called the **Great Compromise**.[30] Under this agreement, much like the committee's recommendations, the national legislature would be bicameral. States would be represented in the House of Representatives according to their populations. The people would directly elect these representatives. States would be represented equally in the upper chamber, the Senate. Two senators would be chosen from each state by their state legislatures. Not all of the small-state delegates were satisfied with the agreement; two left in protest. But the rest felt that having the Senate was protection enough, and they became much more cooperative in the weeks that followed. Delaware, for all its threats and opposition early in the convention, was the first state to later ratify the Constitution, which was being hammered out in Philadelphia. (See Table 2.1.)

That the question of representation in Congress was settled first is important as this shaped the political strategies of the delegates going forward. Having secured equal representation in the Senate, small states offered less opposition to a strong national government. They were now less afraid of Congress, even seeing it as a defense against the power of their larger neighbors. Madison, who had wanted popular representation in both houses, began to push to strengthen the other two branches to act as a counter to the Congress that he had proposed but now mistrusted due to the equal state representation in the Senate.[31] The Constitution did not fall out of the sky. It was the result of compromise. But it was also the result of adaptation to earlier compromises and to changes in the political landscape in which the delegates pursued their goals and those of the states that they had been chosen to represent.

Legislative Structures under the Virginia Plan, New Jersey Plan, and Great Compromise

Structure of Legislature	Virginia Plan	New Jersey Plan	Great Compromise
	Bicameral (two chamber)	Unicameral (single chamber)	Bicameral (two chamber)
Apportionment	**Lower House** • Number of seats apportioned by state population • Members directly elected by citizens	**Legislature** • Equal representation for states regardless of state population • Members appointed by the states	**House of Representatives** • States represented according to population • Members directly elected by citizens
	Upper House • Number of seats apportioned by state population • Members elected by lower house (from list supplied by state legislatures)		**Senate** • States represented equally (two senators per state) • Members appointed by state legislatures
Powers	• Legislature has strong powers to enforce national policy	• Legislature has similar power as under the Articles of Confederation but can also levy taxes and regulate commerce	• Legislature has broad powers over commerce and the ability to make laws as necessary • House of Representatives has power to levy taxes

Delegates Work Out Details of the New Government

2.4 Identify the institutions of government established by the Constitution and the distribution of political power among them.

With the bicameral legislature having resolved the first and largest issue of the convention—the distribution of representation among the states—the convention moved on to the structure of the rest of the government and the specific powers of each branch. In doing so, it confronted the second major issue of the convention: the question of national power. Many of the details of the new government were worked out in committees over the rest of the summer and then presented to the full convention for approval.

The Legislative Branch Is Made the Most Powerful

While representation in Congress had been settled, its powers still had to be worked out. To do so, delegates looked to the powers of the Confederation Congress under the Articles of Confederation as well as to state legislatures under the various state constitutions. As the **legislative branch** of government, Congress's purpose was to legislate—to make laws. Both houses had to work together to pass laws, but because of how congressional members were chosen, each house had a slightly different purpose. Members of the House of Representatives, who were elected directly by the people and had to run for reelection every two years, were meant to be more responsive to the people, to directly represent their constituents. Senators, who were chosen by state legislatures and served six-year terms, were there to check the passions of the people. Senators' terms were staggered in two-year shifts so that only about one-third of senators would be up for reelection in any given election year, making it more difficult for any swift change in mood among citizens to quickly affect national policy.

Congress, as expected, was made more powerful than the unicameral legislature under the Articles of Confederation, especially with regard to issues of money and the economy. Congress was given the power to borrow money, collect taxes, and "regulate Commerce with foreign Nations, and among the several states." To preserve its flexibility, Congress was also given the ability "to make all Laws which shall be necessary and proper for carrying into Execution the foregoing Powers, and all the other Powers vested by this Constitution in the Government of the United States." The necessary and proper clause, combined with the commerce clause, paved the way for a dramatic expansion in Congress's power over national policy in the centuries following ratification.

The Executive Branch Puts the Laws into Effect

Neither the Virginia nor the New Jersey Plan had been very specific about the **executive branch** of government. Madison had not given it as much thought as he had Congress—at least until he decided he needed to build in more protections against equal state representation in the Senate. Initially there was not even a consensus over how many chief executives the country should have, much less over how powerful the branch should be. Alexander Hamilton, young, ambitious, self-made, and not trusted by many delegates, proposed a powerful president who would be elected for life. His plan made the Virginia Plan look moderate. Though it was not voted on, Hamilton's suggestion of an "American king"[32] followed him for the rest of his political career. Most delegates expected Washington would serve as an, if not *the*, executive of the country. Some wrote that confidence in Washington reduced anxiety about how powerful the executive would become.

In the end, the delegates settled on a single executive—a president—who would serve for four-year terms. As head of the executive branch, the president was there to execute, or carry out, the laws that had been passed by Congress. The president was given some, but not unlimited, power over Congress with the ability to veto a piece of legislation that Congress had passed. Congress could, however, override the veto with a two-thirds vote in each of the two houses. The president was named commander in chief of the army and navy. Again, though, power was to be shared. Congress, not the president, was given the power to declare (and raise money for) war. Presidents were given power to oversee the people working in the executive branch and to obtain from them the information needed to govern the country, which has led to the growth of a large and influential federal bureaucracy. Finally, the president was given the power to make foreign policy, though, again, this responsibility was to be shared with the Senate.

More controversial than what powers the executive would have was how the president would be elected, raising once again the question of how states would be represented in the new government. In the end, delegates settled on a complicated compromise for electing the president—one that is still not fully understood by many Americans. Citizens would not vote directly for the president. Instead, an Electoral College consisting of electors awarded to states based on their representation in Congress would select the president. Each state received two electors (for their senators) plus one each for their members of the House of Representatives. Each state would decide how its electors were to be chosen, and successful candidates would need to win the votes of a majority of electors to become president. The system of the Electoral College continues to incite criticism and suggestions for reform. In the minds of the delegates, however, the complicated structure managed to avoid reigniting the disagreements between small and large states over representation.

The Judiciary Is Designed to Interpret Constitutional Conflicts

The Virginia and New Jersey Plans were even less specific about the **judicial branch** of the government, the system of federal courts. Delegates decided on one Supreme Court to be the highest in the land and a system of lower federal courts whose structure and composition would be determined by Congress. Unlike the judiciary under the Articles, the federal courts would have jurisdiction—the authority to hear and decide cases—over all disputes between states and the national government, between two or more states, and between citizens of different states. Combined with the supremacy clause of the Constitution, which declared that national treaties and laws "shall be the supreme law of the Land," the federal court emerged as superior to state courts.

Not included in the Constitution was an explicit description of the power of judicial review, which gives the judicial branch of government the authority to determine if a law, part of a law, or an act of government is or is not in violation of the highest law of the land and, if it *is* in conflict, declare it thus invalid. In the United States, that supreme law is the Constitution, and the power of judicial review rests ultimately with the U.S. Supreme Court. While state supreme courts may exercise judicial review on state laws and actions, the supremacy clause of the Constitution ensures that the exercise of judicial review by the Supreme Court includes the authority to use that power over both national and state laws and actions.

In exercising this power, the Supreme Court does not claim to be above the executive or legislative branch. Instead, the Constitution and the people are above all three branches, and it is the role of the Court to act as the interpreter of conflict between the Constitution and governmental action. As with the other two branches, the judiciary was not to exist in isolation. Congress, not the Supreme Court, had the authority to create the lower federal courts. Congress would determine the number of Supreme Court justices, and the Senate had the power to confirm justices (with a majority vote), who first had to be nominated by the president.

Separation of Powers Allows for Checks and Balances on Government

In drawing up the powers of each of the three branches, the delegates tried to make sure that no one branch could become too powerful on its own. The idea of **separation of powers** was widely supported by delegates at the convention and well known to those who had studied the writings of Baron de Montesquieu. Under this system, branches are not meant to preside over their own spheres. Rather, a system of "separated institutions sharing power" was created.[33] Each branch, whose members tended to represent a different group of people, has to work with the other branches to make things happen, though not on every issue all the time (see Table 2.2). This was the central blueprint around which the national government was structured. Popularly known as the system of checks and balances, the idea of overlapping (but not perfectly overlapping) spheres of influence also applies to relations between the states and the federal government. Federalism, or the sharing of power over some aspects of governance between the states and the nation, is as central to American government as checks and balances, and it has been the source of much conflict and controversy throughout its history.

Delegates Address the "Unfinished Parts" but Leave the Problem of Slavery Behind

At the beginning of September 1787, the Committee on Unfinished Parts[34] reported back to the convention on its efforts to address issues that had been left unresolved. Not all of these issues were ironed out, and the question of slavery threatened to break up the proceedings.

In an attempt to clear up commercial relationships between states, the delegates decided that "full faith and credit shall be given in each State to the public Acts, Records, and judicial Proceedings of every other State." The full faith and credit clause was designed to ensure that each state recognized contracts and other legal proceedings from other states. It has become an important constitutional element in the question of same-sex marriage and marriage equality in the United States (see Chapter 4). The structure of the Electoral College was finalized, as was the office of

Separated Institutions Sharing Powers

	INSTITUTIONS		
	Executive Branch	Legislative Branch	Judicial Branch
Lawmaking Authority	• Executes laws • Has veto power • Nominates judges to the federal judiciary and key executive branch officials • Shapes legislative agenda	• Writes nation's laws • Has veto override • Senate confirms judicial nominees and key executive branch officials • Determines number of Supreme Court justices • Creates lower courts	• Interprets contested laws • Can declare both federal and state laws unconstitutional* *(Formally established in later Supreme Court decisions)
National Security and Foreign Policy Responsibilities	• President acts as commander in chief of the military • Sets foreign policy agenda	• Declares war • Senate ratifies treaties with other nations	
Oversight Responsibilities	• Oversees federal bureaucracy	• Holds power of impeachment • Holds budgetary authority and power of oversight over executive branch agencies	• May declare laws or executive branch actions in conflict with the Constitution* • *(Formally established in later Supreme Court decisions)
Sovereignty	Sovereignty rests with the people. The Constitution is the supreme law of the nation.		

vice president of the United States, whose constitutional powers are quite limited but who plays an important role in presidential elections.

In important ways, however, the Constitution remained unfinished even after the delegates completed their deliberations in September. This was partly by design, partly due to political compromises made during the convention itself. By making provisions for changing the Constitution through a process of **amendment**, the Framers acknowledged that it would always be unfinished, that it would need to be adaptable if it were to endure. By *adaptable*, however, the delegates did not mean easily changed. They purposefully designed a system for amending the Constitution that made this very difficult to achieve. Once again, divisions over representation of states emerged, with small states arguing that states should have the power to approve amendments and the nationalists arguing that it should be left to the people to decide.

In the end, another complicated compromise emerged, with both the people—through official proposal in Congress—and the states—through the process of final ratification—being necessary to alter the Constitution. Amending the document is a two-stage process, with two possible routes to completion of each of the two stages needed for amendment. First, the amendment has to be officially proposed, which involves much more than someone just suggesting an idea. Proposal can happen in one of two ways, only the first of which has ever been used: (1) passage by a two-thirds vote in both the House and the Senate or (2) passage in a national convention called at the request of two-thirds of the states. After formal proposal, the proposed amendment must be ratified by one of two ways: (1) by a majority vote in three-fourths of the state legislatures or (2) acceptance by ratifying conventions in three-fourths of the states. The second method for ratification has been used only once.

Of the thousands of suggestions for amending the Constitution presented in Congress since its founding, only twenty-seven amendments have been formally ratified. The first ten of these, which make up the Bill of Rights, became part of the debate over ratification itself and are often thought of as part of the "original" Constitution. Two others—an amendment prohibiting the sale and consumption of alcoholic beverages and one repealing that prohibition—canceled each other out. Since the passage of the Bill of Rights, therefore, the Constitution has had only fifteen lasting changes. Though the Constitution has rarely been amended, some scholars argue that important decisions by the Supreme Court and major changes in how the American people view themselves have at critical times in history led to changes in government just as significant as formal amendments.[35]

The Founders Reach a Fateful Compromise on Slavery. At the time of the convention, nearly one out of every six individuals living in the thirteen states was enslaved. Most, but not all, lived in the southern states. Southern plantation owners, many of whom were politically powerful in their state legislatures and some of whom were delegates to the Philadelphia convention, had no intention of seeing their institution outlawed or heavily regulated. Plantation owners were not the only interests who benefited from slavery. The slave trade and the trade in goods they produced some powerful shipping interests as well, especially in the Northeast. About one-third of the delegates to the convention, including Madison and Washington, enslaved peoples. A few others, however, saw the preservation of slavery as a moral failure and spoke out at the convention about the hypocrisy of trying to preserve liberty in a document that allowed slavery.

In spite of a few speeches on the floor of the convention, however, the question of slavery was not generally debated in terms of morality or of liberty but rather in terms of states' representation, the same issue that affected so many others at the convention: Would enslaved peoples count when it came time to tally a state's population? In the end, the question of slavery was settled on practical, political considerations.

The final document dealt with slavery in three ways. The word *slavery* never appears—a minor tactical victory for those who did not want the Constitution to appear

SLAVERY, POPULATION, AND THE BALANCE OF POWER BETWEEN SOUTHERN AND NORTHERN STATES

Basic to the use of data in political science is the idea of *counting*. It is far more consequential than it may sound at first. Counting is not a neutral thing. By assigning numbers to individuals or their actions, those who use numerical data to study political processes and outcomes can draw systematic conclusions about them.

However, how we count people is also a political act, one with profound consequences. Today, for example, there is a strong debate about how we should count Americans in the national census conducted every ten years. Are the racial and ethnic categories used in the census forms sufficiently reflective of our diversity or of any one individual's identity?

▼ FIGURE 2-A

Percentage of Slave Population by State

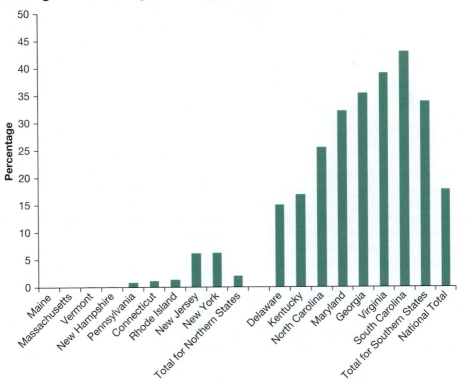

Source: Data from U.S. Census Bureau, https://www.census.gov/library/publications/1793/dec/number-of-persons.html

Free and Slave Population Totals by State

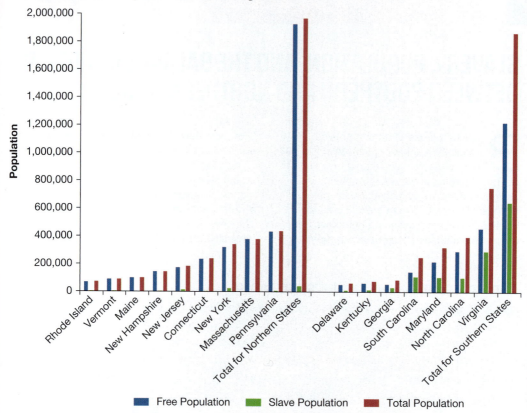

Source: Data from U.S. Census Bureau, https://www.census.gov/library/publications/1793/dec/number-of-persons.html (accessed August 15, 2016).

What about counting undocumented Americans? Doing so may help us better understand our changing population; however, asking individuals to reveal their undocumented status may put them at risk of deportation. Fear of deportation may lead some to avoid being counted at all.

One of the most important divisions between the states during the Constitutional Convention was on the issue of slavery. It was a moral issue to be sure, but how slavery was handled during the proceedings, as all delegates knew, would have serious implications for the balance of political power in the federal government,

especially in the House of Representatives. While states would be equally represented in the Senate, their representation in the House would depend upon their population. Did that population include slaves?

Figure 2.2-A shows the percentage of each state's population that was enslaved in 1790, three years after the drafting of the Constitution. The divisions between northern and southern states are striking. What might this mean for representation in the House?

Figure 2.2-B presents the same data, but it does so in a way that breaks down the population—free, slave, and total—of each state and the two regions. Note the red bars, which represent the total population of the states and regions. Looked at this way, the balance of population between the northern and southern states is roughly equal, with just under two million individuals in each region. However, when one separates out the enslaved population (the green bars), the northern states have a population advantage of more than six hundred thousand people (the dark blue bars). It was this math that drove much of the bargaining over slavery and representation in the convention.

....

WHaT Do You Think?

What information does Figure 2.2-B convey that Figure 2.2-A does not? Have you encountered different charts and tables that present the same or similar data in different ways, thus allowing you to draw different conclusions?

to approve of it. On the question of slavery and representation in Congress, the **Three-Fifths Compromise** ensured that an enslaved person—called an "other person" in the Constitution—would count as three-fifths of a person for a state's representation.[36] Enslaved persons could not vote or be represented, but their numbers would boost the influence of the slave states in which they were held; since enslaved peoples were counted among the population, slaveholding states would be allotted more members of Congress. In a second facet of the compromise, Congress would not be allowed to restrict the slave trade until 1808 at the earliest. Third, enslaved peoples who had successfully escaped would have to be returned to their owners, regardless of the laws of individual states.

Historians and political scientists have debated how the delegates could have agreed to preserve slavery when some observed that it went against the very idea of natural rights upon which the Constitution is based and at a time when some states were beginning to restrict or outlaw it on their own. There are several reasons, and they are not mutually exclusive.

The first reason is that enslaved peoples had not voted for their state legislators. Some delegates did oppose slavery, but enslaved peoples had no direct representation in the Constitutional Convention. While enslaved peoples were not represented, enslavers were, and their delegates used the threat of leaving the convention to secure their interests. Had the southern states pulled out, the Articles of Confederation, which contained no restrictions on slavery, would have remained the law of the land. Politics during the convention also played a large role. The question of slavery had been handed to the Committee of Detail, chaired by John Rutledge of South Carolina. Rutledge's committee proposed to give the slave states everything they demanded. In his notes, Madison commented on the political implications of this slave-state delegate being in charge of the committee that would set the agenda for debate on the issue of slavery.

Others have argued that the preservation of slavery was the result of a **logroll**, or a trading of votes, between the slave states and the northeastern commercial states. Northeastern states received the strong commercial policy they wanted in return for protections on slavery for the southern states. Evidence from the records of the convention supports the idea of a logroll.

Regardless of the reasons, the question of slavery was temporarily handled but fundamentally unsettled. Not until the country was literally torn apart in the Civil War eighty years later would the issue of slavery ultimately be decided. It would take nearly another century and a great deal of sacrifice and strategic political activity to make equality for Black Americans a reality, or at least more of a reality, on the ground rather than just in words. Today, the question of whether Americans are all truly equal in the Republic endures.

James Madison Holds Contradictory Views on Slavery. Although his views on slavery evolved over time, James Madison was never able to completely resolve the contradictions inherent in a Constitution and government that, although based on natural rights and liberties, permitted slavery. Some of his writings dating from the time of the drafting of the Constitution indicate that he understood that enslaved peoples were considered, contradictorily, as both property and as humans with rights under law.[37] Later in his life, Madison wrote out a plan for ending slavery that involved a "gradual" emancipation. Compensation would be made to the enslaver for his "loss," the enslaved person would explicitly acknowledge preferring freedom to bondage, and all former enslaved peoples would be relocated to a region not "occupied by or allotted to a White population."[38]

Madison never did free his own slaves or provide for their freedom upon his death.

The Constitution Is Finished but Not Yet Made the Law of the Land. By proposing a system for amending the Constitution, the Framers ensured that it would always be unfinished so that it could adapt over time. More immediately, however, the Constitution was unfinished because the states had yet to approve it. The document that emerged from Philadelphia was just a proposal. It carried no force until the states chose to adopt it. That would be determined by the battle over ratification.

A skillful move by Benjamin Franklin at the convention's conclusion required only that delegates sign their names as witnesses to their state's endorsement, which allowed some delegates to sign the Constitution even knowing that they would soon speak out against it. Franklin's move, and the departure over the summer of delegates who did not approve of the outcomes, made the delegates appear to be in greater agreement than they really were. In fact, many did have strong reservations, and three refused to sign.

The delegates also used a bit of trickery to get around another issue. The Articles of Confederation stipulated that amendments to the Articles required the approval of the Confederation Congress and all thirteen state legislatures. This, members of the Constitutional Convention knew, was going to be very difficult. Rhode Island had refused to participate in the convention, and public opinion in many states was closely divided. So the delegates declared that the Constitution would become the law of the land if ratifying conventions in nine out of thirteen states approved it, bypassing Confederation Congress as well as the requirement for unanimous approval by the state legislatures. Even with this somewhat unconventional ploy—breaking the spirit if not the law of the Articles—it was still far from certain that the Constitution would be adopted.

Federalists and Anti-Federalists Argue over Ratification

> **2.5** Compare and contrast the arguments put forth by the Federalists and Anti-Federalists during the ratification debates.

The fight between those in favor of the Constitution and those opposed to it was America's first national—and first *negative*—political campaign. Both sides issued dire premonitions of what might happen if the Constitution was or was not ratified. The debate was carried out through the printing presses, which had become widespread enough to allow both sides to carry their messages to the people.

The supporters of the proposed Constitution scored the first tactical victory by claiming the name **Federalists** for their group. That was ironic because the proposed government was actually strongly national, whereas the term *federalist* generally meant more of a balance between the power of states and the national government. That forced those arguing against the document to be tagged as **Anti-Federalists** despite the fact that their position was in reality more federalist.

The Anti-Federalists were in the difficult position of having to argue against a proposal, since basing their argument only on what was good about the Articles of Confederation was a tough sell. So they turned negative. They raised fears in the minds of Americans about what this potentially radical change in the government would bring. Mostly, they argued, it would trample on the rights of the people and the states in which they lived.

For their part, the Federalists pointed to the problems that plagued the government under the Articles—inability to deal with foreign powers; economic challenges; and, especially, the threat of anarchy—and warned citizens that the only way to avoid these dangers was through the new Constitution. The Federalists had celebrity on their side in the figures of Washington and Franklin. The Anti-Federalists, with the exception of a few misguided attempts to counter the celebrity endorsements of Washington and Franklin, stayed away from the issue of famous supporters.

In some ways, the Federalists and Anti-Federalists split along distinctions of class (see Table 2.3). Many wealthy merchants favored the strong economic policy that the Constitution would allow, and many wealthy southern plantation owners supported the agreements that had been struck. On the other side, a large number of Anti-Federalists came from rural areas and mistrusted powerful elites in their states' capitals. To say that the Federalists were wealthy elites and the Anti-Federalists small farmers and shopkeepers is, however, an oversimplification. Many Anti-Federalist leaders were educated elites; some of the most prominent had been

Federalists and Anti-Federalists

Both Federalists and Anti-Federalists were interested in a politically and economically secure nation, but they differed in how they thought that would best be achieved.

Differed in Terms of . . .	Federalists	Anti-Federalists
View of Proposed Constitution	Supporters	Opponents
Proponents of . . .	A strong national government	A stronger state government
Concerned About . . .	The tyranny of the majority	The tyranny of the minority
Proposed . . .	The idea of an extended republic to limit the problem of faction and help to resolve the tyranny of the majority	Strong restrictions be placed on branches of government to help solve the problem of too-strong national government
Supporters Included . . .	Wealthy merchants and southern plantation owners George Washington, Benjamin Franklin, Alexander Hamilton, James Madison, John Jay	People in rural areas, more farmers and shopkeepers Fewer well-known supporters but leadership that included educated elites, Revolutionary War heroes, and convention delegates

heroes in the Revolutionary War, delegates to the convention itself, or important members in state politics.

Though the Federalists tried to associate the threat of anarchy and Shays' Rebellion with their opponents, the Anti-Federalists were just as concerned as their opponents with securing a stable future for the country. The divisions between the two sides represented fundamentally different visions for how to do so.

Three main issues divided the Anti-Federalists and the Federalists on a vision of this future: (1) how to best protect individual liberties against **tyranny** (the suppression of the rights of a people by those holding power), (2) the relative power of states and the nation, and (3) the lack of a bill of rights (a list of rights and liberties that people possess and that governments cannot take away) in the Constitution. Each of these issues was closely related to the others.

Will This Experiment Work? Federalists and Anti-Federalists Debate the Dangers of Power in a Large Republic

The Federalists made their case for the Constitution in a collection of eighty-five essays written primarily for the New York papers from the fall of 1787 to the spring of 1788. **The Federalist Papers** were written under the collective name *Publius* but were actually written by Alexander Hamilton, James Madison, and John Jay. They are now considered some of the most important writings in American political history.

They laid out the theory behind the Constitution (which itself does not directly speak to the reasons behind its own provisions), showing how a large republic could be constructed in a way that would prevent it from growing so self-interested and powerful that it would trample on the rights of states and their citizens.

Many of Madison's essays are now considered to be among the most important in the collection. Two essays in particular, *Federalist* No. 10 and No. 51, tackle Anti-Federalist critiques by laying out the reasons behind the proposed constitutional

The fate of the Constitution was decided in the state ratifying conventions (nine states had to ratify for the Constitution to take effect), but it was the subject of intense debates everywhere—in homes, taverns, coffeehouses, and newspapers.
The Granger Collection, New York

republic. From his research, Madison knew that in a republic one must not assume that people will always act in noble ways, putting their own needs behind what is best for the republic. Instead, a republic must be constructed to account for self-interest and selfish motives.[39]

In American political history, there is no one work that encapsulates Anti-Federalist thought in the same way that *The Federalist Papers* did for Federalists. There are no *Anti-Federalist Papers*; rather, as scholars have pointed out, "the Antifederalist literature is immense and heterogeneous, encompassing speeches, pamphlets, essays and letters."[40] Publishing under pseudonyms—often chosen from ancient Roman politicians and thinkers such as Cato or Brutus—the Anti-Federalists agreed that a nation cannot rely on enlightened self-interest to protect the people from tyranny; however, they disagreed with the Federalists over *how* best to do that.

A Republic Must Be Able to Handle the Problem of Faction. The danger in the view of both sides was not only that people would act according to their self-interest but also that they might join forces with others who had the same motives. Collectively, this group of people, however large or small, could try to use the government to get what it wanted, trampling the rights of others in the process. Such a group of self-interested individuals would constitute what Madison called a **faction**, the most dangerous challenge to a republic.

Long before Karl Marx wrote about the inevitability of class conflict in capitalist societies, Madison made it clear in *Federalist* No. 10 that inequality of wealth is the primary driver of factionalization, asserting that "those who hold and those who are without property have ever formed distinct interests in society."[41] Madison included slave ownership as a source of faction, as slaves were considered a form of property during the discussions in the Constitutional Convention. However, this issue was not addressed in *Federalist* No. 10.

Madison saw several ways to solve the problem of faction. The first was tyranny—factions emerge under conditions of liberty, not tyranny—but tyranny was an unacceptable option. The second was to create a totally unified, factionless society where everyone has "the same opinions, the same passions, and the same interests."[42] This second solution was unrealistic, especially in a large republic like the United States. Indeed, the American Republic has had factions since its origin. Political parties can be thought of as factions, as can interest groups and social movements. Madison concluded that factions were inevitable, so he turned to the question of how a republic can keep them in check.

The superior way to check their power, Madison argued in *Federalist* No. 10, is through an **extended republic**—a republic so large and diverse, with so many factions vying for power, that no one faction is able to assert its will over all the others. Tactically, this was a clever argument. The Anti-Federalists had claimed that the American Republic would be too large to govern effectively, whereas Madison argued that the only solution to the dangers of faction was precisely to have such a large republic. Madison, however, was no populist; his design for government placed brakes on popular passions, insulating representatives from the desires of their citizens.

Anti-Federalists argued that the national government would grow more distant from the people over time and would eventually begin to oppress them. Congress having the power to tax would only make this danger greater, they claimed. Therefore, the Anti-Federalists asserted, more restrictions needed to be placed on the national government and more power reserved for the states. To the Anti-Federalists, those in power in a too-strong national government would eventually, inevitably, come to form their own faction. They noted that many of the Enlightenment writers that Madison had drawn his ideas from had argued that republics had to be small to work properly, and all expected this one to grow even larger over time, making the challenges even worse.

Federalists and Anti-Federalists Fear Different Forms of Tyranny.

Federalists and Anti-Federalists did not disagree in their mistrust of government and the harm that could be inflicted by a self-interested few. Rather, both sides acknowledged that tyranny could take two forms. In a **tyranny of the minority**, a small number of citizens trample on the rights of the rest of the larger population. In a **tyranny of the majority**, a large number of citizens use the power of their majority to trample on the rights of a smaller group. The two sides disagreed on which was the greater danger and, therefore, on how a republic should be structured.

Given Madison's earlier observations about property and the panic associated with Shays' Rebellion, one of the dangers the Federalists saw was a majority of poorer people using their power to redistribute wealth in a more equal way. In *Federalist* No. 10, Madison did not argue for direct democracy, in which citizens vote directly on policies, because he saw that form of government as too unstable, with too few protections for personal security or private property.[43] Instead he argued for the delegation of power to representatives by the people and for power to be divided across government institutions. In *Federalist* No. 51, Madison laid out the blueprints of such a structure. Separation of powers is the guiding principle, with power divided and parsed between the states and nation, among the three branches of the national government, and within each branch.

The Anti-Federalists focused more on the dangers of a tyranny of the minority. Shays and the Regulators had viewed the government of Massachusetts as becoming dangerously disconnected from the people and controlled by wealthy elites. The Anti-Federalists feared the government of the United States would follow a similar path. While acknowledging the dangers of minority tyranny, Madison and the Federalists focused more on the dangers of majority rule and its necessary counters. A majority of people, if in control of all of the levers of power, might use that power to oppress a minority of citizens. Slavery could be thought of as a tyranny of the majority, though in fact enslaved people outnumbered whites in many areas of the country.

Federalists and Anti-Federalists Debate Where Power Should Be Concentrated

Debates over the relative power of the states and the nation were central to the political battles over ratification of the Constitution. The Federalists tried to convince American citizens that the proposed form of government was necessary to preserve their rights and liberties. The Anti-Federalists argued against the proposed increase in national power and warned Americans of what might come to pass over time as the advantages given to the national government in the Constitution might allow it to infringe more and more on the authority of the states.

Federalists Argue for a Strong National Government. In their campaign to defend the proposed Constitution, the Federalists highlighted the problems and dangers of a government in which the states were strong and the nation was weak, pointing out failures of past republics as well as the problems experienced under the Articles of Confederation.[44] In *Federalist* No. 16, Hamilton argued that, for instance, if the national government in a confederacy were ever forced to use military might against one of its members, it would surely result in the "violent death of the confederacy."[45]

In his contributions to *The Federalist Papers*, Madison took a more moderate approach, emphasizing the balance between state and national power in the proposed Constitution. Across numerous papers, Madison argued that the Constitution divided the people's sovereignty in such a way as to preserve the integrity of both states and nation and to guard against the dangers of faction, with checks and balances built into both the legislative and executive branches.

Anti-Federalists Fear Losing Representation at the National Level. The Anti-Federalists were not convinced by the arguments in *The Federalist Papers*. They feared what they saw as a radical increase in national power, not only in the proposed Constitution but in how the government might evolve over time. They feared the distant future as much as the immediate present. They were, in many ways, conservative, trying to preserve the power of the states as enjoyed under the Articles of Confederation.

Many Anti-Federalist concerns centered on how representation of the people's interests could be maintained as the country grew in size, population, and power. They "feared that, once elected and comfortable in their jobs, the representatives would not relinquish power," creating the possibility of a new, elected, American aristocracy.[46] This "democratic" aristocracy, an Anti-Federalist essay warned, would be accompanied by an irresistible trend toward a large and complex national government, driven by the demands of a growing nation, ending in "despotism."[47]

The economic power of the national government to tax and regulate interstate commerce was one of the Anti-Federalists' greatest worries, and it was only made worse by the necessary and proper clause of the proposed constitution. In one Anti-Federalist essay, the author argued that "this power, given [to] the federal legislature, directly annihilates all the powers of the state legislatures."[48]

A Bill of Rights Is a Key Issue in the Ratification Debates

Strategically, the most effective Anti-Federalist charge against the Constitution was that it lacked a bill of rights—a list of rights and liberties with which people are born and which governments cannot take away. Many state constitutions already had them. Motions to include these statements were raised during the convention, but they did not pass; a proposed clause guaranteeing the freedom of the press failed by just one vote. To Madison and other opponents of a bill of rights, such a statement was simply not necessary. In the republic that the delegates had fashioned, the people were already sovereign, and the government was already limited. There was no need to limit Congress's power over things that the Constitution gave it no control over in the first place. Some questioned if it was possible or even desirable to try to make a complete list of rights and liberties. What about the ones that were left out? Would Congress respect rights if they were not part of the official list?

Some, however, both during the convention and after, remained strongly in favor of a bill of rights. A bill of rights, they argued, was necessary to check the tendency of government to infringe on the rights and liberties of citizens over time. They pointed out that one should be concerned with what the government might become in the future, not just what it was in the present, as the prospect of tyranny loomed large in their minds. In addition, the Anti-Federalists argued that a bill of rights served an important educational function in a republic.[49] It would serve to remind citizens of their natural rights and remind them to assert those rights when governments might, often slowly, try to take them away.

As the state ratification conventions took up the debate, the lack of a bill of rights in the document became a powerful political tool for the Anti-Federalists, and the Federalists shifted gears in response. During the ratification campaign, sensing the realities of the political landscape, Madison promised to introduce a bill of rights as proposed amendments during the first session of the new Congress after the Constitution had been ratified.

As the conventions began to vote in the fall of 1787, Delaware, Connecticut, and New Jersey, which had supported the New Jersey Plan during the Constitutional Convention— satisfied by their equal representation in the Senate under the Great Compromise—were among the first to vote in favor of ratification. Georgia and Pennsylvania were quick to follow suit. The outcome in larger states, however, was uncertain.

A nineteenth-century steel engraving depicting Anti-Federalist author Mercy Otis Warren. Publishing anonymously, and often assumed to be a man, Warren warned against the omission of a bill of rights in the proposed Constitution.
The Granger Collection, New York

In February 1788, the Federalists won a narrow victory in Massachusetts, the sixth of nine states needed for ratification, but only after the proconstitutional forces agreed to propose a bill of rights once the original document had itself been ratified. Three months later, South Carolina also ratified, also contingent on a set of amendments that would be offered in the First Congress. On June 21, 1788, with the help of some shrewd procedural tactics on the part of Federalists in the state convention, New Hampshire became the ninth state to ratify.[50] The Constitution of the United States would become the supreme law of the land the following year.

Even after New Hampshire, James Madison continued to worry about the four states that had not yet ratified. It was not North Carolina or Rhode Island that worried him the most, but if Virginia and New York continued to hold out, it might lead to deep divisions within the new country. To Madison's relief, Virginia ratified in June, and New York followed in July. North Carolina and, finally, Rhode Island ratified within a year. Madison kept his word, and in 1791 ten of the amendments that he proposed in the new federal Congress became part of the Constitution. We will examine the Bill of Rights in detail in Chapter 4.

Conclusion: The Motives of the Framers and the Effects of the Constitution Are Still Being Debated

While the delegates to the Constitutional Convention were debating and negotiating behind the closed windows of the Pennsylvania State House, many Americans wondered what they were really up to. And we still do.

To some scholars, constitutions give order to disorder. They make progress in a society possible but only if the people place in them credible, enforceable restrictions on the power of those who would abuse such power.[51] The Constitution drew from the religious traditions and individual constitutions of the colonies. It is a document that creates—or constitutes—a people.[52] It sets out who those people are and why they are doing what they are doing.

To other scholars, American reverence for the Constitution is a dangerous thing. Faith in the Constitution as a symbol of liberty misdirects citizens from the fact that some persons, past and present, have been able to enrich themselves under its protections at the expense of others.[53] Inequality in all its forms has survived, and at times thrived, in the American Republic. Is the Constitution antidemocratic? Does it go against or restrain the will of the majority of the people? Yes, sometimes it is, and sometimes it does. The Constitution was intentionally designed to put brakes on popular desire to change public policy quickly. The result—incrementalism in public policy development whereby policy changes tend to be small and come slowly—has important implications for the United States.

James Madison's studies of the untimely deaths of republics helped to shape the longest-lived written national constitution in the history of human experience. That document did not ban slavery or the trade in enslaved peoples. It did not affirm or institutionalize the natural-born rights and liberties of women, Native Americans, enslaved or formerly enslaved peoples, or many others. It did, however, affirm the rights of citizens to worship as they saw fit, to speak out and organize against tyranny, and to expect that their government would exist to protect and promote their rights and liberties. It created mechanisms to enforce these expectations, should those in power forget whom they were there to represent. And, intentionally or not, it provided a platform and a path for those ignored or oppressed by the original document to change it, to make it acknowledge their natural rights and liberties as well.

The Founders of the American Republic were practical, tactical, strategic men. Their compromises may have been necessary, but they had enormous consequences for people's lives. The document that emerged from the Pennsylvania State House was unfinished and imperfect. Would it allow for a remedy of its defects? Would it create, as Madison had hoped, a republic that would last? The answers to these questions cannot be found in studies of the motives of the Founders or even of the document itself. The answers have come not from words penned in quill and ink but from the efforts of political actors—sometimes generations later—using their own skills in strategic politics, developing their own ideas, and making their own compromises and mistakes. And having done their own homework.

CHAPTER REVIEW

This chapter's main ideas are reflected in the Learning Objectives. By reviewing them here, you should be able to *remember* the key points and *know* these terms that are central to the topic.

2.1   Describe the ideas and historical context that shaped James Madison's thinking about republics.

Remember . . .
- James Madison wanted to form a republic that would last. He and other delegates to the Constitutional Convention met and debated how best to strengthen their union and avoid significant political and economic problems.

Know . . .
- *constitution* (p. 31)
- *republics* (p. 32)

2.2   Explain the challenges faced by the nation following the American Revolution in trying to form a government strong enough to rule effectively but not so strong as to oppress the rights of Americans.

Remember . . .
- James Madison wanted to form a republic that would last. He and other delegates to the Constitutional Convention met and debated how best to strengthen their union and avoid significant political and economic problems.

Know . . .
- *Articles of Confederation and Perpetual Union* (p. 34)
- *Shays' Rebellion* (p. 37)

2.3   Describe the role that compromise over states' interests played in shaping the government during the Constitutional Convention.

Remember . . .
- The delegates to the Constitutional Convention were not charged with drafting a new Constitution but only with proposing possible changes to the Articles of Confederation.

Know . . .
- *Constitutional Convention* (p. 40)
- *Great Compromise* (p. 44)
- *New Jersey Plan* (p. 43)
- *Virginia Plan* (p. 42)

2.4   Identify the institutions of government established by the Constitution and the distribution of political power among them.

Remember . . .
- The idea of separation of powers influenced the decision to create three separate but connected branches of the federal government.

Know . . .
- *amendment* (p. 49)
- *executive branch* (p. 46)
- *judicial branch* (p. 47)
- *legislative branch* (p. 46)
- *logroll* (p. 53)
- *separation of powers* (p. 48)
- *Three-Fifths Compromise* (p. 53)

2.5   Compare and contrast the arguments put forth by the Federalists and the Anti-Federalists during the ratification debates.

Remember . . .
- The proposed Constitution had to be ratified by nine of the thirteen states in order to replace the Articles of Confederation.
- Proponents and opponents of the Constitution tried to rally others to their side and convince individuals of their position.

Know . . .
- *Anti-Federalists* (p. 55)
- *extended republic* (p. 58)
- *faction* (p. 57)
- The Federalist Papers (p. 56)
- *Federalists* (p. 55)
- *tyranny* (p. 56)
- *tyranny of the majority* (p. 58)
- *tyranny of the minority* (p. 58)

CHAPTER 3

FEDERALISM

The Changing Boundaries between the Nation and the States

A sign at the Oregon State Fairgrounds in Salem advertises the dates of the Oregon Cannabis Growers' Fair. Growing and using marijuana are legal under the Oregon law but illegal under federal law, thus illustrating the tensions inherent in federalist systems of government.

AP Photo/Ben Margot

After reading this chapter, you will be able to do the following:

3.1 Explain the tension in American federalism between state and federal laws.

3.2 Identify the elements of the U.S. Constitution that shape American federalism.

3.3 Describe the development of American federalism from the founding to the New Deal.

3.4 Examine the role that the New Deal played in fundamentally reshaping American federalism.

3.5 Discuss changes to American federalism in the modern era and how it might continue to evolve.

On one fundamental issue the Constitution of the United States is absolutely clear: In its opening words, "We the People of the United States," it establishes that ultimate political authority rests with the people. We, and not the government, are sovereign and have supreme political authority.

What the Constitution is much less clear on are the precise mechanisms through which this supreme authority is vested in the government.

Under the Articles of Confederation, the vast majority of the people's authority had been placed in state governments, which left the Confederation Congress constantly struggling to secure cooperation from these multiple governments. That changed with the ratification of the Constitution, but the issue was not settled once and for all. The new system of government divided the people's authority between two levels of government—the nation and the states—with some powers exercised by one level alone, some powers denied to both levels, and some powers shared by both levels. In doing so, a system of **federalism** was created.

The Constitution created much of the basic framework of this division but did not delineate the boundaries between the specific powers of the national government and those of the state governments. The process of setting these boundaries continues even today. Many of the most important and controversial issues in our representative democracy involve difficult questions of American federalism.

In this chapter, we will engage with the stories of Angel Raich and Diane Monson, who sought to secure access to medical marijuana, tracing the roots of their conflict back to the Great Depression and Roosevelt's New Deal. In doing so, we will explore the tensions inherent in American federalism, how it has changed over time, and where American federalism stands in the twenty-first century.

Marijuana Policy Today Reveals Tensions between State and Federal Law

3.1 Explain the tension in American federalism between state and federal laws.

The year 2020 promised to be a big one for cannabis in the United States—even bigger than 2019.

As the new decade dawned, states across the nation were either preparing to roll out recreational consumption that had been legalized the previous year, give their voters the chance to weigh in on legalizing recreational or medical marijuana, or have their state legislatures consider legalization in the future.

In Illinois, beginning on January 1, all those twenty-one and older were able to legally obtain recreational cannabis at one of roughly thirty dispensaries established after passage of the state's Cannabis Regulation and Tax Act in June the previous year. Certain medical marijuana patients were allowed to grow up to five plants.[1]

On New Year's Eve, in anticipation of the law's implementation the next day, Illinois governor J. B. Pritzker "granted 11,017 pardons for individuals whose low-level cannabis convictions have held them back from good jobs, housing and financial aid for college," expunging those convictions from their records.[2] No other state had yet taken such a large step toward addressing the massive fallout—disproportionately affecting people of color—of cannabis laws. "Illinois is going where no other state has gone before," Juliana Stratton, lieutenant governor, announced, "admitting the unjust errors of the war on drugs and giving so many Illinoisans greater opportunities to build good lives for themselves and the people they love."[3]

In Colorado—the first state to legalize recreational cannabis, in 2012—certain businesses, such as restaurants and cannabis cafes, could as of 2020 apply for licenses allowing cannabis consumption on-site. Also included were "mobile 'marijuana hospitality establishments,' such as tour buses," giving the state's hospitality and tourism industries more options to attract out-of-state visitors.[4]

New Jersey voters would get their chance, in November of 2020, to change their state constitution. After the state legislature approved the referendum in December 2019, voters were set to decide if New Jersey, by state constitutional amendment, would become the twelfth state to legalize recreational cannabis.[5]

In December 2019, Major League Baseball announced that it was removing marijuana from the banned substances list—the first major American sports league to do so. Starting with spring training, the league would treat cannabis in the same way it does alcohol.

Finally, in Nevada—which legalized recreational cannabis in 2017—Democratic governor Steve Sisolak "greenlit a law to begin a three-year pilot program of a closed-loop payment system for marijuana purchases." The governor's office hoped to launch the "Venmo-like app" by July 2020.[6]

It is this last, small change in state policy that launches our exploration and frames the central questions that drive this chapter. Nevada and other states are not exploring alternative payment systems because they are cool or new. They are doing so because they have to—as federal law shuts cannabis businesses out of the regular consumer banking system, forcing them to operate on a cash basis, which is far from ideal or efficient.

For all of the changes in cannabis use, cultivation, and distribution going on across the states, one thing remains the same: Marijuana is still illegal at the national level. The federal government considers cannabis to be as dangerous as heroin and LSD.

American cannabis policy in 2020 is untenable and unsustainable, and the ball is in the federal government's court. The states are showing no signs of slowing down. Public opinion is moving steadily toward acceptance of, or at least ambivalence to, legalization.

Where does the U.S. Congress get the power to override state laws in areas such as cannabis policy? It is to this question that we turn, beginning with two individuals who fought all the way to the Supreme Court for their right to legal medical cannabis and lost.

Two Californians Sue for Access to Medical Marijuana

In 2002 Angel Raich and Diane Monson filed suit in a California federal court against the government of the United States. They argued that their use of medical marijuana, which was legal under the laws of California and eight other states at the time but illegal under federal law, was protected by the laws of their state and by the Constitution of the United States.

Both women were trying to cope with significant health issues, the treatment of which, they argued, was helped by the use of cannabis. Raich was struggling against an "inoperable brain tumor, seizures, endometriosis, scoliosis and a wasting disorder. She [weighed] only 97 pounds and said without pot she'd starve to death."[7] "I am not a criminal," Raich declared. "I do not deserve to be behind bars."[8] Monson used cannabis as part of her treatment for chronic back pain and spasms and grew her own plants to provide her medication: "Without cannabis, these spasms would be tortuous and unbearable no matter what other medications were available," she testified in federal court.[9]

Both women were using marijuana under the supervision of their doctors and in compliance with a California state law, the Compassionate Use Act of 1996. This act made the use and cultivation of marijuana for medical purposes legal if undertaken under the supervision of a licensed physician and in accordance with state regulations. However, Raich and Monson feared that the federal government might restrict their future ability to obtain medical cannabis. The reason for their fears was the fact that the use, cultivation, or possession of marijuana was illegal under a federal law, the Controlled Substances Act (CSA; 1970).[10] Under that law, marijuana was classified as a Schedule I drug, among the most dangerous substances, such as heroin and LSD. Raich and Monson were caught between the laws of their state and those of the nation. As such, they found themselves front and center in one of the most enduring debates in American political life—that of federalism.

In August 2002, "county deputy sheriffs and agents from the federal Drug Enforcement Administration (DEA) came to Monson's home. After a thorough investigation, the county officials concluded that her cultivation and use of marijuana was entirely lawful as a matter of California law. Nevertheless, after a three-hour standoff, the federal agents seized and destroyed all six of her cannabis plants."[11] "As I stood by and watched," Monson later testified, "the DEA agents chopped down my medicinal plants. I was crying and my back began to tighten up; for the rest of the week I experienced debilitating back spasms. . . . We do not feel safe; we have had our civil rights and our rights under California law taken from us in our own back yard."[12]

In *Gonzales v. Raich*, the Supreme Court Sides with Federal Law

Facing a threat to their continued access to medical marijuana, the two women filed suit, and their case eventually made its way to the U.S. Supreme Court. In their case, Raich and Monson based their claims upon the laws of California and the Constitution of the United States. In restricting access to marijuana, they argued, the federal government was in violation of several amendments to the Constitution as well as of certain specific powers granted to Congress in the founding document.

In 2005, the Supreme Court decided to take up the case of Angel Raich and Diane Monson, weighing their rights against the authority of the federal government under the CSA and the commerce clause of the Constitution. For their part, representatives of the federal government and the DEA insisted that they were rightfully upholding federal law and federal authority. "Everything we're doing is according to the law," said Richard Meyer, a San Francisco–based DEA spokesman.[13] By enforcing federal law, however, the DEA agents were restricting actions that were legal under California state laws, which begs the central question, when it comes to pot and patients, does federal or state law rule?[14]

In his skeptical questioning of the women's attorneys, Justice Antonin Scalia, a conservative, challenged their assertion that growing and distributing cannabis—even if it stayed within California's borders—would not contribute to the nationally problematic underground market in marijuana. Justice Stephen Breyer, considered one of the liberal members of the Court, suggested that a better course of action for medical cannabis advocates was to change federal law itself, rather than using federal courts to challenge federal policy.[15]

In its decision in *Gonzales v. Raich* (2005), by a 6–3 vote, the Court sided with the power of the federal government and ruled against Raich and Monson. The majority opinion explaining that the Court's logic reached back more than sixty years, to a case during the nation's most severe financial crisis.[16] In that case, an Ohio dairy and cattle farmer, Roscoe Filburn, cultivated a small crop of winter wheat, some of which he used to feed his livestock and some of which he used to feed his family. Under federal laws of the time, Filburn was required to restrict his wheat acreage. Filburn, however, cultivated much more than was legally allowed by quota but, according to his testimony, only for use on his farm, not for sale.

Filburn argued that the federal government was exceeding its constitutional authority under the commerce clause, which allows Congress to regulate interstate commerce (see below), since his activities were local, limited to his farm, and "their effects upon interstate commerce [were], at most, 'indirect.'"[17] The Supreme Court, in a unanimous decision in *Wickard v. Filburn*, disagreed. The Court found that even though the wheat never left the farm or the state, the quotas were a constitutional use of Congress's power under the commerce clause. According to one scholar of American federalism, "With such a definition of interstate commerce, nothing was local."[18]

If a product grown on a local farm for local consumption or marijuana grown at home for use in the home can be considered interstate commerce, then what *can't* be? In the debates over American federalism, defining the proper limits of the commerce clause remains a hotly contested issue.

Conflict between State and Federal Policy on Marijuana Continues

Today, the landscape has changed from the time of *Gonzales v. Raich*, but the central challenge to American federalism remains. Most states have passed laws allowing the use of marijuana for certain medical conditions, though these laws vary considerably both in terms of the medical conditions covered and in the restrictions placed upon its use. Others have decriminalized the possession of small amounts of marijuana, substituting civil fines for criminal penalties. By the beginning of 2020, eleven states and the District of Columbia have legalized marijuana for recreational use. Federal law, however, has not changed, nor has the Supreme Court reversed its upholding of Congress's power to prohibit the growth, use, or possession of marijuana under the authority of the commerce clause.

Plaintiff Diane Monson, shown at her California home, smokes marijuana from plants she grew herself to help alleviate back pain. In 2005, the Supreme Court ruled the federal government does have the authority to prohibit marijuana, despite state laws allowing it.
AP Photo/Max Whittaker

This has put recent administrations in a very difficult spot. During President Barack Obama's second term in office, fully enforcing the CSA in the states had become impossible. In December 2015, in a federal suit brought by neighboring states against Colorado (one of the four states in which recreational use had been made legal), Obama's solicitor general argued in a brief presented to the Supreme Court that it should not decide to hear the case. To some observers, the administration's position, though based on specific legal grounds, implied a position "that marijuana should be federally legalized—even for recreational use."[19] The Justice Department, under the president's direction, however, retained authority to prosecute the CSA, though it was to focus on drug trafficking and not on prosecuting "individuals who were in 'unambiguous compliance with existing state laws.'"[20]

With the election of Republican Donald Trump as president in 2016, many observers thought that federal policy might shift toward letting the states regulate medical and recreational marijuana use, possibly reclassifying or even removing marijuana from the list of controlled substances under the federal law.

What determines the boundaries between the nation and the states? The short answer is the Constitution. The long answer is nearly two and a half centuries of laws, court cases, and political action. The final answer is that there is no final answer; the boundaries between the nation and the states are not ever fully settled. To understand these dynamics more fully, we turn to the Constitution and its incomplete delineation of these boundaries.

The Constitution Divides Power between the Nation and the States

3.2 Identify the elements of the U.S. Constitution that shape American federalism.

One of the most important innovations of the U.S. Constitution was the division of the people's sovereignty between two levels of government: the national government and the states. Each level retained some exclusive powers and had some powers denied to it, and in some areas both levels were empowered to act on behalf of the people.

There Is More Than One Way to Divide Power between Levels of Government

The American Republic created by the Constitution is only one of several possible ways of working out the relationship between different levels of government. The difference between these models is the way in which the people's sovereignty is divided between different governmental units (see Figure 3.1). In **unitary systems**, citizens place their power in one central government that then exercises authority over the subnational governments (such as states and provinces). Most policies are then actually carried out by these subnational governments that derive their power from the national government. Great Britain, France, and Japan are examples of democratic governments operating as unitary systems.

At the opposite end of the spectrum are **confederal systems.** Here, citizens limit the authority of the national government, instead placing most of their sovereignty in the subnational governments, such as states, which then grant power and authority to the national government. In confederal systems, national governments are heavily dependent upon the states to carry out and pay for public policies. The United States under the Articles of Confederation was an example of a confederal system.

Finally, in **federal systems**, citizens divide their sovereignty between two or more levels of government, each of which may have exclusive authority to act in certain areas of policy, be denied from acting in an area of policy, or be required to share authority with another level in some areas. Key to a true federal system is the existence of constitutional protections for each level against encroachment on its powers by the other level(s). The United States, Canada, and India are examples of countries with federal systems.

The Division of Power under Different Systems of Governance

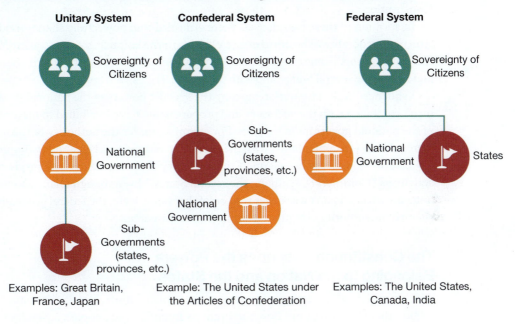

Examples: Great Britain, France, Japan

Example: The United States under the Articles of Confederation

Examples: The United States, Canada, India

The Constitution contains a set of provisions—the supremacy, necessary and proper, and commerce clauses—that shape the relative authority of the state and national governments. At the same time, however, it does not outline a perfectly clear vision of how the system of federalism would actually work.

The Supremacy, Necessary and Proper, and Commerce Clauses Are the Keys to American Federalism

One of the Constitution's most important statements about where the people's sovereignty is located is the **supremacy clause**, which reads, "This Constitution, and the Laws of the United States . . . shall be the supreme Law of the Land."[21] The supremacy clause is a powerful statement of national power. It means that the laws that Congress passes must be executed by the states, even if state constitutional provisions conflict with them. It means that states must abide by national treaties, and it also binds state courts to the Constitution.

In another key clause, Congress is given the power to "make all Laws which shall be necessary and proper for carrying into Execution . . . Powers vested by this Constitution in the Government of the United States."[22] This **necessary and proper clause**, also called the elastic clause, is a critical source of power for the national government, granting Congress the authority to legislate as necessary for carrying out constitutionally granted powers. "Elastic" here refers to the flexibility that it grants Congress, particularly in the authority to pass laws under powers that are implied, but not necessarily textually granted, by the Constitution.

In addition to these two clauses, there is a third that powerfully shapes modern American federalism: the **commerce clause**. In the language of the Constitution, this clause grants Congress the power to "regulate Commerce with foreign Nations, and among the several States, and with the Indian Tribes."[23]

Vagueness in the language regarding the specific powers of the national government, combined with the necessary and proper clause, has contributed to the growth of the national government's power. For example, under the authority of the commerce clause—in combination with the necessary and proper clause and the supremacy clause—Congress has claimed the authority to define nearly any productive activity as "Commerce . . . among the several States." Even though Diane Monson's homegrown marijuana was never sold or left her home state, the federal government claimed the authority to regulate it as interstate commerce.

The Constitution Describes the Powers Belonging to the Nation and the States

The word *federalism* does not appear in the Constitution. Nor is there any one section that clearly lays out how the Framers intended the people's sovereignty to be divided between the states and the national government. Instead, in various sections in the document, powers are given or denied to each level or allowed to be shared by both.

Most Powers of the National Government Are Explicit. In general, the powers of the national government are explicitly listed and described by the Constitution. With a few exceptions, the state governments' powers are assumed to encompass those not explicitly given to the national government. **Enumerated powers** refer to those powers explicitly granted to the national, or federal, government in the Constitution, and especially to Congress. These include the power to tax, coin money, declare war, raise and support an army and navy, make treaties, provide for the naturalization of American citizens, and "regulate Commerce with foreign Nations, and among the several States, and with Indian Tribes."[24]

Implied powers are those not textually granted to the federal government but assumed to be given to it as a result of its need to make all laws "necessary and proper." For example, the Constitution does not give the national government the authority to create an air force. That authority, however, is assumed as part of its power to raise and support a military.

In addition to describing the enumerated and implied (or delegated) powers of the national government, the Constitution denies certain powers to it, especially if the residents of the states have not given their consent, usually through the approval of the state legislatures. The national government may not pass laws that violate the rights and liberties expressed in the Bill of Rights (or other later amendments). The national government may not admit new states to the Union, nor can it change state boundaries without the consent of the state's citizens. It also cannot impose taxes on goods and services exported and imported between states.

The Powers of State Governments Are Less Explicit. The Constitution is much less specific about the powers allocated to the states. Much of the protection for state authority comes from the Tenth Amendment to the Constitution, which states, "The powers not delegated to the United States by the Constitution, nor prohibited by it to the States, are reserved to the States respectively, or to the people."

Called **reserved powers** because of the text of the Tenth Amendment, these are powers that were not given to the national government and are, therefore, reserved to the states. Among the most important of these are **police powers**, which state governments use to protect residents and provide for their safety, health, and general welfare. While law enforcement is an important example of police powers, the scope is much broader, including other activities such as setting health standards and building codes. States are also authorized to conduct elections, including those for national office.[25] No amendments may be made to the Constitution without the consent of three-fourths of the states, either by their legislatures or by ratification conventions in the states.[26] States are also empowered to establish local, town, county, and regional governmental bodies.

The Constitution also denies certain powers to state governments. States are prevented from entering into treaties or alliances with foreign powers—a real concern to the Framers who saw the potential for the European powers to divide the states for their own economic or political gain. States may not print their own money, tax imports or exports, or declare war.[27]

Finally, both the nation and the states are given the authority to act in certain areas of public policy. These **concurrent powers** allow national and state authority to overlap—an example of the concept of "separated institutions sharing power."[28] The power to tax, already given to states under the Articles of Confederation, was extended to the new national government. Both levels are allowed to borrow money, though states have more restrictions on their own ability to go into debt than the federal government has. The nation and the states may both pass and enforce laws, create and operate a system of courts, and charter banks and corporations (see Figure 3.2).

Members of Indigenous Nations Have a Relationship with the Federal Government That Is Different from American Federalism. As citizens both of the United States and their indigenous Native American nations, members of those nations have experienced a complicated and often tragic relationship between the federal government and their indigenous national governments, though one that is

Enumerated, Concurrent, and Reserved Powers in American Federalism

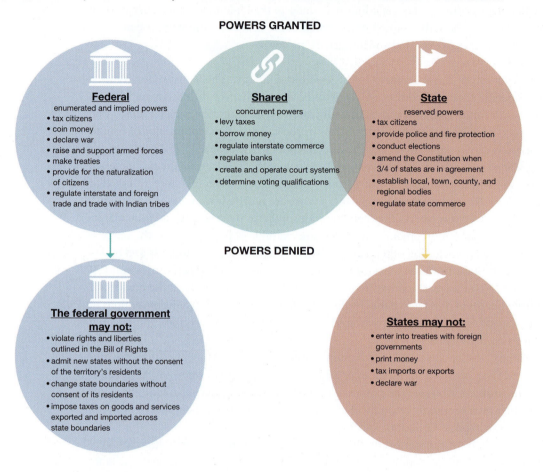

POWERS GRANTED

Federal
enumerated and implied powers
• tax citizens
• coin money
• declare war
• raise and support armed forces
• make treaties
• provide for the naturalization
  of citizens
• regulate interstate and foreign
  trade and trade with Indian tribes

Shared
concurrent powers
• levy taxes
• borrow money
• regulate interstate commerce
• regulate banks
• create and operate court systems
• determine voting qualifications

State
reserved powers
• tax citizens
• provide police and fire protection
• conduct elections
• amend the Constitution when
  3/4 of states are in agreement
• establish local, town, county, and
  regional bodies
• regulate state commerce

POWERS DENIED

**The federal government
may not:**
• violate rights and liberties
  outlined in the Bill of Rights
• admit new states without the consent
  of the territory's residents
• change state boundaries without
  consent of its residents
• impose taxes on goods and services
  exported and imported across
  state boundaries

States may not:
• enter into treaties with foreign
  governments
• print money
• tax imports or exports
• declare war

different from American federalism. The rules governing these relationships have been set down through centuries of treaties, laws, and Court decisions, which establish indigenous nations' governments as entities not formally part of the states in which they are located but with some degree of autonomy, which may supersede state or federal laws where they exist.

These differences in autonomy and governance came to the foreground during the Dakota Access Pipeline protests explored in Chapter 1. One legal tactic that the Standing Rock protesters unsuccessfully pursued was to argue that tribal autonomy called for "government to government" consultations between the Standing Rock Sioux Nation and the federal government to limit construction on lands near the reservation considered by its members to be "tribal land."[29]

DOES MARIJUANA LEGALIZATION AFFECT CRIME RATES?

One of the strongest arguments made against the legalization of marijuana is its potential to increase rates of crime. That potential is only heightened by the fact that American marijuana businesses are usually cash only. Since marijuana remains illegal federally, dispensaries and growers are generally shut out from most banking services and must deal in—and have on hand—large amounts of cash. Commenting on criminal activity in California's Mendocino County—an area known for illegal marijuana cultivation in the past—a sheriff's office official observed, "We're seeing more robberies and more gun violence."[30]

Proponents of legalization counter that these policies will actually decrease criminal activity. Theirs is an argument based on economics. Legalization in this view acts as a "supply shock," increasing the marijuana supply and driving down drug cartel's profits, along with their incentives to "invest" in smuggling, violence, and other criminal activity.[31] Even today, up to half of the marijuana consumed in the United States is believed to come from Mexico and other nations. In Washington, state representative David Sawyer of Tacoma noted that many state officials expected crime rates to rise following legalization, but that did not happen: "I think what more people are realizing is violent crime is linked to keeping marijuana illegal."[32]

So, which is it?

As the legalization of recreational marijuana is still a relatively recent phenomenon, the data are still sparse, and studies continue. That said, most rigorous studies have not found evidence of significant increases in crime, especially violent crime, as a result of legalization. A few have even reported decreases. Other areas, of course, also need more data and analysis, such as the effect of legalization on behaviors such as driving while impaired and increases in use by minors. The most basic challenge to evaluating the effects of legalization on crime, however, is one commonly encountered by political scientists: the lack of controlled experiments.

In a *controlled experiment*, the researcher tries to control as many factors as possible other than the treatment—the factor being tested. Subjects are randomly assigned to a treatment or nontreatment group, and if the two groups are otherwise similar, any differences in outcomes are attributed to the treatment. Political scientists do make use of controlled experiments. One might, for example, show different political advertisements, one of which has been intentionally altered in some way, to individuals in two randomly assigned groups to assess the impact of the alterations on the reception of those advertisements.

Most of the time, however, political scientists cannot do this—especially in the world of public policy. Instead, we rely on *quasi-experiments*, which are not truly random. In a quasi-experiment, the researcher ascribes an outcome to a treatment—here marijuana legalization—whose introduction was not random. States that legalize—or the cities in

(Continued)

(Continued)

them—did not randomly pull a ball from the bingo machine that read, "Yep, marijuana is now legal in your jurisdiction" or "Nope, not this time."

The lack of random assignment means that we cannot be 100 percent sure that some other unobserved factor hasn't led to the outcome that we observe—here an increase or decrease in crime rates. Moreover, that factor may also have had something to do with passage of the law in the first place. Political scientists do have statistical tools to try to account for nonrandomness, but we can never be completely sure.

WHAT Do You Think?

When reading studies reporting changes in crime rates in states that have legalized marijuana, what kinds of other, unobserved factors might be causing these outcomes? If a state legalizes marijuana in reaction to a drug-related crime wave, for example, and violent crime subsequently goes down, was it legalization that caused the drop, or might the crime rate just have been reverting back to some longer trend? On the other hand, if crime rates go up, what other social and economic factors might account for this apart from the change in marijuana laws?

For Much of American History, the Boundaries between the Nation and the States Were Sharper Than They Are Today

> 3.3 Describe the development of American federalism from the founding to the New Deal.

Federalism is not one clean and unchanging concept, and there is no one set way to divide the people's sovereignty between levels of government. Defining the relative power of the two levels, as well as deciding how closely they will be intertwined, happens through the political process, and this has changed over the course of American history. In this section we will look at different types of federalism up through the early twentieth century and see how those relate to specific eras of American political history.

Early Supreme Court Decisions Shape the Division between State and National Power

The void left by the Framers of the Constitution in precisely defining the boundaries of American federalism was quickly filled by the Supreme Court—a role that it continues to pursue actively today. Perhaps the most important figure in shaping American federalism after the ratification of the Constitution was John Marshall, chief justice of the United States from 1801 to 1835 and the longest-serving chief justice in American history. During his tenure as chief justice, Marshall secured and issued several of the most important decisions in the area of American federalism.

McCulloch v. Maryland Relies on the Necessary and Proper Clause to Assert the Power of Congress.

The first of these major decisions was in *McCulloch v. Maryland* (1819).[33] The case involved the Second Bank of the United States, a national bank chartered by Congress. Several states, including Maryland, passed laws to tax the state branches of the Second Bank. They had a variety of reasons for doing this, including to try to kill the branches, to defend their own state's banks, or just to raise money. *McCulloch* centered on two questions: Did Congress have the authority to establish the bank in the first place? And did individual states have the authority to tax the bank's branches operating within their borders? Marshall, writing for a unanimous Supreme Court, came down firmly on the side of the authority of the national government in both questions. Citing the necessary and proper clause of the Constitution, Marshall affirmed the right of Congress to establish the bank and denied the right of Maryland and other states to tax the bank's state branches.

Gibbons v. Ogden Uses the Commerce Clause to Affirm the Power of Congress to Regulate Trade.

In *Gibbons v. Ogden* (1824), the Marshall Court weighed in on the powers of Congress under the commerce clause of the Constitution.[34] As with the *McCulloch* decision, in *Gibbons* the Court affirmed national power. Known as the "steamboat monopoly case," *Gibbons v. Ogden* arose from a battle between two powerful businessmen in the steamboat industry in New York and New Jersey. Aaron Ogden had been granted a monopoly by a New York state law that protected his routes within New York and between New York and New Jersey. Thomas Gibbons filed suit to block the monopoly.

Marshall's decision in the case reaffirmed national power but on a different constitutional principle. While *McCulloch* involved the necessary and proper clause, *Gibbons* focused on the power of Congress to regulate trade "among the several States" as part of its authority under the commerce clause. Marshall also cited the power of the national government under the supremacy clause of the Constitution. Marshall and the Court, again unanimously, struck down the steamboat monopoly between the two states and the part of the New York law that had made the monopoly possible. In doing so, Marshall affirmed the exclusive authority of Congress to regulate interstate commerce.[35]

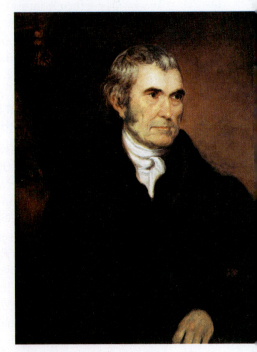

Chief Justice John Marshall's decisions are widely held to be among the most important for shaping the powers and limits of federalism even today.
The Granger Collection, New York

Barron v. Baltimore Rules That the Due Process Clause Applies Only to the National Government.

The third major federalism case decided by the Marshall Court was *Barron v. Baltimore* (1833).[36] *Barron* dealt with yet another part of the Constitution, the portion of the Fifth Amendment called the due process clause, which states, "No person shall . . . be deprived of life, liberty, or property, without due process of law; nor shall private property be taken for public use, without just compensation." John Barron, the owner of a wharf in Baltimore, sued the city for the cost to his business caused by sand that had accumulated in the waters off his wharf as a result of the city's development policies, thus depriving him of property without "just compensation." The Marshall Court issued another unanimous decision; however, in this case, it limited rather than expanded the power of the national government. The Court ruled that the Fifth Amendment's protections were aimed exclusively at restraining the power of the national government and were not intended to apply to the states.[37]

Lurking in the background during this time were the interconnected and unresolved problems of slavery, states' rights, and American federalism. The delegates to the Constitutional Convention had given in to the demands of the slave states to preserve their institution, in spite of the fact that slavery violated the essential principles of natural rights upon which the Constitution was based. In the nineteenth century, as the American Republic expanded to fill the continent, the question of slavery and its implications for the relationship between the nation and the states could no longer be ignored.

The Era of Dual Federalism Separates the Powers of the Nation and the States

For much of the history of the American Republic, the model of the relationship between states and the nation was one of **dual federalism**, which divided the people's sovereignty between the nation and the states. Dual federalism presumes a distinct, though not complete, separation between the two levels of authority, as if both operate side by side with relatively little interaction between the two. Dual federalism, according to an observer of American government in 1888, "is like a great factory wherein two sets of machinery are at work, their revolving wheels apparently intermixed, their bands crossing one another, yet each set doing its own work without touching or hampering the other."[38]

The Supreme Court drew a similar image of two separate systems in the nineteenth century: "The government of the United States and the government of a state are distinct and independent of each other within their respective spheres of action, although existing and exercising their powers within the same territorial limits. Neither government can intrude within the jurisdiction, or authorize any interference therein by its judicial officers with the action of the other."[39] In fact, however, the division of authority between the nation and the states has never been this clean and neat. Even in areas of public policy that have been traditionally handled by the states, such as education, the federal government has been involved.[40]

States' Rights Grow during the Civil War and Reconstruction. The expansion of national power under the Marshall Court did not mean that this new balance of power would be permanent or go unchallenged. Efforts to assert the authority of states continued during the middle decades of the nineteenth century. As the original Federalist justices retired or passed away, many of their replacements felt that more power should be held by the states. Increasingly, the question of federalism also became linked with the issues of slavery, **states' rights**, and the threat of secession. In the 1830s, South Carolina senator John Calhoun argued for the right of states to "nullify" federal laws that were in conflict with those of the states.

In December 1860, South Carolina seceded from the nation. Within six months, ten more southern states had followed to form the Confederate States of America. When the American Civil War finally ended in 1865, more than six hundred thousand soldiers had died, and an unknown number of civilians had been killed.

The Civil War and the process of Reconstruction had settled the issues of secession and of legalized slavery; however, the question of how forcefully the national government would act to preserve the civil rights (the personal rights guaranteed to citizens or residents) of former slaves and their descendants was far from decided. As the government of the United States began to turn its attention to the expansion of the nation's empire toward the Pacific Ocean, the rights of African Americans received less and less consideration and protection.

Under Dual Federalism, the Supreme Court Restricts African Americans' Rights after the Civil War.

Following the Civil War, the Supreme Court did not emerge as a defender of African American civil rights. Instead, it affirmed a vision of federalism that recognized state authority, even if that authority was used to restrict the rights of state citizens based only on their racial identity. Three amendments to the Constitution following the Civil War—called the Reconstruction amendments in reference to the time of their ratification—abolished slavery (Thirteenth Amendment), required states to ensure "equal protection of the laws" (Fourteenth Amendment), and guaranteed the right to vote to African American men (Fifteenth Amendment). While slavery had been abolished, the textually strong protections for the rights of African Americans in the Fourteenth and Fifteenth Amendments did not result in strong protections on the ground, as states restricted them in practice, and the Supreme Court chose not to press the states for more robust action. We will explore these amendments and their role in securing civil rights in detail in Chapter 5.

Plessy v. Ferguson (1896) was a landmark case in restricting the rights of African Americans following the Civil War and asserting states' rights.[41] Homer Plessy, an African American man, had been arrested and fined for violating a Louisiana law requiring separate railroad facilities for whites and African Americans.[42] In its decision in *Plessy*, the Supreme Court held that Louisiana's law did not violate the Fourteenth Amendment, establishing the precedent of constitutionally permissible racial segregation, a precedent that would not be overturned until 1954. We will explore the efforts—first in the states, later in the Supreme Court—of individuals to overturn this doctrine in detail in Chapter 5.

U.S. deputy marshals escort six-year-old Ruby Bridges from William Frantz Elementary School in New Orleans, Louisiana, in 1960. Schools remained explicitly segregated for nearly sixty years following the "separate but equal" ruling in *Plessy v. Ferguson* (1896). Ruby's court-ordered enrollment prompted some white parents to boycott the school and withdraw their children.
AP Photo

In the Age of Industry and National Expansion, Cooperative Federalism Emerges. During the latter part of the nineteenth century and the early decades of the twentieth, the Supreme Court adopted a complex role toward the growing economy. On the one hand, important decisions during this time supported the ability of American businesses to pursue their interests without large amounts of regulation, especially by state and local governments. Workers' rights and food safety, for example, were two areas of business activity that would not see significant federal involvement for several decades. On the other hand, some decisions began to empower the national government to set broader regulatory rules. In many cases, states were happy to have the federal government take more of a leading role in regulating increasingly large and powerful corporations. As American corporations grew in size and power, states began to realize that they could not, on their own, "mobilize sufficient power to regulate wealthy railroads that could cut them off from the rest of the country in retaliation [for regulations], or deal with great industrial combines that could pull up and go elsewhere."[43]

Confronting the challenges and opportunities of economic growth together, the nation and the states began to forge what is called **cooperative federalism**, in which both levels work together in the same areas of public policy. Under this type of federalism, the two levels do not generally play the same roles. Instead, the national government tends to be "responsible for raising revenues and setting standards," while state and local governments remain "primarily responsible for administering the programs."[44]

While both national and state governments began to build the foundations for cooperative federalism in the late nineteenth century, the dominant theme was one of not interfering with American business and the economy, at either the national or state level. Under this approach, government took little action to regulate or restrain private economic activity, even if it resulted in unequal relationships between workers and owners or even dangerous workplace conditions, including the employment of children in factory work. In decisions that restricted the ability of the national government to regulate economic activity, the Supreme Court supported the philosophy of noninterference in the economy.[45]

While some of the seeds of the later growth in national power were planted during the era of big business, it would take a massive economic crisis, the inability of state governments to cope with the crisis, and the response of the national government to the crisis's challenges to fully realize this growth. To understand how major these changes would be, we need to understand the crisis itself: the Great Depression.

President Franklin Roosevelt's Response to the Great Depression Reshapes American Federalism

> 3.4 Examine the role that the New Deal played in fundamentally reshaping American federalism.

During the boom of the 1920s, speculators made risky investments, farmers moved on to riskier land, and debts piled up. During the Great Depression, all of that collapsed into a prolonged period of deflation. Money became scarce, loans were hard to come by or pay back, and prices fell. Faced with the simultaneous disasters of drought, falling prices, and unpayable debts, millions of farmers faced foreclosure. The collapse in farm prices was especially hard on tenant farmers, many of whom were racial and ethnic minorities and whose for-hire labor was no longer needed by their landlords. In one of the largest migrations in American history, millions of displaced farmers and their families abandoned the Dust Bowl and headed West in search of whatever work they could find.

The hardship brought with massive dust clouds over American's heartland was only one of many in the nation. In October 1929, America's stock market crashed, a very visible signal of an industrial economy grinding to a halt. This signaled the start of the **Great Depression**, the most significant economic crisis in the nation's history. The nation's banking system nearly failed. Industrial production collapsed. Workers were laid off or had their wages cut. Foreclosures swept through cities, driving families into homelessness and hunger. The most vulnerable members of the American economy—children, women, and members of racial and ethnic minorities—often suffered the most.

The crisis of the Great Depression strained American federalism. During the boom times of the 1920s, states had increased their spending, especially to expand the highways for the nation's growing fleet of automobiles. To do so, states had borrowed large amounts of money. When the economic crisis took hold, many state governments themselves faced shortfalls and were unable to respond to their residents' needs. Local governments were similarly overwhelmed, unable to care for millions of unemployed workers. Faced with challenges that they could not meet and citizens they could not assist, state and local governments appealed to the national government for help.

President Roosevelt Greatly Expands the Role of the National Government

At his inaugural address in 1933, President Franklin Delano Roosevelt made it clear that he was prepared to bring the full power of the executive branch to bear on the Great Depression. Should Congress not take proper action to assist, he said "I shall ask Congress for . . . broad Executive power to wage a war against the emergency, as great as the power that would be given to me if we were in fact invaded by a foreign foe."[46]

Roosevelt meant what he said, and he would back up those promises and threats as one of the most powerful presidents in U.S. history. Within his first few months in office, Roosevelt secured the passage of fifteen major laws covering large areas of the nation's economy. Called the Hundred Days, this period in Roosevelt's administration resulted in the creation of a host of agencies; thousands of pages of regulations and rules; and a new, stronger role for the national government. It was part of the **New Deal**, Roosevelt's plan for tackling the Great Depression.

Roosevelt was able to use his sensibilities as a canny strategic political actor to exert a powerful influence on the country in a short amount of time. Roosevelt knew that state governments simply did not have the resources to handle the massive problems they faced. They were in no position to refuse the massive amount of federal aid that Roosevelt offered, even if accepting the aid meant trading away some state authority. This dynamic fundamentally changed the relationship between the states and the national government, dramatically strengthening the role of the national government in the economy. In terms of American federalism, it was a true revolution.

Roosevelt's first priority was the nation's crumbling banking system.[47] He officially closed the country's banks for a week and introduced a series of bills to regulate the nation's economy and create a set of federal organizations to carry out and enforce these policies.[48] One of the most important, and controversial, was the National Industrial Recovery Act (NIRA). Its purpose was to "drive prices up and put people back to work."[49] To do so, the act created an administrative agency, the National Recovery Administration (NRA), which became involved in regulating the American economy in ways few would have thought possible before the economic crisis hit. The primary tool of the NRA was a code (or set of rules) created by the NIRA governing prices, outputs, wages, working hours and conditions, management-labor relations, and the employment of children that American businesses pledged to follow.

The code was detailed. It "determined the precise components of macaroni; [it] determined what tailors could and could not sew. In the poultry industry the relevant line of code had banned customers from picking their own chickens."[50] The implementation of the code created political opposition both from business owners who were frustrated by their inability to raise prices and by workers and labor leaders who felt that the law's protections for workers' rights did not go far enough.[51] The complexity of the code also entangled government in the smallest details of businesses, about which individual code inspectors often had little or no knowledge. Roosevelt was himself said to be nervous about wading so forcefully into workers' rights, but he later became more enthusiastic "in part because it strengthened workers' loyalty to the New Deal and the Democratic Party."[52]

The Supreme Court Pushes Back against President Roosevelt's New Deal Expansions

In 1934, Martin Schechter and his three brothers, operators of two kosher Jewish butcheries in New York, found themselves the target of the federal government's NRA regulators. The Schechter brothers' butcheries followed a set of practices that were "both a matter of religious observance and good business."[53]

Franklin Delano Roosevelt's inaugural address, March 4, 1933. In the address, President Roosevelt asserted, "This great Nation will endure as it has endured, will revive and will prosper. So, first of all, let me assert my firm belief that the only thing we have to fear is fear itself—nameless, unreasoning, unjustified terror which paralyzes needed efforts to convert retreat into advance."
Franklin D. Roosevelt Presidential Library & Museum

Those practices placed the Schechter brothers at odds with the administration of President Franklin Delano Roosevelt. The brothers were charged with violating the NIRA federal code, including one charge that centered on the sale of "unfit chickens" not suitable for human consumption. All four brothers were indicted for violating the new laws, and all four were convicted and imprisoned. Instead of backing down, however, the Schechter brothers sued, and their case made it all the way to the Supreme Court. Their case, *Schechter Poultry Corp. v. United States* (1935), shook the foundations of Roosevelt's plan to fight the Great Depression.

The Schechter brothers celebrate with their attorney, Joseph Heller, center, in his law offices in New York on May 27, 1935, upon learning of the Supreme Court's ruling in their favor in the case of *Schechter Poultry Corp. v. United States*. In this case, the NIRA was determined to be unconstitutional.

The policy at the center of the battle was the code the NIRA created and the NRA was tasked to implement. The power of the NRA, its code inspectors, and the federal government seemed to the Schechter brothers and others overbearing and relentless. As they put it, "the NRA code did not make sense."[54] Their lawyers argued that the federal government overstepped its powers in claiming authority over commerce that it did not possess under the Constitution.

The Supreme Court agreed; it was in no mood to allow the new president to expand federal authority in such an unprecedented way.[55] In its opinion in *Schechter*, the Supreme Court struck at the heart of Roosevelt's New Deal, arguing that his administration's policies had gone far beyond the authority granted by the Constitution and especially by the commerce clause. How, a majority of justices asked critically, could the butchery of chickens in New York City be considered "commerce . . . among the several States"?

In his arguments before the Supreme Court, Joseph Heller, the chief litigator on behalf of the Schechter brothers, argued that the federal government had exceeded its implied powers in its expansion of the commerce clause. In its regulation of the slaughter and sale of chickens in Brooklyn, the federal government, Heller asserted, had gone far beyond any reasonable interpretation of the word *among*. Almost all of the chickens, he argued, had been purchased in New York, processed in New York, and sold in New York. Since no state boundary was crossed, the commerce clause could not have been violated.

In a unanimous opinion, the Supreme Court overturned the convictions of the Schechter brothers and, by implication, the NIRA and perhaps the entire New Deal. The code-making and enforcing authority of the NRA, the Court found, violated the commerce clause and was therefore invalid. Without such authority, the NIRA was powerless.

The *Schechter* case was just the beginning. Chief Justice Hughes was far from done, and "between 1933 and 1936, the Court overturned acts of Congress at ten times the traditional rate"—actions that "created an atmosphere of crisis in Washington."[56]

President Roosevelt Strikes Back with a Court-Packing Plan

The challenge to the president's authority would not go unanswered, however. In the months following the Supreme Court's invalidation of the core of his New Deal, Roosevelt pushed ahead with his legislative agenda, called the Second New Deal.

This period in Roosevelt's presidency saw passage of some of the most important New Deal programs.

The Social Security Act of 1935 created a set of programs to support vulnerable groups of Americans. It established unemployment insurance for American workers. It set up old-age insurance and elderly assistance programs, which were later supplemented with disability insurance. In addition, it established Aid to Dependent Children.[57] These programs were designed to be self-funding so as not to force the government to raise taxes and further depress the economy.

President Roosevelt would continue to struggle with what he saw as an obstructionist Court standing in the way of his reforms. In response, the president continued to press ahead with his legislative agenda, even if it meant more conflict with the judicial branch. Following his landslide reelection in 1936, in a move that alarmed even his closest advisers, Roosevelt decided to take on the Supreme Court directly. The president sought to use Congress's constitutional authority to increase the number of justices on the Court from nine to as many as fifteen, thus allowing him to appoint enough pro–New Deal justices to tip the balance of power decisively in his favor. Known as the "Court-packing plan," Roosevelt's gambit was constitutional but very bold and very risky.[58]

In the end, Roosevelt's bill died in the Democratic Congress. The Court-packing plan ultimately divided his own party, driving many conservative Democrats to side with Republicans in Congress, a split heightened over issues of civil rights for African Americans. Roosevelt eventually nominated replacements for most of the justices but only because his unprecedented four terms in office allowed him to outlast the tenure of many of them. Roosevelt would have a much friendlier Court in the later years of his presidency—but not because of Court-packing.

In the New Deal, Cooperative Federalism Replaces Dual Federalism

In the end, the Court did change its opinions, reversing in several key rulings its previous opposition to the constitutionality of Roosevelt's New Deal and similar state measures to regulate businesses and the economy. Scholars continue to debate the role that the president's threats played in shaping subsequent Court decisions, or even if the Court was as unilaterally obstructionist as Roosevelt believed it to be. Whether shaped by public opinion, Roosevelt's threats, or changes in the attitudes of justices themselves, the Supreme Court moved away from its earlier unilateral opposition to the president's agenda. The New Deal survived, and it fundamentally altered the boundaries between the activities of the federal government and those of the states.

The expansion of national power under Roosevelt's New Deal—especially Congress's authority to regulate interstate commerce—permanently altered the relationship between the states and the nation. Cooperative federalism, in which both levels of government are involved in setting policy, firmly replaced earlier models of dual federalism and made the national government at least a coequal in many areas of public policy traditionally handled by the states.

This change did not just happen. Nor was it necessarily inevitable. Roosevelt's popularity, political skill, and miscalculations all played a role. So did the decisions and the shifting opinions of the members of the Supreme Court. However, the revolution was also made possible by the severe economic crisis facing the nation and the inability of states to handle its fallout. States did not always fight Roosevelt's policies, desperate as they were for help in handling the impact of the Great Depression.

Modern American Federalism Remains Cooperative but Faces Challenges

> 3.5   Discuss changes to American federalism in the modern era and how it might continue to evolve.

During the second half of the twentieth century, the expansion of national involvement in the American economy initiated by Roosevelt continued and was in fact strengthened and expanded. Many federal agencies created during the New Deal stayed in place, and some grew larger. As the American economy recovered from the Great Depression and World War II, from which the United States emerged as a global superpower, cooperative federalism remained the dominant model. The dual federalism of the nineteenth and early twentieth centuries was long gone—and, barring a major economic or social crisis, it is not coming back.

One of the primary tools that the federal government can use to achieve its policy objectives within the states is the **grant-in-aid**, money provided to states by the federal government in order to carry out a policy that the national government has decided is important. Though the use of grants-in-aid goes back to the early days of the Republic—especially in grants of land to support public education in the states and territories—they became a common tool in a variety of policy areas during and after the New Deal.

The main form of grant-in-aid under cooperative federalism following the New Deal was the **categorical grant**, a grant provided to states or to local or regional governments for specific policy objectives and with certain conditions attached. (See the left-hand column of Figure 3.3.) These conditions might be a requirement that the state, local, or regional authority provide matching funds in order to receive the federal monies. They might also include specific instructions on how the grant funds are to be used. Sometimes categorical grants are awarded based on formulas that allocate federal money according to factors such as population, income, and need.

Categorical grants-in-aid are an important source of national power. Though state, local, and regional governmental authorities are often not required to accept these funds, once they do they accept the national regulation that goes along with taking the money. Once a state establishes a program based on the receipt of a categorical grant-in-aid, it depends on the continued provision of those funds by the national

Grants-in-Aid

Categorical Grant

Money provided by the national government to state, local, or regional governments that is tied to specific policy objectives and that carries certain conditions for receipt or expenditure.

- National government controls purse strings.
- Once a program is established, states depend upon national government for continuation of that program.
- Can mean that wealthier states "subsidize" poorer ones; but can also mean that inequalities between states are reduced and citizens in poorer states have access to benefits they might not otherwise have.
- Can make it harder for states to control their own budgets.
- Can lead to expansion in size of national and state government.

Block Grant

Money proved to state, local, or regional governments over which subnational governments have greater control.

- State, local, or regional governments have greater say in how funds are spent.
- Subnational governments given greater flexibility in long-term budget planning.
- States can have more authority in setting and enforcing welfare rules.
- Can mean that states decide what priorities to select for their population and are more "in touch" with their needs; but also can mean that federal oversight is reduced and the ability to compare outcomes across states is more limited.
- Can mean that localities with greater need lose out to localities with greater political clout in the allocation of funds.

government, along with any attached strings, to avoid a potentially serious disruption of the provision of services to its citizens and residents. State legislators opting out of these funds may be forced to find the money to replace these services from the state budget or explain to state voters why they are no longer being provided. Federal funding for education in recent decades, for example, has often come with such strings—such as requirements for widespread standardized testing—that have proven very difficult for states to cut, reliant as they are for the education monies to which the strings are attached.

In this way, categorical grants act as both a carrot—to encourage states to carry out national policy objectives—and a stick—to threaten states with the withholding of funds if they fail to carry out the federal government's policy objectives. According to critics of national power, categorical grants pose several problems for American federalism. They may act as "bribes to induce subnational governments to execute national policies" at the expense of their own authority.[59] Officials and citizens of wealthier states may feel that their taxes are being used to subsidize lower-spending state governments. The uncertainty surrounding the continued provision of the grants can make it harder for states to plan their own budgets. Finally, the administration of these programs requires a further expansion of the size of both national and state government.

Those who argue in favor of the use of categorical grants as a tool of national policymaking emphasize the degree to which the redistribution of monies between states can act to reduce inequality between the states. Also, these monies can help state, local, and regional governments improve the lives of their citizens in ways that might not be possible without the help of the federal government.[60]

President Lyndon Johnson's Great Society Expands Cooperative Federalism

The most significant expansion of national power through the use of categorical grants-in-aid in the post–New Deal era occurred during the presidency of Lyndon Johnson. His Great Society program created a new set of administrative agencies aimed at improving social welfare in the United States. Social welfare involves citizens' health, safety, education, and opportunities. Under the old system of dual federalism, social welfare policies were typically thought of as lying within the scope of the police powers of the states and, therefore, mostly under state control.

Although Roosevelt's policies had already involved the federal government in the provision of social welfare policy—for example, by addressing working conditions, unemployment relief, and income security—Johnson's policies expanded this role, aided by strong Democratic Party majorities in both the House and the Senate. Most of his initiatives were grants-in-aid to states and communities.

The Medicare program (1965) supplemented the Social Security program that had been created as part of the New Deal by providing health insurance coverage to individuals aged sixty-five and older. The Medicaid program (1965) provided health care assistance to individuals receiving other forms of aid as well as to those "who were medically indigent but not on welfare."[61] As with many Great Society programs, Medicaid was set up to be funded partly by the federal government and partly by the states. The Elementary and Secondary Education Act of 1965 (ESEA) "provided for the first time, general federal support for public elementary and secondary education."[62] Title I of the ESEA provided federal assistance to children from low-income families in both public and private schools.

With New Federalism Comes Devolution and Attempts to Roll Back National Power

Some backlash followed on the heels of Johnson's Great Society programs and the expansion of national authority that they produced. When Richard Nixon was elected president in 1968, he promised to roll back the expansion of national authority and return at least some of the power to the states. He called his project "new federalism."

One of Nixon's main tools to try to reduce national authority was the **block grant**. Though they are also a type of grant-in-aid, block grants provide federal money for public policies in a way that tries to increase state, local, and regional authority over how that money is spent and decrease national authority in deciding which states, localities, or regions receive those funds. (Look back at the right-hand column in Figure 3.3.) The main difference between block grants and categorical grants is one of flexibility. The strings attached to categorical grants give federal policymakers considerable authority in shaping how the policies are enacted on the ground. Block grants, in contrast, give state policymakers a greater say in how these monies are allocated and, therefore, what the policies actually look like when they are enacted.

Efforts to restore more authority to the states continued under the presidency of Ronald Reagan, who, in his speech accepting the Republican Party's nomination in 1980, promised, "Everything that can be run more effectively by state and local government we shall turn over to state and local government, along with the funding sources to pay for it." As part of his program, Reagan reduced funding for several social welfare programs and increased the use of block grants for those that continued to be funded.

The goal of returning authority for federal programs back to the states is called **devolution**, in the sense that authority is devolved, or returned to, the states. Efforts at devolution aim to increase states' autonomy in economic and social policy by decentralizing control and administration of programs. One of the most important of these efforts focused on social welfare policies. Democratic president Bill Clinton signed into law the Personal Responsibility and Work Opportunity Reconciliation Act of 1996 (PRWORA). PRWORA replaced a Roosevelt-era aid program with Temporary Assistance for Needy Families (TANF), which limits how long people are eligible to receive welfare assistance and added work requirements. In addition, block grants and other changes to the administration of the program gave states more authority in setting and enforcing the rules of welfare programs.

In terms of returning America to the dual federalism of its early history, however, none of the policies of the twentieth-century presidents even came close. At this point in American political history, there has been no going back to the stricter separation between state and national authority that operated prior to Roosevelt's revolution. However, as the United States confronts a new set of challenges in the twenty-first century, calls for a fundamental reexamination of American federalism have gained more and more attention.

State Governments Have Several Tools to Preserve Their Interests

In spite of efforts to restrain the power of the national government during the periods of new federalism and devolution, the New Deal legacy of national involvement in state policy has not fundamentally changed, nor is it likely to. For states to opt out, rejecting the involvement of the federal government that comes with accepting federal funds would require rejecting the funds themselves and either replacing them or explaining to that state's citizens why certain services will no longer be provided. While individual states may do this in regard to individual programs, a national, wholesale withdrawal is almost unthinkable.

State and local governments, however, have not necessarily been passive players in cooperative federalism, and strategic political actors at the various levels have played a role in trying to shape the balance of power between the two levels of the American federalist system. That is likely to continue and may result in an increased use of tools to assert state power, even confrontationally. States have a handful of tools they can use to shape how they participate in cooperative federalism.

One tool is tax policy, especially state sales taxes on e-commerce, where states are increasingly setting policies to collect tax revenues from products purchased online and are coordinating their policies with other state governments. Another tool is **intergovernmental lobbying**, where states and localities mobilize to influence legislation and regulation. Examples of intergovernmental lobbying organizations include the National Governors Association, the National Conference of State Legislatures, and the National League of Cities. Finally, states shape how policies are put into effect on the ground in the process of implementation, by filling in smaller details, definitions, and regulations contained in the laws.

The fact that states actually implement many federal policies provides an important source of state power. In *Federalist* No. 46, James Madison argued that states would have considerable power to resist the carrying out of an "unwarrantable measure of the federal government" by making it difficult, if not impossible, for those unpopular policies to actually be carried out.[63] In fact, according to one scholar of American federalism, "state governments have indeed succeeded tremendously in resisting, delaying, or altering the implementation of federal policies at the state level."[64]

Challenges to Cooperation

While states have opportunities under the modern system of cooperative federalism to try to preserve their authority and influence over policymaking, the relationship between states and the national government is not always cooperative. At times, state governments have objected to federal regulations that, from the point of view of the states, are attempts to make the states pay for federal policies. Such unpaid or underpaid requirements are called **unfunded mandates** or, sometimes, underfunded mandates.

From the point of view of Congress, there are strong incentives to make policies whose costs have to be carried by the states: "The legislator gets the credit for benefitting needy constituents, but the cost is paid by a lower governmental tier."[65] State, local, and regional governments have complained to Washington about the imposition of unfunded mandates in a variety of policy areas, including environmental policy, education policy, and the provision of health and social welfare benefits for low-income and disabled Americans.

One strategy that states use to try to reduce the impact of unfunded mandates is to pressure the federal government for waivers from certain provisions of a given law. Coordinated state pressure on the federal government can lead to exemptions from implementing—and paying for—certain unpopular provisions of a law. This kind of pressure is exactly what happened in

Adrienne Kosewicz, online business owner, shown in her home office in Seattle, Washington, in 2018. Kosewicz pays $3,600 a year for tax collection software to handle payments and reports to her home state. Her business sells toys through Amazon, which handles computation and collection.
AP Photo/Elaine Thompson

response to the federal requirements for standardized testing under the No Child Left Behind Act of 2002. Pressured by the states for more flexibility, the Department of Education during the Obama administration began to grant sweeping state-by-state waivers of some of the law's most stringent provisions. This flexibility was later enacted legislatively by Congress, in No Child Left Behind's successor. We will explore these issues, and education policy more generally, in detail in Chapter 14.

Another tactic that states have occasionally used, and may continue to use in the future, is to pass a state law that is in direct violation of a federal law or policy, perhaps amending the state constitution in order to do so. State laws legalizing recreational and medical cannabis use are a notable example of this tactic. In Chapter 5 we will explore ways in which southern state governments attempted to prevent or delay the desegregation of their states' public schools using similar tactics, prompting strong responses by the federal government.

As the American Republic enters the first decades of the twenty-first century, new state challenges to federal authority are emerging. One tool that many states have used to do this is the sovereignty resolution. Passed by state legislatures, **state sovereignty resolutions** affirm the sovereignty of states under the Tenth Amendment to the Constitution. Variations of these resolutions have been passed or considered in response to a variety of federal laws, including those covering education, immigration, and health care. They are often a response to mandates that state legislators believe are unfunded or underfunded. They are typically only statements of protest, stopping short of actually nullifying a law but asserting the rights of states to do so in the future if necessary.

Though sovereignty resolutions are largely symbolic, the Tenth Amendment has become a more prominent tool in asserting state authority in recent decades, especially in the area of gun control, as several Supreme Court decisions have cited the amendment in the logic of their decisions. In 1995, in *United States v. Lopez*, the

Court struck down a federal law banning the carrying of firearms near schools.[66] On March 10, 1992, Alfonso Lopez Jr. began yet another day of his senior year at Edison High School in San Antonio, Texas. However, this day he entered his high school with an unloaded .38 special revolver and five cartridges in his pocket. His task was to deliver the revolver and ammunition to another student in exchange for $44. Through anonymous sources, school authorities were made aware that Lopez was carrying an unloaded revolver and confronted him. After admitting he was carrying a firearm and ammunition, Alfonso Lopez Jr. was charged with violating the Gun-Free School Zones Act of 1990.

Lopez subsequently moved to dismiss the charges, claiming that the 1990 act was unconstitutional, as Congress did not have the power to regulate public schools. However, the trial court denied the motion, claiming that the act was within the powers enumerated to Congress under Article I, Section 8, Clause 3 of the U.S. Constitution, as activities within elementary, middle, and high schools are components of interstate commerce. After being tried and convicted, Lopez appealed to the Fifth Circuit Court of Appeals in hopes of reversing the decision by the trial court, as he and his representation felt that Congress had overstepped the enumerated powers granted in the commerce clause. The Fifth Circuit agreed, and the conviction was reversed.

The U.S. government was required to prove that the act was constitutional under the commerce clause and that the act dictated a significant portion of interstate commerce. The question presented to the Supreme Court was this: "Is the 1990 Gun-Free School Zones Act, forbidding individuals from knowingly carrying a gun in a school zone, unconstitutional because it exceeds the power of Congress to legislate under the Commerce Clause?"[67] This issue of Congress overstepping the power of the commerce clause had not been reviewed by the Supreme Court since World War II.

In a 5–4 decision, the Supreme Court upheld the ruling of the Fifth Circuit, claiming that "the possession of a gun in a local school zone is not an economic activity that might, through repetition elsewhere, have a substantial effect on interstate commerce. The law is a criminal statute that has nothing to do with 'commerce' or any sort of economic activity."[68] The majority opinion was delivered by Chief Justice William Rehnquist, with concurring opinions delivered by Justice Anthony Kennedy and Justice Clarence Thomas.

The majority opinion was based on four key factors: whether the activity in question was an economic activity, whether the firearm had been transported in interstate commerce, whether there was a link between firearms and education, and whether there was a correlation between the activity and interstate commerce. Justice Stephen Breyer delivered the main dissenting opinion in which he concluded that gun violence could influence interstate commerce and education. He reasoned that a court should not examine a lone isolated case of regulation but rather the overarching effect of firearms on school property.

The decision in *Lopez* was the first time that the Court had strongly limited the power of Congress under the commerce clause since President Roosevelt's battles with it during the New Deal. Following the *Lopez* decision, Congress amended the Gun-Free School Zones Act in 1994 to cover only firearms that had been transported across state lines, placing the law on a stronger constitutional footing, with the explicit focus on interstate commerce in its language.

Conclusion: The Evolution of Federalism Continues

The year 2020 did not turn out to be a big one for cannabis in the United States. It did, however, prove to be a very important one for American federalism, and the reasons are closely connected. COVID-19 upended many state legislative plans that had been set for the year, including cannabis reform initiatives. While nearly two dozen state legislatures had cannabis reform on the agenda earlier in the year, cannabis reform was generally placed on the back burner. State legislatures focused their efforts and energies instead on containing and responding to the outbreak. Pro-cannabis activists struggled to mobilize public support for new state initiatives in the face of social distancing and stay-at-home orders.

Those states that had already legalized recreational cannabis, however, found that the industry thrived in 2020. All recreational-use states except Massachusetts declared cannabis dispensaries to be essential businesses during the pandemic. The cannabis industry witnessed unprecedented demand for dispensaries offering curbside pick-up and delivery options in both recreational- and medicinal-use states. According to a cannabis market research director, in San Francisco, "purchases of edibles like gummy candies surged to levels typically only seen around April 20, or '4/20', the annual, if unofficial, marijuana appreciation holiday. Women and young people—Generation Z—accounted for much of the sales growth."[69] Long lines formed outside of dispensaries in San Francisco and other cities in the hours before stay-at-home orders went into effect, prompting another marketing executive to tweet, "#SanFrancisco goes on lockdown tonight…and the entire marina is buying weed."[70]

While the importance of cannabis as an issue in American federalism receded, the pandemic—and state and federal responses to it—brought federalism to the forefront of public debate. On the positive side, scholars noted that many states undertook closely-coordinated campaigns with neighboring states to control the pandemic. New York, New Jersey, Connecticut, and Pennsylvania, for example, worked together to coordinate school and business closures and other stay-at-home policies. Groups of states in the West and Midwest followed suit. The benefits of forming these kinds of interstate collaborations were one of the primary arguments that the Federalists offered during the ratification debates. Far less positively, directives from many state governments were unclear, confused, or in direct conflict with those of other, even neighboring, states.[71] Tensions between states—especially those with governments under Democratic Party control—and the Trump administration flared up constantly during the pandemic and further politicized state and governmental responses.

American federalism has always been an evolving and contested thing. Its dynamism is offered as one of its greatest strengths. However, in critical moments, the benefits of state experimentation and autonomy may run counter to the need for strong and coordinated national public policy. As the nation confronts, responds to, and recovers from the pandemic, the health of its federalist system will also bear close monitoring.

CHAPTER REVIEW

This chapter's main ideas are reflected in the Learning Objectives. By reviewing them here, you should be able to *remember* the key points and *know* these terms that are central to the topic.

3.1 Explain the tension in American federalism between state and federal laws.

Remember . . .
- The ultimate political authority in the American representative democracy rests with the people, but this authority is divided between two levels of government: the nation and the states.
- The use of medical marijuana in California was legal under the laws of the state but illegal under federal law.
- In *Gonzales v. Raich* (2005), the Supreme Court upheld the power of the federal government to set policy on the use and possession of marijuana and other controlled substances.
- Today, more and more states are legalizing recreational cannabis, yet marijuana remains illegal under federal law.

Know . . .
- *federalism* (p. 65)

3.2 Identify the elements of the U.S. Constitution that shape American federalism.

Remember . . .
- The Constitution lays out much of the framework of American federalism but not in one clear, neatly defined section. Instead, multiple clauses and sections attempt to define its basic boundaries.

Know . . .
- *commerce clause* (p. 72)
- *concurrent powers* (p. 73)
- *confederal systems* (p. 70)
- *enumerated powers* (p. 72)
- *federal systems* (p. 70)
- *implied powers* (p. 72)
- *necessary and proper clause* (p. 71)
- *police powers* (p. 73)
- *reserved powers* (p. 73)
- *supremacy clause* (p. 71)
- *unitary systems* (p. 70)

3.3   Describe the development of American federalism from the founding to the New Deal.

Remember . . .

- The boundaries between the authority of national and state governments have changed over time. Many of these changes have come about as a result of Supreme Court decisions in interpreting the Constitution.
- The New Deal fundamentally reshaped American federalism, but the program was not without challenges, especially by the Supreme Court.

Know . . .

- *cooperative federalism* (p. 80)
- *dual federalism* (p. 78)
- *states' rights* (p. 79)

3.4   Examine the role that the New Deal played in fundamentally reshaping American federalism.

Remember . . .

- Subsequent administrations, especially that of President Lyndon Johnson, expanded upon the promises and programs of the New Deal. However, later presidents, such as Ronald Reagan, attempted to restrict the power of the federal government and turn over more administrative authority to the states.

Know . . .

- *Great Depression* (p. 81)
- *New Deal* (p. 82)

3.5   Discuss changes to American federalism in the modern era and how it might continue to evolve.

Remember . . .

- State and local governments continue to be active in asserting their governmental authority.

Know . . .

- *block grant* (p. 89)
- *categorical grant* (p. 86)
- *devolution* (p. 89)
- *grant-in-aid* (p. 86)
- *intergovernmental lobbying* (p. 90)
- *state sovereignty resolutions* (p. 91)
- *unfunded mandates* (p. 90)

CHAPTER 4

CIVIL LIBERTIES

Building and Defending Fences

A woman checks her cell phone as she waits to enter the U.S. Supreme Court to attend the oral argument in the case of *Carpenter v. United States.* The Court was asked to decide whether the use of location tracking data from cell phone towers constituted a "search," which would compel law enforcement to obtain a warrant before acquiring it.

Alex Wong/Getty Images

By reading this chapter, you will be able to do the following:

4.1 Define *civil liberties,* and understand the key role they play in American political life.

4.2 Describe the civil liberties outlined in the Constitution, the amendments to it, and the process by which they were incorporated.

4.3 Explain the First Amendment protections granted to religion.

4.4 Outline the First Amendment protections concerning freedom of expression.

4.5 Summarize the civil liberties that are guaranteed by the Bill of Rights to those accused of crimes.

4.6 Understand the role that the Ninth and Tenth Amendments play in shaping the protection of freedoms in the nation and across the states.

The American Republic was founded upon the idea that people are born with certain fundamental rights and freedoms. In this representative democracy, citizens enter into a compact with their government: They willingly allow some restrictions upon their actions and expression of their rights in order to create a functioning political body, provided that government preserves and protects citizens' innate rights and liberties. This has always been an uneasy and shifting bargain. The scope of individual freedoms and the acceptable restrictions placed upon those freedoms is perpetually in dispute.

The rights that citizens possess that are protected from unreasonable governmental restriction are referred to as **civil liberties**. In contrast, the term *civil rights* refers to the fundamental rights of individuals to be treated equally under the laws and policies of the government, regardless of their identities and experiences. We will explore civil rights and the challenges present in their protection and establishment in the next chapter.

Civil liberties are often called **negative freedoms.** because protecting them involves restricting—*not* allowing—government actions. The First Amendment to the Constitution begins with "Congress shall make no law. . . ." It is this affirmation of the *limits* on the proper powers of government that helps to protect the fundamental freedoms of Americans. Most of the constitutional protections for American civil liberties reside in the **Bill of Rights**—the first ten amendments to the U.S. Constitution.

The stories in this chapter are about struggles to define and protect fundamental liberties and about building fences, especially around the power of government to restrict the expression of those liberties. One of the longest-running struggles in this area involves the tension between the need to have a safe and orderly society and the need to protect Americans' civil liberties. As we will explore in this chapter, the boundary lines between the rights and freedoms of individuals and the power of the U.S. government and its states are far from clear, fixed, or even agreed upon.

Cell Phone Tracking Capability Challenges the Boundary between Public and Private

4.1 Define *civil liberties*, and understand the key role they play in American political life.

It is entirely possible that your cell phone has a better memory of where you've been lately than you do. More detailed, almost certainly.[1]

We carry these devices around willingly and habitually; people even sleep with them. Yet, if some supervillain were to set out to invent a device that could create a detailed map—in both time and space—of where everyone is, where everyone has been, and with whom they've been, a cell phone would be a very good candidate. Add in some artificial intelligence software, and one could possibly do a fair job of predicting where a specific person will be in the future.

We may or may not have reached this point, but these technological capabilities—and what to do about the massive amounts of personal data mobile devices collect—are posing fundamental questions about how much personal privacy Americans can reasonably expect in the twenty-first century, especially in relation to law enforcement.

Under what conditions should it be acceptable for law enforcement to vacuum up all of the location data that we transmit constantly? What restrictions should be placed on the collection, analysis, and sharing of these data? What safeguards should be put in place? These are the questions that we take up as we consider the challenge of setting boundaries between personal freedoms and the need to have a safe and orderly society.

While exploring these issues, there is another—even trickier—question for us to consider: Are American political institutions sufficiently adaptable to handle the massive changes in communications technology that are taking place? As we will see, even members of the Supreme Court have their worries about this one.

We turn to Detroit and a Supreme Court ruling arising from a criminal case. Ironically, it involves stolen smartphones.[2]

The Supreme Court Places Restrictions on the Use of Cell Phone Tracking Data

In 2011 police arrested four men in connection with a series of armed robberies of RadioShack and T-Mobile stores in the Detroit area. One of the suspects confessed. He also identified fifteen of his accomplices and gave the FBI some of their cell phone numbers. Timothy Carpenter, he alleged, was the ringleader. Other accomplices would later identify Carpenter as the leader as well.

Based on the suspect's information, prosecutors obtained nearly thirteen thousand data location points (101 per day) recorded by cell phone towers, tracking Carpenter's location, movements, and calls. During the trial, an FBI agent with expertise in the use of this kind of surveillance technology produced maps "that placed Carpenter's phone near four of the charged robberies" while they were taking place.[3] Carpenter was found guilty on multiple counts of armed robbery and sentenced to more than one hundred years in prison.

Authorities had obtained the tracking information under the provisions of the federal Stored Communications Act (1986), which "permits the Government to compel the disclosure of certain telecommunications records when it 'offers specific and articulable facts showing that there are reasonable grounds to believe' that the records sought 'are relevant and material to an ongoing criminal investigation.'"[4]

The language in the law is key here. The phrase "reasonable grounds to believe" does not set the same standard that law enforcement must follow when it seeks to obtain other kinds of evidence in a criminal investigation. Typically, when law enforcement wants to conduct a search, investigators must obtain a search warrant. To do so, they must convince a judge that they have probable cause—a reasonable belief that a crime has been committed or that there is evidence of a crime—to conduct the search. Obtaining the cell phone tracking data under the Stored Communications Act, however, did not require a search warrant; officers only needed reasonable grounds to believe they would find evidence, not establish probable cause in front of a judge.

Prior to his trial, Carpenter's attorneys argued that the cell phone location data—as it had not been obtained with a search warrant—was inadmissible and violated rights affirmed by the Fourth Amendment to the Constitution: For "the people to be secure in their persons, houses, papers, and effects," they are protected from "unreasonable search and seizures." The judge was not convinced, and Carpenter was convicted. Following his conviction, Carpenter and his attorneys sued, and the case ended up before the Supreme Court.

In its ruling in *Carpenter v. United States* in 2018, the Court, by a 5–4 margin, sided with Carpenter, determining that the acquisition of his location history through the cell tower data did constitute a search and that "the Government must generally obtain a warrant supported by probable cause before acquiring such records."[5] The Court, however, also stated that there may be justifications for releasing cell tower data without a warrant, such as in cases of "bomb threats, active shootings, and child abductions."[6]

The Court Continues to Wrestle with the Challenges to Civil Liberties Posed by Technological Change

Following the Court's ruling, many civil liberties advocates celebrated the decision. "'This is a groundbreaking victory for privacy rights in the digital age,' said Carol Rose, executive director of the American Civil Liberties Union (ACLU) of Massachusetts, adding that it 'provides a framework for safeguarding other sensitive digital information—from our emails and smart home appliances to technology that has yet to be invented.'"[7] Prosecutors, however, were concerned. "Cell site information is often gathered earlier in an investigation," noted a former federal prosecutor,

"It's one of the building blocks to establish probable cause and support obtaining things like search warrants and, eventually, charges."[8]

The case, however, also illustrates a deep and ongoing question, not just about the boundaries of protection around civil liberties but also about the ability of American political institutions to properly delineate them in the face of technological change. This is not a new question.

In coming to its decision in *Carpenter*, the Court looked back to its ruling in a case from 1928: *Olmstead v. United States*.[9] In that case, federal agents—without judicial approval—installed a wiretap in the office building of a suspected bootlegger and used the evidence to obtain a conviction on conspiracy to violate the National Prohibition Act. The suspect's attorneys argued that the wiretap evidence was inadmissible and constituted a violation of Fourth Amendment protections. The Supreme Court disagreed and ruled that the wiretap did not constitute "search and seizure."

Not all of the justices were convinced. Writing in his dissent, Justice Louis Brandeis warned that the technological innovations known in 1928 would only continue to advance and would present future Supreme Courts with even trickier problems.

In the twenty-first century, justices were still concerned. During the oral arguments phase of the *Carpenter* case, Justice Sonia Sotomayor worried about government's ability to monitor individuals even more intrusively. "As I understand it," she said, "a cellphone can be pinged in your bedroom. It can be pinged at your doctor's office. It can ping you in the most ten intimate details of your life. Presumably at some point even in a dressing room as you're undressing. So I am not beyond the belief that someday a provider could turn on my cell phone and listen to my conversations."[10]

That day, according to some observers, is already here. Interviewed in Moscow in 2014, Edward Snowden—who, if he should return to the United States, will face prosecution for divulging details of the extensive monitoring of Americans by the National Security Agency (NSA)—revealed that the government has the remote capability to make your phone "play dead," leaving the microphone and camera on and recording even after you think you have turned the phone off. "The only way you can tell," according to a former cybersecurity researcher who has worked with the CIA, "is if your phone feels warm when it's turned off."[11]

Rapid advances in surveillance capability pose fundamental and unavoidable questions to Americans and their political institutions, questions about boundaries and who gets to set them. At what point does location data become private and protected from unauthorized governmental access? And, following directly from that question, which political institutions should have the authority to delineate this boundary between public and private in the digital realm? Each of the three branches of the federal government *can* play a role in setting boundaries—either through federal legislation, executive branch enforcement, or judicial action; however, there is no guarantee that they will do so or that they will do so effectively. This raises one more tricky question: Are American political institutions up to the task of digital fence-building in the face of such rapid technological change?

These issues are not going away, and American political institutions are going to continue to face the challenge of delimiting and protecting American civil liberties in an era where technology is redefining what private and public mean. And the boundary between digital privacy and security is only one of many that will need to be drawn and redrawn around Americans' civil liberties. We turn now in detail to those fundamental freedoms as laid out in the Constitution and the Bill of Rights.

The Bill of Rights Establishes Protections for Americans' Civil Liberties

4.2 Describe the civil liberties outlined in the Constitution, the amendments to it, and the process by which they were incorporated.

One of the main concerns the delegates to the Constitutional Convention in 1787 brought with them was how they would secure the protection of individual rights. Following independence, most of the state governments had included some protections for individual rights in their own constitutions.[12] However, those protections varied considerably and often lacked key components that Americans today typically think of as fundamental rights, such as freedom of the press or religion. The delegates agreed to place within the original document certain protections, such as a strict limit on the definition of treason as well as restrictions on punishments available for those convicted of it.[13] They did not, however, include a bill of rights—a list of fundamental individual rights that a government cannot restrict or intrude upon except under specific circumstances.

The Bill of Rights Takes Center Stage in the Ratification Debates

During the ratification campaign following the Constitutional Convention, the Anti-Federalists seized upon the lack of a bill of rights in the proposed document. Their motives for highlighting the issue were diverse. Some used the lack of a bill of rights as a tactical weapon, hoping to defeat the Constitution entirely. Some were opposed to the federal powers of taxation and regulation of commerce and wanted a bill to protect the rights of states.[14] Others argued that a list of fundamental rights was a necessary protection against the inevitable growth of centralized power in what was sure to become a large republic.

Against the Anti-Federalists' charges, the Federalists offered several counterarguments. In *Federalist* No. 84, Alexander Hamilton argued first that a bill of rights was unnecessary. The proposed Constitution, he noted, already contained provisions guaranteeing specific rights.[15] Second, Hamilton argued that including a bill of rights would be dangerous to individual liberty, not supportive of it. His central concern was that any list of individual rights would necessarily be incomplete. What about those rights not enumerated? Might the lack of their textual protections encourage a tyrant to deny them? As we will discuss later in the chapter, the question of protections for rights not specifically enumerated remains one of the most important topics in the study and application of American civil liberties today.

The Anti-Federalists' strategy proved to be a winning one—in a way. They failed to defeat the new Constitution, but on Monday, June 8, 1789, during the first session of Congress, James Madison, as promised during the ratification debate, introduced a draft of the Bill of Rights.[16] After reworking and revising his proposed list, Congress proposed twelve amendments to the Constitution and sent them to the states for ratification. Of these, ten were formally ratified on December 15, 1791.[17] The Bill of Rights had become part of the Constitution.

The list of rights was carefully crafted, covering a wide swath of issues. The First Amendment prevents the legislative branch from passing laws restricting a variety of individual rights, including religion, speech, the press, and assembly. The next two amendments deal with powers generally under the authority of the executive branch involving firearms, state militias, and the quartering of soldiers in people's homes and on their property.

The Fourth through Eighth Amendments guarantee rights of Americans involved with the judicial system: those accused of, arrested for, tried for, and convicted of crimes as well as certain noncriminal cases. The Ninth Amendment arose from concerns that any list of individual rights might be thought of as exhaustive. Therefore, it specifies that the list in the Bill of Rights does not presume or imply a lack of protection for those not enumerated. Finally, the Tenth Amendment declares that those powers not specifically delegated to the federal government are "reserved to the States" or, in a confounding addendum, "to the people." We will explore specific amendments in detail below. Table 4.1 summarizes the main provisions of the Bill of Rights.

The Bill of Rights Establishes Civil Liberties Protections, and Selective Incorporation Applies Them to the States

The text of the Bill of Rights does not place restrictions upon the actions of state governments. It only restrains the powers of the federal government. For example, the First Amendment begins, "Congress shall make no law," and not "Congress and the Legislatures of the several States shall make no laws."

So, for much of the nation's history, the explicit protections contained within the Bill of Rights did not apply to state laws and actions, and the Supreme Court upheld this strict, textual reading of the Constitution. The foundation for extending the protections of the Bill of Rights to state laws and actions was laid in the Fourteenth Amendment, ratified in 1868, specifically by its guarantee against the deprivation by any state of "life, liberty, or property without due process of law"—called the **due process clause**. This process, however, is ongoing.[18]

An Overview of Protections Contained within the Bill of Rights

Amendment	Protection
First	Restricts the lawmaking powers of Congress in the areas of religion, speech, the press, assembly, and petitioning the government
Second	The right to keep and bear arms
Third	No forced quartering of troops in homes
Fourth	Protects against unreasonable search and seizure and establishes the right to have warrants issued prior to arrest or search
Fifth	Right to a grand jury indictment in criminal cases, protection against double jeopardy and self-incrimination, the right to due process of law, and the right to just compensation when private property is taken for public use
Sixth	Protections during criminal prosecutions for a speedy and public trial by an impartial jury, the right to confront witnesses, the right to compel favorable witnesses to testify in one's defense, and the right to the assistance of defense counsel
Seventh	Right to a trial by jury in certain civil suits
Eighth	Protections against excessive bail, excessive fines, and cruel and unusual punishment
Ninth	Nonexclusion of rights not listed in the Constitution
Tenth	Affirms that rights not granted to the federal government are held by the states or the people

In a process called **selective incorporation** because of its selective, piecemeal development, the Supreme Court has, over time, used the due process clause of the Fourteenth Amendment to expand the protections of the Bill of Rights to also apply to state laws and actions. Initially, however, the Court refused to do so when given the chance. In *The Slaughter-House Cases* (1873), the Supreme Court interpreted the Fourteenth Amendment's protections as applying only to African Americans and reaffirmed sharp distinctions between state and federal citizenship.[19] It was not until 1925 with *Gitlow v. New York* that the Court began to shift its position.[20]

In its decision in *Gitlow*, the Supreme Court formally incorporated the First Amendment, declaring that there were limits on the states' ability to restrict expression and the press. In doing so, it signaled that the freedoms of speech and the press constituted *fundamental freedoms* that could not be legitimately restricted by the states without a compelling reason to do so.

Over the two decades following *Gitlow*, the Supreme Court issued a series of decisions incorporating most of the First Amendment's protections for speech, the press, assembly, and religion. Several decades later, in another burst of activity, the Court incorporated the protections for those accused of, arrested for, tried for, and convicted of crimes under state laws. Most recently, in 2019, the Court incorporated the Eighth Amendment's prohibition of excessive fines.[21] As of 2020, most but not all of the protections within the Bill of Rights had been incorporated (see Table 4.2). We will explore many of these cases in detail in this chapter as we consider specific amendments, the protections that they affirm, and the tensions and controversies arising from trying to delimit the boundaries of their promises.

TABLE 4.2

Selective Incorporation of the Bill of Rights

Amendment	Right Incorporated	Supreme Court Decision
First	Freedom from establishment of religion	*Everson v. Board of Education*, 330 U.S. 1 (1947)
	Freedom of religious expression	*Cantwell v. Connecticut*, 310 U.S. 296 (1940)
	Freedom of speech	*Gitlow v. New York*, 268 U.S. 652 (1925)
	Freedom of the press	*Near v. Minnesota ex rel. Olson*, 283 U.S. 697 (1931)
	Right to peaceably assemble	*De Jonge v. Oregon*, 299 U.S. 353 (1937)
Second	Right to keep and bear arms	*McDonald v. Chicago*, 561 U.S. 742 (2010)
Third	Right not to have soldiers quartered in homes	Not incorporated
Fourth	Protection against unreasonable searches and seizures	*Wolf v. Colorado*, 338 U.S. 25 (1949; illegally obtained evidence is still permissible in trial, however)
	Warrant needed for search and seizure	*Mapp v. Ohio*, 367 U.S. 643 (1961; illegally obtained evidence cannot be used in trial)
Fifth	Right to indictment by grand jury in cases involving a serious crime	Not incorporated
	Protection against double jeopardy	*Benton v. Maryland*, 395 U.S. 784 (1969)
	Protection against self-incrimination	*Malloy v. Hogan*, 378 U.S. 1 (1964)
	Right of just compensation for private property taken	*Chicago, Burlington, and Quincy Railroad v. City of Chicago*, 166 U.S. 226 (1897)
Sixth	Right to a speedy and public trial	*In re Oliver*, 333 U.S. 257 (1948); *Klopfer v. North Carolina*, 386 U.S. 213 (1967)
	Right to trial by an impartial jury	*Parker v. Gladden*, 385 U.S. 363 (1966)
	Right to confront witnesses	*Pointer v. Texas*, 380 U.S. 400 (1965)
	Right to compel witnesses to testify in the defendant's favor	*Washington v. Texas*, 388 U.S. 14 (1967)
	Right to counsel in cases involving capital punishment	*Powell v. Alabama*, 287 U.S. 45 (1932)
	Right to counsel in felony cases	*Gideon v. Wainwright*, 372 U.S. 335 (1963)

Amendment	Right Incorporated	Supreme Court Decision
Seventh	Right to trial by jury in civil cases	Not incorporated
Eighth	Protection against excessive bail or fines	*Timbs v. Indiana*, 586 U.S. ___ (2019)
	Protection against cruel and unusual punishment	*Robinson v. California*, 370 U.S. 660 (1962)

The Relationship between Members of Indigenous Nations and the Bill of Rights Has Evolved over Time

As citizens of two governments—their nations and the United States—indigenous Americans' civil liberties are defined by the laws of both. Through a long legal and judicial history—one that took place against an even longer backdrop of displacement, disenfranchisement, and use of force—most but not all of the protections of the Bill of Rights have been extended to indigenous Americans, placing limits on the actions of both the federal government and tribal governments.[22] Many indigenous nations also have their own tribal constitutions.

The Constitution of the Standing Rock Sioux Tribe, for example, includes a bill of rights that affirms many of the same fundamental liberties as the American Bill of Rights. Unlike the federal Constitution, however, that of the Standing Rock Sioux also orders its government to "recognize and promote the economic and educational opportunities of the Standing Rock Sioux Tribal members in a fair and impartial manner."[23]

The process of selective incorporation has made clear that both state and tribal governments are restricted in their ability to infringe upon Americans' fundamental rights and freedoms. But the boundaries around those rights and freedoms are still being drawn. To investigate these issues, we will consider the amendments and the liberties affirmed within them in turn.

The First Amendment's First Two Protections Both Involve Religion

4.3   Explain the First Amendment protections granted to religion.

The third suggested amendment in James Madison's list of seventeen ended up as the First Amendment to the Constitution. The First Amendment restricts what most delegates to the Constitutional Convention thought would be the most powerful, and potentially the most dangerous, entity of the federal government: Congress, the legislative branch.

The Establishment and Free Exercise Clauses Ensure Separation of Church and State

The first two civil liberties affirmed and protected in the Bill of Rights involve religion. The First Amendment begins with "Congress shall make no law respecting an establishment of religion, or prohibiting the free exercise thereof." These two statements, or clauses, form the constitutional bases for protections of religious freedom and expression in America. The first is called the **establishment clause**, as it prohibits governmental establishment of, or support for, religion. The second statement is referred to as the **free exercise clause** because it guards the rights of individuals to exercise and express their religious beliefs.

As with so many other areas of civil liberties, these clauses involve situations that are clear-cut as well as those that are not so easy to evaluate. For example, any attempt by the federal government or one of the states to declare an official religion would be a clear violation of the establishment clause. Similarly, any attempt to prohibit Americans' expressions of their religious faiths in their own homes, provided they did not violate others' fundamental rights and freedoms, would also be unconstitutional.

What about the more difficult cases, however? Consider a student who wants to say a prayer in their valedictory address at her public high school's graduation ceremonies. For the school, as a public institution, to appear to condone her prayer implies a violation of the establishment clause. For it to restrict their right to say a prayer, however, implies a violation of the free exercise clause. How should this situation be handled? That is a question, again, for the Supreme Court.

Courts Have Tested the Establishment Clause over Funding for Religious Schools.

One of the most important Supreme Court decisions dealing with government support for or involvement with religion, and the one that incorporated the establishment clause, was *Everson v. Board of Education* (1947). The case considered a New Jersey law that authorized payment by local school boards of the costs of student transportation to and from private schools, including Catholic ones. A New Jersey taxpayer filed suit claiming that these payments constituted impermissible government support for religion. In its decision, a divided Court ruled that the program was acceptable as it was a "general program to help parents get their children, regardless of their religion, safely and expeditiously to and from accredited schools."[24]

Courts Have Also Tested the Establishment Clause over Prayer in School.

Perhaps no establishment clause issue has been more vexing to the Supreme Court than that of prayer in public schools. In 1962, in *Engel v. Vitale*, the Court ruled unconstitutional the voluntary reading in New York's public schools of the prayer, "Almighty God, we acknowledge our dependence upon Thee, and we beg Thy blessings upon us, our parents, our teachers and our Country."[25] Although the policy's supporters argued that the prayer was nondenominational and permitted students to remain silent or be excused from the classroom during the reading, the Court found that it violated the establishment clause. The next year, in *Abington School District v. Schempp*, the Court struck down a program that involved the reading of ten verses from the Bible and a recitation of the Lord's Prayer at the beginning of each day in Pennsylvania's public schools.[26] In his opinion, Justice Tom C. Clark quoted Madison's warnings about the dangers of enmeshing government and religion, even in seemingly small ways, noting that "it is proper to take alarm at the first experiment on our liberties."[27]

Courts Have Addressed the Boundaries of the Establishment of Religion.

In trying to set guidelines for what is and is not permissible under the establishment clause, the Court has at different times employed various litmus tests for federal and state laws and actions. Proponents of a strict separationist approach to deciding the issue argue for a close textual reading of the establishment clause and say no forms of government support for

Students at Royal High School in Simi Valley, California—a public school—in prayer during a lunchtime meeting. As long as such meetings occur outside instructional time and are both initiated and led by students, they are constitutionally permissible.

Anne Cusack/*Los Angeles Times* via Getty Images

religious institutions are permissible. However, given policy objectives—such as in helping students receive a good education—and the history of religion in American political life, strict separation can be difficult to achieve in the real world. For example, in its decision in *Everson v. Board of Education*, in which it cited Jefferson's metaphor of a "wall of separation," the Court allowed taxpayer funds to be used for transporting students to and from religious schools.

One of the most important tools that the Court has used is the **Lemon test**, named after the Court decision in which it was laid out: *Lemon v. Kurtzman* (1971).[28] The case dealt with Rhode Island and Pennsylvania programs that supplemented the salaries of teachers and provided educational materials (though only the same ones used in the public schools) in religiously based private schools for the purpose of teaching nonreligious subjects. The Court struck down both programs as violating the establishment clause. In doing so, it set out a three-pronged test for permissible government involvement. First, the underlying statute must have a "secular legislative purpose." Second, its effect "must be one that neither advances nor inhibits religion." Third, it must not foster "excessive entanglement between government and religion."

Courts Have Addressed the Boundaries of the Freedom of Religious Expression.

Important cases concerning religious establishment have also often involved the second of the First Amendment's two guarantees on religious freedom: freedom of religious expression. While Americans are free to hold any religious beliefs, they are not always free to act on them. As is the case with the establishment clause, the Supreme Court has had to wrestle with the boundaries of free exercise.

Mauro Morales, shown in front of his business sign in Rio Grande City, Texas, is one of three "Peyoteros," Texans licensed to sell peyote that grows near the border with Mexico, to tens of thousands of Native American Church members across the United States. The Supreme Court has decided that the use of peyote, a hallucinogen, is a constitutionally protected part of Native Americans' exercise of their First Amendment rights of free exercise of religion in spite of its classification as an illegal substance.

AP Photo/LM Otero

The free exercise clause was incorporated in *Cantwell v. Connecticut* (1940). The case involved the distribution of religious materials and playing of religious messages on a phonograph by two members of the Jehovah's Witnesses in a predominantly Catholic neighborhood. The two men, Jesse Cantwell and his son, were arrested under a town ordinance that gave local government officials the authority to decide if such solicitation was legal or not. In its decision, the Supreme Court distinguished between "freedom to believe and freedom to act. The first [the Court noted] is absolute, but, in the nature of things, the second cannot be."[29] While the Court upheld the principle that the state might have a valid interest in restricting the actions involved in religious expression—to maintain safety and public order, for example—in this case the Cantwells' actions posed no threat other than being offensive to some. Their convictions were overturned.

More recently, in *Employment Division v. Smith* (1990), the Court adopted a **neutrality test** in deciding on conflicts between religious expression and legitimate state action. In that case, two individuals had been fired from their jobs as rehabilitation counselors for using the sacramental religious drug peyote in violation of Oregon state law. They were also denied unemployment benefits as a result of their termination. The two men argued that the use of peyote was within their First Amendment rights of free expression as members of the Native American Church.[30] In its opinion, the Court ruled that the state law banning the use and possession of peyote was not targeted toward individuals as a result of their beliefs but that it represented a valid, compelling state interest and was religiously neutral, even if it restricted the religious expression of individuals.

The First Amendment Also Protects Expression: Speech, Press, Assembly, and Petitioning the Government

> 4.4 Outline the First Amendment protections concerning freedom of expression.

Although they come after the two clauses about religion in the text, those parts of the First Amendment that deal with **freedom of expression** are often considered the most fundamental affirmations of Americans' rights and liberties. They involve the expression of political beliefs and opinions. The right to express one's thoughts, especially in being critical of those in power, is one of the cornerstones of American civil liberties.

Free Expression Was Challenged in the Early Years of the Republic

Those who argued for the importance of freedom of expression had good reason to want to protect it. Shortly after the new nation was founded, it was confronted with the question of how far a government could go to restrict these rights. Like many other cases since, this one revolved around questions of national security. The situation involved laws known as the **Alien and Sedition Acts**, which were passed by Congress—controlled by the Federalist Party—and signed into law by Federalist president John Adams in 1798. These laws attempted to suppress Anti-Federalist opposition to the policies of the president and Congress. Among other provisions, the acts authorized severe restrictions on the rights of free speech and the free press. Any behavior that was judged by a federal court (usually controlled by Federalist Party judges) to be part of a conspiracy against the government of the United States, or any publication or speech that was deemed to be "false, scandalous, [or] malicious . . . against the government of the United States, or either house of the Congress of the United States, or the President of the United States," was punishable by fines and imprisonment.[31] Under the power of these acts, newspaper editors opposing Adams and the Federalists "were quickly indicted, and ten were brought to trial and convicted by juries under the influence of Federalist judges."[32]

Courts Have Attempted to Balance Political Expression against the Needs of National Security

One of the most difficult issues in the protection of political expression is balancing that fundamental right with the needs of national security. In 1917, Charles Schenck

Clarence Brandenburg (left), a Ku Klux Klan leader, with Richard Hanna, an admitted member of the American Nazi Party, in Cincinnati, Ohio, in August 1964. Brandenburg's case established a high standard of permissible speech, up to advocating for the legitimacy of violent action, but not organizing for it.

AP Photo

and Elizabeth Baer oversaw the printing and distribution of antiwar leaflets encouraging young men not to comply with the military draft. They were convicted under the Espionage Act of 1917, which made it a crime to interfere with military recruiting. In *Schenck v. United States* (1919), a unanimous Court ruled against the defendants, arguing that the restrictions on expression under the Espionage Act were permissible.

In its decision, the Court established the **clear and present danger test** to evaluate restrictions on political speech, ordering that the context of such expression must be taken into account. The danger, so to speak, with the clear and present danger test is its subjectivity. If a government can restrict urgings not to comply with a draft, then the scope of restricted speech might be interpreted quite widely.

Several cases in the early twentieth century upheld the right of government to restrict such speech in the national interest. However, in a dissent in one of those cases, Supreme Court justice Oliver Wendell Holmes would go on to establish the idea that ideas should compete, as in a marketplace. He wrote, "The best test of truth is the power of the thought to get itself accepted in the competition of the market."[33] Holmes's words did not reflect the mindset of the majority, but his language has been cited by justices in subsequent Courts as they wrestled with the need to balance free political expression with national security.

The modern standard for restrictions on political speech was set in 1969 in *Brandenburg v. Ohio*. At a Ku Klux Klan rally, Klan leader Clarence Brandenburg made a speech threatening that "if our President, our Congress, our Supreme Court, continues to suppress the white, Caucasian race, it's possible that there might have to be some vengeance taken."[34] The Supreme Court ruled for Brandenburg, establishing a two-pronged test of acceptable restrictions on such political speech: Speech that merits restriction must be "directed to inciting or producing imminent lawless action and [must be] likely to incite or produce such action."[35] The test that the Court developed placed a much higher standard on permissible restrictions of political speech, even allowing speech that advocates for the legitimacy of violent action, though it must not actually organize for it. While Brandenburg suggested that "vengeance" might need to be taken, he did not actually organize or incite specific action. If he had, for example, called on a group of rally attendees to join him in committing a violent act, then his speech would have been seen as properly subject to legal restrictions and consequences.

Courts Have Weighed Press Freedoms against National Security

The tension between national security and limits on free expression also applies to the press. One of the key questions in this arena is whether the government may take action only after an article has been published or whether it may exercise **prior restraint** by preventing it from being published at all. Although the Alien and Sedition Acts restricted the ability of the press to criticize the federal government, the Supreme Court did not weigh in on the issue of prior restraint until the twentieth century.

The question of the permissibility of prior restraint during wartime came up during the Vietnam conflict and centered on attempts by the Nixon administration to prevent the *New York Times* and the *Washington Post* from publishing classified materials describing—often unflatteringly—high-level decision making on the part of U.S. officials in conducting the war. In *New York Times v. United States* (1971), the Supreme Court, in a highly divided opinion, ruled that the government did not demonstrate a sufficiently pressing interest to justify such prior restraint; this set a very high bar for the ability of government to prevent publication.[36]

Symbolic Speech Is Protected as a Form of Political Expression

The Supreme Court has extended its protection of political expression to **symbolic speech**, such as images, signs, and symbols used as forms of political expression. In 1968, in *United States v. O'Brien*, the Court ruled against David Paul O'Brien and three other individuals in Boston who had burned their draft cards and encouraged others to do the same in protest against the Vietnam War. In doing so, it set out a three-pronged test of acceptable restriction of symbolic speech under such circumstances: (1) the government must have a substantial interest in doing do, (2) the government's interest must not be the suppression of speech, and (3) the "incidental restriction" of the First Amendment rights should be "no greater than is essential" to accomplish the government's goal.[37] In this case, the Supreme Court held that the government's need to have young men register for the draft passed such a test.

The burning, alteration, or destruction of the American flag in protest has also received Supreme Court protection as a form of symbolic political expression. In *Texas v. Johnson* (1989), the Court overturned the conviction of a man who had

A man burns an American flag in Portland, Oregon, during a protest in January 2017 against the inauguration of President Donald J. Trump. The Supreme Court has made the symbolic act of flag burning a form of protected speech.

Sipa via AP Images

burned the American flag in protest during the 1984 Republican National Convention. "The Government," the Court held, "may not prohibit the verbal or nonverbal expression of an idea merely because society finds the idea offensive or disagreeable, even where our flag is involved."[38]

Other Forms of Expression Have More Limited Protection

While political expression (in speech, writing, symbols, and of the press) has secured considerable protection, the Supreme Court has ruled that other types and forms of speech and publications do not have the same privilege, though it has often set a high bar for restrictions on them.

Expression that defames a person's character, whether in writing or similarly published media (**libel**) or in spoken form (**slander**), is not protected in the same way as political expression and may leave the actor responsible for such statements in legal trouble.[39] To win a case based on libel or slander in the United States, an aggrieved party must show that the statements, publications, or even gestures were made public, that they were untrue, and that they caused harm. For statements and publications about public figures, the standard is even higher, with the plaintiff (the public figure) having to prove that the communication was made with malice, and not, for example, out of a disagreement over the public figures' actions.[40]

Hate speech is another form of damaging expression upon which limits have been placed and for which the Court has struggled to define the proper boundaries. Hate speech is speech that has no other purpose but to express hatred, particularly toward members of a group identified by racial or ethnic identity, gender, or sexual orientation. In *R.A.V. v. St. Paul* (1992), the Court overturned a hate speech ordinance on the grounds that it impermissibly focused on the content of the speech.[41]

Another form of expression that receives weaker protection under the First Amendment is **fighting words**—expression that is likely to incite violence or disrupt the peace. In *Chaplinsky v. New Hampshire* (1942), the Court upheld restrictions on words that "by their very utterance, inflict injury or tend to incite an immediate breach of the peace," but it also affirmed that such restrictions must be narrowly targeted so as not to constitute an undue restriction of First Amendment rights.[42]

Finally, the Supreme Court has upheld restrictions on **obscenity and pornography**, though it has not always been clear just what constitutes an obscene statement or publication. In *Roth v. United States* (1957), the Court defined the standard for judging obscenity—and, therefore, constitutionally permissible restrictions on its expression—as "whether, to the average person, applying contemporary community standards, the dominant theme of the material, taken as a whole, appeals to prurient interest."[43] Marking the boundaries this way raises another challenge, however. What, exactly, are "contemporary community standards," and who gets to define them?

In *Miller v. California* (1973), the Supreme Court attempted to more clearly define obscenity. It set out three criteria that all must be met for material to be considered obscene and, therefore, legitimately subject to restriction. First, the material must be "patently offensive." It must also be "utterly without redeeming social value." Finally, in determining the applicability of the first two parts of the test, "contemporary community standards" must be applied, meaning that different locales may have different standards.[44]

Even this new test, however, is highly subjective. And when one considers material published over the Internet, things become even more challenging. For example, how does one define *community* when considering online material? In 1997, the Court struck down provisions of the Communications Decency Act of 1996, which had been designed to protect minors from viewing obscene or pornographic material on the Internet. The Court held that the restrictions in the act were too vague and restrictive and that they carried the danger of having a "chilling effect on free speech."[45] Depictions of sexual material involving minors, however, have carried no similar First Amendment protections and are subject to full restriction and criminalization.

Freedom of Assembly Is Broadly Protected

The final two rights within the First Amendment—the right to peaceably assemble and to petition the government—have received relatively little Supreme Court attention. When the Court has ruled on them, however, it has generally done so in a way similar to how it has treated political expression, regarding them as cornerstones of civil liberties and rights that should be broadly protected.

The right to peacefully assemble was incorporated in 1937 in *De Jonge v. Oregon*. In that case, the Court overturned an Oregon law under which a member of the Communist Party had been convicted and sentenced to seven years in prison for holding a public meeting. In his opinion, quoting an earlier case, Chief Justice Charles Evans Hughes noted, "The very idea of a government, republican in form, implies a right on the part of citizens to meet peaceably for consultation in respect to public affairs and to petition for a redress of grievances."[46]

As is probably clear by now, there has been a great deal of struggle, controversy, and Supreme Court action throughout American history with regard to freedom of religion, speech, the press, and assembly—and these all involve only the First Amendment.[47] In the Bill of Rights, many other liberties are also addressed.

PRACTICING POLITICAL SCIENCE

INTERPRETING THE SECOND AMENDMENT IN THE TWENTY-FIRST CENTURY

Although firearms ownership by Americans is a highly charged topic of debate in politics today, for most of its history the Supreme Court said very little about the Second Amendment. In 1939, the Court upheld restrictions on private ownership of certain types of weapons—sawed-off shotguns and machine guns—as a result of gangland violence during the era of Prohibition.[48] In his opinion in *United States v. Miller*, Justice James McReynolds stated that "in the absence of any evidence tending to show that possession or use of a 'shotgun having a barrel of less than eighteen inches in length' at this time has some reasonable relationship to the preservation or efficiency of a well regulated militia, we cannot say that the Second Amendment guarantees the right to keep and bear such an instrument."[49]

Not until 2008 did the Court rule directly on laws prohibiting personal possession of firearms generally, as opposed to specific types of them. In a 5–4 decision in *District of Columbia v. Heller*, the Court overturned a District of Columbia ban on handgun ownership for the purpose of self-defense within an individual's home.[50] As *Heller* involved Washington, DC, and not a state, it was decided based on the Second Amendment directly. Incorporation to the states happened two years later, in *McDonald v. Chicago*. In this case, the Court—again splitting 5–4—overturned a Chicago ban on handgun ownership and incorporated the Second Amendment to the states.[51]

In these cases (and the other cases in this chapter), the Supreme Court was engaged in constitutional interpretation—reviewing laws and actions in light of the meaning of the Constitution, which is the highest law of the land. We will explore how the Supreme Court got this power in the first place, as well as how individual justices go about using it, in more detail in later chapters. For now, however, it is important to remember that all Americans are given a similar task in that our understandings of the Constitution inform our political preferences and shape our actions in making our representatives understand what we think it means. So what should we consider?

We start with the words of the Second Amendment, which is stylistically a bit different from the rest of the Bill of Rights in that it gives its own justification in its first clause:[52]

> A well regulated Militia, being necessary to the security of a free State, the right of the people to keep and bear Arms, shall not be infringed.

Different readings of these words—of their *plain meaning*—continue to lead to very different interpretations of how broad the Second Amendment's protections on firearms ownership are in the twenty-first century. Those skeptical of the Second Amendment's scope often point out that the term *militia* does not describe individual firearm ownership. Activities such as hunting and target shooting are not carried out by militias such as the National Guard.

Another place to look for guidance is the *historical context* in which the amendment was

Second Amendment supporters hold signs at a rally in support of gun ownership at the Colorado State Capitol in Denver in 2013. Although their signs quote the Constitution in support of their position, the plain meaning of these words is open to interpretation.

Marc Piscotty/Getty Images

and do look to the decisions of their predecessors in similar cases, to the precedents that those Courts set. Also, justices may consider their own understandings and preferences, although the degree to which they *should* do this is a contested question. A justice might, for example, conclude that the fence between personal freedom and collective security on the issue of firearms ownership needs to be moved, given the costs of gun violence.

WHaT Do You Think?

Firearms laws are among the consequential in the nation, as are policies governing firearms ownership and use. They also raise a fundamental constitutional challenge, similar to that posed by cell phone tracking: As members of a constitutional republic, Americans agree to abide by a set of written rules that "they" created in a very different time. For this to work, the people must have political institutions—like the Supreme Court—that are flexible enough to adapt to changing circumstances, stable enough to govern with coherence and authority, but not so strong as to trample on individual rights.

How bound should we be to the text of our constituting document? To what degree should we apply our own circumstances and understandings in creating new constitutional meanings? How much power to tell us what the Constitution means do we want to give to our political institutions?

written and ratified. Arguably the biggest threat the Framers saw to the republic they were designing was that posed by a standing army. During ratification, in 1788, New Hampshire's convention proposed adding this language: "Congress shall never disarm any citizen, unless such are or have been in actual rebellion."[53] In this contextual reading, the Second Amendment was meant as a counter to a national government that might grow tyrannical. Proponents of a broader scope of Second Amendment protections point to these arguments as establishing a clear intent to restrict the national government's authority over people's right to own firearms.

The text and time of the document are not the only possible sources of guidance. Courts can

The Constitution Also Protects Individuals Involved with the Criminal Justice System

4.5 Summarize the civil liberties that are guaranteed by the Bill of Rights to those accused of crimes.

As its defenders pointed out during the ratification debates, one area in which the proposed Constitution (prior to the adding of the Bill of Rights) did address civil liberties was in protecting the rights of the accused and convicted. Article I, which lays out the powers of Congress, prohibits that branch from passing laws—called *ex post facto* laws—that make conduct retroactively illegal, and therefore punishable. Any new criminal laws cannot apply to events that occurred before the law is passed. It also prohibits bills of attainder, which punish individuals without a trial.[54]

Article I also establishes the right of an individual to petition for a **writ of habeas corpus** upon their arrest or detention (except in the case of rebellion or invasion). Such a writ, if granted by a court, demands that authorities in charge of the person's detention establish the reasons for that detention. If the authorities fail to do so, the person is free to go. This has become one of the central issues in defining and debating the limits on presidential power as America engages in the war on terror in the twenty-first century (see Chapter 11).

All these protections, however, were not sufficient for many of the opponents of the proposed Constitution, who feared that the federal government would use its power to ignore the actions of state courts or violate the rights of individuals. Ultimately, fully half of the ten amendments in the Bill of Rights set boundaries for federal governmental action in dealing with the breaking and enforcing of the laws. Central to the protections for those accused, tried, and/or convicted of a crime is the idea of **procedural justice**, in which the standard of fairness is applied to all participants equally.[55] Most but not all of these standards have since been applied to the actions of the states themselves through the process of incorporation.

The Fourth Amendment Protects against Unlawful Search, Seizure, Warrants, and Evidence

Under British rule, the American colonists had gained a vivid understanding of the potential dangers of allowing a government to stop or inspect individuals or to search citizens' homes without oversight or procedural protections for those who were targeted. Under what conditions can a government legitimately search a person? Even at the time of the adoption of the Bill of Rights, this was not an easy question to answer. With the development of modern technology, the question has only grown more complicated.

In *Katz v. United States* (1967), the Supreme Court established a standard for procedures for obtaining evidence of a crime and wrestled with the challenges that technology poses to setting such boundaries.[56] The case involved an individual, Katz, who had been convicted of operating a gambling operation based on evidence obtained from a police wiretap. While the Court found there was ample reason for a judge to issue a **warrant**—a writ issued by a judge authorizing some activity, such as tapping a phone line or searching an apartment—the officers had not requested one in this case. The Court overturned Katz's conviction and established the need for officers to obtain a warrant from a judge based on probable cause, or reasonable suspicion that a crime has been committed or that there is evidence indicating so.

As we explored at the beginning of the chapter, *Carpenter v. United States* reexamined the issue of warrants in light of new technology and established the need for law enforcement officials to obtain a search warrant for cell phone location data, with certain exceptions such as the threat of imminent danger.

A closely related issue is whether or not evidence that has been obtained without following proper procedures can be used in a trial. The **exclusionary rule** governs the inadmissibility of evidence obtained without a proper warrant.

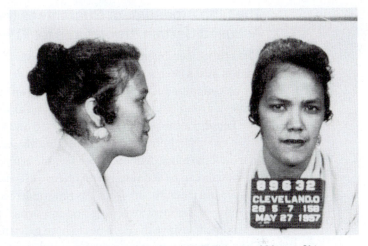

Dollree Mapp at the time of her arrest in 1957. The case of *Mapp v. Ohio* extended Fourth Amendment protections to the states by establishing that evidence gathered via illegal search and seizure is inadmissible in criminal trials in a state court.

AP Photo

The case through which the Fourth Amendment's protections were extended to the states, *Mapp v. Ohio* (1961), dealt with just such an issue. While investigating a different crime (a recent bombing), police found "certain lewd and lascivious books, pictures, and photographs," in the dwelling of Dollree Mapp, placing her in violation of an Ohio anti-obscenity law.[57] The officers, however, did not possess a warrant. The Court threw out Mapp's conviction and declared, "All evidence obtained by searches and seizures in violation of the Federal Constitution is inadmissible in a criminal trial in a state court."

As it has wrestled with the trickier issues in interpreting the exclusionary rule, such as electronic communications and transportation, the Court has ruled that the Fourth Amendment's protections are not absolute. In 1989, the Court upheld the conviction of a suspected drug dealer whose luggage had been searched without a warrant based on his behavior—he had paid cash for his ticket; checked no bags; and appeared nervous, among other "tells." The Court found that the DEA agents conducting the search had "reasonable suspicion" of criminal activity "based on the totality of circumstances."[58]

The Court has also upheld the admissibility of evidence (such as a weapon) connected with a crime (such as an armed robbery) that was not named in the warrant but that was discovered in plain sight while lawfully searching for a different type of evidence (such as the stolen property).[59] In 1996, the Court upheld the introduction of illegal drugs as evidence in a case, though the drugs had been obtained as a result of a traffic stop in which the officers were found to have had "reasonable cause" to believe that a traffic violation had occurred.[60]

The Fifth Amendment Guarantees the Accused Certain Procedures for Their Defense

The Fifth Amendment also provides protections for those accused of crimes, especially in guaranteeing processes and procedures for their defense. Those suspected of having committed serious crimes must have an indictment handed down by a **grand jury**—a group of citizens who, based on the evidence presented to them, decide whether or not the person is to be indicted and subsequently tried in a court of law. It also establishes protections against **double jeopardy**, which is the prosecution of an individual more than once for the same crime in the same jurisdiction. However, individuals can be acquitted of an offense in a state court but then tried for the same incident in a federal court—but this time under federal charges.

Some of the most sweeping and important protections described in the Fifth Amendment involve the right not to have to testify against oneself in a criminal case. These protections have been extended and strengthened by the Court over time.

One of the most important cases in delineating the protections of those accused of crimes was *Miranda v. Arizona* (1966). In that case, Ernesto Miranda had been convicted of kidnapping and rape, based partly on evidence obtained while he was being questioned by officers without an attorney present. During this questioning, he signed a confession. In its ruling, the Supreme Court overturned Miranda's conviction, declaring, "Prior to any questioning, the person must be warned that he has a right to remain silent, that any statement he does make may be used as evidence against him, and that he has a right to the presence of an attorney, either retained or appointed. The defendant may waive effectuation of these rights, provided the waiver is made voluntarily, knowingly and intelligently."[61] Police officers now routinely inform individuals suspected of criminal activity that they have the right not to speak and to have an attorney present during questioning; these rights are commonly referred to as **Miranda rights**.

The Sixth Amendment Guarantees the Accused Certain Rights to Trials and Representation

The Bill of Rights guarantees those accused of committing crimes the right to a speedy trial—a right that was extended to the states in 1963.[62] It also ensures the right to be tried in front of an impartial jury, which is more and more of a challenge given the instantaneous spread of news and opinion with modern technology. These protections, however, may not be of much use to a defendant if they do not have access to a qualified attorney during the complex legal process. While the Sixth Amendment guarantees the right to have counsel present at trial, for most of the nation's history that meant the right to hire an attorney if you could afford one.

In 1932, the Court extended this right, requiring the government to provide attorneys for defendants who couldn't afford them in federal capital murder cases that carried the possibility of the death penalty.[63] In 1938, the Court extended these protections to all federal criminal cases.[64] It was not until 1963—in one of the most famous cases in Supreme Court history—that the Court extended the guarantee of counsel for those unable to afford it to state criminal cases. That decision, in *Gideon v. Wainwright*, involved the conviction for robbery of Clarence Gideon, who had resorted to defending himself in a Florida court when his request to the judge for an attorney was denied.[65] More recently, the Court has strengthened these protections to try to ensure that criminal defendants receive "effective" legal representation and not just legal representation.[66]

The Eighth Amendment Guards against Cruel and Unusual Punishment

While a criminal defendant is awaiting a speedy trial before a jury, they may be able to post **bail**—an amount of money paid as a kind of security deposit to allow the charged individual to be freed while awaiting trial. Although the Eighth Amendment protects against "excessive bail," not every criminal defendant is entitled to bail at all. Those who are deemed to pose a sufficient risk of flight or further criminal activity may legitimately be denied the ability to post bail.

Much more contentious is the question of "cruel and unusual punishment," especially as it applies to the imposition of the death penalty, which some people regard as inherently cruel and unusual. The death penalty was allowed at the time of ratification of the Constitution and the Bill of Rights, and the Fifth Amendment to the Constitution refers to circumstances in which individuals are "deprived of life." Proponents of its use argue that the death penalty can be an effective deterrent against the most heinous crimes. Opponents point to the potential for errors in conviction, discriminatory sentencing, and the movement away from its use in other democracies. While the Supreme Court has not declared the death penalty to be inherently in violation of the Eighth Amendment, it has imposed restrictions on its imposition.[67] For example, the Court has prohibited its use on convicted defendants with significant cognitive disabilities[68] and on juveniles.[69]

The Ninth and Tenth Amendments Help Shape Freedoms in the Nation and across the States

4.6 Understand the role that the Ninth and Tenth Amendments play in shaping the protection of freedoms in the nation and across the states.

In 2009, Edith Windsor's wife, Thea Spyer, passed away from a progressive neurological disease. They had been married in Canada two years before, and their same-sex marriage had been recognized as valid by New York, their state of residence at the time of Spyer's passing.

Windsor and Spyer's marriage, however, was not considered legal under U.S. federal law. As such, after her wife's passing, Windsor was not entitled to the same federal tax provisions granted to surviving spouses in opposite-sex, federally recognized marriages. Therefore, Windsor had to pay more than $350,000 in federal estate taxes. With help, especially from the Lesbian, Gay, Bisexual, and Transgender

Thea Spyer (left) and Edith Windsor (right), whose same-sex marriage was legally recognized by the State of New York but not by the federal government. Following the passing of her wife, Windsor successfully fought to overturn a portion of a federal law that defined marriage as only between opposite-sex couples.

Neville Elder/Corbis via Getty Images

(LGBT) Community Center in New York City, she sued the federal government, claiming her right to have her marriage recognized as legal under federal law and to "the equal protection principles that the Court has found in the Fifth Amendment's Due Process clause."[70]

The Defense of Marriage Act Restricts the Rights of Same-Sex Couples to Marry

At issue were a federal law and a right that Windsor claimed. The law was the Defense of Marriage Act (DOMA), passed by Congress during the presidency of Bill Clinton in 1996 by opponents of marriage equality. It was a reaction to an increasing belief that some states and state courts were likely to legalize same-sex marriages in the coming years. DOMA had two substantive sections. One section stated that for purposes of federal law, marriage meant a legal union between a man and a woman: "In determining the meaning of any Act of Congress, or of any ruling, regulation, or interpretation of the various administrative bureaus and agencies of the United States, the word 'marriage' means only a legal union between one man and one woman as husband and wife, and the word 'spouse' refers only to a person of the opposite sex who is a husband or a wife."

Another section reaffirmed the power of the states to make their own decisions about marriage: "No State, territory, or possession of the United States, or Indian tribe, shall be required to give effect to any public act, record, or judicial proceeding of any other State, territory, possession, or tribe respecting a relationship between persons of the same sex that is treated as a marriage under the laws of such other State, territory, possession, or tribe, or a right or claim arising from such relationship." This section of DOMA tried to clarify, or delimit, the Constitution of the United States, specifically the **full faith and credit clause**, which states, "Full faith and credit shall be given in each state to the public acts, records, and judicial proceedings of every other state. And the Congress may by general laws prescribe the manner in which such acts, records, and proceedings shall be proved, and the effect thereof."[71]

Under the full faith and credit clause, a state is generally required to recognize and honor the public laws of other states unless those laws are contrary to the strong public policy of that state. Full faith and credit is why, for example, a driver's license from one state authorizes you to drive anywhere in the country. However, under DOMA, states were not required to give full faith and credit to same-sex marriages.

In a 5–4 decision in *United States v. Windsor* (2013), the Supreme Court ruled that the section of DOMA classifying only opposite-sex marriages as legal under federal law was unconstitutional.[72] In his majority opinion, Justice Anthony Kennedy decried the intent of DOMA, stating, "The history of DOMA's enactment and its own text demonstrate that interference with the equal dignity of same-sex marriages, a dignity conferred by the States in the exercise of their sovereign power, was more than an incidental effect of the federal statute. It was its essence."[73] One of the most consequential results of the Court's decision in *Windsor* was the provision of the same rights in immigration procedures to same-sex married couples as those granted to opposite-sex married couples when one spouse is not an American citizen.

Two years after her landmark case, Windsor continued to work for LGBTQIA (lesbian, gay, bisexual, transgender, queer, intersex, or asexual) causes and had turned her focus to transgender identity and at-risk youth. She stated, "I think we have a lot to do. A lot. There are a million things to still be done to make it equal. . . . First of all, I have a lot of feeling for trans people. They are making gorgeous progress, but it's a very painful progress. . . . We also have somewhere between 40 and 50% of kids living on the street who are gay. This is a whole chunk of us who also took the courage to come out but were thrown out of their homes and forced to live in the street.[74] After Windsor had made constitutional history, she stated, "Honey, you've got to be loud and proud."[75]

While the Supreme Court in *Windsor* had validated state-recognized same-sex marriages for *federal* purposes, it did not strike down the other substantive clause of DOMA, which allowed states to not give full faith and credit to same-sex marriage licenses from other states. Many Americans wondered when, or if, it ever would.

The Ninth Amendment and Privacy, a Right Not Enumerated

While each of the first eight amendments in the Bill of Rights places literal, textual limits on the power of the federal government, the final two do not. Instead, the Ninth and Tenth Amendments more broadly structure the inclusion and exclusion of rights as well as powers of national and state governments.

One of the concerns raised by opponents about including a list of rights in the Constitution was that such a list would be necessarily incomplete. What about those rights assumed but not specified? Would future federal government officials recognize or try to restrict them? The Ninth Amendment was included to address these fears as well as general concerns by Anti-Federalists about the future growth of federal governmental power.

Part of Windsor's constitutional claims rested on a right not enumerated in the Bill of Rights: **privacy**. Because of this, Windsor was also resting her claim upon previous cases in American constitutional law. In its decisions in past cases, the Supreme Court had affirmed the right to privacy and applied it to several areas of Americans' private lives, such as birth control, abortion, and sexuality.

John Lawrence (right) and Tyron Garner greet supporters at a rally where people had gathered to celebrate the landmark Supreme Court decision in the *Lawrence v. Texas* case on June 26, 2003. The court struck down a Texas sodomy law, a decision applauded by gay rights advocates as a historic ruling that overturned sodomy laws in thirteen states.

AP Photo/Michael Stravato

Early Affirmation of Rights to Privacy Involved the Use of Contraceptives.

The foundational case regarding privacy was *Griswold v. Connecticut* (1965).[76] In it, the Court overturned a Connecticut law that prohibited the provision of contraceptives and medical advice about contraceptive techniques to married couples. In striking down the law, Justice William O. Douglas cited allusions to privacy in several amendments to the Constitution, including the First, which "has a penumbra where privacy is protected from governmental intrusion."[77] *Penumbras* here refers to the implications of textually protected rights that involve private life—such as being secure from having soldiers quartered in one's home—for similarly private behaviors that are not textually listed—such as those involving sexuality.

Expansions of Privacy Rights Involved Sexual Conduct between Consenting Adults.

In later decades, the Supreme Court clarified that the right to privacy extended beyond the use of contraception. One area in which the Court affirmed privacy in the penumbras, or shadows, created by the Constitution's other protections was the right of consenting adults to express their sexuality. In 2003, in *Lawrence v. Texas*, the Court struck down a Texas law making same-sex sexual conduct illegal.[78] In his decision, Justice Kennedy stated, "Liberty presumes an autonomy of self that includes freedom of thought, belief, expression, and certain intimate conduct."[79]

Privacy Rights Also Include a Woman's Decision to Terminate a Pregnancy.

In a series of decisions, the Court has also affirmed and upheld the right of a woman to terminate a pregnancy. In this area of privacy, the foundational case was *Roe v. Wade* (1973).[80] In that case, the Court struck down a Texas law that made abortion illegal. In affirming the right of a woman to obtain an abortion during the first three months of pregnancy, Justice Harry Blackmun drew on the Court's previous ruling in *Griswold*, stating, "This right of privacy is broad enough to encompass a woman's decision whether or not to terminate her pregnancy."[81]

In subsequent decisions, the Court has continued to uphold the fundamental right of a woman to have an abortion, but it has also allowed state legislatures to place certain limits upon this right. Examples of this are state laws requiring minors to obtain parental consent, assuming those laws do not place an "undue burden" on the woman, and certain restrictions upon late-term abortions.[82] Despite the Court's rulings, abortion remains a very contentious issue in American politics. Since *Roe v. Wade*, trying to ascertain a nominee's position on the constitutionality of abortion has become a standard part of the Senate's confirmation process for members of the Supreme Court and federal judiciary.

The Tenth Amendment Is Intended to Protect State Powers

The inclusion of the Tenth Amendment in the Bill of Rights was a direct response to the fears and

James Obergefell in 2015, two and a half months prior to the Supreme Court decision that would guarantee marriage equality for all Americans.

Maddie McGarvey/For *The Washington Post* via Getty Images

demands of the Anti-Federalists during the ratification debates. Many of them wanted a direct statement of the limitation of national power to those powers explicitly listed in the text of the Constitution. All other powers were to be reserved to the individual states, which is why we call most state powers under the Constitution "reserved powers." As it has turned out, however, and as we have already explored in our discussion of the development of American federalism, the Tenth Amendment has not proven to be as strong a protector of state power as some might have thought. That is not to say that it is irrelevant, however. States and their legislatures are increasingly protesting the power of the federal government—especially when they feel that it is requiring them to enact policies without fully funding their implementation—using the Tenth Amendment as their constitutional justification for doing so.

The Final Blow to DOMA

While the Supreme Court's decision in *United States v. Windsor* required the federal government to recognize same-sex marriages from states where they were legal, it did not require states to give full faith and credit to same-sex marriages from other states. Nor had it legalized same-sex marriages generally. One person who would change that was James Obergefell. Though the actual Court decision bundled several cases together, Obergefell's was listed first, which placed his name on the decision. The facts of his case were, sadly, somewhat similar to those of Edith Windsor's.

In 2011, after a decades-long commitment to each other, Obergefell married John Arthur on the tarmac of a Maryland airport. The two men were residents of the state of Ohio, which did not recognize marriage equality, so they flew to Maryland, which did. Arthur was struggling with amyotrophic lateral sclerosis (ALS), a progressive neurological degenerative disease. (ALS is often called Lou Gehrig's disease after the famous and widely respected baseball player who died from it in 1941.) The two men flew to Maryland in a medical transport plane, seeking to get married while they still could. In an interview with BuzzFeed News, a few months before the Court's decision in his case, Obergefell described their ceremony: "We landed at Baltimore, sat on the tarmac for a little bit, said 'I do,' and 10 minutes later were in the air on the way home."[83] John Arthur passed away in 2013.

Obergefell and Arthur's state of residence did not recognize their marriage. As Justice Anthony Kennedy eventually put it in the Supreme Court's decision in the case, "Ohio law does not permit Obergefell to be listed as the surviving spouse on Arthur's death certificate. By statute they must remain strangers even in death, a state-imposed separation Obergefell deems 'hurtful for the rest of time.'"[84] Rather than accept Ohio's refusal to recognize their marriage, Obergefell sued. "This case," he said, "was another way to take care of him and to respect him and to respect our relationship."[85]

In 2015, in its decision in *Obergefell v. Hodges*, the Supreme Court, in yet another 5–4 vote, affirmed the legality of Obergefell and Arthur's marriage and guaranteed the right of all couples to marry. Citing many of the cases that we have discussed, constitutional protections of fundamental civil liberties, and the right to privacy, Justice Kennedy, in his majority opinion, affirmed that "the right to marry is a fundamental right inherent in the liberty of the person." The second major section of DOMA had been declared unconstitutional. More fundamentally, marriage equality had become the law of both the nation and the states.

Reflecting on his case in an interview with *USA Today* two months before the Court's decision, Obergefell recalled how he felt about having to fly, given his husband's serious medical issues, to another state just to get married: "All I thought was, 'This isn't right, I'm p—ed off.'"[86] In the same interview, on a much lighter note, he added, "I chuckle about law students and other people just having to learn how to pronounce Obergefell."[87]

Conclusion: Civil Liberties Involve Fences Still under Construction

The stories regarding civil liberties in the United States are stories about tensions—tensions between one individual's fundamental rights and freedoms and those of another and tensions between individual freedoms and the evolving needs of a society. They are stories about courage and political action. They are also stories about change and adaptation, as generations of activists, Supreme Court justices, and politicians have weighed in on the proper boundaries of American rights and freedoms.

Defining and defending civil liberties in American democracy have always been and will always be controversial and challenging; that is why they are so essential to the nation.

CHAPTER REVIEW

This chapter's main ideas are reflected in the Learning Objectives. By reviewing them here, you should be able to *remember* the key points and *know* the terms that are central to the topic.

4.1 Define *civil liberties*, and understand the key role they play in American political life.

Remember . . . • Protecting civil liberties involves placing restrictions upon the ability of government to limit them.

Know . . . • *Bill of Rights* (p. 97) • *negative freedoms* (p. 97)

  • *civil liberties* (p. 97)

4.2 Describe the civil liberties outlined in the Constitution, the amendments to it, and the process by which they were incorporated.

Remember . . . • The Bill of Rights enumerates a list of fundamental freedoms that the federal government cannot infringe upon.

  • The protections set out in the Bill of Rights as written applied to the actions of the federal government and not those of the state governments. A decades-long process, in which the Supreme Court played a key role, changed this.

Know . . . • *due process clause* (p. 102) • *selective incorporation* (p. 103)

4.3 Explain the First Amendment protections granted to religion.

Remember . . . • The first two clauses in the First Amendment to the Constitution both involve religion; they prevent the federal government from establishing religion and protect Americans' rights to exercise their religious freedoms.

Know . . . • *establishment clause* (p. 106) • *Lemon test* (p. 107)

  • *free exercise clause* (p. 106) • *neutrality test* (p. 108)

4.4 Outline the First Amendment protections concerning freedom of expression.

Remember . . . • Political speech and expression are considered particularly important fundamental freedoms.

  • Since the early years of the American Republic, the federal government has struggled with protecting these freedoms while also ensuring a secure and orderly society.

Know . . . • *Alien and Sedition Acts* (p. 109) • *libel* (p. 112)

  • *clear and present danger test* (p. 110) • *obscenity and pornography* (p. 112)

  • *fighting words* (p. 112) • *prior restraint* (p. 111)

  • *freedom of expression* (p. 109) • *slander* (p. 112)

  • *hate speech* (p. 112) • *symbolic speech* (p. 111)

4.5 **Summarize the civil liberties that are guaranteed by the Bill of Rights to those accused of crimes.**

Remember . . .
- The Bill of Rights guarantees a set of protections for those accused of, investigated for, tried for, and convicted of crimes.

Know . . .
- *bail* (p. 119)
- *double jeopardy* (p. 118)
- *exclusionary rule* (p. 117)
- *grand jury* (p. 118)

- *Miranda rights* (p. 118)
- *procedural justice* (p. 116)
- *warrant* (p. 116)
- *writ of habeas corpus* (p. 116)

4.6 **Understand the role that the Ninth and Tenth Amendments play in shaping the protection of freedoms in the nation and across the states.**

Remember . . .
- The Ninth and Tenth Amendments more broadly structure the inclusion and exclusion of rights as well as powers of national and state governments.
- The Supreme Court, drawing upon the Ninth Amendment, which states that the Bill of Rights does not contain an exhaustive list of fundamental liberties, has affirmed a right of privacy in areas such as reproductive rights, sexuality, and marriage.

Know . . .
- *full faith and credit clause* (p. 120)
- *privacy* (p. 121)

CHAPTER 5

CIVIL RIGHTS

How Equal Is Equal?[1]

Judith Heumann, special adviser for international disability rights at the U.S. State Department, talks with a girl at the Guangzhou Library in Guangzhou, China, about her experiences. A disabled American herself, Heumann has spent a lifetime advocating for the rights of people with disabilities in America and across the globe.

Liang Xu/Xinhua/Alamy Live News

By reading this chapter, you will be able to do the following:

5.1 Understand that securing civil rights requires both actions by individuals and groups to claim them and actions by governments to protect them.

5.2 Trace the history of racial segregation in America and the ratification of the Fourteenth Amendment to the Constitution, which laid the foundation for later struggles to secure civil rights.

5.3 Explain efforts to end legal segregation based on racial identity as well as the strategies used in those efforts.

5.4 Trace the history of efforts to secure civil rights for American women.

5.5 Evaluate the ways the diversity of Americans' identities shapes efforts to secure civil rights in the twenty-first century.

The preamble to the Declaration of Independence makes clear a central purpose of a representative government: to guard and protect the fundamental rights and freedoms of its citizens. However, it does not offer many specifics on the processes and structures needed to make this happen. The rules and institutions set out in the Constitution and later amendments to it have given detailed form to a federal government that would help to secure these rights. Even so, the institutions of American government do not run on autopilot. They require action, both by those within the government to carry out their responsibilities and by Americans to define, advocate for, and protect their **civil rights**—the fundamental rights of individuals to be treated equally under the laws and policies of governments, regardless of their identities and lived experiences.

Civil rights are not binary. By law, one has them or not; however, when those laws are put into practice it becomes more complicated than that. Recall the discussion of civil liberties from Chapter 4. As a rule, the protection of civil liberties requires that a government refrain from certain things—that it not pass laws that might restrict the expression of fundamental rights and freedoms. As with civil liberties, the Framers of the Constitution assumed that citizens possessed civil rights upon birth, though many Americans were excluded or ignored at that point in history. Unlike civil liberties, however, civil rights require *positive* action, both by individuals acting to secure them and by governments in taking action to ensure their expression. For this reason, civil rights are sometimes called **positive freedoms**.

The challenge with civil rights comes from deciding how vigorously a government should act to protect them, how assertively to enforce. How much action does a government need to take? How strongly does government have to act? How equal is equal? There is no single answer to these questions. Americans have always disagreed on how strongly government should act to protect the civil rights of its citizens. In this chapter, we will examine the efforts of individuals such as Judith Heumann and other disability rights protesters, Thurgood Marshall and members of the National Association for the Advancement of Colored People (NAACP), American women, as well as many other people acting alone or in concert to achieve a broader, more robust vision of Americans' civil rights.

Protesters Act to Secure Rights for Americans with Disabilities

In January 2016, writing in celebration of the American holiday devoted to Dr. Martin Luther King Jr., Judith Heumann, a special adviser for international disability rights with the U.S. Department of State, posted an article to the State Department's official blog. In it, she looked both to the past and to the present:

> A stable, prosperous democracy succeeds when individuals can fully partici- pate in political and public life. As we celebrate MLK Day and reflect on past struggles fought by Americans determined to uphold their individual rights, Dr. King's message of inclusion lives on. Dr. King encouraged everyone to participate when he said, "It is not possible to be in favor of justice for some people and not be in favor of justice for all people."

> While change takes time, we must take action to: establish disabled people's organizations; adopt and enforce strong laws; create and enforce standards that advance inclusion of disabled people; and remove barriers—physical and attitudinal in all areas of life.[2]

In writing about the struggles to secure rights and freedoms for persons with dis- abilities, Heumann knows what she is talking about. She has spent a lifetime advocat- ing, protesting, and changing American laws that affect those with disabilities.

As a very young child in 1949, Heumann contracted polio, which has since required her to use a wheelchair for mobility. In the 1950s, administrators at her local public elementary school in Brooklyn, New York, refused to allow her to attend. They cited her inability to access the building since it had no ramps, which was pretty much universal at the time. They refused to relent even when her mother offered to carry her up and down the school's steps. "I was considered to be a fire hazard," Heumann recalled.[3] In spite of these obstacles—imposed not by her disability but by others' actions—Heumann earned two degrees, including a master of arts from the University of California, Berkeley, in 1975. After graduation she applied to become a teacher with the New York City schools but was rejected based on her disability. Instead of backing down, however, "she filed suit against them and won."[4]

But Heumann was far from done.

In the spring of 1977, a group of protesters gathered in San Francisco outside a regional office of the federal Department of Housing, Education, and Welfare (HEW). They consisted of people with disabilities and their supporters, seeking to force the Carter administration to finally and fully implement Section 504 of the Rehabilitation Act of 1973, which stated, "No otherwise qualified handicapped individual in the United States . . . shall, solely on the basis of his handicap, be excluded from the participation in, be denied the benefits of, or be subjected to discrimination under any program or activity receiving Federal financial assistance." Though applying only to programs and activities receiving federal funding, effective implementation of Section 504 would put pressure on other firms and organizations to follow suit.

In his presidential campaign, President Jimmy Carter had promised to redress the lack of funding for and attention to the act under the Ford administration. However, in the view of many Americans with disabilities, President Carter was backtracking. Officials in the executive branch had not signed key regulations of the act, likely because of how much it would cost to put them into effect. In particular, the protesters sought to put pressure on the secretary of HEW, Joseph Califano Jr., who had recently proposed greater flexibility in making federal buildings accessible, suggested that segregation of students with disabilities would be acceptable, and stated that individuals who were disabled and battling substance abuse could be legitimately denied access and services.

On April 5, having announced their intentions beforehand, the individuals who would come to be known as the "Section 504 protesters" moved into the San Francisco HEW building and occupied it. There were also sit-in protests at HEW offices in nine other cities, including Washington, DC. On the eve of the sit-in, one local reporter commented, "Thousands of handicapped Americans may risk being wheel-chaired off to jail in a militant attempt to shut down government offices in 10 cities."[5] Judith Heumann was one of their leaders.

The takeovers were extremely taxing and often dangerous. Protesters with significant physical disabilities and illnesses in particular risked their health, cut off from the medical support upon which they relied. In the nation's capital, the protesters were forced to give up after being denied food. Lack of supplies, strong and effective leadership, or community support all undermined the protest efforts, and most of the sit-ins ended quickly. In San Francisco, however, the 504 protesters maintained their occupation.

According to one news account, "By the late '70s, Americans were used to seeing civil rights marches. But this one was something new: people in wheelchairs, people on portable respirators, deaf people, people with mental retardation. And most were fighting mad."[6] In addition to the occupation, the 504 protesters held rallies, joined by activists from workers' and civil rights organizations. They issued a constant flow of press releases designed to gain support from the community and pressure local, state, and federal politicians to act to remove barriers to accessibility in public spaces, transportation, and access to employment, educational and housing opportunities. They flew to Washington, DC, to testify at committee hearings.

The 504 protesters undertook strategic political action in the service of claiming their civil rights. They were also, however, challenging the perception that people with disabilities were weak and dependent. They sought to show Americans and political figures that they were strong. "We want our rights now," Judith Heumann, then deputy director for the Center for Independent Living, stated in a press release. "We will wait no longer!! The Administration is forcing us to take to the streets and we will."[7]

Demonstrators converge on the offices of the HEW department in San Francisco in April 1977. They were part of a "504 sit-in" to urge that civil rights law for disabled Americans be fully implemented. In the center, a woman briefs the group in American Sign Language.
AP Photo/JP

The 504 protesters received telegrammed support from César Chávez, president of the United Farm Workers of America: "Greetings and best wishes in your struggle. . . . Viva la Causa."[8] Chávez, Dolores Huerta, and other leaders and members of the United Farm Workers had led and organized a yearslong series of strikes and boycotts to call attention to the working conditions of American agricultural workers, a large percentage of whom were Latino and Latina. Leaders and members of civil rights movements for African Americans also supported the 504 protesters. Rev. Jesse Jackson spoke in support, as did members of the Black Panthers, who helped to provide food and supplies during the takeover. In this way, the 504 protesters drew not only on the tactics and lessons from these other civil rights movements but also on their organization, logistics, and voices.

On April 28, after more than three weeks, Secretary Califano endorsed a set of regulations contained within the law. The 504 protesters had succeeded in securing their immediate policy demands. Theirs remains the longest takeover of a federal building in American history. Reflecting on that time, Heumann recalled the personal risks that the activists were willing to take: "People weren't going to work, people were willing to risk arrest, people were risking their own health. Everybody was risking something. . . . Through the sit-in, we turned ourselves from being oppressed individuals into being empowered people. We demonstrated to the entire nation that disabled people could take control over our own lives and take leadership in the struggle for equality."[9]

The Americans with Disabilities Act Expands Protections for People with Disabilities

A later piece of legislation on which Heumann also worked tirelessly was the Americans with Disabilities Act (ADA), signed into law in 1990, which protected individuals with disabilities from discrimination in public life. Among its provisions, the ADA offered protections for Americans with disabilities against discrimination in the workplace and improved their access to public transportation, public services, and other areas of public and commercial life.[10] ADA's accessibility requirements go beyond federal buildings and include private buildings and businesses that are generally open to the public, such as restaurants and doctor's offices. "The ADA was like the Emancipation Proclamation for disabled individuals," Heumann said in 2015, referring to the Civil War proclamation by President Abraham Lincoln that freed the slaves in the states that had rebelled.[11]

In her remarks on Martin Luther King Jr. Day in 2016, Heumann also referred to the words of Supreme Court justice Thurgood Marshall—the first African American appointed to the highest court in the land—in an opinion that he wrote in 1985. The case involved the denial of a permit to build a facility to house and serve people with cognitive disabilities in Cleburne, Texas. The Court unanimously ruled against the city's actions, saying that the permit denial violated those individuals' constitutional rights.[12] In his opinion, Marshall directly connected the struggles to secure civil rights for Americans with disabilities to those of African Americans. The "mentally retarded," Marshall noted, "have been subject to a 'lengthy and tragic history' . . . of segregation and discrimination that can only be called grotesque."[13]

When he used the word *grotesque*, Marshall was not exaggerating. Throughout much of its history, the nation has discriminated against people with disabilities in restrictive, even violent ways. In addition to being excluded from the workplace, schools, transportation, and other forms of public and private life, Americans with disabilities—especially those with cognitive disabilities—have been forcibly institutionalized and even sterilized.[14]

Many advocates for the rights of Americans with disabilities intentionally drew connections between their struggles and those of African Americans decades before. A 1999 position paper for the American Civil Liberties Union (ACLU)—which noted that "people with disabilities are the poorest, least employed, and least educated minority in America"—pointed to a long history of discrimination against Americans with disabilities.[15] "Finally," the report noted, "thanks in part to the inspiration provided by the civil rights struggles of the 1960's, disability rights advocates began to press for full legal equality and access to mainstream society. Through lobbying and litigation, laws were passed and rights established; public education and advocacy were used to promote reason and inclusiveness rather than fear and pity."[16] Heumann had helped to lead that charge.

Civil Rights Amendments Emerge from the Civil War—but Provide Limited Protection in Practice

> **5.2** Trace the history of racial segregation in America and the ratification of the Fourteenth Amendment to the Constitution, which laid the foundation for later struggles to secure civil rights.

Judith Heumann and the 504 protesters, Huerta and Chávez, Thurgood Marshall, and many others whom we've not yet met in this chapter, claimed their civil rights. But on what basis did they do so? The short answer is the Constitution or, more precisely, amendments to it. A more complete answer involves a longer story and an often difficult and troubling part of American history—a part, however, that also includes brave and strategic political action by many individuals.

As we explored in Chapter 2, neither the ratified Constitution of the United States nor the Bill of Rights abolished slavery. Three of the provisions of the original Constitution—though they did not mention slavery by name—served to protect it. Slaves were counted as three-fifths of a person for purposes of states' representation, Congress was forbidden from regulating the slave trade for two decades following ratification, and nonslave states were required to return escaped slaves to bondage. Many delegates and Americans at the time, however, knew and argued that slavery violated the foundations of the Republic itself. Many felt that these unresolved contradictions would eventually tear the nation apart. Slavery, however, endured.

The Supreme Court Denies Citizenship Rights to African Americans, Helping to Spark a War That Splits the Nation

The early and middle decades of the nineteenth century saw the young republic undergo many changes: rapid westward expansion (often catastrophic to the indigenous peoples in those lands), a growing population, technological change, and economic growth. The question of slavery—unresolved during the Constitutional Convention—however, remained. The slave states of the South and the free states of the North were becoming increasingly different economically and socially. But what about the West? Would these new states be slave or free? In a representative democracy, and a federalist one, it was more than a moral question. It would also be decisive in determining the balance of political power in the federal government.

In 1857, in *Dred Scott v. Sandford*, the Supreme Court ruled that Scott, formerly enslaved peoples, and their descendents were not citizens of the United States, even if they were residents of free states or territories. The natural rights proclaimed in the Declaration of Independence and protected in the Constitution, Justice Roger Taney wrote in his opinion, did not extend to individuals "whose ancestors were negroes of the African race," who, at the time of the founding, were considered an "inferior class of beings who had been subjugated by the dominant race, and, whether emancipated or not, yet remained subject to their authority, and had no rights or privileges but such as those who held the power and the Government might choose to grant them."[17] Natural rights, according to the Court, had been selectively bestowed.

Scott's inability to sue for his freedom or that of his family was not the only effect of Taney's majority opinion in *Dred Scott*. In addition, the Court—five of whose nine members were from the South—ruled that the Missouri Compromise, which was a plan that had been created by Congress in 1820 to maintain a balance of slave and nonslave states in the Senate, was unconstitutional. The Court's ruling in *Dred Scott*, though, threatened the constitutionality of any state laws against slavery, as enslaved peoples were considered property subject to the Constitution's protections. The Court's decision served to further polarize public opinion on the question of slavery and galvanize both proslavery and antislavery forces in the United States.

The threat that states might secede from the Union was not a new

A wood engraving depicting Dred Scott and his family on the front page of a newspaper in 1857. The Supreme Court ruled in *Dred Scott v. Sandford* that Scott could not sue for his freedom as he was not considered to be a citizen of the United States, even though he had resided in free territory for a time.

Courtesy of the Library of Congress, Prints and Photographs Division

one. During the Constitutional Convention, a delegate from Delaware had raised it as an implicit threat against the American confederation, though in the context of state representation in Congress rather than over the regulation of slavery. For the southern states in the convention, however, the preservation of slavery in their states had been a precondition to their ratification of the Constitution.

Secession Ensues, and Then Civil War

In December 1860, South Carolina made the long-simmering threat of secession a reality. Within six months, eleven southern states had seceded from the United States to form the Confederate States of America. In April, they fired on a federal fort in

Charleston Harbor. To reunite the Union, President Abraham Lincoln had to take what remained of the American Republic to war. Like many times before and since, leaders, soldiers, and citizens on both sides thought that the war would be over quickly. And like many times before and since, they were wrong.

When the American Civil War finally ended in 1865, more than six hundred thousand soldiers had died. An unknown number of civilians were killed as well. Historians continue to debate the relative roles of slavery, politics, and economics as causes of the Civil War. In many ways, it is difficult to disentangle these causes from each other. Similarly, stories of the Reconstruction—the years after the Civil War when the rebellious southern states were brought back into the Union—have shifted in their focus over time.

During the war, President Lincoln signed the Emancipation Proclamation, which in 1863 declared that all slaves in the states under rebellion were "henceforward and forever free." However, it took the actions of Union troops and enslaved peoples themselves to make that proclamation a reality on the ground. Excluded from the proclamation were enslaved peoples in the border states still loyal to the Union and territories in the South already under federal control. This was a political move, designed to preserve the loyalty of the border states while also putting pressure on Europe not to come to the aid of the Confederacy.

As the war dragged on, African Americans were increasingly brought into the Union war effort. Although forced to serve in segregated units and often assigned to labor detachments, many of the nearly two hundred thousand African Americans who served in the Union Army used their experiences to gain education, advancement, and a claim of equal status as citizens in the victorious Union. African American combat units quickly gained a reputation for effectiveness and bravery under fire.

Constitutional Amendments Abolish Slavery and Affirm Voting and Citizenship Rights for African Americans during Reconstruction

At the conclusion of the war, southern states began to pass laws to preserve the pre-defeat status quo between whites and African Americans. Known as the Black codes, these pieces of legislation attempted to restrict the economic and political rights of freedmen, to "make Negroes slaves in everything but name."[18]

President Andrew Johnson, who succeeded Lincoln upon his assassination, pushed for quick readmission of the southern states with relatively little regard for the preservation of African American political rights. The Republican-controlled Congress, however, was more assertive. Some Republicans were staunch abolitionists based on moral grounds, while others also had strategic political calculations in mind. Making sure that African American men could vote—and, it was expected, vote Republican—was seen as a way to avoid an unbreakable and dominant political alliance of northern and southern Democrats.

Within five years of the conclusion of the Civil War, three amendments had been added to the Constitution, although not without considerable opposition. In 1865, the **Thirteenth Amendment** to the Constitution prohibited slavery within the United States. To ensure the power of the national government to make this provision a reality, and to prevent a Supreme Court from overturning antislavery laws as it had done in *Dred Scott*, Section 2 of the amendment stated that "Congress shall have the power to enforce this article by appropriate legislation."

In 1868, the **Fourteenth Amendment** affirmed the citizenship of all persons "born or naturalized in the United States" and, for the first time in the history of the Constitution, placed explicit restrictions on the laws of states: "No State shall make or enforce any law which shall abridge the privileges and immunities of citizens of the United States; nor shall any State deprive any person of life, liberty, or property, without due process of law; nor deny to any person within its jurisdiction the equal protection of the laws."

The **equal protection clause** of the Fourteenth Amendment served as the constitutional basis for the assault on educational segregation in the courts and for the assertion of civil rights for Americans of many different identities in many different areas of public and private life. In addition to addressing issues of state debts and office holding for former Confederate leaders, the Fourteenth Amendment also rescinded the three-fifths rule for representation in the original Constitution.

Faced with southern resistance to the Fourteenth Amendment—southern states rejected or ratified modified versions of it—the Republican Congress, having won major victories in the 1866 elections, passed the First Reconstruction Act of 1867. This act disbanded southern governments, thus voiding their rejection of the Fourteenth Amendment, and replaced them with military rule. It gave freedmen the right to vote and took that right away from Confederate veterans, and it made ratification of the Fourteenth Amendment a necessary condition of readmission to the United States.

The **Fifteenth Amendment**, ratified in 1870, affirmed the voting rights of all free men, again giving Congress the power to make necessary laws: "The right of citizens of the United States to vote shall not be denied or abridged by the United States or by any State on account of race, color, or previous condition of servitude."

In addition to these Reconstruction amendments, Congress in this period passed several pieces of legislation aimed at securing the civil rights of African Americans. In 1865, Congress created the Freedmen's Bureau, which took steps to provide former slaves with the two things they desired most: land and education. (This was not always done in the interests of freedmen, however. The bureau sometimes forced African Americans to work for whites.[19]) The Civil Rights Act of 1866 affirmed the legal and property rights of former slaves, while the Civil Rights Act of 1875 affirmed "the equality of all men before the law" and the duty of government to enforce that equality. The latter also acknowledged the rights of all to "the full and equal enjoyment of the accommodations, advantages, facilities, and privileges of inns, public conveyances on land or water, theaters, and other places of public

amusement" regardless of race or "previous condition of servitude."

Racial Oppression Continues despite New Protections

These efforts did not go unopposed. As the Democratic Party gained political power in the southern states and the will of the Republican Party to make civil rights a reality on the ground faded, the early gains made by African Americans began to disappear. Southern states passed laws to preserve segregation and prevent African American men from exercising their Fifteenth Amendment right to vote. Known as **Jim Crow laws**, these efforts enforced segregation across all aspects of daily life, including

Jim Crow laws persisted across the United States long after the civil rights acts of the late nineteenth century were passed. Separate facilities in public spaces, including bus terminals like this one, were a common sight in the American South.

transportation, entertainment, business, and education. While **legal segregation** (racial segregation by law) had been enforced in the North before the Civil War, by the time of Reconstruction it had largely disappeared there but remained deeply entrenched in the post–Civil War South. Selective enforcement of poll taxes, which required voters to pay a tax at polling places to vote, and literacy tests, which were used by registrars to determine whether citizens were "qualified" to vote, combined to prevent African American men from voting.

Backing up the laws and statutes were violence and the persistent threat of violence against African Americans who tried to exercise their rights and against whites who tried to help them. The violence against African Americans, especially former soldiers, was often organized, sometimes random: "In Texas, one woman reported that it was a common sight to see the bodies of freedmen floating down a river."[20] Schools that educated former slaves were seen as especially dangerous to the white order. Many were burned; their white teachers were beaten and ostracized. Across the South, the Ku Klux Klan terrorized and murdered African American politicians and civic leaders. Thousands of African Americans were murdered, often to send a message that the racial order was not to be challenged. As in other times and places, terrorism in the postwar South was used as a political weapon.

Opponents of Jim Crow Attempt to Use the Judiciary to Challenge It, but Fail

In the decades following the Civil War, the Supreme Court proved to be an enabler of racial oppression rather than a protector against it. In 1896, it upheld the constitutionality of legalized racial segregation, dealing a further blow to fading Reconstructionist dreams.[21] ***Plessy v. Ferguson*** was a test case organized by the

African American community in New Orleans to challenge Louisiana's Jim Crow laws.[22] Homer Plessy, "a light-skinned man who described himself as 'seven-eighths Caucasian,'"[23] had been arrested and fined for violating a state law requiring separate railroad facilities for whites and African Americans. In the racialized math of the time, his ancestry placed Plessy just over the legal boundary between white and African American in Louisiana. After losing in the state courts, he appealed his case to the U.S. Supreme Court.

In the decision in *Plessy*, Justice Henry Billings Brown declared that Louisiana's law did not violate the Fourteenth Amendment to the Constitution. Arguing that "social prejudices cannot be overcome by legislation," Brown upheld Plessy's conviction and declared that "**separate but equal**" facilities did not violate the Constitution. Justice John Marshall Harlan, the lone dissenter on the Court, correctly, as it turned out, saw *Plessy* as a dangerous and damaging ruling, one that would "prove to be quite as pernicious as the decision made by this tribunal in the *Dred Scott* case." His charge, however, was only a dissent; Brown's majority opinion set policy. The doctrine of "separate but equal" remained constitutional for almost sixty years.

Challenges to Legal Segregation Achieve Successes but Face Resistance

> 5.3 Explain efforts to end legal segregation based on racial identity as well as the strategies used in those efforts.

By the morning of December 9, 1952, hundreds of Americans—far more than the chamber could hold—had already lined up outside the Supreme Court of the United States. Those lucky enough to get seats would not give them up lightly; the better prepared had brought food, knowing someone else would take their place if they left. The line of people standing under the motto of the Supreme Court, "Equal Justice under Law," was integrated. African Americans and whites stood together for a chance to witness history.

In the audience was the president of Howard University, a predominantly African American university whose law school had trained a generation of civil rights lawyers, including the man leading the legal team attempting to challenge segregated education: Thurgood Marshall. Marshall was the chief litigator for the Legal Defense Fund of the NAACP, and he and his team of lawyers were arguing five cases in front of the Court that day.[24] These five cases had been gathered together under the name of the first one on the list, *Brown v. Board of Education of Topeka*. Though differing in their details and pathways through the legal system, the cases dealt with the same question: whether or not legal segregation, in this particular case the separation by law of African American and white children in the public schools based only upon their race, was constitutionally permissible.

It had been a long journey through the courts for Marshall and the NAACP. They had been waging a legal attack on segregation in the United States for decades. The individuals who had filed the lawsuits, those who helped organize them, and the lawyers who had prepared and argued the cases had often done so in the face of genuine personal danger. Some were threatened and assaulted. Many lost their jobs. Some had been shot at. In some cases, their homes and churches had been burned.

Thurgood Marshall and the NAACP Devise a Strategy to End School Segregation

Marshall had shown up in Washington ten days before the trial began to coordinate his team and make sure that they were as prepared as they possibly could be. Their main concern was that the Supreme Court might agree that the African American children in the five cases had been treated unfairly but only because their schools were not equal to the schools of the white children, not because they were segregated. It was not enough to have the Court declare that the educations of the African American children in the cases were unequal. That ruling would have forced the NAACP to try for remedies on a case-by-case basis, to sue to force thousands of school districts to equalize their educational facilities, with districts, counties, and states digging in their heels and trying to slow things down all along the way.

Marshall's legal team needed the Court to overturn its previous decisions—something that it is often hesitant to do—and declare that segregation itself was unequal. Merely showing that the educational facilities in the areas named in the cases were not equal for white and African American children might be a small tactical victory, but it would be a major strategic defeat. What Marshall and his team were trying to prove was that there was no possibility for equality in the presence of segregated education. They needed the Court to declare that segregation based on racial identity was *inherently* unequal and that it violated the Constitution of the United States.

The fact that Marshall and his team were fighting segregation in the courts—indeed, that they were fighting segregation at all—was not inevitable. Given the history of the Supreme Court with respect to the rights of African Americans, the NAACP strategy was not promising. On several occasions in its history, including *Plessy*, the Court had issued rulings that severely restricted the rights of African Americans.

There were other possible strategies that would not have involved the courts. Marshall and his team could have tried to get new laws passed by focusing their efforts on Congress or the state legislatures. Some voices within the NAACP and in many African American communities also felt that the scarce resources available would be better spent on economic development, on building communities and businesses, rather than on the courts or the legislatures. In the end, however, the NAACP adopted a judicial strategy, deciding to focus much of its resource base on attacking segregation through the courts, especially the Supreme Court, with the hope of making lasting social change.

The NAACP's choice to base much of its strategy on winning in the Supreme Court was a risky move. Even if its lawyers succeeded, they had to confront the fact that the judicial branch of the United States was not designed to be a strong instrument of public policy. Though no one branch was supposed to be too powerful on its own, the Founders generally regarded the judiciary as the weakest of the three and had not given it powers to enforce its decisions. Justice Tom Clark, commenting on the decision in *Brown v. Board of Education*, cautioned that "we don't have money at the Court for an army and we can't take ads in the newspapers, and we don't want to go out on a picket line in our robes. We have to convince the nation by the force of our opinions."[25]

Thurgood Marshall (center), special counsel for the NAACP in *Brown v. Board of Education*, and two other members of his legal team in front of the Supreme Court following their landmark victory in 1954.
Bettmann/Contributor

Charles Hamilton Houston oversaw the NAACP's early efforts in guiding educational segregation cases through the courts, a complicated and lengthy process even when things went well. Hamilton had been an officer in an African American artillery regiment in World War I and, as a law student, was the first African American editor of the *Harvard Law Review*. Later, as the dean of Howard University School of Law, he reorganized the school to make it a center of African American legal thinking, training a new generation of civil rights lawyers. After Houston joined the NAACP in 1935, many of the cases brought by the organization focused on segregation in graduate schools. One reason for this was that "plaintiffs were more readily available in these cases than in cases involving elementary and secondary education, where becoming a plaintiff meant putting one's job or one's children at substantial risk."[26]

Another important step during this time was the appointment of Thurgood Marshall as the NAACP's chief counsel for the desegregation cases. A star student of Houston's, Marshall was a skilled litigator and adept at coordinating many different cases. Perhaps most importantly, Marshall was very thorough in his preparation, attending to all the details of the cases himself, knowing that cases could be won or lost over seemingly small points. Marshall showed up early and prepared, just as James Madison had done at the Constitutional Convention nearly two centuries before.

Using what had been learned in earlier cases, Marshall and the NAACP won two important legal victories in 1950, one originating in Texas, the other in Oklahoma. Texas's NAACP staff recruited Heman Sweatt, an African American applicant to the all-white University of Texas School of Law. Trying to comply with the ruling in *Missouri*, Texas quickly put together an all-Black law school and told Sweatt that he should apply there because of his race. Sweatt and the NAACP filed suit instead.[27] Key to the NAACP's case in *Sweatt v. Painter* was the sociological argument that Marshall put forward. He reasoned that one could not look only at the physical facilities when evaluating educational equality. Things like job networks, contacts, career support, and reputation could never be equal in segregated graduate schools. Intangibles mattered just as much as buildings and books. In its decision, the Supreme Court did not directly weigh in on the concept of "separate but equal"; however, it agreed that the intangible aspects of segregated education were destructive and impermissible, and it ordered the state to admit Sweatt to its larger, more established all-White law school.

On the same day that the Supreme Court ruled in *Sweatt*, it handed down a similar decision on the Oklahoma case, *McLaurin v. Oklahoma State Regents for Higher Education*. Though admitted to the state's graduate school, George McLaurin "was made to sit at a desk by himself in an anteroom outside the regular classrooms where his course work was given. In the library, he was assigned a segregated desk in the mezzanine behind half a carload of newspapers. In the cafeteria, he was required to eat in a dingy alcove by himself and at a different hour from the whites."[28] Again, the Court refused to directly address "separate but equal," but it did rule that separate treatment within Oklahoma's graduate school violated McLaurin's civil rights.

Having laid the groundwork in graduate schools and armed with the sociological argument, Marshall and his team were ready to take on segregated elementary and secondary public education in the United States. In doing so, they sought to overturn *Plessy v. Ferguson*, "separate but equal," and Jim Crow itself.

The Supreme Court Rules That "'Separate but Equal' Has No Place"

Oliver Brown of Topeka, Kansas, was a railroad welder, a part-time minister, and a reluctant symbol for desegregation.[29] He had attempted to enroll one of his three daughters, Linda, in an all-white elementary school that was both closer to their house than the all-Black school and did not require Linda to walk among the busy and dangerous Rock Island railroad yards in order to get there. Brown's request was denied, so, with the help of the local NAACP, he and seven other parents sued. After losing in the state courts, they appealed all the way to the Supreme Court. The Kansas case was joined with four others, and they collectively bore the name ***Brown v. Board of Education of Topeka***.

Arguing the case, Marshall got to the heart of the NAACP's arguments. All evidence, including evidence that had been accepted by the Court in earlier cases, had shown that Black and white children were equal in their educational potential. Educational segregation, therefore, had no legitimate basis. Moreover, it violated the Fourteenth Amendment to the Constitution, which had been made part of the Constitution specifically to protect freed slaves from violations of the state legislatures.

In addition to the legal and sociological arguments, psychological evidence was a part of the NAACP's strategy to show that segregation was inherently discriminatory. One piece of evidence introduced was a set of earlier research findings by psychologists Kenneth Clark and Mamie Clark. In those studies, the Clarks presented young African American and White children with a set of brown and white dolls. A majority of children stated that they preferred the white dolls over the brown dolls,

George McLaurin, the plaintiff in one of the two major graduate school cases, sits in a room apart from the main lecture room at the University of Oklahoma. Consider the sociological argument advanced by the NAACP in relation to this photograph. Thurgood Marshall and his team argued that intangible effects of segregation were damaging even when the physical facilities were identical.
Bettmann/Contributor

and many had negative comments about the brown dolls, leading the researchers to conclude that discrimination and prejudice created a feeling of inferiority among African American children.

On May 17, 1954, the last day of the Supreme Court's term, Chief Justice Earl Warren read the Court's decision on *Brown*, years after the case first came before the Court: "Does segregation in public schools solely on the basis of race, even though the physical facilities and other 'tangible' factors may be equal, deprive the children of the minority groups of equal educational opportunities? We believe that it does."[30] Arguing that the premise of *Plessy*—that separation based on race caused no harm in those so separated—was flawed, Warren overturned the 1896 decision, saying, "We conclude that in the field of public education the doctrine of 'separate but equal' has no place. Separate educational facilities are inherently unequal. . . . We have now announced that such segregation is a denial of the equal protection of the laws." The Court was unanimous, a point that Warren inserted into his reading of the official decision.[31] It had to be; a deeply divided Court would not have had the legitimacy that it needed to take on segregation. The unanimous verdict, however, had taken Warren a long time and several compromises within the Court to achieve.

The reaction of the nation was strong and immediate, but not uniform. Many cheered the moral stance the Court had taken. "What the Justices have done," declared a Cincinnati newspaper, "is simply to act as the conscience of the American nation."[32] Many voices in the African American community were supportive but measured; history had shown that white support for their cause had not always been sustained. "As Charles [Hamilton] Houston had said years earlier, 'Nobody needs to explain to a Negro the difference between the law in books and the law in action."[33] In the South, there was discussion among moderates on how to make the required adjustments. But there was also anger. Mobs blocked schools and universities. South Carolina governor James F. Byrnes proclaimed, "Ending segregation [will] mark the beginning of the end of civilization in the South as we have known it."[34]

The South Resists Desegregation

Legal segregation began to disappear in southern states, such as Maryland and Tennessee, that were closest to the North in the old Union/Confederate divide. Washington, DC, one of the five defendants in *Brown*, also moved relatively quickly to end legal segregation. States in the Deep South, however, actively resisted. In 1956, Virginia's legislators passed a resolution of interposition, which argued that the state was "duty bound" to impose itself between children's education and the Supreme Court decision. Several other state legislatures also forbade their state officials from enforcing **desegregation**—the intentional reversal of segregated educational facilities based on children's race or ethnicity.

The Court's decision in *Brown* had intentionally avoided setting a strict timeline on achieving integration. In response to resistance to its efforts, the Court issued a follow-up decision the next year, in 1955. In what is now known as *Brown v. Board of Education of Topeka II*, the Warren Court urged compliance with *Brown I* "with all deliberate speed," a curious choice of words, hardly inflammatory, likely crafted out of political necessity. In addition, the Court dealt with questions of implementation— making a policy a reality on the ground—by placing the federal district court judges in charge of actual desegregation efforts. Some southern district court judges were not sympathetic to the Court's ruling and tried to slow down compliance with it.[35] In general, in spite of the urging in the second *Brown* decision, compliance across the South was slow at best. Fears on the part of Supreme Court justices that their decision would not be obeyed proved to be well founded. In 1964, ten years after the Court's ruling in *Brown v. Board of Education*, 98 percent of African American children still attended completely segregated schools.

The decisions of the Supreme Court did not by themselves end the practice of segregation in the South. As was discussed in Chapter 2, the Constitution set up the American system of government to prevent one branch from having that kind of power. And, for a time, the Court found itself acting alone. According to law professor Gerald Rosenberg, "For ten years the Court spoke forcefully while Congress and the executive did little."[36] There were a few exceptions to this, however. In 1957, President Eisenhower sent federal troops to Little Rock, Arkansas, to enforce a Supreme Court order to segregate the schools against the will of the state's governor. The troops escorted nine African American students through an angry white mob. Also that year, Lyndon Johnson, senator and future president, sponsored the Civil Rights Act of 1957, the first piece of civil rights legislation to pass since Reconstruction. Its primary purpose was to put pressure on the states through the cost of litigation by supporting the lawsuits of African Americans who had been denied the right to vote. Though it did not effect significant policy change, it showed that civil rights legislation could make it past the southern Democrats in Congress.

Citizens Engage in New Forms of Civil Disobedience and Protest

Citizens themselves took increasingly strong action to end segregation in schools, workplaces, and the community. African American community leaders organized boycotts in which people refused to buy services or products from an organization in order to force policy changes. Notable among these was the Montgomery bus boycott, which sought to put economic pressure on the city of Montgomery, Alabama, to end its policy of segregating bus passengers based on their race. At first, Montgomery community leaders tried to pressure the city into changing its policy, but this had no effect. In 1955, Claudette Colvin, an African American high school student, refused to move to the "Negro section" of a Montgomery bus. She was not sitting in the "white section" but in "no man's land," a vaguely defined buffer between the two sections that, according to segregationists, was created "to give the driver some discretion to keep the races out of each other's way."[37] Colvin refused to move and was handcuffed and placed under arrest. That year, other African American women in Montgomery were arrested for the same act of protest. Their case eventually resulted in the bus segregation law being declared unconstitutional.[38]

In December, Rosa Parks also refused to give up her bus seat and was later arrested. The decisions of Colvin and Parks were not taken lightly; they faced the prospect of criticism within their own communities and physical violence at the hands of whites. "When she [Rosa] was allowed to call home," one historian has noted, "her mother's first response was to groan and ask, 'Did they beat you?'"[39] Upon word of Parks's arrest, English professor Jo Ann Robinson and other community leaders organized a boycott, getting the word out with the help of African American churches in the city. They printed flyers in secret in the middle of the night at Alabama State College, where Robinson taught. Dr. Martin Luther King Jr. was selected to lead the boycott. Addressing the community in a Montgomery church, King captured the simple, courageous reason behind the actions of the women of the city: "And you know, my friends, there comes a time when people get tired of being trampled over by the iron feet of oppression. . . We are here—we are here because we are tired now."[40] After lasting for more than a year, the boycott ended with the Supreme Court's 1956 decision in the case of Colvin and three others that declared the bus law unconstitutional. Not only had they won in the Court, but it was a public victory—a citizens' victory.

There were many other acts of **civil disobedience** in the struggle against segregation. Individuals chose to disobey segregation laws despite the dangers they faced in order to point out the injustice inherent in those laws. In 1960, four African American college students sat down at a lunch counter reserved for whites at a Woolworth's in

CAN THE SUPREME COURT EFFECT SOCIAL CHANGE?

Alexander Hamilton, in *Federalist* No. 78, argued that the Supreme Court had little power acting on its own "and must ultimately depend upon the aid of the executive arm even for the efficacy of its judgments." One scholar has collected data on the pace of integration in the South following *Brown v. Board* to make a similar argument: The Supreme Court cannot, acting on its own, produce social change on the ground. His data are displayed in the chart below.

It was not until 1970 that more than half of African American children in the South were attending integrated schools (and many of these were far from fully integrated). During this period, citizens took action through events such as the Montgomery bus boycott, in which African Americans in Montgomery, Alabama, refused to ride city buses in protest over segregated seating; the executive and legislative branches became more involved in the desegregation process; and the Court issued more related rulings. The data in the graph indicate that the decision of *Brown v. Board* did not immediately result in desegregation of schools in the South. To say that the Supreme Court is powerless, however, might be too strong a statement to make based on these data alone.

First, the branches were not designed to act alone but in concert with (and sometimes in opposition to) each other. This is

the principle of separation of powers discussed in Chapter 2. Second, *Brown* was only the first in a string of decisions on school desegregation handed down by the Court—decisions that became stronger and stronger during the time period covered in the graph. See Figure 5.1.

WHAT Do You Think?

For ten years after *Brown*, southern public schools remained segregated. Considering all that you have read so far, why might this have been unsurprising? Do these data confirm that the Supreme Court cannot effect social change? Was the NAACP's decision to adopt a judicial strategy a wise one? Why or why not?

▼ FIGURE 5.1

Percentage of African American Children Attending Integrated Schools in the South

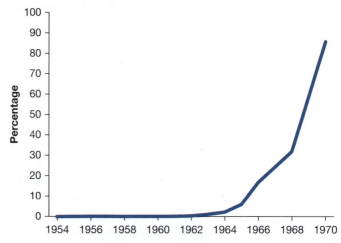

Source: Data from Gerald N. Rosenberg, *The Hollow Hope* (Chicago: University of Chicago Press: 2008), 50–51, Table 2.1.

Greensboro, North Carolina, and requested service. They were denied. They returned the next day, and their numbers began to grow. College students, both African American and white, continued the sit-ins. Over the next months, with the organizational help of the Student Nonviolent Coordinating Committee (SNCC), similar protests occurred across the American South. Some protesters met with arrest, others with violence and intimidation.

In 1961 a group of African Americans and whites undertook another series of protests aimed at pressuring the administration of President John F. Kennedy to enforce Supreme Court decisions banning

Four young Black men sit in at a segregated lunch counter at a drugstore in Jackson, Mississippi, in 1961. They are about to be arrested by police officers (rear) for refusing an order to leave. The efforts of those involved in the lunch counter protests helped call attention to the injustices of segregation in the American South.

The Granger Collection, New York

segregation in public facilities involved with interstate travel. These Freedom Riders also faced arrest and violence. In one case a bus was firebombed, and many protesters were beaten with baseball bats and iron pipes.

The actions of these activists—and their often harsh treatment at the hands of local law enforcement, which was broadcast to Americans on their televisions—began to change public opinion toward the civil rights struggle. By voting in larger and larger numbers, African Americans also began to make their presence felt in Washington, DC. Close elections during the period highlighted to politicians the importance of securing the African American vote, which might tip an election in their favor.

Aware of changing political realities, Congress, under intense pressure from President Johnson, passed two major pieces of civil rights legislation, finally giving its support to efforts that had begun in the Supreme Court and on the streets. A version of the Civil Rights Act of 1964 had been part of President Kennedy's civil rights efforts prior to his assassination in 1963. The legislation that Congress passed in 1964 authorized the federal government to withhold grants from districts that did not integrate their schools. The act outlawed racial segregation in schools and public places and authorized the attorney general of the United States, and therefore the federal government, to sue individual school districts that failed to desegregate. In addition, the act outlawed employment discrimination based on race or ethnicity and also on religion, national origin, or gender. The provisions of the Civil Rights Act of 1964 proved to be as valuable to women and members of other minority groups in their efforts as the civil rights decisions in the Supreme Court. The Voting Rights Act of 1965 outlawed literacy tests for voters and authorized the Justice Department to send federal officers to register voters in uncooperative cities, counties, and states. The effects on African American voter registration were immediate and significant.

The Court Delivers New Decisions Aimed at Strengthening Civil Rights

In a series of decisions over the decade and a half following its decision in *Brown*, the Court spoke with an increasingly firm voice. Like *Brown*, many of these cases involved the public schools. In them, the Court confronted policies in the southern states that tried to get around the ruling in *Brown* without appearing to openly defy it.

Over the next several years, the Supreme Court reached a high-water mark in the scope of its desegregation decisions. In 1971, in *Swann v. Charlotte-Mecklenburg Board of Education*, the Court ruled that busing—the use of transportation to desegregate public schools, even if it meant sending students to schools farther away from their homes—was constitutionally permissible.[41] Busing efforts stirred up considerable political opposition in both the North and the South. Those in favor argued that such efforts were necessary given the deepness of the roots of segregation. Those opposed argued that the role of government in securing equal protection was only to strike down unjust laws, not to produce integration on the ground. The debate over civil rights had moved on from laws to policies, to how strongly government should act to contest segregation that exists even when there are no laws that support or maintain it.

The Court Limits Itself in Addressing Segregation in Practice Rather Than by Law

While the Court had affirmed the constitutionality of robust policies to remedy segregation in *Swann*, it would also place certain limits on its own powers to address the legacy of racial segregation. The difference lies in the sources of segregation. The southern segregation that Thurgood Marshall and the NAACP had challenged in the courts was written into law—sometimes even into state constitutions. These laws did not just allow segregation; they often required it. This type of segregation is called **de jure segregation**, meaning that it is written into law. The efforts of activists and citizens had largely eliminated racially based de jure segregation by the end of the 1960s. Attention now focused on **de facto segregation**, segregation based not on law but on private choices or the lingering social consequences of legal segregation. Addressing de facto segregation has proven to be even more complicated than addressing de jure segregation, and the Supreme Court has been less assertive in remedying it than it has with de jure segregation.

In 1974, in *Milliken v. Bradley*, the Court considered a case of educational segregation that had been caused not by law but by residential housing patterns in and around Detroit, Michigan.[42] The question in *Milliken* was of responsibility. How much action should be taken, and who should be required to take it, when there was no law to point to? In this case, the Court ruled that there was no requirement to try to desegregate the region's schools, since the district boundaries had not been drawn up for the purpose of segregating them. The suburban districts did not have to participate in a plan that would move students across school district boundaries. Limits on the Supreme Court's willingness to require remedies in the presence of de facto segregation had been set.

Questions about how far the Court is willing to go to secure equality in the absence of discriminatory laws have arisen in other aspects of political and economic life as well. **Affirmative action**—a policy designed to address the consequences of previous discrimination by providing advantages to individuals based upon their identities—continues to be a subject of debate in American political life. The Court has issued a much less clear set of guidelines on the use of affirmative action than it has with legal segregation. Many of these cases have involved admissions practices at American colleges and universities that have sought to boost the enrollment of African Americans and members of other racial and ethnic minorities. Again, it boils down to what one means by *equal*. To those who argue for less government intervention, *equal* only means removing any legal barriers to college admissions for members of racial and ethnic minorities. To those who argue for stronger government involvement, it means taking steps to ensure equality of representation that might selectively benefit certain individuals based on their identity, whether in schools or workplaces. In recent years, the Court has tried to navigate among these approaches, but it has not always done so in a clear-cut way.

A 1978 Supreme Court decision in *Regents of the University of California v. Bakke* concerned the use of quotas, or the setting aside of a number of school slots, contracts with the government, or job opportunities for groups who have suffered past discrimination.[43] In the case, Allan Bakke, who identified himself as white, had sued the University of California, Davis, after having been denied admission to its medical school. Bakke argued that his academic record was superior to the group of sixteen minority applicants for whom seats had been set aside. He brought his suit under the Fourteenth Amendment, claiming that the quota system violated his rights under the equal protection clause of the Constitution. In its ruling, the Court agreed that the quota system had violated Bakke's rights and those of other white applicants and instructed the school to admit him. However, the Court also affirmed the worthiness of the goal of increasing minority student enrollment, leaving open the possibility for plans that did not involve strict quotas.

In the years after *Bakke*, the Court issued several rulings that attempted to define the limits of permissible affirmative action. In a series of cases in the 2000s and 2010s, the Court outlawed defined points systems in ranking applicants to increase the diversity of schools' student bodies.[44] But the Court ruled that universities can use race as a factor as long as they could show that they had a "compelling interest" to do so. Ensuring a diverse student body, the Court concluded, is sufficiently compelling.

American Women Work to Secure Their Civil Rights

5.4 Trace the history of efforts to secure civil rights for American women.

Though they constitute a slight majority of the American population, women have also struggled to secure their civil rights throughout the nation's history. Scholars often frame these efforts as having taken place in two waves. The first wave was focused on winning the right to vote and was closely tied to the efforts of nineteenth-century American women to secure their rights in education and to end the practice of slavery. The second wave, which began in the middle of the twentieth century, extended the scope of civil rights protections to women's participation in the classroom and the workplace, their freedom from sexual harassment, and their control over their bodies and their sexuality.

Women's Early Civil Rights Efforts Focus on Enfranchisement

The suppression of women's rights was often justified by claims that women needed to be protected from, and therefore shut out of, elements of public life. This "protection" had legal aspects. Rights of women were severely restricted in the public space, and married women had no legal identity outside their marriage. For the purposes of the courts, they did not exist. The restriction of women's rights was as much social as it was legal. Part of the effort to secure women's rights, therefore, involved redefining what was considered acceptable behavior for a woman. Taking action in the public space—by speaking out, organizing, and mobilizing public opinion—was as political in its challenge to the boundaries of acceptable behavior as was the act of actually changing laws.

Early efforts by women to secure their rights often focused on education, which was considered an acceptable political space for a nineteenth-century white woman to inhabit. But early activists for women's rights quickly began to push the boundaries of that political space and many became active in the **abolitionist movement**—the movement to end the practice of slavery

The efforts of sisters Sarah and Angelina Grimké to organize and speak out against slavery in the 1830s challenged both the institution of slavery and the less visible institution of protection of women from public life. Daughters of a prominent South Carolina slaveholding family, the Grimké sisters set out in 1837 on an antislavery speaking tour in New England. In doing so, they helped to change public perception about a woman's proper role in public life. Their campaign drew much of its strength from their own Christianity—and drew much of its opposition from Christian churches. Their audiences included women and men, African Americans and whites. Their speeches highlighted the cruelty at the heart of the institution of slavery, and they expressed solidarity with enslaved women.

A few of the male leaders of the abolitionist movement welcomed women's participation in the abolitionist struggle and supported their efforts in securing white women's voting rights. Frederick Douglass published on the masthead of the newspaper that he edited, "Right is of no sex—Truth is of no color."[45] Others urged these advocates to drop their push for "a woman's rights," as it was called, fearful that the controversy might detract from the goal of abolition, but the proponents refused. However, the male-dominated abolitionist movement continued to prevent women from assuming public roles as leaders. Sometimes women were allowed to join antislavery conferences, but only as observers in segregated seating, without the right to speak or vote.

Shut out of prominent antislavery conventions in the mid-nineteenth century, abolitionist women organized their own. Lucretia Mott and Elizabeth Cady Stanton met at an antislavery convention in London in 1840 and on their way back to the United States began to plan a separate conference on women's rights. The conference met in a Methodist church in Seneca Falls, New York, over two days in July 1848. On the first day of what would come to be known as the Seneca Falls Convention, Stanton read a list of eleven resolutions, known as the Declaration of Sentiments. These resolutions derived their legitimacy from an appeal to higher law, just as the Declaration of Independence had done 72 years earlier and Dr. Martin Luther King Jr.'s "Letter from Birmingham Jail" would do 115 years later.[46]

Support for the women's declaration was not universal, even among activists. Only one-third of the delegates to the convention signed it. Some thought that it was too bold, especially in its call for suffrage (the right to vote) for women. The convention, however, had given energy to the movement. In the years following Seneca Falls, "a cascade of women's rights conventions . . . carried the movement into towns and villages throughout the Northeast and the Midwest."[47]

Women's rights activists organized rallies and protests, including this march on Labor Day in 1912.
New York Public Library/Science Source

Similar to the struggle for African American rights, the women's movement did not speak with a unified voice. Debates over goals and strategy led to sharp divisions within it. In the last national convention held before the Civil War, Stanton spoke out against marriage laws and in favor of new resolutions making it easier for a woman to obtain a divorce. Many reformers felt that she "had gone too far."[48]

These divisions continued after the Civil War, when giving the right to vote to freed African American men came onto the national agenda. Some women's rights activists wanted to include suffrage for women in the Fifteenth Amendment. Others feared that trying to obtain the right to vote for African Americans and women at the same time might stir up too much opposition. There was often a stated racial bias against African Americans on the part of white women's rights advocates, and far less attention was paid to the rights of African American women than either those of African American men or white women. According to one historian, the issue of suffrage was often portrayed as "a choice between black men and educated white women."[49]

Wyoming Territory granted women the right to vote in 1869. When Wyoming became a state in 1890, it became the first state to grant women the right to vote. By 1918, fifteen states had passed laws allowing women's suffrage. The right was secured at the national level in 1920 with the ratification of the **Nineteenth Amendment** to the Constitution, which had been drafted by Susan B. Anthony and Stanton more than forty years earlier. The amendment stated, "The right of citizens of the United States to vote shall not be denied or abridged by the United States or by any State on account of sex. Congress shall have power to enforce this article by appropriate legislation."

Though the constitutional right to vote came later for women than it did for African American men, women did not face the same kinds of tactics of resistance aimed to keep the legal right from becoming a practical right. As they began to exercise their right to vote, however, the broader vision of equality that many of the pioneers in the American women's movement hoped for was far from secured.

The Second Wave Focuses on Ongoing Inequalities

The second wave of the movement to secure the civil rights of women in the United States began in the 1960s. Like the first wave, much of the strategy involved changing laws. However, the focus went far beyond the voting booth and addressed inequalities at work and in the home as well as protection from violence and sexual harassment.

Crucial to these legislative and legal efforts was the Civil Rights Act of 1964. Title VII of the act prohibits discrimination in employment based on race, color, religion, national origin, or sex. While some scholars have argued that women were added to the act as an attempt to mobilize enough opposition to kill it, the southern congressman who introduced the amendment to add women to the legislation claimed that his motives were sincere.[50] Regardless of the truth, Title VII has proved to be an important tool in the fight for equal rights for women and the basis for several rulings about gender discrimination by the Supreme Court.

One of the early leaders of this second wave was Betty Friedan. Her 1963 book, *The Feminine Mystique*, highlighted the ways in which American society assumed that domestic roles for women were "natural" and argued for a "dramatic reshaping of the cultural image of femininity that will permit women to reach maturity, identity, completeness of self, without conflict with sexual fulfillment."[51] Friedan also served as the first president of the National Organization for Women (NOW), a women's rights advocacy group that pushed for change in both the legislature and the Supreme Court. NOW initially organized largely to pressure the federal government to enforce the antidiscrimination provisions of Title VII. The organization's goals, however, became much more sweeping: "The purpose of NOW is to take action to bring women into full participation in the mainstream of American society now, exercising all the privileges and responsibilities thereof in truly equal partnership with men."[52]

In the 1960s and 1970s, women's rights activists secured several important pieces of legislation. They also lobbied to ensure that these laws were vigorously enforced— to make sure that equal meant equal in the workplaces and schools and not just in the laws. Through these pieces of legislation, women secured the legal right to receive equal pay for equal work in the same workplace and protections against discrimination based on gender, pregnancy, or childbirth. Many of these laws contain language that makes it illegal to retaliate against employees who file or participate in the filing of discrimination claims. The threat of retaliation can be a powerful disincentive for individuals to file discrimination claims, and, therefore, a powerful tool to preserve discrimination.

Protections against gender discrimination apply not just to workplaces but also to schools, states, and local governments. One of the most notable provisions is contained in a set of amendments to the Higher Education Act of 1965; they were passed in 1972. Title IX of these amendments states, "No person in the United States shall, on the basis of sex, be excluded from participation in, or denied the benefits of, or subjected to discrimination under any educational program or activity receiving federal aid."[53] While its provisions apply equally to curriculum, health care, and residential life, Title IX has had a public impact on the provision of athletic programs and, more recently, on the efforts of students who are women and/or lesbian, gay, bisexual, and transgender (LGBT) to overcome harassment based on sexual or gender identity.

One of the most important elements of the legislative campaign for women's rights was an attempt to secure ratification of the **Equal Rights Amendment (ERA)** to the U.S. Constitution. The proposed amendment read, "Equality of rights under the law shall not be denied or abridged by the United States or by any state on account of sex."

Activist Alice Paul had written the original version of the amendment in 1923, and it had been submitted to Congress for official acceptance (the first stage of the two-stage amendment process) every year since. Partly due to the help of NOW, the proposed amendment easily cleared the two-thirds vote requirement of the House of Representatives in 1971 and the Senate in 1972. Submitted to the states for ratification, the ERA got off to a good start, outpacing other recent amendments with its speed of state ratifications. By 1977, thirty-five of the needed thirty-eight states had ratified the ERA. No more states, however, would ratify. In spite of having its ratification deadline extended by Congress, the clock ran out on the ERA in 1982, and the amendment died.

Scholars continue to debate why the ERA failed. Part of the reason is that the Framers designed the amendment process in such a way that most proposals to amend it do fail. The Constitution was designed to be amendable, but the two-stage process for ratification is a very high hurdle. Other explanations have focused on the possibility that proponents did not mobilize as successfully at the state level as they had done in Congress during the first stage of the process. Additionally, the controversy surrounding the Supreme Court's decision on abortion in *Roe v. Wade* in 1973 (see Chapter 4) may have mobilized opponents to the ERA.[54] The fact that so many states ratified early on also allowed opponents to concentrate their resources on a smaller number of remaining states than if they had had to wage a counterstrategy nationwide.[55]

Though the Equal Rights Amendment was not ratified, the debate over its ratification did help increase the visibility of women's rights issues and place them on the national agenda. And, as it turns out, the Fourteenth Amendment to the Constitution and Title VII of the Civil Rights Act of 1964 provided a sufficient basis for the Supreme Court to act in the absence of the Equal Rights Amendment.

The Supreme Court Uses Different Standards of Scrutiny on Gender Discrimination and Sexual Harassment

Although part of the strategy for women's rights advocates was to use the Supreme Court, as African American rights activists had done, they did so under a slightly different standard. Due to the nation's history of slavery, the Court has treated protection of civil rights based on racial identity differently than protection for other groups. Historically, the Court has used three different standards to decide if a law or policy that treats people differently based on some aspect of their identity is allowable or not. In the case of racial identity, the Court applies a standard of **strict scrutiny** to any attempt to provide different or separate treatment. Under such scrutiny, a government has to show a "compelling interest" to justify the unequal treatment, a high standard that is difficult to meet.

At the other end of the spectrum is the **reasonableness standard**, which means differential treatment must be shown to be reasonable and not arbitrary. It is also called the "rational basis" standard as one merely has to show that there is a rational reason for the distinction.[56] This is a much lower bar legally. Under the application of the reasonableness standard, for example, government may tax people at different rates based on their incomes or impose a curfew on minors that does not apply to adults.

Cases involving the rights of women have generally been considered by applying a standard in between these two extremes, one of **intermediate scrutiny**. In general, the Court has found most forms of differential treatment for men and women to be unconstitutional, except when such treatment can be justified as serving important objectives or necessities. In 1996, for example, the Court struck down the male-only admissions policy of the public Virginia Military Institute as a violation of the equal protection clause of the Fourteenth Amendment.[57] Public schools are, however, allowed to have gender-separated physical education classes if they involve physical contact as well as classes dealing exclusively with human sexuality. The standard of intermediate scrutiny has evolved in recent years and continues to be a source of conflict and disagreement between the justices themselves.

Cases involving sexual harassment have generally been evaluated on the basis of the discrimination provisions of Title VII of the Civil Rights Act of 1964 rather than the Fourteenth Amendment. Though Title VII does not specifically mention sexual harassment, the Court has ruled in several recent cases that sexual, or gender-based, harassment does violate the act's antidiscrimination provisions. The Court has identified two types of harassment. *Quid pro quo* harassment occurs when employers request or demand sexual favors in return for advancement or employment. A *hostile working environment* involves actions, statements, or conditions that unreasonably interfere with the ability of employees to do their jobs. In cases of quid pro quo harassment, employers can be found liable for the behavior of their offending employees, even if that behavior was not known at the time it occurred. In cases involving hostile working environments, employers are generally held liable only if they knew about the offending behavior but did nothing to stop it. As with other forms of gender-based discrimination, the Court's treatment of sexual harassment is still evolving and is the source of considerable disagreements within the Court itself.

Americans Confront Overlapping Forms of Discrimination

5.5 Evaluate the ways the diversity of Americans' identities shapes efforts to secure civil rights in the twenty-first century.

African American women's rights activists had been hard at work in the decades before the Civil War. For example, Maria W. Stewart, an African American essayist, activist, and orator from Boston, was the "first American woman to speak in public to a mixed audience of men and women, addressing a gathering at Boston's Franklin Hall in 1832."[58]

In 1851, Sojourner Truth, an orator, activist, and former slave, addressed a women's rights convention in Akron, Ohio. Her speech, only a few paragraphs long, drew from her own experiences as a person confronting more than one form of oppression:

I have plowed and reaped and husked and chopped and mowed, and can any man do more than that? I have heard much about the sexes being equal; I can carry as much as any man, and eat as much too, if I can get it. I am as strong as any man that is now...

But the women are coming up bless be God and a few of the men are coming up with them. But man is in a tight place, the poor slave is on him, woman is coming on him, and he is surely between a hawk and a buzzard.[59]

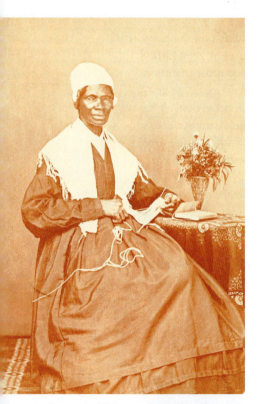

A portrait of Sojourner Truth. Her efforts to call attention to the multiple forms of oppression facing African American women in the nineteenth century highlighted what scholars now call challenges of intersectionality.

Time Life Pictures/Timepix/LIFE Picture Collection/Getty Images

Truth's speech has resonated throughout the history of civil rights and succinctly and eloquently captures the reality that many Americans have been confronting more than one form of inequality in their lived experiences. Scholars of identity and politics call the presence of multiple and overlapping identities and inequalities **intersectionality**.[60] This approach recognizes that multiple forms of oppression are not just additive; they interact with each other to present individuals with complex challenges to the assertion of their own rights.

This concept is more than the subject of academic study. Confronting inequalities based on both race and gender shaped the choices and strategies of early African American women activists. Some chose to focus their efforts primarily on abolition, confronting the very different expectations of "proper" behavior for white and Black American women. Others focused their efforts within their own communities, challenging realities of poverty and poor education at the local level.[61] In the slave states, many African American women focused on keeping their families together and alive. This complex set of choices and challenges continues to present itself to Americans working to secure equal rights against multiple and overlapping forms of discrimination.

Civil Rights Challenges Persist for Other Groups as Well

In this chapter, we have focused on efforts to secure civil rights for Americans with disabilities, African Americans, and women. Throughout the nation's history, however, members of many other groups have acted to secure their own rights. Some of these struggles also go back to the early decades of the American Republic. To give proper attention to all of these efforts would require an entire book at least; therefore, we have focused on only some of them. The guiding principle of this necessary omission is that we cover many of these issues in other parts of this book.

As we explored in Chapter 1, the members of the Standing Rock Sioux Nation based their right to protest on civil liberties protected by the First Amendment to the Constitution. They also, however, did so in order to secure their civil rights. Similarly, the Supreme Court decision that established marriage equality, *Obergefell v. Hodges* (2015), was based upon the Fourteenth Amendment's guarantee of equal protection of the laws.

Many Latinos and Latinas have employed and continue to employ tactics of protest, organization, education, and mobilization to challenge discrimination against members of their communities, especially on issues such as immigration and labor policy. The question of treatment of Americans of color by law enforcement has gained considerable attention in recent years. We will explore this issue in detail in Chapter 6. Individuals and groups have also mobilized to secure the rights of gay, lesbian, and transgender Americans.

In the United States in the twenty-first century, the concept of racial identity is becoming complicated as well. Multiracial Americans, or those with more than one distinctive racial heritage, have increasingly been carving out a space for themselves in discourse and policies involving race and ethnicity. In 2000, the U.S. Census allowed, for the first time, individuals to select more than one racial category. Slightly more than 2 percent chose to do so. By 2010, the number of Americans self-identifying as multiracial increased by 32 percent, to about nine million Americans. Where the most common combination in 2000 was "white and some other race," by 2010 the most common combination was "black and white." In addition, over the same ten-year period, the population of multiracial children increased by 50 percent, "making it the fastest growing youth group in the country."[62]

The increase in Americans who self-identify as multiracial is more than an issue of numbers. Traditional racial and ethnic identifications have been used as the basis for evaluating compliance with Title VII of the Civil Rights Act of 1964, the Voting Rights Act, and educational desegregation policies. Broadening the categories will impact all of these regulations, and some African American rights advocates have expressed concern that it might take away from gains in equality that have been achieved since the civil rights era.[63] Proponents of having multiracial classification argue that it more accurately reflects the changing realities of racial identity in the United States. Testifying before Congress, one parent of a multiracial child stated, "In my opinion, the most traumatic experience related to racial identification for the multiracial child occurs when he/she is asked to deny racial connectedness with one parent."[64]

Conclusion: Have Americans' Civil Rights Been Secured?

The actions involved in claiming and securing civil rights are not isolated things. In addition to confronting social, political, and economic inequalities, members and leaders of civil rights movements often draw support from others' efforts and learn from their successes and failures. Securing civil rights also speaks to the foundations of American democracy, forcing people to consider what full equality truly means. If they are to be successful, these efforts must involve strategic political action and use a variety of tools, including organization, protest, and the media. Equally fundamentally, securing civil rights is also about telling stories that resonate, stories that challenge the idea—often unspoken—that the exclusion of some Americans from full and equal participation in society is somehow natural, appropriate, or inevitable.

The struggle to achieve equality under the laws of the United States has never been simple or clear, and it has only grown more complex. Whatever future attempts to secure civil rights in the United States bring, however, this much is certain: Those attempts will require drawing upon the lessons of past struggles, well-planned action, and courage.

CHAPTER REVIEW

This chapter's main ideas are reflected in the Learning Objectives. By reviewing them here, you should be able to *remember* the key points and *know* the terms that are central to the topic.

5.1 Understand that securing civil rights requires both actions by individuals and groups to claim them and actions by governments to protect them.

Remember . . .
- Securing civil rights requires action—both on the part of individuals to advocate for their rights and on the part of government to protect those rights.

Know . . .
- *civil rights* (p. 129)
- *positive freedoms* (p. 129)

5.2 Trace the history of racial segregation in America and the ratification of the Fourteenth Amendment to the Constitution, which laid the foundation for later struggles to secure civil rights.

Remember . . .
- While the conclusion of the Civil War settled the question of secession and three amendments established a set of constitutional rights for African Americans, struggles to secure their rights continued, often under threats of economic and physical violence.

Know . . .
- *equal protection clause* (p. 137)
- *Fifteenth Amendment* (p. 137)
- *Fourteenth Amendment* (p. 137)
- *Jim Crow laws* (p. 138)
- *legal segregation* (p. 138)
- Plessy v. Ferguson (p. 138)
- *separate but equal* (p. 139)
- *Thirteenth Amendment* (p. 137)

5.3 Explain efforts to end legal segregation based on racial identity as well as the strategies used in those efforts.

Remember . . .
- The NAACP's choice to focus its efforts on ending legal segregation was not preordained, nor was the strategy of using the courts instead of focusing on changing the laws in the states.
- The federal judiciary is only one of three branches and faces many challenges in changing public policy on the ground.

Know . . .
- *affirmative action* (p. 149)
- Brown v. Board of Education of Topeka (p. 142)
- *civil disobedience* (p. 145)
- *de facto segregation* (p. 148)
- *de jure segregation* (p. 148)
- *desegregation* (p. 144)

5.4 Trace the history of efforts to secure civil rights for American women.

Remember . . .
- Early efforts to secure civil rights for African Americans and those to secure civil rights for American women often overlapped—but with differences in their goals and tactics.

Know . . .
- *abolitionist movement* (p. 150)
- *Equal Rights Amendment (ERA)* (p. 153)
- *intermediate scrutiny* (p. 155)
- *Nineteenth Amendment* (p. 152)
- *reasonableness standard* (p. 154)
- *strict scrutiny* (p. 154)

5.5 Evaluate the ways the diversity of Americans' identities shapes efforts to secure civil rights in the twenty-first century.

Remember . . .
- Americans may face multiple forms of discrimination that may act to reinforce each other.

Know . . .
- *intersectionality* (p. 156)

POLITICAL BEHAVIOR AND MASS POLITICS

CHAPTER 6

PUBLIC OPINION

....

How Are Americans' Voices Measured, and Do They Matter?

A protester holds up a sign during a demonstration in Ferguson, Missouri. Eighteen-year-old Michael Brown was killed in a confrontation with a police officer, sparking a series of protests that led to a nationwide conversation about the treatment of Blacks by law enforcement officials and that seems to have influenced the public's view of the issue.

Bilgin Sasmaz/Anadolu Agency/Getty Images

LEARNING **OBJECTIVES**

After reading this chapter, you will be able to do the following:

6.1 Understand how public opinion is dynamic and contested.

6.2 Discuss differing theories about public opinion formation and expression and the degree to which it is meaningful.

6.3 Describe the issues involved in transmitting and measuring American public opinion and constructing the instruments used to do so.

6.4 Examine the contributors to individual attitudes and public opinion.

6.5 Evaluate the power of individuals, events, and people's interpretations of events to make lasting change in American politics.

In a representative government, citizens must have some knowledge of what their elected representatives are up to in order to keep watch on their activities, hold them accountable, and punish them at the voting booth if those representatives are no longer serving their interests. Conversely, elected representatives need to know what citizens' preferences are in order to appeal effectively to voters and to carry out their wishes once in office.

Nothing about that exchange of information can be taken for granted. Why? For starters, the act of conveying opinions to candidates or elected officials requires that people (as individuals and collectively) have preferences on issues in the first place and that these preferences are coherent and meaningful.

This is the central challenge of **public opinion**, the sum of individual attitudes about politics, government, and policies. Scholars debate the degree to which people have individually coherent and meaningful opinions about the issues with which government deals. When these individual bits of information become the collective thing that we call public opinion, they also wonder whether that produces anything meaningful or is just noise.

In this chapter, we will focus on American public opinion in one specific area: the treatment of young Black men by law enforcement officials and protests aimed at calling attention to the issue. We will deal primarily with the difficult story of the shooting death of Michael Brown by a police officer in Ferguson, Missouri, and the events that followed. We will question whether or not these events have produced meaningful changes in American public opinion on the topic of police-community relations.

Public Opinion May Be Moved by Important Events Like Ferguson

6.1 Understand how public opinion is dynamic and contested.

On August 9, 2014, white law enforcement officer Darren Wilson killed Michael Brown, an unarmed eighteen-year-old Black man, during a police stop in Ferguson,

Missouri. Some eyewitness accounts asserted that Brown had his hands raised in surrender when he was shot six times by Wilson.[1] His death sparked a massive public outcry. The day after Brown's death, protesters gathered in Ferguson. "Tension . . . flared off and on through the evening" as protesters cycled between peaceful prayer circles and candlelight vigils and more intense street demonstrations where they chanted "'We are Michael Brown' as wary police officers stood nearby with assault rifles."[2] By nightfall, there was violence: "After a candlelight vigil, people smash[ed] car windows, carr[ied] away armloads of looted goods from stores and burn[ed] down a Quick Trip."[3] By the time the first wave of violence ended, "more than two dozen businesses in Ferguson and neighboring Dellwood were damaged or looted."[4] The protests, some peaceful and some violent, continued for weeks.

Many of the protesters and other residents of Ferguson began to call for the arrest and prosecution of the officer who had shot Brown. Some chanted. One of their common refrains was "black life matters," a reference to the social movement #BlackLivesMatter, which began following the 2013 acquittal of George Zimmerman in the shooting death of Trayvon Martin in Florida. After Ferguson, however, Black Lives Matter became part of the national conversation in ways it had never been before. *Time* magazine included the protesters of Ferguson in its list of candidates for "Person of the Year."[5] The movement gained even more visibility in the public eye as numerous other unarmed African Americans were killed by police officers during the year following. In Dayton, Ohio, police shot and killed twenty-one-year-old John Crawford inside a Walmart. Crawford was handling an air rifle, which officers thought was a firearm.[6] Roughly three weeks before Brown was killed, Eric Garner "died from a police chokehold in Staten Island, N.Y., after telling the arresting officers that he could not breathe."[7]

The Black Lives Matter movement began after the death of Trayvon Martin, an unarmed Black Florida teenager who was shot to death by a white neighborhood watch volunteer in 2012. The group continued protesting in Ferguson after Michael Brown's death.

NICHOLAS KAMM/AFP/Getty Images

At the same time, the views of police officers involved were also shaping the public's perception of the events. In an interview with ABC News in the fall of 2014, Darren Wilson, who had announced his resignation from the Ferguson Police Department, argued that he had acted in self-defense in killing Brown: "I had to. If I don't, he [Brown] will kill me if he gets to me."[8] Ferguson police chief Thomas Jackson relayed to the public Wilson's suspicions that Brown and a friend were suspects in a convenience store robbery that had occurred shortly before the encounter.[9]

Public Opinion Reflects Different Fergusons

After Michael Brown's death, deep divisions emerged, with Americans' views on the shooting split according to racial and ethnic identity. Ferguson, Missouri, was quickly becoming many Fergusons. A *New York Times* article stated that "where once there was only one Ferguson—an anonymous suburb of St. Louis—now there is another: a small city whose name has become known for civil unrest, racial division and police harassment."[10] It was not only the shooting that caused controversy. The different "Fergusons" did not exist only in the streets of the city. The opinions of the community's reactions were as divided as the opinions over the event itself. To some, the protests were a justifiable expression of inequalities and injustices too long ignored; to others, they represented violence and anarchy.

To many Americans, especially whites, the protesters' anger over the events in Ferguson came as a surprise. To large percentages of African Americans, however, the death of Brown was not unique—only another tragedy in a long history of tragedies when young Black men came face-to-face with the American law enforcement system. To individuals within African American communities across the country, the only surprising thing about the fallout from Ferguson was that the issue had not been more debated, more talked about. According to Rep. John Conyers (D-MI), cofounding member of the Congressional Black Caucus, "There are virtually no African-American males—including congressmen, actors, athletes and office workers, who have not been stopped at one time or another for driving while black."[11]

Less than two weeks after Brown's death, the Pew Research Center published the results of a **public opinion survey**, which is a systematic attempt to make inferences about the opinions of large numbers of individuals by carefully sampling and asking questions of a small, randomly assigned sample of the larger population. Pew was looking at Americans' responses to what Ferguson and racial identity meant in the larger national conversation. To conduct the survey, researchers had contacted a random sample of one thousand American adults, half via landlines and half via cell phones. The divisions between African Americans and whites on what Ferguson meant were clear. A full 80 percent of Blacks said that Brown's shooting raised "important issues about race." But only 37 percent of white respondents agreed. Furthermore, 47 percent of Whites said that "race [was] getting more attention than it deserves" (see Figure 6.1). Clearly Americans were deeply split about whether Brown's death reflected important issues about the state of race in America. The idea that there were two Fergusons, one African American and one white, seemed to extend beyond the city limits and apply to the whole of the American public.

Although public opinion was deeply divided especially along lines of racial identity, there were some, perhaps unexpected, complications to these divisions.

Opinion about Ferguson Divided by Racial Identity

Thinking about the police shooting of an African American teen in Ferguson, Missouri, percentage saying . . .

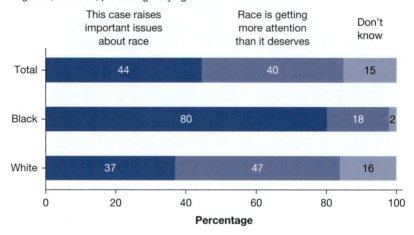

Source: Pew Research Center, "Stark Racial Divisions in Reactions to Ferguson Police Shooting," August 18, 2014, www.people-press.org/2014/08/18/stark-racial-divisions-in-reactions-to-ferguson-police-shooting.

Note: Survey conducted August 14–17, 2014. Whites and Blacks include only those who are not Hispanic. Figures may not add to 100% because of rounding.

For example, a 2012 survey by the Pew Research Center concluded that 48 percent of Americans agreed with the following statement: "Guns do more to protect people than place them at risk." In a similar survey in December 2014, the number of Americans agreeing with that statement had increased to 57 percent. Most strikingly, "the shift [in agreement] was even more substantial among African-Americans, going from 29 percent in early 2013 to 54 percent [in 2014] (though with a margin of error of almost 10 percent due to small sample size)."[12] Critics of the poll, however, questioned the wording of the survey items, suggesting that the pollsters may have shaped their findings by the way in which they posed the questions. (We will explore issues in constructing and administering surveys later in the chapter.)

As we will see in the chapter, in the years following Brown's death, the national conversation about race in America has changed. Of all the critical questions that arose from the events in Ferguson, these are the ones that we will explore: Did the events in Ferguson meaningfully shape American public opinion? If these events did have an impact on American public opinion, what effect did the resulting change in attitudes have on representation and the American political process? Did these changes endure, or did the national conversation go back to the way it was before, divided sharply by racial identity? Did leaders and government officials pay attention to these shifts in the opinion landscape?

LOOKING FOR A "BREAK IN TREND" IN DATA AND DRAWING CONCLUSIONS OVER TIME

In public opinion polls conducted by the Pew Research Center and the *Washington Post* in 2009, 2011, and March 2014, the percentage of Americans who agreed that the nation had "made the changes needed to give blacks equal rights with whites" did not change much. In each poll, roughly half of Americans overall expressed the opinion that the nation had made these changes. Individual attitudes, however, diverged sharply by racial identity.

Higher percentages of white Americans felt that the nation had made the necessary changes, but the vast majority of African American survey respondents (constituting a smaller part of the sample) felt that it had not. See Figure 6.2.

By the late summer of 2015, however, something appeared to have changed.[13] Between the polls conducted in March 2014,

▼ FIGURE 6.2

Majority Says Nation Needs to Make Changes to Give Black Individuals Equal Rights

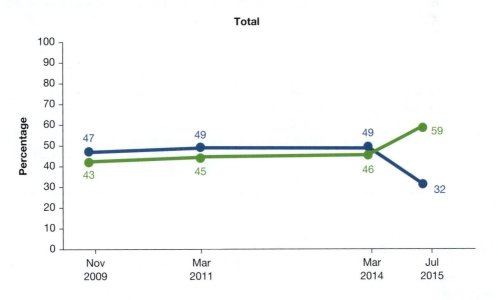

Total

(Continued)

(Continued)

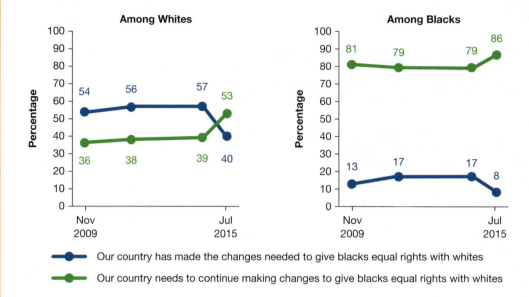

Among Whites / **Among Blacks**

Among Whites data points:
- Our country has made the changes needed to give blacks equal rights with whites: 54, 56, 57, 40
- Our country needs to continue making changes to give blacks equal rights with whites: 36, 38, 39, 40, 53

X-axis: Nov 2009 to Jul 2015

Among Blacks data points:
- Our country has made the changes needed to give blacks equal rights with whites: 13, 17, 17, 8
- Our country needs to continue making changes to give blacks equal rights with whites: 81, 79, 79, 86

X-axis: Nov 2009 to Jul 2015

━━●━━ Our country has made the changes needed to give blacks equal rights with whites

━━●━━ Our country needs to continue making changes to give blacks equal rights with whites

Note: Survey conducted July 14–20, 2015. Whites and Blacks include only those who are not Hispanic.

Source: Pew Research Center, "The Partisan Divide on Political Values Grows Even Wider," October 5, 2017, https://www.people-press.org/2017/10/05/the-partisan-divide-on-political-values-grows-even-wider. 2018 data from Pew Research Center, "2018 Midterm Voters: Issues and Political Values," October 4, 2018, https://www.people-press.org/2018/10/04/2018-midterm-voters-issues-and-political-values.

six months before Brown's shooting, and July 2015, nearly a year after, there appeared to be what political scientists call a "break in trend"— and a sharp one at that. In the 2015 survey, the percentage of Americans surveyed who felt that the nation had done enough to achieve equal rights appeared to have changed. This was true overall and for both Whites and African Americans.

However, when drawing conclusions about the causes of this change in public opinion— including whether that cause was Ferguson— some caution is warranted. Other events between the 2014 and 2015 surveys may have contributed to the observed findings. A debate about the display of Confederate flags, for example, also made it onto the national political agenda during this time, as did more shootings and tragic events. We cannot, based on these data alone, confirm that the events in Ferguson were behind the change in opinion but only that there is a potentially meaningful correlation between the two. That said, this change in American public opinion, how quickly it happened, and how substantial it was are not things to be quickly dismissed.

WHaT Do You Think?

Do these results lead you to conclude that the shooting deaths in Ferguson and other cities and the protests in response actually changed American public opinion? What other evidence might you want to make a firmer conclusion?

Public Opinion Is the Sum Total of Individual Beliefs and Attitudes

6.2 Discuss differing theories about public opinion formation and expression and the degree to which it is meaningful.

One of the most important debates about American public opinion is whether or not there is such a thing. Of course, many Americans *have* thoughts and ideas about politics and policies, but many others do not have well-formed views on these topics. Some people might not care at all and wonder what all the fuss is about. And what do we really learn by asking Americans what they think? Recall the definition of *public opinion* presented previously: the sum of individual attitudes about politics, government, and policies. Public opinion, by definition, involves two components: an individual's own beliefs and attitudes as well as the accumulation of all of these individual preferences into something that we then call public opinion. Either of these two pieces—individual attitudes and the aggregation of individual attitudes—can make American public opinion difficult to understand. This is because individuals may not actually have meaningful preferences on any given issue, and, even if they do, the aggregation of these individual preferences might not yield meaningful and useful information.

These are more than just academic concerns. A representative democracy cannot function without meaningful public opinion. If our elected representatives do not know what we want, then how can they hope to represent us?

There Are Competing Views about the Meaning of Public Opinion

Arguments about the meaning of public opinion in American political life fall into two general camps. One perspective holds that the average citizen either doesn't have or is unable to express meaningful opinions on the vast array of issues with which they are confronted. Maybe there are simply too many issues for any of us to have well-informed and meaningful opinions about all of them. The other perspective holds that even though individuals sometimes lack the information they need to form opinions, they can find ways to overcome or work around these challenges by, for example, making inferences based on their attitudes about other policies and questions, responding to messages from political parties, and/or relying on friends. Perhaps these shortcuts and cues help us arrive at an opinion. Aggregating individual opinions—even if they are individually unclear or inconsistent—can send a useful and impactful signal to elected representatives and government officials.

The Minimalist Paradigm Holds That Most People's Opinions Consist of Stereotypes and Nonattitudes. Proponents of what political scientists have called the **minimalist paradigm** emphasize how most people fall short of what we expect them to know, think about, and pay attention to in the complicated world of politics and policy.[14] Most people, according to this perspective, pay minimal attention to issues and have minimal information about them. Additionally, the opinions that they *do* have are minimally stable; they change over time or in response to attempts to control or shape them.

One of the earliest and most influential expressions of the minimalist argument was Walter Lippmann's *Public Opinion* (1922). A prominent journalist and political observer, Lippmann was concerned about how malleable (or flexible) and receptive Americans' attitudes appeared to be under the pressure of political propaganda leading up to the nation's involvement in World War I. If, in the mind of many observers of American public opinion, a nation could be led into a war most felt had nothing to do with American interests, then what *couldn't* the American people be talked into?

For Lippmann, a key concept was the **stereotype**, a preconceived, often oversimplified idea about something that people apply as a filter to the world. Stereotypes do not filter based upon a rational **consideration** of the issues but upon emotions, and in the world of politics they are easily manipulated by those who seek to shape American public opinion for their own political purposes.

Lippmann described a public that is dangerously unreflective and vulnerable to attempts to shape its opinions. To him, part of the reason why the Framers of the Constitution instituted so many checks and balances in the federal government, so many roadblocks to making major policy change, was mistrust of individuals' haphazard, shifting, and malleable stereotypes.

Inherent in the minimalist critique is the idea that not all Americans have the same amount of political information. A small number of individuals, the **elites**, may have well-informed and well-reasoned opinions, but the majority of individuals, the **masses**, do not. In an early study using large sample surveys, a group of researchers painted a grim picture of the majority of American voters. Most are not politically involved and have only a limited awareness of political events.[15] Instead, voters often rely on their identification with a political party—an identification that itself might not be the result of careful, thoughtful, conscious deliberation.

In 1964, political scientist Philip Converse extended this critique to question whether masses can and do learn from elites, become more informed, and produce responses to surveys that are stable over time. Generally, Converse found, masses do not learn from elites.[16] Instead, most voters have **nonattitudes**. The opinions that most people express in, for example, a public opinion survey, might be vulnerable to the efforts of propagandists, as Lippmann feared, and, frankly, might just be random.

Concerns about a lack of coherent opinions in the American electorate and the challenges that this poses to American representative democracy have not gone away. Recently, two researchers found that significant percentages of Americans were not able to answer basic questions about American government, such as being able to name one or more branches of the federal government or name constitutional protections in the Bill of Rights.[17] At least as troubling was their finding that political knowledge was predictably and unequally distributed. Younger Americans, women, lower-income Americans, and members of racial and ethnic minorities were consistently less able to correctly answer such factual political knowledge questions. These gaps have remained consistent over the past few decades. Researchers with the Pew

Research Center periodically administer a "News IQ" quiz to a random sample of Americans. The test contains questions regarding political figures, knowledge of current issues in domestic and international politics, and geography. While the number of Americans who can correctly answer a question varies within and across these knowledge tests, significant numbers are unable to answer the questions correctly. To what extent does this information gap matter? Can Americans with unequal knowledge of, or access to, information about American politics express their desires with voices as impactful as those of informed Americans? And what implications does this have for the policies that the government enacts and who those policies are designed to benefit?

Another Perspective Says That People Can Overcome Information Gaps.

While more recent scholarship acknowledges the challenges posed by proponents of the minimalist paradigm, it also emphasizes the ways in which the public can still make sense of their opinions and transmit those opinions to their representatives, both collectively and individually. On the most basic point—that Americans often lack opinions on many issues in politics and policy—these scholars agree. Where they disagree is on the need for any one person to have an encyclopedic set of policy preferences so that they are able to offer an opinion on any topic. The aggregation of individuals' opinions, according to some scholars, can produce useful information even in the presence of noise at the individual level. How do individuals answer survey questions? Do they act as file cabinets, carrying around preformed opinions and waiting to pull out the relevant opinion when prompted? Or do they construct at least some of their opinions when asked to do so—opinions that are based on their own understandings but also perhaps shaped by the survey and the context in which they answered the survey's questions? If that is how individual opinions might be "formed," then one might reasonably expect to see changes in answers to surveys over time and in different situations, since the administration of the survey will vary.

For political scientist John Zaller, opinions are constructed things, composed of the facts with which we are presented, but also our predispositions, such as the political party with which we identify and what we think.[18] When presented with a statement by, for example, a political candidate, individuals accept or reject the statement based as much on cues such as political party of the person giving the message as its actual substantive content. Basically, Zaller's theory says that our knowledge, emotions, and predispositions all come into play when we form and express an opinion. We are not file cabinets, but we are also not the modeling clay that Lippmann worried about. We are something in between.[19]

Other research focuses on the ability of voters with low levels of specific political knowledge to make effective use of **cues and information shortcuts** to form meaningful opinions. These informational helpers may come from a variety of sources. One such cue is our evaluation of the person making a statement, rather than the statement itself. Do we trust them? Do they share our values? Our evaluation of the messenger is just as important as our evaluation of the message they are putting out there. This is especially true when we are asked to evaluate highly technical arguments rather than those that often provoke a "gut" response, like whether or not it is acceptable to burn a U.S. flag. Individuals' own personal experiences and interactions with government, accumulated over a lifetime, can also help them make sense of an issue or problem. This "gut rationality" may not help on a political knowledge quiz, but it can assist people in making meaningful political choices.[20] In addition, individuals might rely on advice from friends and colleagues.[21]

Identification with a particular political party (called party identification) is a powerful informational shortcut that voters frequently use when evaluating candidates and forming opinions about specific issues.[22] If I identify as a Republican, I'm likely to be more favorable toward the Republican candidate than the Democratic candidate, even without knowing anything other than their party affiliations. Or if I identify as a Democrat, I am more likely to oppose a policy option that Republicans endorse than one Democrats endorse.

Finally, some political scientists have emphasized the possibility of the "wisdom of crowds"[23] in which individuals, imperfectly informed, can come up with a meaningful assessment of a problem or situation. Benjamin Page and Robert Shapiro emphasized the possibility for a public to be collectively rational even in the presence of individually inconsistent and shapeable opinions: "While we grant the rational ignorance of most individuals, and the possibility that their policy preferences are shallow and unstable, . . . public opinion as a collective phenomenon is nonetheless stable (though not immovable), meaningful, and indeed rational . . . : it is able to make distinctions; it is organized in coherent patterns; it is reasonable, based on the best available information; and it is adaptive to new information or changed circumstances, responding in similar ways to similar stimuli."[24]

Public Opinion Is Transmitted and Measured in Several Ways

> 6.3 Describe the issues involved in transmitting and measuring American public opinion and constructing the instruments used to do so.

The act of representation in a republican form of government has two basic, and crucial, informational requirements. First, voters must have opinions and preferences that can be communicated to their elected representatives. Second, elected officials must respond to, or be forced to respond to, these expressed preferences. We have already considered the debates about whether or not Americans have meaningful opinions. The second part of the equation is just as important. How can Americans effectively communicate their preferences to their government? How do elected representatives learn about the preferences of their constituents? What tools can we use to make sure we are correctly gauging their responses?

Citizens' Opinions Are Transmitted to Public Officials through Direct and Indirect Channels

One method that citizens use is to directly communicate with their elected officials through phone calls or emails. The challenge with direct communication as a tool of representation is that elected officials know that those who call or write do not represent their constituents as a whole but are only a motivated subset of people, often those who are unhappy about something. While direct communication can signal to an elected official the intense preferences of a small group of individuals, it does not convey a sense of the overall preferences of the citizens as a whole.

A tool that does give elected officials this broader knowledge is an election. While we may not think about an election as a tool for measuring public opinion, that is precisely what it is. However, in this regard, elections have their own limitations, starting with the fact that many eligible voters do not vote. In terms of measuring the preferences of constituents, the greater challenge with elections is that they tend to revolve around a small set of issues, albeit ones about which voters have intense preferences. For the majority of public policy issues with which elected officials will have to contend, elections are too broad a tool to reveal useful information.

Therefore, rather than waiting for individuals to contact them or trying to decipher the results of an election, public officials may go directly to the citizens to find out what they think and want. One tool used for this is the **focus group**, in which a small group of individuals is assembled for a directed conversation during which one hopes to uncover patterns of thinking about issues and individuals. Focus groups can offer insight into how individuals come to understand the political issues with which they are contending. However, by their nature, focus groups cannot paint a picture of the constituency as a whole and are therefore limited in their utility.

Another, deeper concern about focus groups and other tools for measuring public opinion comes from their origin in product marketing in which companies use these tools to try to get a sense of which products will sell best and why. This textbook, in fact, as well as most others, involved the use of focus groups in its development. The challenge for representative democracy is whether or not we want our elected officials to think of their role as creating "products" like breakfast cereals. In one sense, we might. We want our elected representatives to care enough about our opinions to find out what they are. On the other hand, there is a danger that our elected representatives might be too concerned with taking the nation's pulse, too hesitant to make difficult decisions that might be unpopular but necessary. The Framers most certainly did not intend for elected representatives to consistently bend to the will of voters. That is part of the reason why they set up so many roadblocks to making major and sweeping changes to American public policy.

Even so, a candidate whose eyes are on the next election will use any tools that they have to gauge the opinions of the voters. The most effective of these is the **scientific poll**. With this tool, pollsters try to gain an understanding of the thoughts and preferences of a large group by obtaining the opinions of a carefully chosen small sample of the group although they are aware of the limitations of the effort.

Scientific Polling Is Based on Efforts to Accurately Sample Representative Populations

A key question in considering how useful a scientific poll is involves its **validity**, the degree to which an instrument accurately measures what it is designed to. In theory, scientific polling is simple. Given the challenges and costs of having to ask everyone in a House district, a state, or the nation what they think, pollsters instead select a smaller representative subset of that constituency and ask its members what they think. That subgroup is called the **sample**. For some political polls, the sample population may be the entire voting-age population of the United States or of an individual state or congressional district. However, there are many other possible populations of interest in a survey, such as individuals with specific racial or ethnic identities or the student population of a college or university.

A key challenge in sampling is **random selection**. For the sample to be useful, it must represent the larger population as well as possible—with no systematic errors. Some errors in sampling are not a problem. If your **respondents**, or those individuals who respond to your survey, are more likely to choose blue over green socks, that is probably not an issue. If, however, a poll systematically oversamples or undersamples individuals based on characteristics that are relevant to what the poll is trying to measure—for example, support for a presidential candidate from the Democratic or Republican Party—then you have a problem. Pollsters are well aware of these challenges. Often, they use the technique of **weighting** to adjust the results of a survey. Put very simply, if pollsters know that, for instance, women make up 50 percent of the population, but only 40 percent of their sample, they will adjust their results to compensate.

Unless one can survey every single person in a population, community, or nation, no researcher can ever know what the "true" opinion of that population is. The goal is to minimize the uncertainty as much as possible while also conducting a poll that does not cost vast sums of money or take an unacceptable amount of time to conduct. When pollsters present their results, they include a measure of the **sampling error** (or margin of error) in their surveys. In larger national polls, which typically aim for about 1,500 respondents, the sampling error is often plus or minus three points, meaning that they can assert that about 95 percent of the time, the true number—which is never known—lies within three points on either side of the measured number. In American politics, the number of citizens on either side of an issue might be closely divided. If, for example, an opinion survey with a margin of error of three points finds that one party's candidate for president has the support of 49 percent of Americans and the other party's candidate the support of 47 percent, then one could not confidently say that the first candidate would win in a national election. Increasing the size of the sample decreases the error, but it also increases the cost. In addition, the greater the variation in the population that one samples, the larger the sampling error.

Public Opinion Survey Validity Varies by Type

In choosing how to administer a survey, a researcher has several options. The degree of confidence that one can place in the findings, however, depends critically upon the ways in which the sample is selected. One popular type of survey is a **straw poll**—an unofficial tally of opinion or support at a meeting or event, such as a political party meeting or caucus. While straw polls can be useful in exploring which individuals support a candidate and why, their target population is not randomly selected. The fact that people have chosen to attend the event at which the straw poll is conducted means that the sample was not randomly chosen and, therefore, cannot be relied upon to draw conclusions about general public opinion.

A **self-selected listener opinion poll** (**SLOP**), in which respondents choose to respond to a survey prompt on their own, suffers from the same disadvantage. SLOPs are quite common. When individuals respond to a radio talk show host's requests to call in, or when a person fills out a quick survey after reading an article or watching a video on the Internet, they are participating in a SLOP. Because more involved and motivated individuals choose to participate—and these individuals do not represent a randomly selected subset of the overall population—one cannot confidently say that their opinions reflect the distribution of them in the larger population.

An **exit poll** is a survey conducted outside a polling place in which individuals are asked for whom or what they just voted and why. While there is much to be gained for a news organization that can call a race before other news outlets based on its exit poll results, there are risks as well. Individuals do not vote at random times, and an exit poll may unintentionally be sampling from a group that over- or underrepresents overall public opinion on an issue or candidate. Also, announcing the results of exit polls while polls are still open runs the risk of influencing an election. Learning that one candidate is supposedly winning may discourage another candidate's supporters from turning out to vote because they believe their votes will not matter. To avoid that problem, news networks have voluntarily committed to not releasing exit poll results until all of a state's polling places have closed. Exit polls can be useful, though, in understanding patterns of voting—for example, what issue was most on the minds of voters who voted for one candidate or another.

Because of the challenges posed by nonrandom selection, news organizations, media outlets, and research organizations rely primarily on the telephone when trying to gauge American public opinion. They may draw from lists of phone numbers or employ **random digit dialing** in which phone numbers are generated randomly by computer. That has the added advantage of potentially including unlisted numbers or those generally not in pollsters' (or marketers') databases, such as numbers for cell phones. Even with random digit dialing, however, there are always risks that a sample is not truly representative of the overall population. Are some people more likely to answer the survey than others? Might patterns of willingness or unwillingness to answer the survey bias the findings? Though pollsters are aware of and try to account for these issues, it is always a potential problem.

How Public Opinion Surveys Are Constructed Affects Their Validity

In addition to sample selection, pollsters must confront other issues that are important for informed consumers of public opinion surveys—such as the students reading this book—to note. We have explored the challenge that Americans may have non-attitudes on some issues, and there is also the risk that individuals may be unwilling to admit a lack of information or opinion and make up responses on the spot. In one survey of Americans, political scientist George Bishop asked respondents about their opinions of the Public Affairs Act of 1975. The trick was that the act never existed. In spite of this small fact, significant percentages of respondents offered an opinion on the piece of fictitious legislation, casting doubt on the reliability of results of surveys of Americans on specific public policies and policy proposals.[25] In light of this phenomenon, well-constructed survey questions focus on issues with which their respondents will be familiar and have opinions about.

Even on issues for which respondents have actual preferences, other factors may shape the results of a public opinion survey. First, the **question order** might have an impact. Consider a question about whether or not individuals should be permitted to burn an American flag in protest. If the flag-burning question were preceded by a question about the importance of patriotism, it might produce more opinions opposed to flag burning. Alternatively, if the flag-burning question followed a question on the importance of free speech in American democracy, it might prime a different pattern of responses. In this way, the same question can produce substantially different results depending on the specifics of the survey.

Similarly, the **question wording** might, intentionally or not, guide respondents to a specific answer. For example, in a 2003 Pew Research Center survey about attitudes toward military action in Iraq, 68 percent of respondents said they favored action when asked if they would "favor or oppose taking military action in Iraq to end Saddam Hussein's rule." However, when asked if they would "favor or oppose taking military action in Iraq to end Saddam Hussein's rule even if it meant that U.S. forces might suffer thousands of casualties," only 43 percent of respondents favored military action.[26] Finally, the interviewers themselves may affect the results of a survey, especially one conducted in person. Political scientists have, for example, documented **race of interviewer effects** in which the outcomes of surveys, even on questions asking only for political knowledge and information, may depend partly upon the racial identities of respondents and surveyors.[27]

Individual Opinions Vary According to Direction, Intensity, Stability, and Salience

Political scientists and scholars of political psychology and mass communication not only need to think about the various techniques and types of instruments they can use to measure public opinion but they also need language they can use to describe that individual's opinions. To do this, they have defined four distinct components of an opinion. The first is the **direction** of the opinion, which is what we commonly focus on. Is the person for an issue, against it, or neutral? Does the person think favorably about a political candidate, unfavorably, or remain neutral? A second dimension of an opinion is the **intensity**, or strength, of involvement and preference, with which an individual holds that opinion. Does the person feel passionately about the issue or is it of minor concern? Another component describes the **stability** of the opinion. Stable opinions tend not to change over time, in different contexts, or in response to differently worded survey questions. Some opinions, such as which political party one prefers, tend to be stable, while others, such as views of a specific water or transportation policy, tend to be much more variable over time and across different surveys—if the individuals have opinions at all. Intensity and stability of an opinion are related. Intense opinions are more likely to be stable than those held with less intensity. Finally, there is the **salience** (or centrality) of an opinion. Opinions with more salience shape expressed opinions on other issues or candidate evaluations. For example, a strongly held belief about the need for an active and involved government might shape a person's opinions about workplace safety regulations or the need to provide universal prekindergarten education. Salient opinions tend to be more intense and stable.

One topic that continues to evoke intense, stable, and salient opinions is the treatment of individuals by law enforcement officers and the relationship between that treatment and the racial and ethnic identity of those individuals. As residents of Ferguson and other communities in which young men of color had been killed by law enforcement officers reacted, protested, and expressed their anger, it quickly became clear that opinions about race and treatment by law enforcement officials were often highly intense and salient. These opinions, however, were sharply divided by race, ethnicity, age, and partisan affiliation.

Polls Are Used for Commercial, Academic, and Political Purposes

Many different individuals and groups make use of public opinion polls. Media outlets work with major polling organizations when covering Americans' support or opposition to a candidate or policy proposal. Academic researchers rely on more in-depth polls to test theories about politics and public opinion. One tool that political scientists and other researchers may employ is the survey experiment, in which individuals are randomly assigned different surveys, perhaps with different question wording or framing. The goal here is not to try to measure the opinions of a larger population but to use the randomized experiments to better understand how people form opinions.

Polls also play key roles in political campaigns. The media may use tools such as exit polls to predict the outcomes of political races or to better understand why people voted one way or another in a given election. Candidates themselves may employ polls to better understand voters' interests and concerns or to gauge public support for themselves or their opponents as a campaign progresses. One controversial tool that candidates or those supporting them may employ is a push poll, which is not really a poll but a negative campaign tactic. Disguised as a survey, a **push poll** presents voters with negative or damaging portrayals of opposing candidates, sometimes with false or exaggerated information.

Political Socialization and Political Ideology Shape Public Opinion

6.4 Examine the contributors to individual attitudes and public opinion.

For all of us, our lived experience contributes profoundly to what we believe and the political attitudes we hold. But there are several other key factors that shape our views,

In an exercise in civic education, high school senior Aaron Levine asks a question of council members during a mock city government election in Wellington, Florida.

Allen Eyestone/ZUMA Press/Newscom

including our political ideology, the groups we belong to, and other influential organizations and actors. Political scientists have long studied how those attitudes are formed in the first place, how they may be altered over time, and how they are influenced by others.

Political Socialization Shapes Individual Attitudes

The formation and modification of opinions and attitudes toward politics, public policy, and political figures is a lifelong process. **Political socialization** refers to the variety of experiences and factors that shape our political values, attitudes, and behaviors.

Families, Schools, and Peers Are Early Shapers of Information and Opinion. The first and most important contributor to the process of political socialization is the family, especially when it comes to shaping children's views about political figures and political authority.[28] **Party identification**—the degree to which an individual identifies with and supports a particular political party—is highly transmitted through families. Families provide, after all, the first source of political information for those who are seeking out information.[29]

Schools often intentionally play a role in political socialization through processes of **civic education** that aim to introduce students to politics and help them develop the ability to interpret and make sense of this knowledge.[30] Families inform political learners first; then schools and educational experiences leave their mark. As such, an individual's civic education does not occur on a blank canvas but one that has already been at least partially painted by their upbringing.

Personal Experience and Focusing Events Affect Individual Attitudes over Time. Individual political opinions are never set in stone. While families, schools, and peers play important but different roles in our political socialization, so do later experiences in life. Our interactions in daily life may also shape our opinions on both individual and national levels, especially when we experience **focusing events**, such as times of crisis.

We see this effect in several ways in the aftermath of Ferguson as individuals across the nation began to take a greater interest in politics and policy and became more informed and involved. One of the individuals attending a protest march at the end of August was forty-four-year-old Ian Buchanan. According to a reporter for the

St. Louis Post-Dispatch, Buchanan, "a former principal in the St. Louis and Normandy school districts, drove to Ferguson from his home in Memphis, Tenn., to attend Saturday's march. 'I came here because I want to be part of the spirit of the movement,' he said. He spent part of the day talking to his former students about how to voice their concerns about injustice. 'The older generation usually wants to write off the younger generation, but to effect change, it comes from the young people,' Buchanan said."[31]

Sometimes the cumulative effect of a series of crises makes a difference at the national level in shifting public opinion. Indeed, public opinion polls conducted in the weeks and months following the deaths of Michael Brown and Eric Garner found that a large majority of Americans, regardless of racial or ethnic identity or political party affiliation, expressed support for the use of body cameras by law enforcement officers to record their interactions with the public.

American public opinion in the twenty-first century is more instantaneously shapeable than has ever been previously possible. Social media allows, in theory, a national conversation between people of very different lived experiences and political attitudes.

Partisan Identification, Individual and Group Identities, and Elite Attitudes Inform Our Views

As we have seen, families, schools, and events (either over the course of a lifetime or focusing ones) play a major role in shaping public opinion. But other factors play important roles as well. How we identify politically, as well as how we define ourselves in terms of gender, race, or ethnicity, can form clear, consistent, and persistent patterns of similarity and division in American public opinion.

Political Ideology. One of the single most effective predictors of public opinion is an individual's identification with a political party. Partisan identification is closely connected to one's **political ideology**, which describes a person's beliefs about political goals, public policies, and acts to shape political choices. In the United States today, two political ideologies tend to dominate. **Liberalism**, in the modern usage of the term, refers to support for more robust governmental action to ensure equality of opportunity, particularly in regulation of the economy, as well as environmental regulation. **Conservatism** highlights a reduced role for the government and an emphasis on individual liberty, again, especially in economic matters.

While these two political ideologies do shape much of the landscape, there are others. **Socialism**, closely related to liberalism, emphasizes an even stronger role for the government in economic matters, including advocating for governmental control over entire sectors of the economy, such as health care. **Libertarianism**, on the other hand, shares an emphasis on individual liberty with conservatism but often takes it further, arguing that governmental involvement in the lives of Americans should be reduced as much as possible.

These ideologies map onto partisan affiliation, with liberals, and some socialists, identifying with the Democratic Party and conservatives and many libertarians identifying with the Republican Party. These mappings, however, are not always neat and clear. As we will explore in our discussion of political parties later in the book, tensions *within* political parties are often as consequential as debates *between* them.

Americans' response to Ferguson was no different. On the question of whether or not local law enforcement agencies could be trusted to administer the laws of the nation impartially and without regard to racial and ethnic identity, Americans were sharply divided according to the political parties to which they attached themselves. Similar divisions emerged in polls showing that over two-thirds of Republicans thought that race was getting too much attention in the media coverage of Ferguson whereas nearly 70 percent of Democrats thought that the shooting raised important issues about race in American society.[32]

Gender.   American public opinion is also often divided along gender lines. On many issues, such as comparative levels of spending on social welfare programs versus national defense, polls have consistently found differences between men and women. These differences in opinion translate into differences in support for American political parties. The term **gender gap** describes the fact that American women are more likely to identify with and vote for Democratic Party candidates than men, who are more likely to vote for Republican Party candidates (see Figure 6.3).

▼ FIGURE 6.3

The Gender Gap in American Politics

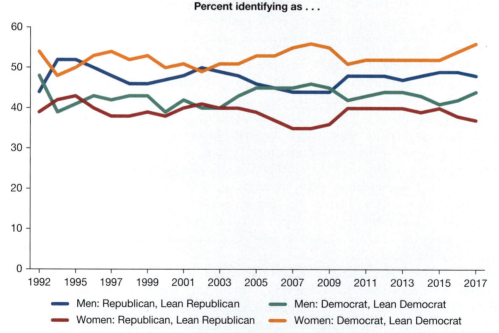

Percent identifying as . . .

— Men: Republican, Lean Republican   — Men: Democrat, Lean Democrat
— Women: Republican, Lean Republican   — Women: Democrat, Lean Democrat

Sources: Pew Research Center, "The Gender Gap: Three Decades Old, as Wide as Ever," March 29, 2012, www.people-press .org/2012/03/29/the-gender-gap-three-decades-old-as-wide-as-ever; Pew Research Center, "Party Identification Trends, 1992–2016," www.people-press.org/2016/09/13/party-identification-trends-1992-2016.

Racial and Ethnic Identity. American public opinion is also often divided on the basis of racial and ethnic identity. Members of American racial and ethnic minorities emphasize the importance of social justice and equality of opportunity more than white Americans,[33] patterns that are correlated with the fact that racial and ethnic minorities are more likely to experience economic challenges and poverty.[34] In addition, scholars of race and gender in American politics have found evidence to support the notion of **linked fate**, in which individual members of a group accept "the belief that [their own] life chances are inextricably tied to the group as a whole."[35] In the days following the shooting in Ferguson, public opinion surveys revealed sharp racial divisions on the event (see Figure 6.4).[36] To say that any community (as defined by the sum of their common experiences) would be united would be far too simplistic. Bernie Frazier, an African American speaker and career strategist from Ferguson, told the *New York Times*, "I've had moments where I feel violated by the protesters. To be honest, I feel violated by the media. I read a headline that said, 'Ferguson under siege.' I saw an article that described Ferguson as 'impoverished.' I've just stopped reading comments online. I'm done."[37]

▼ FIGURE 6.4

Racial and Ethnic Divisions in Opinions of Authorities' Handling of the Ferguson Investigation

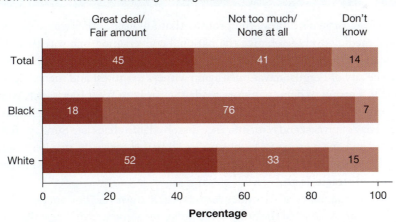

How much confidence in shooting investigations?

Source: Pew Research Center, "Stark Racial Divisions in Reactions to Ferguson Police Shooting," August 18, 2014, www.people-press.org/files/2014/08/8-18-14-Ferguson-Release.pdf.

Notes: Survey conducted August 14–17, 2014. Whites and blacks include only those who are not Hispanic. Figures may not add to 100% because of rounding.

Government and Media Influence Public Opinion

To many of the protesters in Ferguson, the treatment of young African American men by the American political and legal system had been a critical issue for a very long time. One of the many tasks of the president is to act as a "communicator in chief"—to focus attention on specific issues and events and to make sense of tragedies and challenges. In this role, President Barack Obama addressed the shooting of Brown in a speech at the White House, saying, "In too many communities around the country, a gulf of mistrust exists between local residents and law enforcement. . . . In too many communities, too many young men of color are left behind and seen only as objects of fear."[38]

Advancements in technology have also affected public opinion. As we explored in the last chapter, social media and online information sharing are changing the ways in which Americans participate in politics. In the interconnected, live, and unfiltered world of social media, Ferguson made this point very clear. Following the death of Brown and the decision by the grand jury not to indict Wilson, social media lit up. According to the *Washington Post*, "'Black Twitter' . . . emerged as a powerful forum for activism and debate regarding Ferguson, helping sway public opinion by challenging racially biased interpretations of Brown's killing."[39] We will explore the power of the media in the next chapter.

Ferguson and the Effects of Public Opinion on Democratic Representation

> 6.5 Evaluate the power of individuals, events, and people's interpretations of events to make lasting change in American politics.

Did Michael Brown's killing, the protests that followed, other tragic events, and national media coverage change the national conversation in a way that affected American public policy? In 2015, on the one-year anniversary of Michael Brown's death, the city of Ferguson was once again witness to protest and then violence. On August 9, a group of demonstrators made their way to West Florissant Avenue in Ferguson, Missouri, shouting, "Hands up, don't shoot!"[40] News reports noted, "A peaceful day of protest and remembrance dissolved into chaos late Sunday after shots were fired and one person was hit by gunfire."[41] In that sense, the two Fergusons, the peaceful daytime and troubled nighttime Fergusons, had not changed in the year since Brown's tragic death.

Certain behaviors and attitudes *had* changed, however. For one, even though there was some violence at the protest, the police response was different. As reported by the *New York Times*, "No police officers in riot gear emerged Friday night when protesters arrived, a tactic that has drawn criticism. Rather, a small handful of officers calmly walked out and spoke with demonstrators. Many of the Ferguson police on the scene wore white polo shirts rather than their regular uniforms," an effort to deescalate potential tensions by projecting a less military-style profile.[42] Second, there was clear evidence that Black Lives Matter had registered their policy concerns on the national stage. Political leaders and candidates for the 2016 presidential election were paying attention to the protests. They began to talk about Ferguson and what it

Protestors prepared to march in downtown St. Louis on August 10, 2015, to mark the one-year anniversary of Michael Brown's death. The police response to the march was markedly different from previous protests and was much more measured and low key.

REUTERS/Rick Wilking

meant for the nation going forward. During the first Democratic Party presidential candidate debate in October 2015, one of the invited members of the public asked, "My question for the candidates is, do black lives matter, or do all lives matter?" Sen. Bernie Sanders (I-VT) immediately replied, "Black lives matter," and the crowd applauded.[43] When pressed by a moderator, former Maryland governor Martin O'Malley "expressed solidarity with the phrase."[44] Both Sanders and O'Malley had been confronted with public disruptions on the campaign trail challenging them to be more outspoken in their support for criminal justice reform.[45] Following the debate, members of Black Lives Matter were encouraged by the attention and conversation but wanted more specifics about how each candidate would make the words a reality.

Members of Congress were paying attention as well. In January 2015, as reported by the *St. Louis Post-Dispatch*, "On the eve of the Martin Luther King holiday, leading Black members of Congress squeezed into a packed Ferguson church to deliver a specific message: We've got your backs. . . . There, they vowed to push for criminal justice reform."[46] The article quoted Rep. André Carson (D-IN), who said, "We're not here to tell you what to do . . . [but] just to let you know you've got some firepower in Washington, D.C. Ferguson is a clarion call. Ferguson is the new Selma."[47] In August, the *St. Louis Post-Dispatch* reported that "prominent Ferguson protesters announced on Friday Campaign Zero, a policy platform to end killings by the police in the United States, and a website to help voters keep track of where political candidates stand on police brutality."[48] Political science professor Terry Jones, an expert on urban politics and policies interviewed for the article, said, "This is an effort to put some policy meat on the protest bones and say, 'We're not simply for or against that, but here's what our policies would look like.'"[49]

National Anthem Protests in the NFL Draw on #BlackLivesMatter

In August 2016, during the team's first preseason game of the National Football League (NFL) against the Green Bay Packers, San Francisco 49ers quarterback Colin Kaepernick had his own answer, and it would not go down without controversy.[50] He refused to stand during the pregame rendition of the national anthem in protest of racism, especially in police-community relations. "I am not going to stand up to show pride in a flag for a country that oppresses Black people and people of color," Kaepernick later told a reporter. "To me, this is bigger than football and it would be selfish to look the other way. There are bodies in the street and people [police officers] getting paid leave and getting away with murder."[51]

Rather than continuing to sit on the bench during the anthem, Kaepernick decided that he would kneel instead to show respect for the flag and military while protesting. During the 2016 season, other NFL players, athletes in other men's and women's professional sports, and even high school students began to protest in similar

NFL quarterback Colin Kaepernick (center) kneels with fellow players during the national anthem in a regular season game against the Seattle Seahawks in 2016, protesting against police violence.
Steve Dykes / Stringer

ways.[52] Protests expanded and continued into the 2017 NFL season. The level of tension only grew, and so did the politics. While Kaepernick, who had become a free agent after the 2016 season, remained unsigned by any NFL team, President Donald Trump, in a series of tweets and public statements, did not mince words: "Wouldn't you love to see one of these NFL owners, when somebody disrespects our flag, to say, 'Get that son of a bitch off the field right now, he's fired!' You know, some owner is going to do that."[53] Players, and some NFL owners, sharply criticized the president's stance. At a game between the 49ers and the Indianapolis Colts, Vice President Mike Pence left the game after several 49ers players kneeled during the anthem.

In 2017 public opinion researchers with the Pew Research Center released the results of a survey asking Americans the degree to which they felt that racism was a "big problem" in American society. While, unsurprisingly, racial divisions continued, what was especially notable was the sharp increase in divisions based on party identification, perhaps reflecting the degree to which racism, the NFL protests, and President Trump's comments highlighted deep divides in American public opinion. See Figure 6.5.

▼ FIGURE 6.5

Wide Partisan Gap in Views of Racism as a "Big Problem" Grows Even Wider

Percent who say racism is a "big problem" in our society today . . .

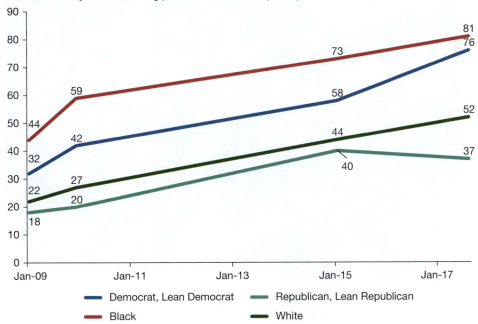

Source: Data from Pew Research Center, "Wide Partisan Gap in Views of Racism as 'Big Problem' Grows Even Wider; Racial Divisions Persist," August 29, 2017, http://www.pewresearch.org/fact-tank/2017/08/29/views-of-racism-as-a-major-problem-increase-sharply-especially-among-democrats/ft_17-08-29_racismproblem_2/.

A Tragedy in Charlottesville Focuses the Nation's Attention on Deep Divisions in American Society

While the political rhetoric surrounding national anthem protests continued to ratchet up, another tragic event shook the nation. Once again, the question of police-community interactions was at the forefront. A series of protests in Charlottesville, Virginia, in the spring and summer of 2017 ultimately ended in tragedy. Just as the NFL protests galvanized and polarized American public opinion, so did the question of removing or keeping in place statues from military and political leaders from the Confederate South.

On August 11, 2017, a group calling themselves "Unite the Right" prepared to protest the removal of Confederate statues, having obtained a permit to do so. Early on August 12, James Fields drove his vehicle into a crowd of counterprotesters, killing one of them, thirty-two-year-old Heather Heyer, and injuring nineteen others. The authors of an independent study found that a single school resource officer had been assigned to maintain order between the protesters and counterprotesters in the area. They concluded that "the City of Charlottesville protected neither free expression nor public safety on August 12 . . . which has led to a deep distrust of government within this community."[54] Speaking before an event for military veterans, President

Protesters march near the Minneapolis 1st Police precinct during a demonstration against police brutality and racism on August 24, 2020 in Minneapolis, Minnesota. Demonstrations also continued for the second day in Kenosha, Wisconsin, after local law enforcement officers shot Jacob Blake multiple times in the back, seriously injuring him.
ZACH GIBSON/AFP/Getty Images

Donald Trump "blamed the unrest 'on many sides,'" prompting members of his own administration to issue clarifications condemning the murder of Heather Heyer.[55]

A Marist College Institute for Public Opinion survey conducted immediately following the Charlottesville murder found that a majority of Americans were not satisfied with the president's response, including a plurality of whites. As we have explored, tracing the causal effects of any one event, even one as tragic and focusing as Ferguson, on American public opinion is difficult to do. However, there is one other way in which events may serve to shape public opinion. They may serve as lenses through which future events are viewed and interpreted. For many Americans, it was not possible to try to come to terms with Charlottesville without placing it in the larger context of the question of not just two Fergusons but two Americas.

Protests, Unrest, and Anger Spread across the Nation after the Killing of George Floyd by a Minneapolis Police Officer

On May 25, 2020, George Floyd, an African-American man, died while in the custody of the Minneapolis police. Mr. Floyd had been "handcuffed and pinned to the ground by a white police officer's knee."[56] Racial justice and police accountability protests followed immediately in Minneapolis and spread rapidly nationwide. On one day alone in June, an estimated "half a million people turned out in nearly 550 places across the United States."[57]

There had been other recent police-involved deaths of Black Americans, and more would follow—Breonna Taylor by the Louisville, Kentucky police in March, and Jacob Blake by the Kenosha, Wisconsin police in August. The shootings, and frustration over the process of prosecuting the officers involved in the killings, brought out more anger and protesters. Taken together, the 2020 Black Lives Matter protests may very well have constituted "the largest movement in the nation's history," even more remarkable as they were more organic and de-centralized in origin than events such as the Women's March of 2017.[58]

The effects of George Floyd's killing and the protests that followed had an immediate and sharp effect on American public opinion. In a June *Pew Research Center* survey, sixty-seven percent of Americans said they "strongly or somewhat support the Black Lives Matter Movement."[59] By September, however, support had dropped among Hispanics and whites, by more than ten percentage points, but remained strong among Black Americans, with eighty-seven percent expressing support. Acts of arson and looting that had followed peaceful protests in several cities across the nation likely contributed to a decline in public support.

Within weeks or months of George Floyd's death, several states and localities had enacted police reform measures or placed them on the agenda. As we will examine later in the book, however, the American policymaking process is, by design, deliberate and incremental. It is, therefore, far too soon to evaluate the full impact of Black Lives Matter on American public policy.

Conclusion: How Meaningful Is Public Opinion?

Political scientist John Kingdon once asked, "But what makes an idea's time come?"[60] That is a very good question and one to which individuals must attend if they are trying to shape laws and policies to get their voices heard. In terms of public opinion, we might rephrase Professor Kingdon's question as this: But what makes *a change of public opinion's* time come? And, we might add, does it even matter if public opinion changes at all?

Reflecting upon Ferguson, other protests inspired by Black Lives Matter, and more recent tragic events, one thing has clearly changed, and that is the list of issues on the national political agenda. To that list has been added the treatment of African Americans, especially young African American men, by the American law enforcement system: "'I live in one of the poorest zip codes in Missouri,' said Ferguson protester Tory Russell in a conference call with reporters . . . adding that fellow African-Americans in the area experience high rates of mortality and murder. 'I never heard any of my elected officials declare those things a state of emergency,' said Mr. Russell, who started the group Hands Up United after Mr. Brown's death to seek justice in Ferguson and beyond."[61] In this chapter, we have explored debates over the coherence and impact of what we call American public opinion by focusing mostly on one tragic event. While the ultimate effects of the tragedy—as well as the protests and efforts at political mobilization that followed—are not yet certain, at the very least the nation's political conversation has been altered.

In October 2014, "Lesley McSpadden, Mr. Brown's mother, made one of her regular visits to the place where her son was killed. . . . She comes to the memorial all the time, she said, even though visits to the site of her son's death deepen her pain. . . . Gazing down at the memorial, Ms. McSpadden pondered the question of how long it should stay in place. 'Forever,' she said."[62]

CHAPTER REVIEW

This chapter's main ideas are reflected in the Learning Objectives. By reviewing them here, you should be able to *remember* the key points and *know* these terms that are central to the topic.

6.1 Understand how public opinion is dynamic and contested.

Remember . . .
- Public opinion is characterized as the aggregation of individual beliefs and attitudes.
- Public opinion is not fixed or static.

Know . . .
- *public opinion* (p. 163)
- *public opinion survey* (p. 165)

6.2 Discuss differing theories about public opinion formation and expression and the degree to which it is meaningful.

Remember . . .
- Public opinion is characterized as the aggregation of individual beliefs and attitudes.
- Representative democracy depends upon individuals having meaningful preferences on issues. Only when constituents are able to convey meaningful opinions can they be adequately represented by public officials.
- The minimalist paradigm emphasizes that most people pay minimal attention to issues and have minimal information about them. Additionally, the opinions that they *do* have are minimally stable; they change over time or in response to attempts to control or shape them.
- Other scholars emphasize the ways in which the public can still make sense of and transmit their opinions to their representatives, both collectively and individually. No single individual needs to have fully formed policy preferences and political views because when taken in the aggregate, public opinion is meaningful.
- Still others have emphasized the possibility for a public to be collectively rational even in the presence of individually inconsistent and shapeable opinions.

Know . . .
- *consideration* (p. 170)
- *cues and information shortcuts* (p. 171)
- *elites* (p. 170)
- *masses* (p. 170)
- *minimalist paradigm* (p. 169)
- *nonattitudes* (p. 170)
- *stereotype* (p. 170)

6.3 Describe the issues involved in transmitting and measuring American public opinion and constructing the instruments used to do so.

Remember . . .
- Americans need to be able to communicate their preferences to government, and their representatives need mechanisms that allow them to learn what those preferences are.
- Individuals can communicate directly with representatives, but people who do so tend to represent subgroups with intense preferences rather than the constituency as a whole.
- Elections give representatives information about the public's views. But since not all eligible voters do vote, that information is imperfect.
- Sometimes elected officials solicit the public's views directly through mechanisms such as focus groups.
- Types of surveys include straw polls, SLOPs, and exit polls.
- In order to achieve random selection in polling, surveyors often reach individuals via telephone using random digit dialing.
- Even when people's opinions are well informed or when enough opinions are sampled to make them meaningful in the aggregate, the instruments used to measure opinion can themselves be flawed, making survey results not meaningful.
- When poorly constructed or deliberately flawed, public opinion surveys can shape survey results and thus deliver misleading findings.
- In some cases, people are unwilling to admit a lack of information or opinion and so make up responses to survey questions.
- The way questions are ordered and worded can also affect survey results.

Know . . .		
• direction (p. 176)		• respondents (p. 174)
• exit poll (p. 175)		• salience (p. 177)
• focus group (p. 173)		• sample (p. 174)
• intensity (p. 176)		• sampling error (p. 174)
• push poll (p. 177)		• scientific poll (p. 173)
• question order (p. 176)		• self-selected listener opinion poll (SLOP) (p. 175)
• question wording (p. 176)		• stability (p. 176)
• race of interviewer effects (p. 176)		• straw poll (p. 174)
• random digit dialing (p. 175)		• validity (p. 173)
• random selection (p. 174)		• weighting (p. 174)

6.4   Examine the contributors to individual attitudes and public opinion.

Remember . . .
- Forming and changing political opinions and attitudes is a lifelong process. The process by which our experiences and other personal factors shape our attitudes toward political issues and public policies is called political socialization.
- There are many sources of political socialization.
- Families convey political attitudes and shape party identification.
- Schools deliver political information and values via civic education.
- People's personal life experiences, including focusing events, affect their views.
- Gender, race, and ethnic identity also affect people's attitudes.
- Political knowledge is predictably and unequally distributed. Younger Americans, women, lower-income Americans, and members of racial and ethnic minorities have consistently fared worse in their answers to factual political knowledge questions.
- How we identify politically as well as how we define ourselves in terms of gender, race, or ethnicity can form clear, consistent, and persistent patterns of similarity and division in American public opinion.
- On some issues we see opinions that cut across identities.

Know . . .		
• civic education (p. 178)		• linked fate (p. 181)
• conservatism (p. 179)		• party identification (p. 178)
• focusing events (p. 178)		• political ideology (p. 179)
• gender gap (p. 180)		• political socialization (p. 178)
• liberalism (p. 179)		• socialism (p. 179)
• libertarianism (p. 179)		

6.5   Evaluate the power of individuals, events, and people's interpretations of events to make lasting change in American politics.

Remember . . .
- Important events can shape public opinion.
- Individuals may filter their interpretation of these events through lenses such as partisan identification, gender, or racial or ethnic identity.
- How the media portray these events may also play a role in opinion formation and change.

CHAPTER 7

THE MEDIA

Truth, Trust, and Power

Donald Trump has been a prolific tweeter throughout his presidency and has used the platform to bypass traditional media—and often denigrate critical coverage of him as "fake news."

The Photo Works/Alamy Stock Photo

By reading this chapter, you will be able to do the following:

7.1 Examine how recent controversies over foreign interference in electoral politics raise questions about the trustworthiness of the American news media.

7.2 Trace the historical development of the American news media.

7.3 Understand the issue of bias in the American media.

7.4 Explain the different perspectives of media ownership and media content.

7.5 Explain the different perspectives on the power of the media to shape political understanding and behaviors.

Americans' political knowledge is sometimes gained directly through experiences like going to a school board meeting, talking with a political candidate, or attending a rally or protest. More often, however, it is mediated, filtered through the news outlets that inform us of political issues. Collectively, this group of outlets is called the **news media**, a broad term that includes newspapers, magazines, radio, television, Internet sources, blogs, and social media postings, all in service of informing or persuading. The word *media* is plural as it refers to a universe of venues and outlets. As we will explore, the way those news sources are produced, who their audiences are, and what technological capabilities they possess all shape the presentation, reception, effect, and even the definition of the news itself.

The American news media is in a period of radical flux. Technology-driven change, partisan politics, ownership, trustworthiness, bias, and objectivity are front and center in debates about the current, or proper, role of the American news media in our political lives. Americans are simultaneously witnessing a major decline in daily newspaper readership, the rise of social media, and increasingly divisive language in political talk shows. What do these changes in the media landscape mean for political representation and participation in the twenty-first century?

We will explore that question and others primarily through the prism of two stories: the controversy surrounding media coverage of accusations of Russian involvement in the presidential election of 2016 and a radio-broadcasted fictional Martian invasion in 1938. Why these two stories, separated by nearly eighty years? Because they are united by two enduring questions: How effective are the news media in shaping Americans' views? And can we trust our news media sources?

These are not separate questions, in fact. At their core, both point directly to Americans' role not only as receivers of the news but as shapers of the media that they choose as their sources. This issue returns us to questions raised in our study of public opinion: How shapeable are Americans' attitudes and preferences? Are we filing cabinets with a set of predetermined and firm attitudes and opinions? Or are we pieces of clay, vulnerable to outside forces to shape as they see fit? For all of the drama we have seen in recent years, these are not new questions, and the answers to them are still unsettled.

Can a Foreign Government Use the American Media to Influence a Presidential Election?

"Weaponized information."[1]

These were the words that Hillary Clinton used to describe what she thought contributed to her loss to Republican Donald Trump in the 2016 presidential election. Interviewed before a live audience at a May 2017 conference, Clinton and her interviewers talked about how domestic or foreign political actors might use the media, especially social media, to influence or undermine a political candidate. They returned time and again to the idea that under certain conditions news stories could be made powerful enough to become political weapons—vastly more destructive than in earlier campaign cycles.

Hillary Clinton speaks at a conference in March 2017, where she leveled charges that the Russians had weaponized news stories against her, costing her the 2016 election.

John Lamparski/Contributor

The specific weapons Clinton was talking about were the release late in the campaign of a series of emails, without authorization and allegedly stolen, from the Democratic National Committee (DNC). Some of the most incendiary emails involved alleged exchanges among Clinton's campaign chairman, John Podesta; his aides; Clinton family members; and influential donors. In those unflattering emails, Podesta and others talked about the perception of Clinton's close ties to Wall Street, reactions to the controversy surrounding Clinton's use of a private email server to conduct official business while serving as secretary of state (which would later come under Federal Bureau of Investigation [FBI] review but result in no charges), and plans to attack the policy positions and record of Sen. Bernie Sanders (I-VT), Clinton's rival for the Democratic presidential nomination.

Many speculated about who was behind the leaked emails and the news stories they generated. Clinton pointed directly to the Russian government, saying, "If you look at Facebook, the vast majority of the news items posted were fake. They were connected to, as we now know, the 1,000 Russian agents who were involved in delivering these messages."[2] Secretary Clinton noted, "I take responsibility for every decision I made, but that's not why I lost. So I think it's important that we learn the real lessons from this last campaign because the forces that we are up against are not just interested in influencing our election and our politics, they're going after our economy and they're going after our unity as a nation."[3]

Indeed, a January 2017 intelligence community assessment involving members of the Central Intelligence Agency (CIA), the FBI, and the National Security Agency (NSA) concluded that "Russian President Vladimir Putin ordered an influence campaign in 2016 aimed at the US presidential election. Russia's goals were to undermine public faith in the US democratic process, denigrate Secretary Clinton, and harm her electability and potential presidency."[4]

Not everyone agreed, most especially President Donald Trump, who challenged the certainty of these conclusions. In a tweet from January 2017, President Trump asserted, "Julian Assange [the founder of WikiLeaks, the website to which the emails were leaked] said 'a 14 year old could have hacked Podesta'[;] why was DNC so careless? Also said Russians did not give him the info!"[5] The presidential election of 2016 was a very close one, decided by perhaps 80,000 votes in a few key battleground states. If only a tiny percentage of Americans had been influenced by outside forces, it could have made the difference in the outcome. The idea that Russia might have used the American media to tip the election was not a welcome one and potentially undermining for a new administration. It should be noted, too, that Clinton was not the only candidate facing negative press. Candidate Trump was hardly the darling of most mainstream newspaper and television outlets and faced plenty of negative coverage of his own: "He was subject to not just relentless partisan attacks but also to overwhelmingly negative media coverage, much of it due to his own endless gaffes and scandals."[6]

While a Special Counsel Investigates, the Cable News Media Go All in on Russia

In May 2017, President Trump dismissed FBI director James Comey over what the president felt was poor handling of an investigation into the possible Russian interference in the election. Code-named "Crossfire Hurricane," the investigation examined "whether individuals associated with the Donald J. Trump for President Campaign were coordinating, wittingly or unwittingly, with the Russian government's efforts to interfere in the 2016 U.S. presidential election."[7] Just over a week after Comey's dismissal, and under pressure from Congress, Deputy Attorney General Rod Rosenstein appointed Robert S. Mueller III (a former FBI director himself) to take over the investigation.

In March 2019—nearly two years after he began—special counsel Mueller presented his findings to Attorney General William Barr. Barr then released a version to Congress and the public, with significant redactions to protect national security. On the question of Russian attempts to influence the election of 2016, the Mueller report concluded that Russia had, in fact, tried to shape the outcome. The special counsel, however, did not find sufficient evidence of collusion by President Trump or his campaign to warrant indictment.

In a public response to the findings and the special counsel's work, President Trump, in an interview with Fox News, railed against the investigation. "This is an absolute catastrophe for our country," he said. "This was a fake witch hunt, and it should never be allowed to happen to another president again."[8] In the same interview, the president added that he had, in fact, watched the ongoing congressional proceedings, albeit

Donald J. Trump ✔
@realDonaldTrump

Now that Russian collusion, after one year of intense study, has proven to be a total hoax on the American public, the Democrats and their lapdogs, the Fake News Mainstream Media, are taking out the old Ronald Reagan playbook and screaming mental stability and intelligence.....

4:19 AM · Jan 6, 2018 · Twitter for iPhone

32.7K Retweets and comments   **127.2K** Likes

Donald Trump tweeted a *Game of Thrones*-style image to declare himself fully vindicated in the investigation into Russian election meddling and alleged collusion with his campaign—despite the fact that special counsel Robert Mueller's report had not yet been made public.

Mandel Ngan/AFP via Getty Images

sporadically. "And I've never seen anything like it, actually. It was sort of good television," he admitted.[9]

The nation's news media outlets agreed. During this time, the American news media—cable television in particular—presented what seemed to many to be round-the-clock coverage of the investigation's twists and turns, prognosticating on likely outcomes along the way. A 2017 report by the Media Research Center showed that during a five-week period that spring, of all news coverage of President Trump, a full 55 percent was devoted solely to the Russia investigation, with the remainder devoted to a range of other issues.[10]

MSNBC's Rachel Maddow, according to the *New York Times* in 2019, had been a fixture on the network for years, "But over the past three, her figure has ascended, in the liberal imagination, from beloved cable-news host to a kind of oracle for the age of Trump. . . . Maddow had used her hour on television to spin out Russiagate into its own extended universe, and a fandom assembled to step into that world every night. . . . With the help of her storytelling, heavily redacted court documents read more like a novel narrated in the close third person. Ever-more-stunning revelations always seemed to be waiting just on the next page."[11]

"Fake News" Highlights the Power of Both the Media and Consumers

In 2017, President Donald Trump declared war.

It was not on Russia but on the media covering the story about his administration's alleged ties with that nation—CNN in particular. In a series of tweets that escalated to the boiling point that summer, the president accused CNN, MSNBC, the *New York Times*, and other mainstream media outlets of broadcasting "fake news" with the goal of undermining his presidency.

In February, President Trump took on the *New York Times* and the rest of the mainstream American media directly, using his Twitter account. "Fake News" became an often-repeated phrase in his tweets. The president's accusation was initially based upon allegations that the *New York Times* had run an inaccurate and poorly sourced story about his ties to the Russian government.[12] However, as the president's war with the mainstream media raged on, it became an increasingly frequent theme.

The term **fake news** is thrown about frequently today, but what does it really mean? To some, it means the intentional use of the media to support a political party, something that would have been hardly surprising to editors of nineteenth-century newspapers. To others, it means the intentional presentation of material that the news agency knows to be untrue, or at least unverified. To others, it means the intentional use of the mass media to change political outcomes by intentionally deceiving the public. In reality, it can be any or all of these. Finally, the term can be used to discredit something that is actually true or to undermine its source. The challenge for consumers of the American media is to determine fact from fiction. It is not an easy task, especially in a new media environment so politically charged and one that moves at warp speed.

In June 2017, independent news agency Project Veritas released what it claimed was undercover footage from an interview with a supervising producer of CNN. In it, the producer allegedly claimed that the 24/7 coverage of President Trump's possible ties with Russia was all about ratings: "Trump is good for business right now."[13] Asked if the Russia story was "bullsh*t," the producer was recorded as saying, "Could be bullsh*t. I mean it's mostly bullsh*t. Like we don't have any big giant proof."[14] In another video, widely watched CNN political commentator Van Jones was recorded as saying, "The Russia thing is just a big nothing burger."[15] Later that month, three journalists resigned from CNN "after the cable news network was forced to retract and apologize for a story on its website involving a close ally of President Trump."[16]

For its part, CNN countered that Sean Spicer, President Trump's press secretary at the time, misrepresented the story. CNN's Jake Tapper reinforced the conclusions of members of the intelligence community that asserted Russian influence in the 2016 elections.[17] In the end, however, all of it—from President Trump's tweets to CNN's round-the-clock coverage of the controversy—was, in spite of their starkly partisan differences, often driven by the same objective: attracting an audience.

Our focus in this chapter, however, is not on the intent of Russian agents but more broadly on the capability of media in general: Do the media really have the power to determine the outcome of an event as important as a presidential election?

That question speaks very much to how fair and trustworthy media sources are in their coverage and the power they wield as organizations. But it also speaks to Americans' potential vulnerability to the media's power, especially in the era of new media.

However, the relationship between Americans and their news media is not a one-way street. To only look at the power of the media over viewers misses the power of viewers over the media, which is just as significant. News media must attract an audience, and that reality gives news consumers power over the product. What if some consumers of news have already made up their minds and look to their trusted sources for confirmation rather than investigation? What if fake news is what the audience demands? If it is the case that the market—or at least a financially important part of it—demands predetermined story lines and analyses that simply reinforce pre-existing conclusions, then Americans are very much a part of this equation. Rather than being victims of the media, in this light, they may be demanding the media to give them the "news" they want, even if it might be fake.

Truth, trust, and power. These are the issues with which consumers of the American news media have always had to contend. Technology may have changed the medium, but the same questions have endured throughout the development of the American media.

The Evolution of American Media Shows That Issues of Power and Trustworthiness Are Not New

7.2   Trace the historical development of the American news media.

The news media have played an important role in shaping American political culture and Americans' attitudes toward their political leaders and institutions from before the country's founding to today. Throughout this history, the connection between the nation's media and American politics has also been shaped in important ways by technological change, politics, and the tension between the rights of a free press and other demands, especially the desire to preserve national security.

Early Newspapers and Pamphlets Shape a New Nation

The pamphlet, a loosely stitched booklet made on a hand-cranked printing press, was the first type of media to shape American attitudes, mobilizing support for the cause of independence from Great Britain. While printing had become cheaper and more widespread in the years leading up to the Revolutionary War, publishing was far from easy. The British colonial administration recognized the pamphlet for what it was, a potentially powerful and revolutionary tool. According to one historian, the British seized some printer's presses, "while still others hid their presses or fled their homes with their families, taking their presses with them. Others closed their shops before the British could."[18]

The number of weekly and then daily newspapers grew in the years following the Revolutionary War, and the newspaper took its place as the primary source for information about American politics. First published in 1783, the *Pennsylvania Evening Post, and Daily Advertiser* was the nation's first daily newspaper; its young salesmen were instructed to shout out to passersby, "All the news for two coppers."[19] Like the pamphlets, early newspapers were hand printed, one sheet at a time, which made them expensive and restricted their reach, even among those who could read them.

Four years later, the nation's second daily newspaper, the *Pennsylvania Packet, and Daily Advertiser*, published just blocks away from where the *Evening Post* had started out, was the first to print the full text of the proposed Constitution of the United States. The delegates to the Constitutional Convention had been very careful to prevent any leaks during the proceedings, thus starving the weeklies and dailies of raw materials for their stories. With the publication of the proposed Constitution, which spurred a flood of editorials for and against the document, newspapers took their place at the center of American political life in the late 1780s.

Freedom of the Press Becomes Enshrined in the Constitution through the Bill of Rights

With memories of British colonial suppression of freedom of the press fresh in their minds, the delegates to the Constitutional Convention were well aware of the need to preserve and protect this freedom. On August 20, 1787, Charles Pinckney from South Carolina proposed the inclusion of this guarantee: "The liberty of the Press shall be inviolably preserved."[20] A guarantee of freedom of the press and other specific rights did not end up in the original Constitution, which became one of the most convincing arguments presented against the proposed document in the ratification debate.

A promise to introduce a set of amendments guaranteeing specific rights and freedoms—a Bill of Rights—during the session of Congress in 1789 proved crucial to securing the ratification of the Constitution. Included in the first of the ten ratified amendments was language very close to Pinckney's initial proposal: "Congress shall make no law . . . abridging the freedom of speech, or of the press." This provided the foundation for press freedoms.

The press also played a pivotal role in the ratification debates themselves, as proponents and opponents of the document made their cases through the nation's newspapers, often writing under pseudonyms. *The Federalist Papers*, the classic statement of the theory behind the Constitution, authored by Alexander Hamilton, James Madison, and John Jay, first appeared as a series of essays written under the pseudonym *Publius* in the New York newspapers. For their part, the Anti-Federalists produced essays warning of the dangers to liberty presented by the proposed Constitution.

The Media Go "Mass" with the Penny Presses in the Eighteenth and Nineteenth Centuries

In the late eighteenth and early nineteenth centuries, however, the dailies and weeklies reached only a fraction of the population, in no small part because they were expensive and often available only through an annual subscription, which required putting down a large sum of money all at once. Political and financial elites were the main consumers, not the mass public. Much of the space in newspapers was taken up by advertisements, and the stories were often overtly political, a fact that was neither hidden nor controversial. Political parties and candidates often supported the presses financially in addition to providing them with essays, stories, and content.[21] By taking political positions and supporting candidates and parties, these papers were acting as a **partisan press**. James Madison and Thomas Jefferson supported the founding of the *National Gazette* in 1791 in response to the partisan coverage presented by the Federalist *Gazette of the United States*.

As the cost to produce and, therefore, buy a newspaper fell during the 1830s, readership grew rapidly. The **penny press**, so labeled because an individual paper cost one penny, could be purchased on the street from newsboys. Within just a few months of its introduction as the nation's first penny press, the *New York Sun* was the city's top-selling paper; by 1834 the *Sun* "was selling 15,000 copies a day."[22] The penny press was truly an example of the **mass media**—sources of information and entertainment (including newspapers, television and radio broadcasts, and Internet content) designed to reach large audiences.

The content in the penny press was sometimes overtly political, but these papers depended far less on political parties for funding or support. They had a new boss: the public. Newspapers depended on sales and on providing an audience for the advertisers, so they often focused on dramatic stories, of crime, riots, and scandalous behavior.[23] Instead of relying on parties, candidates, or politicians for their content, the penny papers hired reporters to dig up the kind of stories that would lure readers and advertisers. **Yellow journalism**, the use of sensational headlines, cartoons and graphics, and emotional language, had a very commercial reason behind its emergence: It worked, boosting sales and profits.

Sensationalism was not confined to stories of crime, misdeeds, and moral failures. In skilled hands, bold headlines, enticing ledes, and emotional language could also be put to political purposes. William Randolph Hearst, publisher of the *New York Journal*, harnessed yellow journalism to advocate war with Spain in the late 1890s. While the Spanish-American War had many causes, Hearst's efforts helped to shape public opinion about the prospect for war. This example of the power of the press to influence public opinion raised the specter of a malleable American public at the mercy of presses and publishers with their own political agendas.

Journalists Become Investigators and Activists in the Nineteenth Century

A faster and cheaper printing press was not the only technological development that shaped the newspaper in the nineteenth century. The telegraph allowed news to travel instantaneously over distances that might have taken days or weeks otherwise. The papers benefited tremendously from the technology and helped to finance and spread it. The Associated Press took advantage of the telegraph to create a **wire service**, an organization that gathers the news and offers it for sale to other media outlets. The nineteenth century also witnessed a new approach to news coverage, **investigative journalism**, in which journalists actively dug up and dug into stories rather than simply conveying the speeches and opinions of political leaders. During the Progressive Era in the early twentieth century, an important group of investigative reporters became known as *muckrakers*; the name was a reference to a tool used to collect manure. Muckrakers used their investigative tactics to bring to light corruption and scandal and also to shape public opinion in support of business or governmental reforms.[24]

Since the nineteenth century, large news outlets have traditionally employed the **beat system**, in which reporters are assigned to specific types of news, policies, and events. Covering politics is a major beat and an important one for news outlets. For major news organizations, there can be many sub-beats, with one journalist covering, say, American foreign policy while another correspondent focuses on economic policy. From the standpoint of efficiency and expertise, the beat system makes a lot of sense. Journalists can be more informed reporters if they become familiar with the lay of the land in a specific area.

There can be issues with using the beat system to organize coverage. First, many sub-beats do not get much attention: transportation policy, for example. Of course, news consumers demand coverage of some beats more than others, so outlets are happy to focus on these. Journalists operating on the beat system have to balance access to their sources with the need to be objective, to prevent being used by those sources. This can be a delicate balance for a journalist, especially when covering something like alleged corruption. Finally, journalists from different news outlets operating on the beat have working relationships with others on the beat, and they share perspectives and interpretations with each other. There is a danger here of "pack journalism," which is when journalists on the same beat collectively shape the coverage.[25] This can involve pushing a certain political perspective, but it can be even more fundamental than that. Journalists on the same beat may come to a consensus on which stories are important and which ones are not, thereby shaping the agenda.

The Twentieth Century Brings Radio and TV News Directly into Americans' Homes

Technological advances during the twentieth century brought political figures into Americans' lives and homes in a direct way, first providing their voices with the advent and widespread adoption of radio and then adding their faces and actions with television. Radio and television, which are examples of **broadcast media**, offered political news to citizens directly and immediately. Its consumption was often a shared experience, with only one radio or television set in the home or in the neighborhood, and the news could be consumed while doing other things, such as driving, doing chores, working, or eating a meal. These forms of media were also truly "mass"—they were experienced simultaneously by audiences across the country. In breaking down geographic barriers, the broadcast media were truly national in scope.

As an instrument of conveying political news, radio came into its own in the 1930s, and no public official was more adept in its use than President Franklin Delano Roosevelt. Beginning in March 1933, Roosevelt began broadcasting speeches to the American public; these speeches became known as "fireside chats," a term coined by a bureau chief with CBS News, even though there was no fireplace.[26] The broadcasts

President Franklin Delano Roosevelt at a fireside chat in 1936. Roosevelt's broadcasts to the nation during times of crisis helped calm a worried population and enabled him to successfully pitch his policies.

were designed to calm anxious Americans during the depths of the Great Depression; present Roosevelt's Depression-fighting policies; and, later, guide citizens through the travails of World War II.

Today, the nation's radios crackle with political commentary from one side or the other of a highly polarized debate. Many of these shows lean Republican, such as *The Rush Limbaugh Show*, but there are liberal examples as well. These talk radio broadcasts have been criticized for their efforts to "provoke emotional responses (e.g., anger, fear, moral indignation) from the audience through the use of overgeneralizations, sensationalism, misleading or patently inaccurate information, ad hominem attacks, and belittling ridicule of opponents."[27]

If the 1930s signaled the emergence of radio as a powerful new force in political news, the early 1960s did the same for television. Television's version of Roosevelt was also a president: John F. Kennedy. Even though most American homes had a television by the 1950s, newspapers remained the primary source of news and coverage of political events. In September 1960, candidates Kennedy and Richard Nixon participated in the first televised presidential debates in American history. While experts and radio listeners did not declare a clear winner at the time, Kennedy's image on television came across as robust and energetic, while Nixon, who had been fighting the flu, appeared pallid and sweaty. In 1961, Kennedy, having won the presidency, gave the first live televised news conference.

As television news broadcasts lengthened and more and more Americans relied upon the major networks for their news and coverage of political events, television news anchors became trusted figures in relaying, describing, and interpreting these events.

The 1990s witnessed the rise of a new outlet for television and television news. First broadcasting in 1980, CNN, the Cable News Network, offered Americans twenty-four-hour news for the first time. But it was CNN's coverage of the Persian Gulf War that placed it squarely on the news media map. In 1991, CNN broadcast video coverage of the bombing of Baghdad by American and coalition forces live, in real time, and unconstrained by a set news broadcast schedule typically employed by the major broadcast networks.

Cable television news changed more than just the schedule of coverage; it changed the form itself. Operating under looser regulatory constraints than the broadcast networks and in a time when those constraints were being relaxed (see next section), television news became more avowedly partisan, less "objective." To some, this overt partisanship seemed like a new and dangerous thing. In fact, it was not new—questions of the objectivity of network news had long been a common source of commentary and conversation. Cable television news coverage became more like what newspapers had been during much of the nation's history: unapologetically partisan.

New Media Have Reinvented the Media Landscape

The Internet revolutionized the media landscape in the late twentieth and early twenty-first centuries. The adoption of broadband reception, the Internet, and other communications technologies enabled Americans to receive and send text, sound, and video at increasing speeds and in increasing volumes.

These new forms of media communication have revolutionized far more than the speed of delivery, or even the content, of political news available to consumers of the news and politics. In the era of 24/7 news coverage and the merging of entertainment and social media, private individuals can be journalists, citizens can be editors and commentators, and members of the media can be and often are pressured to be celebrities. Throughout much of the nation's history, most Americans had a limited number of choices in their news media outlets—generally, one or two daily newspapers, several radio stations, and a few major television broadcast networks. The rise of cable television expanded the number of options; then the Internet increased these options even further.

The rise of **social media** put these trends into hyperdrive. However, the story was not only about the rise of *new* media outlets but also about the need for *old* media outlets, such as broadcast television, to stay relevant. One strategy was to create a greater presence of traditional network broadcast journalists in other venues and highlight their visibility, even celebrity, in order to reach larger audiences in an age of intense competition. In 2018, according to a survey by Pew Research, the percentage of American adults who rely on social media for much of their news surpassed print newspapers for the first time. See Figure 7.1.

Much of the news content transmitted through social media is generated in traditional ways—previously produced stories, videos, and commentaries linked to on Facebook, posted on YouTube, or tweeted to members of one's social network. Other content, however, is generated by **citizen journalists**, nonprofessionals who cover events, say, through filming them on their cell phones or by providing their own commentaries and analysis. The Internet and modern communications technologies did not create the idea of citizen journalism, but they did provide the ability to capture, report on, and transmit citizen-generated news content more quickly and cheaply than has ever been possible. While citizen journalists operate in a variety of contexts, one of the most extreme is combat and military operations abroad. Some scholars of the news media point to the benefits of its democratization, but others worry because citizen journalists lack the ability to fact-check that large news organizations possess.

Changes in American Political News Consumption

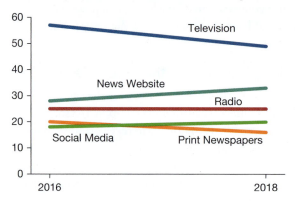

Source: Elisa Shearer, "Social Media Outpaces Print Newspapers in the U.S. as a News Source," Pew Research Center, December 10, 2018, https://www.pewresearch.org/fact-tank/2018/12/10/social-media-outpaces-print-newspapers-in-the-u-s-as-a-news-source/.

One of the most important developments in the Internet age has been the rise of social media outlets, such as Facebook and Twitter. These interactive media environments allow individuals to create or share text, image, and video as well as comment on the content and forward it to other members of their own personal networks. We have already discussed the effects of new technologies in supporting citizen journalism and addressed concerns about the ability to verify such reports for accuracy. Skillful political actors can take advantage of the power of social media to advance their own goals and policy objectives; however, they must be cautious. As they are often acting and speaking amid a sea of cell phone cameras, they must always be aware that any spontaneous, off-the-cuff remarks might find their way onto YouTube or Facebook within minutes.

Questions of Bias Challenge Americans' Trust in the Media's Objectivity

7.3   Understand the issue of bias in the American media.

Understand the issue of bias in American media. During the 2020 presidential campaign, questions of Russian interference arose once again. This time, though, the story focused not on President Trump or the Republicans but on the Democratic presidential nomination. In February, the *Washington Post* reported that "U.S. officials have told Sen. Bernie Sanders that Russia is attempting to help his presidential campaign as part of an effort to interfere with the Democratic contest, according to people familiar with the matter."[28] The allegation was that in doing so, Russia was trying to ensure four more years of President Trump. Sanders was adamant in rejecting any foreign assistance and admonished Russia to stop sowing divisions in the American political process.

No details on how Russia was trying to do all of this emerged. When asked why the information came out a month after Senator Sanders had been briefed—and one day before what portended to be a pivotal Nevada caucus— "Sanders pointed to a [*Washington*] *Post* reporter and said sarcastically: 'It was the *Washington Post*? Good friends,'" implying that the *Post* had its own political agenda.[29] A reporter for the *Nation* later pointed out, "If Russian methods

The day before the pivotal Nevada caucuses, the *Washington Post* had reported on Russian attempts to influence the 2020 Democratic primary in favor of Bernie Sanders. Following his big win in Nevada, however, media coverage focused on Sanders' momentum heading into South Carolina.
Richard Levine/Alamy Stock Photo

are undetectable, how can U.S. officials detect them? Perhaps there is nothing to detect . . . Critical issues that affect regular people's lives are relegated to the margins, replaced by breathless panic that presupposes them to be malleable enough to be duped by Russian memes and bots."[30] News media outlets later downplayed the initial characterization of the classified information in press reports, and the story faded into the background.

Whether or not the *Washington Post* had an agenda in releasing the story when it did, and without more concrete details about the plot, many of Sanders's supporters were upset by the implications put forward by American media outlets. To them, the media appeared to be biased not in favor of one political party over another in this case but against an insurgent candidate with whom the establishment Democrats had never been completely comfortable. We will explore the Sanders's candidacies of 2016 and 2020 in the next chapter. This brief incident during Sanders's campaign, however, highlights the degree to which journalists and news providers may be political actors themselves and raises questions about the degree to which they are able, or willing, to exercise this power objectively.

Bias and the Perception of Bias Is a Problem in Media Coverage

Accusations of bias in news coverage are far from new. Typically, the charge, especially against the nation's largest newspapers and mainstream television news outlets, has been that a **partisan bias** is demonstrated, and a liberal one at that. Many studies and critiques of journalists have focused on the fact that a majority of them self-identify as liberal.[31] So are the media politically biased? This is a complicated question.[32]

Journalists are more likely to self-identify as liberal than members of the general population, but they also tend to have higher levels of educational attainment, which may contribute to these patterns. However, journalists also operate under norms and professional expectations that reward objectivity. Finally, the perception that the media are politically biased might itself be partly shaped by certain media outlets that run stories on the "biased media," thereby encouraging their readers, listeners, or viewers to believe a bias exists.[33] Perhaps unsurprisingly, an individual's view on bias breaks down differently depending upon that person's own political viewpoints. While Americans are more likely to cite political leaders and activist groups than journalists as the source of "made-up news and information," a majority view fixing the problem as the news media's responsibility. These beliefs, however, differ sharply by individuals' partisan affiliations.

Concerns about bias in the media has been accompanied by a lack of trust in the news sources. Confidence in television news, in particular, has fallen dramatically (see Figure 7.2). To the reader of a penny press publication in the nineteenth century, the idea that a particular news outlet pursued a partisan agenda would probably not have been all that surprising; it was an accepted part of the format. The modern view of the proper role of the media, however, was based on trust in

▼ FIGURE 7.2

The Decline in Confidence in Television News

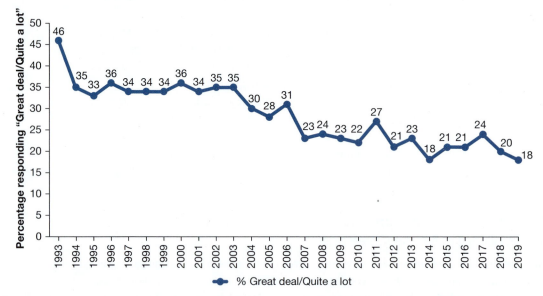

The percentage of Americans expressing a "great deal" or "quite a lot" of confidence in television news has declined dramatically over the past twenty years.

Source: Gallup, "Media Use and Evaluation," accessed April 21, 2020, https://news.gallup.com/poll/1663/media-use-evaluation.aspx.

its objectivity. Twentieth-century television news anchors, for example, were not expected to provide political commentary along with their stories. Viewers trusted their facts.

When thinking about bias in news coverage, one cannot ignore one of the most important potential sources of the problem: us. The news media—even outlets that are operated as nonprofit entities—need to attract an audience. They need us to consume their products, and they may shape their coverage accordingly. This creates the possibility of **commercial bias** in which some news outlets might pursue inflammatory, sensational coverage to secure their niche in the marketplace, while others might choose to play it safe for fear of upsetting their audience.

Commercial bias may shape not just *how* stories are covered but also *which* stories are covered. Stories, for example, about government regulation or public policies are often far from the compelling narratives that will attract a large audience, unless, of course, a major disaster or event shines a spotlight on some underlying problem. In a competitive marketplace, news, including political news, is based on providing compelling narratives.

The News Can Function as Entertainment

Commercial demands upon mainstream news providers have changed the approach many network executives take toward not just their anchors and reporters but the news divisions themselves. According to one communications scholar, "Once upon a time, news was a money loser, but was kept separate from the other divisions of the networks so that the journalists in their employ could operate without much attention to the bottom line. No more."[34] In the run-up to the election of 2016 and in its aftermath, CNN, Fox News, and MSNBC saw substantial increases in viewership as audiences became glued to coverage of the debates and the developments in the early months of the Trump administration.

The pressure of attracting an audience in a marketplace with so many easily accessible alternatives has led many news outlets to focus on **infotainment**, a merging of information and entertainment designed to attract viewers and gain market share. This dynamic includes pressures to provide **soft news**—stories that focus on celebrities, personalities, and entertaining events rather than on topics of local, national, or international political or economic significance.

Scholars continue to debate the effects of soft news on Americans' political knowledge and understanding. Candidate appearances on talk shows might engage viewers who otherwise would not have been exposed to their candidacy or the campaign in general. As a result, voters may be more likely to select candidates who more closely resemble citizens' political preferences.[35]

Soft news can act to engage individuals with foreign policy issues. Dramatic human-interest stories, for example, may engage viewers to think about a foreign crisis in ways that coverage of diplomatic maneuvers does not.[36] On the other hand, scholars have found that viewership of political comedy shows such as *The Daily Show with Trevor Noah* may decrease individuals' support for and engagement with political institutions, exposing them to political issues but increasing cynicism in the process.[37] There are also concerns that soft news may decrease consumers' knowledge of public affairs—knowledge that is necessary for effective democratic governance.[38]

Contemporary Pressures Affect How the Media Cover Campaigns and Elections

The drive to attract an audience also shapes how media outlets cover political campaigns and elections, and it affects how candidates try to present themselves. When covering political campaigns, news outlets may focus on the drama of the race rather than on the policy differences between candidates, a tendency often called the **horse race phenomenon**.

Scandals also sell, as we have explored, tempting media outlets to focus on them and often crowding out discussions of policy, a pattern that political scientist Larry Sabato has called a "feeding frenzy."[39]

Candidates and politicians are not bystanders in the coverage of politics; they actively try to shape the news agenda and the content of the stories covered. They and members of their staffs try to get their message out and shape its reception. The goal is to control the message, sometimes seemingly obsessively, by focusing on one message per news cycle, or day. Allowing or restricting journalists' access is also a strategic decision, made according to what strategy seems best able to "spin" a story in the desired way. Timing the release of statements can be a strategic choice as well. There are incentives for, say, presidents, to comment on unavoidable but unflattering stories on Friday afternoons, hoping they will fade away over the weekend. Aaron Sorkin devoted an entire episode of his (2000) television drama, *The West Wing*, to the phenomenon, calling it "Take Out the Trash Day."[40]

Media Ownership and Content Are Subject to Regulation

> 7.4 Explain the different perspectives of media ownership and media content.

Although the media serve, in part, to try to exercise control over elected officials and government employees, the media are themselves subject to regulation and control by the government. While the challenges to effective and fair regulation have often been specific to certain times, places, and technologies, elected officials' desire to shape the landscape of media coverage is long-standing. These efforts have focused primarily on regulating two things: media ownership and media content.

Regulation Affects Who Owns the Media and How We Consume It

With the technological revolutions of radio and television in the twentieth century came demands from both citizens and content providers themselves for the federal government to regulate the broadcast media. The business logic behind these regulations was based upon the fact that the nation's radio and television frequencies were finite, like rivers, canals, and federal grazing lands.[41] There were also calls to regulate the morality of the content of the material that beamed directly into Americans' homes. And there were calls to regulate the political content of radio and television broadcasts to ensure that multiple political viewpoints were all represented.

Regulation Affects Media Technologies and Ownership

The Radio Act of 1927 established the Federal Radio Commission and required broadcasters to obtain a license to broadcast on specific frequencies in an attempt to bring order to "the utter confusion within the broadcasting band."[42] The Communications Act of 1934 expanded the federal role in governing the nation's broadcast media, creating the Federal Communications Commission (FCC) to oversee its implementation.

In the latter half of the twentieth century, spiking demand from content providers and marketplace competition as well as changes in the ways news stories were created and distributed, forced government once again to rethink the rules governing telecommunications. New legislation was needed to help overcome what was an increasingly messy traffic jam in the nation's telecommunications systems. The Telecommunications Act of 1996 essentially brought deregulation to media ownership (see Figure 7.3). While deregulation might have been expected to increase the diversity of the nation's major news outlets, it had the opposite effect. It led to increasing consolidation as news firms tried to maximize their profits in the face of declining

▼ FIGURE 7.3

Consolidation of Media Ownership

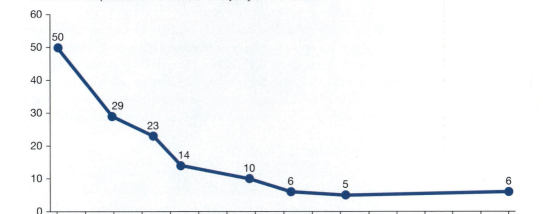

Number of Corporations that Control a Majority of U.S. Media

Source: Modified from Ben H. Bagdikian, *The New Media Monopoly* (Boston, MA: Beacon Press, 2004). Available online at www.corporations.org/media.

sales on things like printed classified advertisements, long a mainstay of traditional newspaper revenue, made obsolete by the Internet.

The concentration of ownership of major media outlets is not only due to relaxation of regulations. There is also a logic to it. Media outlets largely fund their operations through advertising revenue. Advertisers, for their part, want to reach as many consumers as possible. Therefore, media outlets try to expand their reach as far as they can, whether by attracting the largest audiences possible or by purchasing smaller content providers. This has consequences for the content of media coverage as well. Providers may shape their coverage to attract as wide an audience as possible.

The twenty-first century has also witnessed a marked decline in consumption of printed newspapers. Does that mean overall consumption of *news* has declined? The story is more complicated than that. Traditional papers have gone online, sometimes for free and with advertisements, sometimes behind paywalls that require registration and/or a subscription fee. Nontraditional Internet news sources often get their stories from a process called **aggregating**. In this process they still rely on the basic reporting that newspaper journalists do, but then they disseminate and comment on the original coverage.

During this era of proliferation of media outlets and the federal government's relaxation of many of the regulations first introduced during the days of radio, and later, television, the problem of private use of limited public resources has come up again. This time bandwidth is the resource in danger of "overgrazing." **Net neutrality** is the idea that Internet service providers should treat all data and content providers equally and not discriminate based upon content or bandwidth demands. However, some feel that companies that provide the highways of the Internet and broadband age should be able to charge more to content providers whose "livestock" chew up more bandwidth. Streaming movie and television show distributors like Netflix are relatively bandwidth-heavy content providers. Critics who support net neutrality say that allowing firms to price discriminate based on bandwidth use will stifle the expression of multiple and diverse views.

Pro-net neutrality laws that had been advanced by the Obama administration appeared to be targets for opponents to net neutrality within the Trump administration. Under Obama, in June 2016, the DC Circuit Court of Appeals upheld the FCC's net neutrality rules, but several major telecommunications companies promised to appeal the decision. In 2017 President Trump nominated a series of anti-net neutrality commissioners to the FCC's board, signaling relaxed enforcement of those rules.

Regulation Also Affects Content

While the federal government plays only a small role in providing media content—with exceptions such as the Corporation for Public Broadcasting, created by Congress in 1967—it has played an important role in regulating its content. The Communications Act of 1934 led to the establishment of several rules designed to shape news media content to serve the public at large. One of these, the **equal time rule**, requires licensees—companies that have paid for the right to broadcast their programs over the public airwaves—to guarantee political candidates equal time to present their views and opinions. This rule does not apply to cable networks, which use private wired connections to customers' homes to reach their audiences.

One of the more controversial aspects of the equal time provision was an implicit—and perhaps unintended—incentive for broadcasters to avoid presenting the platforms of candidates at all, for fear of running afoul of the law. According to media and politics scholar Doris Graber, the equal time provision may have acted to restrict rather than expand political information as a station may choose not to cover candidates at all, especially those in local races, in which many candidates are vying for office.

The rise of social media has also challenged the ability to ensure equal coverage. Political candidates who are also celebrities, for example, can obtain disproportionate attention based on their celebrity status alone. In the 2016 presidential campaign, Republican candidate Donald Trump used his large following on Twitter to obtain coverage without having to purchase as much airtime as other candidates.

The **fairness doctrine**, introduced in 1949, expanded regulations for American political news coverage beyond just the provision of time for candidates to the content of the coverage itself. It required "that every licensee devote a reasonable portion of broadcast time to the discussion and consideration of controversial issues of public importance" and that broadcasters "affirmatively endeavor to make . . . facilities available for the expression of contrasting viewpoints held by responsible elements with respect to the controversial issues presented."[43] Again, scholars and broadcasters have questioned the unintended consequences of the fairness doctrine. In trying to avoid the appearance of being unfair, political news media providers might decide to play it safe "to shy away from programs dealing with controversial public issues to avoid demands to air opposing views, in place of regular revenue-producing programs."[44] The fairness doctrine had ceased to be rigorously enforced and was largely repealed in the 1980s. In 2011, the FCC formally scrapped it. However, debates about its potential reinstatement (and how the Supreme Court would rule on such an action in the age of the Internet) continue.

The Power of the Media to Affect the Public Is Tested

> 7.5 Explain the different perspectives on the power of the media to shape political understanding and behaviors.

It was fake news, intentionally so.

On Sunday, October 30, 1938, the night before Halloween, Orson Welles, who would later gain notoriety for directing movies, served up a bit of mischief to

American audiences. Welles was that night directing a radio adaptation of the H. G. Wells 1897 science fiction novel *The War of the Worlds*, which centered on an invasion of England by Martians, for the CBS radio program *Mercury Theatre on the Air.*

It was a play, on radio, meant to entertain. The problem was that many Americans did not realize that fact at the time, and it caused a panic.[45]

Welles and his collaborators had decided to set their adaptation not in England but in Grover's Mill, New Jersey. During the process of creating the teleplay, a secretary who had transcribed the original novel, was reported to have remarked, "Those old Martians are just a lot of nonsense! It's all too silly!"[46] Welles, with little more than twenty-four hours before the broadcast, was worried that his radio play would be far from good theater.

So he made a choice: He would make it seem real, drawing on the horrific commentary and screams that accompanied the true coverage of the explosion of the airship *Hindenburg* the year before. Welles also decided to mimic the real "news flash" interruptions of Americans' regular comedy or music broadcasts, tapping into the fears of an already very worried nation that had become used to those kinds of announcements. At the time, reporters would often break into the entertaining radio broadcasts of the day with news of the Great Depression or the rise of Hitler's Nazi Party. With those trappings of "real news" in place, the broadcast went live.

During the program's climax, a fake announcer recounted, "Now the whole field's caught fire. (Explosion) The woods . . . the barns . . . the gas tanks of automobiles . . . it's spreading everywhere. It's coming this way. About twenty yards to my right . . . (CRASH OF MICROPHONE . . . THEN DEAD SILENCE . . .)."[47] Six seconds of complete silence followed.

Another announcer followed: "Ladies and gentlemen, due to circumstances beyond our control, we are unable to continue our broadcast from Grover's Mill. Evidently, there's some difficulty with our field transmission."[48]

As theater, it was genius. To many listeners, the absurdities of the scenario were obvious, so it was nothing more than captivating entertainment. To an unknown

DAILY NEWS

FAKE RADIO 'WAR' STIRS TERROR THROUGH U.S.

"War" Victim

"I Didn't Know". Orson Welles, after broadcast expresses amazement at public reaction. He adapted H. G. Wells' "War of the Worlds" for radio and played principal role.

A respected newspaper coverage of the "fake news" broadcast of *The War of the Worlds.*

NY Daily News Archive via Getty Images

number of Americans, however, it seemed real: "All they knew was that something horrible was happening on the Eastern Seaboard—and that, perhaps, it was coming their way."[49] At the conclusion of the broadcast, Orson Welles stepped out of his persona as a fake Princeton University professor and assured his audience, "This is Orson Welles, ladies and gentlemen, out of character to assure you that THE WAR OF THE WORLDS has no further significance than the holiday offering it was meant to be."[50]

Some Americans missed Welles's disclaimer. The aftermath was intense. Stories of frightened Americans were everywhere, especially in the newspapers on Halloween day. Welles received sharp criticism. Some have asserted that the panic over the broadcast was deliberately overblown by newspapers "to attack their newfangled rival, the radio."[51] Perhaps it was not a "War of the Worlds" but a battle between two media outlets—newspapers and radio—for legitimacy.

In the aftermath of *The War of the Worlds*, one thing was clear: the power of the news media—whether or not they could convince Americans that they were under attack by Martians—was not fake.

Scholars Have Differed on the Media's Effects

When it comes to democratic representation, none of the topics that we have explored in this chapter matter unless one thing is true: that the media can actually shape individuals' political knowledge and understanding. Why regulate the political media, for instance, unless it can affect people's political beliefs and understanding?

But just how much power does the media have? Are they major players in the national political drama or just commentators on it? As with so much else about the American news media, the answers to these questions are evolving. Scholars' views of **media effects**—the power of the news media in shaping individuals' political knowledge, understanding, and preferences—have evolved along with the media itself.

In the early decades of the twentieth century, many observers of American political life considered the media a powerful and potentially dangerous force. The effectiveness of World War I propaganda posters and efforts, which helped to mobilize the nation in support of intervention in a European conflict about which many Americans were ambivalent, seemed to indicate that the public was like political Play-Doh: shapeable and malleable. In this view, media were thought to have a direct effect on a public.

This model of the direct effects of the media began to fall out of favor in later decades as scholars, employing empirical techniques and focusing primarily on the effects of the media in vote choices, found important but limited effects of the media on political outcomes. Though playing an important role in citizen information about candidates and their policy positions, the media were found to be only one factor in an individual's ultimate choice about which candidates to vote for in a given election.[52]

The current view of most scholars of the relationship between the media and American politics lies somewhere between those of the direct and limited effects models. The model of subtle effects focuses not so much on how the media may or may not change—for example, the partisan affiliation or vote choice of a given individual—but on the ways in which the media may shape the overall conversation taking place in the public sphere.

How the media place a story in a larger context—the textual or visual cues that they present along with a particular story—may cause individuals to focus on particular considerations when consuming a media product, an effect known as **framing**. According to political scientists James Druckman and Kjersten Nelson, "For example, if a speaker describes a hate-group rally in terms of free speech, then the audience will subsequently base their opinions about the rally on free speech considerations and, perhaps, support the right to rally. In contrast, if the speaker uses a public-safety frame, the audience will base their opinions on public-safety considerations and oppose the rally."[53] Similarly, a particular media source's coverage of a candidate or issue may highlight specific contextual details in providing the coverage, thereby **priming** individuals to draw on those details when forming opinions.

The power of the media to select which stories are covered cannot be understated. In the choice of coverage, the media may exert an agenda-setting role by highlighting which issues are worthy of coverage and, as a consequence, worthy of the public's attention. The question of **agenda-setting** gets to the very purpose of the role of the media in a representative democracy. According to political scientist Harold Lasswell, the media perform three important and interconnected functions: to survey and report on political events and outcomes, to interpret those events and outcomes to the public, and to educate citizens.[54] To these three, media and politics scholar Doris Graber has added a fourth function: to deliberately manipulate the political process.[55]

Lasswell's assertion that the media survey and report on the political world is often what we think about when we consider the media's role in American representative democracy—hard-hitting journalists asking hard-hitting questions and acting as a watchdog for, or, perhaps more accurately, a watchtower over, American politics. The role of watchdog is well entrenched in Americans' understanding of the role of journalists, editors, and anchors. Objective, aggressive interviews designed to get to the truth are very much a part of the ideal of the American news media. The tricky questions, however, are these: On what issues does the watchtower shine its light? Corruption? Scandal? Infrastructure? Cats? Who controls its aim and focus? To whom does the watchtower's controller answer? Corporate interests, powerful politicians, fellow journalists, or the American consumer? They are important questions with no easy answers.

Who decides where the light is to shine, and what are the consequences of those decisions?

PRACTICING POLITICAL SCIENCE

DO THE MEDIA MAKE US SMART (OR NOT SO SMART)? OR DO WE MAKE THEM LOOK GOOD (OR NOT SO GOOD)?

In 2007, the Pew Research Center reported the findings of a study of Americans' political knowledge and media usage.[56] Part of the study was a political knowledge quiz in which the roughly 1,500 respondents were asked to identify individuals and answer questions about American government. Based on how well they did answering these questions, researchers divided the respondents into three groups: high knowledge, moderate knowledge, and low knowledge.

Another part of the survey asked respondents to identify which sources of political news they

▼ FIGURE 7.4-A

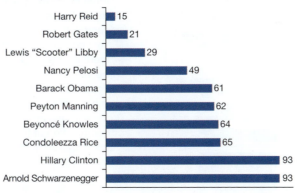

Percentage of Survey Respondents Who Can Identify . . .

Harry Reid	15
Robert Gates	21
Lewis "Scooter" Libby	29
Nancy Pelosi	49
Barack Obama	61
Peyton Manning	62
Beyoncé Knowles	64
Condoleezza Rice	65
Hillary Clinton	93
Arnold Schwarzenegger	93

Percentage of Survey Respondents Who Can Recall the Name of . . .

The president of Russia	36
Their state's governor	66
The vice president	69

Source: Pew Research Center, "What Americans Know: 1989–2007," April 2007, http://www.people-press.org/files/legacy-pdf/319.pdf.

(Continued)

(Continued)

Knowledge Levels by News Source

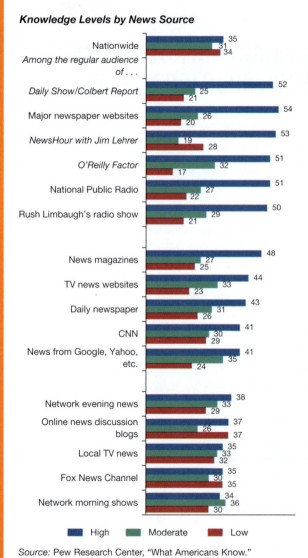

Source: Pew Research Center, "What Americans Know."

regularly consumed, including print, radio, television, cable, and Internet sources. The sources themselves were then scored based on how knowledgeable their regular consumers were. While no one technology emerged as being more or less consumed by more or less knowledgeable individuals, there were some considerable differences between specific sources.

The Daily Show and *The Colbert Report*, along with newspaper websites, had the most knowledgeable consumers. The conservative *Rush Limbaugh Show* and *O'Reilly Factor* also had relatively knowledgeable consumers. Fox News Channel and the network morning shows had the least knowledgeable consumers. See Figures 7.4-A and 7.4-B.

· ·

WHAT Do You Think?

What conclusions can we draw from these data? This is where it is important to be careful. It may be that *The Daily Show* is very educational, making its consumers more informed. On the other hand, it may be that it attracts more informed consumers, as much of the show's humor is not that funny without some background information. Or it may be a combination of these two causes. What additional information might be useful in making stronger conclusions?

Americans May Be Separated by a Digital Divide

At first glance, the proliferation of news sources in the twenty-first century might provide scholars of the news media with a source of optimism. Perhaps, through infotainment, the diversity of perspectives on cable stations, and the spread of social media, Americans who were previously disconnected from the political process might be brought into it and prompted to think about issues and to connect friends and family in their own social networks to American politics. Again, it may not be that simple; the story might not be so neat and inspiring. All Americans do not make use of the new technologies and outlets in the same way. According to the work of political scientist Markus Prior, the new technologies and media avenues may be dividing Americans, making them more partisan.[57] We call those gaps the **digital divide**.

Americans with the resources and skills to navigate this media landscape that contains many options and unclear editorial standards may benefit tremendously, but those who cannot, or choose not to, may be left behind. The Internet, according to Prior, "has widened gaps in news exposure, political knowledge, and turnout between those who like news and those who prefer entertainment."[58] Older, low-income, rural, Spanish-speaking, and disabled Americans are among those less likely to make use of the Internet, as are those with lower levels of educational attainment.[59]

Conclusion: Debates about the Power of the Media Continue

By 2020, fake news was hardly a new story. *The War of the Worlds* had long since passed into American history. The war of words, however, raged on. Secretary Clinton continued to argue that Russian interference, especially through social media, helped to tilt the 2016 election in Trump's favor. Throughout 2020, President Donald Trump's war with the American media had only intensified. Many expected a major escalation over the course of the presidential campaign and election. Which is exactly what happened. Twitter, for example, began to apply content advisories to the President's tweets over concerns of inaccurate claims, particularly over electoral processes. President Trump, in turn, held up these decisions as evidence of election interference. Two days after the election, most cable and broadcast media outlets cut away from a presidential address shortly after it began, in order to fact-check his claims of widespread voter fraud in real time.

How powerful are American media sources in the twenty-first century?

The challenges of filtering the truth of the images, issues, and arguments with which they are bombarded is a major task for Americans. This is as true today in the multilayered media environment of the twenty-first century as it was for listeners tuning in to hear about a Martian invasion in 1938 and for pamphlet readers at the start of the nation. Because so much of our knowledge about the political world comes indirectly from the media and not from direct interaction with politicians, policymakers, or the political process, Americans are tasked with the challenge of needing to be very savvy about the media they consume. Why are we being bombarded with one set of specific issues and not others? What issues are being ignored, and why?

CHAPTER REVIEW

This chapter's main ideas are reflected in the Learning Objectives. By reviewing them here, you should be able to *remember* the key points and *know* these terms that are central to the topic.

7.1 Examine how recent controversies over foreign interference in electoral politics raise questions about the trustworthiness of the American news media.

Remember . . .
- The news media include newspapers, magazines, radio, television, Internet sources, blogs, and social media postings, all in service of informing or persuading.
- Questions about the trustworthiness of the American news media are closely connected to debates about their proper role in American politics.

Know . . .
- *fake news* (p. 197)
- *news media* (p. 193)

7.2 Trace the historical development of the American news media.

Remember . . .
- Since the nation's founding, there has been tension between the constitutional right to freedom of speech and of the press and constraints on those rights.
- Pamphlets and later weekly and daily newspapers were among the first print media in the United States.
- As time went on, costs to produce newspapers decreased, making the news more affordable and available and able to reach a mass audience.
- For much of the history of the American media, the press has been partisan—funded by and disseminating the point of view of particular political factions.
- Sensationalism was also used to sell news, a practice that continues today.
- The nineteenth and twentieth centuries saw the rise of other technologies, such as the telegraph and radio and television.

Know . . .
- *beat system* (p. 201)
- *broadcast media* (p. 201)
- *citizen journalists* (p. 203)
- *investigative journalism* (p. 200)
- *mass media* (p. 200)
- *partisan press* (p. 200)
- *penny press* (p. 200)
- *social media* (p. 203)
- *wire service* (p. 200)
- *yellow journalism* (p. 200)

7.3 Understand the issue of bias in the American media.

Remember . . .
- Cable news offers round-the-clock news coverage, often with a partisan slant.
- Newer technologies, such as the Internet, broadband, and social media, have not only increased the pace and volume of news content but have also blurred the lines between information, entertainment, citizens, and journalists.
- Americans increasingly perceive the media as politically biased and less trustworthy.
- Scholars' views of the power of the media to shape political understanding and behaviors have changed over time.
- A growing digital divide separates Americans along partisan lines as well as by race, class, and ethnicity.

Know . . .
- *commercial bias* (p. 207)
- *horse race phenomenon* (p. 208)
- *infotainment* (p. 207)
- *partisan bias* (p. 205)
- *soft news* (p. 207)

7.4   Explain the different perspectives of media ownership and media content.

Remember . . .
- Some efforts to regulate the news media have focused on ownership; others have focused on its content.
- The Radio Act of 1927 established the FCC and required broadcasters to obtain licenses.
- The Telecommunications Act of 1996 modified regulations on media ownership and led to a period of consolidation.
- The principle of net neutrality calls for Internet service providers to treat data streams equally.
- The equal time rule and fairness doctrine sought to ensure a level playing field for political candidates; however, recent regulatory and technological changes have reduced their impact and raised questions about their relevance.

Know . . .
- *aggregating* (p. 210)
- *equal time rule* (p. 211)
- *fairness doctrine* (p. 211)
- *net neutrality* (p. 210)

7.5   Explain the different perspectives on the power of the media to shape political understanding and behaviors.

Remember . . .
- How has the need to attract an audience shaped the coverage of political news?
- What are possible sources of bias in coverage of political news? Which of these do you think are the most significant?
- Can the media shape Americans' political understandings?

Know . . .
- *agenda-setting* (p. 214)
- *digital divide* (p. 217)
- *framing* (p. 214)
- *media effects* (p. 213)
- *priming* (p. 214)

CHAPTER 8

PARTIES, ELECTIONS, AND PARTICIPATION

Making Representative Democracy Happen

Bernie Sanders started his political career as an outsider, describing himself as an independent socialist and refusing to formally join the Democratic Party when he was elected to Congress in 1991. His message about income inequality further set him apart from the mainstream of the party, but it won him a devoted following who flocked to rallies like this one in Chicago when he ran for president in 2016 and 2020.

John J. Kim/*Chicago Tribune*/Getty Images

By reading this chapter, you will be able to do the following:

8.1 Reflect on the obstacles that insurgent candidates face and the challenges that they present to their party establishments.

8.2 Identify the roles the political parties play in supporting and nominating candidates for office.

8.3 Understand the rules and institutions that structure national elections.

8.4 Describe the traditional and nontraditional forms of political participation in American representative democracy.

American representative democracy involves a great deal of uncertainty—not just in which candidates might win an election but also in how citizens figure out which candidates to support. How can voters be sure they are selecting individuals who will advocate for their interests, act on issues they care about, and govern effectively?

Given the wide variety of governmental policies, it is extremely challenging for even the most attentive voters to know all the details of what a candidate stands for or hopes to accomplish once in office.

Making representative democracy work requires organization—a lot of it. Enter the **political party**. By organizing and supporting candidates running for office, parties provide labels to those candidates—shortcuts for voters, really—that cut through the noise and signal to voters that this is a candidate who deserves their support. Once in office, those candidates work, with the support of other party members, to advance a set of policies. Party leaders face another challenge: creating an attractive and consistent message that gets their candidates elected and maintains party cohesion. American political parties have often been successful in doing this, but not always. Once in a while, a party finds itself challenged not by another party but by members within its own ranks who have felt that their voices are being ignored by party leaders.

National **elections** are the tools with which the American political system chooses its representatives—its presidents and members of Congress. National **campaigns** are the tools that would-be representatives use to connect to American voters. Candidates use them to introduce themselves and to convince voters that they—and not any of their opponents—are the best choice for making the people's wishes known in Washington and enacting these wishes in legislation and policies.

As we will explore, however, campaigns and elections are both composed of many moving parts. The rules governing them, the people who choose to run, and the composition of the electorate all may shift over time, sometimes with profound and long-lasting consequences. Candidates, even those who have been in elected office for years, need to be aware and flexible, ready to change message or strategy if necessary. American political campaigns are no place for dinosaurs . . . not in the long run.

By its nature, representative democracy also requires action. It cannot survive without it.

Representatives act in the space of government to enact their constituents' concerns and preferences in the laws and policies of a nation. For their part, citizens must act to make their wishes known. They must find candidates they feel good about supporting and help those candidates achieve political office; they must also hold those representatives accountable after they are elected. In addition, individuals must rally others to their causes and speak as a member of a group rather than as a lone voice in the political wilderness. But how? What tools can people use to accomplish all of these weighty goals? That is where **political participation** comes in. Through its many avenues, people act to shape the laws and policies of the nation.

Bernie Sanders Challenges the Democratic Party to Become More Progressive, Twice

> 8.1 Reflect on the obstacles that insurgent candidates face and the challenges that they present to their party establishments.

Sen. Bernie Sanders (I-VT) had been to this rodeo before. On February 22, 2020, Senator Sanders packed the Cowboys Dancehall in San Antonio, Texas, to capacity, propelled by a win in New Hampshire, a technical second in a glitchy Iowa caucus, successful fundraising, and a lot of enthusiasm. The Nevada caucuses had not even declared their official results yet, but Bernie was already on to Texas, eyeing Super Tuesday and seeing a real shot at the Democratic Party presidential nomination. Bernie would win Nevada, due to a strong performance (as expected) with younger voters but also with Latina and Latino voters, which boded well for California and beyond.

Not backing away from his support for gun control and rapid action on climate change, controversial anywhere, but even more so in Texas, Sanders gave the crowd his greatest hits: racial, social, and economic justice; eliminating the financial burdens of college; protecting *Roe v. Wade*; and attacking President Trump's immigration policies. "The vibe resembled more of an outdoor concert than a political event. . . . The music thumping through the PA skewed contemporary, though it also included a few shoutouts for non-Millennials and Gen Zers."[1] That night, Sanders tweeted, "I've got news for the Republican establishment. I've got news for the Democratic establishment. They can't stop us."[2]

Four years before, not quite to the day, Sanders was holding a similarly raucous rally, across the state line in Henderson, Nevada. In 2016 Sanders was riding a wave of enthusiasm, grassroots fundraising and support, and Americans' frustration with economic inequality, just as he would in 2020. He was taking on the Democratic Party's top establishment candidate, former secretary of state Hillary Clinton, just like he would in 2020, when he faced former vice president Joe Biden. "The campaign is gaining momentum because we are listening to the pain of the people," he told the crowd in Nevada. "We are listening to the workers...who are telling us they can't make it on $9 an hour. We are listening to our brothers and sisters in the Latino community who are demanding to get out of the shadows and want a path towards citizenship. We are listening to our African American brothers and sisters who are telling us they are tired of a criminal justice system which is broken. We are listening to the women who say...'We are tired of working [for] 79 cents on the dollar compared to men.'"[3]

Bernie Sanders would not become the Democratic Party presidential nominee in 2016 or 2020. In the postmortems that followed each campaign, there were a few similar themes. Perhaps, primarily, Sanders had not sufficiently broadened his coalition: "In 2016, Sanders built a passionate bloc of supporters who crowded his rallies and flooded his campaign with money, but lost to Clinton, a more centrist, establishment Democrat who had greater appeal among black, Southern, and older voters. In 2020, Sanders built a passionate bloc of supporters who crowded his rallies and flooded his campaign with money but lost to Biden, a more centrist, establishment Democrat who had greater appeal among black, Southern, and older voters."[4]

What some analyses paid less attention to, though, was how Sanders himself had helped to change the party's ideological focus in the intervening four years. In 2016, he was out on a limb, largely alone among prominent Democrats in pushing the party toward economic, racial, and social justice. By 2020, he had quite a bit of company. In helping to win the battle of the party's future, he had made it more difficult to stand out among voters as the only candidate who really got it.

Thinking about how parties deal with internal challenges gives us purchase on a much deeper question: How *powerful* are they? How much leverage political parties exercise over the selection and behavior of the candidates is an important one in the study of American politics today. In thinking about the power of political parties, it is also useful to note that many of those involved in framing or ratifying the Constitution—whether they were for it or against it—had misgivings about political parties. They are, after all, examples of the factions that James Madison warned about in *Federalist* No. 10 and No. 51, and potentially dangerous ones at that.

In 2016, Bernie Sanders Pushes the Democratic Party, and the Party Pushes Back

Though he had been a senator since 2007, and a member of the House for sixteen years before that, Bernie Sanders was still an outsider. He didn't even belong to the Democratic Party when he announced he was running for that party's nomination in the 2016 presidential election. Instead, Sanders described himself as an "independent socialist," strongly in favor of the idea that government and society should meet the needs of the public, increasing taxes on the wealthiest Americans to pay for these programs. He was known for criticizing so-called corporate welfare—government benefits, such as special provisions in the tax code, provided to businesses in the hopes of enabling them to succeed and keep workers on their payrolls. Sanders has proposed

A supporter of Bernie Sanders voices his displeasure with the Democratic National Committee (DNC) at a rally in June 2016. Some Sanders supporters, like Sanders himself, were not Democrats, or at least were highly critical of the Democratic Party, and felt that the primary was "rigged" in Clinton's favor.

Alex Wong/Getty Images

a tax on Wall Street transactions to fund tuition-free college and student debt forgiveness.

Though Sanders was not the first, or only, candidate to call attention to economic inequality in the country in the twenty-first century, his message that the playing field was unacceptably tilted toward the top 1 percent of Americans resonated with many voters, especially young adults struggling with student loan debt or seeking to stake their claim on the American dream. Sanders often made an issue of how much money his main Democratic opponent, former secretary of state Hillary Clinton, received from Wall Street firms—more than $15 million in campaign donations as of early 2016, according to the nonpartisan watchdog group Center for Responsive Politics.[5]

In 2016, Bernie Sanders advanced far in the electoral process due to voters' profound disgust with "politics as usual." Unlike other contenders, he did not count on courting the best-known activists and leaders in the Democratic Party—the so-called party establishment or party elites, who are the most powerful insiders in party politics. In fact, he frequently called the party out for not going far enough—especially in addressing an economy that had reached levels of inequality not seen since the 1920s.

He did not, however, win. Hillary Clinton had been seen as the almost inevitable nominee for the Democratic Party. Despite a close race, by June, Clinton had secured enough pledged delegates to win the nomination. At the Democratic National Convention in July, Sanders called on the committee to select Secretary Clinton by acclamation.

The Democratic Party provided Clinton with other advantages over Sanders. The most obvious was that she actually belonged to the party; he did not. That gave her a broad network of prominent supporters who coalesced ahead of primary voting to warn of what they saw as the danger of a Sanders candidacy affecting other races in which Democrats were running. "Here in the heartland, we like our politicians in the mainstream, and [Sanders] is not—he's a socialist," said Democratic Missouri governor Jay Nixon two months before his state's primary. "He's entitled to his positions, and it's a big-tent party. But as far as having him at the top of the ticket, it would be a meltdown all the way down the ballot."[6]

During the primary and caucus season of 2016, many Sanders supporters argued that the party's superdelegate system provided Hillary Clinton with an unfair advantage. Even though Sanders actually won some state primaries and caucuses, the party's rules for how delegates were allocated boosted Clinton's pledged delegate totals and, therefore, her momentum. The Democratic Party had developed a specific set of rules precisely because it wanted to be able to pick presidential nominees strategically. They believed that the elected officials and party leaders would have an interest in backing the strongest possible candidates and that giving those officials the power to switch their votes could avoid messy fights over the nomination.[7]

Sanders's message, however, had gotten through. Sanders succeeded in forcing Clinton to take positions similar to his on trade and jobs. For example, when she first declared her candidacy, Clinton vowed to be "president for the struggling, the striving and the successful."[8] But after losing the Michigan primary, she said, "I don't want to be the president for those who are already successful—they don't need me. I want to be the president for the struggling and the striving."[9] She also expressed a greater willingness to raise taxes on the wealthy to keep Social Security from going broke.[10]

After having finally endorsed nominee Hillary Clinton during the summer's Democratic National Convention, Bernie Sanders continued to campaign on her behalf. Some observers, however, wondered if Sanders could have beaten Donald Trump in the general election by drawing out voters who ended up staying home on Election Day, especially in key battleground states like Michigan. Bernie Sanders wondered as well. He would try again in 2020.

In 2020, Bernie Sanders Runs against the Establishment Again and Finds the Party Has Moved Closer to Him

Bernie Sanders hadn't changed much in four years, but his party had, and it was partly his own fault. Ideas on which Sanders had focused for decades were becoming more mainstream within the Democratic Party. The midterm elections of 2018 continued a trend of growing diversity among Democratic members of Congress (see Chapter 10). Sanders easily secured his third term in the Senate, running as an independent.

The February Nevada caucuses would prove to be the high point of Senator Sanders's presidential prospects in 2020. Two weeks after Sanders rallies across Texas, on Super Tuesday (March 3)—in which fourteen states held primaries with about one-third of the delegates at stake—Sanders underperformed. Though Sanders won in California, former vice president Joe Biden won in the South, as expected, but also in Texas and Minnesota. Biden would defeat Sanders in Michigan a week later. Afterward, Democratic Party elites began to endorse Joe Biden's candidacy at a rapid pace, and his nomination was all but assured.

Sharing the stage during the televised debates, and competing directly with Sanders for at least a part of the electorate—was Massachusetts senator Elizabeth Warren. Sanders and Warren shared some big policy goals, addressing economic inequality in particular. The implementation of a wealth tax to address economic

Joe Biden for President of the United States.

Although Bernie Sanders had appeared dominant during the early primaries, a strong showing on Super Tuesday followed by a string of victories put Joe Biden in the lead. The Democratic establishment then threw their support behind Biden, including former president Barack Obama, in a livestreamed message.

UPI/Alamy Stock Photo

inequality was one proposal on which they agreed. After Super Tuesday, some Sanders supporters suggested that Warren's candidacy had split the progressive vote. Had it consolidated into a bloc behind Sanders, they argued, he could have prevailed on Super Tuesday.

Just as in the postprimary analyses of 2016, questions about Bernie's ceiling and his base came up in 2020. Was Bernie's campaign capable of drawing from outside his enthusiastic base? Would it have been broad enough to defeat Donald Trump? Here again, Sanders's 2016 success emerged as one of the culprits. "Perhaps," according to FiveThirtyEight's Nate Silver, "Sanders was a victim of his own success in 2016. That is, he did such a good job of turning out voters in 2016 that it was hard to *improve* on his performance in 2020. Still, there was never really any recognition that his base alone might not be enough to win—and there were never many efforts to expand beyond the base. Indeed, it's interesting that Sanders *doubled down even more* on his screw-the-establishment messaging amidst his success in the first three states—rather than trying to pivot to a more inclusive campaign and unify the party behind him."[11]

The enthusiastic crowds would keep showing up for Sanders, until COVID-19 forced all campaigns to suspend their rallies in March. By June, Joe Biden had secured enough delegates to clinch the party's nomination, though Bernie Sanders held on to his delegates, hoping to use them to shape the party's agenda during the convention.

Parties Act to Identify, Support, and Nominate Candidates for Elected Office

> 8.2 Identify the roles the political parties play in supporting and nominating candidates for office.

The Constitution of the United States does not mention political parties. In fact, many of the Framers and early leaders of the young Republic feared the potential consequences from parties grown too powerful. The parties have "baneful effects," President George Washington warned in 1796, because they are rooted "in the strongest passions of the human mind," causing splits that lead to political conflict and stagnation.[12] Parties are, after all, factions, with all of the dangers that a group of like-minded citizens can inflict upon others.

Political parties, however, have long been central to democracy and serve several functions. A healthy party serves as a credible check on the opposition, promoting ideas and candidates that differ from the other party's so that voters can choose how they want to be represented. In 1950, a committee composed of members of the American Political Science Association reflected upon the importance of parties for most Americans, noting that "the most valuable opportunity to influence the course of public affairs is the choice they are able to make between the parties in the principal elections."[13]

In developing what is now called the **responsible party model**, the report's authors called for changes in the organization and function of America's political parties. They highlighted the need for parties to take clear positions on issues (to give voters clear choices on policy alternatives), be cohesive both when in power and when in opposition, resist pressures from interest groups, and deliver on the promises that they make. Party members, for their part, should also act strongly to hold their party leadership accountable in fulfilling those promises.[14]

In 1964, political scientist V. O. Key Jr. identified three primary roles that political parties play in American representative democracy:[15] As organizations, political parties recruit, nominate, and support candidates for political office. In the electorate, parties act as labels for candidates and officeholders that voters can use as shortcuts in identifying candidates closer to their own political ideologies and advocating similar policy positions. In government, a party enacts the policy positions of its members and acts as an opposition to the majority party when it is in the minority.

Parties Unite People as Organizations

A political party seeks to unite people under a shared banner of social, economic, and ideological goals. It finds and supports candidates to run for federal, state, and local offices, which includes mobilizing voters and potential voters to support its candidates. Parties raise money to fund campaigns and provide other forms of assistance to try to get their candidates elected. If those candidates win, the parties then try to make sure the politicians stay in office. The parties also come up with themes and principles that they want their candidates to follow in appealing for votes.

Political Parties Are Decentralized. When some people think of political parties, they think of big shots in Washington, DC, commanding the armies of supporters below them. The reality is that parties are basically a large collection of state organizations that, in turn, are loose collections of local groups. This is because the system of federalism dictates that power should not just be concentrated at the top. As reporter Jonathan Rauch explained it, "State parties play a key role. They recruit and cultivate political talent, building a farm team of candidates for higher office. They coordinate campaigns up and down the ballot, connecting politicians to each other and discouraging rogue behavior. They build networks of volunteers, connecting leaders with the party base. They gather voter data and make it available to all candidates, building a library of knowledge about the electorate."[16]

Party Leaders Are Advisers, Not Rulers. The president generally chooses the chair of their national party. The national party chair raises money and serves as a prominent spokesperson on television and other media. But the national party organization's power over the state and local parties is advisory; it can't tell them what to do. Each state has a central committee made up of people from that state's counties and legislative districts who run for office and are elected to terms just like politicians in public office. They help shape the national party's governance, or how it manages its money and runs its operations.

Parties Shape Elections by Recruiting and Supporting Candidates

One way a party tries to shape elections is through **recruitment**, which is considered one of its central tasks. The parties seek candidates who best reflect the party's philosophy and who can attract the voters the parties seek to mobilize.

In recruiting, parties also try to discourage prospective candidates within their own ranks who aren't seen as having a good chance of winning. They fear that those candidates could end up drawing votes away from their preferred choice.

Parties Select Candidates through the Nomination Process

After recruiting and supporting candidates, parties shape the process of **nomination**, in which a party officially selects one candidate to run for one office against the nominees from other parties. In some races and in some states, the electoral process may pit members of the same party against each other in the general election.

Once the official presidential campaign process kicks off, declared candidates vie with others in their own party for that party's nomination. Beginning early in the election year, candidates seek to get the support of party **delegates**, whose votes they will later need to secure the party's nomination. While many of the rules governing the nomination process are set by federal and state laws, most of the details about *how* things actually work are hammered out by the parties themselves. There remain key differences across states and between the parties themselves.

Most states hold **presidential primary elections** wherein a state's voters choose delegates who support a particular candidate. In some states, these elections are **open primaries**, in which all eligible voters may vote in a party's primary election, regardless of that voter's partisan affiliation. Others hold **closed primaries**—open only to registered voters from a particular political party.

Some states hold caucuses wherein eligible voters gather to discuss candidates and issues and to select delegates to represent their preferences in later stages of the nomination process. The rules for taking part in a **caucus** are also more complicated, as they involve more than simply marking a ballot to record the selection of a candidate. Because of their complexity and time commitment, caucuses tend to draw fewer participants than primaries and attract those who are more committed to a candidate or cause.[17]

The schedule of primary elections and caucuses also matters to the ultimate outcomes of the nomination process. Party leaders in a state have a strong incentive to hold their primary election as early as possible in order to garner media attention as well as candidate attention. To take advantage of this, states try to engage in a process of **front-loading**—pushing their primaries or caucuses as early in the season as possible.

By tradition, the Iowa caucuses have been the first on the schedule, followed by the New Hampshire primary. While neither state has a large number of delegates to award, their early position gives them outsize power in creating at least the perception of a front-runner. But both states have larger white, non-Hispanic voting populations than much of the rest of the nation, creating a concern that the diversity of American voices will not be heard until the narrative of the nomination campaign has already been established.

The final phase of the nomination process takes place in the **national conventions** held by the parties in the summer of the presidential election year. During the conventions, delegates vote to select the party's nominee. For much of American history, national conventions were sources of high drama, with many rounds of delegate voting required to select a nominee; in recent decades, the final outcome is already known or expected.

The two major political parties have differed in how they award delegates based on primary elections and caucus results. One of these differences is the existence of **superdelegates**. Superdelegates are members of the Democratic Party—usually elected officials or party activists—who are not pledged to any specific candidate based on the outcomes of their state's primary or caucus. They can support any candidate they choose and can announce their support before any primaries or caucuses have taken place. This can give a candidate the appearance of a formidable lead in the race.

Political Scientists Debate the Power of Parties to Choose the Nominees

In 2008, in the influential book *The Party Decides*, four political scientists argued that party leaders serve as powerful gatekeepers. The parties—whom the political scientists defined not just as senior party officials but the organized advocacy and interest groups that make them up—"scrutinize and winnow the field before voters get involved, attempt to build coalitions behind a single preferred candidate, and sway voters to ratify their choice."[18]

Parties have strong incentives to try to steer the nomination process toward selecting the most "electable" candidates in the general election. At times, however, voters may feel disconnected from their parties and party leaders, feeling that they are not getting the message about what issues matter and what should be done about them.

Voters who identify with a party have a few options if this happens. They can defect and vote for a candidate from another party—uncommon but possible. They might not turn out to vote, which is a very real but not new worry for both major parties in 2020.

Disaffected party members may also use the primaries and caucuses to try to impose their vision of the party's proper focus on its leaders, by choosing nominees other than the party establishment's preferred options. Who wins this showdown? In both 2016 and 2020, there were more than a few Bernie Sanders supporters who would argue that the Democratic Party did, in fact, decide, and they were not happy about it. What that might mean for turnout in 2020 was a major concern for Democratic leaders heading into the elections.

Political Polarization, Gridlock, and Two-Party Dominance Are the Defining Features of Parties in Government Today

If they have been successful in mobilizing citizens to vote for the candidates they have selected and supported, a party's members take office and begin the process of governing. This usually means they attempt to enact their **party platform**, a declaration of the party's general stance on issues and the policies that its members will pursue. Party members write, argue over, and agree on the platform during presidential nomination conventions.

Polarization Leads to Gridlock in American Governance.

Although Americans often say they want politicians to compromise, some experts have found that, in reality, they generally prefer the other side to accede to their wishes. As one scholar of political beliefs stated, "Few people march under a banner that says, 'We may be right, we may be wrong, let's compromise!' You know, that's not good politics."[19]

In general, the parties try to make their case to the public by offering sharp contrasts to each other. Both the Republican and Democratic National Committees constantly put out news releases, videos, tweets, and other social media presentations that seek to further a single larger point: The other side is wrong. In this sense, both parties have a partisan agenda: They are less interested in fostering cooperation than they are in criticizing their opponents.

The pressures that parties face to point out sharp differences between their positions and those of the opposition have led to increasing **political polarization**. Polarization isn't the result of a flaw in our constitutional system, but the Constitution's separation of powers has made it worse. In Washington, increased polarization has led to **gridlock**, which occurs when parties are unable to find any common ground to work together, an increasingly common occurrence over the past few decades.

An ongoing debate among political scientists who study American political parties and elections has been about the sources of partisan polarization in Congress. It used to be common for bills to pass with bipartisan support. Members of Congress are increasingly voting with members of their own party. Why? It is not clear if this trend represents an increasingly polarized environment among political elites, political masses, or both, or if some other factor or factors are at play.[20]

While the Landscape of Parties in Government Has Changed, It Has Historically Been Dominated by Two Major Parties. Almost since the moment the nation was founded, the political establishment has been divided between two political parties. For about the past 150 years, these have been the Democratic or Republican Party. Since then, control of government has shifted back and forth between the parties in periods of **realignment**, which occur when public support shifts substantially from one party to the other. Periods of realignment may be ushered in by **critical elections** (or critical eras), which are followed by periods of stability.[21] Political scientists call the more or less stable eras **party systems**. They often divide American political history into six party systems.

America's Early Party Systems Introduce Two-Party Competition and National Campaigns. America's first president, George Washington, was not a member of a political party and indeed had warned the nation about the dangers partisanship posed to the young Republic. However, during his tenure, Washington's administration split into two factions: those supporting a strong federal government and those who believed that individual states should be given more authority over their own affairs. These groups coalesced into two parties: the Democratic-Republicans (Jefferson and Madison) and the Federalists (Adams and Hamilton), signaling the first party system.

The Democratic-Republican Party had largely dissolved by 1824, with many of its members moving to form what became known as the Whig Party. Due to the granting of suffrage to large numbers of white men who had previously been excluded because of their lack of wealth or property, this era saw the rise of the Democratic Party at the expense of the Federalists. The election of Democrat Andrew Jackson as president in 1828 marked the start of the second party system.

Slavery and the Civil War Shape the Democratic and Republican Parties. The unresolved issue of slavery led to the third party system, with both parties divided internally. The new Republican Party stressed a belief in the potential of the individual Whig free-market principles and argued against slavery on moral grounds.[22] The Democratic Party became a primarily regional party, strong in the South and protective of slavery.

During the fourth party system, Democrats and Republicans continued to dominate. Slavery had ended, but the two parties were divided by the politics of Reconstruction and differences of opinion about how strongly the federal government should act to secure civil rights.

Democratic Party Dominance Emerges from the Great Depression. In 1932, the Great Depression and the New Deal that followed ushered in the fifth party system. The election of Franklin Roosevelt in 1932 and in three subsequent elections led to a period of Democratic Party dominance. Between 1930 and 1994, the Democrats held a majority in the House for all but four years.[23]

The Current Party System Is Marked by Partisanship and Gridlock.
The sixth party system has defined party politics for the past fifty years. The Democratic Party has remained focused on a vigorous federal government in the service of securing civil rights and support for affirmative action and a woman's right to choose. Republicans have remained focused on a smaller federal government, advocating conservative policies on social issues, lower taxes, and fewer restrictions on American businesses. What changed were the coalitions of voters supporting the parties, especially with regard to the geography of partisan support in the nation. Much of this had been driven by the realignment of large numbers of southern white voters from the Democratic Party to the Republican Party during the civil rights era.

The sixth party system has been one of the longest in the nation's history. The Democratic and Republican Parties are trying to stay relevant in an age of intense and increasing polarization. That polarization has led some voters to become engaged not just because they support their party but out of an intense dislike of the other side. It remains to be seen what this means for the parties, particularly when combined with changing demographics, particularly the rising number of Latina and Latino Americans.

America's Electoral System Leads to Two-Party Dominance.
There is no law requiring that American national politics be dominated by two major political parties. Other countries have one, two, or many political parties, or none at all, dominating national politics, with more than two being the norm. With a few very important exceptions, a two-party system has been dominant for most of America's political history. Why?

To explain America's two-party dominance, scholars usually point to the standard U.S. method of voting—a **single-member plurality system** in which voters have a single vote for one candidate and the candidate with the most votes wins. Other countries have **proportional representation systems**. Although there are many differences between nations in the details, proportional representation systems award party representation in legislative bodies based upon percentage of votes overall, which makes it easier for small or new parties to capture a few seats in the legislature.

The winner-take-all system allows the largest politically cohesive groups—the Democrats or Republicans—to elect almost every office in a jurisdiction. Proponents of the system say this promotes stability; if people are happy with the job that a representative from one of those parties is doing, they can keep voting for that representative's party even after they leave office.

Critics say it doesn't do much to help people who are stuck in an area in which one party dominates, such as Republicans in cities and Democrats in rural states. They say that this can be a significant barrier to encouraging greater numbers of people, including minority groups and young people, to take part in politics. Instead, candidates can run divisive campaigns aimed at turning out only the most partisan voters, since the winner-take-all system provides little incentive to reach out to opponents.

Minor Parties May Challenge the Two Major Parties. The Democratic and Republican Parties have occasionally had some competition. Candidates from a **third party (minor party)** usually focus on a single issue that they don't think the major parties are emphasizing enough.

Third-party candidates do sometimes make fairly big splashes. In the 2000 election, consumer activist Ralph Nader captivated many liberals when he ran for president under the Green Party banner. He won 2.74 percent of the popular vote—just enough, many Democrats continue to believe, to deny the presidency to Al Gore.[24] The tendency among some voters to conclude that a vote for a third-party candidate is a vote wasted, essentially helping someone they oppose, has made it difficult for third-party candidates to win national elections.

Although increasing numbers of Americans support the idea of more viable and competitive third parties, the Democratic and Republican Parties have worked to discourage third-party candidacies by making it difficult for them to qualify for presidential debates or to appear on ballots.

The Rules Governing National Elections Shape the Transmission of Americans' Preferences into Laws and Policies

8.3 Understand the rules and institutions that structure national elections.

Because of American federalism, and the provision in the Constitution that requires states, and not the federal government, to set most of the rules for elections, there are significant differences between states on electoral rules. In most states, for example, a candidate needs a **plurality** of votes, meaning that to win the candidate must receive more votes than any other candidate. In other states, a candidate needs a **majority** of votes, meaning more than 50 percent, which may lead to a **runoff election** between the two with the highest total if no one candidate scores a majority.

In Congressional Elections, Constituency Is Key

At the most basic level, the rules governing the division of voters into **constituencies**—bodies of voters in a given area who elect a representative or senator—are laid out in the Constitution. However, the process of this division, especially for the House of Representatives, is often controversial. Even the Supreme Court has had to weigh in on the process in the past.

Senators Represent Their Entire States. The size of the Senate depends only on the number of states in the Union, since two senators represent each state. Since the admission of Hawaii as the fiftieth state in 1959, therefore, the Senate has been composed of one hundred members, each representing the entire state from which they were elected. Because the Senate was divided into three "classes" in order to stagger the elections of senators, no two Senate seats from the same state will be up for grabs in the same election unless a retirement or other event has opened up one of the seats ahead of schedule.

Members of the House Represent Their Districts. In spite of the potential repercussions of equal state representation in the Senate, determining one's potential constituents is a very simple matter for that chamber. When it comes to the House of Representatives, however, things are a bit more complicated—and political.

While initially the size of the House was allowed to grow with the population, it is now fixed at 435 members.[25] The size of a state's representation in the House depends upon its population. The process of determining the number of representatives for each state is called **apportionment**; through this process, the number of representatives is allocated based on the results of the census that is conducted every ten years. As part of the process of apportionment, each state is divided into one or more congressional districts, with one seat in the House representing each district and each state guaranteed one representative, no matter how small its population.

Given that the size of the House is capped, changes in population can produce "winners and losers" among the states following each census (see Figure 8.1). Trends in population growth and distribution in recent decades have produced a clear pattern of gains in House seats for states in the South and the West and losses for states in the Northeast and Midwest.

Redistricting and Gerrymandering Shape Constituencies and Elections in House Races

While the process of apportionment has important consequences for the representation of states in the House, it also has important consequences for the boundaries of constituency. Following each census (and occasionally more often), states enter into the process of **redistricting**, meaning they redraw the electoral district boundaries. Seven states have only one representative; therefore, their district boundaries are the same as the boundaries of the state (though this could, of course, change if these states grow or others shrink).

The stakes involved in redistricting are high, and the process is often very political and controversial. The intentional use of redistricting to benefit a specific interest or group of voters is referred to as **gerrymandering**.

Partisan Gerrymandering Involves Strategic Calculations. Partisan gerrymandering aims to increase the representation of one political party at the expense of another. The idea is to concentrate the opposing party's supporters in a small number

Apportionment Gains and Losses after the 2010 Census

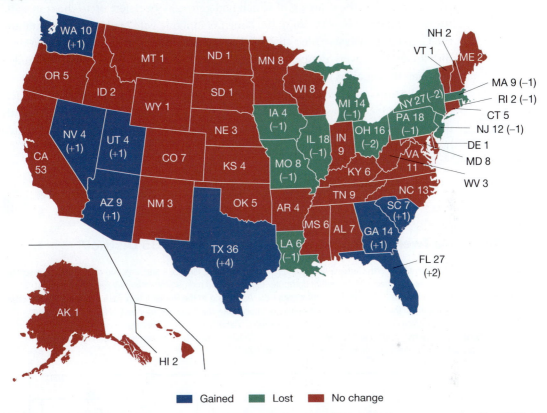

Gained | Lost | No change

Source: U.S. Census Bureau, "Congressional Apportionment," November 2011, https://www.census.gov/prod/cen2010/briefs/c2010br-08.pdf.

Note: Numbers to the right of the state names show the total number of representatives allocated to the state. Numbers in parentheses show the change as either a gain (+) or a loss (–).

of districts, which that party will win easily. By doing so, the party in charge of redistricting is able to "waste" many of the votes of its opposition, since there is no more of an advantage—in terms of the number of House seats a party has—to winning 90 percent of the votes in any one district than there is to winning 55 percent. The party in control then tries to maximize the number of districts that its candidates will win comfortably but not by huge margins.

Racial and Ethnic Gerrymandering Aims to Increase Minority Representation.

A second form of gerrymandering aims to increase the likelihood of electing members of racial and ethnic minorities as representatives by concentrating voters of minority ethnicity within specific congressional districts. Racial and ethnic gerrymandering results in **majority-minority districts** in which voters of *minority* ethnicity constitute an electoral *majority* within the electoral district.

The Supreme Court Continues to Weigh in on Gerrymandering. In recent decades, the Supreme Court has become more active in ruling on congressional district boundaries, the drawing of which had generally been left up to the states and the political process. Affirming the "one person, one vote" rule of representation, the Court in two cases ruled that **malapportionment**—where the population is distributed in uneven numbers between legislative districts—is unconstitutional as it violates the equal protection clause of the Fourteenth Amendment.[26]

While the Court has highlighted potential problems with partisan gerrymandering in several recent cases, it has not gone so far as to declare the practice inherently unconstitutional. The Court has held that voters in these districts are still represented but by members from different political parties. See Figure 8.2.

▼ FIGURE 8.2

North Carolina's Twelfth Congressional District: The "I-85 District"

The Twelfth Congressional District in North Carolina was put in place for the 1992 elections and was one of the primary districts at issue in *Shaw v. Reno*. It was designed with the aid of computer technology to merge predominantly African American communities. The narrow parts of the district followed Interstate I-85. According to the Redistricting Task Force for the National Conference of State Legislatures, "the laboratory that made this birth possible was the computer technology that became available for the 1990s redistricting cycle. The progeny won no Beautiful Baby contests. A *Wall Street Journal* editorial described the 12th as 'political pornography.' Known as the 'I-85 district,' the 12th stretched 160 miles across the central Piedmont region of the State, for part of its length no wider than the freeway right-of-way."

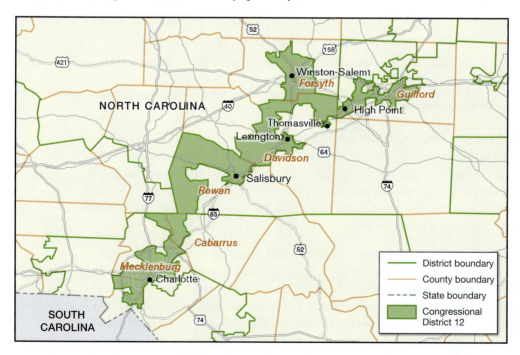

WHAT ARE WE REALLY HOPING TO ACHIEVE IN DRAWING DISTRICT BOUNDARIES?

Political battles over redistricting, intentional efforts to redraw district boundaries in order to increase representation for Americans of color, and Supreme Court wrangling over these efforts all illustrate that House district boundaries matter a great deal to electoral outcomes. As it is now, the "several states," as the Framers would have put it, employ a political and policy hodgepodge in their policies governing redistricting. State legislatures have the final say in the majority of states, but even they vary on whether or not the governor can veto the plan. Some states involve many actors in the map-drawing effort—elected and appointed officials for sure, but in some states members of the public are also allowed to weigh in. It's often very messy.

Rather than having district boundaries be drawn as a result of political battles, what if we added a bit more intentionality to the process by deciding *first* what the goals of the redistricting process should be and *then* establishing the rules for it? While handing control of the redistricting process over to computers is not on the table, thinking about what those boundaries would look like if different criteria were employed is a very useful exercise. That is precisely what the reporters and analysts for the political (and sometimes sports and logic puzzle) website FiveThirtyEight did with "The Gerrymandering Project."[27]

Key to their analysis was examining how different redistricting goals would impact how competitive the races were between Democrats and Republicans. To measure competitiveness, they used the Cook Report's "Partisan Voter Index," which compares how a district has voted compared to the national average in the most recent two presidential elections, to divide the districts into three groups: usually Democratic, highly competitive, and usually Republican.[28]"

That current district boundaries are messy and often driven by politics rather than democratic ideals is a given. So is the fact that gerrymandering has led to a patchwork of often oddly-shaped House districts. The problem, according to the analysts at *FiveThirtyEight* (and many others) is that fixing all of this requires more than just better maps. It involves decisions over priorities and goals, decisions that are inherently contested. It is more than a geometry problem; it is one of priorities.

Figure 8-A (below) represents the current state of affairs in terms of party competitiveness in House districts. In districts labelled "highly competitive" candidates from each of the two major parties have at least a one in six chance of winning the election.

▼ FIGURE 8-A

USUALLY DEM. DISTRICTS	HIGHLY COMPETITIVE	USUALLY REPUBLICAN
168	72	195

As is evident in Figure 8-A, most House districts—as currently drawn—are not competitive. In only 72 of the 435 House districts do candidates from the minority party

(Continued)

(Continued)

in that district (whether Democrat or Republican) have at least a one in six chance of winning there. Moreover, those odds (of roughly 17 percent) for minority-party candidates in competitive districts represent a generous (though analytically-valid) definition of "highly competitive." If one were to set the bar higher—say minority party candidates have a 40 percent chance of winning—then the number of highly competitive districts would shrink considerably.

So how much better could we do if we intentionally tried to maximize competitiveness? The analysts at *FiveThirtyEight* used their algorithms and simulations to draw district boundaries in order to maximize district competitiveness, that is, to give as many voters as possible a chance, or at least belief, that their vote might matter, even if their political party is in the minority among district voters (Figure 8-B).

▼ FIGURE 8-B

USUALLY DEM. DISTRICTS	HIGHLY COMPETITIVE	USUALLY REPUBLICAN
94	242	99

According to these simulations, it is possible to maximize competitiveness. In this scenario, 242 House districts become highly competitive. An interesting side effect, if one thinks about national competitiveness, is that Democrat and Republican districts are more evenly balanced, with 94 districts "usually" voting for a Democratic House candidate and 99 districts for a Republican.

Finally, a third option might be to draw the boundaries as *compactly* as possible, avoiding the uneven shapes that have been the subject of criticism, such as the North Carolina district that came under scrutiny in *Shaw v. Reno*. Figure 8-C, below, displays the simulated results when district compactness is the guiding principle in redistricting.

▼ FIGURE 8-C

USUALLY DEM. DISTRICTS	HIGHLY COMPETITIVE	USUALLY REPUBLICAN
155	99	181

According to the results of this simulation, even geometry is better than politics and the status quo when it comes to district competitiveness. Maximizing the compactness of district boundaries would also result in an increase in highly competitive districts, though far less than when the goal is to maximize competitiveness directly.

WHAT Do You Think?

The creators of the Gerrymandering Project simulated a few other goals as well. Without (or before) going over to their site, think of a few possible alternative goals. Why are these worthwhile objectives? How do you think drawing districts lines with these goals would affect competitiveness?

The Court has also weighed in on the proper role of racial and ethnic considerations in drawing district boundaries—most recently ruling that states are allowed to use race as a consideration but not as the predominant factor in drawing district boundaries.[29]

In 2020, state elections promised to shape district boundaries and how Americans are represented. While national media focused on the drama and implications of the 2020 national elections (see below), there were many state and local elections with federal implications as well, most notably battles for control over state legislatures. One of the most important outcomes of 2020 state legislative battles would be control over the process of redrawing House district boundaries that would follow the 2020 census. The Constitution requires a census of the population every 10 years, which is then used to reapportion the 435 seats in the House. In the 2010 national elections, after the last census, Republicans gained control of a majority of state legislatures, a majority they had held onto ever since. Victorious state Republican parties successfully used that power to attempt to maximize party representation in Congress.

While we have already examined the ways in which state legislatures are not the only or the final arbiters of House district boundaries, we have also explored how important they are. The fact that the Supreme Court has not declared partisan gerrymandering to be inherently unconstitutional all but ensures that each party—should it find itself in control of a state undertaking redistricting—will try to shape the process in order to strengthen the party's representation and influence in Congress going forward. As we have just explored, the power of partisan gerrymandering is not absolute and is still subject to judicial review. The Supreme Court may examine new state redistricting plans, evaluating whether or not the boundaries that they create violate the voting rights of African Americans, the constitutional requirement that House districts be roughly equally apportioned in terms of population, or other rights of Americans to be equally represented in Congress.

One of the most consequential outcomes of the 2010 elections was the subsequent redrawing of House district boundaries in North Carolina, Texas, and Wisconsin, which increased Republican party representation in Congress in three states whose electorates had been moving toward the Democratic party. Following 2010, Democratic party leaders had come under sharp criticism for failing to attend to the importance of state legislative elections, especially those following the decennial census. Insufficient devotion of resources to state elections was cited as the primary failing. Riding a Democratic wave against Donald Trump, in 2018 Democrats regained control over eight state legislatures that had been held by Republicans and aimed to use their new majorities to correct the failings of 2010. In 2020, neither party would ignore state legislative races and their potential impact on control of the House going forward, impacts that would outlast many of the other consequences of the 2020 elections for American politics and public policy for years.

Congressional Incumbents Have Significant Institutional Advantages

Political scientist David Mayhew explained the strategic logic of incumbents and how they use their institutional advantages to maximize their chances of reelection. For Mayhew, legislators are "single-minded seekers of re-election" who make the most of their institutional advantages.[30] These advantages include the free use of the mail for communication with constituents. Incumbents also usually enjoy higher levels of name recognition than their challengers, which is increased by more media coverage than that available to most potential challengers. In that media coverage and at public events, incumbents claim credit for what they have done in Washington and announce their positions on key pieces of legislation of interest to their constituents.[31] Finally, incumbents perform casework for individual constituents, especially in helping them deal with the federal and state bureaucracy.

All of this adds up to a substantial **incumbency advantage**, which has only grown stronger in recent decades. The vast majority of congressional incumbents who seek reelection succeed. Incumbent senators and members of the House have reelection rates of 80 to 90 percent.[32]

If incumbents are usually in no danger, then why do they spend so much time and energy trying to secure reelection? Incumbents maximize their resources to try to ensure that they will not face qualified challengers. Knowing the odds, credible challengers often wait for their chance to run for an open seat where there is no incumbent to face.

Presidential Elections Have Many Stages and Moving Parts

Presidential elections, like congressional campaigns, have two official campaign phases: the nomination campaign, in which candidates try to secure the nomination of their political party, and the general election campaign, in which successful nominees compete for the presidency.

Candidates Lay the Foundations for Their Campaigns Long before Formal Nomination. Nomination campaigns begin long before the actual events at which the nominees are picked. Presidential hopefuls may work on laying the foundations for their bids years before the official process begins. They begin raising money and set up an **exploratory committee**, which allows a potential candidate to "test the waters," to travel around the country, conduct public opinion polls, make outreach phone calls, and raise money to pay for all of this. If a candidate decides to press ahead, their campaign will become official, a status that can be triggered through a potential candidate's statements and fundraising or other activities.

Candidates Try to Secure Their Party's Nomination. Once the official campaign process kicks off, declared candidates vie with others in their own party for that party's nomination. While many of the rules governing the nomination process are set by federal and state laws, most of the details about *how* things actually work are hammered out by the parties themselves. Key differences exist across states and between the parties themselves. As we discussed earlier in the chapter, most states hold presidential primary elections in which a state's voters choose delegates who support a particular candidate. The concluding phase of the nomination process takes place at the national conventions held by each party late in the summer of the presidential election year.

Nominees Compete in the General Election. Once selected by their parties, the nominees proceed to the general election campaign. At this point, candidates need to pivot from speaking mainly to their core supporters and begin to try to appeal to independent and undecided voters. This can be a trap. Voters who participate during the nomination campaigns trend toward the wings of their parties, but there are not often enough of them to win a general election.

The Rules of the Electoral College Decide the Presidency.

The dynamics of the Electoral College system present another significant challenge. Technically speaking, American voters do not vote for the president. Instead, they vote for a slate of electors pledged to vote for a nominee in the presidential election. These electors are chosen by party leaders within their respective states in a system called the **Electoral College**. It is their vote that actually chooses the president.

From left, Democratic presidential candidates Sen. Amy Klobuchar (D-MN), Sen. Cory Booker (D-NJ), South Bend mayor Pete Buttigieg, Sen. Bernie Sanders (I-VT), former vice president Joe Biden, Sen. Elizabeth Warren (D-MA), Sen. Kamala Harris (D-CA), entrepreneur Andrew Yang, former Texas representative Beto O'Rourke, and former Housing and Urban Development secretary Julián Castro participate in a Democratic primary debate in Texas in September 2019.
AP Photo/Eric Gay

Presidential candidates need to obtain 270 Electoral College votes to win. Each of the fifty states is allocated one electoral vote for each of its two senators and one for each of its members of the House of Representatives, guaranteeing each state at least three electoral votes. Adding the three electoral votes allocated to the District of Columbia brings the total to 538. In all but two states, Maine and Nebraska, electoral votes are awarded in a winner-take-all system. In those states, the nominee who wins the popular vote in the state receives two electoral votes; the remaining electoral votes may be split, with one going to the winner of the popular vote in each congressional district.

This system has significant consequences. Given that all but two states award their electoral votes in a block, candidates tend to focus their campaigns on states with a large number of electoral votes and those whose electoral votes seem to be in play, largely ignoring other states. A presidential candidate can win the presidency without actually winning the popular vote. That can happen when a third-party candidate poses a serious challenge, preventing a candidate from winning a majority of the popular vote even if they win a plurality of it, as was the case in President Bill Clinton's victory in 1992. Another example is when a candidate wins by large margins in some states but loses narrowly in others, racking up large popular vote totals but not enough electoral votes, which happened in 2000 when George W. Bush defeated Al Gore and again in 2016 when Donald Trump defeated Hillary Clinton.

Regulating Campaign Spending Has Proved Tricky

The basic challenge of using national policy to regulate campaign spending involves a philosophical question: Is money speech? In other words, is a person's financial contribution to a campaign a form of political expression? If so, then the First Amendment puts some serious brakes on government's ability to restrain and regulate it. Activists, the Supreme Court, and the federal government have long struggled to define and enact proper limits of regulation.

The Federal Election Commission (FEC) is a bureaucratic entity charged with overseeing and implementing national campaign finance laws. Federal law also requires the disclosure of the source of campaign funds, places limits on campaign contributions, and provides public financing for presidential elections. In 1976, in *Buckley v. Valeo*, the Supreme Court upheld the constitutionality of restrictions on campaign contributions by individuals, though not on monies spent independently, monies spent by the candidates themselves, or the total amount of contributions.[33]

When it comes to money and elections, however, controlling the influence of money has often been like handling a balloon—squeeze it in one place and it seems to pop up somewhere else. In 2002, in an effort to more effectively control the balloon, Congress passed the Bipartisan Campaign Reform Act (BCRA), which placed stricter limits on campaign contributions. In *Citizens United v. Federal Election Commission* (2010), in a divided 5–4 decision, the Supreme Court struck down portions of the BCRA, ruling that independent, uncoordinated political contributions by corporations during political campaigns is protected by the First Amendment.[34]

The "new world" of campaign finance in the United States is thorny. Although limits on individual campaign donations remain in place, groups of individuals may contribute, but the rules are complicated. **Political action committees (PACs)** may contribute higher dollar amounts than individuals, though, again, there are limits. In the wake of *Citizens United*, so-called **super PACs** are allowed to spend unlimited amounts on a political campaign; however, that spending must not be coordinated with that campaign.

Political Participation Can Take Many Forms

8.4   Describe the traditional and nontraditional forms of political participation in American representative democracy.

While Americans often equate political participation with voting, and for good reason, casting a ballot is only one of many forms that political participation can take. While voting serves to choose elected representatives, other forms of participation may serve to influence the choices of those in office and the attitudes and actions of other citizens.

In their foundational study of American political participation, Sidney Verba and Norman H. Nie sorted acts of political engagement into four categories: (1) voting, (2) supporting or participating in political campaigns, (3) contacting or pressuring

Categories of Political Participation

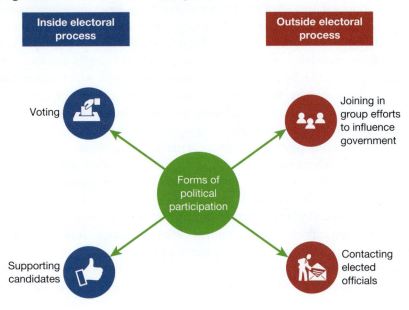

politicians in office, and (4) volunteering or organizing in concert with fellow citizens.[35] The first two of these forms of participation take place within the electoral process; the second two take place after its outcomes have been determined or are outside of it. (See Figure 8.4.)

In 2020, all four of these pathways are undergoing significant changes. COVID-19 has led to conversations and debates about *how* Americans can or should vote in a time of social distancing. While vote-by-mail and the use of absentee ballots had been expanding prior to the viral outbreak, the possibility of much wider use of vote-by-mail in the 2020 general elections became part of the national conversation. While many leading Democratic Party politicians and candidates called for widespread voting by mail, President Trump and other Republicans pushed back, highlighting the potential for fraud in such a system.

Political participation outside of the traditional electoral process is also changing—partly in response to the pandemic but also in response to broader shifts in society that had already been underway. Individuals have traditionally had a variety of tools with which to initiate contact with their elected representatives. Apart from contacting them directly by phone, mail, or email, individuals may testify at congressional hearings, organize petitions to state or federal lawmakers, or encourage and help others to do so. Again, these connections were under strain in 2020, as opportunities for direct contact with elected representatives were lessened, and avenues for elected officials to receive feedback came under stress.

Finally, the landscape of working together outside of the voting process is also changing. Individuals have at their disposal a diverse set of tools with which to work cooperatively for a shared set of political goals. They may, for example, undertake volunteer work, help to organize members of their community, or work with members of their religious communities. Individuals may join with others in organized interest groups, whose collective efforts may try to change policies from the inside or outside. They may join together by taking part in a social movement, which occurs when a group of people come together to make social and political change and place ideas and issues on the political agenda and make their voices heard. The key question, of course, is how influential individuals acting in concert can be compared to powerful groups with closer connections to the inside of the political process.

Technology is driving significant changes in how Americans reach out to others in order to persuade or mobilize. We will take up what is called digital participation, and how effective it can really be, later in the chapter.

Most fundamentally, when participating in any of the diverse forms of political action, Americans express their commitment to **civic engagement**, which is working to make society better through political and nonpolitical action. While Americans participate at the voting booth at lower rates than individuals in other democracies, their rates of nonelectoral participation are equal to or higher than their counterparts in other nations.[36]

Americans' Civic Engagement Can Be Fluid

While it is useful to consider various forms of civic engagement as distinct from each other—especially since it helps us think about political involvement in ways that do not only include voting—in reality, the process is much more fluid than that. Consider the issue of sexual violence on college campuses, for example. Individuals may undertake any one or more of these various forms of participation and civic engagement. Their involvement might encourage others to do so.

In considering all of this, we also need to think about the flip side: *not acting*. We will explore voting and nonvoting in more detail in the next section. However, it is important to note that individuals may choose to act in one space precisely because they have decided that acting in another space will not lead to real change. Struggles to secure fundamental rights and freedoms have often involved such calculi. The protesters at Standing Rock, for example, acted in part out of frustration with elected federal officials and those agencies under their control.

Parties Strive to Get Voters to Identify with Them

Parties contain more than just elected officials and party leaders. Voters are also part of a political party—at least that is what its leaders are trying to achieve. Parties try to bring in the *electorate*—those who are eligible to vote. They hope to connect with voters (and win their votes) by providing candidates with labels that signal to voters a set of goals, priorities, and policy objectives. This is a powerful informational shortcut for voters, who may know little about the candidates, especially in elections that are not as high-profile as a presidential, gubernatorial, or Senate race.

As we discussed in Chapter 6, *party identification* is the degree to which a person self-identifies with a political party. The parties consciously strive to cultivate, maintain, and expand this connection they have with voters. One of the most important things that parties do is signal that they will advance the agendas associated with a particular set of political beliefs, which is key to their role in providing candidates with labels and voters with cues and shortcuts.

In Chapter 6, we also discussed the concept of *political ideology*, which refers to a person's beliefs about political goals and public policies and acts to shape individual electoral choices. It is important to remember, though, that political ideology and party identification are not the same thing. Individuals' political beliefs, including party identification, have many contributors and sources, including family, education, and life experiences.

In the United States, two political ideologies, liberalism and conservativism, have long dominated. Other ideologies, such as socialism and libertarianism, have fewer adherents. Recall, too, that these ideologies map onto partisan affiliation, with liberals and some socialists identifying with the Democratic Party and conservatives and many libertarians with the Republican Party. However, divisions between socialists and Democrats on one hand, and between libertarians and Republicans on the other, can cause severe frictions *within* the two major parties (see Figure 8.5).

Since the 1980s, more people have identified themselves as Democrats than as Republicans. One frustration for both parties, however, is that increasing numbers of people consistently have not identified with either party.[37] Instead, the percentage of Americans self-identifying as independent has grown sharply. Why? A big part of it is Americans' deep frustration with the inability of the federal government to enact policies. Note, though, that when those who "lean" Democrat or Republican are included in the party identification numbers for the two parties, the observed decline in party support does not look as strong. As we explored in Chapter 7, the wording of the questions asked in public opinion surveys can act to shape our interpretation of the "facts on the ground."

Voters have shown less inclination in recent decades to back candidates of different parties in a single election, a practice known as **split-ticket voting**. Still, Americans have become less attached to political parties in recent years. At the same time, the country has grown increasingly polarized by political ideology. More conservatives hold strongly conservative views than in the past, and more liberals hold strongly liberal views. The party organizations have shouldered much of the blame for creating and fostering an environment in which the two sides seem forever locked in combat. Despite this ongoing battle, the parties haven't become any stronger. According to journalist Jonathan Rauch, "Here is the reigning political paradox of our era: Partisanship is strong, but parties are weak."[38]

Political Ideology: How Democrats and Republicans Differ

Democrat		Republican
Pro-choice	Abortion	Pro-life
Maintain race-based preferences	Affirmative action	Abolish race-based preferences
Protect the rights of the accused	Crime	Punish offenders more strictly
Increase regulation and worker protection	Business	Ease regulation and keep government out of business
Ban	Death penalty	Maintain
Decrease or maintain	Defense spending	Increase
More regulation	Gun control	Protect gun ownership
Maintain or expand the Affordable Care Act	Health care	Repeal the Affordable Care Act
Amnesty for undocumented immigrants, allow undocumented people to obtain driver's licenses	Immigration	Prevent amnesty, no driver's licenses, create a national ID card, add border fences
Increase	Minimum wage	Lower or eliminate
Legalize	Same-sex marriage	Ban
End	School vouchers	Expand
Increase taxes, especially for wealthy	Taxes	Cut taxes, especially for businesses

Liberalism — Conservatism

The Decision to Vote or Not Vote Involves Many Factors

When Americans consider the concept of political participation, they often think about voting—and for many good reasons. Participation in the electoral process is an essential component of a representative democracy. Voting gives expression to individuals' voices and serves to hold elected representatives accountable for their promises and actions. It is foundational to what James Madison called the "democratic remedy" to the dangers of faction and the tyranny of the minority that we examined in Chapter 2.

The fact, however, is that large percentages of Americans do not vote. In 2016, a presidential election year, only an estimated 58 percent of eligible voters showed up at the polls, placing the United States near the bottom of democratic nations in terms of **voter turnout**. Turnout in midterm elections is often even lower.

Americans' relative lack of voting participation raises two immediate questions: Why? And does it matter?

For political scientist Anthony Downs, writing in 1957, the decision not to vote might very well be a rational one, given the costs of voting in terms of an individual's time and intellectual effort and the infinitesimally small probability that any one vote will prove to be decisive, especially in national elections. If all potential voters make a rational calculation not to vote, however, then the mechanism of representation would fall apart.

Individual Factors Shape Electoral Participation

Many factors shape a person's decision to vote or not. Some contributors to voter turnout are institutional, shaped by the laws and procedures surrounding the electoral process. Others depend upon the particulars of an election—for example, whether or not it takes place during a presidential election year. A third category of contributors centers on the potential voters themselves, their characteristics and lived experiences. Political scientists count a set of individual factors as among the most important determinants for voting: economic status, level of education, age, race or ethnicity, sex, and partisan attachment.

Socioeconomic Status and Educational Attainment. Voting is costly. It takes time, commitment, and intellectual engagement. Not all voting-eligible Americans have the same resources with which to engage in the process of voting.[39] A key factor in voter turnout is an individual's **socioeconomic status (SES)**, which is a measure of an individual's wealth, income, occupation, and educational attainment. A clear and consistent pattern in electoral participation is that Americans with higher SES participate in electoral activities at higher rates. There are several reasons for this, but there are two key ideas. The first is that individuals with higher SES may be more incentivized to vote. Those with more financially at stake in a given election may be more inclined to participate.

The second key reason that people with higher SES are more likely to participate in the electoral process is that having a high SES lowers the barriers to voting. A core contributor to the measure of an individual's SES is the person's level of educational attainment. Not only are higher levels of educational attainment associated with higher incomes but they also reduce the "costs" of voting, in the sense of making it easier to navigate the issues involved in an election and the process of becoming a voter itself.

Education also plays a role in shaping how individuals think about themselves as political actors and potential voters. The intellectual resources and skills that higher levels of education produce also increase an individual's sense of **political efficacy**, or one's confidence that they can make effective political change.

Age. Another trend is also clear: Young adult voting-eligible Americans vote at lower rates than members of older generations (see Figure 8.6).[40] Why? Again, like income and education, age is connected to many other factors. Older Americans are more likely to have higher levels of income and wealth. Other factors may be the twin challenges of learning about voter registration requirements and meeting them, especially if the young adult voter is in college or has recently moved to a new state.

Racial and Ethnic Identities. The turnout of voting-age Americans is also highly correlated with racial and ethnic identity (see Figure 8.7), which, again, is often connected to SES. Latina and Latino American turnout rates lag far behind those of Americans with other racial and ethnic identities. While some Latina and Latino Americans are undocumented immigrants and therefore ineligible to vote,

Historical Patterns of Voter Turnout by Age

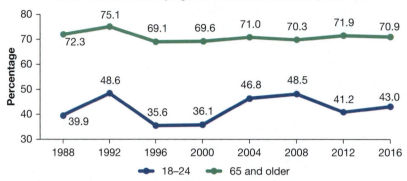

Voter Turnout Rates by Age in Presidential Elections, 1988–2016

Source: Pew Research Center, "Six Take-Aways from the Census Bureau's Voting Report," May 2013, http://www.pewresearch.org/fact-tank/2013/05/08/six-take-awaysfrom-the-census-bureaus-voting-report/; U.S. Census Bureau, "Voting and Registration in the Election of November 2016," May 2017, https://www.census.gov/data/tables/time-series/demo/voting-and-registration/p20-580.html.

Note: Data for those ages twenty-five to sixty-four not shown.

American Voter Turnout in Midterm Elections by Racial and Ethnic Identity

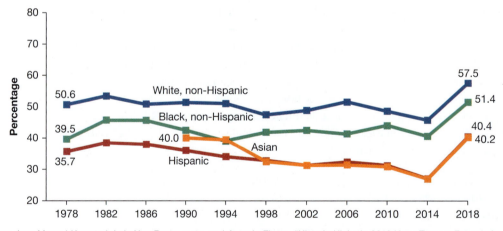

Source: Jens Manuel Krogstad, Luis Noe-Bustamante, and Antonio Flores, "Historic Highs in 2018 Voter Turnout Extended across Racial and Ethnic Groups," Pew Research Center, May 1, 2019, https://www.pewresearch.org/fact-tank/2019/05/01/historic-highs-in-2018-voter-turnout-extended-across-racial-and-ethnic-groups/..

they are also as a group younger, and, as we have discussed, younger voting-eligible Americans vote in far fewer numbers than their older counterparts.

Gender. Since the presidential election of 1980, women have voted at a slightly higher rate than men—typically a difference of a few percentage points.[41] The differences between men's and women's modern voting patterns hold true across racial and ethnic identities, with the largest percentage difference between Black men and women.

Partisan Attachment. Individuals with strong attachment to a political party are more likely to vote than those without one.[42] Efforts by members of American political parties to turn out the vote matter as well, and individuals with strong partisan attachment may find themselves more likely to be on the receiving end of party activities. **Political mobilization**, such as efforts to "get out the vote" (GOTV), can be decisive in an election.

Legal and Institutional Factors Enable and Constrain Voter Turnout

Other factors that affect voter turnout are systemic or institutional. Since the ratification of the Twenty-Sixth Amendment to the Constitution in 1971, all American citizens eighteen years old or older have been guaranteed the right of **suffrage**. The practical exercise of this basic right, however, is complicated. As noted previously, undocumented American immigrants are not granted the right of suffrage, and, in most states, otherwise eligible voters who have been convicted of felonies are also denied the right to vote, either temporarily or permanently, in what is called **felon disenfranchisement**.

State **registration requirements** may also help or hinder the ability of voting-age Americans to participate in the electoral process. Voting actually involves two actions. The second is the casting of a ballot on Election Day. But the first is the act of registering to vote. In some states, a voter may register on Election Day. In most states, however, would-be voters need to register prior to the election, often as many as thirty days before; otherwise they will not be allowed to vote.[43]

In addition, in order to register to vote, Americans need to show identification and/or proof of residency in their state. As of 2020, seven states require a photo identification in order to vote.[44] Others require another form of documentation of residency, such as a lease or utility bill, and some accept a vouching of residency by another registered voter. Even in states that allow same-day registration, however, residency requirements may serve to disenfranchise certain Americans, such as the homeless.

The scheduling of national presidential and congressional elections, by tradition held on the first Tuesday after the first Monday of November, may also serve to discourage participation, as work schedules may make it more challenging for some Americans to make it to the polling place. Although states are increasingly allowing voters to cast **absentee ballots**, some reformers have proposed that national elections be held on weekends or that Election Day be declared a national holiday.

Finally, some advocates of electoral reform have focused on the process of registration itself. In contrast to most modern representative democracies, in the United

States there is no governmental action to register voters automatically. The National Voter Registration Act of 1993, commonly called the **motor voter law**, tried to make voter registration less difficult by allowing Americans to register to vote when applying for or renewing their driver's licenses and making it easier for Americans with disabilities to register to vote. As of 2020, thirty-nine states and the District of Columbia had established systems of online voter registration.[45]

#MeToo Highlights the Possibilities and Challenges of Digital Political Participation

It began with listening.

In 1997, Tarana Burke—at the time "a youth worker, dealing with predominately Black children and children of color"—was approached by a young woman, Heaven, who shared with Burke heartbreaking stories of sexual abuse at the hands of her mother's boyfriend.[46] At the time, Ms. Burke later recalled, the young woman's story was so upsetting that Ms. Burke was overwhelmed and felt powerless to help.

That would change. Burke continued to work on behalf of young women of color, focusing on empowerment and social and political change and continuing to listen. Ten years later, she founded a nonprofit organization, Just Be Inc., devoted to helping survivors of sexual assault and harassment. She also "gave her movement a name: Me Too."[47]

In 2017, actress Alyssa Milano used the hashtag #MeToo on Twitter after reading about allegations of sexual assault by powerful Hollywood film producer Harvey Weinstein. "Suggested by a friend," Milano tweeted, "if all the women who have been sexually harassed or assaulted wrote 'Me too.' as a status, we might give people a sense of the magnitude of the problem."[48] Within a year, the hashtag had been used nineteen million times, more than fifty-five thousand times per day.[49] While Milano credited Tarana Burke with originating the term, its use by white women, especially powerful white women, led some feminists of color to question whether #MeToo was truly inclusive, or if "#MeToo [was] a white women's movement?"[50]

Tarana Burke began using the phrase "Me Too" in her work with survivors of sexual assault and harassment. It was catapulted into the public consciousness as the many allegations against Hollywood producer Harvey Weinstein came to light in 2017. Burke told the story at an event at Calvary Episcopal Church in Pittsburgh in 2018.

Stephanie Strasburg/*Pittsburgh Post-Gazette* via AP

In its use of information sharing through social media in the effort to bring about political change, #MeToo is perhaps the most widely known example of **digital participation**, in which users of social media and other Internet-based platforms strive to use these tools and the interconnectivity that they facilitate in order to make political change.

Scholars Debate the Differences between Digital and Traditional Political Participation.

#MeToo raised public awareness of sexual assault and harassment and highlighted the need to educate, investigate, and act. However, many questions about the impact of participation in politics through social media remain, both in terms of #MeToo specifically and digital participation in general. While it takes time for research to catch up to new and evolving trends, such as political participation through social media, scholars are increasingly examining the ways in which digital participation is, or is not, different from other, more traditional forms.

First, online participation may be more continuous than more traditional forms of political participation. Elections, for example, are relatively discrete events, and they structure participation accordingly. For example, knocking on doors or making phone calls to inform voters of a candidate or issue, or to sway voters' minds, often happens in the context of an upcoming election, and then drops off after the election is over.[51] Digital participation, in contrast, may be more like an "ongoing campaign," which may draw heightened attention during a given election but may be less bound to specific events.[52]

Second, digital participation is often less costly than other forms of political engagement, especially in terms of the investment of time required. Social media use offers individuals a chance to participate in politics and try to shape political debates in ways that may take less time and effort than, say, volunteering on a political campaign. Does the fact that it is often easier to act online necessarily mean that it is less effective? Scholars continue to debate this question.

Immediacy and Interactivity Bring Conversations into Politics, and Politics into Conversations.

As is the case with other forms of media today, politics—and sharp and heated political divides—are strongly present in social media debates and conversations. More concerning, though, significant percentages of social media users appear to be unhappy with how those conversations are going, reporting that they are "worn out" by political content and are stressed out and frustrated in conversations on political issues (see Figure 8.8).

The public and often divisive tenor of American political conversations presents particular opportunities as well as challenges to digital sharing of stories of surviving sexual assault and harassment. Scholars of what is termed *hashtag feminism* have explored the ways in which the public sharing—and opening to comments—of personal stories of surviving sexual assault and harassment offers survivors the opportunity to share and connect with other survivors. One individual who shared her

Users Are Dissatisfied with Political Discourse in Social Media Outlets

% of social media users who say they . . . about politics on social media

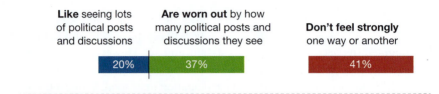

Like seeing lots of political posts and discussions

Are worn out by how many political posts and discussions they see

Don't feel strongly one way or another

20% 37% 41%

When discussing politics on social media with people they disagree with, % of social media users who say these things

They find it to be . . .

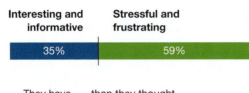

Interesting and informative **Stressful and frustrating**

35% 59%

They have . . . than they thought

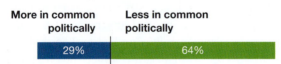

More in common politically **Less in common politically**

29% 64%

Source: Pew Research Center, "The Political Environment on Social Media," October 25, 2016, https://www.pewresearch.org/internet/2016/10/25/the-political-environment-on-social-media/.

experience on #BeenRapedNeverReported highlighted the personal empowerment that resulted from choice to share:

> For me, [sharing] was kind of the strength to say I can report this. And so it gave me the option and the power to actually go through to campus security. . . . I'm not sure if it was because I finally put my name to it [the assault] or because I had seen so many other stories. There was a solidarity with it where I felt comfortable and ready to.[53]

While such sharing can be empowering and build communities of strength, it is also risky. Another survivor interviewed in the study recounted the abusive trolling that the public space of digital sharing made possible:

I've had men be aggressively hostile, abusive and trolling—all unprovoked. I rarely enter into a dialogue, yet have had to block men who deliberately searched keywords and were randomly abusive.[54]

In March 2020, Harvey Weinstein was sentenced to twenty-three years in prison, convicted on one count of committing a criminal sexual act and one count of rape. #MeToo had become part of the national culture and retweeted across the globe. Burke was still listening, but not just to stories of assault and harassment. Now there were also stories of survival and healing.[55]

In 1969, Carol Hanisch penned a memo about the relationship between "therapy and politics" that would be published under the title "The Personal Is Political."[56] In it, Hanisch challenged the assumption that sharing and participation in conversations among feminists were done with the objective of therapy for those who participated. The "patient" in need of a cure was patriarchy—the underlying power structures in society that serve to objectify, silence, and disempower women: "Women are messed over, not messed up! We need to change the objective conditions, not adjust to them."[57] Writing about #MeToo sixty years later, feminist scholar Catharine A. MacKinnon credited the digital sharing in #MeToo and other hashtag movements—themselves "built on decades of collective work against sexual abuse"—with making survivors' experiences unavoidably public and therefore political: "This unprecedented wave of speaking out has begun to erode the two biggest barriers to ending all forms of sexual abuse in law and in life: the disbelief and the trivializing dehumanization of victims."[58] In the realm of social media, the personal may become political in new ways—with old challenges and risks—but, perhaps, also with new tools for changing the politics themselves.

Conclusion: The 2020 Elections

The political direction of the nation is on course to change in 2021. We know that. What we do not yet know is by how much. At the time of this writing (November 19, 2020), enough races had been called to secure victory for Joe Biden, with 306 electoral votes to Donald Trump's 232. President Trump's legal team challenged electoral processes and results in key battleground states; however, the barriers to such a judicial strategy materially altering the outcome were exceedingly high.

Democrats also retained their majority in the House of Representatives, though by a smaller margin than they had before. Control of the Senate remained undecided when the votes were counted in November, and the possibility of unified Democratic control over Congress remained on the table pending early January runoffs in two races, both of them in Georgia. In state legislative and gubernatorial races, the status quo held. Republicans gained one governorship (in Montana) and retained control of a majority of state legislatures heading into the redistricting battles ahead.

While the outcome of the presidential election of 2020 was obviously different from 2016, there were many striking similarities between the two elections. In 2016, fewer than one hundred thousand votes in the Midwest decided the presidency. In 2020, perhaps two or three hundred thousand votes in primarily the same geographic region did the same thing. The landscape of political polarization in the electorate, and the ways in which political institutions such as the Electoral College powerfully shape outcomes, remained.

The tensions within the Democratic Party are not new in 2020 either, nor are they going away. Intra-party negotiation over how strongly to pursue a more progressive political agenda on issues such as climate change and social and economic justice will shape the party's agenda and policies going forward. It will also shape political strategy in Congress, for both parties.

CHAPTER REVIEW

This chapter's main ideas are reflected in the Learning Objectives. By reviewing them here, you should be able to *remember* the key points and *know* these terms that are central to the topic.

8.1 Reflect on the obstacles that insurgent candidates face and the challenges that they present to their party establishments.

Remember . . .
- Political parties help citizens figure out which candidates to vote for, send cues about policy positions, and help translate platforms into policy.
- Bernie Sanders challenged the Democratic Party on progressive liberal ideas in his unsuccessful presidential nomination attempts in 2016 and 2020.

Know . . .
- *campaigns* (p. 221)
- *elections* (p. 221)
- *political participation* (p. 222)
- *political party* (p. 221)

8.2 Identify the roles the political parties play in supporting and nominating candidates for office.

Remember . . .
- Ideally, political parties provide clear positions on issues the parties are strongly committed to, demonstrate internal cohesion both while in power and when in opposition, and have the ability to resist interest group pressure.
- Parties recruit candidates to run for offices at all levels, selecting people who reflect the ideals of the party and who would make strong challengers for office.
- In conjunction with federal and state laws, state parties establish the rules by which their candidates are nominated for the presidency, including what type of primary election process that state will have and when it will be held.
- Parties shape the nomination process by setting rules for how candidates are picked and selecting candidates to run on their tickets.

Know . . .	• *caucus* (p. 228)	• *party systems* (p. 231)
	• *closed primaries* (p. 228)	• *political polarization* (p. 230)
	• *critical elections* (p. 231)	• *presidential primary elections* (p. 228)
	• *delegates* (p. 228)	• *proportional representation systems* (p. 232)
	• *front-loading* (p. 229)	• *realignment* (p. 231)
	• *gridlock* (p. 230)	• *recruitment* (p. 228)
	• *national conventions* (p. 229)	• *responsible party model* (p. 227)
	• *nomination* (p. 228)	• *single-member plurality system* (p. 232)
	• *open primaries* (p. 228)	• *superdelegates* (p. 229)
	• *party platform* (p. 230)	• *third party (minor party)* (p. 233)

8.3 Understand the rules and institutions that structure national elections.

Remember . . .

- In the general election, the system of the Electoral College determines the winner, with states being awarded electoral votes according to their representation in Congress.
- The rules of congressional elections vary by state, and these differences can affect candidate strategies.
- The redrawing of congressional district lines, typically done following a census, can be a very political process in state politics and can have significant electoral consequences.

Know . . .	• *apportionment* (p. 234)	• *majority-minority districts* (p. 235)
	• *constituencies* (p. 233)	• *malapportionment* (p. 236)
	• *Electoral College* (p. 241)	• *plurality* (p. 233)
	• *exploratory committee* (p. 240)	• *political action committees (PACs)* (p. 242)
	• *gerrymandering* (p. 234)	• *redistricting* (p. 234)
	• *incumbency advantage* (p. 240)	• *runoff election* (p. 233)
	• *majority* (p. 233)	• *super PACs* (p. 242)

8.4 Describe the traditional and nontraditional forms of political participation in American representative democracy.

Remember . . .

- Individuals and groups undertake many different kinds of political activities to shape America's laws and public policies. Participating in one way may lead an individual to act in other political spaces as well, or it may shape the behavior of actors in other venues.
- By participating politically, either in traditional or nontraditional ways, Americans express their commitment to civic engagement—to making society better.
- Voter turnout is affected by several factors—some of which are individual-level ones. Other factors that affect voter turnout are not individual but rather systemic or institutional.

Know . . .	• *absentee ballots* (p. 249)	• *political mobilization* (p. 249)
	• *civic engagement* (p. 244)	• *registration requirements* (p. 249)
	• *digital participation* (p. 251)	• *socioeconomic status (SES)* (p. 247)
	• *felon disenfranchisement* (p. 249)	• *split-ticket voting* (p. 245)
	• *motor voter law* (p. 250)	• *suffrage* (p. 249)
	• *political efficacy* (p. 247)	• *voter turnout* (p. 246)

CHAPTER 9

INTEREST GROUPS AND SOCIAL MOVEMENTS

Collective Action, Power, and Representation

More than a decade after the financial crisis of 2008, tensions still exist between interests representing Wall Street and the financial industry and the social movements representing people who want financial reforms to benefit those who are not wealthy. Here, demonstrators in 2011 protest the bank bailouts, foreclosures, and high unemployment of the recession.

Emmanuel Dunand/AFP/Getty Images

LEARNING OBJECTIVES

After reading this chapter, you will be able to do the following:

9.1 Understand how interest group members try to wield the levers of political power to shape policy.

9.2 Summarize the challenges associated with interest group activity.

9.3 Discuss the types of interest groups in the American political landscape and the different tactics that they use.

9.4 Explore the challenges individuals face and the strategies they employ to overcome problems of collective action as members of social movements.

9.5 Analyze the tactics social movements use to advocate on their members' behalf, and contrast them with those of interest groups.

When we think of the people who represent the interests of citizens in government, we tend to think of the leaders those citizens have elected. Elected officials, however, are not the only people who try to represent American interests. The people themselves come together to shape policy or to call attention to issues as well. They form **voluntary associations**—groups and communities who join with each other in pursuit of collective interests and common goals.

In this chapter, we will dive into two related stories: the first is of lobbyists acting on behalf of America's banks and financial firms following the financial collapse of 2007–2008 and the other of a group of protesters who came together a few years later under the name Occupy Wall Street (OWS) to call attention to the issue of income inequality. Both groups were acting on behalf of someone and representing that someone's interests. However, the financial firms and their representatives in Washington acted as **interest groups**, voluntary associations of people who come together with an agreed-upon set of political and policy objectives and who attempt to pull the levers of political power in service of these defined goals. By contrast, OWS attempted to spark a **social movement**. Social movements (sometimes referred to as political movements) are associations of individuals who also come together to change things or keep things from changing, but they often do so by calling attention to a set of injustices in order to get policymakers to act. They also work to educate the public about a set of issues.

As we will explore, members of interest groups and social movements often resort to different tactics to achieve their goals. They do so because they have to. Their choices depend upon a rational determination of what will work to achieve their objectives and of what tools they can bring to bear. Though there are important distinctions between an interest group and a social movement, they are often connected. A social movement, for example, may spawn one, or many, interest groups over the course of its development and expression. For example, the National Association for the Advancement of Colored People (NAACP), in its efforts to end legal segregation (see Chapter 5), was acting as an interest group but also as part of a larger social movement in the struggle for civil rights.

What typically distinguishes these types of associations are questions of power and tactics.

There is, however, a danger inherent in both interest groups and social movements: faction. How can one be sure that a group or movement does not trample on the rights of others? As the stories you will explore show, some voices do get heard more clearly than others.

A Housing Bubble Bursts, and Interest Groups Pop Up

> 9.1 Understand how interest group members try to wield the levers of political power to shape policy.

In the early 2000s, a small number of individuals grew unimaginably rich selling what had once been a very ordinary product: the home mortgage, a type of loan issued by a financial firm to cover the purchase of a home. They did so by turning the humble home loan into a financial monster that nearly wiped out the global economy. How that happened, and what happened in the aftermath, gives us important insight into the power of interest groups.

Financial Engineering Sows the Seeds for a Major Crisis

In the economic boom years of the 2000s, lenders started to issue loans to people who would not have qualified for them under older rules and with terms that were very dicey. Even Americans with very low incomes enjoyed much easier access to home loans, envisioning them as springboards for sending their children to college and moving their families a few rungs up the economic ladder. Banks at the time issued these subprime mortgages with full confidence that the government would cover for them if things went south.

As lenders got busy lending, prominent banks and investment firms also started creating remarkable new investment products based on those risky mortgages. Local banks would sell their subprime and other mortgages to larger financial firms, who would then chop the loans into little bits (the process is really complicated) and reconstitute them into financial products called mortgage-backed securities (MBSs). By the time they were sufficiently chopped, those MBSs couldn't be traced back to the assets that secured them in the first place, so their real value was unclear, and the relationship between the borrower and the holder of the loan was by that point totally disconnected. While MBSs had been invented decades prior, during the housing boom of the early 2000s, firms began to find ever more creative, lucrative, and riskier variations on them, and investors gobbled them up. MBSs ultimately became so complex that the banks themselves did not fully understand the risks they posed. What they *did* know was that there was a lot of money to be made from buying and selling these new financial

Frankenfoods. Banks started to take bigger and bigger risks and issue more and more loans. Between 2000 and 2005, those risks seemed to be paying off for investors who got very, very rich.

For all of this to keep going, however, home prices had to keep going up, and homeowners had to keep making their payments. That was not to be the case. In 2006, home sales peaked and prices began to decline; foreclosure rates began to spike as the people who were least likely to be able to repay their loans *did not* repay those loans. The market began to crash. The housing bubble was popping.

The attraction of flipping houses proved irresistible to many Americans in the years leading up to the subprime mortgage crisis and recession.
AP Photo/ *Las Vegas Sun*, Christopher DeVargas

By 2007 one of the main lenders, Freddie Mac, announced that it was going to stop buying the riskiest subprime mortgages and MBSs, sending shock waves through the markets. Other banks that had issued those loans started failing. Some analysts started to suspect that the party was about to end. Others saw less cause for concern. Ben Bernanke, then chair of the Federal Reserve, reassured a congressional committee in March 2007 that things would not get out of hand, saying, "At this juncture . . . the impact on the broader economy and financial markets of the problems in the subprime market seems likely to be contained."[1]

Bernanke was wrong. By late 2008, a total of nine major U.S. banks were teetering on the brink of ruin, and nearly $20 trillion of Americans' wealth had been vaporized (see Figure 9.1).[2] The Wall Street bankers and investment firms behind the mess plunged into a panic as global markets imploded.

The Lobbyists' Pressure Play Begins

Powerful interest groups stepped in immediately. Wall Street insiders and the interest groups acting on their behalf quickly realized that it was time to scramble for seats on whatever financial lifeboat the U.S. government might launch. The financial firms wanted a bailout—a big one. Appearing on the Sunday morning political news talk shows that month, Henry (Hank) Paulson warned the public "of an economic doomsday if Congress [did not] immediately okay a colossal Wall Street bailout."[3]

Privately, behind closed doors in Washington, DC, Paulson and Bernanke together spoke to members of Congress "in such apocalyptic terms that lawmakers were struck dumb with horror."[4] They argued that the only way to stop the collapse was with taxpayer money—$700 billion, to be exact—and it needed to be delivered

The Crash of the American Housing Market

Foreclosures and Housing Prices

Source: Ben Beachy, "A Financial Crisis Manual: Causes, Consequences, and Lessons of the Financial Crisis," Global Development and Environment Institute Working Paper No. 12-06, Tufts University, December 2012, http://www.ase.tufts.edu/gdae/Pubs/wp/12-06BeachyFinancialCrisis.pdf.

immediately. Such a transaction would transfer these riskiest loans out of the hands of the suddenly imperiled financial giants and place them firmly in the hands of American taxpayers.

As the Senate considered how, or whether, to bail out financial firms and home-owners, lobbyists from America's financial firms were hard at work. Representatives of major banks spent days on Capitol Hill in private conversation with members of Congress and their staffs, and their efforts appeared to pay off.[5] The Bush administration's originally more limited plans to bail out the financial firms evolved in short order into a situation where Wall Street was effectively dictating the terms. The "Securities Industry and Financial Markets Association, Wall Street's main trade and lobbying group, [was by then holding] conference calls to discuss 'your firms' views and priorities related to Treasury's proposal,' according to an e-mail message sent to members."[6]

Counterpressure Arises from Outside Groups

At the same time, opposition to a Wall Street bailout was emerging from other groups, and some wondered just how well Americans' interests were being represented by Paulson and other financial insiders. Messages from Americans to their members of Congress were clear and came in heavy volume. "The phone calls into the district office are about 75 percent saying: Don't do this. They think this is about Wall Street" and not about helping average homeowners, reported a Republican member of the House.[7] In addition to average Americans, organized interest groups joined the chorus of voices expressing concerns about the possible effects of the proposals on struggling Americans. Groups representing farmers, senior citizens, and undocumented Americans as well as civil rights advocates began to put pressure on Washington to advocate for *their* members' interests.[8]

As the congressional negotiations reached a critical point in September 2008, calls to include help for average homeowners grew louder. "We will not simply hand over a $700 billion blank check to Wall Street and hope for a better outcome. Democrats will act responsibly to insulate Main Street from Wall Street," House Speaker Nancy Pelosi (D-CA) promised.[9] The Speaker's promise was made, no doubt, partly because "rank-and-file members were getting an earful from their constituents—and showing signs of a populist revolt."[10]

The Bailout Begins

In October 2008, the Senate passed a bailout bill. Included in the bill were tax breaks for consumers to purchase energy-efficient appliances, $500 million in tax breaks for film producers, breaks for rum producers and Alaskan fishermen, and a "$10 million credit to help employers defray the costs of storing the bicycles of their employees who commute to work."[11] The strategy, which was designed to peel off enough of the "no" votes in the House so that the bill could proceed to the Senate, worked. The bailout bill ultimately made it to President George W. Bush's desk wherein it became law. Along the way, however, the tab had grown to $850 billion, inflated by lawmakers' efforts to extract concessions for their constituents and for interest groups important to their electoral fortunes. One of the small, but noted, additions to the bailout bill— no doubt a result of members of Congress acting on requests from their constituents and interest group actions—was an elimination of a tax on "wooden archery arrows used by kids."[12]

Wall Street breathed a sigh of relief; the stock market stabilized. In the aftermath of the financial crisis and the Wall Street bailout, many Americans clamored for financial reforms to make sure that what many saw as a taxpayer-backed reward for excessive risk-taking by financial firms would not be repeated. In May 2009, President Barack Obama urged Congress to act on legislation that would provide more oversight over the riskiest of Wall Street's complex financial instruments, called swaps and derivatives. As the *New York Times* noted, however, lobbyists were already on the move to curtail reforms that would limit their group's interests: "Hinting at a lobbying campaign to come . . . the chief executive of the International Swaps and Derivatives Association, a trade group, said his organization 'looked forward to working with policy makers to ensure these reforms help preserve the widespread availability of swaps and other important risk management tools.'"[13]

To some, preserving the availability to freely market the very securities whose collapse had nearly brought the global financial system to a dead stop was worrisome.

A study published in 2011 by the National Bureau of Economic Research concluded that those firms involved in the greatest risk-taking leading up to the crisis were among the most active in lobbying for the bailout program Congress passed and benefited the most from it.[14]

Congressional action on financial reform once again brought interest groups into the mix. According to a Politico report in 2010, "Wall Street has dramatically expanded its influence on Capitol Hill over the past year, using a lobbying army that includes nearly 1,500 former federal employees and 73 former members of Congress who have been deployed during debate on financial reform legislation. . . . 'Wall Street hires former members of Congress and their staff for a reason,' said Public Citizen Congress Watch director David Arkush. 'These people are influential because they have personal relationships with current members and staff. It's hard to say no to your friends.'"[15]

Americans Face Challenges in Acting Collectively in a Representative Democracy

9.2   Summarize the challenges associated with interest group activity.

As we have seen with our story about the Wall Street bailout, groups of people acting on behalf of different interests engaged in efforts to get the policies they preferred adopted and to make their points of view heard. Their efforts require massive coordination, however. How do such groups form in the first place? On what basis might they make their claims? Regardless of their differences, members of voluntary associations do share some common traits. Their rights to organize and press their claims upon government are protected in the Constitution—specifically in the First Amendment's restrictions on Congress's ability to impinge upon free expression: "Congress shall make no law . . . abridging the freedom of speech . . . or the right of the people peaceably to assemble, and to petition the Government for a redress of grievances."

In exercising these fundamental rights, people create what James Madison described in *Federalist* No. 10 as a faction: a group of individuals, large or small, who come together to get what they want out of the political process. Madison recognized that factions were potentially dangerous. Their actions risk trampling upon the rights of others or damaging the political community as a whole. Yet, paradoxically, the freedoms protected under the Constitution virtually guarantee the formation of factions. We can eliminate faction at its source, Madison argued, but only by preventing individuals from coming together, speaking, writing, and pressing their government to address their concerns. While effective, such restrictions upon liberty go against the very principles of a representative democracy. If you have freedom, Madison concluded, you will have faction. The challenge is not how to eliminate it but how to make sure that no one faction can do too much damage.

Madison developed a theory as to how the effects of faction would be moderated in an extended republic. He believed many factions would compete with each other in the large political space of the American Republic, making any one faction less of a danger to the nation as a whole. Given that so many competing factions would all fight to achieve their goals in a system that allowed each a voice, the most dangerous consequences of their inevitable formation could be contained.

But . . . can they *really* be contained? In the history of the American Republic and, for certain, with regard to the financial crisis of the twenty-first century and the federal government's response to it, no question has been more important or more controversial.

Theories of Interest Group Formation Focus on the Challenges of Faction

In Frenchman Alexis de Tocqueville's *Democracy in America*, his book recounting his observations while traveling the country from 1831 to 1832, Tocqueville famously called America a "nation of joiners," so struck was he by the passion with which Americans made use of the "powerful instrument" of association.[16] His idea of a nation of joiners is a compelling one, provoking some key questions. Who joins? What does it mean to join? What do people get from joining? And, most crucially, are the opportunities to join—and the results of doing so—equally effective for all Americans?[17]

One of the primary and enduring causes of faction is inequality of wealth. James Madison wrote, "The most common and durable source of factions has been the various and unequal distribution of property. Those who hold, and those who are without property, have ever formed distinct interests in society."[18] Nearly two centuries later, political scientist Robert Dahl confronted the same basic problem: "How does a 'democratic' system work amid an inequality of resources?"[19] Drawing upon Madison's theory of the extended republic, Dahl explored the theory of **pluralism**, in which the distribution of political power—unequal as it may be—among many competing groups serves to keep any one of them in check. Such a widely contested and competitive political space also gives groups that might otherwise be excluded an entry into the political process, helping to ensure the representation of the interests of the less powerful—although not their success.

Not all of Dahl's contemporaries agreed with his pluralist framework or its optimistic conclusion that democratic societies can function effectively despite the presence of inequality of resources and wealth. The debate continues today. In contrast to pluralist perspectives, **elitist theory** focuses on the advantages that certain interests have in the political process based on the unequal distribution of economic and political power. For C. Wright Mills, writing in 1956, a **power elite** composed of the top echelons of people in the business world, government, and military could "look down upon . . . and by their decisions mightily affect, the everyday worlds of ordinary men and women."[20] To Mills, the nation's defense industry and its allies in government posed the greatest danger. Many Americans in the twenty-first century would add the nation's financial firms to a list of power elites.

In his study, Mills also noted that the exercise of power may be seen not only in those actions that are taken but also in inaction or in preventing actions to which the elites are opposed. A few years later, E. E. Schattschneider explored the ways in which elites used power to shut down opposition, including preventing organization from happening in the first place, preventing ideas from being discussed at all, and exercising power to keep certain ideas off the **policy agenda**, which is the set of issues to which policymakers attend.[21] These debates were not settled in the 1960s, and they still have not been. While some scholars point to the dominance of business- and corporate-focused interest groups in campaign contributions (as we will see later in the chapter), others point out that elite-oriented interest groups are often competing against each other.

Theories of Interest Group Formation Also Explore the Challenges of Collective Action

David Truman's *The Governmental Process* is one of the most important early works that systematically examines the dynamics of interest groups in American political life.[22] While exploring the pluralist theory of interest group operation, Truman's study also highlighted the fact that interest groups can wield a considerable amount of power in American political life. How each group wields that power—and how much power it has—depends upon organization within the group itself. Interest groups, after all, are not monolithic entities but collections of individuals, each with their own goals and desires. Successful interest groups harness those energies and direct them toward the group's goals. In doing so, however, leaders and members of voluntary associations—interest groups and social movements alike—have to overcome challenges to successful organization and coordination.

In getting organized and acting for the interests of their members, advocates for American financial firms and (as we shall see) the members of OWS both had to contend with one similar basic challenge, that of **collective action**—getting individuals to contribute their energy, time, or money to a larger group goal. However, the members of these two voluntary associations did not necessarily solve this problem in the same way. Differences in size, wealth, and political power all shape the strategies available to the leaders of voluntary associations as they try to overcome the challenges of collective action.

Economist Mancur Olson developed one of the most influential theories of the logic of interest group participation, or, more precisely, the logic of choosing *not* to participate. According to Olson, "rational, self-interested individuals will not act to achieve their common or group interests . . . unless there is coercion to force them to do so, or unless some separate incentive, distinct from the achievement of the common or group interest, is offered to the members of the group individually on the condition that they help bear the costs or burdens involved in the achievement of group objectives."[23]

A key concept in this framework is the **collective good** (also called a public good), which is some benefit or desirable outcome that individuals can enjoy or profit from even if they do not help achieve or secure it.[24] The problem with collective goods comes from the fact that people can enjoy their benefits without contributing to their provision. Since, in this framework, individuals are completely rational with how they allocate their time, energy, and resources, there is no incentive for them to help out as they know they will receive the benefits of others' efforts. A strong national defense, clean air, or a really nice fireworks display may all be thought of as examples of collective goods. Those individuals who enjoy collective goods without helping to secure them are called **free riders**, and they pose a serious challenge to the efforts of any voluntary association to work toward collective goals. Note that free riders are acting rationally in this framework. Based upon a pure cost-benefit logic, individuals should "free ride" and devote their energies elsewhere, knowing that others will make up for their inaction.

In the absence of some way to force individuals to contribute, therefore, public goods will be underprovided. Taxes, laws, and other forms of coercion are tools that governments use to overcome the challenges of public goods provision.[25] Voluntary associations of individuals, however, do not generally have the coercive power of government behind them, yet people still join and contribute, even at great personal cost and risk. Why? One explanation, which Olson discussed, is that a given group might be small and homogenous enough that the payoffs for individual participation and the collective risks of nonparticipation are obviously clear and compelling.

Other explanations for how interest groups can overcome the challenges of collective action focus on the incentives such groups offer to individuals to join or contribute.[26] These inducements may include **selective benefits**, which are made available only to those who join or contribute to the group, in contrast to public goods, which are available to all. One set of selective benefits is **material rewards**, which may include discounts on goods and services, access to group publications and information, special offers, travel opportunities, or a host of other tangible benefits available only to members and contributors. Professional associations or trade unions may provide their members with the credentials needed to operate in their profession or achieve for their members higher wages or better benefits.

Other rewards that may be available only as a result of participation are **social benefits**, which might allow members to network with other individuals with similar interests and goals. Social benefits may come in the form of personal relationships and the benefits individuals attach to forming such relationships for their own sake, or they may take the form of job opportunities and other avenues for personal advancement. A third type of selective benefits arises from the satisfaction of working with others to achieve a common goal or purpose. For this reason, these inducements are referred to as **purposive benefits**.

Interest Groups Vary by Type and Tactic

9.3 Discuss the types of interest groups in the American political landscape and the different tactics that they use.

While representatives from Wall Street firms mobilized in force during and after the financial crisis, they were not the only ones acting. Other interest groups advocated as well, although many of their members were less connected to the corridors of political power than the titans of the American financial services industry. AARP, for example, argued that in the wake of the crisis, "the social safety net needs to be strengthened and extended. Workers should not have to worry about losing their health and pension benefits when they lose a job."[27] In this section, we will explore the landscape of interest groups in the United States and the varied tactics they use to advance their members' goals.

Americans with a wide variety of political goals join, hire, or support interest groups in order to make their wishes known. Interest groups are often categorized and analyzed according to the broader goals they set out to achieve and for which they are advocating. Though scholars differ on specific classification schemes, the central idea is to examine what kinds of benefits the groups are seeking.

Economic interest groups, as their name implies, advocate for the economic interests of their members. These groups form the largest category of interest groups and are responsible for the largest amount of campaign donations. Within the category of economic interest groups, the largest and generally most influential subcategory is business groups, which advocate for the policies that favor their particular firms or industries. Labor groups, such as trade unions, advocate on behalf of the workers they represent. Finally, farm groups have a long historical tradition of acting in American politics on behalf of farmers.

In contrast, **public interest groups** act on behalf of the collective interests of a broad group of individuals—many of whom may not be members or contributors to the organization. Groups advocating in the areas of civil rights, civil liberties, social welfare, education, or the environment are all examples of public interest groups. Many of these associations focus on one specific area of public policy and are, therefore, often called single-issue groups. A key subcategory of public interest groups advocates for their members with regard to issues of identity and lived experiences. The actions of the NAACP in challenging legal segregation, of the National Organization for Women (NOW) on behalf of gender equality, and of groups acting to secure equality for lesbian, gay, bisexual, and transgender (LGBT) Americans are all examples of public interest groups whose efforts you may be familiar with.

Finally, **governmental interest groups** act on behalf of state, regional, local, or even foreign governments to keep their members apprised of policy discussions;

weigh in on the regulatory process; and generally act on behalf of the relevant government, especially during the appropriations process in Congress, which we will explore in detail in the next chapter.

"Inside" Interest Groups Lobby to Influence Policymaking

All interest groups share the same ultimate goal: to influence public policy on the ground. To do so, they may try to influence any stage of the policymaking process at the federal, state, or local level.

When one pictures organized interest group activity, one of the first things that often comes to mind is the act of **lobbying**, or interacting with government officials to advance a group's goals in the area of public policy. Lobbying in America is as old as the Republic itself. The stereotypical idea of lobby-

ing is often of powerful interest group members contacting members of Congress and pressuring them to act on the group's behalf. Though that is part of the story, lobbying is actually a much more complex and nuanced process. In the first place, interest group members lobby all three branches of the federal government, not just Congress, though the tactics they use may vary depending on which branch is being lobbied. It may involve efforts to shape policy across all three branches: Legislative lobbying seeks to influence how legislation is written, executive branch lobbying focuses on how these laws are implemented, and judicial lobbying centers on how the laws are interpreted.

Second, even when they do approach Congress, lobbyists' tactics are varied and complicated and often focus as much on providing information to representatives, senators, and congressional staff members as they do on pushing for a specific position directly.

Rather than being a single effort, lobbying is most accurately thought of as an ongoing process, in which a lobbyist "seldom does only one specific thing at one specific time . . . but multiple things over a period of time."[28]

Young people rally at an event in Seattle in October 2018 in support of a climate change lawsuit are being heard in federal court. The environment can be freely enjoyed by everyone—a classic public good—and is therefore unlikely to be protected without policy action.
AP Photo/Elaine Thompson

Today's Lobbyists Are Professionals. The First Amendment to the Constitution guarantees the right of any citizen to lobby—"to petition the Government for a redress of grievances." Modern lobbying, however, is very much a professional undertaking. It involves large numbers of people and a lot of money. The Center for Responsive Politics calculated that in 2018 more than 11,654 paid lobbyists spent a total of $3.46 billion lobbying Congress and federal agencies.[29]

Successful lobbyists must be able to provide a service to their clients, the people and firms that hire and pay them. To do so effectively, lobbyists need solid, useful knowledge about the particular policy area and the ability to be heard by those in government. For this reason, former government officials are often in high demand by lobbying firms. And government agencies themselves may recruit individuals from lobbying firms and the private sector for their experience and expertise. The movement of individuals between government and lobbying positions is called the **revolving door phenomenon**. Those who argue that the revolving door is a good thing point to benefits that agencies receive from the experience and expertise of former lobbyists and argue that effective lobbying depends on the kind of knowledge and experience that former government officials can bring to the table. Others, however, have raised concerns about the degree to which those groups capable of paying high prices for well-connected lobbyists tilt public policy in favor of the wealthy and powerful.

Members of interest groups know that their organizations are not all created equal with regard to their wealth, political clout, and access to powerful governmental officials. As such, they may modify their particular lobbying strategies to make the best use of the resources and advantages they have. Consideration of whether or not all these strategies are equally effective, however, also raises questions about the degree to which Americans are fairly and competently represented . . . or represented at all.

Lobbyists Influence Legislation in Congress. Because it writes the nation's laws, Congress is a natural target for lobbyists, who employ several strategies in their efforts to influence legislation. One method, and the one that many people think of when they think of the term *lobbying*, is when lobbyists contact members of Congress or their staff directly to advocate for their group's position. This kind of direct contact is an example of **inside lobbying**, and it takes many forms, which is not surprising given how complex the legislative process is.

In addition to direct contact with representatives, senators, and congressional staff members, lobbyists may prepare research reports and briefs, work to shape the legislative agenda by bringing more attention to their issues of interest, or help coordinate a legislative strategy on an issue.[30] All of this is considered inside lobbying. These efforts may focus on the content of a piece of legislation and also on the levels of funding for agencies and programs through the appropriations process. Lobbyists may try to influence the total amount of funding available to an agency, spending priorities within that agency, earmarks for specific projects, or riders to appropriations bills, which may specify how money *cannot* be spent and are often a powerful weapon in shaping the implementation of the laws that Congress passes.[31]

Successful inside lobbying often depends on personal relationships, access to decision makers, and financial resources—something not all interest groups possess. Much of the power of inside lobbying, however, also relies on the provision of useful and timely information, such as research that might save a congressional staff valuable time, specific language or wording that may shape or find its way into a bill, or studies that convincingly portray the group's position as one that a member's constituents care about and agree with. Testifying at committee or subcommittee hearings and providing members of Congress with research reports and summaries are two common ways interest groups use information to try to advance their positions.

Lobbyists Influence Executive Branch Implementation. From the point of view of interest groups and their lobbyists, winning or losing the battle in Congress is only part of the war. As it is tasked with executing the laws that Congress writes—shaping legislation through the process of implementation—the executive branch also finds itself the target of lobbying efforts. Congress cannot account for every detail within the policy areas covered by its laws. Some flexibility needs to be built in to allow for effective implementation, and legislators eyeing reelection may prefer not to specify certain provisions in too much detail. In trying to influence the appropriations process in Congress, members of organized interest groups try to shape the implementation of the laws by the executive branch. In some cases, they do so directly by lobbying the president (or, more realistically, members of their executive staff) or members of the federal bureaucracy.

Federal law requires executive branch agencies to notify the public and solicit feedback when establishing rules and procedures, an opening into which organized interests happily step.[32] The detailed nature of most proposed legislation provides an advantage to interest groups armed with data and knowledge of the minutiae of the legislation and the affected policy.[33] Interest groups may work to increase the prominence of their goals in the executive branch agenda, and they may also use the courts to challenge federal rules to which they are opposed.

Closely connected to the idea of the revolving door is the risk of **agency capture** (also called regulatory capture), in which those agencies tasked with regulating businesses, industries, or other interest groups are populated by individuals with close ties to the very firms they are supposed to regulate. This can result in ineffective oversight or regulatory actions that favor the firms over the general interests of society or those not so strongly represented.[34]

Lobbyists Influence Judicial Actions. Interest groups and their lobbyists may also try to shape how the nation's laws are interpreted by targeting the federal judiciary. As the thought of a lobbyist badgering an individual member of the Supreme Court about a group's position seems somehow unseemly and, depending on the justice, might backfire, groups generally use other methods to try to shape the activities of the federal judiciary, especially the Supreme Court.

Interest groups may try to influence judicial appointments, either through the presidential nomination or Senate confirmation processes. Given the importance of the federal judiciary and its influence over a host of issues, interest groups often have a very strong desire to shape the appointment process.

The Supreme Court has two decisions to make on each case that comes before it: whether or not to hear the case and how to rule should it decide to hear it. Interest groups may try to influence each of these decisions—typically by filing amicus curiae briefs, which describe a group's position and the arguments for it. There is evidence that a high number of amici can increase the chances that justices will hear a case,[35] though some scholars have pointed out that this does not necessarily mean that interest groups have any particular advantage when it comes time for the Court to rule on the merits of the case.[36]

Interest groups may sponsor litigation, guiding a case through the judiciary, but this is an expensive and time-consuming task, even when it goes well. In the 1950s, the Legal Defense Fund of the NAACP undertook a lengthy, expensive, and risky strategy in trying to use the federal judiciary to bring an end to legal segregation in the United States (see Chapter 5). To do so, the group had to find individuals willing to bring suits in court, which could, and did, subject many of them to physical and economic violence. The litigators and staff of the Legal Defense Fund also had to conduct the research and legal analysis that formed the bases of these lawsuits, which was also a personally risky undertaking.

Lobbying Activities Are Regulated. Given the potential influence of lobbyists on shaping public policy, it is not surprising that attempts have been made over the years to regulate their activities. This is not, however, a simple task. First, the Constitution protects the fundamental rights of interest groups to act on their members' behalf, which includes lobbying activities. Second, there are incentives for members of Congress not to overregulate these activities since representatives and senators may benefit from the information and campaign support that interest groups provide. Most recent efforts to regulate lobbying have focused on making the process more transparent.

Interest Groups Exert Influence through Webs and Networks. One of the classic, and worrisome, depictions of the connections between interest groups and government is the **iron triangle** (see Figure 9.2). As the term suggests, the iron triangle consists of three parts—interest groups, Congress, and the bureaucracy—each of which works with the other two to achieve their shared policy goals, even if achieving those goals runs counter to the general interests of society or specific groups within it. In doing so, the members of the triangle act as factions, each helping the other two members and receiving benefits for doing so.

Interest groups provide electoral support to members of Congress, who use their influence, especially on committees and subcommittees, to advance legislation favorable to the interest groups and reduce oversight of interest group activities. These same interest groups lobby on behalf of the relevant bureaucratic agencies to secure the agencies' desired funding and policy goals. In return, the agencies conduct their job of regulation in ways favorable to interest group objectives. Finally, members of Congress determine funding levels and pass legislation desired by the bureaucratic agencies, which, in turn, implement the laws passed by Congress in ways desired by those members of Congress.

Due to the growth in the number of interest groups and an increasingly fluid and complex policy landscape in recent decades, political scientists have employed the concept of the **issue network** to describe the webs of influence among interest groups,

The Iron Triangle

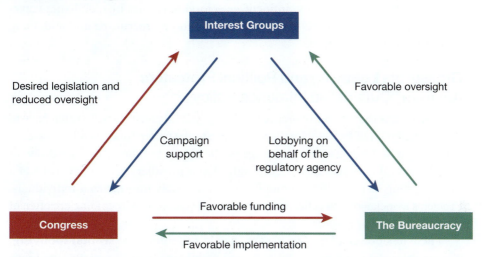

The iron triangle illustrates the linkage of benefits that each of the three members provides to the other two. While all members help each other, it is their common interest in the overall policy goal that drives individual decisions.

policymakers, and policy advocates. In contrast to iron triangles, issue networks are often temporary, arising to address a specific policy problem. Any one issue may give rise to competing issue networks, each of which advocates on a different side of the issue. In this way, issue networks are closer to the idea of pluralism than iron triangles.

Interest Groups Are Involved in Election-Related Activities. Interest groups are often heavily involved in the electoral process. First, and perhaps foremost, their participation revolves around the targeted distribution of financial resources. Money is a powerful strategic tool as it can fund media coverage, a solid ground campaign, and research. Money can also act as a weapon to discourage others from even running for election. Campaigns are often won or lost long before the actual vote.

How and under what conditions interest groups contribute to political campaigns is often determined by the status under which they file with the Internal Revenue Service (IRS). Those classified, for example, as 501(c)(3) organizations, whose contributions are tax deductible, cannot contribute directly to campaign activities but may do so for voter education and mobilization efforts. Political action committees (PACs) may spend more money on campaigns than individuals and may solicit funds from their members to do so, but they also operate with strict limits. Following an important Supreme Court decision in 2010, American politics has seen the emergence and rapid rise of the so-called super PAC, which is allowed to raise and spend money without financial limits but only in ways that are uncoordinated with a campaign.[37]

Efforts to regulate interest group spending on campaigns and elections are ongoing and not always successful. In addition to financial contributions and spending, interest groups also try to influence electoral outcomes by mobilizing voters through get-out-the-vote (GOTV) campaigns and by recruiting and endorsing candidates.

Grassroots Lobbying and Political Protesters Act from "Outside" to Influence Policy

Interest groups that attempt to represent less powerful constituencies often have to use a different set of tactics than those available to the better-funded and better-connected groups. They also aim to change public policy, but they often face different challenges and have to adjust accordingly. Their members generally consist of a diverse group of previously immobilized and possibly unorganized individuals. Problems associated with collective action and the dangers of free riding are often of more concern to such groups.

These less powerful groups may engage in **outside (grassroots) lobbying**, which focuses on reaching constituents and mobilizing them to pressure their representatives rather than pressuring the representatives directly. A group may decide that outside lobbying is its best course of action, or it may have no other choice and have to use this tactic "out of desperation when an 'inside' strategy has failed."[38]

Interest groups may also influence policy through their activities in state and local elections. A **referendum** is a direct vote on a policy proposal or change that is put on the ballot as a result of the actions of a state legislature or other state or local government body. An **initiative** is a direct vote on a policy proposal or change that has been placed on the ballot by citizens or organized groups. States and localities vary on the use of referenda and initiatives, and this option is not available at the national level, as federal elections do not include these electoral processes. Interest groups are often quite active in these forms of outside lobbying.

In some cases, when grassroots support does not really exist, or would not exist if it hadn't been "purchased" by a lobbying firm, an interest group will present the facade of grassroots support. This is referred to as **Astroturf lobbying**; the term alludes to the fact that the "grassroots" drawn upon are made out of fake grass and thus do not reflect genuine public support. While Astroturf lobbying is widely criticized, the lines between genuine grassroots support and Astroturf lobbying are not always entirely clear. As political scientist Ken Kollman has questioned, "If two interest groups mobilize the same number of people to contact Congress, but one of them relies on volunteers and its own members and the other pays a consulting house to generate telephone calls and letters, who is to say which is real and which is artificial?"[39] Astroturf lobbying can be effective, and according to political scientist Kenneth Goldstein, its increasing use may be contributing to a new wave of citizen participation that would not exist if not for the fact that "interest groups and lobbying firms inside the beltway are increasingly utilizing new and sophisticated techniques to water the grass roots outside the beltway."[40]

Interest Groups Face Challenges in Representation

Writing in the 1960s, Grant McConnell pointed out that corporations and private interest groups do not rule themselves democratically and that there are far fewer protections provided within them than those afforded to citizens.[41] McConnell's critique of the exercise of power within interest groups also raises questions about representation within social movements themselves—even those that attempt to speak for the less powerful.

In recent decades, political scientists have come back to the questions of power and representation raised by scholars such as Robert Dahl, C. Wright Mills, and E. E. Schattschneider. They have done so often empirically, using the tools of quantitative analysis to get a better understanding of the dynamics of representation among and within interest groups. In general, in spite of a proliferation of groups and movements devoted to the less well-represented members of society, such as minorities, women, and the elderly, much of the evidence points to a continuation of overrepresentation of the elite, powerful, and wealthy.

Exploring data involving nearly seven thousand interest groups, political scientist Kay Lehman Schlozman concluded that in spite of the growth of public interest groups since the 1960s, business and commerce interest groups still account for the majority of associations, a fact that she attributes to their staying power in the face of all the pressures on a group to maintain its membership and influence.[42] Political scientist Dara Strolovitch concluded that even in interest groups devoted to representing more marginalized members of American society, the relatively better-advantaged members within those groups receive more attention and political effort.[43]

Occupy Wall Street Illustrates the Struggles, Successes, and Failures of Social Movements

> 9.4   Explore the challenges individuals face and the strategies they employ to overcome problems of collective action as members of social movements.

In September 2011, almost three years after the financial collapse, about a thousand people gathered in New York's Zuccotti Park, just blocks from Wall Street and the New York Stock Exchange in lower Manhattan, to protest the concentration of wealth at the very top of American society and what they saw as a deep and structural lack of fairness, made far worse by the bailout of Wall Street. This disparate and evolving group of protesters became known as Occupy Wall Street, or OWS; the movement's message, one fueled by disillusionment and frustration, eventually spread around the globe via strategic use of social media.

The OWS protest in New York City prompted supportive rallies across the country, including this one, in Tampa, Florida, in October 2011, which drew 400 people.

AP Photo/Chris O'Meara

Many observers attribute the origins of OWS to a blog entry posted in July 2011 by the Canadian activist group Adbusters.[44] The founder of Adbusters, Kalle Lasn, told the press that "his group originally proposed one demand—to separate money from politics." According to an article in the *Christian Science Monitor*, "When asked . . . why it was such a slow burn for people to finally protest the financial crisis, Mr. Lasn said that it took some time for people to realize that President Obama," who was by then president, "was not handling the meltdown effectively, going so far as to call him a 'gutless wonder.'"[45]

At that first protest in Zuccotti Park, about eighty individuals were arrested, mostly on charges for blocking traffic, a relatively minor offense. However, in some cases arrests were accompanied by charges of police brutality. Videos that seemed to support those charges went viral on platforms like YouTube. A few weeks later, OWS protesters marched across the Brooklyn Bridge, again leading to arrests, hundreds this time. By this point, however, people were more aware of the movement's existence.

Those who joined OWS did so for a variety of reasons; they were not united by self-interest, as the Wall Street financial firms had been. However, their message that a small faction of the wealthiest Americans was working against the interests of everyone else caught on. According to reporter John Ennis, "'WE ARE THE 99 PERCENT' became the rallying cry of a generation. The simplicity and inclusivity of that message was worthy of the advertising gurus on Madison Avenue."[46]

PRACTICING POLITICAL SCIENCE

DEPICTING INCOME INEQUALITY IN THE UNITED STATES

Using data on wealth and income concentrations in the United States compiled by academic researchers, individuals with OWS created the following image, which found its way into major media outlets and onto T-shirts and posters.

• •

WHAT Do You Think?

How effective do you think this image is in conveying the inequality of wealth in the United States? Though the figure is based on actual data, the creator acknowledges, "I drew the lines in a somewhat impressionistic manner."[47] Does that use of creative license detract at all from the image's power? What other images might one manipulate in a similar way to communicate the central point?

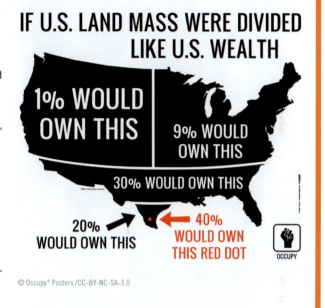

IF U.S. LAND MASS WERE DIVIDED LIKE U.S. WEALTH

1% WOULD OWN THIS

9% WOULD OWN THIS

30% WOULD OWN THIS

20% WOULD OWN THIS

40% WOULD OWN THIS RED DOT

OCCUPY

Early efforts of OWS barely received a mention in the nation's press. What coverage they did get was condescending and dismissive. Though protesters were generally united behind a message of income inequality, OWS as a whole struggled to further define what that message was, a common challenge for those who would start a social movement. It is a particular challenge to successfully mobilize Americans to respond to political and economic inequalities since this depends upon communicating to them an understanding of the messy details of the workings of government. "What do you say about a financial crisis where the villains are obscure and the solutions are obscure?" wondered one critic.[48] While the media may have had a hard time figuring out what OWS was all about, the movement's members felt it was clear that something had gone wrong in the nation. The rich were getting richer, and everyone else seemed to be getting left behind. Change was needed, and Americans needed to be woken up. As Rachel Pletz, a participant in the Zuccotti Park protests who helped to organize similar efforts in Philadelphia, put it, "This is about solidarity. This is about getting people together and figuring it out. We just know something's wrong."[49]

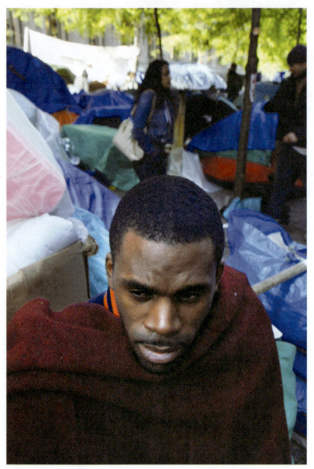

John Hector, one of the relatively few people of color amongst OWS protesters, wraps himself in a blanket against cold temperatures at the group's protest in Zuccotti Park in November 2011. "My concern is the economic situation and particularly police brutality and stop-and-frisk policies in Black and Latino communities," said Hector.

OWS protesters did find a way to make strategic use of social media and other creative protest methods to coordinate and communicate and ultimately got attention from some high-profile celebrity activists who also helped spread word of the cause. The OWS movement quickly went national, even international. In the first week of October, "smaller-scale protests spread . . . to Los Angeles, Chicago, Boston, Denver, Washington, Albuquerque, Portland, Maine, and several other cities. An 'Occupy Toronto' protest [was] planned in Canada."[50]

As the protests gained momentum, some critics claimed that not only did the movement fail to represent the diverse interests of its members but also that it was actively discriminatory, especially toward the American Jewish community. In October 2011, the Republican National Committee issued a memo that "included three videos showing anti-Semitic outbursts by purported Wall Street protestors," though a spokesperson for the Anti-Defamation League countered that these outbursts were "isolated incidents."[51]

The movement was also criticized for failing to sufficiently empower members from traditionally marginalized groups or address their concerns. An article in the *New York Times* in late October 2011, for example, described a sense of alienation felt by a group of organizers from the South Bronx, an area with a high concentration of low-income individuals and those of minority ethnicity. "'Nobody looked like us,' said Rodrigo Venegas, 31, 'It was white, liberal, young people who for the first time in their life are feeling a small percentage of what black and brown communities have been feeling for hundreds of years.'"[52]

Other members of minority groups concluded that a unity of voices—based not on identity but a shared struggle against those in power—might make the social movement stronger. One journalist's account is telling: "Frank Diamond, a 26-year-old-Haitian-American from Jamaica, Queens, who was holding an 'Occupy the Hood' sign at a recent rally, said that many working-class blacks who had originally watched the protests from a distance, were starting to realize they should join. 'It takes a wave to realize that the boat you have been riding is too small,' he said. 'We need to be represented here too. This is about us, too.'"[53]

On September 29, 2011, the NYC General Assembly adopted a declaration of the goals of the movement. One of many participation-based assemblies across the globe, the New York assembly operated on consensus, trying to invite as many voices as was practical into the conversation. The declaration stated that "as we gather together in solidarity to express a feeling of mass injustice, we must not lose sight of what brought us together. We write so that all people who feel wronged by the corporate forces of the world can know that we are your allies."[54] In spite of the theme of solidarity, the list of grievances in the declaration included charges against such disparate entities as Wall Street and home foreclosures, national agriculture policy, labor conditions, health care, money in politics, the death penalty, and American foreign policy.

By November 2011, New York City authorities began to clamp down, stripping the demonstrators in Zuccotti Park of their generators and fuel just as a snowstorm and cold wave "blanketed their tents and tarps with sleet and ice, and left at least one protester hospitalized for hypothermia."[55] Less than two weeks later, Mayor Michael Bloomberg and city authorities evicted the protesters from Zuccotti Park. Reporter Michelle Nichols described the removal: "Wearing helmets and wielding batons, New York police evicted Occupy Wall Street . . . two months after they set up camp and sparked a national movement against economic inequality. Hundreds of police dismantled the sea of tents, tarps, and outdoor furniture, mattresses and protest signs at Zuccotti Park, arresting 147 people, including about a dozen who had chained themselves to each other and to trees."[56] Other cities removed protesters as well.

By the spring of 2012, the tents had mostly disappeared from New York, Boston, Los Angeles, and other cities. Protests continued but without the same level of media coverage. Some debated what had been accomplished. A letter to the editor of the *New York Times* framed the question not in terms of what OWS should do but what America should do, asking, "What will they do now? That question misses the point. Whether the 99 percenters retake Zuccotti Park in New York isn't the issue. The question we should be asking ourselves is, What will we do now? The American democracy—our system of capitalism and free markets, the electoral system and tax policies—has been distorted by moneyed interests. Our challenge is to revive America as a land of equal opportunity."[57]

Other observers had a very different set of suggestions for the movement's leaders. According to one reporter, "Many pundits suggest that it's time for the activists to hire political consultants and assemble a list of demands—in short, to become much more involved in electoral politics."[58] It was time, in other words, for OWS to stop trying to form a social movement and become an interest group.

Social Movements Employ Different Tactics from Interest Groups to Make Change and Educate

> **9.5** Analyze the tactics social movements use to advocate on their members' behalf, and contrast them with those of interest groups.

American political history teaches us that social movements can achieve major policy changes over time: The civil rights movement and the struggle for the rights of women; disabled Americans; and LGBT Americans are all widely acknowledged as social movements that have had significant impact. Though their specific goals were different, those groups often employed similar tactics.

They used **protest**, a public demonstration designed to call attention to the need for action or change. As part of these protests, some members engaged in civil disobedience, the intentional breaking of a law for the purpose of calling attention to an injustice. Protest and civil disobedience can be powerful and effective tactics, especially in altering the political agenda—placing an injustice front and center on the national stage and forcing people to confront it. Both of these tactics are risky, however, not only for the individuals involved but also for the movement itself.

In leading or joining an act of protest or civil disobedience, individuals may endanger their freedom, jobs, physical safety, or even their lives. For the movement itself, there is a chance that these activities may alienate rather than mobilize—that they may further isolate the movement from those who its members hope to convince of the importance of the cause. There is also the risk that the protesters will be ignored. The story of OWS illustrates the power and effectiveness of protest and civil disobedience but also the challenges such movements face.

The Success of Social Movements Is Difficult to Measure

As we have explored, small, homogenous, and economically powerful interest groups have many advantages in overcoming the challenges of collective action. When broad, diverse, voluntary associations of individuals come together to create a social movement, they lack many of the advantages of the more powerful groups. According to Olson, there is a logic to the idea that social movements should not come together at all. Yet some do. Why?

This is not an easy question to answer, either for scholars or for participants in the social movements themselves.[59] Part of the problem lies in the inherent differences in observing success and failure between interest groups and social movements.[60] When an interest group tries to influence legislation in Congress, for example, it is much easier to see if its efforts pay off or if they do not. However, what does it mean for a social movement to succeed, and how would we know if it did or did not? Those social movements that fail are difficult to study, like the proverbial tree that falls in the forest with nobody there to observe. To dive a bit deeper into this question, we have to incorporate insights from both political science and sociology, which is a close relative of political science but focuses more on social processes than on political institutions, processes, and outcomes.

For social movements, success or failure may be best determined not by the final public policy outcomes or by laws that were or were not passed but by the fact that the movement came together at all—that it managed to overcome the problems of collective action and engaged others in its efforts to challenge the political dynamics and that it persuaded the uninvolved to

Lucas Brinson takes on the role of a human microphone, relaying information throughout the OWS encampment in New York's Zuccotti Park days before police cleared out protesters in mid-November 2011.
AP Photo/Bebeto Matthew

become involved, to mobilize, infuriate, and educate. These efforts do not go unopposed, whether by governments, other powerful political players, or the inertia of a public confronted with a new cause or call to combat an injustice.[61] For sociologist Edwin Amenta, some answers, and a better framing of the question itself, may lie in the uneven power relationships that define interest groups and social movements. He argued, "Asking why social movements fail is a little like asking why children do not have backyards full of ponies. Most social movements fail most of the time because they embody a recipe for failure: they combine ambitious goals with severe power deficits."[62]

By some accounts, and not without cause, it is not even clear if OWS created a social movement at all. By the three-year anniversary of the first Zuccotti Park protests, the movement seemed to be over. In comparison to widely acknowledged twenty-first-century movements such as Black Lives Matter, OWS did not appear to have the same staying power or to have built the necessary infrastructure to sustain it over the long haul.

However, in our exploration of political parties, we studied the insurgent candidacy of Sen. Bernie Sanders (I-VT), who most certainly highlighted American economic inequality in his campaign. The efforts of Sanders, Sen. Elizabeth Warren (D-MA), and others to call attention to this issue illustrate one of the primary tools that social movements have: changing the conversation in an effort to influence the political agenda. The idea of "the 99 percent" has taken hold. While OWS tents had long since vanished by 2020, their focus on economic inequality had shaped the Democratic Party's conversation in the presidential elections.

Trying to determine whether or not a social movement has been successful by focusing only on what laws were or were not passed might miss this key contribution.[63] The policy agenda is a shifting and evolving thing; nothing is ever settled, and those who wish to influence political outcomes can never let their guard down.[64] The outcome of any one social movement may teach the members of future movements important lessons about what has worked and what has not. The activities of individuals involved with the civil rights movement, for example, served as lessons to members of future movements, such as those for Americans with disabilities, that sought to call attention to other forms of injustice.[65]

Conclusion: Organizing in American Political Life

Separated in space only by city blocks and in time by only three years, the activities of powerful and well-connected American financial firms in 2008 and the protests of OWS in 2011 might seem as far apart as the citizens they tried to represent. In many ways, they were. The tactics used in these two situations were, to be sure, very different. Insiders—the CEOs of financial institutions and their well-paid lobbyists—worked the levers of the American political system to ensure the survival of the firms they represented. Outsiders—students, opponents of the American capitalist system, advocates for economic equality, and many others without a well-defined agenda—tried to come together and use tools of protest and action to bring about social change.

These two groups, as different as they were, had more in common than even they may have realized. Their leaders and members had to assess where they stood strategically in the real world of American economic and political power, and they had to adjust their strategies accordingly. They had to motivate and coerce members to join and contribute. Most fundamentally, they had to decide exactly whose interests they were trying to represent.

The stories of the financial bailout and OWS are united by two strong and interconnected threads: power and inequality. Even within a social movement that hopes to represent the interests of outsiders, the disconnected, and the less powerful, there is no guarantee that all voices within that movement will be heard. When one compares the activities of interest groups and social movements, the challenges are even greater. The concentration of wealth at the very top of the economic strata is as great as it has ever been in the nation's history.

From these two stories one could draw a simple, neat conclusion: One faction ended up tipping the balance of power in its favor, and the other failed—end of story. However, the complex ways in which social movements have been involved in the American political space are better thought of as seeds. Political seeds—sometimes derided, attacked, or ignored from their beginnings—need two key ingredients: their own potential and the soil upon which that potential falls. Whether or not OWS had a consistent, clear, salable message and what effect that message had on the political process in 2011 or in the years since is not the main concern in this view. What matters is whether or not the efforts of OWS sowed the seeds for a true challenge to the power structure of the American political system in the twenty-first century. And did these efforts fall upon a receptive and fertile soil? Did the political dynamics of Americans' confrontation with the inevitable challenge of faction—and the inevitable contribution of economic inequality to the formation of faction in republican forms of government—change?

CHAPTER REVIEW

This chapter's main ideas are reflected in the Learning Objectives. By reviewing them here, you should be able to *remember* the key points and *know* these terms that are central to the topic.

9.1 Understand how interest group members try to wield the levers of political power to shape policy.

Remember . . .
- In the wake of the financial crisis of 2008, interest groups, especially those representing American financial firms, acted to advocate for the goals shared by their members the ability of Americans to form voluntary associations and make their wishes known.

Know . . .
- *interest groups* (p. 257)
- *social movement* (p. 257)
- *voluntary associations* (p. 257)

9.2 Summarize the challenges associated with interest group activity.

Remember . . .
- The Constitution of the United States ensures the ability of Americans to form voluntary associations and make their wishes known.
- Political scientists have offered a variety of explanations for why Americans choose to join or not join voluntary associations in political life.
- When acting collectively, there are often rational incentives for individuals to allow others to carry the burdens of doing so.

Know . . .
- *collective action* (p. 264)
- *collective good* (p. 265)
- *elitist theory* (p. 263)
- *free riders* (p. 265)
- *material rewards* (p. 265)
- *pluralism* (p. 263)
- *policy agenda* (p. 264)
- *power elite* (p. 263)
- *purposive benefits* (p. 266)
- *selective benefits* (p. 265)
- *social benefits* (p. 265)

9.3 Discuss the types of interest groups in the American political landscape and the different tactics that they use.

Remember . . .
- Interest groups may form to advocate for a variety of goals, including those focused on business and the economy, public issues, and the interests of governmental units.
- Interest groups lobby all levels and all branches of government.
- When lobbying the federal government, interest groups act to influence the actions of the legislative, executive, and judicial branches.
- Interest groups also act to influence campaigns and elections.

Know . . .	• *agency capture* (p. 269)	• *issue network* (p. 270)
	• *Astroturf lobbying* (p. 272)	• *lobbying* (p. 267)
	• *economic interest groups* (p. 266)	• *outside (grassroots) lobbying* (p. 272)
	• *governmental interest groups* (p. 266)	• *public interest groups* (p. 266)
	• *initiative* (p. 272)	• *referendum* (p. 272)
	• *inside lobbying* (p. 268)	• *revolving door phenomenon* (p. 268)
	• *iron triangle* (p. 270)	

9.4 Explore the challenges individuals face and the strategies they employ to overcome problems of collective action as members of social movements.

Remember . . .   • In the presence of increasing economic inequality in the years following the financial bailout, members of OWS attempted to create a social movement.

9.5 Analyze the tactics social movements use to advocate on their members' behalf, and contrast them with those of interest groups.

Remember . . .   • Members of social movements often employ tactics such as protest and civil disobedience to make political change and to educate others.

• It is often more difficult to determine whether a social movement succeeded or failed than it is to evaluate the success of activities of a given interest group.

Know . . .   • *protest* (p. 278)

INSTITUTIONS

CHAPTER 10

CONGRESS

Representation, Organization, and Legislation

"The Squad"—from left, Representatives Rashida Tlaib (D-MI), Ayanna Pressley (D-MA), Ilhan Omar (D-MN), and Alexandria Ocasio-Cortez (D-NY)—was a highly visible symbol of the 2020 "Year of the Woman" in Congress.

Alex Wroblewski/Getty Images

LEARNING OBJECTIVES

After reading this chapter, you will be able to do the following:

10.1 Understand how questions of representation involve political and institutional considerations as well as questions of identity.

10.2 Describe how the Constitution created Congress, including its structure and powers.

10.3 Describe the rules, institutions, and processes that Congress itself has created to carry out its constitutional role.

10.4 Explain the steps of the legislative process and how it can diverge from traditional "textbook" descriptions.

10.5 Connect the issues surrounding the representation of women in Congress to the challenges involving representation of other individuals in America.

Congress is in some ways a story of division. Members are divided into two chambers: the House and the Senate. They are increasingly divided along lines of political partisanship. They sort themselves into various committees and subcommittees to do the actual work of their institution. In spite of those divisions, however, all members of U.S. Congress are united in one thing. They are there to **represent**, to stand for, the interests of the voters who sent them there.[1] It is not, however, a direct transmission, nor was it meant to be.

In Chapter 8, we explored the rules and institutions that shape candidates' electoral chances. What happens after the elections are over, when candidates become representatives? How do the institutions of Congress shape the relationship between those who seek to represent others and those who seek to be represented within the legislative branch?

As we will explore, a study of Congress is also a study in *mediation*, in how that institution shapes the expression of Americans' preferences that were made at the ballot. The formal and informal rules and structures of Congress, political parties and party leaders, and the choices of individual representatives and senators—acting alone, or far more commonly, with others—all serve to transmit voters' preferences into public policy.

Two "Years of the Women" Highlight the Promise and Challenge of More Inclusive Representation in Congress

10.1 Understand how questions of representation involve political and institutional considerations as well as questions of identity.

In this section, we examine two historic congressional elections: 1992 and 2018. Both were described by the American news media at the time as the "Year of the Woman."

Both led to changes in the degree to which Congress reflect a portrait of Americans' lived experiences. By pairing these two elections, we gain insight into the reality that representation in Congress takes time. Getting there is only the beginning. Successful candidates must then navigate the politics of the institution, learn and employ the levers of power within it, and act to change those institutional structures in the service of making the institution more responsive to the diverse lived experiences of their constituents. All of this has to happen if real changes in representation are to occur.

The Election of 1992 Brings New Voices to Congress

The first step in the process of congressional representation is the decision to stand for office. In 1992, a record number of women decided to do just that. They hoped to add to the number of women in Congress, but especially to the Senate, where only two women were serving at the time.[2] In the run-up to the elections, Dianne Feinstein, then a candidate for a Senate seat for California, famously remarked, "Two percent may be good for fat in milk, but it's bad for women in the U.S. Senate."[3] Their collective electoral success meant that 1992 would go down as the "Year of the Woman," with a record fifty-three women in total elected to Congress.[4]

A Singular Event Galvanizes a New Field of Candidates. For many of the women who ran in 1992, one moment in congressional history crystalized their commitment to bringing about change in Congress: the Senate confirmation hearings of Clarence Thomas to the U.S. Supreme Court. Federal judicial confirmations are often politically charged, since appointments have profound and long-lasting consequences (see Chapter 13). Given Thomas's conservative views, the confirmation proceedings were bound to be heated. However, a specific point of controversy emerged during Thomas's hearings: Thomas's former aide, Professor Anita Hill, asserted that Thomas had sexually harassed her while the two were serving in the federal government.

Though many women were concerned about the specific charges of sexual harassment, it was the skepticism displayed by the members of the all-white, male Senate Judiciary Committee toward Hill's testimony—dismissive and condescending in the eyes of many—that galvanized women around the country by "symbolizing the lack of representation for women and their interests on Capitol Hill."[5] In response, "many voters decided that if given the chance they would vote for a woman candidate, in part because she was a woman. . . . [P]arty and grassroots organizations redoubled their efforts to find and fund women candidates. And . . . a number of women decided that they would put themselves on the line and run for local, state, and national office."[6]

In Washington State, Patty Murray, then a state legislator, "watched in disbelief as the committee members questioned Hill's veracity about Thomas' sexual advances and innuendo. Murray found herself asking 'Who's saying what I would say if I were there?'"[7] That evening, at a neighborhood party, as others expressed similar frustration, Murray announced, "You know what? I'm going to run for the Senate."[8]

PRACTICING POLITICAL SCIENCE

GENDER AND METAPHORS OF POWER IN IMAGE

Maureen Keating/The Granger Collection

AP Photo/Joe Rosenthal

Barbara Boxer, Nita Lowey, Eleanor Holmes Norton, Pat Schroeder, Jolene Unsoeld, and the late Patsy Mink, the Democratic women members of the House of Representatives in 1991, marched to the U.S. Senate to voice their concerns about the treatment of Anita Hill and the response to her charges of sexual harassment during the Clarence Thomas confirmation hearings. The American press called their action "the women's Iwo Jima," conjuring up the iconic images of American servicemen during World War II.

For Boxer, "that was an angle tailored by the media. We wanted to try to help the senators rethink their position, and we felt that they might appreciate hearing our perspective. . . . All we were asking was that the Senate take a serious look at Anita Hill's charges."[9]

WHaT Do You Think?

Why do you think a war metaphor was used to describe the efforts of the congresswomen? In what ways might a traditionally male-gendered metaphor shape readers' perceptions of their efforts?

Think about candidates running for Congress. Have you encountered images and portrayals of those you might choose as your representative or senator? How did those depictions reflect your own views of these individuals or your own goals for congressional action? How might they have not?

Murray exemplifies a characteristic that, according to political scientists Linda Fowler and Robert McClure, sets declared candidates apart. That is, she had **political ambition**.[10] Only those with the strongest personal desire to act in politics decide to face the long odds of success, especially if such a bid would mean facing

Five women won seats in the U.S. Senate in 1992—four for the first time—bringing the total number of women in the chamber to six, the most ever at that point. From left, Patty Murray (D-WA), Carol Moseley Braun (D-IL), Barbara Boxer (D-CA), Dianne Feinstein (D-CA), and Barbara Mikulski (D-MD) were part of the wave christened the "Year of the Woman."

Harry Hamburg/*NY Daily News* Archive/Getty Images

a well-resourced incumbent. Where does political ambition come from? The answers are not always neatly categorized by gender, racial, or ethnic identity, or any one simple category. As Murray's example shows, political ambition is as unique to a potential candidate as it is to the constituents they hope to represent.

The Departure of Congressional Incumbents Presents an Opportunity for Women in 1992.

In Chapter 10 we discussed how the power of incumbency—running for reelection as opposed to running for the first time—strongly affects the outcomes of congressional elections. Congressional incumbents possess so many advantages, such as media coverage, a record of providing beneficial service and legislation to a state or district, and name recognition, that qualified challengers often rationally wait until they can run for an open seat, after an incumbent has retired or moved on to another office.

In the 1992 elections, there was an important crack in the normal power of incumbency. For a variety of reasons, there was a record number of open congressional seats. Potential challengers who had been waiting for their chance pounced.

The Class of 1992 Mobilize Significant Resources in Their Electoral Bids.

When challengers do decide to stand for office, they need many things; however, above all else, they need money and experience. Money is inseparable from congressional elections. It buys media spots, funds a ground campaign, and acts to scare off potential opponents. The pressures of fundraising in the modern Congress are relentless.

Experience is hard earned, usually gained by moving up through the layers of local and state politics and becoming professional, polished, and respected. Congressional elections are usually no place for amateurs, who often lack the knowledge, political organization, and well-honed political skills prerequisite to success in the high-stakes enterprise of a national campaign. Looking back on her successful campaign for the U.S. Senate in 1992, Sen. Dianne Feinstein (D-CA) advised congressional hopefuls, especially young women, to "earn your spurs" by starting locally on the school board or town council and building a coherent portfolio that reflects a set of consistent policies "so that people will turn to you."[11]

The opportunity presented in 1992 would not have translated into electoral success without a slate of experienced and well-funded candidates. Carol Moseley Braun had served in the Illinois House of Representatives, and her path to the Senate was paved by the hard-earned experience of Chicago politics—as tough a venue as there is in American government. Moseley Braun saw opportunity not in an open seat but in a Democratic incumbent who had voted to confirm Clarence Thomas. She ousted the incumbent in the primary and then beat the Republican challenger in the general election.

As these new members of Congress arrived in Washington, each had to learn the spoken and unspoken rules that governed the U.S. Congress, figure out how to make their voices heard, and find mentors to show them the way. We will return to how they placed their stamps on what representation means later in the chapter.

In 2018, Women Again Ran in Historic Numbers and, Again, Changed the Composition of Congress

The "Year of the Woman" was declared again in 2018. In some ways, the election highlighted similar themes as 1992—first-time women candidates motivated by strong feelings of injustice and critiques of public policies. Again, a record number of women declared their candidacies in federal, state, and local elections. More than three hundred women ran for the House of Representatives alone, and "36,000 women—nearly 40 times the number from the last election cycle," contacted a women's electoral interest group stating that they wanted to "run or work on campaigns."[12] According to Rep. Anna Eshoo (D-CA), "This is not just a curiosity. It's not an interesting number or statistic. It's historic."[13]

Just as in 1992, the 2018 election campaigns saw a significant jump in contributions by women toward congressional campaigns. According to the nonpartisan Center for Responsive Politics in October 2017, the "number of female donors to federal candidates and committees has skyrocketed by roughly 284 percent," compared to a similar point in the 2015–2016 election cycle, all the more noteworthy given that 2018 was not a presidential election year.[14]

Just as in 1992, in 2018, a sizable majority of women candidates were Democrats. Many first-time candidates in their party stated that their motivation to run came from the policies and antiwomen statements of Republican president Donald Trump. These motivations were also connected to the #MeToo movement that arose in response to revelations of accusations of sexual harassment and rape by famous men in politics, business, and entertainment.[15]

The Diversity of Women's Voices in 2018 Had Grown Since 1992. While the election of 2018 had important parallels to 1992, there were important differences. First, it was not just the number of women candidates that was notable. It was also their diversity of identities and experiences: "It includes more women of color than previous electoral years, as well as a number of immigrants. There are more female veterans in the mix than we've seen before, and they're representing both sides of the aisle."[16]

Included among the winners were the nation's first Muslim congresswomen, Rashida Tlaib (D-MI) and Ilhan Omar (D-MN), and its first Native American congresswomen, Deb Haaland (D-NM) and Sharice Davids (D-KS).[17] Alexandria Ocasio-Cortez (D-NY) became the youngest woman ever elected to Congress.[18] Texas elected its first Latina members of Congress: Veronica Escobar and Sylvia Garcia. Massachusetts elected its first Black congresswoman, Ayanna Pressley, as did Connecticut, Jahana Hayes. Each of these successful candidates, all Democrats, would be hoping to shape Congress but also the direction of their party.

The Women of 2018 Join a Congress Populated by Many Members of the Class of 1992. One reality had not changed since 1992. Women Democrats far outnumbered women Republicans, continuing the sharp gendered split between the two parties in Congress. The fact that the Democratic Party took control of the House of Representatives in the election of 2018 had several major consequences. One of these was the impeachment of President Trump, which we will turn to later in the chapter. Democratic control also meant, however, that women Democrats who had been gaining influence, seniority, and powerful institutional positions over the decades were now part of the majority in the House. As we will see, having a majority in Congress means more than having the most votes; it is also key to holding power in the institutional structures that define how Congress works.

One of those congressional veterans was Rep. Nancy Pelosi (D-CA). Representative Pelosi won her election in 1992, though as a relatively new incumbent rather than a rookie. Narrowly winning a special election in 1987, Pelosi successfully held on to her seat in the House ever since, without even confronting a serious electoral challenge in decades. The elected Speaker of the House, shortly after the 116th Congress convened, found herself under fire—from Republicans to be sure; she was used to that—but also from members of her own party, especially a group of young women of color who were pushing their party to the progressive left. Representatives Ocasio-Cortez, Omar, Pressley, and Tlaib—labeled *the Squad* by Ocasio-Cortez—publicly challenged Speaker Pelosi in 2019 over an appropriations bill that did not include provisions for protections for migrant children. Pelosi fought back, criticizing their lack of party unity and their lack of experience in congressional politics: "All these people have their public whatever and

Rep. Nancy Pelosi (D-CA) reclaimed the Speaker's gavel when the Democrats won a majority in the House of Representatives in 2018. A faction within the Democratic Caucus, especially several of the newly elected women of color, began pushing Pelosi to adopt the more progressive policies that they had campaigned on. Pelosi insisted that the average Democratic voter was more moderate and would not support such an agenda.

Alex Wong/Getty Images

their Twitter world. But they didn't have any following (in the House). They're four people and that's how many votes they got."[19] Pelosi refused to be pushed. "If the left doesn't think I'm left enough, so be it," Pelosi said to a *New York Times* reporter.[20]

How much these internal divisions would damage the Democrats' ability to push a broad agenda going forward was unclear. According to Julia Azari of FiveThirtyEight, the Squad's pushback might have beneficial effects for Democratic turnout in the 2020 elections: "If the goal is to engage young people, women and people of color, and keep the left flank of the party somewhat happy, they seem like a good bet."[21]

To think about what the lasting effects of the congressional election of 2018 may or may not mean for national politics, however, we need to explore the institution that the candidates hoped to join or rejoin. We start with the Constitution, which set the broad structure and power of Congress but left it up to its members to figure out how they would actually go about much of their work.

The Constitution Defines Congress's Shape and Powers

> 10.2 Describe how the Constitution created Congress, including its structure and powers.

The U.S. Congress is called the *first branch* of government for good reason: The Constitution deals with its powers and procedures first, in more detail, and at greater length than it does those of the executive and judicial branches.

The House and Senate Serve Different Roles

The Great Compromise that emerged from the Constitutional Convention in 1787 called for the creation of a bicameral legislature composed of two chambers, the House of Representatives and the Senate. While both the House and the Senate are involved in the legislative process, the Framers of the Constitution saw their roles differently. These differences were designed partly to add checks and balances *within* Congress and not just between Congress and the other branches.

The House of Representatives Is Designed for Greater Accountability.
Members of the House of Representatives are meant to be close to the people and their wishes. At the Constitutional Convention, delegates agreed upon two-year terms for each representative, believing this would keep them close and accountable to the people while also giving them enough time to become competent in their work and familiar with all the relevant laws and issues.

Today, 435 representatives serve in the House, each directly elected by eligible voters in state districts that have been apportioned by population. The Constitution requires that representatives be at least twenty-five years old, a resident of their state, and a citizen of the United States for seven years.[22]

The Constitution did not include property ownership or affiliation in a particular religion as restrictions, because the Framers believed that the requirements for legislative service in the House should be "open to merit of every description."[23] While the Constitution did not explicitly bar women from holding office, the states did. Those that did allow women to hold office restricted it to those with property. Slaves and indigenous peoples were barred from public service, one of many restrictions upon and violations of their natural rights and liberties.

The Senate Is Designed for Greater Stability. Senators, in contrast, are meant to be more insulated from the whims of the public, adding stability to the legislative branch. Elected for six-year terms, the classes of senators are staggered so that about only one-third are up for reelection in a given cycle.

Today, one hundred senators serve in the Senate, two for each state. Senators have to be older than representatives—at least thirty years old—and citizens for at least nine years, and they must live in the state they seek to represent. Missing from the Constitution is any mention of **term limits**—limitations on how many terms a given representative or senator can serve—and today the idea is often debated (see Table 10.1).

▼ TABLE 10.1

The House of Representatives and the Senate Compared

	House of Representatives	Senate
Requirements for Membership	At least twenty-five years old	At least thirty years old
	Seven years of citizenship	Nine years of citizenship
	Resident of the state	Resident of the state
Service	Two-year terms, with unlimited number of terms	Six-year terms, divided into three classes, with unlimited number of terms
Constituency	District, apportioned to states by population	Entire state
Organization	More governed by rules, more institutionally structured, more power to individual leadership positions	Less governed by rules, more power to individual members, more informal
Goals	To be closer to voters' preferences	To be more insulated from voters' preferences

Congress Has Three Key Powers: Lawmaking, Budgeting, and Oversight

The powers of Congress fall into three broad areas: those related to its role as the main lawmaking body, those related to its position at the center of the budgeting process, and those it exerts when exercising oversight of the federal bureaucracy and other public officials.

Legislative Authority Is Key to Congressional Power. The most important power of Congress is its legislative authority—the ability to pass laws in areas of national policy. The body of law that Congress creates is called statutory law as it is written down in the **statutes** that Congress passes. The list of the enumerated powers of Congress is substantial; Congress is authorized to legislate in economic policy, national security, foreign policy, and other policy areas (see Table 10.2).

The Budgeting Process Is Another Key Power of Congress. The second major role of Congress involves its central position in setting a federal budget. Creating a bureaucratic agency requires two steps: First, congressional action authorizes the department or agency. Second, through the process of **appropriation**, Congress funds the agency's activities. Many of the rules governing the budgetary process were first set out in the Congressional Budget and Impoundment Control Act of 1974.[24] The Budget Act created the Congressional Budget Office (CBO), whose role is to provide information and estimates of the likely budgetary consequences of funding the agencies and programs created by Congress. The Budget Act also established the process of reconciliation, whereby congressional committees work out how federal spending will align with the overall congressional budget. Reconciliation bills are passed using a more streamlined process than other bills in Congress. This can make them harder to stop.

Congress Also Has the Power of Oversight. The third major role of Congress in national policymaking is that of **oversight**. Congress uses this authority to ensure that laws are implemented in the way that Congress intended when it passed them. Given the growth in the size and complexity of the federal government, this is not an easy task.

Congressional committees and subcommittees may conduct hearings and investigations into the actions of executive agencies to try to ensure that funds appropriated for programs are being spent efficiently and in accordance with the law's intent and that agents are not abusing their powers. While many committee hearings are routine, some may be called in the event of a perceived breakdown or failure by an executive branch agency.

The calling of hearings in response to a visible crisis is called **fire alarm oversight**, with oversight being triggered only by an alarm call. This is different from **police patrol oversight**, in which Congress continually monitors the actions of

Legislative Powers of Congress in the Constitution

The constitution grants Congress the power to legislate in the following areas:

Enumerated Powers			
	Both Chambers	House	Senate
Economic Policy	Create and collect taxes, coin money, borrow money, regulate the value of currency, borrow money, and regulate commerce.	All bills to raise revenue must be generated in the House.	In practice, the Senate has become a coequal partner in setting national revenue policy.
Foreign Policy	Regulate trade with other nations.		Ratify treaties entered into by a president.
National Security	Declare war, raise and support armies and a naval force and make rules for their governance and regulation, have power to call up the military, and define and punish piracies and felonies committed on the high seas.		
Other Powers Involving the Executive Branch		Impeach the president, vice president, and other executive branch officers.	Confirm presidential nominations of executive branch officers, and try members of the executive branch impeached by the House.
Powers Involving the Judicial Branch	Create levels of the judicial branch below the Supreme Court, and establish the number of Supreme Court justices.	Impeach members of the federal judiciary.	Confirm by majority vote presidential nominees to the federal judiciary, try members of the federal judiciary who have been impeached.
Via Necessary and Proper Clause			
	"To make all Laws which shall be necessary and proper for carrying into Execution the foregoing Powers, and all other Powers vested by this Constitution in the Government of the United States."		
Via Subsequent Amendments			
	Individual amendments (such as the Thirteenth, Fourteenth, and Fifteenth) grant Congress "the power to enforce, by appropriate legislation" those amendments.		

the bureaucracy. Because of the difficulty in continuously monitoring the immense federal bureaucracy, fire alarm oversight is more commonly used than police patrol oversight.[25]

Other Congressional Powers Involve Advice and Consent and Senatorial Courtesy. In implementing the idea of checks and balances, the Constitution gave each of the branches shared authority over some aspects of governance, which allows a kind of oversight of one branch over the other two. As discussed earlier, Congress is given the authority to declare war and the Senate to ratify treaties, thus forcing the executive and legislative branches to work together in important aspects of foreign and national security policy.

Using its power of advice and consent, the Senate confirms presidential nominees to the federal courts by a simple majority. The norm of **senatorial courtesy** has historically involved consultations between the White House and senators from the president's party who represent the states in which those judges will serve. The expectation is that these confirmations will proceed without significant opposition. The increasingly contentious process of confirmation to the federal judiciary has challenged this long-standing norm, however.

Congress also has the power "to constitute Tribunals inferior to [below] the Supreme Court"[26] and set the number of justices on the Supreme Court. In addition confirming presidential nominees to the federal judiciary, the Senate's obligation to advise and consent applies to most presidential nominees to important posts in the federal bureaucracy.

Congress Possesses the Power of Impeachment

Congress is also given the authority to remove federal officials and judges—up to and including the president and Supreme Court justices—through the process of **impeachment**. The House of Representatives votes to impeach if a majority of its members feel that an official has committed "Treason, Bribery, or other high Crimes and Misdemeanors." The vagueness of this language has resulted in debates about just what constitutes an impeachable offense.

If a majority of the members of the House votes to impeach, the trial takes place in the Senate, with a two-thirds majority needed to convict and remove the official from office.[27] Impeachment is a power that has been used rarely. Three presidents have faced successful House resolutions to impeach, but none were removed from office. Andrew Johnson—impeached during the Reconstruction era following the Civil War—survived by a single vote in the Senate. Bill Clinton—charged with lying during and obstructing an investigation into his relationship with intern Monica Lewinsky—was acquitted by a 55–45 vote.

In December 2019, the House of Representatives voted to impeach President Donald Trump on charges of abuse of power and obstruction of justice relating to his interactions with Ukrainian president Volodymyr Zelensky. Trump, the charges stated, had encouraged the Ukrainian president to announce a firm with ties to the son of Democratic presidential candidate Joe Biden in order to damage Biden politically. Linking foreign aid to a politically motivated investigation, the House charged, constituted an abuse of executive power. The vote in the House was largely on party lines, with two Democrats voting against on one charge and three joining the unanimous Republicans on another.

On February 5, 2020, the Senate voted to acquit the president on both charges with, again, the vote mostly following party lines. All forty-five Democratic senators, independents Bernie Sanders (VT) and Angus King (ME), and one Republican, Mitt Romney (UT) voted to convict, falling far short of the two-thirds vote necessary to remove the president from office. In any other election year, the fact that an incumbent president had been impeached, but retained strong support from his party, would have been the story of the campaign. The COVID-19 pandemic and the unrest following the killing of George Floyd by a Minneapolis police officer in May 2020, however, relegated the impeachment saga to the pages of history faster than seemed possible just weeks before.

Congress Is Organized around Formal and Informal Rules

> 10.3   Describe the rules, institutions, and processes that Congress itself has created to carry out its constitutional role.

The congressional elections of 2018 offered the chance for a significant number of newcomers to join the institution—a very diverse group of newcomers. But what would they do once they got there? To be effective, they would quickly have to learn how the institution actually works. Members of Congress must be very familiar with the organizational structure of Congress if they are to succeed in advancing their agenda. Groups may form around a shared set of lived experiences, a shared set of policy goals, or a shared desire to reform how Congress works. In addition, members gain power and influence as their congressional careers develop and they establish seniority within the institution.

While rules and procedures may seem like a dry subject of study, they matter a great deal to what legislation does or does not emerge from Congress. Battles over organization or congressional procedure are often just as heated and consequential as battles over specific policies.

The Constitution is much more specific on what Congress does than on how it is supposed to do it. With a few exceptions, the Constitution does not describe most of the day-to-day processes and procedures of Congress. These rules and details have been created by the chambers themselves, and important modifications have been made over time. Congress includes both formal and informal organizational features. Formally, political parties, party leaders, and the committee system shape much of what happens in the House and Senate. Congressional staff and the congressional bureaucracy are involved as well. Informally, norms and traditional ways of doing things also play a role.

Political Parties Shape How Congress Is Structured

Much of the formal structure of Congress revolves around the role of political parties and party leaders. The majority party, which is the party with the most members in each chamber, and the minority party, which has the second-highest number of members, each control important leadership positions and organize congressional behavior—both to advocate for their preferred policies and to help individual members in their reelection efforts.

In contrast to most modern representative assemblies, party leaders in the U.S. Congress often struggle to make sure that their own members act and vote in support of party positions, especially when a member's constituent preferences clash with those of the member's political party. Leaders, however, are not powerless and have a variety of carrots and sticks with which to steer their members in the desired direction. Party leaders work through party caucuses (Democratic Party) and party conferences (Republican Party), in which party members meet, agree on goals, choose leaders, assign members to committees, and try to present a unified voice to the American electorate through the media.

Party Leaders Play an Important Role in the House of Representatives.

Larger than the Senate since the founding of Congress, the House of Representatives is, by necessity, more formally structured than the Senate, with rank-and-file House members being individually less powerful than their Senate colleagues. The **Speaker of the House**—the only House leadership position described in the Constitution—wields a considerable amount of power, though that power has changed over time in response to demands on the House and strategic political action on the part of its members.

At the beginning of each new Congress (every two years), members of the House elect the Speaker, who has almost always been a member of the majority party. A long history of successful service in the House is usually a prerequisite. Increasingly, the ability to raise money for other members of one's party is considered in selecting a Speaker. The Speaker is second in the line of succession (behind the vice president) to the presidency in the event of death, resignation, removal from office, or inability to conduct the office's duties. In Congress, the Speaker has considerable power over the House agenda and committee assignments.

Assisting the Speaker are the **House majority leader**, the majority **whip** (and other members of the whip system), and various caucus and conference chairs and vice chairs. Members of the whip system collect information about how individual members are planning to vote, corralling their support on key votes and setting party strategy in Congress. The **House minority leader** has far less structural influence in the House than the Speaker but works to coordinate minority party activity, opposition to the majority party, and overall strategy. House minority party leadership also includes its own whips and whip systems.

Party Leaders Also Shape Action in the Senate. Constitutionally, the official leader of the Senate is the vice president of the United States, though they can cast a vote only in the event of a tie. The president pro tempore presides over the chamber's proceedings when the vice president is not present (which is almost all the time) but wields no real power. Typically, junior senators fill in to oversee the day-to-day proceedings.

The most powerful position in the Senate is the **Senate majority leader**, who is chosen by the majority party members in caucus or conference. Although individual senators hold more power than their colleagues in the House, the Senate majority leader is not as powerful as the Speaker. They do play a key role in shaping the legislative agenda, however. The Senate minority leader—chosen by the minority party members—acts as the leader of the opposition in the Senate. Assisting both party leaders are party whips, leadership committees, and party caucuses and conferences.

The Work of Congress Is Done through the Committee System

The work of Congress is considerable and complex. There is no way any one member could be directly involved in each piece of legislation. To divide the workload, both the House and the Senate have established a system of committees and subcommittees that do most of the work of Congress.

Party Leaders and Seniority Shape Committee Membership and Leadership. Committee membership is determined and negotiated by party leaders and generally reflects the ratio of party membership in each chamber. Seniority, or the length of consecutive service on the committee, plays a major role in determining **committee chairs**. These chairs have considerable influence over committee processes, especially in setting the committee's agenda. Because of the differences in the size of the chambers, House committees tend to have more members than Senate committees, while individual senators tend to serve on more committees than their colleagues in the House.

New representatives and senators often try to get appointed to committees that deal with issues of interest to their constituents or that provide benefits to their districts and states. That has the added advantage of helping their prospects for reelection. Requests for committee membership, though, may also be driven by genuine policy interests on the part of members of Congress.[28]

Different Types of Committees Perform Different Roles. Congress has four types of committees: standing, joint, conference, and select. Standing committees are where most of the work of Congress gets done. They are so named because they continue across Congresses, and members tend to serve on them for multiple terms, developing expertise and working to bring benefits to their districts and states. Standing committees consider legislation and exercise oversight of bureaucratic agencies, usually recommending funding levels for them. They are divided by policy areas, with a given committee having jurisdiction over its area of specialization. Standing committees are divided into subcommittees, which specialize even further, usually considering parts of legislation under instructions from their parent committees.

Joint committees contain members of both the House and the Senate. In general they do not have a great deal of power but are used to focus public attention on an issue, gather information for Congress, or help party leaders speed things along in the legislative process.

The conference committee is a temporary joint committee that resolves differences between the House and Senate versions of a bill, which is required by the Constitution before a president can sign the bill into law. Party leaders determine conference committee membership, though members who have been centrally involved in a bill are usually included.

The fourth type of committee is the select or special committee. These temporary bodies are usually called upon to investigate an issue, sometimes in response to a crisis or a scandal. Select committees may be given the authority to report legislation, but their role is usually informational only.

Congressional Staff and the Congressional Bureaucracy Help Members Represent Their Constituents

The third component of the formal organization of Congress consists of the people and institutions developed to help members represent their constituents. Congressional staff assist representatives and senators in conducting casework and give members information about policies, legislation, and constituent preferences. Staff often work closely with members in drafting bills. As the size of the American Republic and the complexity of issues before Congress have both grown, so has the size of the congressional staff.

Congress has also developed nonpartisan bureaucratic organizations to assist its members' efforts. For instance, the CBO provides members with estimates of the likely impact of laws on the national budget, and the Government Accountability Office (GAO) keeps them informed about how well agencies are performing the tasks Congress intended of them.

Norms Are Informal Contributors to Congressional Organization

In addition to the formal structures, less formal processes also play a role in congressional action. Norms are unwritten expectations of how members are supposed to act and help members balance representing their constituents and contributing to the smooth functioning of the House and Senate. Members are expected to be respectful toward their colleagues, to reciprocate help from other members, and to specialize in one or more policy areas to assist the overall level of information and expertise in Congress. Animosity between members of the two political parties has challenged the role of norms in constraining member behavior in recent years, however.

The Legislative Process Is Complex by Design

> 10.4 Explain the steps of the legislative process and how it can diverge from traditional "textbook" descriptions.

By design, the legislative process is complicated and multistepped, with each stage offering another chance to kill a prospective law. Having seen the passions of the people sweep through state legislatures and sometimes trample minority rights, the Framers of the Constitution intentionally placed many hurdles in the path of legislation.

What's more, the modern legislative process rarely follows the traditional, linear "textbook" route that is described in Figure 10.1, especially when it comes to major legislation. Political scientist Barbara Sinclair used the term **unorthodox lawmaking** to describe the realities of the modern legislative process: Whereas "the route to enactment used to be linear and predictable; now it is flexible and varied."[29]

This reality does not mean that legislators are bypassing constitutional provisions—only that the process is much more fluid, complex, and political than any flowchart can adequately describe.

The First Step Is Bill Introduction

The first stage of the legislative process is the formal introduction of a **bill**, a draft of a proposed law, in either the House or the Senate. Any member may introduce a bill, but only members of Congress may do so. Even here we see evidence of unorthodox lawmaking, as other actors often play a role in shaping a bill or encouraging a member to introduce it. For instance, although we often hear presidents talk about legislation they plan to introduce, for all their tremendous power, presidents cannot offer a bill for consideration; only a member of the House can do that. However, presidents can encourage, cajole, and press members of either chamber to get a major piece of legislation on the legislative agenda, whether through discussions with party leaders or though appeals to the American public.

Once introduced, a particular bill must wind its way through the originating chamber and then proceed to the other chamber to begin the process anew. Formally, only the House may introduce revenue bills. In practice, however, both chambers often act simultaneously on similar policies, with frequent communication between party leaders in each chamber. In addition, the Senate (along with the president) has become a coequal partner in the overall revenue and spending process.

The vast majority of bills introduced never become law, and members realize these odds. According to Sinclair, "Members may introduce legislation for a variety of

▼ FIGURE 10.1

The Legislative Process

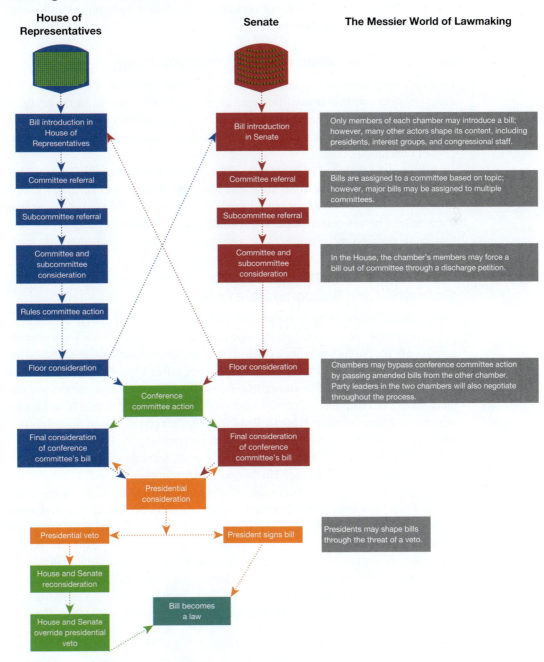

reasons, ranging from placating a pesky interest group in their home state or district to publicizing a little recognized problem or an innovative approach to an acknowledged problem. Members may not expect certain of their bills to pass and, sometimes, may not even want them to."[30]

Referral to Committee Involves Political Strategy

Because committees are so important to the ultimate success or failure of a bill, assignment to committee involves strategic political calculations. In the textbook model, a bill simply goes to the committee that has jurisdiction over that policy area. In practice, committees sometimes fight for bill assignments that would expand or protect their jurisdiction.

Bills may be assigned to more than one committee—a process called multiple referral—especially if the bill is large and complex. The rules governing multiple referral have changed over time, and the practice is more common in the House than the Senate. This process happens sequentially, rather than a bill being before more than one committee at a time.

Bills Are Altered—and Die—Due to Committee and Subcommittee Action

Once referred to one or more committees, legislation is usually sent to one or more subcommittees—more narrowly focused groups of legislators operating under the guidance of the parent committee of which they are a part. Committees and subcommittees hold hearings to gather information about a bill or issue. Outside experts may be brought in to testify. The **markup** session allows committee members to make changes to a bill before the committee sends it to the House or Senate floor for consideration. The committee report follows the bill from committee to floor. It acts as a history of the bill and offers guidance to administrative agencies and (if necessary) courts about the committee's intent regarding the bill. Sometimes early cost estimates of the bill's provisions are included in the conference report.

Congressional committees are the graveyards of most bills. In committee, bills can die because of a committee's refusal to report the bill to the full chamber, changes made to them to make them impassable on the House or Senate floor, or simple neglect. The committee may reject the bill by vote, or it may table the bill with no further action. In the House, a member may file a discharge petition to free a bill from an unfriendly committee and move it to the House floor for a vote if this is agreed to by a majority of representatives. Once they have successfully passed out of committee, bills proceed to consideration on the floors of the House and Senate.

Rules and Institutions Shape Consideration in the House. An important difference between the House and the Senate is the role of the **House Committee on Rules** in the legislative process, which has no equally powerful analogue in the Senate. A majority of the House Rules Committee's members are chosen by the Speaker. This committee determines when a bill will be subject to debate and vote on the House floor, how long the debate will last, and whether amendments will be allowed on the floor. These special rules can play a major role in whether the bill passes the House or not.

Open rules allow all relevant amendments while closed rules prohibit amendments other than those reported by committee. Most bills are considered under rules that fall in between these extremes, with modified open or modified closed rules. The rules about amendments are important because adding amendments to a bill is yet one more way to kill a piece of legislation. Killer amendments are designed to do just that by peeling away support for a bill by adding unpalatable or indefensible language or provisions. Closed rules can occasionally be used to kill a bill as well, if there are enough members who would support a bill only if key amendments were added, which is not allowed under closed rules.

If the House approves the rules governing a bill, then floor debate on the bill begins under those rules. A vote to accept or reject the rules reported out of the Rules Committee can be just as consequential to the fate of a piece of legislation as an actual vote on a bill—though in ways that are less visibly clear to most American voters. If allowed, amendments may be offered and, perhaps, amendments made to amendments. The time allowed for debate and who controls that time will also have been set by the Rules Committee.

A **roll-call vote** is a vote in which each member of the chamber debating a bill indicates "yea," "nay," or "present." In the House, most votes are electronic. Many interest groups keep track of key votes on issues relevant to them, scoring individual members on how friendly or unfriendly their votes have been to the members of that interest group.

Individual Senators Play a Stronger Role in Senate Consideration.
In the Senate, individual senators have more ability to shape outcomes on the floor than their House colleagues. Party leadership still matters, however, and the Senate majority leaders schedule the agenda. While the House was first to adopt more formal procedures for bill consideration, the Senate has also become more formalized—though not to the same degree as the House. In the Senate, most procedures are governed by unanimous consent, in which all senators agree to let a motion proceed to a vote. A simple unanimous consent request may be used on noncontroversial measures. A more complex unanimous consent agreement will be worked out between the parties on major legislation to govern the length of debate and the rules governing amendments.

If an individual senator objects to a bill or part of a bill, that senator may place a hold on the legislation and communicate to the majority leader their reservations about the bill. In their ability to place holds, offer amendments, and debate issues on the floor, individual senators have the ability to consume Congress's scarcest resource: time. While the majority leader does not have to honor the hold request, a hold indicates the possibility of a filibuster on the bill.

A **filibuster** is the use of the power of individual senators to continue to debate issues in order to delay a motion or vote on the floor.[31] Only a successful vote of **cloture**, which requires three-fifths of senators (sixty), can shut down debate and end a filibuster, allowing the Senate to move on to a vote. Therefore, a determined minority party, provided they have at least forty-one seats and are able to maintain party unity, can delay or kill legislation through the use of the filibuster.

The filibuster has a long and controversial history in the Senate. In 1917, under the urging of President Woodrow Wilson, the Senate adopted the rule of cloture. At the time, ending a filibuster required a two-thirds majority; it was changed to three-fifths in 1975. The placing of holds and threats of a filibuster are increasingly common in a closely split but deeply divided Senate. Because of the increased use of the filibuster threat, votes of cloture have become much more numerous as well. Senators have not only threatened to filibuster a bill they object to but they have also at times held up an unrelated vote or confirmation of a presidential nominee in order to extract concessions on something else, a process referred to as hostage-taking.[32]

Changes to Senate rules lowered the cloture threshold to a simple majority for executive branch nominees and lower-level federal judges (by the Democratic-controlled Senate in 2013) and for Supreme Court nominees (by the Republican-controlled Senate in 2017). The ability to filibuster most bills in the Senate, however, remains. During debates over the budget bill in the spring of 2017, President Trump called for the elimination of the filibuster entirely in a set of Twitter posts. "Either elect more Republican Senators in 2018 or change the rules now to 51%," he tweeted. "Our country needs a good 'shutdown' in September to fix this mess!"[33] In a rare, bipartisan response to his comments, "sixty-one senators signed a letter circulated by Senators Chris Coons, Democrat of Delaware, and Susan Collins, Republican of Maine, backing the 60-vote threshold on legislation."[34]

The House and Senate Resolve Differences between Their Bills

The next step in the legislative process is to resolve differences between House and Senate versions of a bill prior to presidential action. The formal structure for reconciling differences between two versions of a bill is the conference committee. Traditionally bipartisan, the Speaker of the House chooses that chamber's members. Because the Senate operates under unanimous consent, leaders from both parties choose its members to conference. Key players in a bill's progress through Congress are usually included as well.

When the differences are over spending amounts, negotiation is usually more straightforward. When they involve major policy differences—especially if one party controls the House and another the Senate—negotiations may be much more difficult. Because the process of sending a bill to conference from the Senate requires several procedural votes, which are subject to filibuster threat, the modern Congress often bypasses conference, though both chambers must still approve identical language for a bill to become law.

On minor bills, or when the differences are small, one chamber may avoid going to conference by simply accepting the other chamber's version of the bill. This especially happens late in a session when time is scarce and can be used by the political opposition as a weapon.[35] Party leaders may also negotiate informally behind the scenes, with the results of these negotiations offered as amendments. The strategy of ping-ponging (also called amendment exchange) is also designed to avoid having to go to conference. House and Senate versions are amended until the process has produced a single text.

Bills Go Back to the Floor for Reconsideration

Once differences between the two versions have been resolved, the single bill goes back to each chamber for reconsideration, without the possibility of amendment. By this point, on major bills, party leaders have already engaged in lengthy negotiations with their counterparts in the other chamber to avoid any surprises.

The President Takes Action

Following successful passage in each chamber, the bill goes to the president. The president then has three choices for each bill that lands on their desk. The president may sign it, in which case the bill becomes a law. They may **veto** it, sending it back to Congress with objections noted. Bills that are vetoed can still become law if two-thirds of both chambers vote to override the president's veto. Veto overrides are not common and signal a deep disconnect between a president and Congress.

As with a filibuster in the Senate, the power of a presidential veto lies as much with the *threat* of its use as with the actual veto. Veto bargaining is a negotiation tactic used by presidents to shape the legislation before it lands on their desk by using the threat of an eventual veto to gain desired concessions or amendments.[36] The president's third option is to do nothing, though what happens next depends on how much time is left in that session of Congress. If the president does nothing and there are ten or more days left in session (Sundays excluded), the bill becomes law anyway. This quiet veto does not change the outcome, but it might signal to American voters presidential displeasure with all or part of the law. If Congress has adjourned that year's session during the ten-day period and the president has not signed it, then the law is vetoed—an outcome that is called a pocket veto. A controversial tactic for Congress to avoid a pocket veto is to leave one or more members behind while everyone else goes home, thus refusing to technically adjourn.

Members Represent Constituents in How They Act and Who They Are

> 10.5 Connect the issues surrounding the representation of women in Congress to the challenges involving representation of other individuals in America.

The most difficult question in the study of Congress is what may seem to be the simplest: What does it mean to represent one's constituents in Congress? Part of the answer lies in *acting*—in the sense of what representatives do. In a representative democracy, citizens choose representatives, to act on their behalf—to vote on the floor and in committee, to sponsor legislation, to negotiate, and to lead. Another part of the answer lies in *being*—in the sense of who the representatives are.

When voters select representatives, they are choosing people who may or may not reflect and share their policy preferences, identities, interests, and lived experiences. They ask that their representatives transmit information about them—the constituents—to the other members of Congress by adding their voices to the debates and deliberations within the institution. In doing so, according to political scientist Richard Fenno, voters are in a sense asking their representatives to take on sometimes competing roles, which he used the term *home style* to denote. Voters want their political representatives to be effective in Washington, which takes them away from home. However, voters also want their members to come home, to present themselves and explain to voters what they have been up to and what they are going to accomplish.[37] More time at home connects representatives and senators to their constituents, while effective representation necessarily involves spending time operating in the intricate machinery of Congress.

Acting in Congress Involves Visible and Invisible Legislative Work

Passing laws—the legislative function—is Congress's most important task, and voting on the House and Senate floor is the most public legislative act members undertake. However, as we have seen, the process of legislation involves many stages and many less visible acts, such as committee work, bill sponsorship, and negotiation, which can pose a challenge to constituents trying to keep tabs on their elected representatives.

Legislators' Voting Decisions Are Affected by Constituents' Interests and Political Parties. When approaching a vote in Congress, members have several factors to consider.[38] First, they must always at least consider their constituents' interests. Though a senator or representative may ultimately decide to vote against the wishes of those who sent them to Washington, no member can ignore voters repeatedly without facing a constituent backlash. If, however, a senator or representative has earned a level of trust from constituents through long and successful service to them, then they may be more willing to act against constituent interests if it feels like the right course of action.[39]

A member's political party also influences how that member will vote. Members may seek input from their colleagues, especially if those colleagues are policy specialists and are known to have a particular expertise relevant to a bill. Input from a member's congressional staff may play a role, as may signals from interest groups, especially if individuals within the interest groups can convince the representative that their constituents agree with the group's position. Finally, the president may try to convince representatives to vote a certain way, especially if they are in the same political party.

Representatives' Actions Are Shaped by Level of Constituent Knowledge.

Elections are the primary tool that voters have to shape the actions of their elected representatives. Voters can pressure candidates to make certain promises during campaigns in exchange for their vote and also threaten backlash in the future if those promises are not kept.[40] Both of these mechanisms, however, require some basic level of information on the part of constituents and representatives. Constituents must have policy preferences to begin with and must communicate those preferences to their representatives. They must also have some basic level of information about the actions of their representatives in Congress to know whether to reward or punish those representatives in the next election.

Unfortunately, a long tradition of research in political science has shown that on most issues the majority of constituents are poorly informed,

Sen. Patty Murray (D-WA) is the ranking member of the Senate Committee on Health, Education, Labor and Pensions; a member of the powerful Senate Committee on Appropriations; and sits on the Senate Committee on the Budget and Senate Committee on Veterans' Affairs. She has risen through the ranks of Congress since her first election in 1992.

Andrew Harrer/Bloomberg via Getty Images

uninterested, or lack any coherent policy preferences. Some constituents are far better informed than others, especially if they have formed themselves into an interest group for the purpose of influencing congressional action. This inequality of information runs the risk of tilting Congress in the direction of acting only in the interests of its most informed and involved constituents to the detriment of the majority of uninformed ones.

Political scientist R. Douglas Arnold's research explored the ways in which Congress might pass laws that benefit the many even if they impose costs on a well-informed and involved few. But this is not easy.[41] First, representatives must shield themselves as much as possible from the backlash of powerful interests, with as few easily traceable votes as possible. Their leaders must frame failure to act as an unacceptable alternative, making it easier for members to explain individually costly votes.

In addition, there must be a real threat that voters who are not currently paying attention might become aware of and involved in an issue in the future. Interest groups may perform the role of "auditing" on behalf of less informed and less aware voters.[42] Congressional challengers may also play a role, bringing up issues in a campaign that incumbents incorporate into their own agendas.[43] Even the most secure incumbents worry about an issue that might cause their constituents alarm or concern. Successfully worrying about what might happen is part of what has kept them in office in the first place.

Key Aspects of Lawmaking Happen outside the Public Eye.

There is another challenge to the ability of constituents to control or influence representatives' actions. While votes on the floor or in committee can usually be traced to a particular member, much of the actual work on legislation happens outside the public eye. The choices that representatives make in allocating their time and energy can have important consequences for the fate of legislation. Members' decisions about how much effort to put into steering a bill through the constitutional obstacle course that is Congress—or how much energy to devote to blocking its progress—can be crucial to success or failure.[44] The challenge for constituents is that these individual choices are difficult to observe and, therefore, reward or punish.

Yet members do act, even when the reelectoral math does not add up. Why? Sometimes the decision to act comes from personal motivations and experiences. Senators Feinstein and Moseley Braun both were involved in one of the most important pieces of legislation taken up by the 103rd Congress: a comprehensive effort to reduce crime and reshape criminal justice policy. Following their elections in 1992, both joined the powerful Senate Judiciary Committee and used their experience and qualifications to translate their influence into legislation. According to one article, in the Senate, "Moseley-Braun . . . highlighted racial concerns while Feinstein led a successful floor fight to add an assault weapons ban to the Senate crime bill."[45] Feinstein had personally witnessed the assassinations of San Francisco mayor George Moscone and supervisor Harvey Milk and became acting mayor in the aftermath of their shooting deaths. Moseley Braun summed up her colleague's efforts: "I'd say that the assault weapons ban is a testimony to her hard work and just doggedness, because at a time when I and every other member of the Committee had concluded that this was a symbolic thing and there was no way we were going to get the votes, Dianne went out and worked and got the votes."[46]

Partisan Polarization Strongly Affects Voting and Cooperation. Representatives do not act in a vacuum. Their behavior is influenced both by the rules and procedures in Congress and by political parties. Political scientists, congressional observers, and some members themselves have become increasingly concerned about trends in partisan polarization in which members of parties vote and act strongly with their own party and become less likely to cross the aisle and cooperate with each other. While scholars disagree about the causes of polarization in Congress, voting records on the House and Senate floor show a clear trend toward intraparty cohesion (see Figure 10.2).[47]

Intense partisanship can lead to more than ill feelings between members. It may contribute to gridlock, a situation in which Congress's ability to legislate is slowed or stopped by its inability to overcome divisions, especially those based on partisanship. Gridlock is made more likely in a period of divided government, which occurs when control of the presidency and one or both chambers of Congress is split between the two major parties.

Descriptive Representation Is about Who Members Are

Many of the Framers and supporters of the U.S. Constitution expected that Congress would be a reflection or "portrait" of the people in the Republic, though the definition of who had the right to be a represented person was highly restrictive.

Visualizing Partisan Polarization

In 2015 a group of researchers mapped the networks of members of the House of Representatives from 1949 to 2011, identifying points of agreement between members on significant issues based on political party. Democratic members are identified in blue and Republicans in red. Each dot represents an individual. The connections represent points of agreement above a specific threshold. Note that over time, the dots have increasingly separated into red and blue groups and are increasingly tightly clustered.

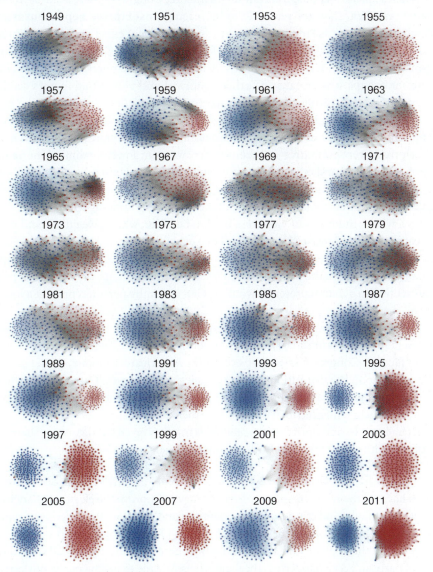

Source: Clio Andris et al., "The Rise of Partisanship and Super-Cooperators in the U.S. House of Representatives," *PloS One* 10, no. 4 (2015), http://journals.plos.org/plosone/article?id=10.1371/journal.pone.0123507.

Several issues and challenges arise when attempting to view Congress as a portrait of America. The first is that no single member can represent each of their constituents' diverse identities, experiences, and interests. Even if somehow possible, this might not be desirable in the extreme. Constituents, for example, might want their legislators to be more knowledgeable about, experienced in, and motivated to act in the messy space of politics than the average American voter.

When scholars and observers talk about making Congress a more accurate reflection of America, they are referring to increasing **descriptive representation**: Members of Congress "mirror some of the more frequent experiences and outward manifestations of belonging to the group."[48] Usually the goal of increasing descriptive representation in Congress is to selectively increase the membership of a particular group or groups who because of other historical and contextual factors remain underrepresented in proportion to their share of the population.[49]

Looking at the modern Congress, it is clear that the members do not come close to presenting a mirror of the American electorate. While Congress has grown more descriptively representative in recent years, women; lower-income Americans; members of racial and ethnic minorities; members of certain religious faiths; and lesbian, gay, bisexual, and transgender (LGRTQIA) Americans remain underrepresented in proportion to their percentage of the American voting-age population.

As a whole, members of Congress tend to be older, whiter, wealthier, and more educated than the American electorate. The lack of descriptive representation raises a complicated set of related questions: Does it matter? Is it necessary for a member of Congress to share the lived experiences of the constituents whom they hope to represent? Can a man represent a woman? Can a wealthy person represent a lower-income person?

Some scholars have argued that there may be benefits to having a descriptively representative legislature apart from what it actually does in Congress. Seeing a diversity of faces in Congress may, in the eyes of the American electorate, confer greater legitimacy upon the institution and the policies that it passes. Other scholars have pointed out that legislators who do not descriptively represent a particular group of their constituents still need to pay attention to their concerns.

A challenge to descriptive representation is that any given legislator may share key attributes with some of their constituents but not others.

Racial and Ethnic Gerrymandering Increases Descriptive Representation.

States have redrawn congressional districts to try to improve the electoral chances of legislators of racial and ethnic minority identities and therefore the descriptive representation of Congress along these characteristics. There is, however, a potential contradiction in the logic of such racial and ethnic gerrymandering. Recall that in the case of partisan gerrymandering, the logic is to isolate the opposing party into a small number of districts, conceding those districts to the opposing party but diluting their votes in a larger number of other districts, thus "wasting" the opposing party's votes.

In the case of racial and ethnic gerrymandering, the tactic is the same, but the goal is different: to concentrate minority voters in a small number of districts in order to help their overall representation in Congress.

Not all scholars agree that creating these majority-minority districts increases the overall representation of minorities in Congress. Political scientist Carol Swain has argued that while creating such districts increases the probability of electing African Americans within those districts, it does not necessarily improve the representation of African Americans overall.[50] Perhaps, Swain argued, it is better to have a larger number of legislators who have to consider the views of their African American constituents than have a small number of descriptively representative legislators who lack enough votes to advocate for their positions.

If the creation of majority-minority districts dilutes the degree to which members have to attend to their minority constituents' interests, then that risk might need to be counterbalanced by having members who have a close connection to specific issues and are willing to undertake the work of making those voices present by, for example, introducing or sponsoring legislation.

Essentialism Problematizes a Focus on Identity. Thinking about constituents in terms of specific characteristics poses another challenge, that of **essentialism**, which political theorist Jane Mansbridge defined as "the assumption that members of certain groups have an essential identity that all members of that group share and of which no others can partake."[51] Essentialism risks masking the complexity of views *within* members of that group, sidelining policy disagreements between them in the name of some shared "women's interest" or "African American interest." Second, it also risks cordoning off members' efforts into a few predefined acceptable issues: the idea that women should only talk about "women's issues" or that Black people should only talk about "Black issues."

Substantive Representation Connects How Members Act and Who They Are

Both the acts that members of Congress undertake and the degree to which they share the lived experiences of their constituents shape representation. It is the connection between acting and reflecting that holds the promise of sorting out some of the contradictions and challenges in each. While it very well may be important for American voters to feel that their Congress is a legitimate portrait of the nation, what really matters is, according to Hanna Pitkin, "the nature of the activity itself, what goes on during representation, the substance of the content of acting for others."[52] Pitkin calls this **substantive representation**.

Substantive representation is important because it holds the promise of linking constituents' lived experiences not just to the actions of their own legislators but to the actions of the institution itself, to the way that the institution works. It has the potential to improve the way that Congress deliberates by expanding the congressional agenda and by facilitating representation across geographical and partisan boundaries.

Deliberation May Be Improved by Substantive Representation. As imagined by those who designed it, Congress is supposed to be much more than just a place to count predecided votes and hear preformed arguments. It is also supposed to be a place for **legislative deliberation**, the considered argument and discussion of the issues. Deliberation is discussion of "which policies are good for the polity as a whole, which policies are good for representatives' constituents, and when the interests of various groups within the policy and constituency conflict."[53]

Deliberation is itself a complicated thing. For viewpoints to be discussed, they must first capture the attention of a large enough number of legislators. Second, deliberation is personal. Individual relationships between members who share interests and experiences can make for a more effective deliberative body. When this occurs, members who share common experiences can work with colleagues in the other party, thereby helping to counter trends in partisan polarization.

In any given session of Congress, there are only so many issues that can be dealt with and discussed—the list of which constitutes the legislative agenda. Why some issues seem to rocket toward the top of the agenda and others languish at the bottom or are ignored is sometimes easily explained—for example, in times of national crisis, some concerns are seen as more urgent than others. However, the setting of the congressional agenda is often unpredictable.[54] By bringing unconsidered issues to Congress's table and making them salient, legislators who share common lived experiences with underrepresented constituents may enlarge the institution's agenda. In doing so, members are acting (in political theorist Jane Mansbridge's analysis) as surrogate representatives: They are representing people who may not live in their district or state but with whom they share common concerns.[55]

Presenting information to one's legislative colleagues is an important part of representation. After the 2000 election, a reporter asked Sen. Kay Bailey Hutchison (R-TX), "Why can't a male senator do everything a woman senator can do?" Hutchison's reply was, "Sometimes, from our experience, there are issues that men just haven't thought about. . . . Most of the time our colleagues are supportive once we've made the case."[56] Research supports Senator Hutchison's assertion.

Members May Choose to Represent Those outside of Their Constituencies. In 1993, Carol Moseley Braun—the only African American senator serving at the time—brought to the chamber's attention the larger implications of an issue that might have seemed trivial to many members, if it was on their radar at all. Sen. Jesse Helms (R-NC) had offered as an amendment a renewal of the patent for the design of the symbol of the United Daughters of the Confederacy, which included the Confederate flag—an image many African Americans found, and continue to find, objectionable but was not seen as problematic by many whites at the time. Had

Moseley Braun been focused only on her reelectoral prospects, this was probably not a battle that needed to be fought. Yet Moseley Braun successfully killed the amendment and in doing so signaled to her own constituents as well as to African American voters across the nation that she intended to voice their shared concerns in the Senate.

Rarely, however, can one legislator reshape the congressional agenda on their own. It requires enough members to join in advocating minority positions. And, as we have seen, the importance of committee action suggests that effective substantive representation requires enough members with shared experiences to make present these voices not just on the floor but behind closed doors in committees.

Carol Moseley Braun greets constituents in her hometown of Chicago, Illinois.
Steve Kagan/The *LIFE* Images Collection/Getty Images

Conclusion: The Complexity of Representation

Today, representation in Congress involves the same issues it always has: standing for constituents, bringing voices and energy to its deliberations and outcomes, and operating within an institution intentionally designed by the Framers of the Constitution to place brakes on the pace of political change.

When the 117th Congress convenes in January of 2021, it will be the most diverse in the nation's history. The Democratic Party will be entering the new Congress with a majority in the House, but a smaller majority than it possessed in the 116th Congress, with Republicans "flipping" at least half a dozen seats in their favor, perhaps several more. Central to that outcome were the collective electoral successes of Republican women, contributing to the largest number of Republican women in Congress in the party's history.

On the Democratic side, there will be new voices as well, including several who campaigned on progressive Democratic platforms, focusing on issues such as climate change, re-examining policing, achieving economic justice, and making substantive changes to the nation's immigration, health, and education policies. House members-elect such as Cori Bush (D-MO-01), Mondaire Jones (D-NY-17), and Jamaal Bowman (D-NY-16) promised to push their parties towards assertive legislative action. The degree to which the growing strength of progressive Democratic voices within Congress will lead to substantive legislative changes, however, is still up in the air.

The Framers of the Constitution did not intend for Congress to be purely and perfectly representative. They mistrusted the ability of *citizens* to avoid the dangers of faction. In recent decades, however, Congress has come to more accurately reflect the American electorate, though it is still far from being perfectly descriptive. These gains have not come about by chance; they are mostly due to the strategic actions of citizens to reshape Congress to better portray the diversity of the nation.

Representation and lawmaking in Congress are complicated, messy, and often uncomfortable. Though the legislative branch is the first branch of government—and viewed as the most powerful by the Framers—it is still only one of three. Over the course of American history, strategic political actors in the other two branches—the executive and judicial—have also tried to shape the power of their institutions, to present their own views of representation in the United States, and to stand for the people.

CHAPTER REVIEW

This chapter's main ideas are reflected in the Learning Objectives below. By reviewing them here, you should be able to *remember* the key points and *know* these terms that are central to the topic.

10.1 Understand how questions of representation involve political and institutional considerations as well as questions of identity.

Remember . . .
- Factors that contribute to a decision to run for election include election-specific ones: adequate funding resources and personal ambition.
- Representation of women in Congress is shaped by sharp partisan divides.
- One of the key issues in the elections was a record number of women running.

Know . . .
- *political ambition* (p. 287)
- *represent* (p. 285)

10.2 Describe how the Constitution created Congress, including its structure and powers.

Remember . . .
- Congress is a bicameral legislature: The House of Representatives and the Senate are divided to establish a set of checks and balances within Congress.
- Members of the House are meant to be closer to the people. Senators are meant to be more insulated from the public to ensure greater stability.
- The House and Senate have legislative authority as well as budgetary and oversight powers.

Know . . .
- *appropriation* (p. 293)
- *fire alarm oversight* (p. 293)
- *impeachment* (p. 295)
- *oversight* (p. 293)
- *police patrol oversight* (p. 293)
- *senatorial courtesy* (p. 295)
- *statutes* (p. 293)
- *term limits* (p. 292)

10.3 **Describe the rules, institutions, and processes that Congress itself has created to carry out its constitutional role.**

Remember . . .
- Political parties exert a good deal of influence in Congress, especially over key leadership positions.
- Congressional committees do most of the work of Congress.
- Norms and traditional ways of doing things also play a role—albeit a more informal one—in the smooth functioning of Congress.

Know . . .
- *committee chairs* (p. 298)
- *House majority leader* (p. 297)
- *House minority leader* (p. 297)
- *Senate majority leader* (p. 298)
- *Speaker of the House* (p. 297)
- *whip* (p. 297)

10.4 **Explain the steps of the legislative process and how it can diverge from traditional "textbook" descriptions.**

Remember . . .
- Before they can become law, bills must be passed by both the House and Senate and then approved by the president.
- Actors other than members of Congress may play a role in influencing whether a bill gets introduced.
- Most bills are never passed.

Know . . .
- *bill* (p. 300)
- *cloture* (p. 303)
- *filibuster* (p. 303)
- *House Committee on Rules* (p. 302)
- *markup* (p. 302)
- *roll-call vote* (p. 303)
- *unorthodox lawmaking* (p. 300)
- *veto* (p. 305)

10.5 **Connect the issues surrounding the representation of women in Congress to the challenges involving representation of other individuals in America.**

Remember . . .
- When taking action in Congress, members must consider the preferences of their constituents, their party, and other influencers.
- Representation in Congress may be descriptive or substantive.

Know . . .
- *descriptive representation* (p. 310)
- *essentialism* (p. 311)
- *legislative deliberation* (p. 312)
- *substantive representation* (p. 311)

CHAPTER 11

THE AMERICAN PRESIDENCY

Individuals, Institutions, and Power

The powers of the American presidency are great, but their boundaries have long been contested. Many recent presidents have pushed what some consider to be the limits of executive authority. President Donald Trump, with his own unique approach to the office, finds himself embroiled in conflicts of power that are both foreign and domestic, political and personal.

11.1 Consider the importance of presidential character in shaping the conduct and effectiveness of an administration.

11.2 Describe the powers of the presidency as defined in the Constitution and the constitutional limitations placed on those powers.

11.3 Discuss institutional and informal sources of and influences on presidential power.

11.4 Understand how presidents have tested the limits of executive power during wartime and other crises.

11.5 Evaluate the tools that presidents use to further expand their power.

As, arguably, the most powerful office-holder in the world, the American president stands alone—and not just at a podium or a press conference but also in comparison to leaders of other democratic nations. The job is unique; no other democratic nation selects, empowers, or limits its top elected leader in quite the same way. However, the American president does not *operate* alone, which is as the Framers of the Constitution intended. The president sits atop a massive collection of organizations, agencies, and bureaus. In the American political system, the president acts as the head of the executive branch of government, which is charged with executing, or putting into effect, the laws of the nation. These many organizations and suborganizations can provide a president with unparalleled information and an ability to shape American public policy on the ground. However, these same organizations can act as a brake on presidential power if they choose to do so.

The American president must also contend with a Congress whose members have their own political goals, even if the majority of those members are from the president's own political party. If the majority of one or both chambers in Congress is not from the president's party, then things get even tougher. And then there are the American people, to whom a president speaks directly. With the American people on their side, a president can be very powerful, especially when dealing with members of Congress. Without this support, presidents are vulnerable.

In this chapter, we will focus primarily on one aspect of presidential power and limitations on that power. We will also explore what it means for one *person* to hold the office and to, at times, push the boundaries of those limits. Throughout, we will consider one critical question: In American representative democracy, how much power should any one person have, even if they are the elected president?

In This Corner...Donald J. Trump: The President as Prizefighter-in-Chief

In 1987, the *Wall Street Journal* published an article about a "flamboyant New York businessman-developer" who was gearing up for battle: "In command central, his spacious Trump tower office high in the sky over Manhattan's posh Fifth Avenue, Donald J. Trump is plotting the overthrow of Las Vegas."[1]

It wasn't a conspiracy theory, or fake news. Donald Trump was in the middle of a battle over professional boxing rights, and he was fighting well. He had just outbid Caesar's Palace for the rights to hold the heavyweight championship between Mike Tyson and Tyrell Biggs—not in Vegas but in Atlantic City, where he owned several casinos. Pressed by the reporter to acknowledge that he couldn't possibly win every one of these battles with Vegas, the future president conceded that he couldn't, "but we'll get more and better fights."[2]

The forty-fifth president of the United States has been defined in many ways by the conflict and confrontation that has been a marker of President Trump's entire professional life. To his opponents, Trump's style, substance, and politics are often abhorrent. To his supporters, combat is what they sent him to Washington, DC, for.

To say that Donald Trump's presidential style is unique is an understatement, to put it mildly. What matters for our analysis, however, is the degree to which it shapes politics and policies. How much does the character of the person holding the office matter? In the case of Donald Trump, the narrative of his presidency is still being written. It is certain, though, that its plot will include quite a few fight scenes.

Conflict Has Been at the Center of President Trump's Presidency at Home

Any president can expect to be involved in multiple conflicts during their tenure of office. It is inherent to the job. Protecting national security, enacting public policy, and taking on the political opposition all involve contestation and opposition. For Donald Trump, however, conflict often seemed to define his presidency. Many questioned if the level of confrontation he displayed was necessary or, more importantly, if it contributed to his presidential power or if it undermined it.

It is hardly surprising when a president uses the position to attack the opposition party, particularly when that party controls one or more chambers of Congress. Donald Trump, however, was at war with the Democrats, and some Republicans, constantly. For the first three years of his presidency he was under an investigation led by special counsel Robert S. Mueller III—former head of the Federal Bureau of Investigation (FBI)—into the role that he was alleged to have played in Russian interference in the election of 2016. That investigation concluded without finding sufficient evidence for charging the president with criminal conspiracy, though several of his associates were charged with crimes. After the conclusion of the inquiry, the president was defiant. Boarding Air Force One, he told reporters, "It's a shame that our country had to go through this. To be honest, it's a shame that your president has had to go through this…This was an illegal takedown that failed."[3]

At the conclusion of the impeachment trial in the Senate, which declined to convict the president, Trump was exultant, celebrating his acquittal and attacking his political enemies at the National Prayer Breakfast.

Oliver Contreras/Sipa/Bloomberg via Getty Images

Within a year of the conclusion of the Mueller investigation, the House of Representatives—under Speaker Nancy Pelosi's (D-CA) leadership—impeached the president over his communications with a Ukrainian ambassador. Trump was accused of threatening to withhold aid to Ukraine unless Ukraine investigated potential corruption involving former vice president—and future Democratic presidential candidate—Joe Biden's son's business dealings with that nation. Although the Republican-controlled Senate voted to acquit the president, House Democrats made no promises that they would not conduct another impeachment inquiry before the end of his term.

President Trump next found himself at odds with many state governors—especially Democratic state governors—over the lockdowns and stay-at-home orders issued to slow the progression of COVID-19. The president pressed governors to loosen their restrictions in order to mitigate the economic fallout from the restrictions. He clashed sharply and publicly with several governors and mayors over their responses to the civil unrest that followed the killing of George Floyd by a Minneapolis police officer. The president urged more robust action, even threatening to deploy the military on American soil. Several governors and mayors resisted.

Conflict on the World Stage Has Also Defined the Trump Presidency

On April 9, 2018, Nikki Haley, then U.S. ambassador to the United Nations, joined other members of the United Nations Security Council (UNSC) to attempt to reach an accord to send a team of chemical weapons inspectors to Syria. Hanging in the balance was a potential American and allied military strike on Syria, a nation caught in a cauldron of civil war, insurgency, and the intervention of global powers (see Chapter 14). The call for inspectors was in response to an alleged chemical weapons attack in Douma, a suburb of Damascus, that was reported to have killed more than forty civilians, many of them children. According to U.S. officials, the Syrian government of Bashar al-Assad was responsible for the attack. An immediate and robust set of inspections, the American administration declared, was the only way to stave off military action.

Syria and its allies, notably Russia, denied that an attack had taken place or that the government was involved.[4] Russian officials issued dire warnings about the military consequences of a U.S. and allied strike on the Assad regime in response to these allegations. Russia's ambassador to Lebanon stated that Russia would respond to any attack by targeting not only the missiles themselves but the ships or bases from which they were launched: "If there is a strike by the Americans then...the missiles will be downed and even the sources from which the missiles were fired," he warned.[5]

This was not the first time that the Assad regime had been accused of using chemical weapons against its own citizens, nor that an American president had used or threatened to use military force in response to the use or alleged use of chemical weapons by the Syrian government. President Trump had ordered a missile attack on a Syrian air base almost exactly a year before. In 2013, President Barack Obama had threatened military strikes in response to an attack; however, they were called off in response to a Russian-led diplomatic effort to secure inspections.

True to form, President Trump took to Twitter.

Portending a potentially massive military response, the president tweeted, "Russia vows to shoot down any and all missiles fired at Syria. Get ready Russia, because they will be coming, nice and new and 'smart!' You shouldn't be partners with a Gas Killing Animal who kills his people and enjoys it!"[6]

Turnover in the President's Administration Raises Concerns. As Nikki Haley prepared to represent the president in the UNSC, there were new faces and missing faces on his national security and foreign policy team, not exactly an unsurprising development given the high rate of turnover in the Trump administration. That very day—Monday, April 9, 2018—was the first day of work for John Bolton, Trump's new and controversial choice for national security adviser, one of a few top posts in a president's formal administration that does not require Senate confirmation. Bolton, who had served in the George W. Bush administration, was himself no stranger to controversy. His previous hardline statements suggesting preemptive strikes on North Korea and Iran worried many observers.[7]

With Trump having recently dismissed Secretary of State Rex Tillerson via a tweet, there was no one in the post to advise and represent the president that week. Trump had nominated Central Intelligence Agency (CIA) director Mike Pompeo for the job, but Pompeo faced a tough confirmation process.[8] Key Republicans such as Sen. Rand Paul (R-KY) expressed their concerns or opposition to Pompeo's confirmation—in Senator Paul's case based upon the nominee's stated "defense of torture and support for the NSA's [National Security Agency's] government spying programs."[9]

The high rate of turnover among high-ranking officials within the president's administration was a source of concern for many, worried that it would hamper effective execution of foreign and domestic policy (see Figure 11.1).

On Friday the 13th, America and key allies launched missile and guided munitions strikes on alleged chemical weapons facilities in Syria. The administration

▼ FIGURE 11.1

Executive Branch Turnover: Major Offices

Turnover in the Trump White House is higher than in past administrations. In his first year in office, there was 34 percent turnover, compared to 9 percent in the Obama administration and 6 percent in the George W. Bush administration.[10]

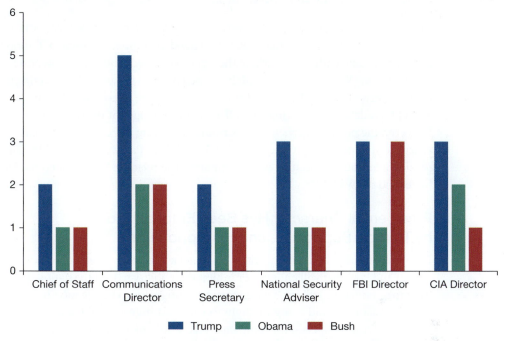

Source: Data from Manuela Tobias, "Comparing Unprecedented Trump White House Turnover with Bush, Obama," PolitiFact, March 15, 2018, http://www.politifact.com/truth-o-meter/article/2018/mar/15/trump-white-house-turnover/.

claimed it was a success. Russia and Iran—with their own military presence in Syria in support of the Assad regime—claimed that Syrian air defenses, provided by Russia, succeeded in taking out most of the missiles. Two weeks later, Russian officials claimed to have captured an American cruise missile intact. No Russian military personnel were reported to have been killed or wounded in the strikes, and a wider war was avoided.

Conflict with His Defense Department over Syria Foreshadows More Confrontation down the Road. Trump's authority to authorize strikes without prior congressional approval came under question that year by members of the legislative branch and his own cabinet. General James Mattis, President Trump's secretary of defense at the time, would later say he had urged the president to obtain congressional approval for strikes before authorizing them but that Trump overruled him.[11]

Mattis resigned over disagreements with the president over his policy toward Syria later that year. In June 2020, the former secretary and Marine Corps general took the highly unusual step of criticizing his former boss over the president's response to nationwide protests and unrest that followed the killing of George Floyd by a Minneapolis police officer in May. Publishing his condemnation in *The Atlantic*, Mattis sharply criticized the president's call to use the United States military in Washington, DC, and American cities. "We must reject and hold accountable those in office who would make a mockery of our Constitution," Mattis said.[12]

President Trump Challenges China and the World Health Organization during the Global Pandemic. As the COVID-19 pandemic spread, President Trump took a combative tone with China, where the virus originated, and with the World Health Organization (WHO), an agency of the United Nations tasked with protecting public health internationally. President Trump was not alone in criticizing China and the WHO for a delay in reporting the full extent and danger of the outbreak in China. However, the president's rhetoric—periodically calling it the "Chinese virus"—was sharply critiqued by many, including key Republican Party strategists.[13] In May, the president announced that he was terminating the relationship between the United States and the WHO.[14]

Presidential Character Has Been Emphasized by Trump's Supporters and His Opponents

During a presidential election, voters try to get a bead on who each candidate is as a person and how that will enhance or inhibit their ability to lead the nation. President Trump's combative style was an important contributor to his election in 2016. The promise that he would bring the fight to the Washington establishment was a key theme in Trump's successful campaign. According to a survey of Americans conducted by the Pew Research Center in the months leading up to the 2016 election, a plurality of those who supported Trump framed their favorable opinions in terms of his style and approach to politics—that he was an "outsider/not a politician" who "tells it like it is" and will "shake things up" in Washington.[15]

Constant conflict and combat defined Trump's successful presidential campaign, and it seemed destined to define his presidency as well. According to a December 2017 article in the *New York Times*, Trump "sees the highest office in the land much as he did the night of his stunning victory over Hillary Clinton—as a prize he must fight to protect every waking moment, and Twitter is his Excalibur."[16] Members of his own party openly questioned the wisdom of the president's leadership style. "The problem he's going to face," according to Sen. Lindsey Graham (R-SC), "is there's a difference between running for the office and being president. You've got to find that sweet spot between being a fighter and being president."[17]

By 2020, many Republicans were growing concerned about the president's often inflammatory statements and the effects that these would have on his own reelectoral prospects—as well as the ability of the party to maintain control of the Senate, not to mention retake the House of Representatives. According to a March 2020 survey by the Pew Research Center conducted during the COVID-19 outbreak, 80 percent of

Republicans Largely Agree with President Trump's Policies, but Worry about His Style of Leadership

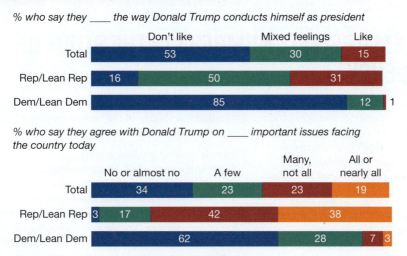

% who say they ____ the way Donald Trump conducts himself as president

	Don't like	Mixed feelings	Like
Total	53	30	15
Rep/Lean Rep	16	50	31
Dem/Lean Dem	85	12	1

% who say they agree with Donald Trump on ____ important issues facing the country today

	No or almost no	A few	Many, not all	All or nearly all
Total	34	23	23	19
Rep/Lean Rep	3 / 17	42		38
Dem/Lean Dem	62		28	7 / 3

Source: Pew Research Center, "Few Americans Express Positive Views of Trump's Conduct in Office," March 5, 2020, https://www.people-press.org/2020/03/05/few-americans-express-positive-views-of-trumps-conduct-in-office/.

respondents described Trump as "self-centered."[18] More problematic for the president's reelectoral bid was the fact that many Republicans expressed unease with his leadership style (see Figure 11.2).

Political scientists have looked to the character and personality of individual presidents to explain their relative effectiveness in office. That individual presidents—their characters, skills, successes, and failures—have all contributed to the development of the American presidency is a point on which most would agree. For scholars of the presidency, however, the challenge is to figure out just how these traits matter to presidential performance. Some scholars have classified presidents based on personal and psychological characteristics as a way of gaining insight into behavior inside the Oval Office.[19] Successfully predicting presidential behavior based on assessments of character is, however, a difficult thing to do. Separating the person of the president from the times and context in which that president governed is never easy. In addition, sudden, unexpected events can thrust a president into situations that none could have imagined or predicted.

Presidential scholar Richard Neustadt painted a strategic, but constrained, portrait of presidential power. For Neustadt, the power of an individual president is not automatic but must be developed, especially through persuasion and skillful political action.[20] He argued that presidential power consists of presenting a credible threat to known and potential political enemies, and convincing allies and opponents that supporting the president is in their own self-interest. According to Neustadt,

PRACTICING POLITICAL SCIENCE

THE PROBLEM OF SMALL NUMBERS IN THE STUDY OF THE PRESIDENCY

How much do the personal characteristics of an individual president matter to their performance in office? Can we say anything systematic about the relationship between character and performance?

Originally published in 1972, James David Barber's *The Presidential Character: Predicting Performance in the White House* applied understandings from psychology to try to predict how presidents would behave—and how successful they would be—by categorizing them into four types based on two separate personality traits: (1) how active or passive they were, in the sense of the energy and innovation they bought to the office, and (2) how positively or negatively they approached their duties, in the sense of the enjoyment they displayed in managing the ship of state.

Based on these determinations, George Washington, for example, was a passive-negative president in that he reluctantly led the nation and preferred stability over dramatic change. Thomas Jefferson, on the other hand, was an active-positive president who actively engaged in the give-and-take of politics in the service of a grand vision for the young nation.

Though it has been influential in political science, Barber's approach has not escaped criticism. Some have argued that the many institutional and political limitations on presidential action overwhelm the ability to define a president's actions. Others have critiqued the validity of the two underlying measures themselves.

There is another challenge in drawing systematic conclusions about individual presidents that goes beyond the issue of character. The reality is that there have not been that many presidents; thus, the question is one of sample size. To demonstrate empirical relationships with confidence, we need a certain number of observations to better ensure that the patterns we observe are indeed representative of the group under study and not due to the unique characteristics of our small sample.

WHaT Do You Think?

How might political scientists get around the problem of the limited number of presidents in making social scientific claims about executive branch politics? One option might be to look at executives across nations, giving us more observations. The problem here is that other systems are typically very different from that of the United States. Another approach might be to look at state governors. The challenge here, though, is that the American federalist system defines very different roles for state and federal executives. This is not to say that such an approach might not be useful—only that we should be careful in using it. What might we learn from examining the behavior of state governors that could translate into a better understanding of the American presidency?

"The essence of a President's persuasive task is to convince such men that what the White House wants of them is what they ought to do for their sake and on their own authority."[21] In future retrospectives, the presidency of Donald J. Trump may very well be used to confirm or challenge Neustadt's analysis. Can the actions of a confrontational President Trump—so to speak, conventional wisdom about the need for consensus-building—be an effective use of executive power?

In this chapter, we explore the American presidency, its awesome power, and the limits on the use of that power. We will discover that institutions, rules, and the American public all act to constrain and bound these decisions. For their part, individual presidents have pushed and tested these boundaries in securing their vision of what it means to make Americans safe and prosperous. We turn next to the Constitution of the United States and the new and unique office that it created.

The Constitution Outlines the Powers of the American Presidency and Places Limits on Those Powers

> 11.2 Describe the powers of the presidency as defined in the Constitution and the constitutional limitations placed on those powers.

James Madison had given more thought to creating a new type of republic than any of the other delegates to the Constitutional Convention. Even so, even he hadn't specified the details for what would become the executive office. Like so much else, the agreement that there would be one president was worked out later in the convention. Some provisions, especially the method of electing presidents, were sources of intense conflict. One reason was that the job that the delegates ended up creating had no real precedent, though delegates looked to the constitutions of the individual states and other sources for its formation.

Delegates to the convention were in general agreement that the new government would have to be more powerful than that under the Articles of Confederation. That confederal government had been in perpetual financial crisis, often unable to coerce individual states to contribute sufficient funds to allow it to operate effectively. While the Framers of the Constitution knew that the executive needed to be powerful enough to lead, they also feared that the office might become too powerful. They were in no mood to recreate the tyranny of the British monarchy with an elected one on American shores.

Delegates Settle Questions of Selection, Qualifications for Office, and Length of Terms

Once they settled on a single president, the most contentious issue facing the delegates was how this person was going to be selected. The factionalized debate between less populous and more populous states that had resulted in the bicameral Congress reared its head once again. Less populous states feared that direct popular election of the president would see their states' interests swallowed up by their more populous neighbors. Most delegates assumed that voters would pick candidates from their own states. Many delegates also mistrusted Americans' ability to responsibly directly elect a president. In the end, the delegates agreed to a method of presidential selection that did not involve direct popular election. Instead, electors, chosen by state legislatures and apportioned to states based on congressional representation, were to choose the president (see Chapter 8).

Delegates also settled on a term of four years with the possibility of reelection. No limits were placed on the number of times a person could be elected president. The nation's first president, George Washington (1789–1797), chose not to seek a third term, however, establishing a precedent that held until Franklin Roosevelt (1933–1945) was elected four times.[22] Ratified largely in response to Roosevelt's multiple terms, the Twenty-Second Amendment (1951) prohibited future presidents from being elected more than twice and allowed election only once if that person had assumed the office (due to a death, resignation, or impeachment) more than two years prior to the end of a partial term.

Delegates set out a number of conditions for eligibility for the office of the presidency. A candidate had to be "a natural born Citizen, or a Citizen of the United States at the time of the Adoption of this Constitution," be thirty-five years old or older, and have been a resident of the United States for at least fourteen years. The Constitution did not explicitly prohibit women from holding the office; however, at the time of ratification, women were generally denied the right to vote or hold political office within their states.[23]

The President Is Granted Considerable Powers

One of the main reasons that the method of selecting the president caused so much debate was that as the summer of 1787 progressed, the office grew in power and scope. The expectation that Washington, trusted and admired throughout the nation, would be the first president may have allayed delegates' concerns about the powerful office they were creating. Although the convention settled on the simple title of President of the United States, Washington was said to have preferred "His High Mightiness, the President of the United States and Protector of their Liberties."[24]

When the delegates hammered out the framework of the American presidency, they created an institution that had never been seen on a national scale. In some ways, there is still no exact equivalent to its scope and complexity in modern democracies. The powers placed in the president's hands are threefold. Expressed (or enumerated) powers are those given to the president explicitly in the Constitution. Implied powers, though not laid out in the text, are assumed as part of the president's expressed powers, as they are necessary to carry out the expressed powers. Delegated powers are those that Congress grants to the president in order to execute, or carry out, the laws that Congress has passed (hence the name the *executive branch*). In wielding these three types of powers, the American president assumes a variety of roles.[25]

As Chief Executive, the President Carries Out the Nation's Laws. As the head of the executive branch, the president is responsible for carrying out the laws of the nation. They oversee what has become a large and complex system of agencies and bureaucracies in order to do so. The Constitution, however, does not offer many specifics as to what it means to execute the laws. Article II, which is devoted to the presidency, begins, "The executive Power shall be vested in a President of the United States of America."[26] When taking the oath of office, the president promises to "faithfully execute the Office of the President of the United States" and is later instructed to "take Care that the Laws be faithfully executed."[27] Other than that, the Constitution does not give much detail on *how* the president is supposed to run the federal government.

Presidents are given some help, however. They are authorized to "require the Opinion, in writing, of the principal Office in each of the executive Departments, upon any Subject relating to the Duties of their respective Offices."[28] Though not mentioned by name, the president's cabinet has evolved into a powerful source of information and a point of contact with the nation's sprawling federal bureaucracy. It also provides a way to reward individuals and members of important interest groups for past (and future) support through their appointment to positions within the cabinet.

Modern presidents have the authority to appoint individuals to thousands of administrative positions, from their closest advisers and heads of large agencies to lower-level administrative staff. Roughly one thousand of these appointments require Senate confirmation. Presidents also nominate individuals to serve as judges and justices in the federal judiciary; each nomination also requires Senate confirmation. A president may make a **recess appointment** without Senate confirmation while Congress is not in session, but the term of the recess appointment ends at the conclusion of that congressional session unless that person is formally confirmed.

As Chief Diplomat, the President Guides Foreign Policy. The president is also responsible for guiding U.S. foreign policy and interacting with the heads of other nations. The president is authorized "to make Treaties," to "appoint Ambassadors," and to "receive Ambassadors and other public Ministers."[29] This diplomatic power is partly symbolic and ceremonial; events like state dinners and parties showcase the power and prestige of the office.

The diplomatic power of the president helps to shape national foreign policy. While Congress, particularly the Senate, plays a major role in foreign affairs, the fact that the president is one person—and not 100 or 435, as is the case for the Senate and House—gives them an advantage over Congress in the ability to act quickly and decisively on the international stage. As one presidential scholar put it, "Secrecy, dispatch, unity, continuity, and access to information—the ingredients of successful diplomacy—are properties of his office, and Congress . . . possesses none of them."[30]

The speed with which presidents can act also gives them a significant advantage over Congress in shaping foreign and domestic policy. As political scientist William

After months of saber-rattling, some diplomacy ensues: Here, North Korean leader Kim Jong-un (left) shakes hands with President Donald Trump during their historic summit in Singapore in June 2018. Trump hoped that the historic meeting would bring an end to decades of hostility and the threat of North Korea's nuclear program.

Handout/Getty Images

Howell has noted, presidents may act first and alone across a wide variety of policy areas, often by issuing directives to the vast federal bureaucracy without waiting for Congress to clarify the laws that it has passed. Acting first and acting alone forces the other two branches to react.

As Commander in Chief, the President Is Responsible for the Nation's Security.

Perhaps the most fateful role that the Constitution creates for the president is their authority as "Commander in Chief of the Army and Navy of the United States, and of the Militia of the several States."[31] The president is at the top of the entire military chain of command, including the strategic nuclear forces of the nation, an awesome responsibility.

Originally, the constitutional war-making power of the presidency was a limited one; it was designed so the president could efficiently lead the American armed forces during a time of war and to allow for quick response to threats when Congress was not in session. Therefore, the president was also given a role in national war making, though "the Commander-in-chief clause remained 'the forgotten clause' of the Constitution for the early decades of the nation's history."[32] President Lincoln's assumption of broad executive powers during the Civil War changed that (see later in the chapter). American presidents continued to seize on the powers offered by their role as commander in chief during the twentieth century, which included two world wars and the Cold War with the Soviet Union that followed World War II.

Following the conflict in Vietnam, Congress attempted to reassert its role in setting American military policy. The **War Powers Resolution of 1973**, passed despite Richard Nixon's veto, has been one of the most enduring and controversial legacies of his presidency.[33] Initially intended by its sponsors to reaffirm congressional authority over the introduction of American armed forces into combat, the resolution is credited by some scholars as being "the high-water mark of congressional reassertion in national security affairs."[34] Passed during the weakening of Nixon's authority as the Watergate investigations unfolded, the resolution was the product of widespread public and congressional dissatisfaction with the Vietnam conflict as well as unilateral presidential actions carried out by Lyndon Johnson and Nixon.

Drawing on Congress's authority under the necessary and proper clause of the Constitution, the resolution's purpose was to recenter war-making authority.[35] Under the terms of the War Powers Resolution, a president may only introduce armed forces into conflict or likely conflict if one of the three following conditions is present:

1. "a declaration of war [by Congress],"

2. "a specific statutory authorization [by Congress]," or

3. "a national emergency created by an attack on the United States, its territories or possessions, or its armed forces"[36]

The president is required within forty-eight hours to notify Congress of "the circumstances necessitating the introduction of United States Armed Forces; . . . the constitutional and legislative authority under which such introduction took place; and . . . the estimated scope and duration of the hostilities or involvement."[37] Unless Congress has declared war, passed specific authorization, extended the notification deadline, or is physically unable to meet, the president must withdraw those forces within sixty days, with a thirty-day extension allowed if necessary to withdraw those forces safely.[38]

The last war officially declared by Congress was World War II in 1941. Since that time, American armed forces have been stationed in more than one hundred countries, though many of these are allies or military partners, and involved in a number of conflicts. Presidents have often held that the War Powers Resolution unconstitutionally restricts their war power, though they have also routinely pursued congressional authorization for the use of military force consistent with the resolution.[39] Some critics of the resolution argue that it actually makes presidents more powerful, since they may feel less constrained during those sixty or ninety days than they would if the resolution did not exist.

Presidents Use the State of the Union Address to Advance Their Goals.
In devising a system where power was to be shared between the three branches, the Framers gave the president a limited and mostly negative role in the legislative process. However, this role has since been extended quite far.

The president is directed to "from time to time give Congress Information of the State of the Union." For much of the nation's history, presidents sent written reports to Congress without actually addressing the legislative branch in person. Today, no president would pass on the opportunity provided by the **State of the Union address** to speak live on television before Congress; members of the Supreme Court; the military; and, most importantly, the entire nation. In the address, a president encourages or cajoles Congress to pass key pieces of their legislative agenda. The real audience, however, is the American people, and presidents use the address to try to mobilize support and pressure members of Congress to act.

The President Has Important but Proscribed Powers in the Legislative Process. The president is also expected to "recommend to their [Congress's] Consideration such Measures as he shall judge necessary and expedient."[40] While, as we saw in Chapter 10, only members of Congress can formally introduce bills, presidents work with party leaders in both chambers to shape the legislative agenda.

Finally, the president is given the power to veto legislation (see Chapter 10), although this veto is subject to a potential override by a two-thirds vote in both chambers. Individual presidents have varied considerably in the use (and successful use) of the veto. Overrides are rare; marshaling the required two-thirds vote in both chambers is usually very difficult to do. The mere threat of a presidential veto is often enough to shape a piece of legislation more to a president's liking.[41] Vetoes are more likely during periods of divided government, when one or both chambers of Congress are under the control of a party other than that of the president.

Presidents Have the Power to Issue Pardons. Another power the Constitution carves out for the president is the ability to issue a **presidential pardon**. The "Power to grant Reprieves and Pardons for Offenses against the United States, except in Cases of Impeachment," allows the president to release individuals convicted of federal crimes from all legal consequences and restore their benefits of citizenship.[42] Presidents often grant pardons in their final days and weeks of office. In cases where it appears that pardoned individuals have close personal or professional ties to the president, this practice can be quite controversial.

The Powers of the Presidency Are Constitutionally Limited

The Framers also placed limitations on the power of the office, primarily by granting specific powers to Congress and the federal judiciary (see Table 11.1).[43] In most circumstances, the judicial branch has little involvement with presidential actions and responsibilities. Congress, however, is a different story. Presidents cannot accomplish most of their objectives without at the very least a lack of opposition by Congress, as the Constitution places in Congress's hands several negative checks on presidential action. Presidents need majority support in Congress to pass the laws, create and fund the programs, and confirm the presidential appointments that are necessary to fully realize their policy objectives. The president must obtain from the Senate majority approval to confirm appointments to the federal judiciary as well as to many executive branch offices. Ratification of a treaty requires a two-thirds vote in the Senate.[44] With a two-thirds vote in each chamber, Congress can override a presidential veto, though veto overrides are relatively uncommon given the high vote hurdle needed to succeed. See Table 11.1.

Congress has the power to impeach the president (as well as "the Vice President and all civil Officers of the United States") for the vaguely defined transgressions of "Treason, Bribery, or other high Crimes and Misdemeanors."[45] A majority vote in the House is needed to pass articles of impeachment. Once an officeholder is impeached, the trial takes place in the Senate. The chief justice of the United States presides over a presidential impeachment, and a two-thirds vote is necessary to convict.[46]

Powers and Limits to Powers of the President

Enumerated, Implied, and Delegated Powers	Limits to Powers
The President may. . . .	*Congress may. . .*
Execute the nation's laws	Investigate or impeach the president
Submit the annual federal budget	Pass the budget
Appoint and seek the advice of cabinet departments	Confirm, delay, or block nominations
Shape foreign policy by enacting treaties, appointing ambassadors, and conducting diplomacy	Ratify treaties
Provide information and make policy recommendations to Congress; veto congressional legislation	Override vetoes
Act as commander in chief of the armed forces	Declare war and fund the armed forces
Deliver pardons but may not pardon individuals who have been impeached	Not override a pardon (and neither can the judiciary)

Three presidents have been impeached, and none have been removed from office. Andrew Johnson barely survived a Senate vote over political battles following the Civil War in 1868, and Bill Clinton avoided conviction over charges of perjury and obstruction of justice during an investigation into his involvement with a White House intern, Monica Lewinsky, in 1998. President Richard Nixon would almost certainly have been impeached and convicted for his role in covering up a break-in at the Democratic Party national headquarters (the so-called Watergate affair) in 1972. He resigned from office in 1974 before a House vote took place, however, and received a pardon from his successor, President Gerald R. Ford, later that year. Donald Trump was impeached by the Democratic-controlled House of Representatives in 2019 on two counts—obstruction of Congress and abuse of power. He was acquitted of both charges by the Republican-controlled Senate.

Institutions and Other Informal Sources of Power Shape the Modern Executive Branch

11.3 Discuss institutional and informal sources of and influences on presidential power.

While the American presidency must feel at times like the loneliest job in the world, no president truly acts alone. Instead, the president operates at the center of multiple organizations and institutions. Like many aspects of the presidency, the size and complexity of the presidential establishment is both a source of presidential power and a constraint on it. The machinery of the presidential establishment allows the president to act in many areas of domestic and foreign policy and provides them with large amounts of information, which is an important commodity in dealing with other nations, Congress, and the many actors in American politics. However, the size and complexity of the executive branch establishment—especially the federal bureaucracy—can act as a powerful brake on presidential initiatives, particularly since most lower-level federal bureaucrats keep their jobs long after any one president has come and gone.

The Vice Presidency Plays a Limited but Important Role

While the Constitution's vague language created an ambiguous but ultimately powerful presidency, it also created a very weak second in command: the office of the vice president. Delegates to the Constitutional Convention were not even sure that the nation needed a vice president. The ultimate inclusion of the position was probably driven by the need to soothe tensions between more populous and less populous states over the presidential election process.[47]

Constitutionally, the vice president has two jobs. They are "President of the Senate, but shall have no Vote, unless they be equally divided."[48] The logic behind the vice president's leadership role in the Senate was to ensure that no state lost its equal Senate representation by virtue of having one of its two senators serving as president of the chamber. Rarely does the vice president actually preside over the Senate. Instead the president pro tempore of the Senate usually presides officially, but junior senators routinely fill this role.

Second, the vice president assumes the office of the presidency should a serving president vacate the office due to death, resignation, or impeachment. The Twenty-Fifth Amendment (1967) established the modern rules of succession and also established a process for replacing a vice president who leaves office during their term. In this process, the president nominates a replacement, and approval is required "by a majority vote of both Houses of Congress."

In addition to addressing succession, the Twenty-Fifth Amendment also established a procedure through which the vice president may temporarily assume the role of acting president in the event "that the President is unable to discharge the powers and duties of his office."

Although the office of the vice presidency is officially weak, any vice president knows that they are a heartbeat away from perhaps the most powerful position in the world. Reflecting on his role as the nation's first vice president, John Adams noted, "I am Vice President. In this I am nothing, but I may be everything."[49] In the nation's history, eight vice presidents have assumed the office of the presidency upon the death of the serving president and one upon the president's resignation.

Historically, most vice presidents have had little impact on national policy, but it has recently become more common for vice presidents to have a larger role in White House deliberations. Other than being ready to take over, the main job of the vice president is to help the president get elected. Vice presidential nominees have often been selected to "balance the ticket" with respect to geographical representation, connections to important blocks of voters, or experience.

The Cabinet and the Executive Branch Bureaucracy Help Advise the President

The president's cabinet consists of the heads of the fifteen major executive branch departments, the vice president, and the heads of other agencies that the president wishes to assign cabinet-level status. In addition to leading their agencies, cabinet department heads, most of whom are called secretaries, advise the president and act as the link between the president and their own bureaucracies. Unlike the majority of people who work for the federal bureaucracy, heads of the executive branch departments typically come and go with each new administration.

In choosing cabinet members, presidents have to juggle several considerations. Presidents need capable, experienced, and strong appointees to provide useful information and to effectively run their departments. However, assertive cabinet secretaries, who often have their own bases of power, can challenge the president or drag their heels if they disagree with a policy objective. Presidents must also consider politics and public opinion in their choices. Cabinet department heads with ties to important interest groups—teachers or members of the business community, for example—can help a president to be informed of the concerns of those groups as policy is shaped. Cabinet appointments can also signal to a diverse constituency of Americans and those who represent them that the president will advance their interests.

The Executive Office of the President Assists the President with Policy

Established in 1939 upon the recommendation of a presidential commission that concluded "the president needs help," the **Executive Office of the President (EOP)** is a collection of agencies and offices that assist the president in both an advisory and policymaking capacity.[50] The White House chief of staff oversees the EOP and is usually a close, trusted, and politically skilled associate of the president. The chief of staff often acts as a protector of the president's scarcest resource: time. Most individuals who work for the various agencies within the EOP are appointed by a president and not expected to serve past that administration; though some of the larger offices do have permanent staff members.

One of these larger offices is the Office of Management and Budget (OMB), which advises and assists the president in crafting the national budget and studies various plans and initiatives designed to increase the efficiency of executive branch departments. The National Security Council advises the president on issues of national security, the military, and foreign policy.

The White House Office (part of the EOP) has grown into an important bureaucracy itself, and its most important members share offices near the president's. The hundreds of staff members in this office are there to support the president in achieving their policy objectives. They achieve this by effectively communicating the president's vision to the American people, building support for goals and polices, and playing the complicated and high-stakes game of Washington politics. In choosing the members of the White House staff, presidents value political skill and loyalty. Many times staff members are individuals who were involved in the campaign or with the president in previous roles. Directors and deputy directors of communication ensure that the president's message is delivered to the American people. The White House press secretary acts as the president's spokesperson to members of the media and conducts press briefings, partly to inform but also partly to shape the national conversation in a way that helps the president achieve their policy goals.

The First Spouse Can Help the President Connect

The spouse of a president occupies no formal role in an administration but is in a unique position to act as an adviser to the president and a public and personal link between the president and the American people.

Edith Bolling Galt Wilson, President Woodrow Wilson's wife, was probably the most powerful First Lady. She helped to organize and run the White House after her husband suffered a serious stroke in 1919, becoming, to some, an acting president. Eleanor Roosevelt spoke and wrote frequently about public policy and had a successful and influential career in public life following Franklin Roosevelt's death in 1945. Modern first spouses often choose one or more policy areas and use their influence and visibility to call attention to issues in those areas and promote solutions.

Political Parties Influence the Power of the Executive

The role that the president plays as "chief of party" is not mentioned in the Constitution. The Framers worried privately and publicly about the dangers of faction—of which political parties were viewed as a particularly dangerous example. Parties, however, are nearly as old as the Republic; divisions between President Washington's closest advisers gave rise to the nation's first political parties.

Modern presidents serve as the unofficial, but real, leaders of their own political parties. They often choose the official leadership of their party, or at least have a major say in it. Presidents must contend with partisan politics in Congress, especially if opposing political party controls one or both chambers of Congress. These periods of divided government are often associated with legislative gridlock in which Congress's ability to pass laws is diminished or grinds to a halt completely.[51]

Presidents expect to have to battle and negotiate with members of the opposing party in Congress. However, support from their own party members can never be taken for granted either. Even when Republicans controlled both chambers of Congress, during the first two years of his term, President Trump found it far from easy to achieve his policy objectives. Presidents and members of Congress serve different constituencies. The American people demand that their presidents keep them safe and prosperous. Demands on senators and representatives are often more local and address the unique characteristics and needs of their states or districts. No member of Congress can ignore the wishes of their constituents without risk, even if a popular president requests it. Skillful presidents are fully aware of these tensions and—working with party leaders in Congress—often try to accommodate individual defections by members of their own party with the expectation that loyalty will be shown on less locally contentious votes somewhere down the line.

Marian Anderson, renowned opera singer, receives the Spingarn Medal from First Lady Eleanor Roosevelt in Richmond, Virginia, in July 1939. Eleanor Roosevelt's efforts to overcome racial discrimination in the United States were among her most important achievements on behalf of her husband's administration.

Keystone-France/Gamma-Keystone via Getty Images

The President Tries to Use the Media to Shape Public Opinion

As the power of the American presidency has evolved, so has the president's relationship to the nation's citizens. Public opinion—the distribution of people's preferences and evaluations of policies and individual political actors—has come to play an important role in expanding or constraining the power of individual presidents. When expertly harnessed, public opinion is a powerful tool in battles with Congress, the judiciary, or too-independent members of a president's own political party. If it is poorly mobilized or understood, however, the unfortunate president, in the words of Clinton Rossiter, "will find himself exposed to all those enemies who multiply like mosquitoes in a [New] Jersey August. The various institutions and centers of power that check the President are inept and often useless without public opinion—and with it are often wondrously armed."[52]

Modern communications technology and ease of travel have significantly contributed to connecting the president to the American public. But long before the

Internet, television, and even radio, individual presidents recognized and tried to harness the latent power of public opinion. Andrew Jackson, who drew on his public support in battles with Congress and the judiciary, commented, "The President must be accountable at the bar of public opinion for every act of his administration."[53] Modern presidents attempt to make full use of communications technologies and public appearances in order to mobilize American public opinion in support of their own goals and policies. Political scientist Samuel Kernell used the term **going public** to describe "a strategy whereby a president promotes himself and his policies in Washington by appealing directly to the American public for support."[54]

Perhaps no president in American history is as tied to public opinion as President Donald Trump. Without question, his use of social media has been more powerful and effective than that of any other candidate, or president. The question, though, is this: Does the immediacy of connection outweigh the risk of poorly timed or, perhaps, not politically savvy tweets? In 2020—with the nation barely over the drama of impeachment—it confronted a global pandemic, widespread protests over the treatment of African Americans by law enforcement officials, and the deep challenge to the status quo that these protests presented. Many on both sides of the political divide questioned the utility of President Trump's strategy of confrontation-by-tweet during a time in which the nation badly needed to heal.

Americans' Evaluations of Presidential Performance Can Affect the President's Policy Agenda

Since Franklin Roosevelt's presidency, pollsters have periodically taken the national pulse on Americans' views of how well their presidents are doing. These presidential approval ratings provide more than just a snapshot of the public's views. A president with high approval ratings is in a more powerful position in relation to Congress than one with low or sinking ratings. Sometimes unanticipated events—and the president's response to them—can produce dramatic changes in presidential approval. A national economic or military crisis, if handled well in the eyes of the American public, can produce a surge in presidential approval. In the months after the 9/11 attacks, President Bush's approval rating rose to 90 percent, the highest ever recorded, but it later declined as the public became increasingly skeptical of his handling of the war in Iraq and of the nation's economy (see Figure 11.3).

Some patterns of presidential approval are more predictable. A new president—especially after a convincing first-term victory—ordinarily enjoys a period of strong public approval, called a honeymoon period. For this reason, presidents often try to secure major legislative victories early in their first terms to capture public support and build momentum for future battles with Congress. Presidential approval, however, usually declines over time as the American public begins to assign blame to the president for things that are not going well, whether this is deserved or not. There is also typically some recovery in presidential approval as the term draws to a close.[55]

Presidential Approval Ratings in Comparison

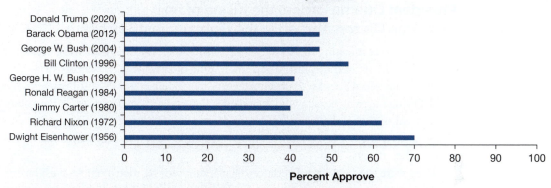

Do you approve or disapprove of the way the president is handling his job as president?

Source: "Presidential Approval Ratings—Donald Trump," Gallup, accessed June 5, 2020, https://news.gallup.com/poll/203207/trump-job-approval-weekly.aspx.

Presidents Have Pushed the Limits of Their Power to Preserve National Security

11.4 Understand how presidents have tested the limits of executive power during wartime and other crises.

In times of crisis, especially economic or military crises, no single actor in the American political system is able to react to the demands of the situation as quickly and decisively as the president: "Under crisis conditions the political system under-goes a drastic change. The White House becomes a command post, Congress and interest groups assume minor roles, the public becomes acutely aware of the threat and looks fervently to the president for authoritative guidance."[56] As we explored in Chapter 3, President Roosevelt's response to the Great Depression fundamentally altered American federalism and increased the power of the national government and the executive branch. It has been in times of military crises and threats to national security, however, when the nation has primarily witnessed the starkest increase in presidential authority and the transformation of the character, scope, and reach of the American president.

Arguing in favor of a single executive in *Federalist* No. 74, Alexander Hamilton saw the potential of and need for presidential power in wartime. He wrote, "Of all the cares or concerns of government, the direction of war most peculiarly demands those qualities which distinguish the exercise of power by a single hand."[57] Writing in 1888, noted observer of American political life James Bryce confirmed the transfor-mative power of war and conflict on the American presidency, saying, "In quiet times the power of the President is not great...In troublous times it is otherwise, for immense responsibility is then thrown on one who is both the commander-in-chief and the head of the civil executive."[58] The ability to act first and act alone is a tool unique to the president. Its power is only magnified during times of threat and crisis.

President Obama Orders the Killing of an American Citizen Abroad in the Fight against Terrorism

On a September morning in 2011, a group of men had just finished eating breakfast in a remote desert in the country of Yemen. One of them was Anwar al-Awlaki, an American citizen who was, to counterterrorism officials, "a rock star propagandist for al-Qaeda's arm in Yemen who recruited followers over the Internet."[59] Patrolling the Yemeni skies that day were American drones launched from an airstrip in Saudi Arabia and remotely piloted from far away. Noticing the drones, the men "scrambled to get to their trucks."[60]

They were too late. Two Predator drones marked the men's trucks with lasers, and larger Reaper drones launched three Hellfire missiles. Al-Awlaki's vehicle "was totally torn up into pieces," according to reports from unidentified witnesses to the strike, the men reduced to "small human parts."[61]

Anwar al-Awlaki Attributes His Radicalization to American Foreign Policy.
About Anwar al-Awlaki, this much was known: Born in New Mexico in 1971 but raised in Yemen, he returned to the United States for undergraduate and graduate education. He was serving as imam of a mosque near Washington, DC, in 2001 at the time of the 9/11 attacks. In the weeks following, al-Awlaki presented a moderate face to Americans trying to understand what had happened and to many Muslim Americans worried about a backlash against members of their faith. However, according to the *New York Times,* "nine years later, from his hide-out in Yemen, [he] declared war on the United States," his primary weapon being the Internet.[62] His "website became a favorite for English-speaking Muslims who were curious about jihad."[63] With his command of the English language and ability to draw on American social and cultural references in his posts and videos, al-Awlaki became a very effective "recruiter and propagandist."[64]

By al-Awlaki's own account, it was U.S. intervention in countries like Iraq, Afghanistan, Pakistan, and Yemen that drove him to follow "the religious obligation to defend his faith."[65] Interviews with others who knew him cited al-Awlaki's eighteen months in a Yemeni prison—much of it in solitary confinement—as the driving force behind his radicalization. He blamed the United States for allowing his detention, and there is some evidence that this was the case. The *New York Times* reported that "John D. Negroponte, then director of national intelligence, told Yemeni officials that the United States did not object to his detention."[66]

The Process Involved in President Obama's Decision Raises Concerns.
For more than a year and a half following the strike, the administration of President Barack Obama remained officially silent on the targets. Under pressure from

members of Congress, including some key Democrats, Attorney General Eric Holder formally acknowledged in May 2013 that the 2011 strike had targeted an American citizen: al-Awlaki. According to the *New York Times*, "For what was apparently the first time since the Civil War, the United States government had carried out the deliberate killing of an American citizen as a wartime enemy and without a trial."[67] Al-Awlaki's name had been placed at the top of the CIA list of individuals to be captured if possible or killed if not. Many of the details about how individuals were on this list were secret, but reporters learned that the target list was vetted and approved, also in secret, by the National Security Council and others on the administration's legal team.[68]

Pilotless drones like this Reaper have allowed the U.S. military to strike targets deep within other countries without risk to American service members. The constitutionality of such measures remains a matter of debate.

Isaac Brekken/Getty Images

It was the "secret" part of the administration's decision to target al-Awlaki that made many uncomfortable. In a public speech in 2012, Obama's top counterterrorism adviser, John Brennan, reassured his audience that individuals, including Americans, were targeted for killing only if capture was not a realistic option and only after careful and thorough review.[69]

Expanding on the comments of other administration officials, in a May 22, 2013, memo informing congressional leaders of the administration's 2011 decision to target and kill al-Awlaki, Attorney General Holder laid out the administration's case for why such measures had been necessary. He based the justification not on al-Awlaki's inflammatory rhetoric but on intelligence that al-Awlaki had moved from the role of terrorist propagandist to one of senior leadership in al-Qaeda in the Arabian Peninsula (AQAP). Holder repeated the administration's position that the decision to target and kill al-Awlaki had been taken only after an extensive review process and only after the conclusion that he could not feasibly be captured alive and brought to a court for a hearing.[70]

In its justification for the targeted killing of al-Awlaki, the Obama administration argued that it was left with no other options to protect national security. Al-Awlaki had, in the estimation of officials, become a clear and present danger to the United States. As one anonymous counterterrorism official in the Obama administration told the *New York Times*, "American citizenship doesn't give you carte blanche to wage war against your own country."[71]

President Obama was neither the first American president to challenge the boundaries of war-making authority in the name of national security nor the last. President Trump's decision to order missile strikes against Syria had been made without explicit authorization by Congress, as part of a broad conception of the war on terror that had been adopted by both President George W. Bush and President Obama.

Abraham Lincoln Pushes the Boundaries of Executive Power during the American Civil War

In April 1861, at the outset of the Civil War, a mob attacked a group of Union soldiers in Baltimore, Maryland, en route to Washington, DC.[72] Someone fired a pistol into the group of soldiers, and the soldiers—frightened and disorganized—fired upon the mob.[73] Four Union soldiers and twelve civilians died in the violence.

Four days later, John Merryman, a prominent and well-to-do Marylander and member of a Southern secessionist group operating in that state, oversaw and led the burning of at least six railroad bridges and the toppling of some telegraph lines that formed one of the key military links between Washington, DC, and the Union states of the North. Merryman claimed he was acting on orders from a former U.S. Army captain. According to witnesses, "Barking orders, repeatedly citing his 'authority,' Merryman proclaimed his intention to stop Northern troops from invading Maryland. . . . 'We'll stop them from coming down and stealing our slaves.'"[74]

President Abraham Lincoln (1861–1865) knew that keeping the border states from joining the South was key to any hope of winning the war and reconstituting the Union, and Maryland was one of the most important of these states. If Maryland was lost, then the Union's capital in Washington, DC, would be nearly impossible to defend, as it would be cut off from supplies and reinforcements by land. Lincoln used the full force of his presidency to ensure the border states remained in the Union: He called up state militias, blockaded Southern ports, expanded the army and the navy, spent $2 million from the U.S. Treasury, "closed the Post Office, . . . suspended the writ of habeas corpus in certain localities, [and] caused the arrest and detention of persons who were 'represented to him as being engaged in treasonable practices.'"[75] Calling up the state militias was within his executive authority. All of his other actions were "without any statutory authorization."[76]

President Lincoln Defies the Federal Judiciary.

On the morning of May 25, 1861, federal troops roused Merryman from his bed and took him to Fort McHenry in Baltimore Harbor, where he was imprisoned. As he was from a prominent family and had powerful political connections in Maryland, Merryman's detention did not go unnoticed. Within hours of his internment at the federal fort, Merryman's lawyers arrived and prepared a petition for his release. Supreme Court chief justice Robert Brooke Taney received Merryman's petition and issued a writ of habeas corpus on his behalf. Taney noted that Merryman had been "imprisoned by the commanding officer, without warrant from any lawful authority . . . upon charges of treason and rebellion, without proof and without giving the names of the witnesses, or specifying the acts which, in the judgment of the military officer, constituted these crimes."[77]

Taney called on the Union general in charge of the fort to produce "the body of John Merryman"[78] so the charges against him could be examined. *Habeas corpus*—from the Latin "you [shall] have the body"—defines a procedure through which a person can challenge what they see as unlawful detention. If Taney's writ of habeas corpus in the case of Merryman was honored, either an arrest warrant would be issued for Merryman or Merryman would be free to go.

The Union commander refused to honor the writ. Instead, he sent an aide, who showed up in Taney's courtroom without Merryman. It became clear to Justice Taney that Merryman was being held under the authority of President Lincoln and was not to be released, not even upon Taney's direct demand. According to Baltimore mayor George William Brown, "A more important question could hardly have occurred. Where did the president acquire such a power? Was it true that a citizen held his liberty subject to the arbitrary will of any man? In what part of the Constitution could such a power be found?"[79]

On Tuesday morning, having been twice rebuffed, Taney prepared to confront the president. He wrote and swiftly delivered an opinion, *Ex parte Merryman* (1861), in which he challenged the president's authority to suspend writs of habeas corpus, even in times of war and rebellion.[80] "The President, under the Constitution and laws of the United States," Taney declared, "cannot suspend the privilege of the writ of *habeas corpus*, nor authorize any military officer to do so."[81]

In his opinion, Taney acknowledged that the Constitution does grant the federal government the power to suspend the writ of habeas corpus during times of rebellion or invasion.[82] However, Taney noted, Article I gives that power to Congress, not the executive branch. And, Taney continued, the judicial branch has the power to issue arrest warrants, not the president or the military under his command. The president, therefore, "has exercised a power which he does not possess under the Constitution."[83]

President Lincoln Defends His Emergency Powers. For his part, Lincoln justified to members of Congress and the Union "these actions of dubious constitutionality by reference to the 'war powers' granted to the executive."[84] In other words, he argued that the war powers granted to the presidency were sufficient grounds for his actions. Congress retroactively approved most of Lincoln's actions taken that year. However, it did not approve the suspension of habeas corpus (with some limits) until 1863, after the president had issued a broader suspension of the privilege the year before.[85]

Such drastic unilateral presidential action in times of war and national crisis led political scientist Edward Corwin to conclude that "the Constitution is an easily dispensable factor of our war effort—perhaps one might say 'expendable' factor,'" transforming it during wartime "from a *Constitution of Rights* into a *Constitution of Powers*."[86]

Taney expected to be impeached or even arrested over his confrontation with Lincoln, and Lincoln is said to have contemplated it. In the end, however, the president simply ignored Taney, prosecuting the war by whatever means he saw necessary to restore the Union. Lincoln continued to defend his suspension of habeas corpus and other measures as valid uses of the constitutional power of the government "when in cases of Rebellion or Invasion the public Safety may require it."[87]

Lincoln believed that the powers he had to assume during the war would no longer be necessary once the crisis of the Civil War was successfully resolved. In this prediction, he proved to be correct. Presidential power did recede in the decades following the Union victory, and Congress once again assumed its position as the strongest of the three branches. But not forever. As America again confronted wars, major crises, and other extraordinary circumstances, successive presidents also tested the limits of executive branch power, as we saw with President Obama and the targeted killing of Anwar al-Awlaki.

When Obama ordered the drone strike that killed al-Awlaki, he did so with the conviction that he was acting within his constitutional powers as the commander in chief of the United States. Some questioned whether this was in fact true.

Since George Washington was inaugurated as the nation's first president in 1789, the institution of the American presidency has undergone a major transformation, one that would likely seem remarkable to the Framers of the Constitution. The office has grown in power, prestige, and complexity, "not smoothly but with great leaps, periods of dormancy, and occasional setbacks."[88]

The President Has Several Tools for Unilateral Action

11.5 Evaluate the tools that presidents use to further expand their power.

Scholars' views of the American presidency and the power of the office have, like the institution itself, changed over time and in response to the individual presidents and the times in which they have governed. Increasingly, political scientists have focused on a unilateral model of presidential action in which presidents attempt to influence both domestic and foreign policy with few or no constraints by Congress or the judiciary. It is, in other words, when presidents act alone. Individual presidents have often tried to defend the power of their office or even push the boundaries of that power, but the scope and frequency of unilateral presidential action in recent administrations has raised questions about the degree to which powers truly remain separated between the three branches of the U.S. government.

Presidents attempt to exercise independent control over information through the assertion of **executive privilege**, in which they try to shield from Congress; the judiciary; and, ultimately, the public the details of debates, discussions, memos, and emails surrounding presidential decisions and actions. Since the administration of George Washington, presidents have asserted that their ability to control information is essential to their effectiveness.[89]

During the investigation of President Nixon and his role in the Watergate affair, Nixon refused to hand over to a special prosecutor audio recordings of his conversations with senior aides as well as other documents relating to the investigation, citing the power of executive privilege. In *United States v. Nixon* (1974), the Supreme Court affirmed the power of executive privilege, finding that "a President and those who assist him must be free to explore alternatives in the process of shaping policies and making decisions, and to do so in a way many would be unwilling to express except privately."[90] However, the Court also demanded that the president hand over the recordings and documents, balancing the need for executive privilege with the need for the rule of law in criminal investigations.

In the area of foreign policy, presidents may sign **executive agreements** with foreign nations without Senate ratification, which is needed for treaties. Though they are not binding upon future presidents in the way that treaties are, executive agreements can give a president a way to shape foreign policy that bypasses the Senate's role of advice and consent. Their details are often kept secret from the public and Congress for reasons of national security.

In the president's role in the legislative process, the use of **signing statements** has gained increased attention recently. When a president signs a bill into law, they may add written comments that convey instructions to the various agencies that will actually carry out the law or that offer the president's interpretation of the law. Sometimes signing statements are far from controversial; they may be offered to try to build a public record of support for an issue, to call attention to an issue, or to offer a slightly different interpretation of a law that a president otherwise supports. However, if the president either interprets the law differently from the way Congress intended or instructs agencies to execute it selectively or differently, then concerns can be raised that the president is taking the lawmaking authority intended for Congress for themselves.

Executive orders are policy directives issued by presidents to the executive branch bureaucracy that do not require congressional approval. Most executive orders constitute a set of instructions given by the president to the executive branch agencies informing them of how they are supposed to go about implementing a law or policy. Often they deal with routine administrative procedures. Presidents have also used executive orders, however, to make major changes in public policy.[91]

In 1942, President Roosevelt issued Executive Order 9066, which authorized the secretary of war to declare certain areas in the United States as "military areas . . . from which any or all persons may be excluded, and with respect to which the right of any person to enter, remain in, or leave shall be subject to whatever restrictions the Secretary of War or the appropriate Military Commander may impose in his discretion."[92] Issued for the declared purpose of "protection against espionage and against sabotage to national-defense material," Roosevelt's executive order led to the internment of more than one hundred thirty thousand individuals, most of whom were Japanese Americans. In *Korematsu v. United States* (1944), the Supreme Court upheld Roosevelt's authority. In a dissent, however, one justice commented about the internment: "I need hardly labor the conclusion that Constitutional rights have been violated."[93]

Conclusion: The Paradoxes of Power Continue

When Joe Biden takes office in January of 2021, he and Vice President-elect Kamala Harris may be well-advised to act quickly. Midterm elections typically bring gains in Congress for the party not in control of the presidency. In 2022 Biden will have to consider the real possibility of losing one or both chambers of Congress to Republican control.

These calculations involve more than future "what ifs." The tools of presidential action depend very much on partisan control in Congress. In the days and weeks following the election, President-elect Biden began to outline one unilateral strategy that he planned to use in the possible presence of divided government: issuing executive orders to reverse Trump-era policies. Rejoining the Paris climate accords, ending a travel ban on residents from certain Muslim-majority nations, and protecting "dreamers" (undocumented Americans who arrived as minors) emerged as top candidates for unilateral presidential action.

The power of the American presidency is not easily defined, nor are sources easily traced or separated. Many factors—constitutional provisions, institutional and political contexts, individual personality and skill, and responses to crises—have all played a role in its development. As scholars have observed, the office of the presidency is full of paradoxes.[94] The Framers wanted a strong and decisive office, yet they were wary of creating an elected monarch. Americans often look to their presidents for leadership above the fray of partisan politics, yet the position is, by design, political and embedded in a system of checks and balances. Americans look to their presidents for leadership yet expect them to follow the will of the people.

The modern American presidency is a massively powerful office. As Americans are confronted with a global war on terror, reshaping of the international balance of power in the face of China's rise, and multiple crises—foreign and domestic—setting the proper limits of presidential power is one of the most important tasks the nation faces today.

CHAPTER REVIEW

This chapter's main ideas are reflected in the Learning Objectives. By reviewing them here, you should be able to *remember* the key points and *know* these terms that are central to the topic.

11.1 Consider the importance of presidential character in shaping the conduct and effectiveness of an administration.

Remember . . .
- Donald Trump's presidential style has been characterized by conflict and contestation.
- Scholars have attempted to define the impact of presidential character on effective execution of the office's powers.

11.2 **Describe the powers of the presidency as defined in the Constitution and the constitutional limitations placed on those powers.**

Remember . . .
- The Framers called for a single executive, the president, with enough power to lead successfully but not so much power to make him susceptible to tyranny.
- As set out in the Constitution, the president serves a four-year term with the possibility of reelection. Candidates must be natural-born citizens, at least thirty-five years old, and a resident of the nation for fourteen years.
- The office of the presidency is granted a set of expressed, implied, and delegated powers.
- Executive power is constitutionally limited by powers granted to Congress and the judiciary.

Know . . .
- *presidential pardon* (p. 330)
- *recess appointment* (p. 327)
- *State of the Union address* (p. 329)
- *War Powers Resolution of 1973* (p. 328)

11.3 **Discuss institutional and informal sources of and influences on presidential power.**

Remember . . .
- The institutions of the presidency can enhance or limit presidential power.
- The size and scale of the executive branch make it possible for the president to act on multiple fronts, but at the same time they can act as a brake on presidential initiatives.
- The president's cabinet and executive office act as sources of information for the president and also can communicate to the citizens a president's commitment to representing all Americans and their interests.
- Public opinion has come to play an important role in expanding or constraining the power of individual presidents. However, a president's approval ratings tend to decline over time.

Know . . .
- *Executive Office of the President (EOP)* (p. 333)
- *going public* (p. 336)

11.4 **Understand how presidents have tested the limits of executive power during wartime and other crises.**

Remember . . .
- The Constitution provides that the U.S. government has certain powers to suspend rights during times of rebellion or invasion. The text granting that power is within Article I, which is devoted to the structure and powers of Congress, not the executive branch. However, presidents have sometimes pointed to the "war powers" granted to the executive as justification for their actions.
- President Lincoln suspended habeas corpus during the Civil War on the grounds that the crisis necessitated it.

11.5 **Evaluate the tools that presidents use to further expand their power.**

Remember . . .
- Presidents sometimes attempt to exercise a degree of unilateral authority through the assertion of executive privilege, signing statements, and executive orders.

Know . . .
- *executive agreements* (p. 343)
- *executive orders* (p. 343)
- *executive privilege* (p. 342)
- *signing statements* (p. 343)

CHAPTER 12

THE FEDERAL BUREAUCRACY

Putting the Nation's Laws into Effect

After Hurricane Maria slammed into Puerto Rico and devastated the island's infrastructure, residents lined up to collect water from a tanker truck. The federal response to the storm was widely criticized, especially when viewed in conjunction with the preparation for and response to Hurricanes Harvey and Irma, which struck the U.S. mainland.

Pedro Portal/El Nuevo Herald/Getty Images

After reading this chapter, you will be able to do the following:

12.1 Understand how federal bureaucratic action involves many different agencies and evolves over time, often in response to lessons learned from past actions.

12.2 Name the key characteristics of bureaucratic organization and the theories that explain why bureaucratic organization happens.

12.3 Outline the historical development of the American federal bureaucracy.

12.4 Describe the structure of the federal bureaucracy, including executive branch agencies, cabinet departments, and regulatory bodies.

12.5 Describe the tools of bureaucratic control, oversight, and reform.

To most Americans, the word *bureaucracy* refers to something that must be dealt with when necessary, complained about at times, and perhaps feared when confronted with its seemingly faceless exercise of power. Bureaucracy, however, simply describes an organization designed to carry out specific tasks according to a prescribed set of rules and procedures. In this chapter, you will learn about the **federal bureaucracy**—what it is, how it is structured, and how it works. Formally, the federal bureaucracy is part of the executive branch of the national government, charged with executing, or putting into action, the laws

that Congress has written. However, the federal bureaucracy is actually a powerful player in the American political scene in its own right, though one that rarely makes the news unless something goes wrong. Whether you realize it or not, this is the part of the federal government that actually impacts your life in a more personal way than the actions of the president, Congress, or the judiciary typically do.

Americans often have contradictory views of bureaucracy and make many demands of it. At times, they complain that bureaucracy is too powerful, capable of making their lives more difficult or expensive—or even that it is corrupt. At other times, they complain that it is powerless to help them, incompetent, wasteful, and inefficient. As you will see, these enduring tensions have spurred periods of reform and change since the nation's founding, in turn shaping the modern bureaucracy.

In this chapter, we will examine the American federal bureaucracy through the lenses of recent natural disasters and the responses to them—three hurricanes that impacted the Caribbean, the Gulf of Mexico region, and the United States mainland in 2017 as well as one extraordinarily destructive hurricane whose effects along the Gulf Coast are still being felt fifteen years after its impact in 2005. The impacts, levels of response, and evaluations of the bureaucratic response to each of these was as unique as each storm and the main challenges it presented.

In considering the federal bureaucracy in the light of these natural disasters, you will gain a deeper understanding of its complexity, how it has changed over time, and efforts to make it more efficient and successful given the myriad tasks Americans place upon it.

Federal Bureaucratic Action Consists of Many Actors and Evolves over Time

> **12.1** Understand how federal bureaucratic action involves many different agencies and evolves over time, often in response to lessons learned from past actions.

We may be inclined to think of the federal bureaucracy as one thing. It is not. As we will explore, it is a machinery constructed from many smaller units, each with its own objectives and administrative structures. We may also be inclined to see federal bureaucratic action as static in time. As we will see, it is not that either. Bureaucracies evolve and learn—unfortunately sometimes because of failure and political pressure applied in response to that failure. To begin to explore these issues, we examine a series of twenty-first-century disasters, hurricanes specifically. We start with three Atlantic Ocean hurricanes that came ashore in different places in the same year: 2017.

Hurricanes Harvey, Irma, and Maria Test the Federal Response

The first of the 2017 Atlantic monsters was Hurricane Harvey. It would become the costliest tropical cyclone in U.S. history. Making U.S. landfall at Rockport, Texas, as a 200-mile-wide but slow-moving Category 4 storm (with Category 5 being the most dangerous), Harvey's main impact was not wind but rain—torrential rain. In places over a large part of South Texas, it dropped almost unimaginable amounts, as much as sixty inches in the areas worst hit.

Houston was especially inundated. The flooding was so severe that, according to a NASA (the National Aeronautics and Space Administration; NASA is a federal agency and part of the bureaucracy) scientist, the weight of the water pushed the earth and bedrock in West Houston and nearby areas down by two centimeters.[1]

To some experts and observers, it could have been far worse. A combination of good advance preparation and community spirit helped. Warnings went out to residents ahead of time, low-lying roads were barricaded, and—as the devastation became clear for all to observe—"thousands of ordinary folks walked out into the rain, some with just a scant idea of how they might be of assistance."[2] Officials and staff for the Federal Emergency Management Agency (FEMA) had sent supplies to Texas ahead of the storm. In addition to members of other agencies and the National Guard, more than 31,000 people delivered millions of meals and millions of liters of water.[3]

However, in the aftermath of the storm, some asked what could have been done better. Two reservoirs constructed by the U.S. Army Corps of Engineers (USACE; yet another part of the federal bureaucracy) in the 1940s to protect Houston residents had proved insufficient to handle the storm waters, as Houstonians had built homes and businesses far beyond the land they were designed to protect. Thousands of homes outside the two reservoirs flooded. Some blamed Congress for not directing the USACE to protect a larger area and for not funding the USACE accordingly.[4]

While the recovery efforts continued from Harvey, Irma landed, and with force. With Irma, unlike Harvey's rains, the main damage was the wind and the "storm surge," the ocean water pushed landward by the power of the storm and the differences in pressure between it and the surrounding ocean water.

At the peak of its power, Irma was a Category 5 hurricane. It devastated the Virgin Islands; the Caribbean; and then Key West, Florida. In the United States, at least ninety people lost their lives.

On the American mainland, from Key West to South Carolina, Irma and its storm surge wreaked havoc. Five million Floridians lost power. Federal and state officials struggled to reach them. "Basically, every house in the Keys was impacted some way," reported a FEMA administrator. The federal response was equally massive. FEMA deployed thousands of people and transferred even more meals and liters of water than it had when Harvey impacted Texas.[5]

And then there was Maria.

That hurricane did not wreak the kind of destruction Harvey and Irma had on the U.S. mainland. Both had caused devastation and loss of lives as they made their way to the United States across the islands and nations of the Caribbean and the Atlantic basin.

Still, Maria wreaked enormous havoc on the United States—in Puerto Rico, a U.S. territory though not a state. For Maria, the consequences were devastating, destroying the entire infrastructure of Puerto Rico.

Much of Puerto Rico remained without power, food distribution, and clean water for months.[6] Many questioned whether President Donald Trump had fully deployed the power of the United States in relief efforts, through its federal bureaucracy, in repairing the damage that Maria brought. President Trump cited the difficulties of reaching the island territory: "It's very tough because it's an island. . . . In Texas and Florida and we will also see on Puerto Rico, but the difference is this is an island sitting in the middle of an ocean, and it's a big ocean."[7]

In June 2018, eight months after Maria made landfall, Puerto Rico was still struggling to recover. It was not even clear how many people had lost their lives in the storm the year before. The official government toll was sixty-four. Researchers from Harvard University, however, calculated it to be much, much larger—as many as 4,645—once deaths due to effects such as delayed medical

Yamiles Vazquez poses with her baby Joy on a section of her family's damaged property. Three weeks after Hurricane Maria hit Puerto Rico, the town had yet to receive any FEMA aid. The area was without running water or grid power for months.
Mario Tama/Getty Images

care were taken into account.[8] That month, protesters gathered in New York City to demand that an *international* bureaucratic organization, the United Nations, investigate the official conclusions of the Puerto Rican government. "They took their shoes off as a symbol of the people who died as a result of the storm but who were not immediately counted."[9] In bureaucratic politics, the act of counting is itself an act of political power.

The 2018 Atlantic hurricane season officially began on June 1, a date established by a federal bureaucracy in the 1960s, largely based on the time when hurricane reconnaissance aircraft began to patrol the ocean in the absence of the widespread weather satellite coverage now employed. Prior to each hurricane season, the National Hurricane Center publishes a list, for different ocean basins and regions, of names to be given to storms as they reach significant status as a tropical storm and/or hurricane (with the World Meteorological Organization controlling the actual procedure). The names are applied alphabetically, reused in six-year cycles until a name gets retired and replaced if that storm resulted in significant death or destruction. The names Harvey, Irma, and Maria have all been retired.

There was another notable storm whose name will not be used again if the list of named storms reaches *K* in 2021 or afterward. Not only did that storm produce devastation that still shapes New Orleans, the Gulf Coast, and many lives fifteen years after its impact but it resulted in one of the deepest questionings of the actions of federal bureaucracies in preparation for and responses to natural disasters in the twenty-first century.

Its name was Katrina.[10]

Katrina Provides Uncomfortable Lessons about the Federal Response

Max Mayfield saw it coming, and he tried to warn as many people as he could. As director of the National Hurricane Center, based in Miami, Florida, Mayfield and the scientists on his team sounded the alarm on August 26, 2005, that a potentially catastrophic hurricane would make landfall on the coast of Louisiana, southeast of New Orleans. In predicting the point of impact for the hurricane's eye, they were off by a mere eighteen miles. As one reporter noted, "In the business of hurricane prediction, that's laser-beam accuracy."[11]

Two days prior to landfall, "Mayfield was so worried about Hurricane Katrina that he called the governors of Louisiana and Mississippi and the mayor of New Orleans. On Sunday, he even talked about the force of Katrina during a video conference call to President George W. Bush . . . 'I just wanted to be able to go to sleep that night knowing that I did all I could do.'"[12]

As the storm approached shore, officials warned that it could make landfall with winds in excess of 130 miles per hour, pushing ahead of it a storm surge of devastating intensity and volume.

Of all the concerns, the most worrisome was the city's system of levees and pumps, designed by the USACE to keep the water at bay. With much of the city below sea level, a failure in any one section of the system would cause New Orleans "to fill up like a bathtub."[13] By the morning of Sunday, August 28, New Orleans was under evacuation orders. The roads were packed. Inbound lanes of the main highways were redirected to handle outbound traffic. Many residents, however, could not or would not leave. In a press conference, Mayor C. Ray Nagin had acknowledged that the Superdome would be needed to temporarily house the one hundred thousand

Hurricane Katrina refugees wait near the Superdome to be evacuated as a helicopter brings National Guard troops. Thousands of troops poured into New Orleans scrambling to reverse a tide of anarchy and to bolster relief efforts that President George W. Bush acknowledged were unacceptably slow.

Robert Sullivan/AFP/Getty Images

or more of the city's residents who lacked the transportation needed to leave the city, a disproportionate number of whom were elderly, poor, or African American.[14] When the Superdome opened to receive those unable to evacuate, "people on walkers, some with oxygen tanks, began checking in."[15]

On the morning of August 29, Hurricane Katrina's eyewall made its first Gulf Coast landfall at Plaquemines Parish, Louisiana. Initially, New Orleans and its mayor were hopeful that a disaster had been avoided. The city had been spared the storm's strongest winds and storm surge. Within hours, however, it became clear that the levee system was failing. Water overtopped the levees in some areas. In others, leaks developed, and the pumps designed to protect the city from the water entering it began to fail. The "bathtub" that included many of the city's poorest neighborhoods began to fill up.

More than one thousand residents of Louisiana died in the storm and the flooding that followed, many of them its most vulnerable. A study of the bodies recovered following the storm concluded that "64 percent of the people who died were elderly."[16] Immediately after the scope of the devastation became clear, calls went out for donations to private relief agencies, such as the American Red Cross and the Salvation Army. Then, in the days, weeks, and months that followed, Gulf Coast residents looked to FEMA to step in and lead recovery efforts. However, as refugees from New Orleans evacuated to nearby states following the storm, they shared not only stories of loss and devastation but plenty of criticism for how public officials had handled the disaster. Some of the sharpest words came from those who sheltered at the Superdome. One woman, Maia Brisco, told reporters the stadium was "a total hell hole."[17]

In the aftermath of Hurricane Katrina, the performance of local, state, and federal officials in predicting, preparing for, and responding to the storm came under intense scrutiny. Figuring prominently in this process was the federal bureaucracy, which is really a small universe of organizations operating across the country. Within this vast system are departments, agencies, and bureaus, which themselves are often divided and subdivided into smaller organizational units. The National Hurricane Center, for example, and Max Mayfield and the members of his team, were part of the National Weather Service, which is part of the National Oceanic and Atmospheric Administration, which, in turn, is part of the Department of Commerce.

As the nation was confronted with scenes of devastation and loss in Katrina's wake, parts of the federal bureaucracy, such as the National Hurricane Center, were singled out for praise. Others, however, such as the USACE and FEMA, received sharp criticism. How could some parts of the vast machinery of the federal government have gotten things right while others seemed to have gotten them so wrong? As Congress, the White House, and the American people asked this very question, it was concluded that the answers were complicated, just like the vast bureaucracy responsible for preparing for and responding to disasters such as Hurricane Katrina.

Did the Bureaucracy Learn from Katrina?

As the affected areas began to clean up and rebuild from the triple monsters in late 2017, two questions were commonly posed: Had the federal and state agencies learned from Katrina? Did they put this dearly paid-for education into practice on the ground?

The year 2017 was not the first time these questions had been asked since Katrina laid waste to New Orleans and the Gulf Coast in 2005. In 2012, Hurricane Sandy spread destruction from the Caribbean up the East Coast of the United States, from Florida to Maine. More than 140 people died as a direct result of Sandy. In the United States, the devastation was worst in New Jersey and New York, mostly due to flooding. While some praised the response to Sandy by the administration of President Barack Obama, others critiqued it.

By some accounts, government had learned and adapted. Enabled by legislation passed in Katrina's wake, President Obama was able to quickly instruct FEMA to coordinate and streamline its rescue response across all responders.[18] Three months after Sandy's landfall, however, when a blast of arctic air hit the Northeast, some critics pointed to families having to rely on space heaters to stave off the cold while still awaiting repairs and rebuilding. The bureaucratic apparatus might have been more responsive in preparation, but in terms of rebuilding, it seemed to be too slow yet again.

In the aftermath of the hurricanes of 2017, there were similarly mixed reviews. Once again, for example, the National Hurricane Center received widespread praise for its work. Though not perfect—a very difficult thing to achieve with hurricanes—the National Hurricane Center developed, and disseminated, shocking predictions of likely rainfall totals associated with Harvey.[19] They were right. Rebuilding efforts in Puerto Rico in the wake of Maria undertaken by federal and territorial agencies, on the other hand, continue to come under sharp criticism.

Differences in evaluations of bureaucratic performance, however, also depend upon competing political demands on the bureaucracy and on Americans' views of its proper role in American public life. And they are shaped by politics. In March 2018, during the administration of President Donald Trump, the agency tasked as a watchdog over FEMA (the Department of Homeland Security's Office of Inspector General) removed from its website twelve reports, many positive, of the handling of natural disasters—including Hurricane Sandy—by the administration of President Obama. A former FEMA administrator from the Obama administration called the removal "curious."[20]

Those who have argued for a reduced role for government in American public policy have highlighted the successes of the private sector in responding to the challenges of rebuilding: "In particular, hurricane-damaged areas should encourage the private sector to play a large role in both disaster response and long-term recovery. Firms like Walmart and Home Depot were crucial to both processes during Katrina and were again at the forefront [in the 2017] hurricane season."[21]

Can bureaucracies learn and adapt? To gain any traction on this critical question, we need to start with two others: Which bureaucracy? Learn what, precisely? We begin by trying to tease out this thing we call bureaucracy.

Theories of Bureaucratic Organization Focus on Rules, People, and Tasks

> 12.2 Name the key characteristics of bureaucratic organization and the theories that explain why bureaucratic organization happens.

Americans' ambivalence about the federal bureaucracy may be partly due to the fact that—unlike Congress, the president, or the Supreme Court—Americans actually have contact with it in their personal or professional lives.

Any American-made product you consume involved federal agencies making sure that the factory was safe for its employees, that it did not discriminate in hiring, that it dealt with labor issues and complaints fairly, and that it did not degrade the environment. For anything you purchase manufactured by a foreign country, the bureaucracy acted to ensure that the country of origin was following rules of fair trade and labor practices promised in trade agreements. Driving much of this bureaucratic involvement in daily life are the demands of Americans themselves—for safe products, fair labor practices, and environmentally conscious factories. Ensuring that these demands are met involves the federal bureaucracy in many areas of the nation's economy and private life. The vast majority of the federal bureaucracy lies within the executive branch of the federal government, which is tasked with executing, or carrying out, federal laws.

In addition to the federal bureaucracy, there is another category of public bureaucracies: **state and local bureaucracies**. These agencies are also involved in the lives of Americans: They made the rules that governed the construction of the houses in which they live; determine the property taxes that they pay; provide the school, police station, and firehouse down the street; and supply the water in the glass next to the alarm clock (the time on which is actually regulated by a federal bureaucratic agency, the Department of Transportation, believe it or not).[22]

What's more, the same products regulated by public bureaucracies—federal, state, and local—have been produced by another category of bureaucratic organizations: **private bureaucracies**. While corporations and companies are not usually called bureaucracies, they in fact are. They share some, though not all, of the characteristics of public bureaucracies. A common critique of public bureaucracies is that they should try to operate more like the makers of consumer products and less like the government, a topic to which we will return later in the chapter. In short, bureaucratic organization is everywhere. It is an elaborate system, but not necessarily a mysterious one.

Before we begin to untangle the complex constellation of federal administrative organizations, we need to consider how bureaucracies operate. The term *bureaucracy* describes an organization or a set of organizations, but it also describes a way of organizing, a way of distributing power. Scholars have offered a variety of theoretical approaches to explaining bureaucratic organization, none of which have to be mutually exclusive. Three approaches, in particular, highlight different aspects of bureaucratic organization: rules, people, and tasks.

Weber's Theory Focuses on Rules

Max Weber (pronounced VAY-ber), a German sociologist, was among the first to define the boundaries and characteristics of bureaucratic organization. Weber saw bureaucracy as a large and complex machine. Each individual in this machine—a bureaucrat—was "only a single cog in an ever-moving mechanism."[23] For Weber, bureaucratic power rested upon what he called "rational-legal authority" in which citizens accept the authority of organizations, or, more precisely, the rules and organizational structures that define that authority and place limits upon it. Once firmly established, Weber concluded that "bureaucracy is among those social structures which are hardest to destroy."[24]

The Weberian bureaucracy is characterized by four main organizational traits. First, bureaucrats have defined tasks and rules governing how these tasks should be carried out. The sets of rules governing the behavior of bureaucrats are commonly referred to as **standard operating procedures**. Second, authority in bureaucracy is hierarchical. Third, individual jobs within the organization are specialized, with workers increasingly selected for specific jobs based on their technical competence. Finally, the modern bureaucracy is divorced from politics and personal relationships, its effective functioning made more likely if "it succeeds in eliminating from official business love, hatred, and all purely personal, irrational, and emotional elements which escape calculation."[25]

Barnard's Theory Focuses on People

Chester Barnard drew on decades of experience with the American Telephone and Telegraph Company in the early twentieth century to outline a theory of the bureaucracy in which people—and not just rules and procedures—mattered to the life of a bureaucracy. For Barnard, the essence of a bureaucracy is that it involves "conscious coordination" of individuals' activities in pursuit of a joint objective.[26]

Whenever people undertake action in pursuit of a common goal, however, they are taking a risk that others involved might not do what they are supposed to do. Political scientists often describe these risks in terms of the **principal-agent problem**. The "principal" in this model is the actor who asks the agent to carry out a task. The challenge in doing so is twofold. First, the agent may have their own goals, which may not be the same as the principal's. Second, the agent may have information that the principal lacks, which opens up the opportunity for the agent to behave in a way that is not in the interests of the principal.

Principal-agent relationships are everywhere. An example from politics is that when voters (the principals) elect members of Congress (the agents), the voters run the risk that their elected representatives will not faithfully carry out their wishes, especially during the parts of the legislative process that are harder to observe and happen out of public view.

According to Barnard, bureaucratic leadership is central to the success of a bureaucracy. The job of the leader is to secure the cooperation of those within the organization.[27] In this effort, **incentives**—those inducements that the leaders of a bureaucracy can offer to their employees—are key to successful performance. Incentives do not always have to involve money. Power, prestige, a sense of accomplishment, and a shared vision of important work can also act as incentives for successful bureaucratic performance.

Wilson's Theory Focuses on Tasks

For political scientist James Q. Wilson, rules and procedures were important, as were individuals. However, his analysis added a third element of bureaucratic organization: tasks, or what different bureaucrats in their organizations actually do. Wilson wrote that "people matter, but organization matters also, and tasks matter most of all."[28] Of special concern in Wilson's analysis was the ability or inability to observe two consequences of bureaucratic action: outputs and outcomes. Outputs are what bureaucratic operators do; outcomes are what changes in the world as a result of their actions. When either outputs or outcomes are difficult to observe with any certainty, problems arise. When both are difficult to discern, "effective management is almost impossible."[29]

Consider the nation's public schools.[30] When a teacher closes the classroom door, that teacher's outputs are largely unseen except by the students. Sure, the principal can observe the teacher, but both know that the observation day is likely not a typical class. More problematically, especially as America is testing its students like never before, it is very difficult and expensive to try to measure a teacher's outcomes, or what a teacher is adding to the mind of one particular student.[31] In order to be effectively managed, both outputs and outcomes must be "visible."

The Bureaucracy Has Developed in Response to Demands and Crises

12.3 Outline the historical development of the American federal bureaucracy.

In the early years of its history, the American bureaucracy was absolutely tiny, reflecting the reality that the autonomous and mostly agrarian society did not place many demands on the young national government. From its beginnings as a small set of departments employing few people, the bureaucracy has grown enormously and today has nearly three million civilian employees working across the country. This growth has not been steady and gradual but—like the power of the national government itself—has experienced periods of relatively little growth and periods of intense expansion.

The Founders Are Skeptical of, and Unclear about, the Role of the Bureaucracy

Although the delegates to the Constitutional Convention wrestled a great deal with the issue of the power and independence of the chief executive, they spent very little time discussing the administrative apparatus itself, and the "Constitution is virtually silent on the subject."[32] Much of the constitutional basis for the bureaucracy lies in Article II, which lays out the functions and processes of the executive branch of government. In it, the president is authorized to "require the Opinion, in writing, of the principal Officer in each of the executive Departments, upon any Subject relating to the Duties of their respective Offices."[33] This section forms the basis for the executive branch departments, special organizations created by acts of Congress to assist the president in executing the laws of the nation. The heads of these departments form the president's cabinet, along with the vice president and the heads of a few other offices given cabinet-level status.

Delegates Aim to Avoid Tyranny but Preserve Efficiency. The delegates to the Constitutional Convention brought with them a deep mistrust of administrative power that was born out of experiences under British colonial rule: Many of the charges against King George III in the Declaration of Independence focused on administrative abuses. The delegates were in no mood to create a homegrown swarm of officers.

On the other hand, the delegates also held the general belief, gained from hard experience, that placing administrative responsibilities entirely in the hands of the legislature would be slow and inefficient. The Continental Congress had done just that with numerous committees handling the business of fighting a revolution. This arrangement worked poorly, and individual members of the Congress were constantly overworked and overburdened.

Trying to steer a course between executive tyranny and legislative inefficiency, the delegates agreed to place in the hands of the president the authority to nominate executive branch officials rather than having a council of officers selected by Congress, which had been discussed in the convention. The Senate, though, was assigned the role of advising on and consenting to presidential nominees by a majority vote.[34] In addition, Congress retained the ability to impeach (in the House) and try (in the Senate) "all civil Officers of the United States" for "Treason, Bribery, or Other high Crimes and Misdemeanors."[35]

How Officers Would Be Removed Remains Unsettled.

Having settled on how executive branch offers would be selected, the most contentious question facing the delegates was how these people were to be removed. Did the president have the authority to remove officers at will, was it Congress's job, or should there be a role for both the president and the Congress? Or were these people to serve for life with no possibility for removal? On this question—other than setting out the rarely used process of impeachment—the Constitution remained silent.

Only weeks after the first national Congress assembled, the issue of the removal of officers came before it in what has become known as the Decision of 1789. Following what became "the first major constitutional debate" in the young Republic,[36] Congress left the power of removal in the hands of the president. The question, however, reemerged with the Tenure of Office Act (1867), which—largely because of the tense politics following the Civil War—restricted the president's authority of removal. Only in 1926, in the case of *Myers v. United States*, which held the Tenure of Office Act unconstitutional, was the question settled. Presidents retained the authority to remove officials in the executive branch, a necessary ability in their role of ensuring that laws are faithfully executed.[37]

Washington Forms the First Administration and the First Cabinet Departments.

President George Washington's cabinet included just four men and three official departments. Secretary of State Thomas Jefferson oversaw the Department of State, handling the young nation's dealings with foreign nations as well as publishing laws and overseeing the hiring of civil officials. The Department of War (later incorporated into the Department of Defense) oversaw the nation's small military with fewer than one hundred civilian employees. Alexander Hamilton used his position as secretary of the Treasury to advance his goal of expanding the role of the federal government in the nation's economic affairs. Finally, Washington's attorney general (later made the head of the Department of Justice) acted as a legal adviser to the president and members of his cabinet. In the centuries since, Congress has created new departments and reorganized others. (See Figure 12.1.)

FIGURE 12.1

Executive Branch Departments: Year of Establishment and Primary Tasks

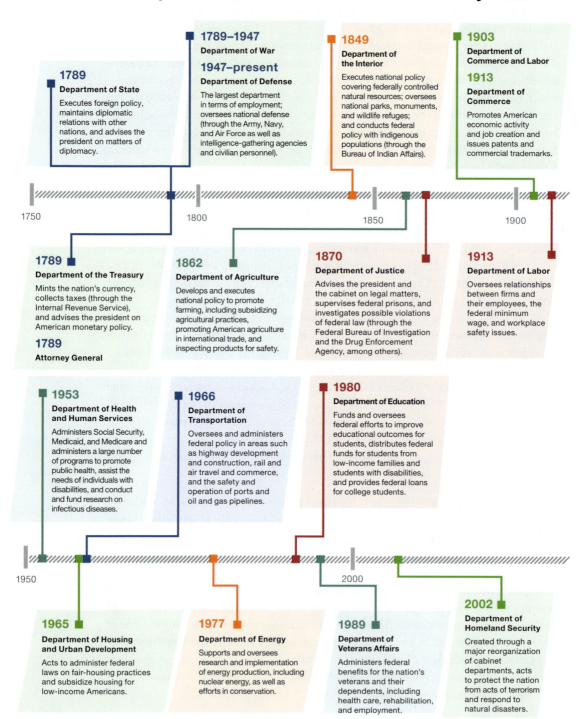

1789
Department of State
Executes foreign policy, maintains diplomatic relations with other nations, and advises the president on matters of diplomacy.

1789–1947
Department of War
1947–present
Department of Defense
The largest department in terms of employment; oversees national defense (through the Army, Navy, and Air Force as well as intelligence-gathering agencies and civilian personnel).

1849
Department of the Interior
Executes national policy covering federally controlled natural resources; oversees national parks, monuments, and wildlife refuges; and conducts federal policy with indigenous populations (through the Bureau of Indian Affairs).

1903
Department of Commerce and Labor
1913
Department of Commerce
Promotes American economic activity and job creation and issues patents and commercial trademarks.

1750   1800   1850   1900

1789
Department of the Treasury
Mints the nation's currency, collects taxes (through the Internal Revenue Service), and advises the president on American monetary policy.

1789
Attorney General

1862
Department of Agriculture
Develops and executes national policy to promote farming, including subsidizing agricultural practices, promoting American agriculture in international trade, and inspecting products for safety.

1870
Department of Justice
Advises the president and the cabinet on legal matters, supervises federal prisons, and investigates possible violations of federal law (through the Federal Bureau of Investigation and the Drug Enforcement Agency, among others).

1913
Department of Labor
Oversees relationships between firms and their employees, the federal minimum wage, and workplace safety issues.

1953
Department of Health and Human Services
Administers Social Security, Medicaid, and Medicare and administers a large number of programs to promote public health, assist the needs of individuals with disabilities, and conduct and fund research on infectious diseases.

1966
Department of Transportation
Oversees and administers federal policy in areas such as highway development and construction, rail and air travel and commerce, and the safety and operation of ports and oil and gas pipelines.

1980
Department of Education
Funds and oversees federal efforts to improve educational outcomes for students, distributes federal funds for students from low-income families and students with disabilities, and provides federal loans for college students.

1950   2000

1965
Department of Housing and Urban Development
Acts to administer federal laws on fair-housing practices and subsidize housing for low-income Americans.

1977
Department of Energy
Supports and oversees research and implementation of energy production, including nuclear energy, as well as efforts in conservation.

1989
Department of Veterans Affairs
Administers federal benefits for the nation's veterans and their dependents, including health care, rehabilitation, and employment.

2002
Department of Homeland Security
Created through a major reorganization of cabinet departments, acts to protect the nation from acts of terrorism and respond to natural disasters.

In forming his first cabinet, Washington tried to reassure members of the experimental nation that his government was competent and representative of all thirteen states. He knew this task would not be easy. A week after his inauguration, the president wrote to a friend, "I anticipate that one of the most difficult and delicate parts of the duty of my Office will be that which relates to nominations for appointments."[38] Three of the members of his small cabinet represented diverse and powerful states: Massachusetts, New York, and Virginia.[39]

Washington was right to be worried. Within the first three years of his administration, "open warfare had broken out" between two powerful members of his cabinet: Alexander Hamilton and Thomas Jefferson.[40] With very different visions of the role of the federal government—especially in the nation's economic life—these men participated in some of the first **turf wars** in the history of the federal bureaucracy, in which each tried to take duties and responsibilities away from the other's department or keep his opponent from doing so.

In choosing individuals to fill out his administration, Washington's primary consideration was what he referred to as "fitness of character," by which he meant integrity, standing in the community, and qualities that would ensure the nation's confidence. Washington's priorities ensured that members of the upper social classes tended to be the ones to fill these positions.[41] Technical competence, except in a few positions, such as those involving legal matters, was not the primary consideration. Washington also viewed his cabinet as very much subordinate to his leadership, sometimes calling on his cabinet secretaries to take dictation.

The Jacksonian Era Sees the Rise of Political Patronage

In the early decades of the nineteenth century, most of the growth of the federal bureaucracy was a result of the geographic expansion of the nation; one particular issue that needed to be addressed was delivery of the mail across the growing territory. The bureaucratic reforms of President Andrew Jackson (1829–1837) sought to separate the person from the office. In his inaugural address, Jackson railed against the sense of "ownership" of important (and sometimes well-paying) administrative positions on the part of the officeholders, who in some cases unofficially handed the positions down to their heirs, as had been done officially in Britain and other European countries.

As part of his reforms, Jackson instituted what is called **political patronage**—filling administrative positions as a reward for support rather than based solely on merit. His use of patronage is commonly referred to as the **spoils system**; the name indicates that part of the "spoils" of a successful election is the ability to clean house of one's opponents and install supporters in their place. Although politics—specifically removing political opponents and installing supporters—played a role in Jackson's reforms, so did a desire to separate the man from the office he held in order to undercut individual power bases as a challenge to Jackson's power and authority.

Ironically, one of the consequences of patronage was to make the federal bureaucracy in some ways closer to what Weber described: impartial, neutral, driven by standard operating procedures and technical expertise. If, after elections, a nation is constantly shuffling people in and out of important administrative positions—people who often have little expertise in the operations of those agencies and departments—then it becomes necessary to standardize procedures. Otherwise, little would get done, or at least done well. Thus, through their overtly political practices, Jackson and his supporters laid the foundations for the modern federal bureaucracy.

Post–Civil War, the Bureaucracy Grows along with the Nation's Territories

As America emerged from the devastation of the Civil War, the nation found itself engaged in relentless expansion of both the nation's boundaries in the West and of agriculture and industry. To cope with the demands placed upon the federal government as a result of this expansion, the bureaucracy grew in size and also in the scope of its involvement with the nation's economy.

As large corporations such as the railroads outgrew the ability of individual states to control and regulate them, demands by the public for a more active federal role in supervising businesses and commerce led to the creation of independent regulatory agencies, which exist outside the major cabinet departments and whose job is to monitor and regulate specific sectors of the economy. Congress created the first, the Interstate Commerce Commission, in 1887 in order to monitor price setting and other practices by the railroads.

In addition to calls for regulation, the federal bureaucracy found itself confronted with the demands of organized interests, such as farmers, who sought to use the power of the federal government to advance and promote their own endeavors. The result was the development of **clientele agencies**, which, as their name implies, act to serve and promote the interests of their clients. The Department of Agriculture (1862) served the interests of farmers—one of the most powerful clientele groups of the time—by, for example, collecting and distributing data about advancements in agricultural practices.[42]

The development and expansion of the federal bureaucracy happened relatively late in the life of the American democracy, especially when compared to European democracies of the period. For most of these nations, a well-developed bureaucracy existed before they became democracies, having developed under the rule of monarchs. For political scientist Stephen Skowronek, the fact that the American bureaucracy had to develop in the shadow of two other, already established, sets of political institutions—the court system and political parties—resulted in a federal bureaucracy that was more fragmented and decentralized than its European counterparts.[43]

Political scientist Theda Skocpol looked to the same period in state development to explain why America never developed the kind of comprehensive social welfare state as Europe, even though America introduced some of the earliest social welfare policies in the world with its system of pensions for Civil War veterans and their survivors. For Skocpol, the well-developed system of federal courts was hostile to large-scale government intervention on behalf of citizens, and American political parties did not want to give up the power they gained by providing benefits in return for political patronage.[44]

Both of these studies highlight the idea of American exceptionalism, in which scholars have examined how the unique histories, paths,

A NAUSEATING JOB, BUT IT MUST BE DONE

A political cartoon depicting President Theodore Roosevelt as a muckraker taking on the meatpacking industry. Muckrakers focused on a variety of abuses in private industry, including working conditions.

North Wind Picture Archives via AP Images

and development of American political institutions may have led to uniqueness in the nation's representative government itself. In doing so, scholars have also stressed the importance of **path dependence** in which a set of political choices at one time produces a set of outcomes that shapes the possibilities for future politics and public policies.

Bureaucratic Expansion in the Progressive Era Focuses on Labor and Eliminating Patronage

The Progressive Era (roughly from 1890 to 1920) is known for the continued expansion of the role of the federal bureaucracy in the nation's economic life and for attempts to take politics out of the bureaucracy itself. Congress created the Department of Commerce and Labor in 1903 to oversee and regulate workplaces, the rights of employees, and working conditions, which had become the focus of reform-minded journalists called muckrakers.[45]

The Progressive Era also witnessed attempts to reform the bureaucracy, especially in trying to alleviate the effects of the patronage system of appointment. The model that these reformers used was one of science and business. Their target was what they saw as a corrupt, inefficient, and too-political bureaucracy. Under President Chester A. Arthur (1881–1885), Congress passed the Pendleton Civil Service Reform Act of 1883, commonly known as the Pendleton Act in reference to its primary Senate sponsor. The Pendleton Act created the first U.S. Civil Service Commission. Its three members, appointed by Arthur, were active reformers. Their task was to draw up and enforce rules on hiring, promotion, and tenure of office within the civil service.

Under these new rules, members of the **federal civil service** were hired and promoted on the basis of the **merit system**, in which competitive testing results, educational attainment, and other qualifications formed the basis for hiring and promotion rather than politics and personal connections. In the early years after the act's passage, only a small percentage of federal bureaucrats were covered by its requirements; by 2016, more than 90 percent were.

Twentieth-Century Crises Expand Clientele Agencies and the Military Bureaucracy

As we discussed in Chapter 3, President Franklin Roosevelt's New Deal efforts to combat the crisis of the Great Depression resulted in an unprecedented expansion of the size of the federal bureaucracy as well as an equally startling expansion of the role of government and the bureaucracy in the American economy. Roosevelt created a host of bureaucratic agencies (despite challenges from the Supreme Court) that were primarily clientele agencies, acting on behalf of specific groups of citizens, such as the unemployed. Their purpose was to increase the provision of social services to affected Americans, including senior citizens, low-income and unemployed Americans, and individuals with disabilities.

Following World War II, the United States and its former ally, the Soviet Union, entered a period of competition for global supremacy known as the Cold War, in which the nuclear-armed superpowers engaged in smaller military confrontations around the globe without directly engaging each other's militaries on a large scale. To fight the Cold War, the federal bureaucracy saw the creation of new agencies. President Harry S. Truman (1945–1953) signed into law the National Security Act of 1947, which created the National Security Council to advise the president on security matters and the Central Intelligence Agency (CIA) to advise the president on intelligence matters and help coordinate intelligence-gathering activities.[46] Not a formal cabinet department, the CIA is an example of an **independent executive agency**. These agencies resemble cabinet departments in many ways, such as having their top administrators appointed by and reporting to the president, but they exist outside the cabinet structure and usually have a narrower focus of mission.

In the Mid-Twentieth Century, the Social Safety Net Grows

Postwar economic prosperity allowed the nation to fund a large expansion in the national bureaucracy in the areas of defense and the provision of social services. Under the umbrella of the Great Society, President Lyndon B. Johnson (1963–1969) proposed a series of expansions to the social safety net with the goal of securing opportunity for more Americans. The Department of Housing and Urban Development (HUD) was created in 1965 and the Department of Transportation in 1966. Efforts to secure civil rights for Americans and battle discrimination based on sex and race led to the passage of the Civil Rights Act of 1964.[47] The act created the Equal Employment Opportunity Commission, which today acts to enforce prohibitions on discrimination in the workplace based on racial identity, sex, religious preference, national origin, age, or disability.

The Late Twentieth Century Brings Reform and Scaling Back

When he was elected president in 1980, Ronald Reagan (1981–1989) promised to reduce the size of the federal government as well as its impact on the daily lives of

Americans. As discussed in Chapter 3, efforts at devolution attempted to return power over implementing public policy back to the individual states. Efforts at deregulation aimed to reduce government oversight of and involvement with specific industries, notably transportation, banking, and utilities. Though Reagan, his Republican successor George H. W. Bush (1989–1993), and his Democratic successor Bill Clinton (1993–2001) all promised some form of bureaucratic reform or improvement, the federal bureaucracy did not undergo a major restructuring during the period. After being elected in 2016, President Donald Trump promised to shrink the American federal bureaucracy and its power over the American economy. According to an article published by *Fortune* magazine, on this he has made progress: "According to the American Action Fund, his actions have reduced regulatory costs by $70 billion."[48]

A Functioning Bureaucracy Depends upon Effective Organization

12.4 Describe the structure of the federal bureaucracy, including executive branch agencies, cabinet departments, and regulatory bodies.

Today, bureaucratic tasks have become increasingly technical and specialized. The organization of authority within the federal bureaucracy and the tasks that agencies undertake matter not just because they are complex but because both can affect how well a bureaucracy functions and how easy it can be to reform one that has gone astray. The individual parts of the federal bureaucracy are people, not bits of a machine, and they have their own priorities and competencies. Politics, competition, and even faction are as present in bureaucratic action as they are in any other endeavor in which individuals work to achieve goals.

The Federal Bureaucracy Is a Web of Organizations

The American federal bureaucracy is not one structure but a complex web of organizations. **Cabinet departments** serve as the primary administrative units in the federal bureaucracy. Congress has the authority to establish and fund the departments, each of which is responsible for a major area of public policy. They are typically divided into subunits based on the policy in which they specialize. The division of tasks among departments does not always follow a clear logic; historical development, politics, and competition among the divisions of the federal bureaucracy over the authority to perform a specific task—and spend the funds Congress has allocated to do so—have all shaped the division of labor among departments. There are currently fifteen cabinet departments.

There is considerable diversity in the size and budgets of the cabinet departments. Sizable budgets do not always mean large numbers of employees. For example, the Department of Health and Human Services (which issues payments for Social Security and Medicare) and the Department of the Treasury (which makes interest payments on the national debt) both have relatively large budgets for the number of

Meeting with members of his cabinet, President Donald Trump shared a thumbs-up with departing Energy secretary Rick Perry.

Mark Wilson/Getty Images

employees in them. Prestige also varies among the departments, including one of its most visible markers: face time with the president.

Cabinet departments are headed by cabinet secretaries (or by the attorney general in the case of the Justice Department) who are nominated by the president and confirmed by a majority vote in the Senate. Cabinet secretaries formally work under the president; however, they also depend on Congress for appropriation of funds and for legislation that sets out specific goals and objectives for their departments. In addition, cabinet secretaries often have to contend with pressure from those affected by the actions of their departments, such as citizens or organized interest groups.

Independent executive agencies like NASA and FEMA function similarly to departments in many ways but are usually narrower in focus and retain more independence in carrying out their goals.

Independent regulatory agencies act to oversee and regulate governmental function, especially in economic affairs. Created by Congress to have enough independence to protect them from political partisanship, they are typically headed by appointed boards with fixed and staggered terms of service, making it more difficult to remove their leadership. The Consumer Product Safety Commission (established by the Consumer Product Safety Act of 1972), the Nuclear Regulatory Commission (established by the Energy Reorganization Act of 1974), and the Securities and Exchange Commission (established by the Securities Act of 1933) are all examples of these kinds of regulatory bodies.

Government corporations act as businesses within the federal government, charging fees for their services but still subject to governmental control and possible financial subsidization. The earliest government corporation was the Federal Deposit Insurance Corporation (FDIC), established as part of the New Deal to avoid a repeat of the bank runs in the Great Depression by insuring deposits in the nation's banks.

Private contractors are not officially a part of the federal bureaucracy, but the government increasingly relies on them to provide goods and services in support of federal activity. The U.S. military, for example, relies on contractors for logistical support. Proponents of contracting argue that it allows the military and federal agencies to focus on their core missions. Opponents worry about a lack of careful oversight of contractor activities.

Bureaucratic Authority Is Hierarchical

Formally, authority across the federal bureaucracy is structured like a pyramid.[49] At the top are the **executive political appointees**, such as cabinet secretaries and deputy secretaries, who serve at the pleasure of the president and are subject to presidential removal. Of the roughly 6,500 political appointees in the executive branch, about 1,500 require Senate confirmation. Compared to the vast majority of federal bureaucrats, these individuals are short-timers. They do not expect to transition from one administration to the next. Presidents must juggle several considerations in selecting who will lead their departments and agencies. Experience and competence are certainly important but so are political calculi and a desire to signal to important constituencies a willingness to work with them. The American people also expect a commitment to representing the wide diversity of their interests, experiences, and backgrounds.

Below these political appointees are the members of the **Senior Executive Service (SES)**. These individuals—most of whom have been promoted up from the lower ranks of the federal bureaucracy—enjoy slightly more job security than high-level appointees and are paid and treated more like vice presidents of businesses than political figures. They are expected to use their authority to achieve concrete results.

The vast majority of employees occupy the bottom of the pyramid. They are the career civil servants, whose job ranks are clearly defined according to the General Service (GS) levels. Entrance into and advancement within the federal civil service are governed by the merit system, which relies on competitive examinations, educational qualifications, and performance reviews. Career civil servants enjoy considerable protections from termination, especially for political reasons. This job security is by design, though it presents presidents with a significant challenge. The federal bureaucracy is not a power station in which a president flips a switch and makes things happen automatically. Instead, it is a complex hierarchy of people, most of whom will still have their jobs long after the president and political appointees have moved on.

Implementation Is Only One of the Bureaucracy's Core Goals

The primary function of the federal bureaucracy is implementing, or putting into action, the laws that Congress has passed. **Implementation** is rarely, if ever, a straightforward process.[50] New policies are not enacted in isolation; they are introduced into a universe of existing policies, sometimes with competing demands.[51]

The technical knowledge required of many federal bureaucrats in order to successfully implement public policies also acts as a brake on the ability of a president or their political appointees to shape bureaucrats' actions. High-level executive branch officials may lack the technical expertise necessary to evaluate or challenge the actions of their subordinates.

In addition, many frontline bureaucrats interact directly with citizens in an environment that makes it difficult to observe and control their behavior effectively. Law enforcement officers, teachers, and social workers are all examples of what are called street-level bureaucrats.[52] Because of their close contact with citizens, street-level bureaucrats may conclude that they need to "bend the rules" to do their jobs as they see them.

When Congress passes laws, it often only sets general goals and targets, leaving many of the details up to the bureaucratic agencies themselves. The complexity involved with implementing policies, the technical and specialized knowledge often required to do so, and the flexibility needed to handle unforeseen circumstances all argue for giving bureaucrats the authority to flesh out parts of the laws in action. By doing so, however, Congress opens up a space for **bureaucratic discretion**, in which the bureaucrats have some power to decide how a law is implemented and, at times, what Congress actually meant when it passed a given law. In addition, those affected by legislation cannot go about planning how they are going to respond to a law or set of regulations until they actually know the details of it. How much will it cost to comply? What changes must be made in order to do so? The answers to these important questions more often than not come from the bureaucracy rather than Congress, the president, or the courts.

Rulemaking Fills in the Blanks. The process through which the federal bureaucracy fills in critical details of a law is called **rulemaking**. By law, agencies must follow a specific set of steps. The first is to announce a proposed set of rules and allow interested parties to weigh in; this process is called notice and comment. Agencies may have to notify the president or Congress about the anticipated impact of a proposed rule or set of rules. Finally, the adopted rules must be published in the *Federal Register*, which is published annually and typically runs more than seventy thousand pages. These rules matter; "they carry the same weight as congressional legislation, presidential executive orders, and judicial decisions."[53]

Adjudication Settles Disputes. Part of the Framers' purpose in establishing the president's cabinet advisers and other executive branch officials was for them to share their expertise and knowledge with the president; Congress; and, increasingly, clientele groups and the public. At times the bureaucracy also acts somewhat like a court. It may settle disputes between parties that arise over the implementation of federal laws and presidential executive orders or determine which individuals or groups are covered under a regulation or program—a role called **bureaucratic adjudication**.

Bureaucrats Can Act as Representatives, But They Are Shielded from Politics. Finally, and perhaps surprisingly, bureaucrats can act as representatives of the American public, especially if they have the ability to act on behalf of their clients in the way that street-level bureaucrats often do.[54] While cabinet secretaries are increasingly representative of the diversity of the American people, they still do not present a complete portrait of the nation. Members of the civil service, in contrast, do represent the nation's diversity in many ways, save perhaps educational attainment (as it factors into the hiring and promotion process). In this view, having a "representative bureaucracy"—a civil service that truly reflects the diversity of the American people—may also act to legitimize its actions.[55]

Their role, however, is also intentionally shielded from regular politics, with legislation limiting the degree to which civil servants can participate in politics. Concerns about political patronage in President Roosevelt's New Deal programs led to the passage in 1939 of what is commonly known as the Hatch Act, which restricted the actions of federal workers in the political realm with exceptions for the highest-level political appointees. Federal workers were prohibited from participating in political campaigns, coercing other employees to participate, raising funds for a campaign, or holding all but a few elective offices. The Federal Employees Political Activities Act of 1993 relaxed some of the restrictions of the Hatch Act, allowing most federal employees to run in nonpartisan elections and contribute to and to participate in fundraising for political campaigns as long as they do not use their official authority to do so.

The Bureaucracy Is Constrained by Oversight and Reform

12.5 Describe the tools of bureaucratic control, oversight, and reform.

While complaints about the bureaucracy are as old as the institution itself, recent decades have seen a renewed focus on highlighting its failures and offering reforms to fix them. One set of critiques focuses on the inefficiency of large and complex bureaucracies. The term *red tape*, derived from "the narrow ribbons used at one time in England and America to tie up packets of legal and government documents," conjures up images of bureaucrats mindlessly following rules and standard operating procedures, whether or not it actually helps get things done.[56] Another line of critique emphasizes the tendencies of federal departments, bureaus, and agencies to be budget maximizers—that is, to seek to continually expand their level of appropriations beyond that necessary for the efficient provision of their services.[57]

Still another accusation points to problems that arise when bureaucracies stray from their established goals and devote their energies and efforts to nonessential tasks, a phenomenon known as **bureaucratic drift**. Worries about straying from the intended mission may apply to individual bureaucrats as well. Individuals may not do their jobs effectively or responsibly, a failing commonly referred to as shirking. Or they may actively work against the stated mission of their agency, substituting their own evaluations of a proper course of action, which is referred to as sabotage.[58] From the point of view of the bureaucrat, sabotage may be for very good reasons—for example, bending the rules to help out a client confronted with a rigid set of rules and procedures.

Another concern, especially for bureaucrats in regulatory agencies, is that individuals may undermine effective regulation if their own interests are more closely aligned with the targets of regulation than the mission of the agency, a problem known as agency capture. If regulators have close ties to the industry being regulated—either through previous employment or, perhaps, expected future employment—then there may be temptations to "look the other way," instruct their subordinates to do so, or conduct their jobs in such a way as to benefit a few preferred clients.[59]

Separation of Powers Makes Overseeing the Bureaucracy Difficult

The system of separation of powers that the Framers designed poses a special challenge to controlling the bureaucracy. As authority over the federal bureaucracy is divided between different branches, federal agencies and bureaus often have to answer to more than one overseer. According to political scientist Joel Aberbach, "Since usually no one set of institutional actors has clear control and signals often conflict, it is difficult to hold the bureaucracy. . . reasonably to account."[60]

The President Is at the Top of the Federal Bureaucracy. As head of the executive branch, the president formally controls most of the federal bureaucracy.[61] They have the authority to appoint and remove individuals at the top layers of the bureaucracy. Presidents can also shape bureaucratic priorities through the annual budgets that they present to Congress and, with congressional approval, by reorganizing agencies. As discussed in Chapter 11, executive orders carry the force of law and typically instruct departments, agencies, and bureaus on how they are to go about implementing policy.

Presidents, however, often confront restrictions in their control over the day-to-day functions of the bureaucracy. Bureaucratic discretion and the bureaucracy's size and complexity all conspire against achieving quick results.

In spite of these constraints, presidents can exert significant influence over public policy through their control over the federal bureaucracy. When the administration of President Trump is evaluated in hindsight, one of its more lasting effects is likely to be the president's rollback of federal bureaucratic oversight in environmental regulation. Rulemaking is an important tool that bureaucracies use to shape policy, and it is here that the Trump administration has placed significant energy in efforts to reduce the level of federal oversight over businesses in their use of natural resources and their impact on the nation's environment. Reducing fuel efficiency standards and emissions regulations on the sourcing and burning of coal are two notable examples of President Trump's bureaucratic agenda.

If they disagree with a president's policies, federal bureaucrats can act to impede their implementation. Some individuals, especially scientists, have taken this route in response to President Trump's rule changes. According to an article in the *New York Times*, "Scientists and lawyers inside the federal government have embedded statistics and data in regulatory documents that make rules vulnerable to legal challenges. These facts, often in the technical supporting documents, may hand ammunition to environmental lawyers working to block the president's policies."[62] Expected lawsuits from state attorneys general are likely to draw on data from an Environmental

Protection Agency (EPA) scientific advisory panel in their efforts to block the agency's deregulation efforts.[63]

Congress Creates and Funds the Federal Bureaucracy.

Congress plays a key role in controlling and guiding the bureaucracy. The Senate has power over confirmation for the higher levels of the federal service. Congress as a whole can pass legislation creating or terminating agencies and programs and, through the process of appropriation, has control over the resources that departments, bureaus, and agencies receive to carry out their tasks. Congressional committees, especially the House and Senate Appropriations Committees, are key players in these processes.

While legislation can be a proactive way to shape bureaucratic behavior by setting goals, priorities, and the overall organizational structure, Congress also has the ability to influence what happens when agencies are up and running through the process of oversight. Congress has established its own bureaucracies to keep tabs on executive branch implementation. The Government Accountability Office (GAO) is an example of this type of agency. Its work can have real bite. One GAO report investigating what had happened after Hurricane Katrina stated, "No one was designated in advance to lead the overall federal response in anticipation of the event despite clear warnings from the National Hurricane Center."[64]

Congress has a choice in how it goes about oversight. It may conduct police patrol oversight—conducting investigations and collecting data to make sure all is well—or fire alarm oversight—responding to crisis with close examination of a department or agency.[65]

To lead the EPA, Donald Trump nominated Oklahoma attorney general Scott Pruitt, seen here at his confirmation hearing. Oklahoma, led by Pruitt, was one of dozens of states that sued to block a regulation giving EPA and the USACE discretion to regulate tributaries and wetlands to protect water quality. The lawsuit contends the rule gives government too much power over private property.

AP Photo/J. Scott Applewhite

The Judiciary, the Media, and Public Opinion Also Influence the Bureaucracy.

Decisions by the federal judiciary can significantly impact bureaucratic behavior. Judicial control is typically negative—not in the sense that it is bad, but in the sense that judicial decisions on, for example, civil liberties and civil rights restrict and constrain the scope of accepted bureaucratic action. One part of the federal bureaucracy may also find its actions constrained by other departments, agencies, and bureaus. Bureaucratic jurisdiction—the authority to act in a certain policy area—is often not clearly or cleanly defined. **Interagency rivalry** occurs when two or more agencies are charged with a similar mandate, an outcome that becomes more likely in times of budget cuts and competition for scarce or dwindling appropriations. Clientele groups and businesses affected by federal rules, whether proposed or finalized, will lobby parts of the federal bureaucracy as well as Congress to get a more favorable outcome according to their perceived interests.

As a rule, the media infrequently cover the workings of the federal bureaucracy. Most Americans are understandably not well informed of the day-to-day workings of the vast bureaucracy, and there are no doubt numerous agencies many Americans don't know even exist. Crises are exceptions to public inattention. When the machinery of government is involved in a major crisis or catastrophe that becomes highly publicized—and especially when it appears that it has failed—the federal bureaucracy might find itself center stage with a full and angry audience in attendance. Such was the case after Katrina. A year after its landfall on the Gulf Coast, thousands of residents were still waiting for federal help, and public opinion had turned against President Bush on his handling of the disaster. A national poll found that only 31 percent of Americans approved of his management of the storm, and 56 percent did not "believe that the country [was] ready for another disaster."[66]

Current Reform Efforts Involve Deregulation and Privatization

In addition to calls for oversight of bureaucracies and the agencies in which they operate, pushes have been made—especially in recent decades—to shrink, overhaul, or eliminate parts of the federal bureaucracy. Ronald Reagan's petitions to roll back the growth in the size and power of the bureaucracy in his successful presidential bid in 1980 focused public attention on these efforts. As discussed in Chapter 3, devolution aimed to transfer power over public policy back to the states and shrink the size of the federal government by allowing states to have more authority to determine how taxpayer dollars should be spent. Proponents of **deregulation** argued that the personnel rules of the civil service, along with excessive red tape, made it difficult to attract "talented energetic potential candidates" to the federal service and restrained their energies once hired.[67] As a result of deregulation efforts beginning in the 1970s, certain federal agencies saw their authority curtailed or were abolished entirely, particularly in the areas of transportation, commerce, and the provision of utilities.

Another set of reforms sought to make the federal bureaucracy work more efficiently—more like the private sector. The National Performance Review conducted under the administration of President Clinton collected detailed data on bureaucratic efficiency and proposed measures to streamline bureaucratic operations as part of an effort to "reinvent government."[68]

Other reform proposals advocate placing control over the provision of certain functions in the hands of the private sector instead of the federal bureaucracy. Proponents of **privatization** argue that many tasks currently handled by the federal service can be more efficiently and more cheaply addressed by private organizations and businesses. Opponents of privatization argue that reducing or eliminating governmental oversight over the provision of these services might lead to waste or fraud or might undermine the larger policy goals of the national government.

Political scientist James Q. Wilson pointed out that there might be valid reasons for the fact that public bureaucracies often act differently and less efficiently than private bureaucracies. By their very nature, public bureaucracies operate under a different set of constraints. Congress, and not the marketplace, sets the goals for, budgets of, and allocation of resources within the federal service. In addition, the American public often demands a higher standard of fairness in the actions of its public bureaucracies than it does of private ones. Public schools, for example, generally face more binding constraints over admission and expulsion of students than do the nation's private schools.[69]

Following Katrina, the Private Sector Comes under Scrutiny.

As we discussed earlier in the chapter, one of the tasks following Hurricanes Harvey, Irma, and Maria was to assess the degree to which the bureaucracy—really multiple bureaucracies—had learned from Katrina. These retrospective analyses were also applied to private bureaucracies—private sector businesses—especially in questioning if these resources were usefully brought to bear to fill the most urgent needs, and in a properly coordinated fashion.

Following Katrina, investigators and members of Congress questioned both the government's reliance on private contractors in relief efforts and governmental interference with private sector efforts. According to a local official in Louisiana, FEMA had blocked private relief efforts as well: "We had Wal-Mart deliver three trailer trucks of water. FEMA turned them back. They said we didn't need them."[70] As it became clear that the effects from Katrina would be felt for years, many private organizations and individuals stepped up to help. Habitat for Humanity dispatched thousands of volunteers to the Gulf Coast to rebuild housing for low-income residents. Mary Gray founded MinnesotaHelpers, a "Mississippi-to-Minnesota arts pipeline" to provide opportunities for Gulf Coast artists to display and sell their work, as they had few such venues in their own devastated communities.[71]

Not all private responses were viewed so positively, however. Some

Trucks from Walmart with relief supplies for residents of the Gulf Coast were turned away by federal officials. FEMA was widely criticized for hampering private efforts at assistance.
NICHOLAS KAMM/AFP/Getty Images

were accused of running scams to take advantage of the federal dollars that flowed into devastated areas, prompting the government to establish the Hurricane Katrina Fraud Task Force to "thwart and prosecute hurricane-related fraud."[72] Some initiatives, though not illegal, seemed to take advantage of the disaster. In January 2006, a local tour bus company planned to operate a "Hurricane Katrina Tour—America's Worst Catastrophe!" to offer tourists the chance to see the aftermath of the storm from air-conditioned buses, though the company promised a portion of the $35 ticket price would benefit recovery efforts.[73]

The Private Sector's Role Is Again Examined after Harvey, Irma, and Maria.

In 2017, after Harvey, Irma, and Maria, the private sector's disaster response came under review again, to examine what had or had not been learned from Katrina. Just as the final grades for the public bureaucracies were mixed, so, too, were those for private businesses and the effectiveness with which they were employed. Many individual business owners received praise for their efforts—owners such as "Mattress Mack," who, following Harvey in Houston, "transformed his two furniture warehouses into emergency relief shelters, giving over 400 displaced Houstonians a warm, safe, dry place to stay as well as free meals."[74] Large businesses had donated more than $270 million to Harvey and Irma recovery efforts within two months of their landfalls, including pharmaceuticals, food, water, and cleaning supplies.[75]

Not all of the reviews, however, were positive. While New Orleans tour bus operators had been chastised for profiting from the disaster, these kinds of charges were again made against certain businesses in 2017. This time, however, they were more serious, especially in Puerto Rico following Maria. Whitefish Energy, "a little-known energy firm based in Montana," secured a $300 million contract to restore power to Puerto Rico.[76] Some lawmakers questioned how and why such a small firm beat out larger utilities. In a press briefing, White House press secretary Sarah Sanders answered, "This is a contract that was determined by the local authorities, not something the federal government played a role in."[77] While the private sector can and does have the capacity to contribute to disaster relief, the lack of centralized oversight can also facilitate private profit at the expense of the public good.

Conclusion: What Does a "Good" Bureaucracy Look Like?

In 2020, the federal bureaucracy was again in the public consciousness. Again the focus was on its ability to flexibly, capaciously, and fairly respond to a national crisis. While the COVID-19 pandemic was different in many fundamental ways from the natural disasters of 2005 and 2017, the central challenge was the same—to bring public and private bureaucratic power to bear effectively and in accordance with the principals of representative democracy. The Centers for Disease Control and Prevention (CDC) will replace FEMA in the spotlight; however, the same basic question will be asked as it was in 2005 and in 2017: What, if anything, had the federal bureaucracy learned?

ANALYZING CONGRESSIONAL TESTIMONY

In her prepared testimony before the Select Bipartisan Committee to Investigate the Preparation for and Response to Hurricane Katrina in December 2005, New Orleans resident Leah Hodges raised troubling concerns about how she and other individuals who sought refuge had been treated.[78] While not all of the witnesses testifying felt that African Americans were treated differently because of their race, Hodges's assessment of the connection between racial identity and equality of treatment echoed the accusations of many others. Hodges testified the following:

I come from a family of musicians. Before Hurricane Katrina, we were planning a musical family reunion. I had taken time off from pursuing my law degree to care for my sick granddad. I was also in the process of working with community leaders on setting up music and art workshops for youths. The manual I was writing for the workshops was severely damaged in the flood. I intend to finish it. . . . But I have also started a new project, which is all about my experience as a detainee at the Highway 10 causeway.

My family was ordered to evacuate our home. We were directed to evacuation points. . . . We were then lured to the so-called evacuation points. This was several days after the hurricane had struck. The city was flooded. Soldiers had showed up with M16s and military weapons. They had declared New Orleans and Jefferson Parish a war zone.

We were just three miles from an airport, but we were detained there for several days. Many of those who were there when we arrived had already been there several days. On any given day there were at least

New Orleans citizens and evacuees (from left) Terrol Williams, Doreen Keeler, Patricia Thompson, Leah Hodges, and "Mama D" Dyan French testify before Congress in December 2005.

AP Photo/Susan Walsh

ten thousand people in the camp. On my last day there, I would estimate there were still three thousand detainees. By that time, nearly all the white people had been selected to evacuate first. They were put on buses and shipped out, leaving the remaining population 95 percent Black.

People died in the camp. We saw the bodies lying there.

They were all about detention, as if it were Iraq, like we were foreigners and they were fighting a war. They implemented warlike conditions. They treated us worse than prisoners of war. Even prisoners of war have rights under the Geneva Convention.

WHaT Do You Think?

Some of the harshest criticism about the response to Hurricane Katrina involved accusations of differential treatment of African Americans. Can you think of other examples where a federal, state, or local agency has been accused of racial and ethnic bias? Have you or people close to you experienced this?

Americans place many demands upon their federal bureaucracy, and it usually only makes the news when something has gone wrong. As we have explored, the federal bureaucracy is not a unified thing, nor is it static. Departments, agencies, and bureaus can learn and adapt; however, they often do not do so quickly—relying on Congress to give them much of the ability to do so—nor efficiently. Equally fundamentally, bureaucracies can adapt and change. However, this change may be slow, given challenges of coordination and the inertia inherent in a large and complex organization. Competing demands on any given department, agency, or bureau can slow the processes of change down further.

Americans want the primary instrument of national policy implementation to be effective and strong. When they feel that it is not—such as was the case with Hurricane Katrina—they demand change. However, Americans do not want the federal bureaucracy to be too strong. When they feel that it has become too powerful, they worry. Both the separation of powers and the realities of American federalism shape the behaviors of the federal departments, agencies, and bureaus. These organizations are not smoothly running machines but a constellation of teams operating in an often political space; they have multiple constraints on their behavior and also must contend with multiple interests and groups trying to shape that behavior. Such is the complex nature of the American federal bureaucracy.

CHAPTER REVIEW

This chapter's main ideas are reflected in the Learning Objectives. By reviewing them here, you should be able to *remember* the key points and *know* these terms that are central to the topic.

12.1 Understand how federal bureaucratic action involves many different agencies and evolves over time, often in response to lessons learned from past actions.

Remember . . .
- The federal bureaucracy consists of organizations and suborganizations within the executive branch that are tasked with putting the laws of the nation into effect.
- Bureaucracies change over time, sometimes as a result of significant failures.

Know . . .
- *federal bureaucracy* (p. 347)

12.2 Name the key characteristics of bureaucratic organization and the theories that explain why bureaucratic organization happens.

Remember . . .
- Most of the federal bureaucracy lies within the executive branch. State and local bureaucracies also make rules that impact people's daily lives.
- Private bureaucracies are companies and corporations that also operate like federal, state, and local bureaucracies.
- Various theories of bureaucracies exist to explain how and why they are organized the way they are.

Know . . .	• *incentives* (p. 355)	• *standard operating procedures* (p. 354)
	• *principal-agent problem* (p. 355)	• *state and local bureaucracies* (p. 353)
	• *private bureaucracies* (p. 354)	

12.3 Outline the historical development of the American federal bureaucracy.

Remember . . .
- The federal bureaucracy has grown exponentially over time, as has the complexity of the tasks it must perform and the demands for services placed upon it by the American people.
- The Constitution calls for executive branch departments to assist the president in executing the laws of the nation. To control the power of the executive, Congress was given the power to approve nominees and impeach executive officers.

Know . . .

• *clientele agencies* (p. 360)	• *path dependence* (p. 361)
• *federal civil service* (p. 361)	• *political patronage* (p. 359)
• *independent executive agency* (p. 362)	• *spoils system* (p. 359)
• *merit system* (p. 361)	• *turf wars* (p. 359)

12.4 Describe the structure of the federal bureaucracy, including executive branch agencies, cabinet departments, and regulatory bodies.

Remember . . .
- The federal bureaucracy is a complex web of organizations and organizations within organizations, headed by the president.
- Congress has the authority to establish and fund the departments—each of which is responsible for a major area of public policy.
- Independent regulatory agencies act to oversee and regulate governmental function, especially in economic affairs.
- The bureaucracy is a hierarchy, with executive political appointees at the top and SES employees with supervisory and administrative responsibilities in the middle. Career civil servants make up the bulk of the employees.
- Implementing the laws passed by Congress is one of the bureaucracy's core tasks.

Know . . .

• *bureaucratic adjudication* (p. 366)	• *implementation* (p. 365)
• *bureaucratic discretion* (p. 366)	• *independent regulatory agencies* (p. 364)
• *cabinet departments* (p. 363)	• *private contractors* (p. 364)
• *executive political appointees* (p. 364)	• *rulemaking* (p. 366)
• *government corporations* (p. 364)	• *Senior Executive Service (SES)* (p. 365)

12.5 Describe the tools of bureaucratic control, oversight, and reform.

Remember . . .
- Perceived inefficiency, bureaucratic drift, agency capture, and interagency rivalry are common complaints and problems of the federal bureaucracy.
- Control over the bureaucracy is challenging given that responsibility and power are shared across the executive, legislative, and judicial branches of government.
- Efforts to reform the bureaucracy include devolving responsibilities to the states, deregulation, and privatizing government responsibilities to increase competitiveness.

Know . . .

• *bureaucratic drift* (p. 367)	• *interagency rivalry* (p. 370)
• *deregulation* (p. 370)	• *privatization* (p. 370)

CHAPTER 13

THE FEDERAL JUDICIARY

Politics, Power, and the "Least Dangerous" Branch[1]

Supreme Court justice Sonia Sotomayor attends a game between the Boston Red Sox and New York Yankees at Yankee Stadium in August 2017 in the Bronx borough of New York City. Sotomayor has said that her experience growing up in New York as the child of Puerto Rican immigrants has informed her judicial decision making. Because they are appointed to lifetime terms, Supreme Court justices are very influential, and their appointment can be a challenging political process.

Rich Schultz/Getty Images

After reading this chapter, you will be able to do the following:

13.1 Explore the role of politics in modern Supreme Court confirmation proceedings.

13.2 Describe the structure and powers of the federal judiciary as laid out in the Constitution.

13.3 Explain John Marshall's development of judicial review in the Supreme Court decision in *Marbury v. Madison.*

13.4 Describe the structure of the American legal system and the federal judiciary.

13.5 Compare theories of judicial decision making as well as arguments for or against judicial restraint and activism in constitutional review.

What is the federal judiciary? As with many questions you are asked to consider in this book, there are both simple answers and deeper ones. In this chapter, we will deal with both. The definition is simple. The **federal judiciary** is one of the three branches of the nation's government. Its role is to interpret and apply the laws of the nation. Sitting atop the federal judiciary is the **Supreme Court,** which was established in the Constitution and serves as the highest court in the nation.

On a deeper level, however, more difficult questions arise. First, how different is the federal judiciary from the other two branches—or, more precisely, how *political* is it? How political should it be? Also, how *powerful* is it? As we have explored, both Congress and the president have at their disposal powerful levers to shape national public policy. Congress writes the laws; it has the power to tax and to fund. The president is the commander in chief of the armed forces and is tasked with carrying out the laws of the nation. What power does the federal judiciary have other than the authority to apply the law to the cases brought before it?

These questions are very much interconnected. The power of the federal judiciary affects how it engages as a political actor. Conversely, the degree to which the federal judiciary chooses to involve itself in political controversies has and will continue to impact its legitimacy in the eyes of the American public.

In this chapter, we will engage with the stories of recent Supreme Court confirmations as well as John Marshall's establishment of judicial review. We will consider why Supreme Court confirmations are so politically charged and how the unique role of the federal judiciary is something its justices and judges have acted to preserve. In doing so, members of the federal judiciary bring with them their own understandings of their roles in it and the role of their institution in American political life.

The Politics of Supreme Court Confirmations Place Nominees on "Trial"

In this section, we consider the official beginning of a justice's career on the Supreme Court—confirmation by the U.S. Senate. Of course, that depends upon a successful confirmation process, which, as we will explore shortly, does not always happen. Even unsuccessful or delayed confirmations, however, are worth studying, because the position for which these individuals were interviewing is both very powerful *and* highly independent, a potentially problematic setup for a representative democracy that prefers to have multiple ways of making personnel changes.

Short of impeachment, there is no process through which the American people can remove justices from office if they don't like how they are performing their duties. Only one justice has been impeached (Samuel Chase in 1804), and he was not convicted by the Senate and thus remained in office. Congress can't even cut their pay; the Framers made sure to establish that fact early in Article III of the Constitution, which establishes the Supreme Court and the federal judiciary. In the second sentence, in fact.

Individual justices may change their views over time—about what guidance the Constitution offers on a given issue or question, for example. They might change their views about the proper relationship between the Constitution and representative democracy itself, or how they think the justices should go about reading the text of the document as a basis for making their decisions. If that happens, there is not a lot that the American people can do about it—certainly not the president who nominated them in the first place, and there have been presidents who ended up not very pleased by the subsequent careers of one of their nominees.

The reason this matters so much is that the decisions that Supreme Court justices make (or do not make, as we will also explore) can be vitally important. Their decisions have the potential to shape national policy in fundamental ways and may have profound implications for what Americans agree that their Constitution says. The power to confirm presidential nominees to the Supreme Court and other levels of the federal judiciary—granted to the Senate in the Constitution—is, therefore, a weighty one. In the modern era, Supreme Court confirmations have often resembled elections more than formal affairs, with nominees choosing their answers to senators' questions carefully. And this is with good reason: There is a tremendous risk inherent in picking this person, knowing that they are about to be both powerful and hard to control.

The fact that they are so contentious makes Supreme Court confirmation proceedings worth studying—whether or not they are successful—because they tend to raise important, basic questions about the proper role of the Supreme Court and its justices in American democracy. That is why we start with a few of them. We will move around in time a little, as the focus here is not on a linear development of the institution but instead on the ways in which these confirmations raised deeper questions about the Supreme Court and American political life.

Sonia Sotomayor's Confirmation Highlights the Role of Lived Experience in Judicial Decision Making

In May 2009, President Barack Obama was presented with his first opportunity to nominate an individual to the U.S. Supreme Court. The retiring justice, David H. Souter, ordinarily sided with the liberal bloc of justices in his decisions, so Obama's appointment, likely a liberal, would probably not shift the ideological balance of the Court. In the intensely partisan world of the modern federal government, that lessened, if only a bit, the tensions surrounding the nomination. Even so, observers and insiders expected an intensely political battle, as justices on the Supreme Court are appointed for life.

Although the nomination of a liberal justice was expected, there were other hopes pinned on the president's selection. With only one woman, one African American, and no Latino or Latina justices on the bench, many urged the president to use the opportunity to expand the diversity of the Court. On Obama's short list was Sonia Sotomayor, the daughter of Puerto Rican immigrants, a graduate of Yale Law School, a former prosecutor and litigator, and a sitting judge with the U.S. Court of Appeals for the Second Circuit. She was, however, according to the *Washington Post*, the "riskiest choice" of the likely nominees, largely because of public remarks she had made on the importance of identity and personal history in approaching judicial decision making.[2]

When Sotomayor's nomination became official, both sides swung into campaign mode, each accusing the other of violating norms of propriety in handling a Supreme Court nomination.

Republicans in the Senate painted Sotomayor as a justice who was "willing to expand constitutional rights beyond the text of the constitution."[3] Given the president's popularity at the time, and with the Senate under Democratic control, defeating Sotomayor was unlikely. Still, Republicans hoped to use the confirmation proceedings to "galvanize a movement demoralized by Republican electoral defeats."[4] Remarks made by Sotomayor at a public lecture in 2001 received particular scrutiny from Republicans during the confirmation proceedings. Sotomayor had highlighted the role that her Latina identity and life experiences played in her judicial career—a perspective that, to her, helped her make just decisions, especially in cases involving equality and discrimination.

Addressing the attendees, Sotomayor stated that, though a "Newyorkrican" who brings her particular set of lived experiences to her judicial decision making, "No one person, judge or nominee will speak in a female or people of color voice."[5] That said, a justice's experiences can and should factor into their decisions. "I would hope that a wise Latina woman with the richness of her experiences would more often than not reach a better conclusion than a white male who hasn't lived that life," she stated.[6]

President Obama urged quick action on the nomination, but the press raised the specter of failed confirmations of the past, wondering if a similar ideological showdown was looming.[7] A leading Republican senator summed up his party's planned line of questioning: "Do I want a judge that objectively applies the law to the facts?"[8]

The Senate Judiciary Committee began its proceedings on the nomination in mid-July. Sotomayor rehearsed her testimony and her answers to expected questions in the week before the hearings. Addressing her critics, Sotomayor affirmed her judicial legacy, stating that in her seventeen years on the bench, she had "applied the law to the facts at hand."[9]

In the end, the vote in the Senate Judiciary Committee was without much drama or surprise. In a 13–6 vote, with one Republican joining the unanimous Democrats, the committee approved her nomination and sent it to the full Senate, wherein an expected filibuster-proof confirmation vote was all but certain. On August 9, the Senate confirmed Sotomayor's appointment to the Supreme Court by a 68–31 vote. Like other supporters gathered at a "vote watch" party nearby, law student Lucy Flores was jubilant, but she offered words of caution for those who might think Sotomayor's confirmation marked an end, rather than just a step forward. "It shouldn't be a historic moment," she said. "Everyone of all races and all backgrounds should be able to get to where she is based on their ability and their desire."[10]

Robert Bork's Unsuccessful Nomination Highlights the Role of Politics in Confirmations

Lurking in the background of Sotomayor's confirmation proceedings was a nomination that failed—that of Robert Bork. In the summer of 1987, even before President Ronald Reagan named his selection to fill a vacant seat on the Supreme Court, the atmosphere was politically charged. Reagan's nominee had the potential to tilt the closely divided Court away from its liberal-moderate majority. It was also a chance for the president, struggling to enact his programs in the face of a Democratic-controlled Congress, to help cement his legacy in American political history.

President Reagan chose Robert H. Bork, then serving on the court of appeals for the District of Columbia. While none questioned Bork's powerful intellect or his legal and professional qualifications, his rulings and statements in many cases involving highly charged social issues, such as abortion, sexuality, civil rights, and rights of the accused, sparked serious concern among liberals, especially since cases in many of these areas were awaiting Supreme Court action.

As the Senate Judiciary Committee scheduled its confirmation hearings for September, its chair, Sen. Joe Biden (D-DE), promised civil rights leaders that "he would lead the battle against Judge Bork in the Senate."[11] A senior administration official promised that President Reagan "would 'use all his resources' to push the Bork nomination."[12] Failed nominations to the Supreme Court are not unprecedented but are also not common. There had been four of them in the twentieth century before Judge Bork, most of which occurred during periods of divided government.[13] Two of those, however, had occurred during Richard Nixon's presidency, and it was likely that President Reagan was looking back to the battles that the last elected Republican in the White House had fought as he looked ahead to the confirmation process. Both sides prepared their arguments "like a championship fight," according to a lobbyist helping Bork to prepare.[14]

At the core of the controversy was Bork's view of constitutional interpretation. Bork believed that a justice should focus on the language and intent of the Constitution rather than supplying their own interpretation of the document—or, more significantly, inventing their own constitutional rights and liberties. The changing norms and values of society over time should have no impact on the Court's interpretation of the Constitution. Many, including key Democrats, were uncomfortable with the potential implications of Bork's approach. He had previously argued that the Supreme Court's decision in *Roe v. Wade* (1973), which recognized a woman's right to an abortion, was unconstitutional because it was based on the right to privacy, which is not mentioned in the text.[15] The death penalty, he argued, as referred to in the original text of the Constitution, was not.[16]

President Ronald Reagan with Judge Robert Bork in 1987.
Rex Features via AP Images

After twelve days of testimony by 110 witnesses, the Senate Judiciary Committee voted 9–5 against confirmation, spelling certain defeat for the nomination in the Democratic-controlled Senate. Republican senators called on the president to withdraw the nomination in order to preserve his dwindling political capital. There were also calls for Bork to withdraw on his own volition. Bork refused, not because he thought there was a chance of a successful outcome but in protest over what he saw as an overtly political process of confirmation to the Supreme Court. He would later write, "Federal judges are not appointed to decide cases according to the latest opinion polls. They are appointed to decide cases impartially according to the law. But when judicial nominees are assessed and treated like political candidates the effect will be to chill the climate in which judicial deliberations take place, to erode public confidence in the impartiality of our judges, and to endanger the independence of the judiciary."[17] In the end, the Senate voted 58–42 against Bork's confirmation, the largest margin of defeat for a Supreme Court nominee in American history.[18]

One Nominee Gets His Opportunity, the Other Does Not: Merrick Garland and Neil Gorsuch

Fast forward nearly thirty years to February 2016: Justice Antonin Scalia had passed away suddenly and unexpectedly, presenting President Barack Obama with the possibility of a third Supreme Court nomination during his tenure. While Sonia Sotomayor's confirmation had been somewhat contested, his second, that of Elena Kagan, had gone relatively smoothly. In March 2016, with ten months left in office, Obama nominated Judge Merrick Garland to fill Scalia's seat. Republicans, with a majority in the Senate, refused even to consider the president's nominee, arguing that the nomination should be made by the next president, a gamble that a Republican might win the White House. As Scalia was one of the staunchest conservatives on the Court, Republicans knew that replacing him with anyone even slightly more liberal would have the potential to shift the ideological balance of the Court for years if not decades.

Donald Trump's win in the presidential election that year and the continuing Republican control of the Senate ensured that Garland would not get his chance. In 2017, Trump secured the nomination of Neil Gorsuch to the bench after Senate Republicans changed the chamber's rules to prevent a filibuster (see Chapter 10). Given that both Scalia and Gorsuch were very conservative, the confirmation did not shift the Court's ideological balance. In fact, three Democrats voted for his confirmation. All three were from states that President Trump had carried in 2016.

Justice Brett Kavanaugh's Confirmation Involves an Investigation and a Potentially Major Shift in the Court

In June 2018, Justice Anthony Kennedy announced his retirement. Though nominated by a Republican president (Ronald Reagan), Kennedy proved to be a moderate, centrist justice. Many of Kennedy's votes proved decisive in a closely divided Court, which issued a host of 5–4 decisions on politically and socially divisive issues during Kennedy's tenure. With the potential to move the Court in a more conservative direction, President Trump's choice for his replacement was sure to draw intense scrutiny, and the process of choosing the individual certain to be contentious.

It proved to be far more than that. In the weeks leading up to the Senate confirmation vote and the midterm elections, Christine Blasey Ford, a California university psychology professor, and several other women alleged that the president's nominee, Judge Brett Kavanaugh, had sexually assaulted them decades prior. Kavanaugh's final vote was delayed a week for an additional Federal Bureau of Investigation (FBI) investigation into the allegations, though critics asserted that it was not thorough enough. In the end, Kavanaugh secured the confirmation by a 50–48 vote, the narrowest margin in more than a century.

There were also questions about how Kavanaugh's confirmation would shift the ideological and interpretive balance of the Court, especially in the area of reproductive rights, along with rights of privacy more broadly. Like many other individuals President Trump nominated to the federal courts, Judge Kavanaugh came with the recommendation of conservative groups such as the Federalist Society and the Heritage Foundation. An article in the *New York Times* lamented the lack of real insight into a nominee's likely decisions on key issues like abortion provided during modern confirmation processes: "Ever since the bitter battle over President Ronald Reagan's failed nomination of Robert Bork in 1987, [the process has] devolved into a second-rate Samuel Beckett play starring an earnest legal scholar who sits for days at a microphone and labors to sound thoughtful while saying almost nothing."[19]

Brett Kavanaugh, nominated to the Supreme Court by President Trump, testified before the Senate Judiciary Committee during his confirmation hearings. The hearings were extended after Kavanaugh was accused of sexual assault, prompting widespread public outcry.
Chip Somodevilla/Getty Images

The Constitution Casts the Judiciary as a Unique but Weaker Branch

13.2 Describe the structure and powers of the federal judiciary as laid out in the Constitution.

The delegates to the Constitutional Convention spent much less time debating the structure and powers of the federal judiciary than they did hammering out the design of the legislative and executive branches. They were in general agreement that the judicial branch would be the weakest of the three, lacking an equivalent to Congress's power of the purse and the president's power as commander in chief. Second, the delegates agreed that the judiciary should retain a degree of independence from the other two branches—especially in the processes of appointment and removal of judges—though the specific details were not worked out until the summer of 1787.[20] That federal judges should have tenure for life with "good behavior" was generally agreed upon, as was the need to protect their salaries from an unhappy or vengeful Congress.[21] Both of these protections made it into the final document.[22] The question of appointment, however, remained unresolved until late in the convention with the delegates finally approving a process through which the president would nominate federal judges and the Senate through its role of advice and consent would confirm the nominations.[23]

Finally, a diverse group of delegates agreed that the judiciary should have the power to strike down laws that were in violation of the Constitution. The federal "courts were not *expressly* given the power to rule on constitutionality," however, that instance of "carelessness" would have a profound impact.[24]

The Constitution Grants the Federal Judiciary Supremacy over Lower State Courts

This issue of constitutionality and the judiciary is not the only instance in which the text of the Constitution is less than thorough. Only the highest level of the federal judiciary—the Supreme Court—is actually described in the document, while the establishment of lower federal courts was left in the hands of Congress: "The judicial Power of the United States, shall be vested in one supreme Court, and in such inferior Courts as the Congress may from time to time ordain and establish."[25]

On one point the Constitution was clear: the federal judiciary, and the Supreme Court in particular, was to be the highest judicial power in the land: "The judicial power shall extend to all Cases, in Law and Equity, arising under this Constitution, the laws of the United States, and Treaties made, or which shall be made, under their Authority."[26] This judicial power, when combined with the supremacy clause of the Constitution, which declared the "Constitution, and the Laws of the United States" to be "the supreme Law of the Land; and [instructed that] the Judges in every State shall be bound thereby," established the federal judiciary as supreme to those of the states.[27]

In defining the scope of the power of the federal judiciary, the Constitution also (briefly) describes one of the most fundamental characteristics of any court: its jurisdiction, or its authority to hear and decide on specific cases.[28] Although there are many types and classifications of jurisdiction, the two most relevant to the study of the American judicial system are original and appellate jurisdiction. If a court has **original jurisdiction** in a case, then that court acts as the originating court, with the authority to hear the case first and to establish the facts pertaining to it. Courts with original jurisdiction are commonly referred to as trial courts. If a court has **appellate jurisdiction** over a case, then it possesses the authority to review the decision of a lower court and, if it so decides, to revise that decision. Courts operating under appellate jurisdiction generally focus on the lower courts' actions and procedures without finding facts on their own. As we will explore, most of the cases that the U.S. Supreme Court hears are done so under appellate jurisdiction.

During Ratification, Concerns about Judicial Abuse of Power Are Addressed

During the ratification debates, those who opposed the Constitution, the Anti-Federalists, raised concerns about potential abuses of power by the proposed federal judiciary. Anti-Federalists feared the growth in power of the national government and an associated subjugation of the rights of states and individuals by an increasingly powerful federal judiciary. In granting the power to overturn legislation to the Supreme Court, Anti-Federalists argued that the nation would run the risk of unconstrained justices imposing their own views of what is constitutional and what is not.

In *Federalist* No. 78, Alexander Hamilton sought to reassure skeptical Anti-Federalists and others that the planned federal judiciary would not trample upon their rights and liberties because it would neither want to nor be able to. In the first place, Hamilton argued, members of the federal judiciary—because of the process of their selection and their lifetime tenure—would stand apart from politics and the dangers that politics might pose to liberties and be able to "secure a steady, upright, and impartial administration of the laws."[29] Second, the federal judiciary was weak—indeed it would be "the least dangerous" branch.[30] Compared to the powers of the executive branch's sword and the legislature's purse, Hamilton reassured, the federal judiciary—exercising only the power of judgment and located outside the arena of political struggle—was not to be feared. He argued that it was in fact the judiciary that needed protection from encroachment on its limited powers by the other two branches.

Congress Fills in the Blanks with the Judiciary Act of 1789

Taking up its constitutional authority to establish "inferior Courts" in the federal judiciary, the first Congress passed the Judiciary Act of 1789 to flesh out "the nature and the organization" of the court system.[31] Only the chief justice of the United States is mentioned in the Constitution; the document does not specify the number of justices in the Court, instead leaving that decision to Congress. The Judiciary Act added five associate judges to the Supreme Court, bringing the total number of justices to six, and it instructed that the Court was to meet in session twice a year in February and August. (Although the number of justices has varied throughout the nation's history, it has been set at nine since 1869.) The act also established two lower tiers to the federal judiciary, as only the Supreme Court had been set out in the Constitution; though changes have been made to their organization since.

The Judiciary Act of 1789 also created the office of attorney general "to prosecute and conduct all suits in the Supreme Court in which the United States shall be concerned, and to give his advice and opinion upon questions of law when required to by the president of the United States."[32] Today, the office of the solicitor general represents the president in the Supreme Court, while the attorney general is head of the Justice Department. Finally, the act gave the Supreme Court the power to review and reverse actions of the state courts if it found them to be in conflict with the Constitution—a power tied to both the Constitution's description of the scope of judicial power and the supremacy clause.

Appointment to the Federal Judiciary Is Often Political

Successfully placing individuals on the federal bench is one of the most important things that a president can do. While most district court nominees are approved, the confirmations of appellate and Supreme Court judges have become increasingly affected by partisan political battles in recent years, though there have been many other periods in American history where this has also been the case. Part of the reason that things tend to run more smoothly at the district court level is the custom of senatorial courtesy, in which presidents (and the high-ranking members of the Justice Department who do much of the actual work of identifying candidates) consult with senators from the state in which the vacant district judgeship is located, especially if those senators are from the president's political party.

The higher two levels of the federal judiciary often witness more direct presidential involvement in the nomination process, and these nominations are more likely to be caught up in partisan battles. While most Supreme Court nominees are confirmed, their confirmation hearings can and have often involved intense scrutiny of the nominee. In addition, recent confirmation votes in the Senate have tended to be closer than those in decades prior. As with other presidential nominees subject to Senate approval, federal judicial nominees have sometimes found their paths blocked by a filibuster or the threat of one. That obstacle began to go away in 2013 when a Democratic-controlled Senate changed the chamber's rules to prevent filibusters of federal district and appellate court judges. In 2017, a Republican-controlled Senate did the same for Supreme Court nominees.

Presidents Balance Legal and Political Considerations in Making Supreme Court Nominations.

Unlike presidents and members of Congress, the Constitution places no requirements on the necessary qualifications to serve in the federal judiciary; judges do not even have to be lawyers. When vacancies occur in the Supreme Court, presidents are presented with an important, though challenging, opportunity to help shape policy for years to come. When the position of chief justice is vacant, a president may nominate a sitting member of the Court for that position and fill the newly vacant position of associate justice (which is how it usually happens), or the president may nominate an individual from outside the Court to the position of chief justice directly.

Because they are such high-profile appointments, nominees to the Court have to be weighed especially carefully. When choosing Court nominees, presidents have to balance both legal and political considerations. Experience, ethical integrity, and legal accomplishment are extremely important factors and can help smooth the confirmation process. Modern Court nominees will have typically already served in the federal judiciary or a similarly high-level position.

Presidents may also strive to nominate individuals who share their judicial philosophies and approaches to constitutional interpretation. Once confirmation occurs, however, presidents have no control over the behavior of their nominees. More than one president has successfully nominated an individual only to be surprised by some of that justice's later decisions. Political calculations come into play as well. Nominees who are considered outspoken on contentious political issues are likely to face careful scrutiny and intense questioning by senators concerned about these stances. As the Court, like Congress, still does not descriptively represent the American people, presents may also consider nominating those with diverse backgrounds to the Court to make it more closely resemble a portrait of the nation.

A Key Part of President Trump's Legacy Will Be Federal Judicial Appointments. For any president, two successful appointments to the Supreme Court is considered a major and impactful accomplishment, and President Trump achieved that outcome in one term in office. While considerable attention was paid to the appointments of Gorsuch and Kavanaugh, also significant is the president's impact on the lower federal courts, the district and appellate courts.

As of January 2018—one year into office—President Trump had secured twenty-three confirmations for these lower federal courts, six of them replacing Democratic-appointed judges. Twelve of these were at the appellate level, the second-highest first-year total for a president since 1912, when the previous appellate system was reorganized into its modern form.[33] Ignoring the ratings of the American Bar Association, which was highly unusual, Trump nominated strong conservatives. Of the twenty-three successful nominees, only nine had prior judicial experience; the rest had backgrounds in litigation, private or public.[34] As he began his fourth year in office, President Trump had appointed 28 percent of serving appellate judges, double the percentage of President Obama at the same point in his administration.[35]

The Supreme Court's Role in National Policymaking Is Defined but Limited

No one branch of the federal government operates in a vacuum, and the federal judiciary, including the Supreme Court, is no exception. When the Court attempts to influence public policy, it does so in the face of multiple constraints on its independent use of authority, but its unique role within the system of shared powers offers it opportunities to shape policy in a way that the other two branches cannot.

There Are Limitations on the Power of the Supreme Court. One constraint on the power of the Court is the legal process itself. A U.S. court, no matter how activist, cannot simply declare unconstitutional a law that it does not like. It can only rule on a specific case that has been properly filed and brought before it. Only plaintiffs who can demonstrate standing can bring suit in court, which requires that they show that they have been wronged by a law or action and that the law in question covers the interests the plaintiff alleges to have been violated or denied. Even when everything works efficiently, the process of moving a case through the federal judiciary takes time. When a case begins in a state judiciary, the process can take even longer.

The legislative and executive branches may also act as a check on the power of the federal judiciary. We have discussed the role of the president in nominating justices and that of the Senate in confirming them. We have also examined the role of Congress in setting the size of the Supreme Court and establishing other federal courts. Congress and the states may collectively amend the Constitution, the results of which are not subject to judicial review. In addition, the Court lacks the tools for implementing public policy and often must turn to the other two branches to add force to its rulings. When a Court goes against the will of the president or Congress, the other branches may be less than supportive in implementing the decisions or even might ignore or defy the Court entirely. Even when the other two branches do not openly defy the Supreme Court, their lack of support of its rulings can limit the Court's power in setting national policy.

Finally, although justices are appointed for life and do not need to worry about being reelected, they do operate in the American political system in which public opinion plays an important role. Political scientists continue to debate the degree to which Supreme Court justices attend to public opinion in crafting specific decisions; however, scholars agree that it is not something that can completely be ignored.[36]

Justices have had to attend to the fact that their power in exercising judicial review is tied to Americans' views of the legitimacy of their branch of government. It is no accident that of all the branches, only the federal judiciary, and the Supreme Court in particular, chooses to retain its costumes, secrecy, and traditional ways of doing things, as out of time as they may seem. The drama of the Court adds to its legitimacy in the view of the American people, and all justices—whatever their own political beliefs—know that they play a key role in preserving the story of the Court and its power.

The Supreme Court Has the Power of Agenda-Setting. While the Supreme Court and the rest of the federal judiciary cannot act as all-powerful, unilateral makers of public policy, their particular position in the nation and the federal government does give them a unique role in American politics: that of setting the national agenda. Because they do not face elections like members of the other two branches, Supreme Court justices are able to bring up in the national conversation issues that need to be discussed. They can act ahead of public opinion—perhaps not *too* far but far enough to force debate on the national stage. Recent Court rulings on marriage equality may be perfect examples of this power. In exercising this power, the Court may not necessarily be acting against the wishes of elected representatives, or at least all of them. A member of Congress or a president who may be afraid to weigh in on an important and controversial issue out of fear of the backlash from public opinion can point to a Court decision and tell the American people they now have to act. Providing political cover for elected representatives who wish to act on an issue may be one of the most important powers of the unelected branch of government.

The "Trial" of John Marshall Establishes the Principle of Judicial Review

> 13.3 Explain John Marshall's development of judicial review in the Supreme Court decision in *Marbury v. Madison*.

In 2017, perhaps no issue in American government was more important than the confirmations of Supreme Court justices. In April 2017, after Republicans in the

Senate had changed the institution's rules to prevent a filibuster of a Supreme Court nominee, Neil Gorsuch joined the bench. As a replacement for the deceased, and highly conservative, Antonin Scalia, that appointment did not cause as much concern as future ones might. If President Trump, however, is able to replace a more liberal or moderate justice, it might have consequences for American policy for decades. But why? Aren't justices supposed to be insulated from politics? That is a very important question to which we will now turn.

The Election of 1800 Gives Rise to a Federalist Judicial Strategy

The election of 1800 was one of the nastiest in American history. The seeds of faction that had been planted during George Washington's presidency came into full bloom in the late 1790s as political parties took root. President John Adams, once Washington's vice president and now seeking his own second term in office, had allied with Alexander Hamilton, who had been Washington's secretary of the treasury, under the banner of the Federalists. In Hamilton, Adams saw a partner who would help him promote a strong national government, especially in the area of economic policy and banking.[37]

They squared off against Thomas Jefferson and the Republican Party.[38] They mistrusted the Federalists' motives and the reach of Hamilton's economic policies. As each side sought support for its views in Congress and in the state legislatures, America's first political parties increasingly gained power, like new planets pulling more and more supporters into their political orbit. Both campaigns were bitter, partisan, and personal right up to the election.

And then there was a tie: Jefferson, the Republican, had unexpectedly tied for votes not with John Adams but with Aaron Burr.

The decision about who would become president would move from the Electoral College to the House of Representatives.

Months of postelection discord followed with accusations of voting irregularities flying and partisan rancor so intense that some feared a civil war would break out. Thomas Jefferson was finally elected president of the United States by the House on the thirty-sixth ballot. Jefferson, in his inaugural address, sought to calm tensions throughout the nation. "We are all republicans," he said. "We are all federalists."[39] Nonetheless, the Federalist Party paid dearly. It had been soundly defeated in both the presidential election and in the congressional elections. Its days in power were numbered.

Trying to preserve their influence within the national government, the Federalists turned to the federal judiciary, the one branch where they might endure, given that the Constitution grants federal judges lifetime job security.[40] In the waning weeks of Adams's administration, the Federalists in the legislature and the executive branches made several changes to the federal judiciary to cement their power.[41]

With the Judiciary Act of 1801, Federalists in Congress changed the Supreme Court's schedule, reduced the size of the Court from six to five justices, and reorganized the lower federal courts in such a way as to create sixteen vacancies. The reduction in the size of the Supreme Court could not force a sitting justice out; that would have been unconstitutional. What it did do was ensure that incoming president Jefferson would not be able to fill the next vacancy with someone the Federalists presumed would be a Republican.

Just before leaving office, Adams filled the vacancies created by the Judiciary Act of 1801. He also set about building up the administration of the nation's new capital in Washington, DC (the seat of government had been recently relocated from Philadelphia). There were many good jobs to fill there, including justices of the peace.[42] One candidate for one of these new jobs was a Mr. William Marbury.

Less than two weeks before Adams signed the Judiciary Act of 1801 into law, the Senate confirmed the president's appointment of his secretary of state, John Marshall, to be the new chief justice of the United States.[43] Marshall was a Federalist and an experienced politician. For the last weeks of the Adams administration, Marshall was also both chief justice and secretary of state. He had a lot on his plate—as it turned out, perhaps too much. In the scramble to complete the paperwork before the Republicans took the reins of government, some of the commissions Adams had signed, including one for William Marbury, had not been delivered and were still sitting on Secretary of State Marshall's desk when Adams's term expired at midnight.

Upon assuming office, President Jefferson did deliver the commissions to some of those hastily approved appointees after he took office. But William Marbury and several others did not receive theirs. Marbury, along with three other men, brought suit against Jefferson's secretary of state, James Madison, requesting that the Court issue a writ of mandamus ("we command") ordering Madison to deliver their commissions as justices of the peace.[44] The men argued that all of the required steps in their appointments had been properly taken: President Adams had nominated them, the Senate had confirmed their nominations, and the commissions had been signed and affixed with the presidential seal. Marshall's failure to deliver the commissions, they insisted, constituted nothing more than a serious breach of etiquette and tradition.

Chief Justice John Marshall Confronts Politics and the Power of the Supreme Court

As he contemplated how the Court would respond to the demands of Marbury and his fellow would-be justices, Marshall confronted two powerful and related sets of questions about the role of the federal judiciary in the life of the American Republic—the same two questions with which we began this chapter: How powerful is the federal judiciary? And how political is it? In *Marbury v. Madison* (1803), the Court found itself involved in an intense partisan battle between the defeated Federalists and the victorious Republicans.[45] That Congress and the executive were highly political branches was obvious to everyone, especially after the election of 1800. The judiciary, however, was supposed to be different. It was constrained and defined by law, not politics. How should such an institution handle its role in the larger political life of the nation?

Chief Justice Marshall could not ignore either of these considerations; both had to be addressed. If his Court waded into the political battle of the time forcefully—ordering Jefferson's administration to deliver the commissions—he risked being rebuffed by the president or even impeached by the Republican-controlled Congress. Marshall *could* choose not to enter the battle. He could deny Marbury's petition, thus preventing a confrontation with Jefferson and his Republicans. However, to do so might send a message that the judiciary was weak in the face of powerful political forces, which could deal a blow to its power, prestige, and independence.[46] Marshall was in a bind, and he knew it. In the decision that he ultimately delivered, Marshall noted the "peculiar delicacy of this case."[47] The way in which Marshall dealt with this dilemma continues to shape the role of the Supreme Court in American political life to this day.

Marbury v. Madison Leads to the Establishment of Judicial Review

Because of the changes to the Supreme Court's schedule brought about by the Judiciary Act of 1801, Marbury and his associates had to wait for nearly two years before the Court heard their request to issue a writ of mandamus to Secretary of State Madison. Both of Chief Justice Marshall's apparent options in the case seemed likely to diminish the power of his judiciary. Either he could order Jefferson's administration to deliver the commissions and risk being refused or ignored, or he could decide not to challenge the president and risk looking weak and timid.

Marshall chose neither option. Instead, in a tactically brilliant move, he broke the decision before him into three separate questions. First, the chief justice asked if the men were entitled to their commissions. To this first question, Marshall, in his opinion, answered yes. The presidential signing of such commissions is the last formal act, and that had been done. Delivery of the commissions, Marshall noted, "is a practice directed by convenience, but not by law."[48] Once this part of the decision was established, Marshall considered whether or not a legal remedy involving the courts was available to Marbury and his fellow plaintiffs. To this second question, Marshall also answered in the affirmative, arguing that "the individual who considers himself [so] injured has a right to resort to the laws of the country for a remedy."[49]

So far, it seemed that Marshall was going to take on Jefferson's administration with all of the risks that such a strategy entailed. But he did not. Instead, Marshall presented a third question for his Court to consider: Were Marbury and the other plaintiffs entitled to the remedy that they sought—the writs of mandamus? To this question, Marshall answered no. The power to issue these kinds of writs in this particular instance, he declared, had been improperly given to the Court by a section of the Judiciary Act of 1789.[50] Though the reasoning is a bit technical, Marshall argued that when Congress had granted the Court the authority "to issue writs of

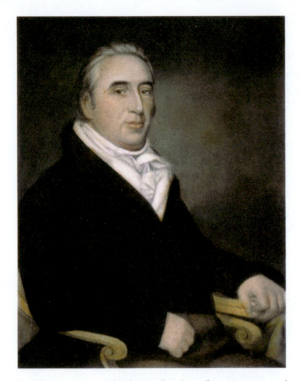

Judicial nominee William Marbury, whose suit against James Madison in *Marbury v. Madison* established judicial review of federal law.

The Granger Collection, New York

mandamus to public officers," it was attempting to expand the scope of the original jurisdiction of the Court, which Congress cannot do. Only the Constitution can. Therefore, the Court did not have the power to give Marbury the remedy he sought.

In stating the inability of his Court to legitimately provide the sought-after remedy, Marshall also found that the part of the Judiciary Act that tried to give his Court such power was in violation of the Constitution and, therefore, invalid: "A law repugnant to the Constitution is void, and . . . courts, as well as other departments, are bound by that instrument."[51]

It proved to be a bold strategic move. Madison did not have to deliver the commissions. Marshall, however, had just asserted what the Constitution had failed to lay out in its brief treatment of the third branch: The Supreme Court had the power of **judicial review**, which is the authority of a court to review laws and actions of other branches and levels of government to decide if they are in conflict with the highest law of the land—in this case, the Constitution—and, if they are, to declare those laws or actions invalid.

In establishing the precedent for judicial review over federal laws, Marshall expanded the Court's responsibility in **constitutional interpretation** in which the judiciary reviews laws and actions in light of the meaning of the Constitution. In exercising judicial review, according to Marshall's logic, the Court does not place itself above the other two branches; it is coequal to them, and the Constitution is supreme to all three.

Under the decades-long tenure of Marshall, the Supreme Court used the tool of judicial review to weigh in on the constitutionality of several state laws, declaring some invalid. Marshall, however, never again used the power of judicial review to strike down an act of Congress. It would be more than fifty years before the Court took such an action again, in its infamous decision in *Dred Scott v. Sandford* (1857). In this case, Justice Roger Taney and his Court overturned the Missouri Compromise, deepening national divisions over the future of slavery.[52]

In the end, William Marbury and his fellow job seekers never received their commissions, and the power of judicial review and the role of the Court in constitutional interpretation remain highly debated issues to this day. Before we can explore the implications of this claimed authority, however, it is necessary to examine the structure and operation of the American judicial system.

The American Legal System Is Defined by Federalism

Each of the two levels in the federalist system—the nation and the states—operates its own system of courts, with a single federal judiciary for the nation and separate state judiciaries in each of the fifty states. While the structure of American federalism defines the basic organization of the nation's legal system, the dual systems of federal and state courts share in common the tradition of the **adversarial system** of justice, in which the opposing parties present their sides of a case in the most persuasive way possible. In this system, a **plaintiff** is the party bringing a complaint, and the **defendant** is the party accused of wrongdoing.[53]

Cases Are Divided into Criminal and Civil Types

Whether or not a specific court has jurisdiction over a specific case may depend on whether that court is a state or a federal court, the details of the case, or where that court lies within the overall structure of the federal or state court system. Both state and federal courts have jurisdiction over two categories of law: criminal and civil.[54] **Criminal law** covers actions determined to harm the community itself, such as committing an act of violence against another person.[55] In a criminal case, the state or federal government acts as the plaintiff and tries to prove the guilt of the defendant, the party accused of a crime. Although many acts (such as murder or assault) are considered to be criminal offenses in all of the states, some acts (such as gambling or recreational use of marijuana) are legal in some states but not in others. The punishments handed out for those convicted of similar crimes may also vary from state to state.

Being convicted under a criminal statute leads to some form of punishment, such as fines; imprisonment; or, in some cases, the death penalty.[56] Most criminal cases are resolved through the process of **plea bargaining**. In this process, a defendant in a criminal case agrees to plead guilty to a lesser charge than the one brought by the prosecutors in order to reduce their punishment. Plea bargaining is also used in civil cases. As is the case with defendants during the arrest and trial phases, those ultimately convicted of crimes have constitutional protections, specifically against the Eighth Amendment's protection against the imposition of "cruel and unusual punishments." Whether or not the death penalty—or specific methods of instituting it—constitutes a violation of the Eighth Amendment's protections continues to be debated today.

Noncriminal law, commonly referred to as **civil law**, covers cases involving private rights and relationships between individuals and groups. In a civil case, the plaintiff is the party who argues that they have been wronged, and the defendant is the party accused of violating a person's rights or breaking an agreement. While in criminal cases a government (state or federal) is always the plaintiff, in civil cases the plaintiff may be a government or an individual. A jury or a judge might decide civil cases—though most are settled before a verdict is rendered—either before the case goes to trial or during the proceedings.

State Courts Handle the Majority of Cases in the United States

While our focus is on the federal judiciary, it is important to note that state courts handle the vast majority of cases in the United States. While states may vary in how their judicial systems are structured and organized—including how judges are selected—the state court systems share a few common traits. State judicial systems handle both criminal and civil cases. Each state has a system of trial courts that does most of the work of the state's judiciary, handles cases arising under that state's laws, and possesses original jurisdiction. More than half of the states have an intermediate system of appellate courts that operate with appellate jurisdiction. Each state has at least one state supreme court, which acts as the highest court in that state's system and as the final level of appeal.[57] A select group of cases may proceed to the federal judiciary from the highest state court of appeals. These cases generally involve a question arising under the Constitution, such as a claim that an individual's constitutional rights have been violated. States also operate systems of specialized courts that typically handle issues like traffic violations, family disputes, and small claims.

Most of the Impactful Cases Are Handled by the Federal Judiciary

While the majority of cases are handled by the state courts, many of the most impactful happen at the federal level. The federal judiciary includes two types of courts: constitutional courts and legislative courts. The term *constitutional courts* refers to the Supreme Court and the lower levels of the federal judiciary that the Constitution authorized Congress to create in Article III. Legislative courts are specialized courts created by Congress under its authority in Article I to handle matters such as tax and trade law. Our focus in this chapter will be on the constitutional court system rather than on the specialized legislative courts.

The Federal District Courts Serve as the Bottom Level of the Federal Judiciary. The constitutional court system is structured as a three-layered pyramid (see Figure 13.1). At the bottom are the nation's **federal district courts**. Congress created the district courts in the Judiciary Act of 1789. In most federal cases, district courts act as the trial courts and possess original jurisdiction. As of 2020, there were ninety-four district courts in the United States, and each state had at least one. District court boundaries do not cut across state lines. The district courts handle most of the work of the federal courts, and their cases are heard by a single federal judge. Cases heard in a district court may or may not include a jury; the Constitution

The Modern Court System

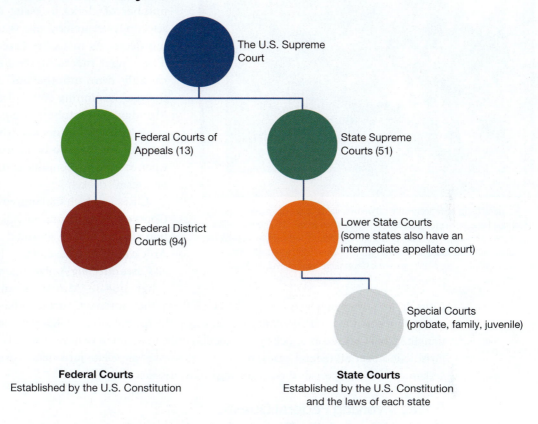

The U.S. Supreme Court

Federal Courts of Appeals (13)

State Supreme Courts (51)

Federal District Courts (94)

Lower State Courts (some states also have an intermediate appellate court)

Special Courts (probate, family, juvenile)

Federal Courts
Established by the U.S. Constitution

State Courts
Established by the U.S. Constitution and the laws of each state

guarantees the right to a jury trial in all federal criminal cases (Sixth Amendment) and in some civil cases (Seventh Amendment).

The Appellate Courts Sit in the Middle. The **federal courts of appeals** occupy the middle level of the constitutional courts. There are thirteen courts of appeals; eleven have jurisdiction over regionally based "circuits," one has jurisdiction over the District of Columbia (which handles appeals involving federal agencies), and the Thirteenth Circuit handles cases arising under international trade and patent law. The courts of appeals exercise appellate jurisdiction only, reviewing decisions made by the federal district courts and certain specialized federal courts.

The Supreme Court Sits at the Top. At the top of the federal judicial system is the U.S. Supreme Court, which, as the Constitution established, is the highest court in the nation. Part of the Court's intended purpose was to resolve differences between the states, which had not effectively been provided for in the government created by the Articles of Confederation. The Court also acts to resolve differing interpretations

The Supreme Court now hears only between seventy and eighty cases a year, but its workload was once much higher. This illustration from 1885 shows the justices of the time inundated with cases from the lower courts. Behind them are closets full of unadjudicated cases from years past that await their attention. Reforms passed by Congress eventually gave the Court more control over its docket.
Library of Congress Prints and Photographs Division

of the law in the lower federal courts. Each justice has a small number of clerks to assist in selecting, researching, and issuing decisions in Court cases. The Court meets in session roughly nine months out of the year, beginning on the first Monday in October. Those cases still on the docket (the schedule of cases to be heard) when a term ends continue to the next term's docket.

Cases in which the Supreme Court exercises original jurisdiction are few and are specified in Article III of the Constitution: "In all Cases affecting Ambassadors, other public Ministers and Consuls, and those in which a State shall be a Party, the supreme Court shall have original jurisdiction."[58] In all other cases in which the federal judiciary has jurisdiction, the Court possesses appellate jurisdiction only. In addition to having appellate jurisdiction over all federal cases, the Court possesses appellate jurisdiction over certain state cases, especially those involving a federal issue.

Cases Involving Federal Questions Proceed through the Federal Judiciary

Those cases that begin in the federal judiciary—in which the federal courts have original jurisdiction—must fall into one of three categories. The first category is cases in which the federal government is a party in a dispute. Second, the federal judiciary possesses original jurisdiction in civil suits involving parties from two different states in which the amount of money in question is more than $75,000. Finally—and, for our purposes, most importantly—the federal judiciary possesses original jurisdiction in cases that involve a federal question, such as a case in which a party files a claim of violations of rights under the Constitution, a dispute involving a federal treaty, or a case involving a federal law. Cases involving federal questions may be either criminal or civil cases. State cases that proceed to the Supreme Court also involve federal questions. Many of the most important federal cases in American history—and most of the cases that we consider in this book—are those involving charges of violations of constitutional rights and liberties. See Figure 13.2.

▼ FIGURE 13.2

How Cases Move through the Court System

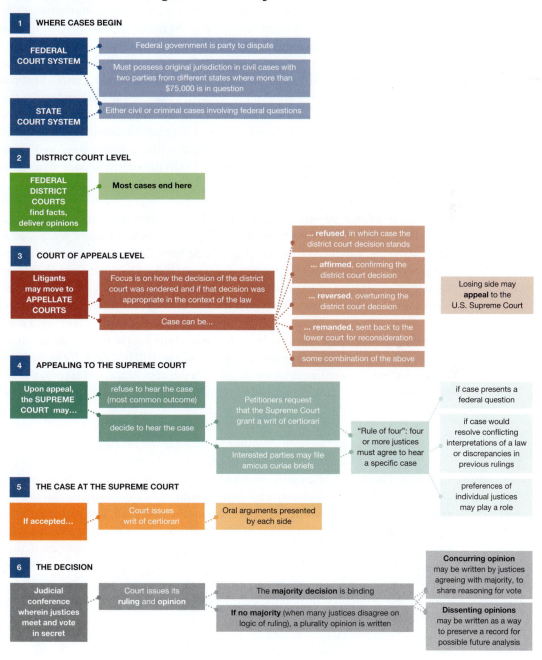

As the courts of original jurisdiction in most federal cases, the federal district courts act as the trial courts, finding facts and delivering opinions on the case. Litigants who lose in a district court have the option to appeal the decision to the appellate courts; if they do, the case moves up to the next level.[59] Most federal cases, however, go no farther than the district courts.

Appellate courts possess appellate jurisdiction only and review cases on appeal with cases typically heard by three-judge panels. Rather than finding facts, the appellate courts focus on how the decision of the district court was rendered and if that decision was appropriate in the context of the law. An appellate court has several options. It may refuse to hear the appeal, in which case the decision of the district court (or specialized federal court) holds. Litigants whose appeal is refused by the appellate court may still appeal to the Supreme Court, though their odds of receiving a hearing by the Court are very small.

If it decides to hear a case, an appeals court may choose to affirm the judgment of the lower court, confirming that court's ruling. It may reverse the decision; if this is the case, it is typically based on questions of how the lower court proceeded or applied the law. Finally, it may remand the case back to the lower court for reconsideration, again often because the appellate court judges had questions about procedure or application of the law. These options are not mutually exclusive for any one case. The court could affirm part of a lower court's decision in a particular case, reverse part of it, and remand yet another part, though this is far from a common outcome. The side that loses in an appellate court has the right to appeal to the Supreme Court, but there is no guarantee that its case will be heard. If the Supreme Court declines to take the case, the decision of the appellate court stands, though any broader rule or principle created in the decision applies only to that circuit, not nationwide.[60]

The Supreme Court Decides Whether to Take Cases on Appeal. In exercising its authority of appellate jurisdiction, the Supreme Court is confronted with two questions. The second of these questions is whether or not the case has been properly decided by the lower courts, which will determine the Court's ruling. But the first question for the Court is whether or not to hear the case at all. The vast majority of cases heard on appeal in the Court originate with a litigant who has lost in a lower court filing a petition to have their case heard. Almost all such petitions are denied, however. The modern Court receives, on average, between eight thousand and nine thousand such petitions a year but hears only about seventy to eighty, less than 1 percent. In recent decades, the Court has gained a much greater degree of control over its docket.

A petitioner who wishes to have the Court accept their case files an argument with the Court in a written **brief**, which presents the arguments for the appeal. Not everyone can file a legitimate brief before the Court. In addition to certain other technical requirements about the facts and merits of a case, a petitioner must demonstrate that they have **standing**, which involves demonstrating an actual or imminent harm from a law or action in question. As we will discuss later in the chapter, the need to establish standing acts as a limitation on the power of the Court to shape national public policy. The opposing party in a case may also file a brief with the Court laying out their arguments.[61]

As the Constitution offers little guidance on which cases the Court does or does not take, justices have adopted the custom of the rule of four, which simply means that it will generally hear a case if at least four of the nine justices vote to do so.

If it decides to hear a case, the Court issues a **writ of certiorari** (from the Latin "to be more informed") to the lower court for the records of the case, a process that is commonly referred to as certiorari, or "granting cert." In its own rules, the Court makes it clear that the hurdle for having a case heard on appeal is high: "Review on a writ of certiorari is not a matter of right, but of judicial discretion. A petition of a writ of certiorari will be granted only for compelling reasons."[62]

The most important factor in the decision to grant or deny cert is if there is confusion about or alternate interpretations of a law or previous ruling among or between lower-level federal courts or state supreme courts. Cases presenting a federal question are also more likely to be heard. The Court does not, however, take all cases in which the lower courts made a mistake or convicted an innocent person. Its role is not the corrector of all lower court mistakes in finding fact or applying the law. Instead, it seeks to answer important federal concerns and constitutional questions that will affect many cases across the country.

Interested parties who are not plaintiffs or defendants may also try to signal to the Court their interest in the decision to grant cert or on the merits of the case should cert be granted. Plaintiffs and defendants are not the only parties that may file briefs. An interested party (such as an interest group) may also submit its opinions to the Court in what is called an amicus curiae brief (from the Latin, "friend of the court").[63] The volume, authorship, and content of these briefs can act as a signal to the Court about how the public or interest groups view an issue.[64] An especially important filer of amici curiae briefs is the **solicitor general**, who is appointed by the president to represent the federal government at the Court. An indication to the Court that the government (or the president, specifically) is interested in a case can be a powerful influence both on whether or not the Court should hear a particular case and on its ruling should it decide to do so.

The preferences of the justices may also play a role in the decision to grant cert. After all, the final decision rests on the votes of the justices themselves. While scholars continue to debate the role that justices' political or policy preferences play in their decisions (which we will examine later in the chapter), a justice who supports a particular view on an issue before the Court must consider how the other justices are likely to vote on the merits of the case. Justices are well aware that the outcome of a Supreme Court case can set a **precedent**, or a judicial decision that acts as a basis for deciding similar cases in the future. An individual justice may be more or less likely to grant cert if they believe that the outcome might set a precedent that the justice desires or wishes to avoid.

Once Cases Are Taken Up, the Supreme Court Considers and Decides Them. If the Supreme Court decides to grant cert in a case, it requests briefs from both sides laying out their full arguments. Court clerks will assist the justices in reviewing these briefs. The case is then scheduled for **oral argument** before the assembled justices, during which each side gets a fixed amount of time (typically half an hour) to present. In exceptional circumstances, filers of amicus curiae briefs may also be given time during oral arguments, but this is not common. During this phase, the justices frequently interrupt and question the lawyers as they present, though some justices tend to interrupt and question more than others. Cameras are not allowed in the courtroom during oral arguments, though sketch artists and audio recordings are.

Scholars debate how influential oral arguments are in shaping justices' rulings in a case.[65] This process, however, is often of intense interest to members of the public, who analyze the content of justices' questions for clues as to how those justices will ultimately vote. After oral argument, the case proceeds to judicial conference in which the justices meet and vote in secret; not even their clerks are present.

Next, the Court must decide who will write the opinions that will announce the Court's decision in the case and its reasoning. If the chief justice is in the majority, then they select the author of the majority opinion. If not, the most senior member of the majority does so. The power to choose the author of an opinion can be a useful strategic tool as even justices who vote together may have differences in their interpretations of certain points brought up in the case. If there is no majority, which typically occurs when many justices disagree on the logic behind a ruling, then a plurality opinion will be written that expresses the views of the largest number of justices who voted together. The process can go on for months (on and off, of course), and individual justices can and do change their votes during this phase.

Finally, the Court issues its decision. The majority opinion consists of the ruling—and the logic behind it—of the majority of justices in the case. When it acts under appellate jurisdiction (which is most of the time), the Court has the same options as other appellate courts. It may affirm the lower court's decision, reverse it, or remand back to the lower court the case or choose some mix of these three for different aspects of a case.[66] The decision and the majority opinion are binding and serve to guide lower courts and future courts in handling similar cases.

A justice voting with the majority may also write a concurring opinion (often called a concurrence). More than one justice may collaborate on a concurrence. Concurrences are common when a justice has some differences in logic or reasoning with the other members of the majority but not enough to cause that justice to side against them. A justice who voted with the minority may write a dissenting opinion, called a dissent, also alone or with other justices. These opinions do not carry the weight of the Court behind them (since the justice writing the dissent was on the losing side). However, if a future court should revisit a precedent with a thought of overturning it, a dissent may provide a useful record and analysis of why at least one justice thought the Court got it wrong the first time.

Judicial Review Raises Questions of Constitutional Interpretation and Judicial Decision Making

13.5 Compare theories of judicial decision making as well as arguments for or against judicial restraint and activism in constitutional review.

Since its inception, the federal judiciary itself has been on trial—in the court of constitutional law, political science, and American public opinion. The chief defendant in this long and sometimes contentious history has been the Supreme Court, and the primary behavior in question has been the use of judicial review. Four main problems lie at the heart of the issue.

The first, and potentially biggest, concern about judicial review arises from the fact that Supreme Court justices, who are not elected, have the power to overturn laws passed by representatives and senators who *were* elected. Alexander Bickel described this **countermajoritarian difficulty** in the exercise of judicial review: the worry that in striking down legislation, the Court "exercises control, not in behalf of the prevailing majority, but against it."[67] Of course, justices are nominated by elected presidents and confirmed by elected senators, but they are not beholden to those elected officials after they are confirmed. Second, there is the concern that Americans may become less vigilant about who they elect, knowing that if they do a poor job in choosing their representatives, the Supreme Court will be there to bail them out. In modern terms, this is called the problem of moral hazard. The term comes from the concept of unwanted incentives created by having insurance. When a person is insured against bad outcomes from their own actions, then the person may take less care in avoiding those outcomes. By acting as a safety net against poor, factious, or tyrannical legislation, the Court might actually make unwanted legislative outcomes more, not less, likely.

Third, the power of judicial review lies as much in its power to affirm as in its power to negate. In upholding the constitutionality of laws, the Supreme Court also exercises power over the legislative process by adding legitimacy in the minds of the American public to those laws passed by Congress.[68] In doing so, the Court risks giving its stamp of approval to tyranny of the majority by validating laws that trample on the rights of minorities.

Finally, there exists the challenge inherent in interpreting and applying the Constitution to a variety of specific cases and circumstances across time and by individuals with their own opinions on what is or is not in accordance with the document, its language, and its intent. To fully consider this issue, however, it is first necessary to explore in more detail how justices go about interpreting the Constitution and applying this highest law of the land to the cases brought before them.

Justices Take Several Approaches to Constitutional Interpretation

Trying to figure out why justices vote the way they do on any specific case is very difficult given all the factors that likely contribute to an individual justice's vote. However,

As executive director of the National Association for the Advancement of Colored People (NAACP) Legal Defense and Educational Fund, Thurgood Marshall was instrumental to the effort to end legal segregation, culminating in the Supreme Court decision in *Brown v. Board of Education.* That decision, hailed as a major victory for civil rights, nonetheless overturned the will of many Americans who had voted for segregationists, an example of the countermajoritarian difficulty.

AP Photo

political scientists have developed several models that describe different approaches to judicial decision making. While a justice may emphasize one approach more than others, these models are best thought of as elements in the overall process and not as approaches that a given justice will use exclusively. Justices themselves likely combine several considerations when approaching a case, especially difficult ones involving constitutional interpretation.

The Legal Model Emphasizes Facts and Previous Decisions.

The legal model focuses on applying the law to the facts of the case. In this model, justices rely on precedent—a previous decision on a similar case that serves as a basis for future decisions. When a justice follows precedent, they are said to be employing the doctrine of **stare decisis** (from the Latin "to stand by things decided").[69] All justices—even the ones who emphasize their own capacity to interpret the Constitution—are bound by and employ the legal model to some extent in their decisions. There is good reason for this. It is, after all, how the legal system operates; similar cases are supposed to be decided in similar ways. To do otherwise would bring an unacceptable lack of uniformity to the legal system. There is also, however, a more strategic concern. A Supreme Court that is constantly ignoring its own precedents would likely not retain much legitimacy and authority in the eyes of the American people. While all justices employ the legal model, especially when deciding criminal cases, when it comes to those cases with significant implications for public policy—when the constitutionality of laws is at stake—other models may factor into judicial decision making as well.

Some justices applying the legal model look to the written text of the Constitution and the intent of the Framers for guidance rather than to their own interpretation of the document's intent. Proponents of original understanding (or originalism) argue that the process of constitutional amendment, not Supreme Court decisions, should be the primary way to make major changes in the fundamental law of the nation.

The Attitudinal Model Emphasizes Policy Preferences.

The attitudinal model describes a process through which the political and policy preferences of individual justices shape their votes on cases rather than a neutral weighing of the facts and the law.[70] This model describes an overtly political approach to judicial decision making, one very far from Alexander Hamilton's reassurances about the nonpolitical federal judiciary in *Federalist* No. 78. Much of the research in this area has focused on explaining and predicting the votes of justices based on what we know about their political ideologies.[71] For scholars who emphasize the role of the individual attitudes and political ideologies of justices, the countermajoritarian difficulty can be especially worrisome. Not only can unelected justices strike down the will of the majority, but they may do so to advance their own political and policy agendas.

The Strategic Model Emphasizes Strategic Calculation. Finally, the strategic model portrays individual justices as strategic political actors who, according to political scientist Walter Murphy, try to make the best use of their "resources, official and personal, to achieve a particular set of policy objectives."[72] Strategic justices do more than just vote according to their individual preferences. They consider the likely behaviors of their fellow justices; understand the national political context and the system of shared powers in which the Court operates; and, when deciding how to act, "compute in terms of costs and revenues whether a particular choice is worth the price which is required to attain it."[73] Strategic considerations may shape whether or not a justice votes to grant cert,[74] how justices vote on cases before them, and how justices craft their opinions.[75]

Justices Exercise Degrees of Judicial Restraint and Judicial Activism

Related to the question of how justices make their decisions is the issue of how willing or reluctant they are to exercise the authority of judicial review. How eager, in other words, should the Court be to overturn the actions of the other two branches of government?

Proponents of **judicial restraint** argue that the Court should use this power rarely and whenever possible defer to the judgment of the legislative and executive branches on decisions that those branches have made. These proponents offer several justifications for their caution. First, they point to the dangers of the countermajoritarian difficulty and the potential antidemocratic consequences of unelected justices overturning the actions of elected representatives. In addition, the Supreme Court's voice in declaring a law to be unconstitutional is more authoritative when used sparingly, sending a clear signal in those times when it is employed. Finally, justices are legal and constitutional specialists; they are not policy specialists, nor are their clerks. The public policies that may be impacted by the use of judicial review may involve complex technical questions the details of which justices may not fully understand.

Proponents of **judicial activism**, on the other hand, argue that justices should be willing to step in and overturn laws when they see a need to do so. Sometimes the other two branches may make mistakes or, worse, trample on individual rights

EXAMINING THE RELATIONSHIP BETWEEN JUDICIAL REVIEW AND JUSTICES' IDEOLOGIES

What role do the political ideologies of Supreme Court justices play in the willingness of justices to overturn federal or state laws? This is a very complex question that political scientists continue to debate. Part of the issue is actually measuring the political ideologies of justices as they are not required to wear a label or announce to the world their personal politics. Many presidents are unhappily surprised to find that a justice they nominated has a different judicial philosophy than expected once the justice is on the Court and serving a lifetime term.

Using data from the Supreme Court Database—created and shared by a group of scholars—we can begin to explore this question. Figure 13.3-A displays the total number of cases in which the Court declared an act of Congress or a state or territorial law (or state constitutional provision) unconstitutional during a specific time in the Court's history: 1953–1968. These years cover the Warren Court, in which Earl Warren served as the chief justice. The Warren Court is often considered to be one of the most liberal Courts in the nation's history. The blue bars indicate a use of judicial review to overturn a law or provision in a liberal direction as defined by the scholars, and the green bars indicate a use that overturned a law in a conservative direction. The largest group of these decisions involved questions of civil rights, followed by First Amendment concerns.

Based on Figure 13.3-A, one might infer that liberal justices are more likely to overturn federal or state laws than conservative justices since nearly 90 percent of the decisions are in a liberal direction, and the Court was considered to be composed of a majority of liberal justices.

However, it is important to remember that these data are from only one Supreme Court era. Figure 13.3-B presents a similar analysis; however, these data are from the tenure of Chief Justice Charles Evans Hughes, when the Court was considered to be a very conservative one.[76] In contrast to the Warren Court, the majority of uses of judicial review to overturn federal or state laws in the Hughes Court era were conservative and focused primarily on economic activity and taxation policy. In terms of federal laws, many of these uses of judicial review focused on challenging President Roosevelt's New Deal, which we discussed in Chapter 3.

The data from Figure 13.3-B present a more complex picture of the connection between judicial ideology and the willingness of justices to overturn federal or state laws, especially before Roosevelt began a series of appointments (some of whom served on the Warren Court) in 1937. These data challenge the assertion that liberal justices are *necessarily* more likely to exercise judicial review to overturn federal or state laws than conservative ones. However, they do support the idea that the political ideologies of the justices can affect patterns of the use of judicial review. This important issue is one scholars will continue to examine.

WHAT Do You Think?

To what extent do you think justices should or should not bring their own political views into the use of judicial review? What responsibility should the Senate exercise in trying to ascertain the politics of Supreme Court nominees during the confirmation proceedings?

▼ FIGURE 13.3-A

Liberal and Conservative Uses of Judicial Review in the Warren Court, 1953–1968

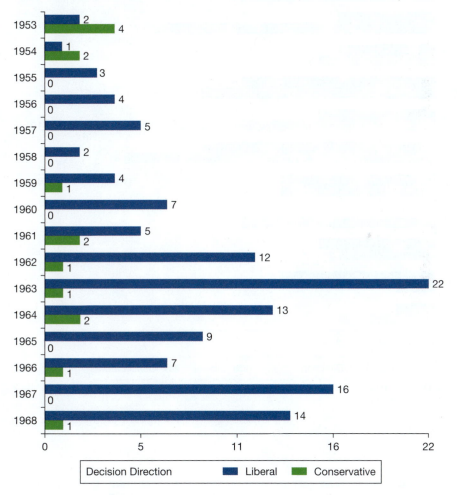

Source: Data from Harold Spaeth et al., "2018 Supreme Court Database," accessed August 11, 2018, http://supremecourtdatabase.org.

(Continued)

(Continued)

Liberal and Conservative Uses of Judicial Review in the Hughes Court, 1929–1940

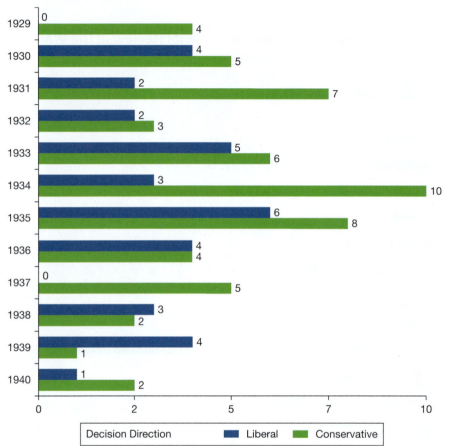

Source: Data from Harold Spaeth et al., "2018 Supreme Court Database," accessed August 11, 2018, http://supremecourtdatabase.org.

and liberties. The very power that fuels concerns about the countermajoritarian difficulty—that the Court can strike down the will of the majority—also gives it the power to protect the rights of minorities. Proponents of activism point to times when the other two branches act in ways damaging to rights and liberties; they also point to the fact that these branches often do not act at all. Free from the need to be concerned about the popularity of their actions, Supreme Court justices can place on the agenda issues that Congress and the president are unwilling to tackle.

Conclusion: The Trial of the Supreme Court Continues

Following the passing of Justice Ruth Bader Ginsburg in September 2020, President Trump nominated conservative judge Amy Coney Barrett to join the Supreme Court. With the election at hand, Democrats argued that confirmation of Justice Ginsburg's replacement should be delayed.

The Senate confirmed Barrett 52-48, with Susan Collins (R-ME) the only Republican opposed. Following Barrett's confirmation, Democrats began to discuss expanding the size of the Supreme Court, should they find themselves in a position to do so.

In this chapter, we have explored two important and closely related questions: How political is the Court? And how powerful is it? In *Federalist* No. 78, Alexander Hamilton—a proponent of a strong national government—tried to reassure a skeptical confederation during the ratification debates that the Court was neither political nor powerful. History has proven Hamilton correct and incorrect on both counts.

The justices of the Supreme Court and the federal judiciary are not political in the ways that presidents, representatives, and senators are, in no small part because they do not have to worry about reelection. They must consider the facts of the case and the letter of the law when ruling on cases. Justices are, however, political people, and their personal views on issues may affect their decisions on impactful cases. They must always be strategic in understanding the role their institution plays in the system of separation of powers and in Americans' views on the legitimacy of the institution.

Theirs is a power that must be nurtured, cultivated, and protected, as John Marshall and subsequent members of the federal judiciary have had to learn. Compared to the legislative and executive branches, the power of the federal judiciary in national policymaking is much less imposing. It cannot write laws; it has no army. It has only the power of its decisions and the willingness of the people and the members of the other two branches to acquiesce to its decisions. It is not powerless; it is just different. How dangerous—or promising—this difference is continues to be a central subject of debate in American politics.

CHAPTER REVIEW

This chapter's main ideas are reflected in the Learning Objectives. By reviewing them here, you should be able to *remember* the key points and *know* these terms that are central to the topic.

13.1 Explore the role of politics in modern Supreme Court confirmation proceedings.

Remember . . .
- Recent Supreme Court confirmation proceedings reveal the importance of the decision for political parties.
- Questions about how much justices should incorporate their own experiences and outlooks into their decisions have played a key role in confirmation debates.

Know . . .
- *federal judiciary* (p. 377)
- *Supreme Court* (p. 377)

13.2 Describe the structure and powers of the federal judiciary as laid out in the Constitution.

Remember ...
- The Constitution contains less detail about the judiciary than about the legislative or executive branches, but it is clear that the Framers intended it to be the weakest of the three and also relatively independent of the other two.
- Article III does not expressly give the judiciary the power to strike down laws that it views as being in violation of the Constitution.

Know ...
- *appellate jurisdiction* (p. 384)
- *original jurisdiction* (p. 384)

13.3 Explain John Marshall's development of judicial review in the Supreme Court decision in *Marbury v. Madison*.

Remember ...
- In part of his ruling in *Marbury v. Madison*, Marshall found that part of the law that Marbury was basing his claim on, the Judiciary Act of 1789, was unconstitutional and thus unenforceable.
- Marshall, therefore, asserted that the Supreme Court had the power of judicial review over federal laws.

Know ...
- *constitutional interpretation* (p. 392)
- *judicial review* (p. 392)

13.4 Describe the structure of the American legal system and the federal judiciary.

Remember ...
- All courts in the American system are based on the adversarial system with plaintiffs and defendants arguing their opposing sides of the case in the most persuasive way possible.
- Criminal law covers actions determined to harm the community itself, whereas civil law covers cases involving private rights and relationships between individuals and groups.
- The federal judiciary is composed of constitutional courts and specialized legislative courts. The constitutional courts are organized into three levels: federal district courts, the federal court of appeals, and the Supreme Court.

Know ...
- *adversarial system* (p. 393)
- *brief* (p. 398)
- *civil law* (p. 393)
- *criminal law* (p. 393)
- *defendant* (p. 393)
- *federal courts of appeals* (p. 395)
- *federal district courts* (p. 394)
- *oral argument* (p. 400)
- *plaintiff* (p. 393)
- *plea bargaining* (p. 393)
- *precedent* (p. 399)
- *solicitor general* (p. 399)
- *standing* (p. 398)
- *writ of certiorari* (p. 399)

13.5 Compare theories of judicial decision making as well as arguments for or against judicial restraint and activism in constitutional review.

Remember ...
- Judicial review raises a series of questions concerning the scope of powers of an unelected group of justices; citizen neglect of civic responsivity; the potential of validating laws that trample on the rights of minorities; and challenges of interpretation and application of the Constitution.
- There are three main models of constitutional interpretation: legal, attitudinal, and strategic.
- Justices may diverge in their approach to decision making, showing either judicial restraint or judicial activism.

Know ...
- *countermajoritarian difficulty* (p. 401)
- *judicial activism* (p. 403)
- *judicial restraint* (p. 403)
- *stare decisis* (p. 402)

POLICY

PART IV

CHAPTER 14

PUBLIC POLICY

Promoting the General Welfare and Advancing Americans' Interests

Mitzi Pena (right), her sister Yaretzi Pena (center), and her cousin Karina Terriquez (left) wait in line to file their applications for the Deferred Action for Childhood Arrivals (DACA) program in August 2012, in Los Angeles, California. Under this Obama administration program, undocumented youth who qualify can file applications for citizenship to avoid deportation and obtain the right to work.

Kevork Djansezian/Getty Images

After reading this chapter, you will be able to do the following:

14.1 Understand the steps in the policymaking process and the different forms of domestic social policy in America today.

14.2 Discuss the politics of American health care policy.

14.3 Understand the approaches to and goals of fiscal policy in the United States.

14.4 Summarize the historical development of America's involvement in international affairs.

14.5 Understand the connection between American immigration policy and the nation's foreign policy.

In this chapter, you will take a deep dive into health care in the United States. This is a primary area in which federal, state, and local governments—as well as the private sector, nonprofit organizations, academics, and political entrepreneurs—all weigh in, pursuing their goals in the realm of American **public policy**, which is the intentional use of governmental power to secure the health, welfare, opportunities, and national security of citizens.

Governmental action involves **domestic policy**, through which policymakers aim to improve the social welfare of the American citizens. It also involves **economic policy**, through which American policymakers try to ensure that all Americans can achieve their futures. Finally, it involves **foreign policy**, through which policymakers try to protect Americans' interests in an uncertain world.

These issues are not separate. As you will discover, American public policy involves connections between domestic, economic, and foreign policy. Throughout this book, we have wrestled with questions of power, politics, and representation. This chapter is no different, except for one thing: We move between Washington, DC; the state capitals; and other nations, as officials at all levels of the American government are tasked to meet the demands of America's citizens and those who strive to become part of the American dream.

Problems, solutions, and politics. In America, now and throughout its history, there has been no shortage of any of these things. Experts, congresspeople, presidents, and members of interest groups have all presented to the public their analyses of problems that need to be solved and their best solutions to those problems. In doing so, all are engaged with the political process, and all must be strategic in this engagement if they hope to succeed.

American Dreamers' Futures Depend upon Whether a Public Policy Will Continue

> **14.1** Understand the steps in the policymaking process and the different forms of domestic social policy in America today.

In an interview with the *New York Times,* Julia Verzbickis told her story. It was part of a series called "American Dreamers."[1] The story focused on the path to inclusion and American citizenship for young immigrants introduced in 2012 through an executive order by President Obama: Deferred Action for Childhood Arrivals, or DACA.[2] Under the order, undocumented individuals who came to the United States before the age of sixteen (as of the enactment of the policy) and who were in school or who had recently graduated could seek a deferment on their deportation.

Julia Verzbickis's arrival in the United States was not without many challenges, but she persevered:

> The lawyer we had turned out to be fraudulent, and as a result, my parents, my sisters and I all lost our status in the country. It was the summer before my first year of high school. The future remained unclear, but I made some choices. I chose to keep my grades up in school. I chose to give myself the opportunity at a future. . . . The week after my twenty-first birthday, I got a notice that my DACA application had been approved. . . . In August 2015, I started teaching. . . . I've been teaching middle school since then, and I love it. My kids are amazing. They drive me nuts on any given day, but I love them.[3]

According to public opinion polls, most Americans believe that undocumented immigrants living in the United States who meet certain requirements should be allowed to stay in the country legally, but more Democrats support that position than Republicans, making the issue a partisan one.[4] As part of a broader effort at immigration reform, DACA was aimed at protecting a group of people who seemed to be both the most vulnerable and least controversial from a policy perspective—the children of undocumented immigrants. As one report put it, "DACA is an important tool for expanding economic and civic contributions from these individuals. Ultimately, these . . . initiatives will benefit places, not just individuals and families."[5]

Changes in Demographics Will Continue to Shape American Public Policy

American public policy is and will continue to be influenced by changes in **demographics**, which are groupings of individuals based on shared characteristics, such as ancestry, race, ethnicity, age, and gender. The composition of the American electorate will be changing over the next several decades. Candidates, parties, and political activists are already very familiar with the changes to the composition of the nation that are coming down the pike. The ways in which American parties and candidates respond to these changes will, to a very large degree, determine their electoral successes and failures and, perhaps, their very survival in their current form.

Driving much of this is the growth in the number of Latino and Latina Americans via immigration, births, and generational change.[6] By 2043, according to analysts with the U.S. Census Bureau, America will be a plural nation, meaning that members of no single traditional racial or ethnic group will make up more than half of the population. This will mark the first time in the nation's history that white, non-Hispanics will not have constituted a majority of Americans and eligible voters.[7] By 2060, Hispanics are projected to make up over 30 percent of the nation's population—nearly doubling the percentage of just a few decades prior. In contrast, the percentage of white, non-Hispanic Americans in the nation's population is projected to decline from more than 60 percent in 2013 to roughly 43 percent (see Figure 14.1).

▼ FIGURE 14.1

Projected Changes in the Racial and Ethnic Makeup of the United States

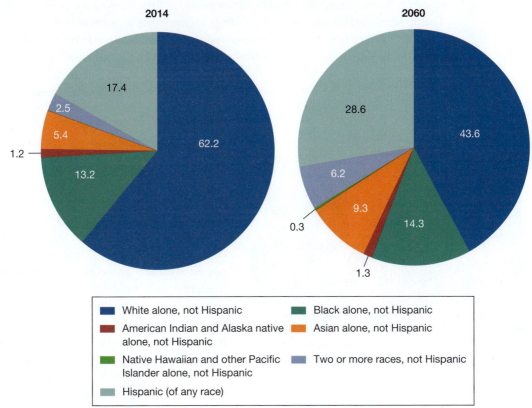

Source: Data from Jonathan Vespa, David M. Armstrong, and Lauren Medina, "Demographic Turning Points for the United States: Population Estimates and Projections for 2020 to 2060," *U.S. Census Bureau*, March 2018, https://www.census.gov/content/dam/Census/library/publications/2018/demo/P25_1144.pdf.

President Trump Acts to End DACA, but the Supreme Court Stays His Hand

With the arrival of the administration of President Donald Trump in 2017, however, many expected that DACA would be rescinded. A spokesperson for the Federation for American Immigration Reform, a group that supports reduced immigration, noted, "This was the crown jewel of illegal executive orders—amnesty for illegal aliens. It doesn't get any more blatant than that."[8] Many Republicans in Congress critiqued President Obama's executive orders on immigration as a way of sidestepping the Republican-controlled Senate and House. Once in office, President Trump acted to terminate DACA via executive order, in September of 2017.[9]

Although both Democrats and Republicans in Congress discussed the need for immigration reform, the Democratic majority in the House after the 2018 election introduced a period of divided government that made passing any legislation, especially on such a contentious topic as immigration, a tall order. In 2020, the U.S. Supreme Court blocked President Trump's rescission of DACA but did so on procedural rather than fundamental constitutional grounds.[10] Because the ruling was based on the reasoning the administration provided for canceling the program, the Trump administration retained the ability to reformulate its termination (in which case the Supreme Court would almost certainly take another look at the new procedures). With the national elections in November, however, the Supreme Court's ruling meant that the immediate future of DACA would be in the hands of voters.

Roberto Martinez, a DACA recipient, chants and cheers outside the Supreme Court building in Washington, DC, following the Court's decision that the Trump administration could not immediately end the program. The monarch butterfly image is one used by activists, organizers, and artists to signal support for immigrants due to the insect's migration pattern that bridges the United States and Mexico.
Drew Angerer/Getty Images.

The Domestic Policy Process Is Dynamic

Domestic policies undertaken with the aim of improving or protecting the health, safety, education, and opportunities for citizens and residents are called social welfare policies. As we discussed in Chapter 3, under the old system of dual federalism, **social welfare policies** were typically thought of as lying within the scope of the police powers of the states and, therefore, mostly under state control and administration. With the transition to cooperative federalism, especially during President Franklin D. Roosevelt's New Deal, the federal government became much more involved in the provision of social welfare policy.

The American policymaking process is often very messy because decisions are made at all levels of government—federal, state, and local—and private organizations are often involved as well. The many stages of the domestic policymaking process are also always political. Every step along the way, from the identification of what needs to be fixed to the presentation of possible solutions to the selection of a policy to implement, involves contestation, mobilization, and controversy.

Federal, state, and local governments aren't the only actors that define and shape social welfare policies. Citizens do, too. Identifying why some policies get enacted and others do not continues to be a subject of study and debate among scholars. At its core, social welfare policy involves redistribution of resources. Providing resources to specific populations necessarily implies diverting those resources from other potential uses and raising funds—typically through taxation—to do so.

The policy process is never finished, therefore, with new participants—and new problems—entering the arena all the time (see Figure 14.2). Scholars of public policy often break down the process into a series of stages or steps. While it is very useful to think in these terms, it is also important to remember that the entire process is fluid;

▼ FIGURE 14.2

The Policymaking Process

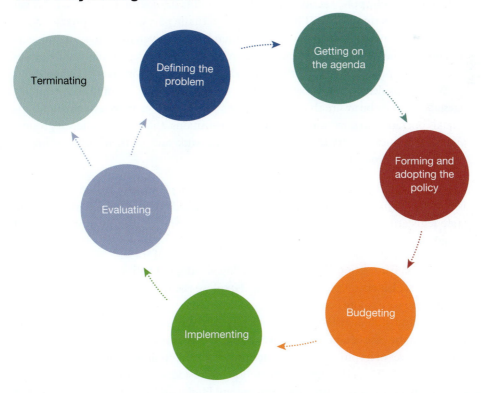

constantly changing; and, above all else, political. Nothing is ever settled, and the American political system is designed to have multiple points of access and contestation throughout.[11]

Step 1: Problem Definition. What may seem like the simplest—and most nonpolitical—part of domestic policymaking may actually be the most significant, the most consequential, and the most contested part of the entire process: defining the problem. Problems point to solutions, opening up specific lines of attack and closing off others. Having one's definition of the problem accepted constitutes a very effective exercise of power in the policy process.

Step 2: Agenda-Setting. Defining a problem is not consequential or powerful if one's ideas do not get discussed or debated. Getting on the policy agenda—the necessarily limited set of issues on which policymakers focus their attention—is crucial for anyone who wants to influence the policymaking process. Getting on the agenda, or keeping an idea off it, is a very effective exercise of political power. The science of getting on the agenda remains, in a sense, somewhat unscientific because the ability to get one's concerns considered depends not only on the merits of the issue but also on the political and economic contexts in which the ideas are offered and on the ways in which the public views the issue, its importance, and the deservingness of those targeted for public policy action. As political scientist John Kingdon queried, "What makes an idea's time come? That question is actually part of a larger puzzle: What makes people in and around government attend, at any given time, to some subjects and not to others?"[12] While trying to get on the domestic agenda may not be a precisely defined process with clear rules, there are some lessons that may be followed.

When considering how ideas do or do not make it onto the national or state policy agenda, we must be aware that people matter, too. **Policy entrepreneurs** are individuals operating in government, academic institutions, think tanks, interest groups, and other venues who try to shape the political agenda and get their solutions implemented on the ground.

Step 3: Policy Formation and Adoption. Getting a policy proposal on the agenda is only the beginning. The policies have to be worked out and passed by either the state legislatures or the federal Congress and signed into law by governors and presidents.

Step 4: The Budgeting Process. Financing an adopted policy is yet another political process. Later in the chapter, we will explore the federal budgeting process in detail when we explore economic policymaking. State governments have to set their budgets, and state legislatures and state executives are important players in this process. In the case of education, however, there is a wrinkle. The federal government uses the power of its purse to push its agendas into other policies generally handled by the states. In 1974, under the administration of President Richard Nixon and during the energy crisis of the time, the Emergency Highway Energy Conservation Act required states to reduce the maximum speed limits on their highways or risk losing federal transportation monies. It is through this financial leverage that the federal government often coerces states to comply with federal policy, especially in areas such as education.

It is by using this financial leverage that the federal government often coerces states to comply with federal policy.

Step 5: Implementation. After being authorized by the relevant federal or state governmental actors, policies have to be implemented, or enacted, in the real world.[13] Once implemented, a public policy may be very different on the ground from the idealized form created in the responsible legislative body or institution.

Step 6: Evaluation. Evaluation—determining if a policy is achieving its stated objectives—is just as consequential as the other stages of the policymaking process and, therefore, just as contested and political. Congress, state legislatures, academic institutions, federal and state courts, and policy entrepreneurs all weigh in on evaluations.

Step 7 (Maybe): Termination. The last step in the policymaking process is one that does not always happen—at least formally—even when there is widespread agreement that a policy is not working. If the political consequences of ending the policy are high, or if the recipients of the "failed" policy are seen as deserving, a policy might endure despite poor evaluations of it.

The authority to formally terminate a policy may reside with Congress or a state legislature. There are, however, other ways in which a policy might be terminated. Courts, especially the Supreme Court, might terminate a policy through the use of judicial review.

American Health Care Policy Has Evolved Significantly since the Great Society

14.2   Discuss the politics of American health care policy.

The federal government involved itself in some areas of health policy in the early decades of the twentieth century, such as instituting inspections of food products and the creation of the Food and Drug Administration (FDA) to monitor food and drug safety. In the 1960s, its involvement grew significantly. President Lyndon Johnson's Great Society program amended the Social Security Act to establish Medicare, which provides health insurance to senior citizens (age sixty-five or older) and the disabled. The various parts of Medicare (some of which are optional and require individual contributions) cover hospitalization, physicians' services, and prescription drugs. Collectively, Social Security and Medicare are massive programs, constituting by far the largest part of federal social welfare spending and much of the federal budget. This is only expected to increase in the coming decades.

The legislation that created Medicare also established the Medicaid program, which covers health services for low-income Americans. While Medicare (along with Social Security) is run by the federal government and supported by federal taxes, Medicaid is jointly funded and administered by the states and the federal government. The idea of national health insurance made it onto the national agenda in the 1970s, with both President Nixon and key Democratic Party leaders proposing competing plans. Political opposition and the Watergate scandal combined to stall any national comprehensive health insurance policies. Incremental tweaks to health care policy continued into the 1990s, when President Bill Clinton tried and failed to achieve national health insurance during his administration.

President Obama Takes on Health Care Reform with the Patient Protection and Affordable Care Act

As Senators Barack Obama (D-IL) and Hillary Clinton (D-NY) squared off in the 2008 Democratic Party presidential nomination season, both agreed on one key point: The nation's health care system needed reforming. As approximately forty-five million Americans were uninsured and millions of others were struggling to pay the costs of care and treatment, both candidates focused on the need to provide affordable access to health care and health insurance for all Americans. Highlighting the connection between the health care crisis and the financial crisis, Obama noted, "This is a cost that now causes bankruptcy in America every thirty seconds. By the end of the year, it could cause 1.5 million Americans to lose their homes."[14]

As both the Senate and the House took up their own health care reform bills in the spring and summer of 2009, Obama, now president, called upon the American people to support his reform proposals and pressure their senators and representatives to do the same. Assisting the president were citizen volunteers from groups such as Organizing for America, who knocked on doors to explain the president's plan and gain support for it.

On November 7, 2009, the Democratic-controlled House of Representatives passed the health care reform bill by a 220–215 vote, with one Republican joining the Democrats. The Senate would prove to be much more complicated. Facing a certain Republican filibuster, the Democrats needed every one of their sixty votes to secure cloture, including liberal Democrats; moderate Democrats; and Bernie Sanders, an independent. Thanks to a series of deals and a lot of horse trading, on Christmas Eve, Senate majority leader Reid had secured the near impossible: sixty filibuster-proof votes in the Senate to pass health care reform, after the longest session of the Senate without a day off since World War I.

Notably, the bill that passed included an individual mandate. This provision was put in the Patient Protection and Affordable Care Act (ACA) to protect the health insurance industry. The act forbade insurance companies from denying coverage or raising premiums for people with preexisting conditions. The companies and their lobbyists argued that the financial strains of this change would force them out of the plans or into bankruptcy. Requiring everyone to have coverage, or face a federal tax penalty for not doing so, was put in to protect companies from having a higher percentage of patients who needed expensive coverage, as otherwise healthy people might just wait until they got sick and *then* apply for coverage, knowing they could not be denied.[15]

President Obama signed the ACA into law in March 2010. With the implementation of most of its key provisions delayed to 2014 or beyond, the ACA resulted in a major overhaul of the provision of health care services in America. See Table 14.1.

▼ TABLE 14.1

Key Provisions of the Affordable Care Act and Related Pieces of Legislation

• A requirement for employers (with more than fifty full-time employees) to provide health care insurance for their employees or pay a penalty
• A requirement for individuals to obtain health care insurance (with some exceptions for religious beliefs or financial hardship) or pay a penalty
• An expansion of Medicaid benefits to more low-income Americans
• The creation of health care exchanges in the states, with federal subsidies, to help individuals and small businesses obtain health insurance
• A requirement for health insurers to allow young adults up to the age of twenty-six on their parents' or guardians' plans
• A prohibition against excluding individuals with preexisting medical conditions in most plans

Efforts to Repeal and Replace the ACA Are Ongoing

The ACA held up against a Republican Congress that opposed the legislation during Obama's second term as well. However, as we explored with the story of Cleveland's school voucher program, legislatures are not the only bodies that can terminate public policies. Courts, especially the Supreme Court, also have that power, so opponents of the president's reforms turned to the judiciary. In 2012, in *National Federation of Independent Business v. Sebelius*, the Court upheld the constitutionality of the individual mandate provision in the law.[16] In 2015, in *King v. Burwell*, the constitutionality of the tax credits in the ACA for federal exchanges as well as those created by the states was also upheld.[17] Reflecting on the Court's decision in *King*, Obama stated that health care reform "has now been woven into the fabric of America."[18]

Having vowed to "repeal and replace" the ACA during his campaign once in office, President Donald Trump went after the law. Though a repeal passed the House, it did so by a narrow margin and faced a tough road in the Senate. Key Republican senators did end up defecting, with Sen. John McCain (R-AZ) casting the decisive vote that ended the possibility for a major legislative repeal.[19]

Although Republicans failed to completely repeal the ACA, they did succeed in making several important changes through the 2017 budget process. Those changes involved a repeal, starting in 2019, of the penalty levied upon those who do not have some sort of health coverage. This effectively repealed the individual mandate; although people were still technically required to have insurance, there was no penalty for noncompliance.[20] Armed with their victory in defanging the individual mandate, conservatives once again turned to the judiciary. In February 2018, twenty Republican state attorneys filed suit in federal court, arguing that the repeal of the mandate rendered all or part of the ACA unconstitutional. Their reasoning was that the Court's determination in *Sebelius* that ACA was constitutional relied upon the existence of the individual mandate. Without the mandate, they argued, the law should fall. For its part, the Trump administration stated that it would not defend the ACA. Democratic state attorneys generally promised that they would. Given, as we have explored, the slow pace of the judicial system, the legal issue is not likely to be resolved soon.

With the House of Representatives switching to Democratic control after the 2018 midterm elections, a major legislative challenge to the ACA was off the table. The Trump administration, however, continued its judicial challenges to the law.

Health Care Is Only One of Many Policies Designed to Protect Americans' Basic Needs

All levels of government are also involved in protecting Americans from poverty, providing access to housing, protecting the environment, and enacting many other areas of domestic policy. Health care policy is only one example of these. **Social insurance programs** are financed by payroll taxes paid by individuals and do not have income-based requirements to receive their benefits. Social Security is one of the most important American social insurance programs.

The Social Security Act of 1935 created a set of programs to support vulnerable groups of Americans. It established unemployment insurance for workers and set up the Old Age Insurance and Old Age Assistance programs, which were later supplemented with disability insurance. In addition, it established Aid to Dependent Children.[21] Social Security was designed to be self-funding so as not to force the government to raise income taxes and further depress the economy. Working people and their employers pay into a fund from which retirees are paid their benefits. Americans do not have individual accounts where the contributions sit until needed. As workers retire, younger generations take their place paying into the program. This was intended to allow the program to run indefinitely, but its ability to be sustained in the twenty-first century—when life spans are significantly longer and birth rates significantly lower than when the program was first enacted—is the subject of much current debate in American politics.

While the Social Security Act created several types of insurance, the term *Social Security* is generally used to refer to old-age insurance, which protects against the loss of income in an individual's later years. The level of benefits received depends upon one's contributions during the working years, or the contributions of one's spouse in the case of survivorship. These programs are often called **entitlement programs**, meaning that if one meets the categorical requirements, such as age or a minimum number of years of payroll contributions, one is entitled to receive the benefits, regardless of income.

While projections vary, the Old-Age, Survivors, and Disability Insurance (OASDI) trust fund—the official name for the reserves underlying Social Security—will be out of money at some point in the coming decades. Fixing this deficit is not just a problem of mathematics; it is also a problem of politics. Reducing benefits to current recipients would produce a massive backlash from a large group of politically active Americans who would mobilize to ensure the program continues with current benefit levels. For this reason, Social Security is often called the "third rail" of American politics, so named for the rail in many subway systems that carries electricity to the trains and would likely cause death if touched. Raising the payroll tax on current workers is another possibility, though, again, one with significant political risk for lawmakers if enacted.

Need-Based Public Assistance Programs Are Tied to Incomes. Unlike entitlement programs such as Social Security and Medicare, which are funded through payroll taxes and do not require a demonstration of need (beyond meeting certain categorical requirements such as age or disability), another major category of social welfare programs requires that individuals demonstrate specific need. As such, they are called **need-based assistance** programs, and they involve a means test that is usually based on income. In assessing who qualifies for need-based assistance, the federal government often employs a concept called the poverty line, which defines an income below which a family is considered poor. In 2020, the federally defined poverty threshold for a family of four was an annual family income of $26,200.[22] Need-based social welfare policies are funded through federal and/or state tax revenues rather than payroll taxes.

In addition to covering health services for low-income Americans, the federal government provides other forms of need-based assistance. Aid to Families with Dependent Children (AFDC) was created in the 1930s to help families support their children in the event that a parent was deceased, disabled, unable to work, or out of work. In the decades following, AFDC was expanded to aid parents as well, increasing the number of covered individuals as well as the cost of the program. AFDC was sometimes accused of cultivating dependency among the families receiving it and creating generations of families that received its benefits.

With the Personal Responsibility and Work Opportunity Reconciliation Act of 1996 (PRWORA), Democratic president Bill Clinton brought the principles of devolution to social welfare programs. The outlines of PRWORA had been part of the Republican Party's "Contract with America," a set of campaign promises made during the congressional elections of 1994, in which Republicans took control of both the House and the Senate.[23] PRWORA replaced AFDC with Temporary Assistance for Needy Families (TANF), which placed time limits on receipt of welfare assistance and added work requirements for beneficiaries.

The Supplemental Nutrition Assistance Program (SNAP), formerly called the Food Stamp Program, assists the poor in meeting their needs for food. The Earned Income Tax Credit (EITC) provides a tax credit to the working poor, one that in many cases results in these Americans receiving a larger refund than the amount of federal income taxes that have been deducted from their paychecks.

Housing Policy Focuses on Affordability and Access.

Many efforts to secure adequate housing for Americans occur primarily at the state and local levels. The federal government, however, has involved itself in housing policy in several ways. One of President Roosevelt's New Deal programs was the establishment of the Federal Housing Administration (FHA) in 1934, tasked with combating widespread foreclosures as a result of the Great Depression. By regulating interest rates and home mortgage terms, the FHA sought to make homeownership more attainable. It also undertook programs to increase the availability of affordable rental units.

In 1965, the FHA was folded into the Department of Housing and Urban Development (HUD). The department administers programs to combat homelessness, oversees programs to provide housing vouchers for low-income Americans (often called Section 8 vouchers), and enforces federal laws against discrimination in housing based on racial and ethnic identity, religion, national origin, sex, disability, and family status. HUD also provides assistance in financing home mortgages.

Environmental Policy Has Long Focused on Cleaning and Protecting the Country's Natural Resources.

Another major area of federal domestic policy involves efforts to clean up and protect the environment. While we have focused on education and health policy in depth in this chapter, it is important to note that the development of and debates surrounding American environmental policy also connect to the larger questions with which we have dealt in this chapter and in this book.

Like other areas of domestic policy, American environmental policy has changed along with the evolution of American federalism. In the era of dual federalism, states took primary responsibility, with a focus on land preservation and conservation. By the turn of the twentieth century, most states had created conservation commissions, charged with conducting inventories of land resources and setting policies to conserve these areas. In 1908, President Theodore Roosevelt appointed the National Conservation Commission, charged with a purpose similar to that of the state organizations, though with little coordination between the federal and state commissions.

With the rise of cooperative federalism, the federal-state relationship in environmental policy changed dramatically. Franklin Roosevelt's New Deal economic reconstruction programs provided conservation-related jobs for large numbers of unemployed Americans. In 1935, Congress created the Soil Conservation Service, increasing federal and state cooperation in response to the destruction of the Dust

Bowl that had contributed to the Great Depression (see Chapter 3). The Clean Air Act (1963), passed under the administration of Lyndon Johnson, sought to address the problem of air pollution.[24] While the concern was not new, the Clean Air Act was notable in that the federal government established national standards and used the leverage of federal money to ensure state compliance.

The Environmental Protection Agency (EPA), established in 1970 during the administration of Richard Nixon, works in coordination with state, tribal, and local governments to enforce federal laws governing environmental standards, monitor pollution and cleanup efforts, and oversee energy conservation measures. Among the federal laws that the EPA is tasked to enforce are the Clean Air Act, the Water Quality Act, and the Endangered Species Act (all of which have had subsequent extensions). While the EPA is not an official cabinet department, the EPA administrator is typically given cabinet-level status.

Debates over how best to address the environmental challenges of the twenty-first century often revolve around questions of the proper role of government and private markets. Tradable discharge permits (TDPs), for example, are designed to address pollution by creating a market for pollution rights. As unused permits can be bought or sold, firms have an incentive to reduce pollution for economic gain. Proponents of market-based solutions to domestic policy problems argue that devices such as TDPs can address environmental challenges more efficiently than government-based oversight and control.

Finally, environmental policy also connects to broader questions about civil rights and liberties in America. We have already explored one example of this in the Standing Rock protests (see Chapter 1). Many of the protesters were motivated, in part, by concerns over land use and the environmental risks of the Keystone oil pipeline. However, the interaction between the protesters and law enforcement officials also raises serious questions about the degree to which rights surrounding evidence gathering, arrest, and detention are fully protected today.

Fiscal Policy Guides the Economy and Responds to Crises

14.3 Understand the approaches to and goals of fiscal policy in the United States.

Managing the nation's economy is not an exact science; there are too many variables at play to know for sure what all of the consequences of any one economic policy decision or set of decisions will be. In spite of these uncertainties, federal authorities can and do act to produce desirable economic outcomes. One major set of governmental activities is called fiscal policy. Through **fiscal policy**, the government attempts to reduce unemployment, support economic activity, and stabilize the economy by using policies of taxation and spending. In the section that follows, we will look at some of the foundational ideas behind the economic decision making that takes place and ask what role government should play in the economy.

The Government Monitors the Health of the Economy

In guiding the nation's fiscal policy, one of the main roles the federal government plays is to monitor the health of the American economy. It collects and distributes data about that health and uses this information to guide future decisions in fiscal policy. To do this, federal fiscal policymakers often rely on a few key indicators.

One of these indicators is the **gross domestic product (GDP)**, which attempts to measure the total value of goods and services produced by American economic activity. A decline or stagnation of the nation's GDP indicates that the country's economy is not firing on all cylinders and could be slipping into an **economic recession**, in which American economic activity slows down. This is not good for American workers—or for their elected representatives should voters place the blame for the recession upon their shoulders.

Economists also focus on the nation's **unemployment rate** to gauge the health of American businesses. A rise in the unemployment rate indicates a private sector that is cutting back, not hiring, or laying off workers based on its own calculations about the health of the economy going forward. A third key indicator of the health of the American economy is the rate of **inflation**, or the rise in the prices of goods and services purchased by individuals. A high rate of inflation, especially if not accompanied by an equal increase in wages, makes American workers poorer, with all the negative electoral consequences for government officials produced by this development. One key measure of inflation is the **consumer price index (CPI)**. The CPI affects not only voters' decisions; many programs that involve mandatory spending, such as Social Security payments, are tied to calculations of the nation's CPI.

The Federal Government Sets the National Budget

Setting the national budget is always contentious, and the modern process almost always misses its own deadlines, with stopgap measures passed along the way until the political parties can reach some sort of agreement.

In setting the national budget, the federal government operates in some ways like an American household, assessing money coming in and money going out. The Budget and Accounting Act of 1921 established the basis of modern federal budgeting processes, particularly with its incorporation of the president as a key part of the process. It also established the **Office of Management and Budget (OMB)** to assist the president in setting national spending priorities. As with other kinds of lawmaking we have covered in this book, setting the federal budget occurs in several stages.

Step 1: The President Proposes a Budget. The Congressional Budget and Impoundment Control Act of 1974, amended since its passage, modified the process of setting the federal budget, requiring that the president's proposed budget be reviewed by congressional committees. The committees are assisted by advice and research from the **Congressional Budget Office (CBO)**. The federal government's fiscal year begins in October, and the expectation is that a president will submit a proposed budget to Congress in February of that year. Formally, the president's proposal carries no constitutional or legal weight, but it does carry a great deal of political weight. The staff of the Council of Economic Advisers (CEA) also assist the president by providing economic analysis and long-range trend forecasting.

The majority of spending in any fiscal year's federal budget, however, has already been allocated or promised. Entitlement programs, such as Social Security, Medicaid, and Medicare, consume the bulk of yearly federal spending. As this spending is "locked in," it is referred to as **mandatory spending**. The actual amount available for **discretionary spending**—spending for programs and policies at the discretion of Congress and the president—constitutes a much smaller slice of the pie (see Figure 14.3).

Step 2: Congress Acts. In response to a president's proposals, Congress is expected to produce a **budget resolution** that provides broad outlines for federal spending. The real action, however, happens in the House and Senate Appropriations Committees, which set the budgets for departments, agencies, and bureaus. These committees then submit budget resolutions that are passed by Congress and sent to the president for approval.

▼ FIGURE 14.3

Revenues, Mandatory Spending, and Discretionary Spending in the President's Proposed Budget, Fiscal Year 2020–2021

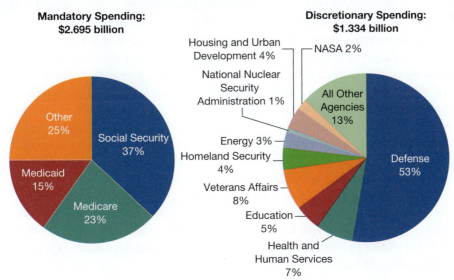

Source: Office of Management and Budget, "Budget of the U.S. Government," accessed June 14, 2020, https://www.whitehouse.gov/wp-content/uploads/2020/02/budget_fy21.pdf. Percentages may not add up to one hundred due to rounding. Amounts are estimated prior to the COVID-19 crisis.

The budgeting process establishes both the amount of money with which the national government has to work and the ways in which that money is allocated. It also sends a signal to other nations and their economic policymakers as well as the international financial markets about the soundness of American economic policy.

Uncharted Waters: American Economic Policy in Response to COVID-19

When economists describe sudden and disruptive changes to economies, they do so in terms of shocks, two kinds. A **supply shock** is an external event or occurrence that "reduces the economy's capacity to produce goods and services, at given prices."[25] A **demand shock** results in a sudden reduction in "consumers' ability or willingness to purchase goods and services, at given prices."[26] Suddenly falling supply and production cause high unemployment, lost wages, and product shortages—that is, if people can still afford to buy them. Suddenly falling demand pressures companies' bottom lines, which in turn stresses the nation's financial system, as defaults spread from bills that can no longer be paid. Either of these shocks can present an economy and its policymakers with tremendous problems.

COVID-19 was both. The quotes in *each* definition just given, in fact, come from the St. Louis Federal Reserve in May 2020, when it described the likely economic impacts of the pandemic. The report's authors concluded that "most economists would agree that the pandemic combines aspects of both supply and demand shocks."[27]

It started in China, at the points of origin in many of the supply chains that constitute the global industrial and consumer machine. In early 2020, with outbreaks spreading to major urban centers beyond Wuhan—the site of the initial outbreak—and the nation's health care system in danger of collapse, Chinese authorities closed down the factories that supply much of the world. Even if they were operating, workers in China were unable to get to the factories, with national travel restrictions in place, leaving millions of rural Chinese citizens unable to return to the cities for work after the Chinese New Year holiday.

Just as China was emerging from the worst of its initial outbreak—making tentative, though risky, steps to restart production—global demand collapsed. In the United States and across the world, stay-at-home orders and concerns about the virus instantly reshaped consumers' spending patterns. Furloughed, laid off, or still employed but worried about their future economic prospects, consumers cut back. There were also far fewer goods and services to buy. Restaurants, hotels, casinos, shopping malls, airlines, ride services, and many other businesses were operating at a fraction of their pre-virus capacity and often with very different business practices, if they were open at all.

One thing there was no shortage of was hockey sticks—not the kind used in sports, though those were likely plentiful with ice arenas closed down, but the kinds of hockey sticks that one observes in charts—and not in a good way. Economic indicators may go up or down over time, or meander around. Those movements convey important information about how an economy is doing, even when they don't change much. Sometimes, however, there is a break in trend so notable that it looks like a hockey stick on an economic chart. That is what the economic indicators were all doing in the spring of 2020. Unemployment rates were already showing signs of real concern—even with the limited data available at the time—and were projected to reach levels not seen since the Great Depression (see Figure 14.4). GDP was collapsing, and the projections equally dire (see Figure 14.5). How *long* this would go on—whether this was a long-term cataclysmic event or a deep but short challenge—was unknown. To tackle these challenges in 2020, national policymakers brought out seemingly every fiscal tool they possessed.

▼ FIGURE 14.4

Unemployment Rates Spike with COVID-19

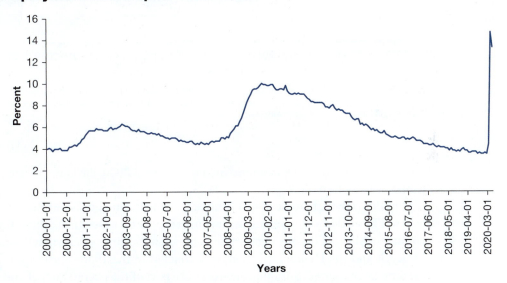

Source: Data from Federal Reserve Bank of St. Louis, "Unemployment Rate," May 2020, https://fred.stlouisfed.org/series/UNRATE.

Congress Passes Coronavirus Relief and Puts It on the National Tab. Another tool the federal government possesses is **fiscal stimulus**—legislative action to stimulate an economy that is underperforming. Stimulus measures may include reducing taxes, increasing federal spending on projects (thus creating new jobs), or even making direct cash payments to individuals or businesses. Prior to 2020, the idea of the federal government making direct cash payments to individuals or businesses broadly was not a mainstream view, though other democracies already

GDP Falls Sharply, and the Estimates Are Worse

Percent Change in Real GDP, Quarterly

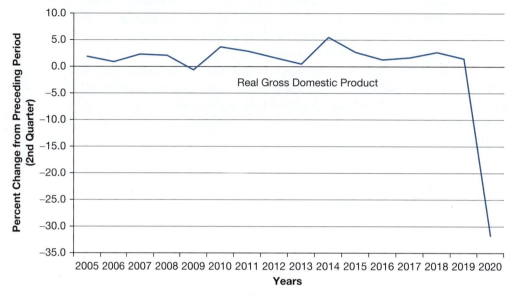

Source: Data from Federal Reserve Bank of St. Louis, "Gross Domestic Product," May 28, 2020, https://fred.stlouisfed.org/series/ A191RL1Q225SBEA. Estimates for 2020 Q2 are from Center for Quantitative Research, "GDPNow," June 9, 2020, Federal Reserve Bank of St. Louis, https://www.frbatlanta.org/cqer/research/gdpnow.

had variants of individual guaranteed income. By April 2020, the United States had (temporarily) done both.

Stimulus is thought to be more effective to combat demand shocks than supply shocks. The goal is to get money in consumers' pockets to rev the nation's financial engine. Many of the most important depression-fighting policies that President Roosevelt and the Democratic Congress enacted in the 1930s consisted of fiscal stimulus measures. Stimulus measures are part of the overall budget and can impact the ratio between money coming into the federal government and money going out.

While partisan politics in the election year of 2020 were as heated as ever, each member knew that they or their party would pay a hefty price in November if they seemed to be putting politics ahead of the crisis. A lot of money, everyone knew, was about to be spent.

The first major legislative response by Congress was the Coronavirus Preparedness and Response Supplemental Appropriations Act, which President Trump signed into law on March 6, 2020.[28] It allocated federal funds to the health care sector and federal bureaucracies involved in health, disease prevention, and vaccination policy. The CBO estimated its total cost over the next ten years at $8 billion, all in new discretionary outlays.[29] On March 18, the Families First Coronavirus Response Act (FFCRA) followed.[30] It provided funding for health care services and coronavirus testing and for fourteen-day paid leave for American workers. The CBO put the total cost of new expenditures and lost tax receipts at $192 billion.[31]

U.S. Federal Reserve chairman Jerome Powell speaks during a news conference on March 21, 2018, in Washington, DC. The Federal Reserve has been a key player in the federal loan programs intended to shore up American businesses during the coronavirus pandemic.

Sarah Silbiger/Bloomberg/Getty Images

The most expensive response by Congress was the Coronavirus Aid, Relief, and Economic Security (CARES) Act, signed into law by President Trump on March 27.[32] The CARES Act established a paycheck protection program to encourage firms to retain employees, authorized funds for small business loans, increased and extended unemployment benefits, and deferred payroll taxes. It also provided a refundable tax credit, or rebate, of $1,200 for individuals and $500 for each dependent child (with exclusions for students in colleges and universities).

The law also included provisions for student debt relief, though only temporarily. Student loan payments were paused until September 30, 2020. Interest accrual on loans was suspended, and funds were allocated to colleges and universities to make emergency grants to students on a financial-need basis. These stimulus measures, however, applied only to federally guaranteed student loans. The estimated cost for the CARES Act in total—including both expenditures and lost tax receipts—was $1.7 trillion.[33]

Finally, the Paycheck Protection Program and Health Care Enhancement Act (PPPHCEA) became law on April 24.[34] It added to the funds for the paycheck protection loan program in the CARES Act as well as to funds for hospitals and virus testing. Its estimated cost to the American taxpayer was $483 billion.[35]

In less than two months, Congress had committed an estimated $2.4 trillion of taxpayer money to counter the pandemic's effects on the economy. As Congress and the president pushed for and argued over specific stimulus measures during the rest of

2020, the final price tag was unknown. It was not even clear how many more stimulus bills would ultimately be passed in response to COVID-19.

Taxation, Deficits, and Debts Are All Part of the National Checkbook. The federal government not only spends but also taxes its citizens to pay for its spending. Aside from a brief period during the Civil War, individual incomes were not taxed until 1913 after the ratification of the Sixteenth Amendment, which instituted a national tax on the incomes of Americans. But how does the government set the national income tax rates? This has always been a politically charged issue. The debate has been about both the rates themselves and income tax deductions and exemptions. The result has been a vast and complicated system of income tax law.

Federal taxation policies, as vexing as they may be to individual taxpayers, determine the amount of money that the federal government takes in to pay for its fiscal policies. If the federal government takes in more money than it spends, then it runs a **budget surplus**. If not, it runs a **budget deficit**, forcing it to borrow from expected tax revenues and the economic activity that will produce these projected revenues (see Figure 14.6).

As any borrower knows, it is not only the money that one borrows in a given year that matters to one's financial health. It is the total amount of debt owed. In the case of the federal government, the **national debt** continues to grow.

▼ FIGURE 14.6

Federal Budget Deficits, Historical and Projected

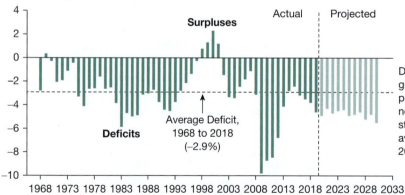

Percentage of Gross Domestic Product

Deficits as a percentage of gross domestic product are projected to increase over the next few years and then largely stabilize. They exceed their 50-year average throughout the 2018–2028 period.

Source: Congressional Budget Office, "An Update to the Budget and Economic Outlook: 2018 to 2028," Figure 4.1: Total Deficits or Surpluses, April 2018, https://www.cbo.gov/system/files/115th-congress-2017-2018/reports/53651-outlook.pdf; Congressional Budget Office, "Budget and Economic Data: 10-Year Budget Projections," March 2020, https://www.cbo.gov/about/products/budget-economic-data#3.

Note: These data are from projections as of March 6, 2020.

PRACTICING POLITICAL SCIENCE

DID THE FEDERAL RESERVE JUST CALL IN THE HELICOPTERS?

While the federal government plays a critical role in guiding and supporting the American economy, it does not do so on its own. The decisions of corporations and other national governments may have their own effects on the nation's economic performance. Another major player is the board of governors of the **Federal Reserve System**, often referred to as "the Fed." The system consists of a seven-member panel of governors, twelve regional Federal Reserve banks, and six thousand member banks. The members of the board of governors are appointed by the president and confirmed by the Senate. They serve fourteen-year nonrenewable terms, except for the chair, who serves for a four-year renewable term. The governors are not removable except for cause so that the Fed can maintain a degree of independence from economic influence.

The Fed is the most important player in charting national **monetary policy**, which regulates the amount of money in the economy (in circulation and in the deposits) and influences **interest rates**, the rates paid to borrow money. The system's primary tools involve buying and selling Treasury securities—through which the federal government borrows money—regulating the amount of deposits that banks must keep as reserves and setting the interest rate at which banks can borrow money from the Fed. By using these three tools, the Fed also influences other interest rates in the economy, since banks and credit card companies usually adjust the rates they charge their own customers in response to the actions of the Fed.

In a speech in November 2002, Ben Bernanke, then chair of the Federal Reserve, discussed the powers of monetary policy in the face of the kind of crushing deflation that gripped the United States during the Great Depression.[36] Bernanke suggested the possibility that in an extreme economic crisis, the Federal Reserve, operating in coordination with the federal government, could print and loan to the government enough money to finance a massive tax cut and economic stimulus. Bernanke was drawing from a 1969 essay published by economist Milton Friedman, in which Friedman suggested that if a helicopter flew over a community and dropped $1,000 in bills from the sky, and individuals were sure that it would be a one-off event, then the unconventional policy might result in fiscal stimulus.[37]

Bernanke's reference, in that speech and in later Federal Reserve responses to the financial crisis that threatened the nation in 2008, drew many sharp rebuttals in images, speeches, and text. In some media circles, he was called "Helicopter Ben."

There are many concerns with the idea of helicopter money. First, all aggressive intervention in the economy by the Federal Reserve can distort interest rates, which reflect the "price" of borrowing money. It might spark bubbles, as that money rushes into the next hot new investment.

(Continued)

(Continued)

Expansion of the Fed's Balance Sheet

Total Federal Reserve Assets (Quarterly)

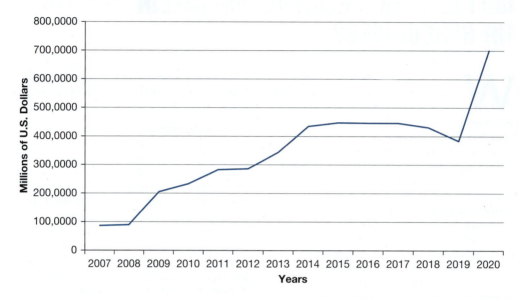

Source: Data from Federal Reserve Bank of St. Louis, "Total Assets," *Board of Governors of the Federal Reserve System*, June 11, 2020, https://fred.stlouisfed.org/series/WALCL#0.

Figure 14.7 shows the total assets of the Federal Reserve as of June of each year. When the Fed expands its assets, it may do so by (digitally) printing the money to buy them. Therefore, significant expansions of the balance sheet might also lead to significant inflation. The first significant jump happened in response to the 2008 financial crisis, and there was (and is) much hand-wringing over that amount. That, however, has been overshadowed by recent asset purchases, especially to help the U.S. government pay for its coronavirus stimulus measures.

The helicopters may not have arrived, but they appear to be warming up at least.

••

WHƏT Do You Think?

What was (and is) troubling to some was that the Federal Reserve is not actually part of the federal government, though it is subject to governmental oversight and control of its appointments. What might you do if a national policy to distribute $10,000 to every American was implemented? What longer-term effects of this action might you anticipate?

And that was before COVID-19. When numbers came in for the initial effects of the pandemic and the government's response to it on the national checkbook, they were concerning to say the least. The budget deficit for May 2020—for that one month alone—came in at $424 billion, more than double that of May 2019.[38] The nation, and the world, had been living with the consequences of the pandemic for months; however, the national economic consequences were only beginning to be felt.

U.S. Foreign Policy Has Changed with the Nation's Place in Global Affairs

14.4 Summarize the historical development of America's involvement in international affairs.

Just as the United States has changed since its founding, so has its relationship to the rest of the world. And just as the national government has grown tremendously, especially in the twentieth century, so have the various parts of the foreign policy decision-making apparatus.

America Was Isolationist for Much of Its History

The first cabinet position established to assist President George Washington in the nation's first administration was that of the secretary of state. In addition to keeping the Great Seal of the United States and overseeing the U.S. Mint, which produced the nation's currency, Thomas Jefferson, the first person to fill the post, spent much of his time overseeing foreign affairs. Jefferson recommended the creation of a corps of ambassadors to manage and promote America's economic interests as well as diplomatic relations with other nations. Congress agreed and paid for the employment of these ambassadors.

In his Farewell Address to the nation, after declining to run for a third presidential term, Washington presented a more muted perspective of American influence: "The great rule of conduct for us in regard to foreign nations is in extending our commercial relations, to have with them as little political connection as possible."[39] Washington's admonishments pointed in many ways to a policy of **isolationism**, in which a nation attempts to stay out of foreign entanglements.

The fact is that the United States has never been a truly isolationist nation, even in its early decades. In 1803, as president, in spite of his worries about the strength of the national government, Jefferson oversaw the successful purchase of the Louisiana Territory from Napoleon Bonaparte of France. This transaction nearly doubled the size of the nation in one $15 million deal.[40] During his administration, Jefferson also expanded and employed the U.S. Navy to Tripoli, part of the Barbary States of North Africa at the time and now part of Libya, to protect American commerce and, eventually, to secure the release of American sailors from the ship *Philadelphia*.[41]

American Influence in the Western Hemisphere Grew in the Nineteenth Century

In 1812, the nation again went to war with Great Britain, partly over trade issues. In 1823, President James Monroe announced what is known as the **Monroe Doctrine**, a policy that asserted American interests in and primacy over actions in the Western Hemisphere. President Theodore Roosevelt expanded upon the Monroe Doctrine in 1904 by issuing the **Roosevelt Corollary**, which asserted that the United States was the guarantor of political, military, and economic stability in Latin America and the Caribbean. The corollary promised the use of American armed forces to back up its provisions.

During the nineteenth century and the early years of the twentieth century, much of American interest focused not on Europe but on securing control over territory west to the Pacific Ocean—a process that was devastating to the indigenous peoples on those lands. Then the government focused on establishing the nation as the dominant power in the Western Hemisphere and securing American economic and military interests at home and abroad. With regard to the many military conflicts in Europe and its colonies, America adopted an isolationist policy until the twentieth century.

The Twentieth and Twenty-First Centuries Have Been Defined by Four Global Wars

The patterns of global involvement that had dominated America's approach for more than a century—defined by economic involvement globally but a lack of military involvement outside the Western Hemisphere—began to change in the twentieth century. Four wars—two "hot," one "cold," and one whose boundaries are still being defined—served as the catalysts for these changes, which redefined not only America's role in the world but the nation itself.

Though the United States had chosen to actively engage with other nations to protect its interests (especially in the Western Hemisphere), arguments for isolationism still shaped much of its foreign policy. In the twentieth century, however, the nation began to adopt a foreign policy defined much more by **internationalism**, an approach that emphasizes closer contact and cooperation between nations.

The first of the four wars, World War I, established the United States as a major player in global economic and military affairs. The second, World War

II, which came after a period in which America had once again withdrawn to its own hemisphere, established the nation as a military and economic superpower. The third, the Cold War, locked America into an ideological, economic, diplomatic, and occasionally military conflict with the other global superpower, the Soviet Union. The fourth, the so-called war on terror, is still being fought today. This conflict is challenging the very notion of what a national boundary is and raising questions of what the limits should be on the use of American military force.

World War I Established America as a Major Global Player. American intervention in World War I (1914–1918) was initially opposed by large numbers of citizens who saw it as a conflict between European monarchies and autocratic governments that did not, and should not, involve the United States. Eventually, after helping convince the people through the intentional use of political propaganda, America entered the war in 1917 and allied with France and Great Britain against Germany and the Austro-Hungarian Empire. Many other nations were involved in the global conflict, including Russia and Japan on the Allied side and the Ottoman Empire (which included the modern-day nation of Turkey) on the side of the Central Powers of Germany and the Austro-Hungarian Empire. It was the most global and destructive war in human history to that point; however, it would not be the last, or the most horrific.

The war—and the Allies' victory—changed the global map, the global balance of power, and the international system in a major way. The United States was established as a global military and economic power. American involvement had major effects at home as restrictions on civil liberties in the name of national security (see Chapter 4) were put in place—restrictions that had not been seen to such an extent since the actions of President Abraham Lincoln during the Civil War (see Chapter 11).

World War II Established America as a Superpower. World War II (1939–1945) surpassed World War I as the largest and most destructive war in human history. The deaths in World War II have never been accurately tallied, especially in the Soviet Union. Civilian deaths were almost certainly far greater than those of combat personnel. Sixty million people is often cited as an estimate of the war's final global toll.

Many of the seeds of World War II were sown by the consequences of World War I. These included the failure of President Woodrow Wilson's concept of a cooperative and transnational global power structure, punitive treatment of Germany by the Allies following victory, economic chaos and hyperinflation in Germany and Austria, and the rise of Adolf Hitler in Germany. As in World War I, the list of participants in World War II was long. Primarily, however, it pitted the Allies (Great Britain; the United States; the Soviet Union; and, until

A man stands amid the ruins of Hiroshima, Japan. The United States dropped the world's first atomic bomb on that city on August 6, 1945, at the end of World War II, killing an estimated seventy thousand people instantly and completely destroying the city. Three days later, the United States dropped a second bomb on Nagasaki. Many thousands more died over the following years due to radiation; the total number of the victims is thought to be approximately 340,000.

it was occupied by Germany, France) against the Axis powers (Germany, Japan, and Italy).[42]

Following grinding island campaigns in the Pacific, the firebombing of cities in Germany and Japan (in which hundreds of thousands of civilians were incinerated), and a nearly unimaginably horrific block-to-block battle in Berlin, the war finally ended with two atomic bombs dropped on Japan by the United States in August 1945—the first on Hiroshima, the second on Nagasaki. World War II had ended, the atomic age had begun, and America had emerged as the world's first **superpower**. For a time, the American economy produced as much industrial output as the rest of the world combined.[43]

The Cold War Involved America and the Soviet Union in Many Regional Conflicts.

Following World War II, two of the victorious allied nations, the United States and the Soviet Union, became ideological, economic, and military adversaries.[44] The world had become bipolar. In the words of former British prime minister Winston Churchill, "From Stettin in the Baltic to Trieste in the Adriatic an iron curtain has descended across the continent. . . . The safety of the world, ladies and gentlemen, requires a unity in Europe, from which no nation should be permanently outcast."[45] On the Western side of this curtain were America and its allies. On the Eastern side, the Soviet Union and its client states dominated, having formed the Warsaw Pact in 1955 in response to the creation of the North Atlantic Treaty Organization (NATO). The possibility of tanks rolling across the iron curtain was very real, as was the threat of nuclear confrontation.

Neither superpower engaged in all-out war against the other in the era of nuclear weapons, though both sponsored governments and rebels in **proxy wars** across the globe in order to undercut the other's influence and power. Rather than fight each other directly, the United States and Soviet Union supported competing factions in places such as Southeast Asia, Africa, and Central America. One disputed area of influence during the war was Cuba, and in 1962 the superpowers nearly went to war over the deployment of Soviet nuclear ballistic missiles in that country. This incident is known as the Cuban missile crisis.

Although the scare of the crisis did lead to efforts between the United States and the Soviet Union to increase dialogue and negotiate limits on nuclear weapons, conflicts continued to erupt, most notably in Vietnam in the 1960s and 1970s. In this clash, East and West battled for ideological supremacy in Southeast Asia, with communist North Vietnam pitted against capitalist and American-supported South Vietnam. Though the Vietnam conflict was not a war formally declared by Congress, it was a major one. Roughly sixty thousand American service personnel were killed, as were more than a million North and South Vietnamese soldiers and millions of civilians in Southeast Asia, either during the war or in the chaos that followed it.

Even after the withdrawal of American forces from South Vietnam in 1973 and the official conclusion of hostilities in 1975, when the United States withdrew and South Vietnam fell to the North, the superpower conflict continued to flare up, though not on the same scale. In the 1980s, President Ronald Reagan put into effect what is known as the **Reagan Doctrine**, which offered American assistance to anticommunist groups, most notably in Nicaragua and Afghanistan. This assistance included military training and weaponry. Citizens in both nations suffered the effects of the conflicts that were fueled and supported by the distant superpowers. In particular, American assistance in the resistance of Afghanis to Soviet occupation in Afghanistan had repercussions that continue today. The Afghani mujahideen, whom America armed most effectively with shoulder-fired missiles that decimated Soviet helicopters, successfully expelled the Soviet military from their nation. Years later, however, some of the mujahideen's former members and leaders, along with new recruits, turned their anger toward the United States and helped plan the 9/11 terrorist attacks.

The United States Adopts a Policy of Containment toward Soviet Expansion.

The goal of these proxy wars and American military policy became one of **containment**, or the restriction of the expansion of Soviet ideological and military influence, using military force if necessary.

Part of America's containment strategy was to rebuild Western Europe as a bulwark against Soviet expansion into the parts of Germany and the rest of Western Europe that the United States, Great Britain, and the Soviet Union had agreed would remain under Western control. A key tool in this policy was the **Marshall Plan**, named after Secretary of State George Marshall, who had been instrumental in mobilizing and organizing American economic and military output during World War II. The plan involved loans and aid to the devastated nations of Western Europe and established organizations of economic cooperation that would eventually lead to the modern **European Union (EU)**.

The American response to threats of Soviet expansion in Western Europe were not just economic; they were also diplomatic, including efforts within multinational institutions, such as the **United Nations**, to gather other countries in support of

Soviet containment. These efforts involved military commitments. In 1949, the North Atlantic Treaty was signed, creating NATO, a mutual defense pact in which member nations agree to "settle any international dispute in which they may be involved by peaceful means in such a manner that international peace and security and justice are not endangered, and to refrain in their international relations from the threat or use of force in any manner inconsistent with the purposes of the United Nations."[46]

The Cold War was a very real and major conflict in which each superpower used its economic, political, and military might to influence nations across the globe.

The Collapse of the Soviet Union Leaves the United States as the World's Only Superpower.

The Cold War ended with the collapse and disintegration of the Soviet Union in 1991. What had been a bipolar world, with two major powers shaping the political, military, and economic landscape of the globe, suddenly became a unipolar one, in which the United States stood alone as the world's unquestioned military and economic superpower.

While the nuclear arsenals of the Cold War posed an existential threat to the planet, its end brought new challenges to nuclear security. **Nuclear proliferation**—the spread of nuclear weapons or capability to other nations or nonstate actors—presents new challenges in the more fluid multipolar global political environment. The Treaty on the Non-Proliferation of Nuclear Weapons, which came into force in 1970, restricted nuclear weapons capability to five nations: the United States, Russia, the United Kingdom, France, and China. The treaty currently has 191 signatory nations; however, other nations are known or thought to be nuclear capable states, including India, Pakistan, Israel (which maintains official ambiguity), and North Korea. In 2015, Iran reached an agreement with world powers, including the United States, to restrict nuclear research and open up facilities for inspections. The Joint Comprehensive Plan of Action (JCPOA) lifted economic sanctions on Iran, which had placed a significant strain on the Iranian economy and people. In 2018, President Trump withdrew the United States from the JCPOA, citing concerns about verifiability under the accord.

The possibility that terrorist organizations might attain nuclear weapons or use nuclear material in conventional explosives remains one of the key threats to international security today.

World War II and the Cold War that followed did not just change America's relationship with other nations; they changed America itself. These two wars resulted in a major expansion of American military, political, and diplomatic engagement across the globe in order to counter the threat of Soviet power whenever possible. They also resulted in a massive expansion of the American military and intelligence-gathering bureaucracy.

The War on Terror Reshapes the Middle East.

The fourth war, the global war on terror, changed things yet again. This conflict drew many nations, including the United States and its allies and Russia and its partners and allies, into the cauldron of civil war in the Middle East and North Africa in a complex and contentious way.

Terrorism was not invented in the twenty-first century. The term refers to the use of extreme and inhumane violence to achieve *political* ends. It is fundamentally a political tool. World War I had some, though not all, of its roots in terrorism. Members of the Black Hand, a secret military society in Serbia, used terrorism to challenge the dominance of the Austro-Hungarian Empire in the Balkans. Their actions helped to set the world on fire and kill the dreams of a united, prosperous, and peaceful global future.

On September 11, 2001, members of the terrorist organization al-Qaeda, under the leadership of Osama bin Laden, hijacked four U.S. commercial aircraft. They crashed two of these planes into the Twin Towers of the

An unidentified New York City firefighter walks away from lower Manhattan after the collapse of the Twin Towers on September 11, 2001. Al-Qaeda terrorists attacked the World Trade Center and the Pentagon using commercial airliners as missiles. George W. Bush called for a war on terrorism in the aftermath of the attacks.
Anthony Correia/Getty Images

World Trade Center in New York City; both towers collapsed shortly afterward. Another plane crashed into the Pentagon in Washington, DC. The fourth crashed in Pennsylvania following a struggle between the hijackers and a group of passengers. Nearly three thousand people died, including over four hundred firefighters, law enforcement officers, and paramedics responding to the attacks on the World Trade Center.

The impact of these attacks was immense and far-reaching. The administration of President George W. Bush declared a war on terrorism and, with congressional authorization, brought American military power to bear. In 2001, Bush sent forces into combat in Afghanistan, the country from which Osama bin Laden had operated, planned, and recruited individuals for the terrorist attacks.

In 2003, the United States invaded Iraq. Though Saddam Hussein's autocratic regime proved not to have been a part of the 9/11 attacks, Bush named the nation as part of an "axis of evil" (along with Iran and North Korea), the defeat of which he argued was necessary to ensure the security of the United States. In a speech at West Point in 2002, Bush articulated a theory of **preemptive war**, in which the United States would use its military might to challenge adversaries before they launched attacks upon the nation or harbored those who might do so.[47]

Bush's decision to move against Iraq in 2003 without a formal declaration of war—but with congressional authorization—remains one of the most controversial and consequential choices in foreign policy in the nation's history. Militarily, the battle was

Iraqi security forces and other allies gather next to a mural depicting the emblem of the Islamic State of Iraq and Syria (ISIS) outside one of the presidential palaces in Tikrit on April 1, 2015. ISIS rose to power during the instability in Iraq and the region as a whole after the American invasion.

AHMAD AL-RUBAYE/AFP/Getty Images

quick and successful, though not without great effort and sacrifice by American service personnel both during combat and in the years that followed. By April 9, 2003, less than a month after the beginning of air and ground operations, America and its coalition partners had captured the nation's capital, Baghdad. In December, Iraq's former leader, Saddam Hussein, was captured, tried by an Iraqi tribunal, and hung.

The decision to go to war against Iraq and the long-term consequences of that decision, however, are still debated. Prior to the war, in February 2003, Secretary of State Colin Powell presented to the United Nations evidence that Saddam Hussein had undertaken efforts to procure weapons of mass destruction. According to Powell, "Indeed, the facts and Iraq's behavior show that Saddam Hussein and his regime are concealing their efforts to produce more weapons of mass destruction."[48] But the truth behind those accusations and the national intelligence that informed Powell's statements were later challenged.[49]

Following victory, the U.S. government chose to disband the Iraqi military, as some commentators have asserted, "without the knowledge or consent of either the Pentagon or the President."[50] Some of the Iraqi army's former officers and soldiers chose to join a radical Sunni Muslim resistance group founded by Abu Musab al-Zarqawi. The militant Islamic organization has many names, including the Islamic State of Iraq and Syria (ISIS) and the Islamic State of Iraq and the Levant (ISIL).[51] The *Wall Street Journal* reported that "after the fall of Saddam, many Sunnis, suddenly out of power and fearing reprisals, turned to Zarqawi's toxic strain of Islamist violence. Look closely at the leaders of ISIS and you will find among them some of Saddam's army officers and secret policemen."[52]

Immigration Connects Foreign Policy to Domestic Policy

14.5 Understand the connection between American immigration policy and the nation's foreign policy.

American foreign policy has both shaped and been shaped by the nation's power status at a particular point in time. Amidst the changing dynamics of global political and economic power competition, national objectives, foreign policy, and domestic policy are unavoidably linked together. Pursuing the objective of maximizing national power and influence, for a nation like the United States, risks critically destabilizing parts of the world, displacing large numbers of those nations' citizens. These displaced individuals may, in turn, make claims upon the United States government to provide pathways to citizenship, given its responsibility for the destabilization. American voters may support those claims, pressuring policymakers to respond.

It is in this way that American foreign policy connects with American domestic policy—by raising the issue of national responsibility for and domestic response to the effects of the nation's foreign policies. Global military competition is only one area in which a nation's pursuit of self-interest may result in the displacement of large numbers of individuals.[53] Climate change policies may also be examined through this lens, though space constraints prevent us from giving that proper attention here. Instead, we will focus on American military policy and involvement in geopolitical power struggles in Syria, the effects of those conflicts on the residents of that nation, and the claiming of rights by displaced Syrians.

The Arab Spring Begins as a Regional Political Movement

On December 17, 2010, Mohamed Bouazizi, a street vendor in the North African nation of Tunisia, poured flammable liquid over his body and set himself on fire. He later died from his burns. By some accounts, Bouazizi made this tragic statement in protest against local police corruption and a lack of response to it by the autocratic government of Tunisian president Zine El Abidine Ben Ali. One journalist recounted, "The abuse took many forms. Mostly, it was the type of petty bureaucratic tyranny that many in the region know all too well. Police would confiscate his scales and his produce, or fine him for running a stall without a permit."[54]

Bouazizi's tragic death sparked a series of protests in the nation of Tunisia. Modern communications technologies played a key role in their spread. "Protesters took to the streets with 'a rock in one hand, a cell phone in the other,' according to Rochdi Horchani—a relative of Mohamed Bouazizi—who helped break through the [government-imposed] media blackout."[55]

More protests followed against authoritarian governments in North Africa and the Middle East, and the governments of some nations were overthrown. The uprisings, which became known as the **Arab Spring**, were rooted in a history of Western control over the region, autocratic governments, and centuries-old tensions between groups of individuals in the nations involved. They were sparked largely by young members of these nations who were connected to the world and to each other through cell phones and social media. As it spread across the affected regions, the Arab Spring led to democratic reforms in some nations, such as Tunisia, and to hope.

In other nations, however, spring led to winter and then chaos. "Almost every Arab country is either worse off than it was in 2011 or no significant positive change has occurred, so the phase that the region is in right now is a brutal winter," said Amy Hawthorne, deputy director of research at the Project on Middle East Democracy.[56]

People demonstrate against Ben Ali's regime in front of the police station in the city of Kasserine, in the south of Tunisia. Following the death of Mohamed Bouazizi, twenty-six, a street vendor who set himself on fire when police tried to prevent him from selling vegetables without a permit, a huge movement of protests erupted in the country against the corrupted regime of President Ben Ali and the family of his second wife, Leila Trabelsi.

Antoine Gyori/AGP/Corbis via Getty Images

A voter shows his ink-stained finger after participating in the second round of Tunisia's presidential election in December 2014. Tunisia is one of the few countries in the Middle East experiencing relative stability and a degree of democratic reform in the aftermath of the Arab Spring.

Marieau Palacio/Anadolu Agency/Getty Images

A Civil War in Syria Draws in Global Powers

Particularly affected was Syria. The country's boundaries had been drawn by the victorious powers after World War I without sufficient consideration of the various factions within the area, and these cleavages resulted in an earthquake.[57] There were protests and calls for democratic reforms, but also atrocities and civil war, which led to the eventual intervention of outside powers, including the United States and Russia. Though both countries had the same goal of fighting terrorist groups in Syria and other nations, they were often on opposite sides of conflicts, especially in Syria.

In 2011, according to news accounts, "peaceful protests inspired by earlier revolutions in Egypt and Tunisia rose up to challenge the dictatorship running [Syria]. The government [of Bashar al-Assad] responded—there is no getting around this—like monsters. First, security forces quietly killed activists. Then they started kidnapping, raping, torturing and killing activists and their family members, including a lot of children, dumping their mutilated bodies by the sides of roads. Then troops began simply opening fire on protests. Eventually civilians started shooting back."[58]

One of the groups fighting against the al-Assad regime was ISIS. The terrorist group's goal was clear: to establish a worldwide caliphate, an Islamic state ruled by a political and religious leader with absolute authority. Its tactics were horrific; it used social media to publicize beheadings as well as burning people alive. ISIS members also, according to widespread reports from Syria and Iraq, sold women and girls into sexual slavery. According to one report, "A price list verified as authentic by the UN confirms the fact that younger is apparently better in the eyes of ISIS. The list showed that children aged one to nine years old are sold for about $165, while women over 40 go for as little as $41."[59]

In the fall of 2014, the United States and its allies in the Middle East began to use military airpower to strike ISIS targets in Syria, though with the stated goal of doing so in ways that would not assist the al-Assad regime. President Trump continued this policy, aiding what were called "moderate" Syrian rebels in efforts to both confront ISIS and challenge the Syrian regime of Bashar al-Assad. Russia, Iran, and Hezbollah fought against rebels and extremists in support of the Syrian government.

American Foreign Policy Contributes to the Displacement of Syrians

In a series of essays published in the *London Review of Books*, Pulitzer Prize–winning journalist Seymour Hersh—noted for his role in exposing the massacre of Vietnamese civilians in My Lai in Vietnam in 1969 as well as the massacre's cover-up by American officials—dropped a series of bombshells about the conduct of foreign policy by the administration of President Barack Obama. These bombshells involved Syria.

Citing unnamed sources, Hersh used a Central Intelligence Agency (CIA) term, the "Rat Line," to describe a presidential policy that was designed "to funnel weapons and ammunition from Libya via southern Turkey and across the Syrian border to [opponents of the al-Assad regime]. Many of those in Syria who ultimately received these weapons were jihadists, some of them affiliated with al-Qaida."[60] Hersh's claim has, not surprisingly, come under intense scrutiny, with critiques focused especially on the fact that his sources were unnamed.

The Syrian cauldron continued to boil. At the end of 2018, it was estimated that there were 6.7 million Syrian refugees worldwide[61] and 6.2 million Syrians who had been internally displaced.[62] Turkey hosted the largest share of refugees, but Lebanon, Jordan, Iraq, and Germany also granted asylum to a sizable number of displaced Syrians.[63] In 2017, the United States took in comparatively few Syrian refugees, 6,557, although that number represented the third largest among nations from which the United States accepted refugees (behind the Democratic Republic of the Congo and Iraq).[64] That number dropped to just sixty-two in 2018.

In Spite of Restrictions under American Domestic Policy, Some Displaced Syrians Arrive to Make Their Claims on the American Dream

According to many accounts, Daraa, Syria, is where the nation's civil war started, after anti-regime graffiti was painted on a wall by teenagers in February 2011 in support of the Arab Spring.[65] The Syrian government's response was reportedly brutal: "In a gloomy interrogation room the children were beaten and bloodied, burned and had their fingernails pulled out."[66] Syrian citizens in Daraa, Damascus, and other cities began to protest. In March, Syrian forces opened fire on protesters in Daraa, killing at least four. By April, the Syrian government laid siege to Daraa. CNN reported that "mass arrests unfolded and tales of torture spread across the country. The protest movement grew and solidified into an opposition."[67]

By 2013, Daraa had become a living nightmare, caught between rebel fighters from the Free Syrian Army (FSA) and government forces. One of the residents of Daraa trying to survive was Faez al Sharaa. He had worked in the health insurance industry in Syria before the chaos; his wife, Shaza, had been a schoolteacher. In March, he ran into soldiers from the Syrian Army. Deciding to flee the war-torn nation, Faez, his wife, and their daughter became refugees, paying smugglers to help spirit them into neighboring Jordan.

While debates about America's immigration policy often focus on individuals arriving from Mexico and Central America, the question of whether or not to receive refugees from Syria has also been a very political one. By 2016, President Obama had publicly committed to resettling ten thousand Syrian refugees in America, a very small fraction of those displaced by the nation's civil war—a civil war fought, in part, by American-supported rebels using American-supplied weapons.

In Paris on the night of November 13, 2015, "gunmen and suicide bombers hit a concert hall, a major stadium, restaurants and bars, almost simultaneously—and left 130 people dead and hundreds wounded."[68] Outside the Stade de France, France's national stadium and one of the places targeted by the terrorists, authorities found a Syrian passport. The passport, most experts agreed, was fake.[69]

In terms of public perception, however, this didn't matter. In France, the rest of Europe, and the United States, there was a backlash against the policy of welcoming refugees from Syria out of fear that terrorists might use the opportunity to enter Western nations. Following the Paris attacks, Republican governors in thirty-one American states declared that they would block the resettlement of Syrian refugees in their states. While final authority over the nation's immigration policy rests with the federal government and not the states, the states' efforts could at the very least present roadblocks to its implementation.[70]

By 2015, Faez al Sharaa was living with his wife and children in Richardson, Texas, just outside Dallas. His youngest daughter, Sara, was born in Dallas and is thus an American citizen. Faez and his family were resettled with the help of the United Nations Refugee Agency. They had been subject to an extensive process of investigation, which included "more than a two-year process of background checks by several government agencies, including the FBI, Department of Homeland Security and the National Counterterrorism Center."[71]

Faez got a job at Walmart, found an apartment for his family, and bought a used car. According to the *Time* article, "Faez came to believe that the U.S. offered the chance for personal growth and prosperity for his children. He worked hard to improve his English, and has laid out a series of long-term goals, including a higher education degree. 'I would like to make sure to provide for my wife and children,' he says, 'so they can live a happy life.'"[72]

Texas had been more welcoming than any other state in the nation to refugees from across the globe, including those from Syria, accepting more Syrian refugees than any state except California. Many Christian, Jewish, and Islamic members of Texas's faith-based agencies advocated welcoming Syrian refugees with open arms and helped them find housing and jobs.

However, in the aftermath of the Paris attacks and in the sharply divided partisan environment of American national politics, Texan hospitality

Khaled Assaf (middle) and Mariam Rastanawi (right) were two of just sixty-two Syrian refugees allowed to enter the United States in the 2018 fiscal year, which enabled them to join their daughter (left) and grandchildren in Indianapolis.

Youngrae Kim/*Washington Post*/Getty Images

came under question. Bee Moorhead, executive director of a faith-based group in Texas working with refugee agencies, said in a *Los Angeles Times* article, "Texans, it is in our DNA to exhibit Southern hospitality. But when politicians ratchet up the rhetoric, the people who maybe are already disposed to bigotry feel like they've gotten the license they need." The same article reported that "Texas Agriculture Commissioner Sid Miller has posted photos on Facebook of refugees and snakes, saying, 'Can you tell me which of these rattlers won't bite you?'"[73]

In December 2015, the attorney general of Texas, under the leadership of Republican governor Greg Abbott, sued the U.S. government—along with a non-profit organization—to block the resettlement of six Syrian refugees in the state, citing security concerns.[74] These six refugees were members of the family of Faez al Sharaa: his half-brother, Tamman; Tamman's wife and two children; and Faez's parents. Faez's efforts to bring members of his extended family to his new home in North Texas had been caught up in the contentious politics of American foreign policy. "The clock is ticking," said the leader of a North Texas nonprofit resettlement and advocacy organization. "What is the state going to do? Are they going to meet Faez's brother at the airport and send him away?"[75] The members of Faez's extended family were ultimately allowed to enter, met at the airport by a caseworker from the International Rescue Committee, and escorted to their new apartment in Dallas.[76]

Reflecting upon his path to the United States, Faez expressed a very practical but profound belief in the American dream: "The best thing [about Texas] is the opportunity for employment. . . . Here, anyone who has a goal to pursue or a dream, it is possible for them to reach that goal and reach that dream here."[77]

Conclusion: The Story of American Politics Continues

We began this book with a narrative about water protectors claiming their rights at Standing Rock. We end with one of a displaced Syrian working at a Walmart in North Texas, making a claim on the American dream. In between we have engaged with many other narratives, not one of them simple. That is why they are in this book. Powerful stories are not simple; they are not supposed to be. That is why they get told and retold.

The stories in this book have all been introduced to drive home and make real this fact: At the end of the day, American government is, and has always been, about people—their hopes, struggles, successes, and failures. The conclusions to these stories were never predetermined, and they were always contested. Even though it may not seem like it, contributing to the quilt of American government is never beyond the reach of those who participate in it. Many of those who offered a patch, or even just a thread, to this quilt probably never expected that they would do so. But they did. In 1892, American poet Walt Whitman asked what good one person could possibly do in such a big, scary, and often impersonal world. He asked what meaning one life, one story, could possibly have. His answer was this: "That the powerful play goes on, and you may contribute a verse."[78]

And so, we end with the most important question of all: What are the pieces that you will contribute to this quilt? When you add your own voice to the stories of American government, you might be surprised by what gets told in chapters not yet written.

CHAPTER REVIEW

This chapter's main ideas are reflected in the Learning Objectives. By reviewing them here, you should be able to *remember* the key points and *know* the terms that are central to the topic.

14.1 Understand the steps in the policymaking process and the different forms of domestic social policy in America today.

Remember . . .
- Social welfare policy consists of governmental efforts designed to improve or protect the health, safety, education, and opportunities for citizens and residents.
- The role the federal government plays in social welfare policy has greatly expanded in the twentieth century.
- The stages of public policymaking include defining the problem, setting the agenda, formulating and adopting policy, budgeting, implementing, evaluating, and terminating.

Know . . .
- *demographics* (p. 412)
- *domestic policy* (p. 411)
- *economic policy* (p. 411)
- *foreign policy* (p. 411)
- *policy entrepreneurs* (p. 416)
- *public policy* (p. 411)
- *social welfare policies* (p. 414)

14.2 Discuss the politics of American health care policy.

Remember . . .
- Recent Supreme Court confirmation proceedings reveal the importance of the decision for political parties.
- Questions about how much justices should incorporate their own experiences and outlooks into their decisions have played a key role in confirmation debates.

Know . . .
- *entitlement programs* (p. 421)
- *need-based assistance programs* (p. 421)
- *social insurance programs* (p. 420)

14.3 Understand the approaches to and goals of fiscal policy in the United States.

Remember . . .
- Programs like Medicare and Medicaid are major federal health policy programs covering retirees, low-income workers, and the disabled. Federal spending on Social Security and Medicare make up a significant part of the federal budget. The ACA expanded Medicare.
- After the 2008 election, President Barack Obama and congressional Democrats secured passage of the ACA.
- Since then, Republicans in Congress and later President Donald Trump have tried to repeal or replace the act.

Know . . .
- *budget deficit* (p. 430)
- *budget resolution* (p. 425)
- *budget surplus* (p. 430)
- *Congressional Budget Office (CBO)* (p. 424)
- *consumer price index (CPI)* (p. 424)
- *demand shock* (p. 426)
- *discretionary spending* (p. 425)
- *economic recession* (p. 424)
- *Federal Reserve System* (p. 431)
- *fiscal policy* (p. 423)
- *fiscal stimulus* (p. 427)
- *gross domestic product (GDP)* (p. 424)
- *inflation* (p. 424)
- *interest rates* (p. 431)
- *mandatory spending* (p. 425)
- *monetary policy* (p. 431)
- *national debt* (p. 430)
- *Office of Management and Budget (OMB)* (p. 424)
- *supply shock* (p. 426)
- *unemployment rate* (p. 424)

14.4 Summarize the historical development of America's involvement in international affairs.

Remember . . .
- Since the nation's founding, U.S. foreign policy has swung between periods of relative isolationism and increased foreign engagement and intervention.

Know . . .
- *containment* (p. 437)
- *European Union (EU)* (p. 437)
- *internationalism* (p. 434)
- *isolationism* (p. 433)
- *Marshall Plan* (p. 437)
- *Monroe Doctrine* (p. 434)
- *nuclear proliferation* (p. 438)
- *preemptive war* (p. 439)
- *proxy wars* (p. 436)
- *Reagan Doctrine* (p. 437)
- *Roosevelt Corollary* (p. 434)
- *superpower* (p. 436)
- *terrorism* (p. 439)
- *United Nations* (p. 437)

14.5 Understand the connection between American immigration policy and the nation's foreign policy.

Remember . . .

- The Arab Spring began in 2010 with protests against governments in North Africa and the Middle East. Some nations moved toward democracy while others descended into civil war and chaos.

- In the twenty-first century, the militant group ISIS took root and expanded its influence and control over territory in North Africa and the Middle East.

Know . . .

- *Arab Spring* (p. 441)

APPENDIX 1 DECLARATION OF INDEPENDENCE

On June 11, 1776, the responsibility to "prepare a declaration" of independence was assigned by the Continental Congress, meeting in Philadelphia, to five members: John Adams, Benjamin Franklin, Thomas Jefferson, Robert Livingston, and Roger Sherman. Impressed by his talents as a writer, the committee asked Jefferson to compose a draft. After modifying Jefferson's draft, the committee turned it over to Congress on June 28. On July 2, Congress voted to declare independence; on the evening of July 4, it approved the Declaration of Independence.

In Congress, July 4, 1776, The Unanimous Declaration of the Thirteen United States of America,

When in the Course of human events, it becomes necessary for one people to dissolve the political bands which have connected them with another, and to assume among the Powers of the earth, the separate and equal station to which the Laws of Nature and of Nature's God entitle them, a decent respect to the opinions of mankind requires that they should declare the causes which impel them to the separation.

We hold these truths to be self-evident, that all men are created equal, that they are endowed by their Creator with certain unalienable Rights, that among these are Life, Liberty and the pursuit of Happiness. That to secure these rights, Governments are instituted among Men, deriving their just powers from the consent of the governed. That whenever any form of Government becomes destructive of these ends, it is the Right of the People to alter or to abolish it, and to institute new Government, laying its foundation on such principles and organizing its powers in such form, as to them shall seem most likely to effect their Safety and Happiness. Prudence, indeed, will dictate that Government long established should not be changed for light and transient causes; and accordingly all experience hath shown, that mankind are more disposed to suffer, while evils are sufferable, than to right themselves by abolishing the forms to which they are accustomed. But when a long train of abuses and usurpations, pursuing invariably the same Object evinces a design to reduce them under absolute Despotism, it is their right, it is their duty, to throw off such Government, and to provide new Guards for their future security. Such has been the patient sufferance of these Colonies; and such is now the necessity which constrains them to alter their former Systems of Government. The history of the present King of Great Britain is a history of repeated injuries and usurpations, all having in direct object the establishment of an absolute Tyranny over these

States. To prove this, let Facts be submitted to a candid world.

He has refused his Assent to Laws, the most wholesome and necessary for the public good.

He has forbidden his Governors to pass Laws of immediate and pressing importance, unless suspended in their operation till his Assent should be obtained; and when so suspended, he has utterly neglected to attend to them.

He has refused to pass other Laws for the accommodation of large districts of people, unless those people would relinquish the right of Representation in the Legislature, a right inestimable to them and formidable to tyrants only.

He has called together legislative bodies at places unusual, uncomfortable, and distant from the depository of their Public Records, for the sole purpose of fatiguing them into compliance with his measures.

He has dissolved Representative Houses repeatedly, for opposing with manly firmness his invasions on the rights of the people.

He has refused for a long time, after such dissolutions, to cause others to be elected; whereby the Legislative Powers, incapable of Annihilation, have returned to the People at large for their exercise; the State remaining in the mean time exposed to all the dangers of invasion from without, and convulsions within.

He has endeavored to prevent the population of these States; for that purpose obstructing the Laws of Naturalization of Foreigners; refusing to pass others to encourage their migration hither, and raising the conditions of new Appropriations of Lands.

He has obstructed the Administration of Justice, by refusing his Assent to Laws for establishing Judiciary Powers.

He has made Judges dependent on his Will alone, for the tenure of their offices, and the amount and payment of their salaries.

He has erected a multitude of New Offices, and sent hither swarms of Officers to harass our People, and eat out their substance.

He has kept among us, in times of peace, Standing Armies without the Consent of our legislature.

He has affected to render the Military independent of and superior to the Civil Power.

He has combined with others to subject us to a jurisdiction foreign to our constitution, and unacknowledged by our laws; giving his Assent to their acts of pretended legislation:

For quartering large bodies of armed troops among us:

For protecting them, by a mock Trial, from Punishment for any Murders which they should commit on the Inhabitants of these States:

For cutting off our Trade with all parts of the world:

For imposing taxes on us without our Consent:

For depriving us in many cases, of the benefits of Trial by Jury:

For transporting us beyond Seas to be tried for pretended offences:

For abolishing the free System of English Laws in a neighbouring Province, establishing therein an Arbitrary government, and enlarging its Boundaries so as to render it at once an example and fit instrument for introducing the same absolute rule into these Colonies:

For taking away our Charters, abolishing our most valuable Laws, and altering fundamentally the Forms of our Governments:

For suspending our own Legislature, and declaring themselves invested with Power to legislate for us in all cases whatsoever.

He has abdicated Government here, by declaring us out of his Protection and waging War against us.

He has plundered our seas, ravaged our Coasts, burnt our towns, and destroyed the lives of our people.

He is at this time transporting large armies of foreign mercenaries to compleat the works of death, desolation and tyranny, already begun with circumstances of Cruelty & perfidy scarcely parallel in the most barbarous ages, and totally unworthy the Head of a civilized nation.

He has constrained our fellow Citizens taken Captive on the high Seas to bear Arms against their Country, to become the executioners of their friends and Brethren, or to fall themselves by their Hands.

He has excited domestic insurrections amongst us, and has endeavoured to bring on the inhabitants of our frontiers, the merciless Indian Savages, whose known rule of warfare, is an undistinguished destruction of all ages, sexes and conditions.

In every stage of these Oppressions We have Petitioned for Redress in the most humble terms: Our repeated Petitions have been answered only by repeated injury. A Prince, whose character is thus marked by every act which may define a Tyrant, is unfit to be the ruler of a free People.

Nor have We been wanting in attention to our British brethren. We have warned them from time to time of attempts by their legislature to extend an unwarrantable jurisdiction over us. We have reminded them of the circumstances of our emigration and settlement here. We have appealed to their native justice and magnanimity, and we have conjured them by the ties of our common kindred to disavow these usurpations, which would inevitably interrupt our connections and correspondence. They too have been deaf to the voice of justice and of consanguinity. We must, therefore, acquiesce in the necessity, which denounces our Separation, and hold them, as we hold the rest of mankind, Enemies in War, in Peace Friends.

We, therefore, the Representatives of the United States of America, in General Congress, Assembled, appealing to the Supreme Judge of the world for the rectitude of our intentions, do, in the Name, and by Authority of the good People of these Colonies, solemnly publish and declare, That these United Colonies are, and of Right ought to be Free and Independent States; that they are Absolved from all Allegiance to the British Crown, and that all political connection between them and the State of Great Britain, is and ought to be totally dissolved; and that as Free and Independent States, they have full Power to levy War, conclude Peace, contract Alliances, establish Commerce, and to do all other Acts and Things which Independent States may of right do. And for the support of this Declaration, with a firm reliance on the Protection of Divine Providence, we mutually pledge to each other our Lives, our Fortunes and our sacred Honor.

John Hancock.

New Hampshire:
Josiah Bartlett,
William Whipple,
Matthew Thornton.

Massachusetts-Bay:
Samuel Adams,
John Adams,
Robert Treat Paine,
Elbridge Gerry.

Rhode Island:
Stephen Hopkins,
William Ellery.

Connecticut:
Roger Sherman,
Samuel Huntington,
William Williams,
Oliver Wolcott.

New York:
William Floyd,
Philip Livingston,
Francis Lewis,
Lewis Morris.

Pennsylvania:
Robert Morris,
Benjamin Rush,
Benjamin Franklin,
John Morton,
George Clymer,
James Smith,
George Taylor,
James Wilson,
George Ross.

Delaware:
Caesar Rodney,
George Read,
Thomas McKean.

Georgia:
Button Gwinnett,
Lyman Hall,
George Walton.

Maryland:
Samuel Chase,
William Paca,
Thomas Stone,
Charles Carroll of Carrollton.

Virginia:
George Wythe,
Richard Henry Lee,
Thomas Jefferson,
Benjamin Harrison,
Thomas Nelson Jr.,
Francis Lightfoot Lee,
Carter Braxton.

North Carolina:
William Hooper,
Joseph Hewes,
John Penn.

South Carolina:
Edward Rutledge,
Thomas Heyward Jr.,
Thomas Lynch Jr.,
Arthur Middleton.

New Jersey:
Richard Stockton,
John Witherspoon,
Francis Hopkinson,
John Hart,
Abraham Clark.

APPENDIX 2
ARTICLES OF CONFEDERATION

To all to whom these Presents shall come, we the undersigned Delegates of the States affixed to our Names send greeting. Articles of Confederation and perpetual Union between the states of New Hampshire, Massachusetts-bay Rhode Island and Providence Plantations, Connecticut, New York, New Jersey, Pennsylvania, Delaware, Maryland, Virginia, North Carolina, South Carolina and Georgia.

Article I

The Stile of this Confederacy shall be **"The United States of America"**.

Article II

Each state retains its sovereignty, freedom, and independence, and every power, jurisdiction, and right, which is not by this Confederation expressly delegated to the United States, in Congress assembled.

Article III

The said States hereby severally enter into a firm league of friendship with each other, for their common defense, the security of their liberties, and their mutual and general welfare, binding themselves to assist each other, against all force offered to, or attacks made upon them, or any of them, on account of religion, sovereignty, trade, or any other pretense whatever.

Article IV

The better to secure and perpetuate mutual friendship and intercourse among the people of the different States in this Union, the free inhabitants of each of these States, paupers, vagabonds, and fugitives from justice excepted, shall be entitled to all privileges and immunities of free citizens in the several States; and the people of each State shall free ingress and regress to and from any other State, and shall enjoy therein all the privileges of trade and commerce, subject to the same duties, impositions, and restrictions as the inhabitants thereof respectively, provided that such restrictions shall not extend so far as to prevent the removal of property imported into any State, to any other State, of which the owner is an inhabitant; provided also that no imposition, duties or restriction shall be laid by any State, on the property of the United States, or either of them.

If any person guilty of, or charged with, treason, felony, or other high misdemeanor in any State, shall flee from justice, and be found in any of the United States, he shall, upon demand of the Governor or executive power of the State from which he fled, be delivered up and removed to the State having jurisdiction of his offense.

Full faith and credit shall be given in each of these States to the records, acts, and judicial proceedings of the courts and magistrates of every other State.

Article V

For the most convenient management of the general interests of the United States, delegates shall be annually appointed in such manner as the legislatures of each State shall direct, to meet in Congress on the first Monday in November, in every year, with a power reserved to each State to recall its delegates, or any of them, at any time within the year, and to send others in their stead for the remainder of the year.

No State shall be represented in Congress by less than two, nor more than seven members; and no person shall be capable of being a delegate for more than three years in any term of six years; nor shall any person, being a delegate, be capable of holding any office under the United States, for which he, or another for his benefit, receives any salary, fees or emolument of any kind.

Each State shall maintain its own delegates in a meeting of the States, and while they act as members of the committee of the States.

In determining questions in the United States in Congress assembled, each State shall have one vote.

Freedom of speech and debate in Congress shall not be impeached or questioned in any court or place out of Congress, and the members of Congress shall be protected in their persons from arrests or imprisonments, during the time of their going to and from, and attendence on Congress, except for treason, felony, or breach of the peace.

Article VI

No State, without the consent of the United States in Congress assembled, shall send any embassy to, or receive any embassy from, or enter into any conference, agreement, alliance or treaty with any King, Prince or State; nor shall any person holding any office of profit or trust under the United States, or any of them, accept any present, emolument, office or title of any kind whatever from any King, Prince or foreign State; nor shall the United States in Congress assembled, or any of them, grant any title of nobility.

No two or more States shall enter into any treaty, confederation or alliance whatever between them, without the consent of the United States in Congress assembled, specifying accurately the purposes for which the same is to be entered into, and how long it shall continue.

No State shall lay any imposts or duties, which may interfere with any stipulations in treaties, entered into by the United States in Congress assembled, with any King, Prince or State, in pursuance of any treaties already proposed by Congress, to the courts of France and Spain.

No vessel of war shall be kept up in time of peace by any State, except such number only, as shall be deemed necessary by the United States in Congress assembled, for the defense of such State, or its trade; nor shall any body of forces be kept up by any State in time of peace, except such number only, as in the judgement of the United States in Congress assembled, shall be deemed requisite to garrison the forts necessary for the defense of such State; but every State shall always keep up a well-regulated and disciplined militia, sufficiently armed and accoutered, and shall provide and constantly have ready for use, in public stores, a due number of filed pieces and tents, and a proper quantity of arms, ammunition and camp equipage.

No State shall engage in any war without the consent of the United States in Congress assembled, unless such State be actually invaded by enemies, or shall have received certain advice of a resolution being formed by some nation of Indians to invade such State, and the danger is so imminent as not to admit of a delay till the United States in Congress assembled can be consulted; nor shall any State grant commissions to any ships or vessels of war, nor letters of marque or reprisal, except it be after a declaration of war by the United States in Congress assembled, and then only against the Kingdom or State and the subjects thereof, against which war has been so declared, and under such regulations as shall be established by the United States in Congress assembled, unless such State be infested by pirates, in which case vessels of war may be fitted out for that occasion, and kept so long as the danger shall continue, or until the United States in Congress assembled shall determine otherwise.

Article VII

When land forces are raised by any State for the common defense, all officers of or under the rank of colonel, shall be appointed by the legislature of each State respectively, by whom such forces shall be raised, or in such manner as such State shall direct, and all vacancies shall be filled up by the State which first made the appointment.

Article VIII

All charges of war, and all other expenses that shall be incurred for the common defense or general welfare, and allowed by the United States in Congress assembled, shall be defrayed out of a common treasury, which shall be supplied by the several States in proportion to the value of all land within each State, granted or surveyed for any person, as such land and the buildings and improvements thereon shall be estimated according to such mode as the United States in Congress assembled, shall from time to time direct and appoint.

The taxes for paying that proportion shall be laid and levied by the authority and direction of the legislatures of the several States within the time agreed upon by the United States in Congress assembled.

Article IX

The United States in Congress assembled, shall have the sole and exclusive right and power of determining on peace and war, except in the cases mentioned in the sixth article—of sending and receiving ambassadors—entering into treaties and alliances, provided that no treaty of commerce shall be made whereby the legislative power of the respective States shall be restrained from imposing such imposts and duties on foreigners, as their own people are subjected to, or from prohibiting the exportation or importation of any species of goods or commodities whatsoever—of establishing rules for deciding in all cases, what captures on land or water shall be legal, and in what manner prizes taken by land or naval forces in the service of the United States shall be divided or appropriated—of granting letters of marque and reprisal in times of peace—appointing courts for the trial of piracies and felonies commited on the high seas and establishing courts for receiving and determining finally appeals in all cases of captures, provided that no member of Congress shall be appointed a judge of any of the said courts.

The United States in Congress assembled shall also be the last resort on appeal in all disputes and differences now subsisting or that hereafter may arise between two or more States concerning boundary, jurisdiction or any other causes whatever; which authority shall always be exercised in the manner following. Whenever the legislative or executive authority or lawful agent of any State in controversy with another shall present a petition to Congress stating the matter in question and praying for a hearing, notice thereof shall be given by order of Congress to the legislative or executive authority of the other State in controversy, and a day assigned for the appearance of the parties by their lawful agents, who shall then be directed to appoint by joint consent, commissioners or judges to constitute a court for hearing and determining the matter in question: but if they cannot agree, Congress shall name three persons out of each of the United States, and from the list of such persons each party shall alternately strike out one, the petitioners beginning, until the number shall be reduced to thirteen; and from that number not less than seven, nor more than nine names as Congress shall direct, shall in the presence of Congress be drawn out by lot, and the persons whose names shall be so drawn or any five of them, shall be commissioners or judges, to hear and finally determine the controversy, so always as a major part of the judges who shall hear the cause shall agree in the determination: and if either party shall neglect to attend at the day appointed, without showing reasons, which Congress shall judge sufficient, or being present shall refuse to strike, the Congress shall proceed to nominate three persons out of each State, and the secretary of Congress shall strike in behalf of such party absent or refusing; and the judgement and sentence of the court to be appointed, in the manner before prescribed, shall be final and conclusive; and if any of the parties shall refuse to submit to the authority of such court, or to appear or defend their claim or cause, the court shall nevertheless proceed to pronounce sentence, or judgement, which shall in like manner be final and decisive, the judgement or sentence and

other proceedings being in either case transmitted to Congress, and lodged among the acts of Congress for the security of the parties concerned: provided that every commissioner, before he sits in judgement, shall take an oath to be administered by one of the judges of the supreme or superior court of the State, where the cause shall be tried, 'well and truly to hear and determine the matter in question, according to the best of his judgement, without favor, affection or hope of reward': provided also, that no State shall be deprived of territory for the benefit of the United States.

All controversies concerning the private right of soil claimed under different grants of two or more States, whose jurisdictions as they may respect such lands, and the States which passed such grants are adjusted, the said grants or either of them being at the same time claimed to have originated antecedent to such settlement of jurisdiction, shall on the petition of either party to the Congress of the United States, be finally determined as near as may be in the same manner as is before prescribed for deciding disputes respecting territorial jurisdiction between different States.

The United States in Congress assembled shall also have the sole and exclusive right and power of regulating the alloy and value of coin struck by their own authority, or by that of the respective States—fixing the standards of weights and measures throughout the United States—regulating the trade and managing all affairs with the Indians, not members of any of the States, provided that the legislative right of any State within its own limits be not infringed or violated—establishing or regulating post offices from one State to another, throughout all the United States, and exacting such postage on the papers passing through the same as may be requisite to defray the expenses of the said office—appointing all officers of the land forces, in the service of the United States, excepting regimental officers—appointing all the officers of the naval forces, and commissioning all officers whatever in the service of the United States—making rules for the government and regulation of the said land and naval forces, and directing their operations.

The United States in Congress assembled shall have authority to appoint a committee, to sit in the recess of Congress, to be denominated 'A Committee of the States', and to consist of one delegate from each State; and to appoint such other committees and civil officers as may be necessary for managing the general affairs of the United States under their direction—to appoint one of their members to preside, provided that no person be allowed to serve in the office of president more than one year in any term of three years; to ascertain the necessary sums of money to be raised for the service of the United States, and to appropriate and apply the same for defraying the public expenses—to borrow money, or emit bills on the credit of the United States, transmitting every half-year to the respective States an account of the sums of money so borrowed or emitted—to build and equip a navy—to agree upon the number of land forces, and to make requisitions from each State for its quota, in proportion to the number of white inhabitants in such State; which requisition shall be binding, and thereupon the legislature of each State shall appoint the regimental officers, raise the men and cloath, arm and equip them in a solid-like manner, at the expense of the United States; and the officers and men so cloathed, armed and equipped shall march to the place appointed, and within the time agreed on by the United States in Congress assembled. But if the United States in Congress assembled shall, on consideration of circumstances judge proper that any State should not raise men, or should raise a smaller number of men than the

quota thereof, such extra number shall be raised, officered, cloathed, armed and equipped in the same manner as the quota of each State, unless the legislature of such State shall judge that such extra number cannot be safely spread out in the same, in which case they shall raise, officer, cloath, arm and equip as many of such extra number as they judge can be safely spared. And the officers and men so cloathed, armed, and equipped, shall march to the place appointed, and within the time agreed on by the United States in Congress assembled.

The United States in Congress assembled shall never engage in a war, nor grant letters of marque or reprisal in time of peace, nor enter into any treaties or alliances, nor coin money, nor regulate the value thereof, nor ascertain the sums and expenses necessary for the defense and welfare of the United States, or any of them, nor emit bills, nor borrow money on the credit of the United States, nor appropriate money, nor agree upon the number of vessels of war, to be built or purchased, or the number of land or sea forces to be raised, nor appoint a commander in chief of the army or navy, unless nine States assent to the same: nor shall a question on any other point, except for adjourning from day to day be determined, unless by the votes of the majority of the United States in Congress assembled.

The Congress of the United States shall have power to adjourn to any time within the year, and to any place within the United States, so that no period of adjournment be for a longer duration than the space of six months, and shall publish the journal of their proceedings monthly, except such parts thereof relating to treaties, alliances or military operations, as in their judgement require secrecy; and the yeas and nays of the delegates of each State on any question shall be entered on the journal, when it is desired by any delegates of a State, or any of them, at his or their request shall be furnished with a transcript of the said journal, except such parts as are above excepted, to lay before the legislatures of the several States.

Article X

The Committee of the States, or any nine of them, shall be authorized to execute, in the recess of Congress, such of the powers of Congress as the United States in Congress assembled, by the consent of the nine States, shall from time to time think expedient to vest them with; provided that no power be delegated to the said Committee, for the exercise of which, by the Articles of Confederation, the voice of nine States in the Congress of the United States assembled be requisite.

Article XI

Canada acceding to this confederation, and adjoining in the measures of the United States, shall be admitted into, and entitled to all the advantages of this Union; but no other colony shall be admitted into the same, unless such admission be agreed to by nine States.

Article XII

All bills of credit emitted, monies borrowed, and debts contracted by, or under the authority of Congress, before the assembling of the United States, in pursuance of the present confederation, shall be deemed and considered as a charge against the United States, for payment and satisfaction whereof the said United States, and the public faith are hereby solemnly pledged.

Article XIII

Every State shall abide by the determination of the United States in Congress assembled,

on all questions which by this confederation are submitted to them. And the Articles of this Confederation shall be inviolably observed by every State, and the Union shall be perpetual; nor shall any alteration at any time hereafter be made in any of them; unless such alteration be agreed to in a Congress of the United States, and be afterwards confirmed by the legislatures of every State.

And Whereas it hath pleased the Great Governor of the World to incline the hearts of the legislatures we respectively represent in Congress, to approve of, and to authorize us to ratify the said Articles of Confederation and perpetual Union. Know Ye that we the undersigned delegates, by virtue of the power and authority to us given for that purpose, do by these presents, in the name and in behalf of our respective constituents, fully and entirely ratify and confirm each and every of the said Articles of Confederation and perpetual Union, and all and singular the matters and things therein contained: And we do further solemnly plight and engage the faith of our respective constituents, that they shall abide by the determinations of the United States in Congress assembled, on all questions, which by the said Confederation are submitted to them. And that the Articles thereof shall be inviolably observed by the States we respectively represent, and that the Union shall be perpetual.

In Witness whereof we have hereunto set our hands in Congress. Done at Philadelphia in the State of Pennsylvania the ninth day of July in the Year of our Lord One Thousand Seven Hundred and Seventy-Eight, and in the Third Year of the independence of America.

Agreed to by Congress 15 November 1777

In force after ratification by Maryland, 1 March 1781

APPENDIX 3
CONSTITUTION OF THE UNITED STATES

The U.S. Constitution was written at a convention that Congress called on February 21, 1787, for the purpose of recommending amendments to the Articles of Confederation. Every state but Rhode Island sent delegates to Philadelphia, where the convention met that summer. The delegates decided to write an entirely new constitution, completing their labors on September 17. Nine states (the number the Constitution itself stipulated as sufficient) ratified by June 21, 1788.

The Framers of the Constitution included only six paragraphs on the Supreme Court. Article III, Section 1, created the Supreme Court and the federal system of courts. It provided that "[t]he judicial power of the United States, shall be vested in one supreme Court," and whatever inferior courts Congress "from time to time" saw fit to establish. Article III, Section 2, delineated the types of cases and controversies that should be considered by a federal—rather than a state—court. But beyond this, the Constitution left many of the particulars of the Supreme Court and the federal court system for Congress to decide in later years in judiciary acts.

We the People of the United States, in Order to form a more perfect Union, establish Justice, insure domestic Tranquillity, provide for the common defence, promote the general Welfare, and secure the Blessings of Liberty to ourselves and our Posterity, do ordain and establish this Constitution for the United States of America.

Article I

Section 1. All legislative Powers herein granted shall be vested in a Congress of the United States, which shall consist of a Senate and House of Representatives.

Section 2. The House of Representatives shall be composed of Members chosen every second Year by the People of the several States, and the Electors in each State shall have the Qualifications requisite for Electors of the most numerous Branch of the State Legislature.

No Person shall be a Representative who shall not have attained to the age of twenty five Years, and been seven Years a Citizen of the United States, and who shall not, when elected, be an Inhabitant of that State in which he shall be chosen.

[Representatives and direct Taxes shall be apportioned among the several States which may be included within this Union, according to their respective Numbers, which shall be determined by adding to the whole Number of free Persons, including those bound to Service for a

Term of Years, and excluding Indians not taxed, three fifths of all other Persons.][1] The actual Enumeration shall be made within three Years after the first Meeting of the Congress of the United States, and within every subsequent Term of ten Years, in such Manner as they shall by Law direct. The Number of Representatives shall not exceed one for every thirty Thousand, but each State shall have at Least one Representative; and until such enumeration shall be made, the State of New Hampshire shall be entitled to chuse three, Massachusetts eight, Rhode-Island and Providence Plantations one, Connecticut five, New-York six, New Jersey four, Pennsylvania eight, Delaware one, Maryland six, Virginia ten, North Carolina five, South Carolina five, and Georgia three.

When vacancies happen in the Representation from any State, the Executive Authority thereof shall issue Writs of Election to fill such Vacancies.

The House of Representatives shall chuse their Speaker and other Officers; and shall have the sole Power of Impeachment.

Section 3. The Senate of the United States shall be composed of two Senators from each State, [chosen by the Legislature thereof,][2] for six Years; and each Senator shall have one Vote.

Immediately after they shall be assembled in Consequence of the first Election, they shall be divided as equally as may be into three Classes. The Seats of the Senators of the first Class shall be vacated at the Expiration of the second Year, of the second Class at the Expiration of the fourth Year, and of the third Class at the Expiration of the sixth Year, so that one third may be chosen every second Year; [and if Vacancies happen by Resignation, or otherwise, during the Recess of the Legislature of any State, the Executive thereof may make temporary Appointments until the next Meeting of the Legislature, which shall then fill such Vacancies.][3]

No Person shall be a Senator who shall not have attained to the Age of thirty Years, and been nine Years a Citizen of the United States, and who shall not, when elected, be an Inhabitant of that State for which he shall be chosen.

The Vice President of the United States shall be President of the Senate, but shall have no Vote, unless they be equally divided.

The Senate shall chuse their other Officers, and also a President pro tempore, in the Absence of the Vice President, or when he shall exercise the Office of President of the United States.

The Senate shall have the sole Power to try all Impeachments. When sitting for that Purpose, they shall be on Oath or Affirmation. When the President of the United States is tried, the Chief Justice shall preside: And no Person shall be convicted without the Concurrence of two thirds of the Members present.

Judgment in Cases of Impeachment shall not extend further than to removal from Office, and disqualification to hold and enjoy any Office of honor, Trust or Profit under the United States: but the Party convicted shall nevertheless be liable and subject to Indictment, Trial, Judgment and Punishment, according to Law.

Section 4. The Times, Places and Manner of holding Elections for Senators and Representatives, shall be prescribed in each State by the Legislature thereof; but the Congress may at any time by Law make or alter such Regulations, except as to the Places of chusing Senators.

The Congress shall assemble at least once in every Year, and such Meeting shall [be on the first Monday in December],[4] unless they shall by Law appoint a different Day.

Section 5. Each House shall be the Judge of the Elections, Returns and Qualifications of its own Members, and a Majority of each shall constitute a Quorum to do Business; but a smaller Number may adjourn from day to day, and may be authorized to compel the Attendance of absent Members, in such Manner, and under such Penalties as each House may provide.

Each House may determine the Rules of its Proceedings, punish its Members for disorderly Behaviour, and, with the Concurrence of two thirds, expel a Member.

Each House shall keep a Journal of its Proceedings, and from time to time publish the same, excepting such Parts as may in their Judgment require Secrecy; and the Yeas and Nays of the Members of either House on any question shall, at the Desire of one fifth of those Present, be entered on the Journal.

Neither House, during the Session of Congress, shall, without the Consent of the other, adjourn for more than three days, nor to any other Place than that in which the two Houses shall be sitting.

Section 6. The Senators and Representatives shall receive a Compensation for their Services, to be ascertained by Law, and paid out of the Treasury of the United States. They shall in all Cases, except Treason, Felony and Breach of the Peace, be privileged from Arrest during their Attendance at the Session of their respective Houses, and in going to and returning from the same; and for any Speech or Debate in either House, they shall not be questioned in any other Place.

No Senator or Representative shall, during the Time for which he was elected, be appointed to any civil Office under the Authority of the United States, which shall have been created, or the Emoluments whereof shall have been encreased during such time; and no Person holding any Office under the United States, shall be a Member of either House during his Continuance in Office.

Section 7. All Bills for raising Revenue shall originate in the House of Representatives;

but the Senate may propose or concur with Amendments as on other Bills.

Every Bill which shall have passed the House of Representatives and the Senate, shall, before it become a Law, be presented to the President of the United States; If he approve he shall sign it, but if not he shall return it, with his Objections to that House in which it shall have originated, who shall enter the Objections at large on their Journal, and proceed to reconsider it. If after such Reconsideration two thirds of that House shall agree to pass the Bill, it shall be sent, together with the Objections, to the other House, by which it shall likewise be reconsidered, and if approved by two thirds of that House, it shall become a Law. But in all such Cases the Votes of both Houses shall be determined by yeas and Nays, and the Names of the Persons voting for and against the Bill shall be entered on the Journal of each House respectively. If any Bill shall not be returned by the President within ten Days (Sundays excepted) after it shall have been presented to him, the Same shall be a Law, in like Manner as if he had signed it, unless the Congress by their Adjournment prevent its Return, in which Case it shall not be a Law.

Every Order, Resolution, or Vote to which the Concurrence of the Senate and House of Representatives may be necessary (except on a question of Adjournment) shall be presented to the President of the United States; and before the Same shall take Effect, shall be approved by him, or being disapproved by him, shall be repassed by two thirds of the Senate and House of Representatives, according to the Rules and Limitations prescribed in the Case of a Bill.

Section 8. The Congress shall have Power To lay and collect Taxes, Duties, Imposts and Excises, to pay the Debts and provide for the common Defence and general Welfare of the United States; but all Duties, Imposts and

Excises shall be uniform throughout the United States;

To borrow Money on the credit of the United States;

To regulate Commerce with foreign Nations, and among the several States, and with the Indian Tribes;

To establish an uniform Rule of Naturalization, and uniform Laws on the subject of Bankruptcies throughout the United States;

To coin Money, regulate the Value thereof, and of foreign Coin, and fix the Standard of Weights and Measures;

To provide for the Punishment of counterfeiting the Securities and current Coin of the United States;

To establish Post Offices and post Roads;

To promote the Progress of Science and useful Arts, by securing for limited Times to Authors and Inventors the exclusive Right to their respective Writings and Discoveries;

To constitute Tribunals inferior to the supreme Court;

To define and punish Piracies and Felonies committed on the high Seas, and Offences against the Law of Nations;

To declare War, grant Letters of Marque and Reprisal, and make Rules concerning Captures on Land and Water;

To raise and support Armies, but no Appropriation of Money to that Use shall be for a longer Term than two Years;

To provide and maintain a Navy;

To make Rules for the Government and Regulation of the land and naval Forces;

To provide for calling forth the Militia to execute the Laws of the Union, suppress Insurrections and repel Invasions;

To provide for organizing, arming, and disciplining, the Militia, and for governing such Part of them as may be employed in the Service of the United States, reserving to the States respectively, the Appointment of the Officers, and the Authority of training the Militia according to the discipline prescribed by Congress;

To exercise exclusive Legislation in all Cases whatsoever, over such District (not exceeding ten Miles square) as may, by Cession of particular States, and the Acceptance of Congress, become the Seat of the Government of the United States, and to exercise like Authority over all Places purchased by the Consent of the Legislature of the State in which the Same shall be, for the Erection of Forts, Magazines, Arsenals, dock-Yards, and other needful Buildings;—And

To make all Laws which shall be necessary and proper for carrying into Execution the foregoing Powers, and all other Powers vested by this Constitution in the Government of the United States, or in any Department or Officer thereof.

Section 9. The Migration or Importation of such Persons as any of the States now existing shall think proper to admit, shall not be prohibited by the Congress prior to the Year one thousand eight hundred and eight, but a Tax or duty may be imposed on such Importation, not exceeding ten dollars for each Person.

The Privilege of the Writ of Habeas Corpus shall not be suspended, unless when in Cases of Rebellion or Invasion the public Safety may require it.

No Bill of Attainder or ex post facto Law shall be passed.

No Capitation, or other direct, Tax shall be laid, unless in Proportion to the Census or Enumeration herein before directed to be taken.[5]

No Tax or Duty shall be laid on Articles exported from any State.

No Preference shall be given by any Regulation of Commerce or Revenue to the Ports of one State over those of another; nor shall Vessels bound to, or from, one State, be obliged to enter, clear, or pay Duties in another.

No Money shall be drawn from the Treasury, but in Consequence of Appropriations made by Law; and a regular Statement and Account of the Receipts and Expenditures of all public Money shall be published from time to time.

No Title of Nobility shall be granted by the United States: And no Person holding any Office of Profit or Trust under them, shall, without the Consent of the Congress, accept of any present, Emolument, Office, or Title, of any kind whatever, from any King, Prince, or foreign State.

Section 10. No State shall enter into any Treaty, Alliance, or Confederation; grant Letters of Marque and Reprisal; coin Money; emit Bills of Credit; make any Thing but gold and silver Coin a Tender in Payment of Debts; pass any Bill of Attainder, ex post facto Law, or Law impairing the Obligation of Contracts, or grant any Title of Nobility.

No State shall, without the Consent of the Congress, lay any Imposts or Duties on Imports or Exports, except what may be absolutely necessary for executing its inspection Laws: and the net Produce of all Duties and Imposts, laid by any State on Imports or Exports, shall be for the Use of the Treasury of the United States; and all such Laws shall be subject to the Revision and Controul of the Congress.

No State shall, without the Consent of Congress, lay any Duty of Tonnage, keep Troops, or Ships of War in time of Peace, enter into any Agreement or Compact with another State, or with a foreign Power, or engage in War, unless actually invaded, or in such imminent Danger as will not admit of delay.

Article II

Section 1. The executive Power shall be vested in a President of the United States of America. He shall hold his Office during the Term of four Years, and, together with the Vice President, chosen for the same Term, be elected, as follows:

Each State shall appoint, in such Manner as the Legislature thereof may direct, a Number of Electors, equal to the whole Number of Senators and Representatives to which the State may be entitled in the Congress: but no Senator or Representative, or Person holding an Office of Trust or Profit under the United States, shall be appointed an Elector.

[The Electors shall meet in their respective States, and vote by Ballot for two Persons, of whom one at least shall not be an Inhabitant of the same State with themselves. And they shall make a List of all the Persons voted for, and of the Number of Votes for each; which List they shall sign and certify, and transmit sealed to the Seat of the Government of the United States, directed to the President of the Senate. The President of the Senate shall, in the Presence of the Senate and House of Representatives, open all the Certificates, and the Votes shall then be counted. The Person having the greatest Number of Votes shall be the President, if such Number be a Majority of the whole Number of Electors appointed; and if there be more than one who have such Majority, and have an equal Number of Votes, then the House of Representatives shall immediately chuse by Ballot one of them for President; and if no Person have a Majority, then from the five highest on the list the said House shall in like Manner chuse the President. But in chusing the President, the Votes shall be taken by States, the Representation from each State having one Vote; A quorum for this Purpose shall consist of a Member or Members from two thirds of the States, and a Majority of all the States shall be necessary to a Choice. In every Case, after the Choice of the President, the Person having the greatest Number of Votes of the Electors shall be the Vice President. But if there should remain two or more who have equal Votes, the Senate shall chuse from them by Ballot the Vice President.][6]

The Congress may determine the Time of chusing the Electors, and the Day on which they shall give their Votes; which Day shall be the same throughout the United States.

No Person except a natural born Citizen, or a Citizen of the United States, at the time of the Adoption of this Constitution, shall be eligible to the Office of President; neither shall any Person be eligible to that Office who shall not have attained to the Age of thirty five Years, and been fourteen Years a Resident within the United States.

In Case of the Removal of the President from Office, or of his Death, Resignation, or Inability to discharge the Powers and Duties of the said Office,[7] the Same shall devolve on the Vice President, and the Congress may by Law provide for the Case of Removal, Death, Resignation or Inability, both of the President and Vice President, declaring what Officer shall then act as President, and such Officer shall act accordingly, until the Disability be removed, or a President shall be elected.

The President shall, at stated Times, receive for his Services, a Compensation, which shall neither be encreased nor diminished during the Period for which he shall have been elected, and he shall not receive within that Period any other Emolument from the United States, or any of them.

Before he enter on the Execution of his Office, he shall take the following Oath or Affirmation:—"I do solemnly swear (or affirm) that I will faithfully execute the Office of President of the United States, and will to the best of my Ability, preserve, protect and defend the Constitution of the United States."

Section 2. The President shall be Commander in Chief of the Army and Navy of the United States, and of the Militia of the several States, when called into the actual Service of the United States; he may require the Opinion, in writing, of the principal Officer in each of the executive Departments, upon any Subject relating to the Duties of their respective Offices, and he shall have Power to grant Reprieves and Pardons for Offences against the United States, except in Cases of Impeachment.

He shall have Power, by and with the Advice and Consent of the Senate, to make Treaties, provided two thirds of the Senators present concur; and he shall nominate, and by and with the Advice and Consent of the Senate, shall appoint Ambassadors, other public Ministers and Consuls, Judges of the supreme Court, and all other Officers of the United States, whose Appointments are not herein otherwise provided for, and which shall be established by Law: but the Congress may by Law vest the Appointment of such inferior Officers, as they think proper, in the President alone, in the Courts of Law, or in the Heads of Departments.

The President shall have Power to fill up all Vacancies that may happen during the Recess of the Senate, by granting Commissions which shall expire at the End of their next Session.

Section 3. He shall from time to time give to the Congress Information of the State of the Union, and recommend to their Consideration such Measures as he shall judge necessary and expedient; he may, on extraordinary Occasions, convene both Houses, or either of them, and in Case of Disagreement between them, with Respect to the Time of Adjournment, he may adjourn them to such Time as he shall think proper; he shall receive Ambassadors and other public Ministers; he shall take Care that the Laws be faithfully executed, and shall Commission all the Officers of the United States.

Section 4. The President, Vice President and all civil Officers of the United States, shall be removed from Office on Impeachment for, and Conviction of, Treason, Bribery, or other high Crimes and Misdemeanors.

Article III

Section 1. The judicial Power of the United States, shall be vested in one supreme Court, and in such inferior Courts as the Congress may from time to time ordain and establish. The Judges, both of the supreme and inferior Courts, shall hold their Offices during good Behaviour, and shall, at stated Times, receive for their Services, a Compensation, which shall not be diminished during their Continuance in Office.

Section 2. The judicial Power shall extend to all Cases, in Law and Equity, arising under this Constitution, the Laws of the United States, and Treaties made, or which shall be made, under their Authority; —to all Cases affecting Ambassadors, other public Ministers and Consuls; —to all Cases of admiralty and maritime Jurisdiction; —to Controversies to which the United States shall be a Party; —to Controversies between two or more States; —between a State and Citizens of another State;[8] —between Citizens of different States; —between Citizens of the same State claiming Lands under Grants of different States, and between a State, or the Citizens thereof, and foreign States, Citizens or Subjects.[8]

In all Cases affecting Ambassadors, other public Ministers and Consuls, and those in which a State shall be Party, the supreme Court shall have original Jurisdiction. In all the other Cases before mentioned, the supreme Court shall have appellate Jurisdiction, both as to Law and Fact, with such Exceptions, and under such Regulations as the Congress shall make.

The Trial of all Crimes, except in Cases of Impeachment, shall be by Jury; and such Trial shall be held in the State where the said Crimes shall have been committed; but when not committed within any State, the Trial shall be at such Place or Places as the Congress may by Law have directed.

Section 3. Treason against the United States, shall consist only in levying War against them, or in adhering to their Enemies, giving them Aid and Comfort. No Person shall be convicted of Treason unless on the Testimony of two Witnesses to the same overt Act, or on Confession in open Court.

The Congress shall have Power to declare the Punishment of Treason, but no Attainder of Treason shall work Corruption of Blood, or Forfeiture except during the Life of the Person attainted.

Article IV

Section 1. Full Faith and Credit shall be given in each State to the public Acts, Records, and judicial Proceedings of every other State. And the Congress may by general Laws prescribe the Manner in which such Acts, Records and Proceedings shall be proved, and the Effect thereof.

Section 2. The Citizens of each State shall be entitled to all Privileges and Immunities of Citizens in the several States.

A Person charged in any State with Treason, Felony, or other Crime, who shall flee from Justice, and be found in another State, shall on Demand of the executive Authority of the State from which he fled, be delivered up, to be removed to the State having Jurisdiction of the Crime.

[No Person held to Service or Labour in one State, under the Laws thereof, escaping into another, shall, in Consequence of any Law or Regulation therein, be discharged from such Service or Labour, but shall be delivered up on Claim of the Party to whom such Service or Labour may be due.][9]

Section 3. New States may be admitted by the Congress into this Union; but no new State shall be formed or erected within the Jurisdiction of any other State; nor any State be formed by the Junction of two or more States, or Parts of States, without the Consent of the Legislatures of the States concerned as well as of the Congress.

The Congress shall have Power to dispose of and make all needful Rules and Regulations respecting the Territory or other Property belonging to the United States; and nothing in this Constitution shall be so construed as to Prejudice any Claims of the United States, or of any particular State.

Section 4. The United States shall guarantee to every State in this Union a Republican Form of Government, and shall protect each of them against Invasion; and on Application of the Legislature, or of the Executive (when the Legislature cannot be convened) against domestic Violence.

Article V

The Congress, whenever two thirds of both Houses shall deem it necessary, shall propose Amendments to this Constitution, or, on the Application of the Legislatures of two thirds of the several States, shall call a Convention for proposing Amendments, which, in either Case, shall be valid to all Intents and Purposes, as Part of this Constitution, when ratified by the Legislatures of three fourths of the several States, or by Conventions in three fourths thereof, as the one or the other Mode of Ratification may be proposed by the Congress; Provided [that no Amendment which may be made prior to the Year One thousand eight hundred and eight shall in any Manner affect the first and fourth Clauses in the Ninth Section of the first Article; and][10] that no State, without its Consent, shall be deprived of its equal Suffrage in the Senate.

Article VI

All Debts contracted and Engagements entered into, before the Adoption of this Constitution, shall be as valid against the United States under this Constitution, as under the Confederation.

This Constitution, and the Laws of the United States which shall be made in Pursuance thereof; and all Treaties made, or which shall be made, under the Authority of the United States, shall be the supreme Law of the Land; and the Judges in every State shall be bound thereby, any Thing in the Constitution or Laws of any State to the Contrary notwithstanding.

The Senators and Representatives before mentioned, and the Members of the several State Legislatures, and all executive and judicial Officers, both of the United States and of the several States, shall be bound by Oath or Affirmation, to support this Constitution; but no religious Test shall ever be required as a Qualification to any Office or public Trust under the United States.

Article VII

The Ratification of the Conventions of nine States, shall be sufficient for the Establishment of this Constitution between the States so ratifying the Same.

Done in Convention by the Unanimous Consent of the States present the Seventeenth Day of September in the Year of our Lord one thousand seven hundred and Eighty seven and of the Independence of the United States of America the Twelfth. IN WITNESS whereof We have hereunto subscribed our Names,

George Washington, President and deputy from Virginia, and thirty-eight other delegates.

[The language of the original Constitution, not including the Amendments, was adopted by a convention of the states on September 17, 1787, and was subsequently ratified by the states on the following dates: Delaware, December 7, 1787; Pennsylvania, December 12, 1787; New Jersey, December 18, 1787; Georgia, January 2, 1788; Connecticut, January 9, 1788; Massachusetts, February 6, 1788; Maryland, April 28, 1788; South Carolina, May 23, 1788; New Hampshire, June 21, 1788.

Ratification was completed on June 21, 1788.

The Constitution subsequently was ratified by Virginia, June 25, 1788; New York, July 26, 1788; North Carolina, November 21, 1789; Rhode Island, May 29, 1790; and Vermont, January 10, 1791.]

Amendments

Amendment I

(First ten amendments ratified December 15, 1791.)

Congress shall make no law respecting an establishment of religion, or prohibiting the free exercise thereof; or abridging the freedom of speech, or of the press; or the right of the people peaceably to assemble, and to petition the Government for a redress of grievances.

Amendment II

A well regulated Militia, being necessary to the security of a free State, the right of the people to keep and bear Arms, shall not be infringed.

Amendment III

No Soldier shall, in time of peace be quartered in any house, without the consent of the Owner, nor in time of war, but in a manner to be prescribed by law.

Amendment IV

The right of the people to be secure in their persons, houses, papers, and effects, against unreasonable searches and seizures, shall not be violated, and no Warrants shall issue, but upon probable cause, supported by Oath or affirmation, and particularly describing the place to be searched, and the persons or things to be seized.

Amendment V

No person shall be held to answer for a capital, or otherwise infamous crime, unless on a presentment or indictment of a Grand Jury, except in cases arising in the land or naval forces, or in the Militia, when in actual service in time of War or public danger; nor shall any person be subject for the same offence to be twice put in jeopardy of life or limb; nor shall be compelled in any criminal case to be a witness against himself, nor be deprived of life, liberty, or property, without due process of law; nor shall private property be taken for public use, without just compensation.

Amendment VI

In all criminal prosecutions, the accused shall enjoy the right to a speedy and public trial, by an impartial jury of the State and district wherein the crime shall have been committed, which district shall have been previously ascertained by law, and to be informed of the nature and cause of the accusation; to be confronted with the witnesses against him; to have compulsory process for obtaining witnesses in his favor, and to have the Assistance of Counsel for his defence.

Amendment VII

In Suits at common law, where the value in controversy shall exceed twenty dollars, the right of trial by jury shall be preserved, and no fact tried by a jury, shall be otherwise re-examined in any

Court of the United States, than according to the rules of the common law.

Amendment VIII

Excessive bail shall not be required, nor excessive fines imposed, nor cruel and unusual punishments inflicted.

Amendment IX

The enumeration in the Constitution, of certain rights, shall not be construed to deny or disparage others retained by the people.

Amendment X

The powers not delegated to the United States by the Constitution, nor prohibited by it to the States, are reserved to the States respectively, or to the people.

Amendment XI
(Ratified February 7, 1795)

The Judicial power of the United States shall not be construed to extend to any suit in law or equity, commenced or prosecuted against one of the United States by Citizens of another State, or by Citizens or Subjects of any Foreign State.

Amendment XII
(Ratified June 15, 1804)

The Electors shall meet in their respective states and vote by ballot for President and Vice-President, one of whom, at least, shall not be an inhabitant of the same state with themselves; they shall name in their ballots the person voted for as President, and in distinct ballots the person voted for as Vice-President, and they shall make distinct lists of all persons voted for as President, and of all persons voted for as Vice-President, and of the number of votes for each, which lists they shall sign and certify, and transmit sealed to the seat of the government of the United States,

directed to the President of the Senate; — The President of the Senate shall, in the presence of the Senate and House of Representatives, open all the certificates and the votes shall then be counted; — The person having the greatest number of votes for President, shall be the President, if such number be a majority of the whole number of Electors appointed; and if no person have such majority, then from the persons having the highest numbers not exceeding three on the list of those voted for as President, the House of Representatives shall choose immediately, by ballot, the President. But in choosing the President, the votes shall be taken by states, the representation from each state having one vote; a quorum for this purpose shall consist of a member or members from two-thirds of the states, and a majority of all the states shall be necessary to a choice. [And if the House of Representatives shall not choose a President whenever the right of choice shall devolve upon them, before the fourth day of March next following, then the Vice-President shall act as President, as in the case of the death or other constitutional disability of the President. —][11] The person having the greatest number of votes as Vice-President, shall be the Vice-President, if such number be a majority of the whole number of Electors appointed, and if no person have a majority, then from the two highest numbers on the list, the Senate shall choose the Vice-President; a quorum for the purpose shall consist of two-thirds of the whole number of Senators, and a majority of the whole number shall be necessary to a choice. But no person constitutionally ineligible to the office of President shall be eligible to that of Vice-President of the United States.

Amendment XIII (Ratified December 6, 1865)

Section 1. Neither slavery nor involuntary servitude, except as a punishment for crime whereof the party shall have been duly convicted, shall exist within the United States, or any place subject to their jurisdiction.

Section 2. Congress shall have power to enforce this article by appropriate legislation.

Amendment XIV
(Ratified July 9, 1868)

Section 1. All persons born or naturalized in the United States, and subject to the jurisdiction thereof, are citizens of the United States and of the State wherein they reside. No State shall make or enforce any law which shall abridge the privileges or immunities of citizens of the United States; nor shall any State deprive any person of life, liberty, or property, without due process of law; nor deny to any person within its jurisdiction the equal protection of the laws.

Section 2. Representatives shall be apportioned among the several States according to their respective numbers, counting the whole number of persons in each State, excluding Indians not taxed. But when the right to vote at any election for the choice of electors for President and Vice President of the United States, Representatives in Congress, the Executive and Judicial officers of a State, or the members of the Legislature thereof, is denied to any of the male inhabitants of such State, being twenty-one years of age,[12] and citizens of the United States, or in any way abridged, except for participation in rebellion, or other crime, the basis of representation therein shall be reduced in the proportion which the number of such male citizens shall bear to the whole number of male citizens twenty-one years of age in such State.

Section 3. No person shall be a Senator or Representative in Congress, or elector of President and Vice President, or hold any Office, civil or military, under the United States, or under any State, who, having previously taken an oath, as a member of Congress, or as an officer of the United States, or as a member of any State legislature, or as an executive or judicial officer of any State, to support the Constitution of the United States, shall have engaged in insurrection or rebellion against the same, or given aid or comfort to the enemies thereof. But Congress may by a vote of two-thirds of each House, remove such disability.

Section 4. The validity of the public debt of the United States, authorized by law, including debts incurred for payment of pensions and bounties for services in suppressing insurrection or rebellion, shall not be questioned. But neither the United States nor any State shall assume or pay any debt or obligation incurred in aid of insurrection or rebellion against the United States, or any claim for the loss or emancipation of any slave; but all such debts, obligations and claims shall be held illegal and void.

Section 5. The Congress shall have power to enforce, by appropriate legislation, the provisions of this article.

Amendment XV
(Ratified February 3, 1870)

Section 1. The right of citizens of the United States to vote shall not be denied or abridged by the United States or by any State on account of race, color, or previous condition of servitude.

Section 2. The Congress shall have power to enforce this article by appropriate legislation.

Amendment XVI
(Ratified February 3, 1913)

The Congress shall have power to lay and collect taxes on incomes, from whatever source derived, without apportionment among the several States, and without regard to any census or enumeration.

Amendment XVII
(Ratified April 8, 1913)

The Senate of the United States shall be composed of two Senators from each State, elected by the people thereof, for six years; and each Senator shall have one vote. The electors in each State shall have the qualifications requisite for electors of the most numerous branch of the State legislatures.

When vacancies happen in the representation of any State in the Senate, the executive authority of such State shall issue writs of election to fill such vacancies: *Provided*, That the legislature of any State may empower the executive thereof to make temporary appointments until the people fill the vacancies by election as the legislature may direct.

This amendment shall not be so construed as to affect the election or term of any Senator chosen before it becomes valid as part of the Constitution.

Amendment XVIII
(Ratified January 16, 1919)

Section 1. After one year from the ratification of this article the manufacture, sale, or transportation of intoxicating liquors within, the importation thereof into, or the exportation thereof from the United States and all territory subject to the jurisdiction thereof for beverage purposes is hereby prohibited.

Section 2. The Congress and the several States shall have concurrent power to enforce this article by appropriate legislation.

Section 3. This article shall be inoperative unless it shall have been ratified as an amendment to the Constitution by the legislatures of the several States, as provided in the Constitution, within seven years from the date of the submission hereof to the States by the Congress.[13]

Amendment XIX
(Ratified August 18, 1920)

The right of citizens of the United States to vote shall not be denied or abridged by the United States or by any State on account of sex.

Congress shall have power to enforce this article by appropriate legislation.

Amendment XX
(Ratified January 23, 1933)

Section 1. The terms of the President and Vice President shall end at noon on the 20th day of January, and the terms of Senators and Representatives at noon on the 3d day of January, of the years in which such terms would have ended if this article had not been ratified; and the terms of their successors shall then begin.

Section 2. The Congress shall assemble at least once in every year, and such meeting shall begin at noon on the 3d day of January, unless they shall by law appoint a different day.

Section 3.[14] If, at the time fixed for the beginning of the term of the President, the President elect shall have died, the Vice President elect shall become President. If a President shall not have been chosen before the time fixed for the beginning of his term, or if the President elect shall have failed to qualify, then the Vice President elect shall act as President until a President shall have qualified; and the Congress may by law provide for the case wherein neither a President elect nor a Vice President elect shall have qualified, declaring who shall then act as President, or the manner in which one who is to act shall be selected, and such person shall act accordingly until a President or Vice President shall have qualified.

Section 4. The Congress may by law provide for the case of the death of any of the persons from whom the House of Representatives may choose a President whenever the right of choice shall have devolved upon them, and for the case of the death of any of the persons from whom the Senate may choose a Vice President whenever the right of choice shall have devolved upon them.

Section 5. Sections **1** and **2** shall take effect on the **15**th day of October following the ratification of this article.

Section 6. This article shall be inoperative unless it shall have been ratified as an amendment to the Constitution by the legislatures of three-fourths of the several States within seven years from the date of its submission.

Amendment XXI
(Ratified December 5, 1933)

Section 1. The eighteenth article of amendment to the Constitution of the United States is hereby repealed.

Section 2. The transportation or importation into any State, Territory, or possession of the United States for delivery or use therein of intoxicating liquors, in violation of the laws thereof, is hereby prohibited.

Section 3. This article shall be inoperative unless it shall have been ratified as an amendment to the Constitution by conventions in the several States, as provided in the Constitution, within seven years from the date of the submission hereof to the States by the Congress.

Amendment XXII
(Ratified February 27, 1951)

Section 1. No person shall be elected to the office of the President more than twice, and no person who has held the office of President, or acted as President, for more than two years of a term to which some other person was elected President shall be elected to the office of the President more than once. But this Article shall not apply to any person holding the office of

President when this Article was proposed by the Congress, and shall not prevent any person who may be holding the office of President, or acting as President, during the term within which this Article becomes operative from holding the office of President or acting as President during the remainder of such term.

Section 2. This article shall be inoperative unless it shall have been ratified as an amendment to the Constitution by the legislatures of three-fourths of the several States within seven years from the date of its submission to the States by the Congress.

Amendment XXIII
(Ratified March 29, 1961)

Section 1. The District constituting the seat of Government of the United States shall appoint in such manner as the Congress may direct:

A number of electors of President and Vice President equal to the whole number of Senators and Representatives in Congress to which the District would be entitled if it were a State, but in no event more than the least populous State; they shall be in addition to those appointed by the States, but they shall be considered, for the purposes of the election of President and Vice President, to be electors appointed by a State; and they shall meet in the District and perform such duties as provided by the twelfth article of amendment.

Section 2. The Congress shall have power to enforce this article by appropriate legislation.

Amendment XXIV
(Ratified January 23, 1964)

Section 1. The right of citizens of the United States to vote in any primary or other election for President or Vice President, for electors for President or Vice President, or for Senator or Representative in Congress, shall not be denied or abridged by the United States or any State by reason of failure to pay any poll tax or other tax.

Section 2. The Congress shall have power to enforce this article by appropriate legislation.

Amendment XXV
(Ratified February 10, 1967)

Section 1. In case of the removal of the President from office or of his death or resignation, the Vice President shall become President.

Section 2. Whenever there is a vacancy in the office of the Vice President, the President shall nominate a Vice President who shall take office upon confirmation by a majority vote of both Houses of Congress.

Section 3. Whenever the President transmits to the President pro tempore of the Senate and the Speaker of the House of Representatives his written declaration that he is unable to discharge the powers and duties of his office, and until he transmits to them a written declaration to the contrary, such powers and duties shall be discharged by the Vice President as Acting President.

Section 4. Whenever the Vice President and a majority of either the principal officers of the executive departments or of such other body as Congress may by law provide, transmit to the President pro tempore of the Senate and the Speaker of the House of Representatives their written declaration that the President is unable to discharge the powers and duties of his office, the Vice President shall immediately assume the powers and duties of the office as Acting President.

Thereafter, when the President transmits to the President pro tempore of the Senate and the Speaker of the House of Representatives his written declaration that no inability exists, he shall resume the powers and duties of his office unless the Vice President and a majority of either the principal officers of the executive departments or of such other body as Congress may by law provide, transmit within four days to the President pro tempore of the Senate and the Speaker of the House of Representatives their written declaration that the President is unable to discharge the powers and duties of his office. Thereupon Congress shall decide the issue, assembling within forty-eight hours for that purpose if not in session. If the Congress, within twenty-one days after receipt of the latter written declaration, or, if Congress is not in session, within twenty-one days after Congress is required to assemble, determines by two-thirds vote of both Houses that the President is unable to discharge the powers and duties of his office, the Vice President shall continue to discharge the same as Acting President; otherwise, the President shall resume the powers and duties of his office.

Amendment XXVI
(Ratified July 1, 1971)

Section 1. The right of citizens of the United States, who are eighteen years of age or older, to vote shall not be denied or abridged by the United States or by any State on account of age.

Section 2. The Congress shall have power to enforce this article by appropriate legislation.

Amendment XXVII
(Ratified May 7, 1992)

No law varying the compensation for the services of the Senators and Representatives shall take effect, until an election of Representatives shall have intervened.

Source: U.S. Congress, House, Committee on the Judiciary, *The Constitution of the United States of America, as Amended,* 100th Cong., 1st sess., 1987, H Doc 100–94.

Notes

1. The part in brackets was changed by section 2 of the Fourteenth Amendment.
2. The part in brackets was changed by the first paragraph of the Seventeenth Amendment.
3. The part in brackets was changed by the second paragraph of the Seventeenth Amendment.
4. The part in brackets was changed by section 2 of the Twentieth Amendment.
5. The Sixteenth Amendment gave Congress the power to tax incomes.
6. The material in brackets was superseded by the Twelfth Amendment.
7. This provision was affected by the Twenty-fifth Amendment.
8. These clauses were affected by the Eleventh Amendment.
9. This paragraph was superseded by the Thirteenth Amendment.
10. Obsolete.
11. The part in brackets was superseded by section 3 of the Twentieth Amendment.
12. See the Nineteenth and Twenty-sixth Amendments.
13. This amendment was repealed by section 1 of the Twenty-first Amendment.
14. See the Twenty-fifth Amendment.

APPENDIX 4
FEDERALIST NO. 10

The Same Subject Continued: The Union as a Safeguard Against Domestic Faction and Insurrection.

From the New York Packet
Friday, November 23, 1787.

Author: James Madison

To the People of the State of New York:

AMONG the numerous advantages promised by a wellconstructed Union, none deserves to be more accurately developed than its tendency to break and control the violence of faction. The friend of popular governments never finds himself so much alarmed for their character and fate, as when he contemplates their propensity to this dangerous vice. He will not fail, therefore, to set a due value on any plan which, without violating the principles to which he is attached, provides a proper cure for it. The instability, injustice, and confusion introduced into the public councils, have, in truth, been the mortal diseases under which popular governments have everywhere perished; as they continue to be the favorite and fruitful topics from which the adversaries to liberty derive their most specious declamations. The valuable improvements made by the American constitutions on the popular models, both ancient and modern, cannot certainly be too much admired; but it would be an unwarrantable partiality, to contend that they have as effectually obviated the danger on this side, as was wished and expected. Complaints are everywhere heard from our most considerate and virtuous citizens, equally the friends of public and private faith, and of public and personal liberty, that our governments are too unstable, that the public good is disregarded in the conflicts of rival parties, and that measures are too often decided, not according to the rules of justice and the rights of the minor party, but by the superior force of an interested and overbearing majority. However anxiously we may wish that these complaints had no foundation, the evidence, of known facts will not permit us to deny that they are in some degree true. It will be found, indeed, on a candid review of our situation, that some of the distresses under which we labor have been erroneously charged on the operation of our governments; but it will be found, at the same time, that other causes will not alone account for many of our heaviest misfortunes; and, particularly, for that prevailing and increasing distrust of public engagements, and alarm for private rights, which are echoed from one end of the continent to the other. These must be chiefly, if not wholly, effects of the unsteadiness and injustice with which a factious spirit has tainted our public administrations.

By a faction, I understand a number of citizens, whether amounting to a majority or a minority of the whole, who are united and actuated by some common impulse of passion, or of interest, adversed to the rights of other citizens, or to the permanent and aggregate interests of the community.

There are two methods of curing the mischiefs of faction: the one, by removing its causes; the other, by controlling its effects.

There are again two methods of removing the causes of faction: the one, by destroying the liberty which is essential to its existence; the other, by giving to every citizen the same opinions, the same passions, and the same interests.

It could never be more truly said than of the first remedy, that it was worse than the disease. Liberty is to faction what air is to fire, an aliment without which it instantly expires. But it could not be less folly to abolish liberty, which is essential to political life, because it nourishes faction, than it would be to wish the annihilation of air, which is essential to animal life, because it imparts to fire its destructive agency.

The second expedient is as impracticable as the first would be unwise. As long as the reason of man continues fallible, and he is at liberty to exercise it, different opinions will be formed. As long as the connection subsists between his reason and his self-love, his opinions and his passions will have a reciprocal influence on each other; and the former will be objects to which the latter will attach themselves. The diversity in the faculties of men, from which the rights of property originate, is not less an insuperable obstacle to a uniformity of interests. The protection of these faculties is the first object of government. From the protection of different and unequal faculties of acquiring property, the possession of different degrees and kinds of property immediately results; and from the influence of these on the sentiments and views of the respective proprietors, ensues a division of the society into different interests and parties.

The latent causes of faction are thus sown in the nature of man; and we see them everywhere brought into different degrees of activity, according to the different circumstances of civil society. A zeal for different opinions concerning religion, concerning government, and many other points, as well of speculation as of practice; an attachment to different leaders ambitiously contending for pre-eminence and power; or to persons of other descriptions whose fortunes have been interesting to the human passions, have, in turn, divided mankind into parties, inflamed them with mutual animosity, and rendered them much more disposed to vex and oppress each other than to co-operate for their common good. So strong is this propensity of mankind to fall into mutual animosities, that where no substantial occasion presents itself, the most frivolous and fanciful distinctions have been sufficient to kindle their unfriendly passions and excite their most violent conflicts. But the most common and durable source of factions has been the various and unequal distribution of property. Those who hold and those who are without property have ever formed distinct interests in society. Those who are creditors, and those who are debtors, fall under a like discrimination. A landed interest, a manufacturing interest, a mercantile interest, a moneyed interest, with many lesser interests, grow up of necessity in civilized nations, and divide them into different classes, actuated by different sentiments and views. The regulation of these various and interfering interests forms the principal task of modern legislation, and involves the spirit of party and faction in the necessary and ordinary operations of the government.

No man is allowed to be a judge in his own cause, because his interest would certainly bias his judgment, and, not improbably, corrupt his integrity. With equal, nay with greater reason, a body of men are unfit to be both judges and parties at the same time; yet what are many of the most important acts of legislation, but so many judicial determinations, not indeed concerning the rights of single persons, but concerning the rights of large bodies of citizens? And what are the different classes of legislators but advocates and parties to the causes which they determine? Is a law proposed concerning private debts? It is a question to which the creditors are parties on one side and the debtors on the other. Justice ought to hold the balance between them. Yet the parties are, and must be, themselves the judges; and the most numerous party, or, in other words, the most powerful faction must be expected to prevail. Shall domestic manufactures be encouraged, and in what degree, by restrictions on foreign manufactures? are questions which would be differently decided by the landed and the manufacturing classes, and probably by neither with a sole regard to justice and the public good. The apportionment of taxes on the various descriptions of property is an act which seems to require the most exact impartiality; yet there is, perhaps, no legislative act in which greater opportunity and temptation are given to a predominant party to trample on the rules of justice. Every shilling with which they overburden the inferior number, is a shilling saved to their own pockets.

It is in vain to say that enlightened statesmen will be able to adjust these clashing interests, and render them all subservient to the public good. Enlightened statesmen will not always be at the helm. Nor, in many cases, can such an adjustment be made at all without taking into view indirect and remote considerations, which will rarely prevail over the immediate interest which one party may find in disregarding the rights of another or the good of the whole.

The inference to which we are brought is, that the CAUSES of faction cannot be removed, and that relief is only to be sought in the means of controlling its EFFECTS.

If a faction consists of less than a majority, relief is supplied by the republican principle, which enables the majority to defeat its sinister views by regular vote. It may clog the administration, it may convulse the society; but it will be unable to execute and mask its violence under the forms of the Constitution. When a majority is included in a faction, the form of popular government, on the other hand, enables it to sacrifice to its ruling passion or interest both the public good and the rights of other citizens. To secure the public good and private rights against the danger of such a faction, and at the same time to preserve the spirit and the form of popular government, is then the great object to which our inquiries are directed. Let me add that it is the great desideratum by which this form of government can be rescued from the opprobrium under which it has so long labored, and be recommended to the esteem and adoption of mankind.

By what means is this object attainable? Evidently by one of two only. Either the existence of the same passion or interest in a majority at the same time must be prevented, or the majority, having such coexistent passion or interest, must be rendered, by their number and local situation, unable to concert and carry into effect schemes of oppression. If the impulse and the opportunity be suffered to coincide, we well know that neither moral nor religious motives can be relied on as an adequate control. They are not found to be such on the injustice and violence of individuals, and lose their efficacy in proportion to the number combined together, that is, in proportion as their efficacy becomes needful.

From this view of the subject it may be concluded that a pure democracy, by which I mean a society consisting of a small number of citizens, who assemble and administer the government in person, can admit of no cure for the mischiefs of faction. A common passion or interest will, in almost every case, be felt by a majority of the whole; a communication and concert result from the form of government itself; and there is nothing to check the inducements to sacrifice the weaker party or an obnoxious individual. Hence it is that such democracies have ever been spectacles of turbulence and contention; have ever been found incompatible with personal security or the rights of property; and have in general been as short in their lives as they have been violent in their deaths. Theoretic politicians, who have patronized this species of government, have erroneously supposed that by reducing mankind to a perfect equality in their political rights, they would, at the same time, be perfectly equalized and assimilated in their possessions, their opinions, and their passions.

A republic, by which I mean a government in which the scheme of representation takes place, opens a different prospect, and promises the cure for which we are seeking. Let us examine the points in which it varies from pure democracy, and we shall comprehend both the nature of the cure and the efficacy which it must derive from the Union.

The two great points of difference between a democracy and a republic are: first, the delegation of the government, in the latter, to a small number of citizens elected by the rest; secondly, the greater number of citizens, and greater sphere of country, over which the latter may be extended.

The effect of the first difference is, on the one hand, to refine and enlarge the public views, by passing them through the medium of a chosen body of citizens, whose wisdom may best discern the true interest of their country, and whose patriotism and love of justice will be least likely to sacrifice it to temporary or partial considerations. Under such a regulation, it may well happen that the public voice, pronounced by the representatives of the people, will be more consonant to the public good than if pronounced by the people themselves, convened for the purpose. On the other hand, the effect may be inverted. Men of factious tempers, of local prejudices, or of sinister designs, may, by intrigue, by corruption, or by other means, first obtain the suffrages, and then betray the interests, of the people. The question resulting is, whether small or extensive republics are more favorable to the election of proper guardians of the public weal; and it is clearly decided in favor of the latter by two obvious considerations:

In the first place, it is to be remarked that, however small the republic may be, the representatives must be raised to a certain number, in order to guard against the cabals of a few; and that, however large it may be, they must be limited to a certain number, in order to guard against the confusion of a multitude. Hence, the number of representatives in the two cases not being in proportion to that of the two constituents, and being proportionally greater in the small republic, it follows that, if the proportion of fit characters be not less in the large than in the small republic, the former will present a greater option, and consequently a greater probability of a fit choice.

In the next place, as each representative will be chosen by a greater number of citizens in the large than in the small republic, it will be more difficult for unworthy candidates to practice with success the vicious arts by which elections are too often carried; and the suffrages of the people being more free, will be more likely to centre in men who possess the most attractive merit and the most diffusive and established characters.

It must be confessed that in this, as in most other cases, there is a mean, on both sides of which inconveniences will be found to lie. By enlarging too much the number of electors, you render the representatives too little acquainted with all their local circumstances and lesser interests; as by reducing it too much, you render him unduly attached to these, and too little fit to comprehend and pursue great and national objects. The federal Constitution forms a happy combination in this respect; the great and aggregate interests being referred to the national, the local and particular to the State legislatures.

The other point of difference is, the greater number of citizens and extent of territory which may be brought within the compass of republican than of democratic government; and it is this circumstance principally which renders factious combinations less to be dreaded in the former than in the latter. The smaller the society, the fewer probably will be the distinct parties and interests composing it; the fewer the distinct parties and interests, the more frequently will a majority be found of the same party; and the smaller the number of individuals composing a majority, and the smaller the compass within which they are placed, the more easily will they concert and execute their plans of oppression. Extend the sphere, and you take in a greater variety of parties and interests; you make it less probable that a majority of the whole will have a common motive to invade the rights of other citizens; or if such a common motive exists, it will be more difficult for all who feel it to discover their own strength, and to act in unison with each other. Besides other impediments, it may be remarked that, where there is a consciousness of unjust or dishonorable purposes, communication is always checked by distrust in proportion to the number whose concurrence is necessary.

Hence, it clearly appears, that the same advantage which a republic has over a democracy, in controlling the effects of faction, is enjoyed by a large over a small republic,—is enjoyed by the Union over the States composing it. Does the advantage consist in the substitution of representatives whose enlightened views and virtuous sentiments render them superior to local prejudices and schemes of injustice? It will not be denied that the representation of the Union will be most likely to possess these requisite endowments. Does it consist in the greater security afforded by a greater variety of parties, against the event of any one party being able to outnumber and oppress the rest? In an equal degree does the increased variety of parties comprised within the Union, increase this security. Does it, in fine, consist in the greater obstacles opposed to the concert and accomplishment of the secret wishes of an unjust and interested majority? Here, again, the extent of the Union gives it the most palpable advantage.

The influence of factious leaders may kindle a flame within their particular States, but will be unable to spread a general conflagration through the other States. A religious sect may degenerate into a political faction in a part of the Confederacy; but the variety of sects dispersed over the entire face of it must secure the national councils against any danger from that source. A rage for paper money, for an abolition of debts, for an equal division of property, or for any other improper or wicked project, will be less apt to pervade the whole body of the Union than a particular member of it; in the same proportion as such a malady is more likely to taint a particular county or district, than an entire State.

In the extent and proper structure of the Union, therefore, we behold a republican remedy for the diseases most incident to republican government. And according to the degree of pleasure and pride we feel in being republicans, ought to be our zeal in cherishing the spirit and supporting the character of Federalists.

PUBLIUS.

APPENDIX 5
FEDERALIST NO. 51

The Structure of the Government Must Furnish the Proper Checks and Balances Between the Different Departments

From the New York Packet.
Friday, February 8, 1788.

Author: James Madison

To the People of the State of New York:

TO WHAT expedient, then, shall we finally resort, for maintaining in practice the necessary partition of power among the several departments, as laid down in the Constitution? The only answer that can be given is, that as all these exterior provisions are found to be inadequate, the defect must be supplied, by so contriving the interior structure of the government as that its several constituent parts may, by their mutual relations, be the means of keeping each other in their proper places. Without presuming to undertake a full development of this important idea, I will hazard a few general observations, which may perhaps place it in a clearer light, and enable us to form a more correct judgment of the principles and structure of the government planned by the convention.

In order to lay a due foundation for that separate and distinct exercise of the different powers of government, which to a certain extent is admitted on all hands to be essential to the preservation of liberty, it is evident that each department should have a will of its own; and consequently should be so constituted that the members of each should have as little agency as possible in the appointment of the members of the others. Were this principle rigorously adhered to, it would require that all the appointments for the supreme executive, legislative, and judiciary magistracies should be drawn from the same fountain of authority, the people, through channels having no communication whatever with one another. Perhaps such a plan of constructing the several departments would be less difficult in practice than it may in contemplation appear. Some difficulties, however, and some additional expense would attend the execution of it. Some deviations, therefore, from the principle must be admitted. In the constitution of the judiciary department in particular, it might be inexpedient to insist rigorously on the principle: first, because peculiar qualifications being essential in the members, the primary consideration ought to be to select that mode of choice which best secures these qualifications; secondly, because the permanent tenure by which the appointments are held in that department, must soon destroy all sense of dependence on the authority conferring them.

It is equally evident, that the members of each department should be as little dependent as possible on those of the others, for the emoluments annexed to their offices. Were the executive magistrate, or the judges, not independent of the legislature in this particular, their independence in every other would be merely nominal. But the great security against a gradual concentration of the several powers in the same department, consists in giving to those who administer each department the necessary constitutional means and personal motives to resist encroachments of the others. The provision for defense must in this, as in all other cases, be made commensurate to the danger of attack. Ambition must be made to counteract ambition. The interest of the man must be connected with the constitutional rights of the place. It may be a reflection on human nature, that such devices should be necessary to control the abuses of government. But what is government itself, but the greatest of all reflections on human nature? If men were angels, no government would be necessary. If angels were to govern men, neither external nor internal controls on government would be necessary. In framing a government which is to be administered by men over men, the great difficulty lies in this: you must first enable the government to control the governed; and in the next place oblige it to control itself.

A dependence on the people is, no doubt, the primary control on the government; but experience has taught mankind the necessity of auxiliary precautions. This policy of supplying, by opposite and rival interests, the defect of better motives, might be traced through the whole system of human affairs, private as well as public. We see it particularly displayed in all the subordinate distributions of power, where the constant aim is to divide and arrange the several offices in such a manner as that each may be a check on the other that the private interest of every individual may be a sentinel over the public rights. These inventions of prudence cannot be less requisite in the distribution of the supreme powers of the State. But

it is not possible to give to each department an equal power of self-defense. In republican government, the legislative authority necessarily predominates. The remedy for this inconveniency is to divide the legislature into different branches; and to render them, by different modes of election and different principles of action, as little connected with each other as the nature of their common functions and their common dependence on the society will admit. It may even be necessary to guard against dangerous encroachments by still further precautions. As the weight of the legislative authority requires that it should be thus divided, the weakness of the executive may require, on the other hand, that it should be fortified.

An absolute negative on the legislature appears, at first view, to be the natural defense with which the executive magistrate should be armed. But perhaps it would be neither altogether safe nor alone sufficient. On ordinary occasions it might not be exerted with the requisite firmness, and on extraordinary occasions it might be perfidiously abused. May not this defect of an absolute negative be supplied by some qualified connection between this weaker department and the weaker branch of the stronger department, by which the latter may be led to support the constitutional rights of the former, without being too much detached from the rights of its own department? If the principles on which these observations are founded be just, as I persuade myself they are, and they be applied as a criterion to the several State constitutions, and to the federal Constitution it will be found that if the latter does not perfectly correspond with them, the former are infinitely less able to bear such a test.

There are, moreover, two considerations particularly applicable to the federal system of America, which place that system in a very interesting point of view. First. In a single republic, all the power surrendered by the people is submitted to the administration of a single government; and the usurpations are guarded against by a division of the government into distinct and separate departments. In the compound republic of America, the power surrendered by the people is first divided between two distinct governments, and then the portion allotted to each subdivided among distinct and separate departments. Hence a double security arises to the rights of the people. The different governments will control each other, at the same time that each will be controlled by itself. Second. It is of great importance in a republic not only to guard the society against the oppression of its rulers, but to guard one part of the society against the injustice of the other part. Different interests necessarily exist in different classes of citizens. If a majority be united by a common interest, the rights of the minority will be insecure.

There are but two methods of providing against this evil: the one by creating a will in the community independent of the majority that is, of the society itself; the other, by comprehending in the society so many separate descriptions of citizens as will render an unjust combination of a majority of the whole very improbable, if not impracticable. The first method prevails in all governments possessing an hereditary or self-appointed authority. This, at best, is but a precarious security; because a power independent of the society may as well espouse the unjust views of the major, as the rightful interests of the minor party, and may possibly be turned against both parties. The second method will be exemplified in the federal republic of the United States. Whilst all authority in it will be derived from and dependent on the society, the society itself will be broken into so many parts, interests, and classes of citizens, that the rights of individuals, or of the minority, will be in little danger from interested combinations of the majority.

In a free government the security for civil rights must be the same as that for religious rights. It consists in the one case in the multiplicity of interests, and in the other in the multiplicity of sects. The degree of security in both cases will depend on the number of interests and sects; and this may be presumed to depend on the extent of country and number of people comprehended under the same government. This view of the subject must particularly recommend a proper federal system to all the sincere and considerate friends of republican government, since it shows that in exact proportion as the territory of the Union may be formed into more circumscribed Confederacies, or States oppressive combinations of a majority will be facilitated: the best security, under the republican forms, for the rights of every class of citizens, will be diminished: and consequently the stability and independence of some member of the government, the only other security, must be proportionately increased. Justice is the end of government. It is the end of civil society. It ever has been and ever will be pursued until it be obtained, or until liberty be lost in the pursuit. In a society under the forms of which the stronger faction can readily unite and oppress the weaker, anarchy may as truly be said to reign as in a state of nature, where the weaker individual is not secured against the violence of the stronger; and as, in the latter state, even the stronger individuals are prompted, by the uncertainty of their condition, to submit to a government which may protect the weak as well as themselves; so, in the former state, will the more powerful factions or parties be gradually induced, by a like motive, to wish for a government which will protect all parties, the weaker as well as the more powerful.

It can be little doubted that if the State of Rhode Island was separated from the Confederacy and left to itself, the insecurity of rights under the popular form of government within such narrow limits would be displayed by such reiterated oppressions of factious majorities that some power altogether independent of the people would soon be called for by the voice of the very factions whose misrule had proved the necessity of it. In the extended republic of the United States, and among the great variety of interests, parties, and sects which it embraces, a coalition of a majority of the whole society could seldom take place on any other principles than those of justice and the general good; whilst there being thus less danger to a minor from the will of a major party, there must be less pretext, also, to provide for the security of the former, by introducing into the government a will not dependent on the latter, or, in other words, a will independent of the society itself. It is no less certain than it is important, notwithstanding the contrary opinions which have been entertained, that the larger the society, provided it lie within a practical sphere, the more duly capable it will be of self-government. And happily for the REPUBLICAN CAUSE, the practicable sphere may be carried to a very great extent, by a judicious modification and mixture of the FEDERAL PRINCIPLE.

PUBLIUS.

APPENDIX 6
POLITICAL PARTY AFFILIATIONS IN CONGRESS AND THE PRESIDENCY, 1789–2020

Year	Congress	House		Senate		President
		Majority party	Principal minority party	Majority party	Principal minority party	
1789–1791	1st	AD-38	Op-26	AD-17	Op-9	F (Washington)
1791–1793	2nd	F-37	DR-33	F-16	DR-13	F (Washington)
1793–1795	3rd	DR-57	F-48	F-17	DR-13	F (Washington)
1795–1797	4th	F-54	DR-52	F-19	DR-13	F (Washington)
1797–1799	5th	F-58	DR-48	F-20	DR-12	F (John Adams)
1799–1801	6th	F-64	DR-42	F-19	DR-13	F (John Adams)
1801–1803	7th	DR-69	F-36	DR-18	F-13	DR (Jefferson)
1803–1805	8th	DR-102	F-39	DR-25	F-9	DR (Jefferson)
1805–1807	9th	DR-116	F-25	DR-27	F-7	DR (Jefferson)
1807–1809	10th	DR-118	F-24	DR-28	F-6	DR (Jefferson)
1809–1811	11th	DR-94	F-48	DR-28	F-6	DR (Madison)
1811–1813	12th	DR-108	F-36	DR-30	F-6	DR (Madison)
1813–1815	13th	DR-112	F-68	DR-27	F-9	DR (Madison)
1815–1817	14th	DR-117	F-65	DR-25	F-11	DR (Madison)
1817–1819	15th	DR-141	F-42	DR-34	F-10	DR (Monroe)
1819–1821	16th	DR-156	F-27	DR-35	F-7	DR (Monroe)

(Continued)

(Continued)

Year	Congress	House Majority party	House Principal minority party	Senate Majority party	Senate Principal minority party	President
1821–1823	17th	DR-158	F-25	DR-44	F-4	DR (Monroe)
1823–1825	18th	DR-187	F-26	DR-44	F-4	DR (Monroe)
1825–1827	19th	AD-105	J-97	AD-26	J-20	DR (John Q. Adams)
1827–1829	20th	J-119	AD-94	J-28	AD-20	DR (John Q. Adams)
1829–1831	21st	D-139	NR-74	D-26	NR-22	DR (Jackson)
1831–1833	22nd	D-141	NR-58	D-25	NR-21	D (Jackson)
1833–1835	23rd	D-147	AM-53	D-20	NR-20	D (Jackson)
1835–1837	24th	D-145	W-98	D-27	W-25	D (Jackson)
1837–1839	25th	D-108	W-107	D-30	W-18	D (Van Buren)
1839–1841	26th	D-124	W-118	D-28	W-22	D (Van Buren)
1841–1843	27th	W-133	D-102	W-28	D-22	W (W. Harrison)
						W (Tyler)
1843–1845	28th	D-142	W-79	W-28	D-25	W (Tyler)
1845–1847	29th	D-143	W-77	D-31	W-25	D (Polk)
1847–1849	30th	W-115	D-108	D-36	W-21	D (Polk)
1849–1851	31st	D-112	W-109	D-35	W-25	W (Taylor)
						W (Fillmore)
1851–1853	32nd	D-140	W-88	D-35	W-24	W (Fillmore)
1853–1855	33rd	D-159	W-71	D-38	W-22	D (Pierce)
1855–1857	34th	R-108	D-83	D-42	R-15	D (Pierce)
1857–1859	35th	D-131	R-92	D-35	R-20	D (Buchanan)
1859–1861	36th	R-113	D-101	D-38	R-26	D (Buchanan)
1861–1863	37th	R-106	D-42	R-31	D-11	R (Lincoln)
1863–1865	38th	R-103	D-80	R-39	D-12	R (Lincoln)
1865–1867[1]	39th	U-145	D-46	U-42	D-10	U (Lincoln)
						U (A. Johnson)
1867–1869	40th	R-143	D-49	R-42	D-11	R (A. Johnson)
1869–1871	41st	R-170	D-73	R-61	D-11	R (Grant)
1871–1873	42nd	R-139	D-104	R-57	D-17	R (Grant)
1873–1875	43rd	R-203	D-88	R-54	D-19	R (Grant)
1875–1877	44th	D-181	R-107	R-46	D-29	R (Grant)

Year	Congress	House Majority party	House Principal minority party	Senate Majority party	Senate Principal minority party	President
1877–1879	45th	D-156	R-137	R-39	D-36	R (Hayes)
1879–1881	46th	D-150	R-128	D-43	R-33	R (Hayes)
1881–1883	47th	R-152	D-130	R-37	D-37	R (Garfield)
						R (Arthur)
1883–1885	48th	D-200	R-119	R-40	D-36	R (Arthur)
1885–1887	49th	D-182	R-140	R-41	D-34	D (Cleveland)
1887–1889	50th	D-170	R-151	R-39	D-37	D (Cleveland)
1889–1891	51st	R-173	D-159	R-37	D-37	R (B. Harrison)
1891–1893	52nd	D-231	R-88	R-47	D-39	R (B. Harrison)
1893–1895	53rd	D-220	R-126	D-44	R-38	D (Cleveland)
1895–1897	54th	R-246	D-104	R-43	D-39	D (Cleveland)
1897–1899	55th	R-206	D-134	R-46	D-34	R (McKinley)
1899–1901	56th	R-185	D-163	R-53	D-26	R (McKinley)
1901–1903	57th	R-198	D-153	R-56	D-29	R (McKinley)
						R (T. Roosevelt)
1903–1905	58th	R-207	D-178	R-58	D-32	R (T. Roosevelt)
1905–1907	59th	R-250	D-136	R-58	D-32	R (T. Roosevelt)
1907–1909	60th	R-222	D-164	R-61	D-29	R (T. Roosevelt)
1909–1911	61st	R-219	D-172	R-59	D-32	R (Taft)
1911–1913	62nd	D-228	R-162	R-49	D-42	R (Taft)
1913–1915	63rd	D-290	R-127	D-51	R-44	D (Wilson)
1915–1917	64th	D-231	R-193	D-56	R-39	D (Wilson)
1917–1919	65th	D-216	R-210	D-53	R-42	D (Wilson)
1919–1921	66th	R-237	D-191	R-48	D-47	D (Wilson)
1921–1923	67th	R-300	D-132	R-59	D-37	R (Harding)
1923–1925	68th	R-225	D-207	R-51	D-43	R (Coolidge)
1925–1927	69th	R-247	D-183	R-54	D-40	R (Coolidge)
1927–1929	70th	R-237	D-195	R-48	D-47	R (Coolidge)
1929–1931	71st	R-267	D-163	R-56	D-39	R (Hoover)
1931–1933	72nd	D-216	R-218	R-48	D-47	R (Hoover)
1933–1935	73rd	D-313	R-117	D-59	R-36	D (F. Roosevelt)

(Continued)

(Continued)

Year	Congress	House Majority party	House Principal minority party	Senate Majority party	Senate Principal minority party	President
1935–1937	74th	D-322	R-103	D-69	R-25	D (F. Roosevelt)
1937–1939	75th	D-333	R-89	D-75	R-17	D (F. Roosevelt)
1939–1941	76th	D-262	R-169	D-69	R-23	D (F. Roosevelt)
1941–1943	77th	D-267	R-162	D-66	R-28	D (F. Roosevelt)
1943–1945	78th	D-222	R-209	D-57	R-38	D (F. Roosevelt)
1945–1947	79th	D-243	R-190	D-56	R-38	D (F. Roosevelt) D (Truman)
1947–1949	80th	R-246	D-188	R-51	D-45	D (Truman)
1949–1951	81st	D-263	R-171	D-54	R-42	D (Truman)
1951–1953	82nd	D-234	R-199	D-48	R-47	D (Truman)
1953–1955	83rd	R-221	D-213	R-48	D-46	R (Eisenhower)
1955–1957	84th	D-234	R-201	D-48	R-47	R (Eisenhower)
1957–1959	85th	D-233	R-200	D-49	R-47	R (Eisenhower)
1959–1961	86th	D-283	R-153	D-64	R-34	R (Eisenhower)
1961–1963	87th	D-262	R-175	D-64	R-36	D (Kennedy)
1963–1965	88th	D-258	R-176	D-67	R-33	D (Kennedy) D (L. Johnson)
1965–1967	89th	D-295	R-140	D-68	R-32	D (L. Johnson)
1967–1969	90th	D-248	R-187	D-64	R-36	D (L. Johnson)
1969–1971	91st	D-243	R-192	D-58	R-42	R (Nixon)
1971–1973	92nd	D-255	R-180	D-54	R-44	R (Nixon)
1973–1975	93rd	D-242	R-192	D-56	R-42	R (Nixon) R (Ford)
1975–1977	94th	D-291	R-144	D-60	R-37	R (Ford)
1977–1979	95th	D-292	R-143	D-61	R-38	D (Carter)
1979–1981	96th	D-277	R-158	D-58	R-41	D (Carter)
1981–1983	97th	D-242	R-192	R-53	D-46	R (Reagan)
1983–1985	98th	D-269	R-166	R-54	D-46	R (Reagan)
1985–1987	99th	D-253	R-182	R-53	D-47	R (Reagan)
1987–1989	100th	D-258	R-177	D-55	R-45	R (Reagan)
1989–1991	101st	D-260	R-175	D-55	R-45	R (G. H. W. Bush)

Year	Congress	House		Senate		President
		Majority party	Principal minority party	Majority party	Principal minority party	
1991–1993	102nd	D-267	R-167	D-56	R-44	R (G. H. W. Bush)
1993–1995	103rd	D-258	R-176	D-57	R-43	D (Clinton)
1995–1997	104th	R-230	D-204	R-52	D-48	D (Clinton)
1997–1999	105th	R-226	D-207	R-55	D-45	D (Clinton)
1999–2001	106th	R-223	D-211	R-55	D-45	D (Clinton)
2001–2003	107th	R-221	D-212	D-50	R-50	R (G. W. Bush)
2003–2005	108th	R-229	D-204	R-51	D-48	R (G. W. Bush)
2005–2007	109th	R-232	D-202	R-55	D-44	R (G. W. Bush)
2007–2009	110th	D-233	R-202	D-49	R-49	R (G. W. Bush)
2009–2011	111th	D-254	R-175	D-57	R-40	D (Obama)
*2011–2013	112th	D-193	R-242	D-53	R-47	D (Obama)
2013–2015	113th	R-232	D-200	D-53	R-45	D (Obama)
2015–2017	114th	R-246	D-188	R-54	D-44	D (Obama)
2017–2019	115th	R-241	D-194	R-52	D-46	R (Trump)
2019–2021	116th	D-232	R-197	R-53	D-45	R (Trump)
2021–[2]	117th	D-219	R-203	Pending	Pending	D (Biden)

Sources: For data through the 33rd Congress, see U.S. Bureau of the Census, *Historical Statistics of the United States, Colonial Times to 1970* (Washington, D.C.: Government Printing Office, 1975), 1083–1084; for data after the 33rd Congress, see U.S. Congress, Joint Committee on Printing, *Official Congressional Directory* (Washington, D.C.: Government Printing Office, 2008), 553–554; for 2008 election data see CQ Politics Election 2008, www.cqpolitics.com/wmspage.cfn?parm1=2. See also http://innovation.cq.com/election_night08?tab2=f; for 2010 election data, see http://www.rollcall.com/politics/. For 2012 election data, see the Office of the Clerk of the U.S. House of Representatives, http://clerk.house.gov/member_info/cong.aspx.

Notes: Figures are for the beginning of the first session of each Congress. Key to abbreviations: AD—Administration; AM—Anti-Masonic; D—Democratic; DR—Democratic-Republican; F—Federalist; J—Jacksonian; NR—National Republican; Op—Opposition; R—Republican; U—Unionist; W—Whig.

1. The Republican Party ran under the Union Party banner in 1864.

2. Data current as of November 19, 2020. Senate control pending two Georgia runoff elections on January 5, 2021. *Source:* National Public Radio, "2020 Election Results," (Aggregated results from AP), https://apps.npr.org/elections20-interactive/? Accessed November 19, 2020.

APPENDIX 7
SUMMARY OF PRESIDENTIAL ELECTIONS, 1789–2020

Year	No. of states	Candidates		Electoral vote		Popular vote	
1789[a]	10	Fed.		Fed.		——[b]	
		George Washington		69			
1792[a]	15	Fed.		Fed.		——[b]	
		George Washington		132			
1796[a]	16	Dem.-Rep.	Fed.	Dem.-Rep.	Fed.	——[b]	
		Thomas Jefferson	John Adams	68	71		
1800[a]	16	Dem.-Rep.	Fed.	Dem.-Rep.	Fed.	——[b]	
		Thomas Jefferson	John Adams	73	65		
		Aaron Burr	Charles Cotesworth Pinckney				
1804	17	Dem.-Rep.	Fed.	Dem.-Rep.	Fed.	——[b]	
		Thomas Jefferson	Charles Cotesworth Pinckney	162	14		
		George Clinton	Rufus King				
1808	17	Dem.-Rep.	Fed.	Dem.-Rep.	Fed.	——[b]	
		James Madison	Charles Cotesworth Pinckney	122	47		
		George Clinton	Rufus King				
1812	18	Dem.-Rep.	Fed.	Dem.-Rep.	Fed.	——[b]	
		James Madison	George Clinton	128	89		
		Elbridge Gerry	Jared Ingersoll				
1816	19	Dem.-Rep.	Fed.	Dem.-Rep.	Fed.	——[b]	
		James Monroe	Rufus King	183	34		
		Daniel D. Tompkins	John Howard				
1820	24	Dem.-Rep	——[c]	Dem.-Rep.	——[c]	——[b]	
		James Monroe		231			
		Daniel D. Tompkins					

Year	No. of states	Candidates		Electoral vote		Popular vote	
1824[d]	24	Dem.-Rep.	Dem.-Rep.	Dem.-Rep.	Dem.-Rep.	Dem.-Rep.	Dem.-Rep.
		Andrew Jackson	John Q. Adams	99	84	151,271	113,122
		John C. Calhoun	Nathan Sanford			41.3%	30.9%
1828	24	Dem.-Rep.	Nat.-Rep.	Dem.-Rep.	Nat.-Rep.	Dem.-Rep.	Nat.-Rep.
		Andrew Jackson	John Q. Adams	178	83	642,553	500,897
		John C. Calhoun	Richard Rush			56.0%	43.6%
1832[e]	24	Dem.	Nat.-Rep.	Dem.	Nat.-Rep.	Dem.	Nat.-Rep.
		Andrew Jackson	Henry Clay	219	49	701,780	484,205
		Martin Van Buren	John Sergeant		54.2%		37.4%
1836[f]	26	Dem.	Whig	Dem.	Whig	Dem.	Whig
		Martin Van Buren	William H. Harrison	170	73	764,176	550,816
		Richard M. Johnson	Francis Granger			50.8%	36.6%
1840	26	Dem.	Whig	Dem.	Whig	Dem.	Whig
		Martin Van Buren	William H. Harrison	60	234	1,128,854	1,275,390
		Richard M. Johnson	John Tyler			46.8%	52.9%
1844	26	Dem.	Whig	Dem.	Whig	Dem.	Whig
		James Polk	Henry Clay	170	105	1,339,494	1,300,004
		George M. Dallas	Theodore Frelinghuysen			49.5%	48.1%
1848	30	Dem.	Whig	Dem.	Whig	Dem.	Whig
		Lewis Cass	Zachary Taylor	127	163	1,233,460	1,361,393
		William O. Butler	Millard Fillmore			42.5%	47.3%
1852	31	Dem.	Whig	Dem.	Whig	Dem.	Whig
		Franklin Pierce	Winfield Scott	254	42	1,607,510	1,386,942
		William R. King	William A. Graham			50.8%	43.9%

Year	No. of states	Candidates		Electoral vote		Popular vote	
		Dem.	Rep.	Dem.	Rep.	Dem.	Rep.
1856[g]	31	James Buchanan	John C. Fremont	174	114	1,836,072	1,342,345
		John C. Breckinridge	William L. Dayton			45.3%	33.1%
1860[h]	33	Stephen A. Douglas	Abraham Lincoln	12	180	1,380,202	1,865,908
		Herschel V. Johnson	Hannibal Hamlin			29.5%	39.8%
1864[i]	36	George B. McClellan	Abraham Lincoln	21	212	1,812,807	2,218,388
		George H. Pendleton	Andrew Johnson			45.0%	55.0%
1868[j]	37	Horatio Seymour	Ulysses S. Grant	80	214	2,708,744	3,013,650
		Francis P. Blair Jr.	Schuyler Colfax			47.3%	52.7%
1872[k]	37	Horace Greeley	Ulysses S. Grant		286	2,834,761	3,598,235
		Benjamin Gratz Brown	Henry Wilson			43.8%	55.6%
1876	38	Samuel J. Tilden	Rutherford B. Hayes	184	185	4,288,546	4,034,311
		Thomas A. Hendricks	William A. Wheeler			51.0%	47.9%

(Continued)

(Continued)

Year	No. of states	Candidates Dem.	Candidates Rep.	Electoral vote Dem.	Electoral vote Rep.	Popular vote Dem.	Popular vote Rep.
1880[o]	38	Winfield S. Hancock	James A. Garfield				
		William H. English	Chester A. Arthur			48.2%	48.3%
1884	38	Grover Cleveland	James G. Blaine	219	182	4,874,621	4,848,936
		Thomas A. Hendricks	John A. Logan			48.5%	48.2%
1888	38	Grover Cleveland	Benjamin Harrison	168	233	5,534,488	5,443,892
		Allen G. Thurman	Levi P. Morton			48.6%	47.8%
1892[l]	44	Grover Cleveland	Benjamin Harrison	277	145	5,551,883	5,179,244
		Adlai E. Stevenson	Whitelaw Reid			46.1%	43.0%
1896	45	William J. Bryan	William McKinley	176	271	6,511,495	7,108,480
		Arthur Sewall	Garret A. Hobart			46.7%	51.0%
1900	45	William J. Bryan	William McKinley	155	292	6,358,345	7,218,039
		Adlai E. Stevenson	Theodore Roosevelt			45.5%	51.7%
1904	45	Alton B. Parker	Theodore Roosevelt	140	336	5,028,898	7,626,593
		Henry G. Davis	Charles W. Fairbanks			37.6%	56.4%
		John W. Kern	James S. Sherman			43.0%	51.6%
1912[m]	48	Woodrow Wilson	William H. Taft	435	8	6,293,152	3,486,333
		Thomas R. Marshall	James S. Sherman			41.8%	23.2%
1916	48	Woodrow Wilson	Charles E. Hughes	277	254	9,126,300	8,546,789
		Thomas R. Marshall	Charles W. Fairbanks			49.2%	46.1%
1920	48	James M. Cox	Warren G. Harding	127	404	9,140,884	16,133,314
		Franklin D. Roosevelt	Calvin Coolidge			34.2%	60.3%
1924[n]	48	John W. Davis	Calvin Coolidge	136	382	8,386,169	15,717,553
		Charles W. Bryant	Charles G. Dawes			28.8%	54.1%
1928	48	Alfred E. Smith	Herbert C. Hoover	87	444	15,000,185	21,411,991
		Joseph T. Robinson	Charles Curtis			40.8%	58.2%
1932	48	Franklin D. Roosevelt	Herbert C. Hoover	472	59	22,825,016	15,758,397
		John N. Garner	Charles Curtis			57.4%	39.6%
1936	48	Franklin D. Roosevelt	Alfred M. Landon	523	8	27,747,636	16,679,543
		John N. Garner	Frank Knox			60.8%	36.5%
1940	48	Franklin D. Roosevelt	Wendell L. Willkie	449	82	27,263,448	22,336,260
		Henry A. Wallace	Charles L. McNary			54.7%	44.8%
1944	48	Franklin D. Roosevelt	Thomas E. Dewey	432	99	25,611,936	22,013,372
		Harry S. Truman	John W. Bricker			53.4%	45.9%
1948[o]	48	Harry S. Truman	Thomas E. Dewey	303	189	24,105,587	21,970,017
		Alben W. Barkley	Earl Warren			49.5%	45.1%
1952	48	Adlai E. Stevenson II	Dwight D. Eisenhower	89	442	27,314,649	33,936,137
		John J. Sparkman	Richard M. Nixon			44.4%	55.1%
1956[p]	48	Adlai E. Stevenson II	Dwight D. Eisenhower	73	457	26,030,172	35,585,245
		Estes Kefauver	Richard M. Nixon			42.0%	57.4%

Year	No. of states	Candidates Dem.	Candidates Rep.	Electoral vote Dem.	Electoral vote Rep.	Popular vote Dem.	Popular vote Rep.
1960[q]	50	John F. Kennedy	Richard M. Nixon	303	219	34,221,344	34,106,671
		Lyndon B. Johnson	Henry Cabot Lodge			49.7%	49.5%
1964	50	Lyndon B. Johnson	Barry Goldwater				
		Hubert H. Humphrey	William E. Miller			61.1%	38.5%
1968[r]	50	Hubert H. Humphrey	Richard M. Nixon				
		Edmund S. Muskie	Spiro T. Agnew			42.7%	43.4%
1972[s]	50*	George McGovern	Richard M. Nixon	17	520	29,171,791	47,170,179
		Sargent Shriver	Spiro T. Agnew			37.5%	60.7%
1976[t]	50*	Jimmy Carter	Gerald R. Ford	297	240	40,830,763	39,147,793
		Walter F. Mondale	Robert Dole			50.1%	48.0%
1980	50*	Jimmy Carter	Ronald Reagan	49	489	35,483,883	43,904,153
		Walter F. Mondale	George H. W. Bush			41.0%	50.7%
1984	50*	Walter F. Mondale	Ronald Reagan	13	525	37,577,185	54,455,075
		Geraldine Ferraro	George H. W. Bush			40.6%	58.8%
1988[u]	50*	Michael S. Dukakis	George H. W. Bush	111	426	41,809,074	48,886,097
		Lloyd Bentsen	Dan Quayle			45.6%	53.4%
1992	50*	William J. Clinton	George H. W. Bush	370	168	44,909,326	39,103,882
		Albert Gore	Dan Quayle			43.0%	37.4%
1996	50*	William J. Clinton	Robert J. Dole	379	159	47,402,357	39,198,755
		Albert Gore	Jack F. Kemp			49.2%	40.7%
2000	50*	Albert Gore	George W. Bush	266	271	50,992,335	50,455,156
		Joseph I. Lieberman	Richard B. Cheney			48.4%	47.9%
2004	50*	John Kerry	George W. Bush	252	286	59,026,013	62,025,554
		John Edwards	Richard B. Cheney			47.3%	50.7%
2008	50*	Barack Obama	John McCain	365	173	69,498,459	59,948,283
		Joe Biden	Sarah Palin			52.9%	45.6%
2012	50*	Barack Obama	Mitt Romney	332	206	62,611,250	59,134,475
		Joe Biden	Paul Ryan			51.5%	48.5%
2016**	50*	Hillary Clinton	Donald Trump	232	306	64,827,442	62,494,402
		Tim Kaine	Mike Pence			(48.2%)	(46.4%)
2020	50*	Joe Biden	Donald Trump	306[v]	232	78,738,112	73,149,296
		Kamala Harris	Mike Pence			50.9%	47.3%

Sources: Harold W. Stanley and Richard G. Niemi, *Vital Statistics on American Politics, 2007–2008* (Washington, D.C.: CQ Press, 2008), 26–30; *CQ Press Guide to U.S. Elections*, 5th ed. (Washington, D.C.: CQ Press, 2006), 715–719; for the 2008 election: for presidential race electoral vote data, see *CQ Politics Election 2008*, http://innovation.cq.com/election_night08?tab2=f. For presidential race popular vote data, see the *New York Times*'s Presidential Big Board, http://elections.nytimes.com/2008/results/president/votes.html. 2012 election data calculated from Politico, 2012 Presidential Election, http://www.politico.com/2012-election/map/#/President/2012/.

Note: Dem.-Rep.—Democratic-Republican; Fed.—Federalist; Nat.-Rep.—National-Republican; Dem.—Democratic; Rep.—Republican.

a. Elections from 1789 through 1800 were held under rules that did not allow separate voting for president and vice president.

b. Popular vote returns are not shown before 1824 because consistent, reliable data are not available.

c. 1820: One electoral vote was cast for John Adams and Richard Stockton, who were not candidates.

d. 1824: All four candidates represented Democratic-Republican factions. William H. Crawford received 41 electoral votes and Henry Clay received 37 votes. Because no candidate received a majority, the election was decided (in Adams's favor) by the House of Representatives.

e. 1832: Two electoral votes were not cast.

f. 1836: Other Whig candidates receiving electoral votes were Hugh L. White, who received 26 votes, and Daniel Webster, who received 14 votes.

g. 1856: Millard Fillmore, Whig-American, received 8 electoral votes.

h. 1860: John C. Breckinridge, southern Democrat, received 72 electoral votes. John Bell, Constitutional Union, received 39 electoral votes.

i. 1864: Eighty-one electoral votes were not cast.

j. 1868: Twenty-three electoral votes were not cast.

k. 1872: Horace Greeley, Democrat, died after the election. In the Electoral College, Democratic electoral votes went to Thomas Hendricks, 42 votes; Benjamin Gratz Brown, 18 votes; Charles J. Jenkins, 2 votes; and David Davis, 1 vote. Seventeen electoral votes were not cast.

l. 1892: James B. Weaver, People's Party, received 22 electoral votes.

m. 1912: Theodore Roosevelt, Progressive Party, received 88 electoral votes.

n. 1924: Robert M. La Follette, Progressive Party, received 13 electoral votes.

o. 1948: J. Strom Thurmond, States' Rights Party, received 39 electoral votes.

p. 1956: Walter B. Jones, Democrat, received 1 electoral vote.

q. 1960: Harry Flood Byrd, Democrat, received 15 electoral votes.

r. 1968: George C. Wallace, American Independent Party, received 46 electoral votes.

s. 1972: John Hospers, Libertarian Party, received 1 electoral vote.

t. 1976: Ronald Reagan, Republican, received 1 electoral vote.

u. 1988: Lloyd Bentsen, the Democratic vice-presidential nominee, received 1 electoral vote for president.

v. Results current as of November 19, 2020. *Source:* The Cook Political Report, *2020 National Popular Vote Tracker,* https://cook political.com/2020-national-popular-vote-tracker. Accessed November 19, 2020.

*Fifty states plus the District of Columbia.

**Election data current as of November 29, 2016.

GLOSSARY

abolitionist movement: a political struggle to end slavery and free all slaves

absentee ballots: votes completed and submitted by a voter prior to the day of an election

adversarial system: a legal structure in which two opposing sides present their case in the most persuasive way possible

affirmative action: a policy designed to address the consequences of previous discrimination by providing advantages to individuals based upon their identities

agency capture: when agencies tasked with regulating businesses, industries, or other interest groups are populated by individuals with close ties to the very firms they are supposed to regulate

agenda-setting: the media's ability to highlight certain issues and bring them to the attention of the public

aggregating: a process through which Internet and other news providers relay the news as reported by journalists and other sources

Albany Plan: a proposal for a union of British colonies in North America in which colonial legislatures would choose delegates to form an assembly under the leadership of a chief executive appointed by Great Britain

Alien and Sedition Acts: four separate laws passed under the administration of President John Adams that, among other things, restricted the freedom of speech and the press

amendment: a constitutional provision for a process by which changes may be made to the Constitution

American dream: the idea that individuals should be able to achieve prosperity through hard work, sacrifice, and their own talents

American exceptionalism: belief in the special character of the United States as a uniquely free nation based on its history and its commitment to democratic ideals and personal liberty

American political culture: a shared set of beliefs, customs, traditions, and values that define the relationship of Americans to their government and to other American citizens

Anti-Federalists: the name taken by those opposed to the proposed Constitution; the Anti-Federalists favored stronger state governments

appellate jurisdiction: the authority of a court to hear and review decisions made by lower courts in that system

apportionment: the process of determining the number of representatives for each state using census data; states are divided into congressional districts that have at least one representative each

appropriation: the process through which congressional committees allocate funds to executive branch agencies, bureaus, and departments

Arab Spring: a series of protests taking place across North Africa and the Middle East beginning in early 2010 that led to democratic reforms in some nations and civil war and chaos in others

Articles of Confederation and Perpetual Union: a constituting document calling for the creation of a union of thirteen sovereign states in which the states, and not the union, were the centers of political power

Astroturf lobbying: when a group presents the facade of grassroots support that does not exist on its own or would not exist without the "purchase" of support by the lobbying firm itself

bail: an amount of money posted as a security to allow the charged individual to be freed while awaiting trial

beat system: the practice of assigning reporters to specific types of news, policies, and events

bill: a draft of a proposed law

Bill of Rights: the first ten amendments to the U.S. Constitution that list a set of fundamental rights and freedoms that individuals possess and that government cannot infringe upon

block grant: a type of grant-in-aid that gives state officials more authority in the disbursement of federal funds

brief: a legal document presented by plaintiffs; defendants; and, at times, other interested parties outlining their arguments in a case

broadcast media: outlets for news and other content that rely on mass communications technology to bring stories directly into people's homes; these media sources are subject to stricter content regulations than cable television outlets and alternative sources of information

Brown v. Board of Education of Topeka: a landmark 1954 Supreme Court ruling that overturned *Plessy v. Ferguson* and declared legal segregation in public education to be in conflict with the equal protection clause of the Fourteenth Amendment

budget deficit: when the federal government takes in less money than it spends

budget resolution: a step in the budgeting process in which Congress provides broad outlines for federal spending

budget surplus: when the federal government takes in more money than it spends

bureaucratic adjudication: when the federal bureaucracy settles disputes between parties that arise over the implementation of federal laws and presidential executive orders or determines which individuals or groups are covered under a regulation or program

bureaucratic discretion: the power to decide how a law is implemented and, at times, what Congress actually meant when it passed a given law

bureaucratic drift: when bureaucracies stray from their established goals and devote their energies and efforts to peripheral tasks

cabinet departments: federal executive departments created and funded by Congress

campaigns: the political process that would-be representatives use to connect to American voters in hopes of winning office

capitalist system: a way of structuring economic activity in which private firms are allowed to make most or all of the decisions involving the production and distribution of goods and services

categorical grant: a grant-in-aid provided to states with specific provisions on its use

caucus: a process through which a state's eligible voters gather to discuss candidates and issues and select delegates to represent their preferences in later stages of the nomination process

citizen journalists: nonprofessionals who cover or document news and events or offer their own analyses of them

civic education: the transmission of information about the political world and civic norms to learners

civic engagement: working to improve society through political and nonpolitical action

civil disobedience: the intentional refusal to obey a law in order to call attention to its injustice

civil law: a category of law covering cases involving private rights and relationships between individuals and groups

civil liberties: fundamental rights and freedoms of citizens, the protection of which involves restricting the power of a government

civil rights: fundamental guarantees ensuring equal treatment and protecting against discrimination under the laws of a nation

clear and present danger test: a Supreme Court tool to evaluate whether or not forms of political expression constitute such a threat to national security as to warrant restriction

clientele agencies: organizations that act to serve and promote the interests of their clients

closed primaries: primary elections in which only registered voters from a particular political party may vote

cloture: a procedure through which senators can end debate on a bill and proceed to action, provided three-fifths of senators agree to it

collective action: political action that occurs when individuals contribute their energy, time, or money to a larger group goal

collective good: also called a public good; some benefit or desirable outcome that individuals can enjoy or profit from even if they do not help achieve or secure it

commerce clause: a part of the Constitution that grants Congress the authority to regulate business and commercial activity

commercial bias: the shaping of the content and focus of news based upon the desire to capture news consumers

committee chairs: leaders of the subunits of congressional committees who have authority over the committee's agenda

communist system: a way of structuring economic activity in which a government exerts complete control over the production and distribution of goods and services

concurrent powers: powers granted to both states and the federal government in the Constitution

confederal systems: structures of governance in which the subnational governments retain the majority of the granted authority

Congressional Budget Office (CBO): the federal agency tasked with producing independent analyses of budgetary and economic issues to support the congressional budget process

conservatism: a political ideology that emphasizes a reduced role for government and emphasizes individual liberty

consideration: a combination of cognition and affect that contributes to any one answer to any one question or evaluation

constituencies: bodies of voters in a given area who elect a representative or senator

constitution: a document that defines and creates a people politically, sets out the fundamental principles of governance, and creates the rules and institutions through which a people choose to self-govern

Constitutional Convention: a meeting held in Philadelphia in 1787 at which state delegates met to fix the Articles of Confederation that would result in the drafting of the U.S. Constitution

constitutional interpretation: the process of applying the Constitution in assessing whether or not a law, part of a law, or an action by a governmental official is or is not in conflict with the Constitution

constitutional republic: a form of government in which people vote for elected representatives to make laws and policies and in which limits on the ability of that government to restrict individual rights are placed in a constituting document that is recognized as the highest law of the land

consumer price index (CPI): an economic measure that is used to assess price changes associated with the cost of living

containment: a Cold War foreign policy strategy designed to restrict expansion of Soviet ideological and military influence, using military force if necessary

cooperative federalism: a vision of American federalism in which the states and the national government work together to shape public policy

countermajoritarian difficulty: the concern that judicial review empowers the Supreme Court to overturn the will of the majority of citizens who have acted through their elected officials

criminal law: a category of law covering actions determined to harm the community itself

critical elections: major national elections that signal change either in the balance of power between two major parties or the emergence of a new party system

cues and information shortcuts: pieces of information individuals pick up that help them form political opinions

Daughters of Liberty: a group of colonial-era women who participated in the boycotting of British goods

de facto segregation: a separation of individuals based on identity that arises not by law but because of other factors, such as residential housing patterns

defendant: a person or group against whom a case is brought in court

de jure segregation: the separation of individuals based on their characteristics, such as race, intentionally and by law

delegates: people who act as voters' representatives at a convention to select their party's presidential nominee

demand shock: a disruption to consumers' willingness or ability to purchase goods and services

democracy: a system of government where power is held and political decisions are made by the people in that society

demographics: the grouping of individuals based on shared characteristics, such as ancestry, race, ethnicity, and gender

deregulation: the reduction or elimination of government power in a particular industry, usually in order to create more competition within the industry

descriptive representation: the degree to which a body of representatives in a legislature does or does not reflect the diversity of that nation's identities and lived experiences

desegregation: the act of eliminating laws or practices that separate individuals based upon racial identity

devolution: a national policy goal of returning more authority to state or local governments

digital divide: divisions in society that are driven by access to and knowledge about technologies; these gaps often fall along the lines of partisanship, class, race, and ethnicity

digital participation: active engagement with political issues through the Internet, including social media, blogs, and other information sharing platforms, and membership in online communities

direct democracy: a form of government in which citizens vote directly on public policies

direction: the focus of an individual's opinion

discretionary spending: spending for programs and policies at the discretion of Congress and the president

domestic policy: policy designed to improve the social welfare of citizens

double jeopardy: the prosecution of an individual more than once for the same crime

dual federalism: a view of American federalism in which the states and the nation operate independently in their own areas of public policy

due process clause: the clause in the Fourteenth Amendment that restricts state governments from denying their citizens the right to due process of law

economic equality: when wealth is relatively evenly distributed across society

economic interest groups: groups that organize to advocate on behalf of the economic interests of their members

economic policy: the efforts of government to regulate and support the economy in order to protect and expand citizens' financial well-being and economic prospects and to support businesses in the global financial system

economic recession: a period of decline in economic activity, typically defined by two consecutive quarters of negative GDP growth

economy: the systems and organizations through which a society produces and distributes goods and services

elections: the political system through which American voters choose their representatives

Electoral College: a slate of individuals apportioned to states who are pledged to vote for a presidential candidate

elites: a small number of individuals (who tend to have well-informed and well-reasoned opinions)

elitist theory: a theory of governmental influence that focuses on the advantages that certain interests have in the political process based on the unequal distribution of economic and political power

entitlement programs: programs wherein one receives a set of benefits regardless of income provided one meets certain categorical requirements, such as age or a minimum number of years of payroll contributions

enumerated powers: powers explicitly granted to the government via the Constitution

equal protection clause: a clause of the Fourteenth Amendment that serves as the constitutional basis for the assault on educational segregation in the courts and for the assertion of civil rights for Americans of many different identities in many different areas of public and private life

Equal Rights Amendment: a proposed but not ratified amendment to the Constitution that sought to guarantee equality of rights based upon sex

equal time rule: a regulation that requires American radio and television broadcast networks to provide equal time for political candidates to present their views on issues

essentialism: the risks posed by linking individuals' lived experiences to policy preferences, whether by identifying those individuals by those policies or by excluding them from advocating different policy objectives

establishment clause: a First Amendment clause protecting individuals from governmental establishment of, or support for, religion

European Union (EU): an association of European countries formed in the 1990s for the purpose of achieving political and economic integration

exclusionary rule: a rule governing the inadmissibility of evidence obtained without a proper warrant

executive agreements: agreements between a president and another nation that do not have the same durability in the American system as a treaty but may carry important foreign policy consequences

executive branch: the institution responsible for carrying out laws passed by the legislative branch

Executive Office of the President (EOP): a collection of offices within the White House organization designed primarily to provide information to the president

executive orders: directions made by presidents to the executive branch departments that often contain nothing more than instructions to be carried out by agencies, bureaus, and departments but may at times be considered acts of presidential lawmaking

executive political appointees: employees at high levels in the federal bureaucracy who serve at the pleasure of the president and are subject to presidential removal

executive privilege: a right claimed by presidents to keep confidential certain conversations, records, and transcripts from outside scrutiny, especially that of Congress

exit poll: a survey conducted outside a polling place in which individuals are asked who or what they just voted for and why

exploratory committee: a group that helps determine whether a potential candidate should run for office and that helps lay the groundwork for the campaign

extended republic: a republic so large and diverse, with so many factions vying for power, that no one faction is able to assert its will over all the others

faction: a group of self-interested people who use the government to get what they want, trampling the rights of others in the process

fairness doctrine: a federal rule that expanded regulations for American political news coverage beyond just the provision of time for candidates to the content of the coverage itself

fake news: a term that may refer to the intentional presentation of news in favor of a political party or the intentional presentation of unverified or inaccurate news

federal bureaucracy: the organizations and suborganizations within the executive branch that are tasked with putting the laws of the nation into effect

federal civil service: the permanent professional branches of government concerned with administrative functions, excluding the armed forces and political appointments

federal courts of appeals: the middle level of the federal judiciary; these courts review and hear appeals from the federal district courts

federal district courts: the lowest level of the federal judiciary; these courts usually possess original jurisdiction in cases that originate at the federal level

federalism: a structure of governance that places the people's authority in two or more levels of government

The Federalist Papers: a series of eighty-five essays written by Alexander Hamilton, James Madison, and John Jay and published between 1787 and 1788 that lay out the theory behind the Constitution

Federalists: the name taken by supporters of the proposed Constitution; the Federalists called for a stronger national government

federal judiciary: the branch of the federal government that interprets and applies the laws of the nation

Federal Reserve System: the central bank of the United States

federal systems: structures of governance that divide a people's sovereignty between two or more levels of government

felon disenfranchisement: the denial of voting rights to Americans who have been convicted of felonies

Fifteenth Amendment: an amendment to the Constitution passed in 1870 affirming the voting rights of all freedmen

fighting words: expression (spoken, written, or symbolic) that is likely to incite violence or disrupt the peace

filibuster: a tactic through which an individual senator may postpone action on a piece of legislation

fire alarm oversight: a term that describes congressional oversight procedures primarily in response to problems or complaints

fiscal policy: a set of activities through which government tries to lower unemployment, support economic activity, and stabilize the economy by using policies of taxation and spending

fiscal stimulus: government policies designed to increase economic activity

focus group: a small group of individuals assembled for a directed conversation during which one hopes to uncover patterns of thinking about issues and individuals

focusing events: sudden and dramatic events that draw individuals' attention

foreign policy: the ways in which political actors in a nation engage others at home and abroad to advance their nation's interests, protect and secure national security, and support their own economies

Fourteenth Amendment: an amendment to the Constitution passed in 1868 affirming the citizenship of all persons born or naturalized in the United States and, for the first time in the history of the Constitution, placing explicit restrictions on the laws of states that sought to abridge the privileges and immunities of citizens of the United States

framing: influencing people's interpretations of news, events, or issues through the presentation of the context

freedom of expression: a fundamental right affirmed in the First Amendment to speak, publish, and act in the political space

free exercise clause: a First Amendment clause guarding the rights of individuals to exercise and express their religious beliefs

free riders: individuals who enjoy collective goods without helping to secure them

front-loading: when a state pushes its primary or caucus to a date as early in the season as possible to become more instrumental in the nomination process

full faith and credit clause: a portion of the Constitution that generally requires states to honor licenses and judicial outcomes of other states

gender gap: a term that refers to the fact that American women are more likely to identify with and vote for Democratic Party candidates than men, who are more likely to vote for Republican Party candidates

gerrymandering: the intentional use of redistricting to benefit a specific interest or group of voters

going public: a strategy through which presidents reach out directly to the American people with the hope that the people will, in turn, put pressure upon their representatives and senators to press for a president's policy goals

government: a system of rules and institutions that defines and shapes the contours of public action

governmental interest groups: organizations that act to secure the interests of local, state, or foreign governments in the political process

government corporations: organizations that act as businesses within the federal government, charging fees for their services but still subject to governmental control and possible financial subsidization

grand jury: a group of citizens who, based on the evidence presented to them, conclude whether or not a person is to be indicted and subsequently tried in a court of law

grant-in-aid: federal money provided to states to implement public policy objectives

Great Compromise: an agreement for a plan of government that drew upon both the Virginia and New Jersey Plans; it settled issues of state representation by calling for a bicameral legislature with a House of Representatives apportioned proportionately and a Senate apportioned equally

Great Depression: a period defined by the most significant economic crisis in American history

gridlock: an inability to compromise and enact legislation that is driven by political polarization

gross domestic product (GDP): a measure of the total value of goods and services produced by a nation's economic activity

hate speech: speech that has no other purpose but to express hatred, particularly toward members of a group identified by racial or ethnic identity, gender, or sexual orientation

horse race phenomenon: coverage of political campaigns that focuses more on the drama of the campaign than on policy issues

House Committee on Rules: a powerful committee that determines when a bill will be subject to debate and vote on the House floor, how long the debate will last, and whether amendments will be allowed on the floor

House majority leader: the head of the party with the most seats in the House of Representatives, chosen by the party's members

House minority leader: the head of the party with the second-highest number of seats in the House of Representatives, chosen by the party's members

impeachment: a legislative process for removing elected and appointed officials

implementation: the bureaucracy's role in putting into action the laws that Congress has passed

implied powers: powers not textually granted to a government but considered valid in order to carry out the enumerated powers

inalienable rights: rights that exist before and above any government or its power

incentives: inducements that leaders of a bureaucracy can offer to their employees to spur successful performance

incumbency advantage: institutional advantages held by those already in office who are trying to fend off challengers in an election

independent executive agency: an agency similar to a cabinet department but existing outside the cabinet structure and usually having a narrower focus of mission

independent regulatory agencies: organizations that exist outside the major cabinet departments and whose job it is to monitor and regulate specific sectors of the economy

inflation: the rise in the prices of goods and services purchased by individuals

infotainment: a merging of information and entertainment in a way designed to attract viewers and gain market share

initiative: a direct vote on a policy proposal or change that has been placed on the ballot by citizens or organized groups

inside lobbying: when lobbyists contact members of Congress or their staff directly to advocate for their group's position

intensity: the strength of involvement and preference of an individual's opinion

interagency rivalry: when two or more agencies are charged with a similar mandate, an outcome that becomes more likely in times of budget cuts and competition for scarce or dwindling appropriations

interest groups: voluntary associations of people who come together with an agreed-upon set of political and policy objectives and who attempt to pull the levers of political power in service of these defined goals

interest rates: the rates paid to borrow money

intergovernmental lobbying: efforts by state and local governments to act in Washington on behalf of their own interests

intermediate scrutiny: a middle-ground standard for determining whether differential treatment is allowable

internationalism: an approach to international affairs that emphasizes close contact and cooperation between nations

intersectionality: the presence of multiple and overlapping identities and inequalities

Intolerable Acts: a term used in the American colonies to refer to a series of laws enacted by Great Britain in response to the Boston Tea Party

investigative journalism: an approach to news gathering in which reporters dig into stories, often looking for instances of corruption or failures to uphold the interests of citizens

iron triangle: the coordinated (and mutually beneficial) activities of interest groups, Congress, and the bureaucracy to achieve shared policy goals, sometimes against the general interests of society or specific groups within it

isolationism: a foreign policy orientation in which a nation attempts to stay out of foreign entanglements

issue network: the webs of influence among interest groups, policymakers, and policy advocates

Jim Crow laws: state and local laws passed after Reconstruction through the mid-1950s by which white southerners reasserted their dominance by denying African Americans basic social, economic, and civil rights, such as the right to vote

judicial activism: a philosophy of constitutional interpretation that asserts justices should wield the power of judicial review when needed

judicial branch: the institution responsible for hearing and deciding cases via a system of federal courts

judicial restraint: a philosophy of constitutional interpretation that asserts justices should be cautious in overturning laws

judicial review: the authority of the highest court in a political system to determine if a law is or is not in conflict with a government's highest law, which in the United States is the Constitution

legal segregation: the separation by law of individuals based upon their racial identities

legislative branch: in a divided government, the institution responsible for making laws

legislative deliberation: the considered argument and discussion of the issues by congressional representatives

Lemon test: a three-pronged test developed by the Supreme Court to determine whether a law or action by the federal or a state government violates the establishment clause

libel: expression in written form or similarly published media that defames a person's character

liberalism: a political ideology that emphasizes more robust governmental action, especially to ensure equality

libertarianism: a political ideology that emphasizes minimal governmental involvement in individual choices

liberty: social, political, and economic freedoms

linked fate: a theory of group identification that describes ways in which individuals tie their own life chances to those of members of a group who share their lived experiences

lobbying: interacting with government officials to advance a group's goals in the area of public policy

logroll: an exchange of political favors, such as when legislators trade votes to support one another's proposed legislation

majority: when a candidate receives more than 50 percent of the vote

majority-minority districts: districts in which voters of a minority ethnicity constitute an electoral majority within that electoral district

malapportionment: the uneven distribution of the population between legislative districts

mandatory spending: spending for programs and policies required by law

markup: a process during which a bill is revised prior to a final vote in Congress

Marshall Plan: a Cold War policy wherein loans and aid were made available to the nations of Western Europe; it also established organizations of economic cooperation

masses: the majority of individuals (who tend to be less informed)

mass media: sources of information that appeal to a wide audience, including newspapers, radio, television, and Internet outlets

material rewards: a type of tangible benefit made available to members and contributors of a group

media effects: the power of the news media in shaping individuals' political knowledge, preferences, and political behavior

merit system: a system of hiring and promotion based on competitive testing results, education, and other qualifications rather than politics and personal connections

minimalist paradigm: a theory of public opinion that emphasizes how most people fall short of what we expect them to know, think about, and pay attention to in the complicated world of politics and policy

Miranda rights: the right not to speak and to have an attorney present during questioning; these rights must be given by police to individuals suspected of criminal activity

monetary policy: a set of economic policy tools designed to regulate the amount of money in the economy (in circulation and in the deposits)

Monroe Doctrine: a policy that asserted American interests in and primacy over actions in the Western Hemisphere

motor voter law: a law allowing Americans to register to vote when applying for or renewing their driver's licenses and making it easier for Americans with disabilities to register to vote

national conventions: meetings where delegates officially select their party's nominee for the presidency

national debt: the sum of all previously incurred annual federal deficits

natural rights: rights that people have inherently that are not granted by any government

necessary and proper clause: a part of the Constitution that grants the federal government the authority to pass laws required to carry out its enumerated powers; also called the elastic clause

need-based assistance programs: social welfare programs whose benefits are allocated to individuals demonstrating specific needs

negative freedoms: fundamental liberties of which protection is ensured by restricting governmental action and authority

net neutrality: the idea that Internet service providers should not be allowed to discriminate based upon content or bandwidth demands

neutrality test: a Supreme Court test for examining questions of free expression that allows restrictions upon religious expression, provided that laws doing so not single out one faith, or faith over nonfaith

New Deal: a set of policies passed during the administration of President Franklin Roosevelt to combat the Great Depression

New Jersey Plan: a plan of government that preserved many of the provisions in the Articles of Confederation, including the unicameral legislature with equal votes for each state, but strengthened the confederal government

news media: the variety of sources providing information and covering events, including newspapers, television, radio, the Internet, and social media

Nineteenth Amendment: a 1920 amendment to the Constitution that prevented states from denying the right to vote based on sex

nomination: the formal process through which parties choose their candidates for political office

nonattitudes: a term referring to the lack of stable and coherent opinions on political issues and candidates

nuclear proliferation: the development of nuclear weapons or nuclear weapons capability among previously nonnuclear states or nonstate actors

obscenity and pornography: text, images, or video that depict sexual activity in ways offensive to the broader community and that lack any artistic merit

Office of Management and Budget (OMB): the executive branch office whose purpose is to assist the president in setting national spending priorities

open primaries: primary elections in which all eligible voters may vote, regardless of their partisan affiliation

oral argument: presentation made by plaintiffs and attorneys before the Supreme Court

original jurisdiction: the authority of a court to act as the first court to hear a case, which includes the finding of facts in the case

outside (grassroots) lobbying: a type of lobbying that focuses on reaching constituents and mobilizing them to pressure their representatives rather than pressuring the representatives directly

oversight: efforts by Congress to ensure that executive branch agencies, bureaus, and cabinet departments, as well as their officials, are acting legally and in accordance with congressional goals

partisan bias: the slanting of political news coverage in support of a particular political party or ideology

partisan press: media outlets or organizations that promote a particular political ideology or support a political party

party identification: the degree to which an individual identifies with and supports a particular political party

party platform: a set of positions and policy objectives that members of a political party agree to

party systems: periods of stability of the composition of political parties and the issues around which they coalesce, brought on by shorter periods of intense change

path dependence: the way in which a set of political outcomes shapes future possibilities for political action

penny press: nineteenth-century American newspapers that sold for only one cent each, thus increasing the size of the audience that could afford to purchase them

plaintiff: a person or group who brings a case in court

plea bargaining: a legal process in which the plaintiff and defendant agree to an outcome prior to the handing out of a verdict

Plessy v. Ferguson: a Supreme Court case in 1896 that upheld legal racial segregation

pluralism: a theory of governmental influence that views the distribution of political power among many competing groups as serving to keep any one of them in check

plurality: when a candidate receives more votes than any other candidate

police patrol oversight: a term that describes congressional oversight as a process of constant monitoring rather than responding to specific crises

police powers: a category of reserved powers that includes the protection of people's health, safety, and welfare

policy agenda: the set of issues to which government officials, voters, and the public attend

policy entrepreneurs: individuals in government, academic institutions, think tanks, interest groups, and other venues who try to shape the political agenda and get their solutions implemented

political action committees (PACs): organizations that raise money to support chosen candidates and defeat others

political ambition: a personal desire to enter politics

political efficacy: a person's belief that she or he can make effective political change

political equality: when members of a society possess the same rights under the laws of the nation

political ideology: a set of beliefs about the desired goals and outcomes of a process of governance

political institutions: rules and structures that shape political action and representation

political mobilization: efforts by members of American political parties to turn out the vote and encourage their members to get others to do so

political participation: the different ways in which individuals take action to shape the laws and policies of a government

political party: an organized group of candidates, officeholders, voters, and activists who work together to elect candidates to political office

political patronage: filling administrative positions as a reward for support rather than based solely on merit

political polarization: a sharp ideological distance between political parties

political propaganda: attempts to shape governmental actions and laws by changing people's beliefs and opinions

political socialization: the variety of experiences and factors that shape our political values, attitudes, and behaviors

politics: the process of influencing the actions of officials and the policies of a nation, state, locality, or community

positive freedoms: fundamental rights and freedoms that require action by individuals to express and by governments to secure

power elite: a group composed of the top echelons of people in the business world, government, and military

precedent: a judicial decision that guides future courts in handling similar cases

preemptive war: a type of war in which a state uses its military might to challenge adversaries before they launch attacks or harbor those who might do so

presidential pardon: the presidential authority to forgive an individual and set aside punishment for a crime

presidential primary elections: elections in which a state's voters choose delegates who support a particular candidate for nomination

priming: shaping individuals' interpretations of news or events by highlighting certain details or contexts

principal-agent problem: the challenge that arises when one actor, the principal, tasks another, the agent, to carry out the principal's wishes in the presence of uncertainty and unequal information

prior restraint: the suppression of material prior to publication on the grounds that it might endanger national security

privacy: a right not enumerated in the Constitution but affirmed by Supreme Court decisions that covers individuals' decisions in their private lives, including decisions regarding reproductive rights and sexuality

private bureaucracies: privately owned corporations and companies that carry out specific tasks according to a prescribed set of rules and procedures

private contractors: nongovernmental workers hired by the federal bureaucracy to provide goods and services in support of federal activity

privatization: shifting control over the provision of certain governmental functions from the federal bureaucracy to the private sector

procedural justice: a judicial standard requiring that fairness be applied to all participants equally

proportional representation systems: structures of electoral representation in which parties are represented in government according to their candidates' overall share of the vote

protest: a public demonstration designed to call attention to the need for action or change

proxy wars: wars in which major powers support different sides but do not directly go to war with each other

public interest groups: groups that act on behalf of the collective interests of a broad group of individuals, many of whom may not be members or contributors to the organization

public opinion: the sum of individual attitudes about government, policies, and issues

public opinion survey: sampling a portion of the public in order to draw conclusions about the larger population's views on an issue

public policy: the intentional use of governmental power to secure the health, welfare, opportunities, and national security of citizens

purposive benefits: rewards in the form of satisfaction from working with others to achieve a common goal or purpose

push poll: a negative campaign tactic disguised as a survey in which a candidate's opponent or opponents are portrayed in an unfavorable way

question order: the ways in which earlier questions in a survey may shape answers to later questions

question wording: the ways in which the phrasing of survey questions may shape answers

race of interviewer effects: the potential impact of the racial identities of surveyors and respondents on the respondents' answers

random digit dialing: when potential survey respondents are selected by computer-generated random numbers

random selection: how participants are selected from the population for inclusion in the study

Reagan Doctrine: a foreign policy agenda under President Ronald Reagan offering American assistance, including military training and weaponry, to anticommunist groups

realignment: a major shift in allegiance to the political parties that is often driven by changes in the issues that unite or divide voters

reasonableness standard: a more relaxed judicial standard in which differential treatment must be shown to be reasonable and not arbitrary

recess appointment: occurs when Congress is not in session and the president appoints a person to fill a position that would normally require the advice and consent of the Senate; unless the person is formally confirmed when the Senate reconvenes, the position ends at the conclusion of the next session of Congress

recruitment: the process through which political parties identify potential candidates

redistricting: states' redrawing of the electoral district boundaries following each census

referendum: a direct vote on a policy proposal or change put on the ballot by a state legislature or other body of government

registration requirements: the set of rules that govern who can vote and how, when, and where they vote

represent: to "stand for" the interests of voters in government

representative democracy: a political system in which voters select representatives who then vote on matters of public policy

republics: governments ruled by representatives of the people

reserved powers: powers reserved to the states if not textually granted to the federal government

respondents: individuals who answer a survey

responsible party model: a proposal for party reform that emphasized cohesive party positions that present voters with a clear set of choices and allow members' voices to be effectively incorporated into party positions on issues

revolving door phenomenon: the movement of individuals between government and lobbying positions

roll-call vote: a recorded vote on a bill

Roosevelt Corollary: a policy that asserted that the United States was the guarantor of political, military, and economic stability in Latin America and the Caribbean

rulemaking: the process through which the federal bureaucracy fills in critical details of a law

runoff election: an election that is held between the two candidates with the highest total votes if no one candidate scores a majority

salience: the centrality of an individual's opinion in the sense of the opinion's ability to shape the individual's views on other issues or candidates

sample: the subgroup of individuals from the larger population of whom one wants to measure the opinions

sampling error: error in a statistical analysis arising from the unrepresentativeness of the sample taken

scientific poll: when pollsters try to gain an understanding of a large group of individuals by obtaining the opinions of a carefully chosen small sample of the group, although they are aware of the limitations of the effort

Second Continental Congress: an assembly of delegates from the thirteen British colonies in America that drafted and approved the Declaration of Independence, conducted the Revolutionary War, and created the governmental structure that followed the war

selective benefits: goods that are made available only to those who join or contribute to a group

selective incorporation: the piecemeal process through which the Supreme Court has affirmed that almost all the protections within the Bill of Rights also apply to state governments

self-selected listener opinion poll (SLOP): a survey in which respondents choose to respond to a survey prompt on their own

Senate majority leader: a chosen senator who speaks for the majority party and helps to shape the Senate agenda

senatorial courtesy: a traditional norm in which presidents consult with senators from the states when considering potential nominees to the lower levels of the federal judiciary

Senior Executive Service (SES): federal employees with higher-level supervisory and administrative responsibilities who are paid and treated more like vice presidents of businesses than political figures

separate but equal: the doctrine that racial segregation was constitutional so long as the facilities for blacks and whites were roughly equal

separation of powers: a design of government that distributes powers across institutions to avoid making one branch too powerful on its own

Seven Years' War: a war principally between France and Great Britain and other European nations that was fought across the globe

Shays' Rebellion: a grassroots popular uprising against the government of Massachusetts that led to calls for reform, or replacement, of the Articles of Confederation

signing statements: text written by a president while signing a bill into law, usually consisting of political statements or reasons for signing the bill but possibly also including the president's interpretation of the law itself

single-member plurality system: a structure of electoral representation in which a candidate and the party that he or she represents must win the most votes in a state or district in order to be represented in government

slander: expression in spoken form that defames a person's character

social benefits: rewards in the form of new connections or access to networks that members of a group receive through their participation

social contract: an agreement in which people give to their governments the ability to rule over them to ensure an orderly and functioning society

social equality: when no individual's social status is inherently higher than another's

social insurance programs: programs such as Social Security that are financed by payroll taxes paid by individuals and that do not have income-based requirements to receive their benefits

socialism: a political ideology that emphasizes an even stronger role for government than liberalism, including government control and ownership of sectors of the economy

socialist system: a way of structuring economic activity in which private firms are allowed to operate and make decisions over production and distribution, but with significant governmental involvement to ensure economic equality

social media: forms of electronic communication that enable users to create and share content or to participate in social networking

social movement: voluntary associations of individuals who come together to change things or keep things from changing, but they often do so by calling attention to a set of injustices or wrongs in order to get policymakers to act and to educate the public about the issue

social welfare policies: governmental efforts designed to improve or protect the health, safety, education, and opportunities for citizens and residents

socioeconomic status (SES): a measure that captures an individual's wealth, income, occupation, and educational attainment

soft news: stories that focus on celebrity and personality rather than political or economic issues

solicitor general: a presidential appointee who represents the federal government in the Supreme Court

Sons of Liberty: a group initially formed of merchants and workingmen in response to the Stamp Act that resisted Great Britain and its tax policies

Speaker of the House: the leader of the House of Representatives, chosen by an election of its members

split-ticket voting: when a voter chooses a candidate from one party for one office and a candidate from a different party for another position on the ballot

spoils system: the practice of cleaning house of one's opponents and installing supporters in their place following a successful election

stability: the degree of change over time, in different contexts, or in response to differently worded survey questions of a particular opinion

standard operating procedures: the sets of rules governing the behavior of bureaucrats

standing: the legal ability to bring a case in court

stare decisis: a doctrine of constitutional interpretation based upon following earlier decisions in similar cases

state and local bureaucracies: public organizations below the federal level designed to carry out specific tasks according to a prescribed set of rules and procedures

State of the Union address: an annual speech before Congress in which the president highlights the administration's achievements and presses a legislative agenda

state sovereignty resolutions: state legislative measures that affirm the sovereignty of states under the Tenth Amendment

states' rights: the idea that American states have the authority to self-govern, even when in conflict with national laws

statutes: written laws established by a legislative body

stereotype: a preconceived, often oversimplified idea about something that people apply as a filter to the world

straw poll: an unofficial tally of opinion or support at a meeting or event

strict scrutiny: the most stringent judicial standard applied for deciding whether a law or policy is allowed to treat people differently

substantive representation: the degree to which elected representatives or senators represent the interests and policy preferences of their constituents

suffrage: the right to vote in political elections

superdelegates: members of the Democratic Party—usually leaders or members of note—who are not pledged to any certain candidate based on the outcomes of their state's primary or caucus

super PACs: political action committees (PACs) permitted to spend unlimited amounts of money in a campaign, though these actions must not be coordinated with that campaign

superpower: an extremely powerful state that is capable of influencing international events and the actions of other less powerful states

supply shock: a disruption to an economy's ability to produce goods and services

supremacy clause: a part of the Constitution that establishes the Constitution and the laws of the nation passed under its authority as the highest laws of the nation

Supreme Court: the highest level of the federal judiciary, which was established in the Constitution and serves as the highest court in the nation

symbolic speech: protected expression in the form of images, signs, and other symbols

term limits: formal limits on the number of times an elected official may serve in a given office

terrorism: the use of violence as a means to achieve political ends

third party (minor party): a political party operating over a limited period of time in competition with two other major parties

Thirteenth Amendment: an amendment to the Constitution passed in 1865 prohibiting slavery within the United States

Three-Fifths Compromise: an agreement reached by delegates at the Constitutional Convention that ensured that a slave would count as three-fifths of a person for a state's representation

turf wars: when bureaucrats compete to take duties and responsibilities away from one another's departments or keep their opponents from doing so

tyranny: the suppression of the rights of a people by those holding power

tyranny of the majority: when a large number of citizens use the power of their majority to trample on the rights of a smaller group

tyranny of the minority: when a small number of citizens trample on the rights of the larger population

unemployment rate: the percentage of the total labor force that is unemployed

unfunded mandates: federal regulations that must be followed by the states but whose costs must also be shouldered by the states

unitary systems: structures of governance that place the people's sovereignty in a national government, with subnational governments deriving their authority from it

United Nations: an international organization formed in 1945 to promote international dialogue and cooperation

unorthodox lawmaking: a term that refers to ways in which legislative activity, especially on major bills, is often more fluid than described in a traditional textbook

validity: the degree to which a tool accurately measures what it is intended to

veto: the power of a president to reject a bill passed by Congress, sending it back to the originating branch with objections noted

Virginia Plan: a plan of government calling for a strong national government with three branches of government and a bicameral legislature, with legislators elected using proportional representation

voluntary associations: groups and communities who join with each other in pursuit of collective interests and common goals

voter turnout: the number of eligible voters who actually participate in an election versus the total number of eligible voters

War Powers Resolution of 1973: a law passed over a presidential veto that restricts the power of the president in committing the nation's armed forces into combat or situations of likely combat

warrant: a writ issued by a judge authorizing some activity

weighting: a procedure in which the observed results of a survey are adjusted according to what is known about specific proportions in the larger population

whip: an individual in the House or Senate, chosen by his or her party members, whose job is to ensure party unity and discipline

wire service: an organization that gathers and reports on news and then sells the stories to other outlets

writ of certiorari: the process through which most cases reach the Supreme Court; after four justices concur that the Court should hear the case, a writ of certiorari is issued to the lower court to request the relevant case records

writ of habeas corpus: a statement demanding that authorities in charge of a person's detention establish the reasons for that detention

yellow journalism: an approach to reporting employed in the nineteenth century that relied on sensational headlines and emotional language to persuade readers and sell newspapers

NOTES

CHAPTER 1

1. Ray Halbritter, "Letter from the Publisher," *Indian Country Today*, Fall 2016, https://ictmn.lughstudio.com/wp-content/uploads/2016/10/DAPL-Magazine-2016_PREVIEW_r1.pdf.

2. "Corporate Overview," Energy Transfer, accessed March 12, 2018, http://www.energytransfer.com/company_overview.aspx.

3. Jack Healy, "Occupying the Prairie: Tension on the Plains as Tribes Move to Block a Pipeline," *New York Times*, August 23, 2016, https://www.nytimes.com/2016/08/24/us/occupying-the-prairie-tensions-rise-as-tribes-move-to-block-a-pipeline.html.

4. Jack Healy, "From 280 Tribes, a Protest on the Plains Speaks Out against an Oil Pipeline," *New York Times*, September 12, 2016, https://www.nytimes.com/interactive/2016/09/12/us/12tribes.html.

5. Healy, "From 280 Tribes."

6. Christopher Mele, "Veterans to Serve as 'Human Shields' for Dakota Pipeline Protesters," *New York Times*, November 29, 2016, https://www.nytimes.com/2016/11/29/us/veterans-to-serve-as-human-shields-for-pipeline-protesters.html.

7. Water Protector Legal Collective, "Mission Statement," accessed March 12, 2018, https://waterprotectorlegal.org.

8. Jack Healy, "Neighbors Say South Dakota Pipeline Protests Disrupt Lives and Livelihoods," *New York Times*, September 13, 2016, https://www.nytimes.com/2016/09/14/us/north-dakota-pipeline-protests.html.

9. Sue Skalicky and Monica Davey, "Tension between Police and Standing Rock Protesters Reaches Boiling Point," *New York Times*, October 29, 2016, https://www.nytimes.com/2016/10/29/us/dakota-access-pipeline-protest.html.

10. Healy, "Occupying the Prairie."

11. Erin Mundahl, "As North Dakota Continues to Try Standing Rock Protesters, Dismissed Cases Pile Up," InsideSources.com, May 29, 2017, http://www.insidesources.com/nd-dismissed-cases-standing-rock/.

12. Jack Healy, "Army Approves Construction of Dakota Access Pipeline," *New York Times*, February 7, 2017, https://www.nytimes.com/2017/02/07/us/army-approves-construction-of-dakota-access-pipeline.html.

13. Mitch Smith, "Standing Rock Protest Camp, Once Home to Thousands, Is Razed," *New York Times*, February 23, 2017, https://www.nytimes.com/2017/02/23/us/standing-rock-protest-dakota-access-pipeline.html.

14. Marty Schladen, "Hearing on Ohio Bill to Limit Protests Ends in Protest," *Zanesville Times Recorder*, January 31, 2020.

15. Schladen, "Hearing on Ohio Bill."

16. Birthright citizenship for indigenous Americans was not protected until 1924, by an act of Congress.

17. Philip Bump, "48 Percent of Millennials Think the American Dream Is Dead. Here's Why," *Washington Post*, December 10, 2015, https://www.washingtonpost.com/news/the-fix/wp/2015/12/10/48-percent-of-millennials-think-the-american-dream-is-dead-heres-why. The authors obtained their data from Harvard Kennedy School Institute of Politics, "Harvard IOP Fall 2015 Poll: Trump, Carson Lead Republican Primary; Sanders Edging Clinton among Democrats, Harvard IOP Poll Finds," December 10, 2015, http://iop.harvard.edu/survey/details/harvard-iop-fall-2015-poll.

18. Samuel Huntington, *American Politics: The Promise of Disharmony* (Cambridge, MA: Harvard University Press, 1983); John Kingdon, *America the Unusual* (New York: St. Martin's Press, 1999).

19. Paraphrasing Eric Foner, *Give Me Liberty! An American History* (New York: W. W. Norton, 2006), 36.

20. George Brown Tindall and David E. Shi, *America: A Narrative History*, brief 2nd ed. (New York: W. W. Norton, 1989), 16.

21. Foner, *Give Me Liberty!*, 43.

22. Global war began in 1756, while conflict in the colonies started two years earlier. Other major

European powers became involved in various theaters in the war.

23. Seven colonies sent representatives: Connecticut, Maryland, Massachusetts, New Hampshire, New York, Pennsylvania, and Rhode Island.

24. Eleven of the thirteen colonies were included in Franklin's proposed plan; Georgia and Delaware were not. Virginia and Massachusetts would each have had seven of the forty-eight total seats, being the largest and wealthiest colonies.

25. Merrill Jensen, *The Founding of a Nation* (Indianapolis: Hackett, 2004), 4–5.

26. Literacy rates varied significantly by gender and race.

27. Philip Davidson, *Propaganda and the American Revolution, 1763–1783* (Chapel Hill: University of North Carolina Press, 1941), xiii.

28. Charles M. Andrews, *The Colonial Background of the American Revolution* (New Haven, CT: Yale University Press, 1924), 64–65.

29. Thomas Paine, *Common Sense* (New York: Buccaneer Books, 1976), 63, 69.

30. Eric Foner, *Tom Paine and Revolutionary America* (New York: Oxford University Press, 1976), 74.

31. Jensen, *The Founding of a Nation*, 99.

32. New York, New Hampshire, Virginia, North Carolina, and Georgia did not send delegates. Support in several of these colonies was strong, but royal governors prevented them from sending delegates.

33. "Newspaper Account of the Boston Massacre," in *English Historical Documents: Volume IX, American Colonial Documents to 1776*, ed. Merrill Jensen (New York: Oxford University Press, 1955), 749.

34. Andrews, *The Colonial Background of the American Revolution*, 157.

35. Jensen, *The Founding of a Nation*, 33. Citing "John Adams to Hezekiah Niles," in *The Works of John Adams*, Vol. X, ed. C. F. Adams (Boston, 1850–1856), 283.

36. Foner, *Give Me Liberty!*, 53.

37. Jackson Turner Main, *The Social Structure of Revolutionary America* (Princeton, NJ: Princeton University Press, 1965), 221–27.

38. Thomas Hutchinson, *Strictures upon the Declaration of the Congress at Philadelphia* (London, 1776), 9–10, quoted in Sylvia R. Frey, "Liberty, Equality, and Slavery: The Paradox of the American Revolution," in *The American Revolution: Its Character and Limits*, ed. Jack P. Greene (New York: New York University Press, 1987), 230.

39. Hutchinson, *Strictures upon the Declaration*.

40. Thomas J. Davis, "Emancipation Rhetoric, Natural Rights, and Revolutionary New England: A Note on Four Black Petitions in Massachusetts, 1773–1777," *New England Quarterly* 62, no. 2 (June 1989): 248–63.

41. Ruth Bogin, "'Liberty Further Extended': A 1776 Antislavery Manuscript by Lemuel Haynes," *William and Mary Quarterly* 40, no. 1 (January 1983): 94.

42. Elaine F. Crane, "Dependence in the Era of Independence: The Role of Women in a Republican Society," in *The American Revolution: Its Character and Limits*, ed. Jack P. Greene (New York: New York University Press, 1987).

43. Joan R. Gunderson, *To Be Useful to the World: Women in Revolutionary America*, rev. ed. (Chapel Hill: University of North Carolina Press, 2006), 23.

44. Mary Beth Norton, *Liberty's Daughters: The Revolutionary Experience of American Women, 1750–1800* (Boston: Little, Brown, 1980), 22.

45. Sara M. Evans, *Born for Liberty: A History of Women in America* (New York: The Free Press, 1989), 48.

46. Carol Berkin, *Revolutionary Mothers: Women in the Struggle for America's Independence* (New York: Alfred A. Knopf, 2005), 21.

47. Berkin, *Revolutionary Mothers*, 44.

48. Berkin, 46.

49. Russell Shorto, *The Island at the Center of the World: The Epic Story of Dutch Manhattan and the Forgotten Colony That Shaped America* (New York: Doubleday, 2004), 50.

50. See, for example, Gail D. MacLeitch, *Imperial Entanglements: Iroquois Change and Persistence on the Frontiers of Empire* (Philadelphia: University of Pennsylvania Press, 2011); Karim M. Tiro, *The People of Standing Stone: The Oneida Nation from the Revolution through the Era of Removal* (Amherst: University of Massachusetts Press, 2011).

51. Richard Hofstadter, William Miller, and Daniel Aaron, *The American Republic*, vol. 1 (Upper Saddle River, NJ: Prentice Hall, 1970), 167.

52. The Articles of Confederation and Perpetual Union (see Chapter 2).

53. "The Virginia Resolutions for Independence," in *English Historical Documents*, ed., Merrill Jensen, vol. IX, *American Colonial Documents to 1776* (New York: Oxford University Press, 1955), 867–68.

CHAPTER 2

1. Madison's two papers were titled "Notes of Ancient and Modern Confederacies," written in the spring of 1786, and "Vices of the Political System of the United States," written in the spring of 1787.

2. Robert Livingston Schuyler, *The Constitution of the United States: An Historical Survey of Its Formation* (New York: The Macmillan Company, 1923), 90.

3. William Waller Hening, "Virginia Laws for Blacks—17C & 18C," in *Laws of Virginia, 1619–1792* (1823), I–III. For more on Madison's ambivalence toward slavery, see William Lee Miller, *The Business of May Next: James Madison and the Founding* (Charlottesville: University Press of Virginia, 1992), 177–84.

4. Charles M. Andrews, *The Colonial Background of the American Revolution* (New Haven, CT: Yale University Press, 1924), 26.

5. Merrill Jensen, *The Articles of Confederation: An Interpretation of the Social-Constitutional History of the American Revolution, 1774–1781* (Madison: University of Wisconsin Press, 1948), 150.

6. Robert W. Hoffert, *A Politics of Tensions: The Articles of Confederation and American Political Ideals* (Niwot: University Press of Colorado, 1992), 86.

7. Andrews, *The Colonial Background of the American Revolution*, 44.

8. U.S. Const. art. II.

9. This idea of term limits is one that we continue to debate today. For a discussion of challenges of coordination under the Articles of Confederation, see Keith L. Dougherty, *Collective Action under the Articles of Confederation* (New York: Cambridge University Press, 2001).

10. Jensen, *The Articles of Confederation*, 240.

11. "We do Each one of us, acknowledge our Selves to be Inlisted. . . in colo Hazeltons Regiment of Regulators. . . for Suppressing of tyrannical government in the Massachusetts State." "Report of the Commissioners, April 27, 1787," in David P. Szatmary, *Shays' Rebellion: The Making of an Agrarian Insurrection* (Amherst: University of Massachusetts Press, 1980), 63.

12. James MacGregor Burns, *The Vineyard of Liberty* (New York: Alfred A. Knopf, 1982), 14.

13. Szatmary, *Shays' Rebellion*.

14. Louise B. Dunbar, "A Study of 'Monarchical' Tendencies in the United States from 1776 to 1801," in *The Papers of James Madison: Volume 9, 9 April 1786–24 May 1787*, ed. Robert A. Rutland and William M. E. Rachal (Chicago: University of Chicago Press, 1975), 162.

15. "Letter from George Washington to James Madison, November 5, 1786," in Rutland and Rachal, *The Papers of James Madison*, 162.

16. George Washington had been reluctant to be a delegate in part because the Society of the Cincinnati, an organization of former Revolutionary War officers of which he had been a president, was to meet in Philadelphia at the same time. The society was viewed with mistrust due to its potential to form a new aristocracy. See Catherine Drinker Bowen, *Miracle at Philadelphia: The Story of the Constitutional Convention, May to September 1787* (Boston: Little, Brown, 1966).

17. Patrick Henry, "Virginia Ratifying Convention, June 4 and 5, 1788," in *The Essential Antifederalist*, 2nd ed., ed. W. B. Allen and Gordon Lloyd (New York: Rowman & Littlefield, 2002), 130.

18. See, for example, Gordon S. Wood, "The Origins of the Constitution," in *This Constitution: A Bicentennial Chronicle*, ed. Paul Finkelman et al. (Washington, DC: The American Political Science Association, 1987).

19. Max Farrand, ed., *The Records of the Federal Convention of 1787, Volume I* (New Haven, CT: Yale University Press, 1911), xi.

20. "Notes of James Madison, May 29, 1787," in Farrand, *The Records of the Federal Convention*, 15.

21. Bowen, *Miracle at Philadelphia*, 22.

22. Bowen, 18.

23. "Notes of James Madison, June 9, 1787," in Farrand, *The Records of the Federal Convention*, 177.

24. "Notes of James Madison, June 9, 1787," 179.

25. Bowen, *Miracle at Philadelphia*, 116.

26. Bowen, 285.

27. Bowen, 492.

28. "Notes of Robert Yates, July 2, 1787," in Farrand, *Records of the Federal Convention*, 519.

29. "Notes of James Madison, May 29, 1787," in Farrand, *Records of the Federal Convention*, 531.

30. It is also known as the Connecticut Compromise, after Roger Sherman, a Connecticut delegate, member of the committee, and author of the proposal. One state delegation was split.

31. For an analysis of Madison's strategic shift, see Miller, *The Business of May Next*, 78–80.

32. Bowen, *Miracle at Philadelphia*, 115.

33. Richard E. Neustadt, *Presidential Power and the Modern Presidents: The Politics of Leadership from Roosevelt to Reagan* (New York: The Free Press, 1990), 29.

34. Also called the Committee of Eleven.

35. Bruce Ackerman, *We the People: Foundations* (Cambridge, MA: Harvard University Press, 1991).

36. Native Americans not paying taxes would not count at all.

37. James Madison, *Federalist* No. 54, in *The Federalist Papers*, ed. George W. Carey and James McClellan (Indianapolis: Liberty Fund, 2001), 283.

38. James Madison, "James Madison to Robert I. Evans, June 15, 1819," Library of Congress, June 15, 1819, https://www.loc.gov/item/mjm018592.

39. James Madison, *Federalist* No. 51, in Carey and McClellan, *The Federalist Papers*, 269.

40. Allen and Lloyd, *The Essential Antifederalist*, xxiii.

41. Madison, *Federalist* No. 10, in Carey and McClellan, *The Federalist Papers*, 44.

42. Madison, *Federalist* No. 10, 43.

43. Madison, 46.

44. Alexander Hamilton, *Federalist* No. 9, in Carey and McClellan, *The Federalist Papers,* 41.

45. Hamilton, *Federalist* No. 16, in Carey and McClellan, *The Federalist Papers,* 76–77.

46. Hamilton, *Federalist* No. 16, xxiii.

47. "Centinel Letter I, October 5, 1787," in Allen and Lloyd, *The Essential Antifederalist,* 102–3. See also Herbert J. Storing, *What the Antifederalists Were For* (Chicago: University of Chicago Press, 1981), 57.

48. "Brutus Essay V, December 13, 1787," in Allen and Lloyd, *The Essential Antifederalist,* 119.

49. See Storing, *What the Antifederalists Were For,* 21.

50. Storing, 12–13.

51. Douglass C. North and Barry R. Weingast, "Constitutions and Commitment: The Evolution of Institutions Governing Public Choice in Seventeenth-Century England," *The Journal of Economic History* 49, no. 4 (December 1989): 803–32.

52. Donald S. Lutz, "From Covenant to Constitution in American Political Thought," in *Covenant, Polity, and Constitutionalism,* ed. Daniel Elezar and John Kincaid (Lanham, MD: University Press of America, 1983).

53. Edward S. Corwin, "The Constitution as an Instrument and as a Symbol," *The American Political Science Review* 30, no. 6 (December 1936): 1071–85. See also Edward S. Corwin, *The "Higher Law" Background of American Constitutional Law* (Ithaca, NY: Great Seal Books, 1928).

CHAPTER 3

1. Paul Armentano, "Illinois: Retail Marijuana Sales Begin Next Week," NORML Blog, December 27, 2019, https://blog.norml.org/2019/12/27/illinois-retail-marijuana-sales-begin-next-week/.

2. Office of the Governor, "Beginning First Wave of Cannabis Expungements, Gov. Pritzker Grants 11,017 Pardons for Low-Level Convictions," Illinois.gov, December 31, 2019, https://www2.illinois.gov/Pages/news-item.aspx?ReleaseID=20988.

3. Office of the Governor, "Beginning First Wave."

4. Jacob Sullum, "New Law Finally Authorizes Cannabis Cafés in Colorado, the First State to Allow Recreational Sales," Reason.com, December 30, 2019, https://reason.com/2019/12/30/new-law-finally-authorizes-cannabis-cafes-in-colorado-the-first-state-to-allow-recreational-sales/.

5. NJ SCR183, "Proposes Constitutional Amendment to Legalize Cannabis for Personal, Non-Medical Use by Adults Who Are Age 21 Years or Older, Subject to Regulation by Cannabis Regulatory Commission."

6. Kaitlin Miller, "These Will Be the Big Changes to Marijuana Law in 2020," *TheActiveTimes,* December 20, 2019, https://www.theactivetimes.com/changes-new-marijuana-laws-2020/slide-11.

7. Dan Reed, "Medicinal Pot Users Renew Legal Challenge," *San Jose Mercury News,* October 10, 2002; available from Lexis-Nexis Academic.

8. Brian Anderson, "Women File Suit for Continued Access to Marijuana," *Contra Costa Times,* October 10, 2002; available from Lexis-Nexis Academic.

9. "Declaration of Diane Monson in Support of Motion for Preliminary Injunction," Raich v. Ashcroft, 248 F. supp 2d 918 (ND Cal. 2003).

10. Comprehensive Drug Abuse and Control Act of 1970, 84 Stat. 1236.

11. Comprehensive Drug Abuse and Control Act of 1970, 84 Stat. 1236.

12. "Declaration of Diane Monson."

13. Anderson, "Women File Suit."

14. Richard Willing, "Medical-Pot Fight Goes to Justices," *USA Today,* November 26, 2004; available from Lexis-Nexis Academic.

15. Richard Willing, "Justices Doubtful about Medical Marijuana," *USA Today,* November 30, 2004; available from Lexis-Nexis Academic.

16. Wickard v. Filburn, 317 U.S. 11 1 (1942).

17. *Wickard,* 317 U.S. 11 1.

18. Paul E. Peterson, *The Price of Federalism* (Washington, DC: Brookings Institution, 1995), 12.

19. Reagan Ali and M. David, "Obama Effectively Tells Supreme Court to Legalize Marijuana," CounterCurrentNews.com, January 17, 2016, http://countercurrentnews.com/2016/01/obama-tells-supreme-court-to-legalize.

20. Ariane de Vogue, "Obama Admin Weighs in on Legalized Marijuana at the Supreme Court," CNN.com, December 16, 2015, www.cnn.com/2015/12/16/politics/supreme-court-marijuana-colorado-obama.

21. U.S. Const. art. VI.

22. U.S. Const. art. I, § 8.

23. U.S. Const. art. I, § 8.

24. U.S. Const. art. I, § 8.

25. U.S. Const. art. I, § 2, 4; art. II, § 1.

26. U.S. Const. art. V.

27. U.S. Const. art. I, § 10.

28. Richard E. Neustadt, *Presidential Power and the Modern Presidents: The Politics of Leadership from Roosevelt to Reagan* (New York: The Free Press, 1990), 29.

29. Elizabeth Bower, "Standing Together: How the Federal Government Can Protect the Tribal Cultural Resources of the Standing Rock Sioux Tribe," *Vermont Law Review* 42 (1996): 605–30.

30. James Graham, "Ending Weed Prohibition Hasn't Stopped Drug Crimes," *The Atlantic,* February 2019, https://www.theatlantic.com/

magazine/archive/2019/01/california-marijuana-crime/576391.

31. Evelina Gavrilova, Takuma Kamada, and Floris Zoutman, "Is Legal Pot Crippling Mexican Drug Trafficking Organizations? The Effect of Medical Marijuana Laws on U.S. Crime," *Economic Journal* 129 (2017): 375–407.

32. Melissa Santos, "What Actually Happened to Violent Crime after Washington Legalized Marijuana?" *News Tribune*, July 26, 2017, https://www.thenewstribune.com/news/local/marijuana/article163750293.html.

33. McCulloch v. Maryland, 17 U.S. (4 Wheat.) 316 (1819).

34. Gibbons v. Ogden, 22 U.S. (9 Wheat.) 11 (1824).

35. *Gibbons,* 22 U.S. (9 Wheat.) 11.

36. Barron v. Mayor and City Council of Baltimore, 32 U.S. 243 (1833).

37. This interpretation would change during the process of incorporation, which began in the twentieth century (see Chapter 4).

38. James Bryce, *The American Commonwealth,* Vol. I (New York: Macmillan and Co., 1888), 432.

39. *Tarble's Case,* 80 Wall. 397 (1871).

40. The Northwest Ordinance of 1787, for example, stated, "Religion, morality, and knowledge, being necessary to good government and the happiness of mankind, schools and the means of education shall forever be encouraged." Henry Steele Commager, ed., *Documents of American History,* 8th ed. (New York: Appleton-Century-Crofts, 1968), 131.

41. Plessy v. Ferguson, 163 U.S. 537 (1896).

42. Mark V. Tushnet, *The NAACP's Legal Strategy against Segregated Education, 1925–1950* (Chapel Hill: University of North Carolina Press, 1987), 21.

43. Elazar, *American Federalism,* 33.

44. Elazar, 33.

45. See United States v. E. C. Knight Company, 156 U.S. 1 (1895); Hammer v. Dagenhart, 247 U.S. 251 (1918).

46. Jean Edward Smith, *FDR* (New York: Random House, 2007), 15.

47. Arthur M. Schlesinger Jr., *The Age of Roosevelt, Vol. II: The Coming of the New Deal* (Boston: Houghton Mifflin Company, 1958), 4.

48. See the Banking Act of 1933, the Securities Act of 1933, and the Securities Exchange Act of 1934.

49. Amity Shlaes, *The Forgotten Man: A New History of the Great Depression* (New York: HarperCollins, 2007), 150.

50. Shlaes, *The Forgotten Man,* 151.

51. Schlesinger, *The Age of Roosevelt,* 121.

52. Alan Brinkley, *Franklin Delano Roosevelt* (New York: Oxford University Press, 2010), 52.

53. Steven Horwitz, "The Story of the Schechter Brothers," George Mason University History News Network, http://historynewsnetwork.org/blog/57574.

54. Shlaes, *The Forgotten Man,* 220.

55. See also *Panama Refining Co. v. Ryan,* 293 U.S. 388 (1935).

56. Jeff Shesol, *Supreme Power: Franklin Roosevelt vs. the Supreme Court* (New York: W.W. Norton, 2010), 2–3.

57. Pub. L. No. 74-271, 49 Stat 620-648 (1935). The programs were collectively called Old-Age, Survivors, and Disability Insurance (OASDI), commonly referred to as Social Security. Aid to Dependent Children was later renamed Aid to Families with Dependent Children (AFDC), which was abolished in 1996 and replaced with Temporary Assistance for Needy Families (TANF).

58. Shesol, *Supreme Power,* 3–4.

59. Joseph F. Zimmerman, *Contemporary American Federalism: The Growth of National Power* (New York: Praeger, 1992), 118.

60. Zimmerman, *Contemporary American Federalism,* 118–19.

61. Lawrence D. Brown, James W. Fossett, and Kenneth T. Palmer, *The Changing Politics of Federal Grants* (Washington, DC: Brookings Institution, 1984), 7.

62. Brown et al., *The Changing Politics of Federal Grants,* 8.

63. James Madison, *Federalist* No. 46, in *The Federalist Papers,* ed. George W. Carey and James McClellan (Indianapolis: Liberty Fund, 2001), 246.

64. John D. Nugent, *Safeguarding Federalism: How States Protect Their Interests in National Policymaking* (Norman: University of Oklahoma Press, 2009), 56.

65. Peterson, *The Price of Federalism,* 45.

66. United States v. Lopez, 514 U.S. 549 (1995).

67. *Lopez,* 514 U.S. at 549.

68. *Lopez,* 514 U.S. at 549.

69. Dan Levin, "Is Marijuana an 'Essential' Like Milk or Bread? Some States Say Yes," *The New York Times,* April 10, 2020, https://www.nytimes.com/article/coronavirus-weed-marijuana.html.

70. *Ibid.*

71. J. Edwin Benton, "Challenges to Federalism and Intergovernmental Relations and Takeaways Amid the COVID-19 Epidemic," *American Review of Public Administration* 50, no 6 (2020): 536–542.

CHAPTER 4

1. Bruce Schneider, "I Spy with My Little Algorithm," *New Internationalist,* July 1, 2016, https://newint.org/features/2016/07/01/i-spy-with-my-little-algorithm.

2. In his majority opinion in *Carpenter,* Chief Justice Roberts noted the irony: "In 2011, police officers

arrested four men of robbing a series of Radio shack and (ironically enough) T-Mobile stores in Detroit. Carpenter v. United States 585 U.S. __ (2018).

3. Carpenter v. United States 585 U.S. __ (2018).
4. *Carpenter*, 18 U.S.C. §2703(d).
5. *Carpenter*, 18 U.S.C. §2703(d).
6. *Carpenter*, 18 U.S.C. §2703(d).
7. Robert Barnes, "Supreme Court Rules That Warrant Is Needed to Access Cell Tower Records," *Washington Post*, June 23, 2018, A1.
8. Barnes, "Supreme Court Rules That Warrant Is Needed," A2
9. Olmstead v. United States, 277 US 438 (1928).
10. Robert Barnes, "Justices Appear to Favor More Restraints on Government Access to Digital Information," *Washington Post*, November 29, 2017, https://www.washingtonpost.com/politics/courts_law/justices-appear-to-favor-more-restraints-on-access-to-digital-information/2017/11/29/5f7aaae2-d499-11e7-b62d-d9345ced896d_story.html.
11. Jose Pagliery, "How the NSA Can 'Turn on' Your Phone Remotely," CNN Business, June 6, 2014, https://money.cnn.com/2014/06/06/technology/security/nsa-turn-on-phone/.
12. Catherine Drinker Bowen, *Miracle at Philadelphia: The Story of the Constitutional Convention, May to September 1787* (Boston: Little, Brown, 1966), 244.
13. U.S. Const. art. III, § 3.
14. Irving Brant, *The Bill of Rights: Its Origin and Meaning* (New York: Bobbs-Merrill, 1965), 39.
15. Alexander Hamilton, *Federalist No. 84*, in *The Federalist*, ed. George W. Carey and James McClellan (Indianapolis: Liberty Fund, 2001), 447.
16. *Annals of Congress*, House of Representatives, 1st Cong., 1st sess. (June 8, 1789), 440–41, http://memory.loc.gov/ammem/amlaw/lwac.html.
17. Two of the proposed twelve did not receive enough votes to secure ratification. The first involved apportionment of seats in the House of Representatives; the second restricted Congress's ability to raise its own pay. This latter amendment was ratified, but not until 1992 (the Twenty-Seventh Amendment). Amendments are typically proposed including a date of expiry, but this was not the case for the two unratified, originally proposed amendments.
18. The Fifth Amendment to the Constitution includes a similar clause asserting that "No person . . . shall be deprived of life, liberty, or property, without due process of law," but the Supreme Court had interpreted the Fifth Amendment as restricting the power of only the federal government.
19. The Slaughter-House Cases, 83 U.S. 36 (1873). The Court also placed limits on the privileges and immunities clause of the same amendment, stating that its protections apply only to national, not state, citizenship.
20. Gitlow v. New York. In Chicago, Burlington & Quincy Railroad Company v. Chicago, 166 U.S. 226 (1897), the Supreme Court had already applied the Fifth Amendment's due process clause to state actions in its reasoning, though ruling against the plaintiffs.
21. Timbs v. Indiana, 586 U.S. ___ (2019).
22. James A. Poore III, "The Constitution of the United States Applies to Indian Tribes," *Montana Law Review* 59 (1998), http://scholarship.law.umt.edu/mlr/vol59/iss1/4.
23. *The Constitution of the Standing Rock Sioux Tribe*, enacted in 1959 and since amended, http://indianaffairs.nd.gov/image/cache/standing_rock_constitution.pdf.
24. Everson v. Board of Education, 330 U.S. 1 (1947). The justices were closely divided 5–4.
25. Engel v. Vitale, 370 U.S. 421 (1962).
26. Abington School District v. Schempp, 374 U.S. 203 (1963). The Pennsylvania case was considered with a similar program in Maryland.
27. James Madison, "A Memorial and Remonstrance," in *The Constitution and Religion: Leading Supreme Court Cases on Church and State*, ed. Robert S. Alley (Amherst, MA: Prometheus Books, 1999), 30, quoted in Abington School District v. Schempp.
28. Lemon v. Kurtzman, 403 U.S. 602 (1971). In establishing the test, the Court drew on the logic of Board of Education v. Allen (1968) and other cases.
29. Cantwell v. Connecticut, 310 U.S. 296 (1940).
30. Employment Division Dept. of Human Resources of Oregon v. Smith, 494 U.S. 872 (1990).
31. "The Sedition Act (1798)," in *Documents of American History*, 8th ed., ed. Henry Steele Commager (New York: Appleton-Century-Crofts, 1968), 177–78.
32. Paul E. Peterson, *The Price of Federalism* (Washington, DC: Brookings Institution, 1995), 8.
33. Abrams v. United States, 250 U.S. 616 (1919).
34. Brandenburg v. Ohio, 395 U.S. 444 (1969).
35. *Brandenburg*, 395 U.S. 444.
36. New York Times v. United States, 403 U.S. 713 (1971).
37. United States v. O'Brien, 391 U.S. 367 (1968).
38. Texas v. Johnson, 491 U.S. 397 (1989). See also Spence v. Washington, 418 U.S. 405 (1974).
39. The definitions of legal terms in this section are informed by Bryan A. Garner, ed., *Black's Law Dictionary*, 8th ed. (St. Paul, MN: Thomson/West, 2004).
40. There are certain types of communication that are privileged and not subject to the legal consequences

of defamation. For example, a witness in a trial may intentionally make a false and damaging statement but not be subject to legal action on the basis of slander, though they might be charged and convicted of perjury.

41. R.A.V. v. St. Paul, 505 U.S. 377 (1992).
42. Chaplinsky v. State of New Hampshire, 315 U.S. 586 (1942).
43. Roth v. United States, 354 U.S. 476 (1957).
44. Miller v. California, 413 U.S. 15 (1973).
45. Reno v. American Civil Liberties Union et al., 521 U.S. 844 (1997).
46. De Jonge v. Oregon, 299 U.S. 353 (1937). See also Edwards v. South Carolina, 372 U.S. 229 (1963).
47. Noting, however, that the process of incorporating these rights has involved the Fourteenth Amendment as well.
48. National Firearms Act (1934).
49. United States v. Miller, 307 U.S. 174 (1939).
50. District of Columbia v. Heller, 554 U.S. 570 (2008).
51. McDonald v. Chicago, 561 U.S. 742 (2010). A similar law in Oak Park, a suburb of Chicago, was also overturned.
52. While some have argued that the justification clause limits the scope of the Second Amendment, such clauses were not uncommon in state constitutions covering other fundamental rights and freedoms.
53. Douglas Walker Jr., "Necessary to the Security of Free States: The Second Amendment as the Auxiliary Right of Federalism," *American Journal of Legal History* 56 (2016): 365–91.
54. U.S. Const. art. I, § 9.
55. John Rawls, *A Theory of Justice* (Cambridge, MA: Belknap Press of Harvard University Press, 1999).
56. Katz v. United States, 389 U.S. 347 (1967).
57. Mapp v. Ohio, 367 U.S. 643 (1961).
58. United States v. Sokolow, 490 U.S. 1 (1989).
59. Horton v. California, 496 U.S. 128 (1990).
60. Whren v. United States, 517 U.S. 806 (1996).
61. Miranda v. Arizona, 384 U.S. 436 (1966). Miranda was retried without the illegally obtained evidence but was convicted based on other evidence, including identification by the victim and the testimony of his girlfriend.
62. Kloppfer v. North Carolina, 386 U.S. 213 (1967).
63. Powell v. Alabama, 287 U.S. 45 (1932).
64. Johnson v. Zerbst, 304 U.S. 458 (1938).
65. Gideon v. Wainwright, 372 U.S. 335 (1963).
66. Wiggins v. Smith, 539 U.S. 510 (2003).
67. The Court's decision in Furman v. Georgia, 408 U.S. 238 (1972), invalidated the use of the death penalty according to the state laws at the time, finding them arbitrary and discriminatory. Rewritten death penalty statutes were held constitutional in Gregg v. Georgia, 428 U.S. 153 (1976).
68. Atkins v. Virginia, 536 U.S. 304 (2002).
69. Roper v. Simmons, 543 U.S. 551 (2005).
70. United States v. Windsor, 570 U.S. __ (2013).
71. U.S. Const. art. IV, § 1.
72. *Windsor*, 570 U.S. __.
73. *Windsor*, 570 U.S. __.
74. Justin Jones, "The Godmother of Gay Marriage: Edie Windsor's Passionate Life," *Daily Beast*, March 18, 2015, http://www.thedailybeast.com/articles/2015/03/18/the-godmother-of-gay-marriage-edie-windsor-s-passionate-life.html.
75. Jones, "The Godmother of Gay Marriage."
76. Griswold v. Connecticut, 381 U.S. 479 (1965).
77. *Griswold*, 381 U.S. at 479.
78. Lawrence v. Texas, 539 U.S. 558 (2003). In its ruling, the Court overturned Bowers v. Hardwick, 478 U.S. 186 (1986).
79. *Lawrence*, 539 U.S. at 558.
80. Roe v. Wade, 410 U.S. 113 (1973).
81. *Roe*, 410 U.S. at 113.
82. See Webster v. Reproductive Health Services, 492 U.S. 490 (1989); Planned Parenthood v. Casey, 505 U.S. 833 (1992); Stenberg v. Carhart, 530 U.S. 914 (2000); Gonzales v. Carhart, 550 U.S. 124 (2007).
83. Chris Geidner, "Two Years after His Husband's Death, Jim Obergefell Is Still Fighting for the Right to Be Married," BuzzFeed.com, March 22, 2015, http://www.buzzfeed.com/chrisgeidner/his-husband-died-in-2013-but-jim-obergefell-is-still-fighting#.ldrnVM0Ag.
84. Obergefell v. Hodges, 576 U.S. __ (2015).
85. Geidner, "Two Years after His Husband's Death."
86. Richard Wolf, "Grieving Widower Takes Lead in Major Gay Marriage Case," *USA Today*, April 10, 2015, http://www.usatoday.com/story/news/nation/2015/04/10/supreme-court-gay-marriage-obergefell/25512405/.
87. Wolf, "Grieving Widower."

CHAPTER 5

1. Harriet Hartman and Moshe Hartman, "How Equal Is Equal? A Comparison of Gender Equality among Israeli and American Jews," *Contemporary Jewry* 14, no. 1 (1993): 48–72.
2. Judith Heumann, "Justice for All: Advancing Dr. King's Call," DIPNOTE, U.S Department of State Official Blog, January 18, 2016, https://blogs.state.gov/stories/2016/01/18/justice-all-advancing-dr-king-s-call.
3. Team Celebration, "Judith E. Heumann—Woman of Action," A Celebration of Women, July 24, 2012,

http://acelebrationofwomen.org/2012/07/judith-e-heumann-woman-of-action/.

4. Team Celebration, "Judith E. Heumann."

5. Jack Anderson and Les Whitten, "Sit-Ins Planned by Handicapped," *Progress Bulletin from Pomona (California)*, March 27, 1977.

6. "A Look Back at 'Section 504,'" Minnesota Governor's Council on Developmental Disabilities, April 28, 2002, http://mn.gov/mnddc/ada-legacy/npr-504.html. The article was drawn from the transcript of "Disability Rights, Part II," National Public Radio, April 28, 2002, http://www.npr.org/templates/story/story.php?storyId=1142485.

7. HolLynn D'Lil, *Becoming Real in 24 Days* (HolLynn D'Lil, 2015), 16.

8. Cesar Chavez, telegram to Judy Heuman [sic], April 2, 1977 (D'Lil, 16).

9. Michael Irvin, "The 25 Day Siege That Brought Us 504," Independent Living Institute, accessed March 17, 2016, http://www.independentliving.org/docs4/ervin1986.html.

10. Lanny E. Perkins, Esq., and Sara D. Perkins, Esq., "ADA Update," Multiple Sclerosis Foundation, accessed March 16, 2016, http://msfocus.org/article-details.aspx?articleID=340.

11. Ginger Adams Otis, "Trailblazing Advocate Judy Heumann Says There's More Work to Do 25 Years after Americans with Disabilities Act Was Signed into Law," *New York Daily News*, July 25, 2015, http://www.nydailynews.com/news/national/ada-advocate-judy-heumann-work-article-1.2304397.

12. City of Cleburne, Texas v. Cleburne Living Center, Inc., 473 U.S. 432 (1985).

13. University of California Regents v. Bakke, 438 U.S. 265, 438 U.S. 303 (1978), *quoted in* City of Cleburne, Texas v. Cleburne Living Center, Inc.

14. David Pfeiffer, "Eugenics and Disability Discrimination," *Disability and Society* 9, no. 4 (1994): 481–99.

15. American Civil Liberties Union, "Disability Rights—ACLU Position/Briefing Paper," no. 21 (Winter 1999), https://www.aclu.org/disability-rights-aclu-positionbriefing-paper.

16. American Civil Liberties Union, "Disability Rights."

17. Dred Scott v. Sandford, 60 U.S. 393 (1857).

18. W. E. B. Du Bois, *Black Reconstruction in America, 1860–1880* (New York: Anthem, 1992), 167.

19. Du Bois, *Black Reconstruction in America*, 167.

20. Richard Wormser, *The Rise and Fall of Jim Crow* (New York: St. Martin's Press, 2003), 11.

21. Plessy v. Ferguson, 163 U.S. 737 (1896).

22. *Plessy* did not deal with education. In 1899, the Supreme Court approved segregated educational facilities in *Cumming v. Board of Education*, 175 U.S. 528 (1899).

23. Mark V. Tushnet, *The NAACP's Legal Strategy against Segregated Education, 1925–1950* (Chapel Hill: University of North Carolina Press, 1987), 21. The section on the NAACP's strategic decision-making processes draws heavily on Tushnet's analysis and Richard Kluger's historical account.

24. The four states were Kansas (*Brown v. Board of Education*, 98 F. Supp. 797 [D. Kan. 1951]); South Carolina (*Briggs v. Elliot*, 103 F. Supp. 920 [E.D.S.C. 1952]); Delaware (*Gebhart v. Belton*, 33 Del. 145, 91 A.2d. 137 [1952]); and Virginia (*Davis v. County School Board of Prince Edward County, Virginia*, 103 F. Supp. 337 [E.D. Va. 1952]). The Washington, DC, case was *Bolling v. Sharpe*, 347 U.S. 497 (1954). As the District of Columbia is not a state, the case was tried under the due process clause of the Fifth Amendment. Thurgood Marshall argued the South Carolina case before the Supreme Court. His legal team divided the oral arguments.

25. Richard Kluger, *Simple Justice: The History of* Brown v. Board of Education *and Black America's Struggle for Equality* (New York: Vintage Books, 1977), 706.

26. Tushnet, *The NAACP's Legal Strategy*, 36.

27. Sweatt v. Painter, 339 U.S. 629 (1950); McLaurin v. Oklahoma State Regents for Higher Education, 339 U.S. 637 (1950).

28. Kluger, *Simple Justice*, 268.

29. Kluger, 395.

30. Brown v. Board of Education of Topeka, 347 U.S. 483 (1954).

31. It was said that Justice Felix Frankfurter told Justice Stanley Reed, who was most likely to dissent, that "a dissent is written for the future, but that there was no future for segregation" (Jack Greenberg, *Crusaders in the Courts: How a Dedicated Band of Lawyers Fought for the Civil Rights Revolution* [New York: Basic Books, 1994], 198).

32. Quoted in Jennifer Hochschild, *The New American Dilemma: Liberal Democracy and School Desegregation* (New Haven, CT: Yale University Press, 1984), 15.

33. Juan Williams, *Eyes on the Prize: America's Civil Rights Years, 1954–1965* (New York: Viking Penguin, 1987), 35.

34. Williams, *Eyes on the Prize*, 34.

35. *Brown.*

36. Gerald N. Rosenberg, *The Hollow Hope: Can Courts Bring About Social Change?* (Chicago: University of Chicago Press, 1991), 49.

37. Taylor Branch, *Parting the Waters: American in the King Years, 1954–63* (New York: Simon & Schuster, 1988), 129.

38. Gayle v. Browder, 352 U.S. 903 (1956).

39. Branch, *Parting the Waters*, 129.

40. Branch, 139–40.

41. Swann v. Charlotte-Mecklenburg Board of Education, 401 U.S. 1 (1971). *See also* Alexander v. Holmes County Board of Education, 396 U.S. 19 (1969).

42. Milliken v. Bradley, 418 U.S. 717 (1974).

43. Regents of the University of California v. Bakke, 438 U.S. 265 (1978).

44. Gratz v. Bollinger, 539 U.S. 244 (2003).

45. Sklar, *Women's Rights Emerges*, 58.

46. *Woman's Rights Conventions, Seneca Falls & Rochester, 1848* (New York: Arno, 1969), 4.

47. Sklar, *Women's Rights Emerges*, 1.

48. Frances Ellen Watkins Harper, "We Are All Bound Up Together," in *Proceedings of the Eleventh Women's Rights Convention* (New York: Robert J. Johnston, 1866). Read more at BlackPast.org, http://www.blackpast.org/1866-frances-ellen-watkins-harper-we-are-all-bound-together-0#sthash.rrwYWPvy.dpuf.

49. McMillen, *Seneca Falls*, 167.

50. See Jo Freeman, "How 'Sex' Got into Title VII: Persistent Opportunism as a Maker of Public Policy," *Law and Inequality: A Journal of Theory and Practice* 9, no. 2 (March 1991): 163–84; Rosalind Rosenberg, *Divided Lives: American Women in the Twentieth Century* (New York: Hill and Wang, 2008), 187–88.

51. Betty Friedan, *The Feminine Mystique* (New York: Dell, 1963), 351.

52. National Organization for Women, "National Organization for Women (N.O.W.) Statement of Purpose, 1966," accessed August 11, 2016, http://coursesa.matrix.msu.edu/~hst306/documents/nowstate.html.

53. Title IX of the Education Amendments of 1972, vol. 20, U.S.C. sec. 1681.

54. Jane J. Mansbridge, *Why We Lost the ERA* (Chicago: University of Chicago Press, 1986).

55. Mark R. Daniels and Robert E. Darcy, "As Time Goes By: The Arrested Diffusion of the Equal Rights Amendment," *Publius* 15, no. 4 (Autumn 1985): 51–60.

56. The distinction originally appeared in a footnote to Justice Harlan Fiske Stone's opinion in *United States v. Carolene Products Co.* 304 U.S. 144 (1938).

57. United States v. Virginia, 518 U.U. 515 (1996).

58. Sklar, *Women's Rights Emerges*, 10. See also Marilyn Richardson, ed., Maria W. Stewart, *America's First Black Woman Political Writer: Essays and Speeches* (Bloomington: Indiana University Press, 1987).

59. In Sklar, *Women's Rights Emerges*, 179–80. Many versions of Truth's speech have been presented. Some were heavily edited by newspapers of the time, which sometimes changed her words to fit racial stereotypes of the period. See Carla Peterson, *"Doers of the Word": African American Women Speakers and Writers in the North (1830–1880)* (New York: Oxford University Press, 1995), 47–55.

60. Kimberlé Crenshaw, "Demarginalizing the Intersection of Race and Sex: A Black Feminist Critique of Antidiscrimination Doctrine, Feminist Theory, and Antiracist Politics," *University of Chicago Legal Forum* 1989, no. 1, http://chicagounbound.uchicago.edu/cgi/viewcontent.cgi?article=1052&context=uclf.

61. See Shirley J. Yee, *Black Women Abolitionists: A Study in Activism, 1828–1860* (Knoxville: University of Tennessee Press, 1992).

62. Susan Saulny, "Census Data Presents Rise in Multiracial Population of Youths," *New York Times*, March 24, 2011, http://www.nytimes.com/2011/03/25/us/25race.html.

63. Molefi Kete Asante, "Racing to Leave the Race: Black Postmodernists Off-Track," *Black Scholar* 23 (Summer/Fall 1993): 50–51.

64. Marvin C. Arnold, "Testimony before the Subcommittee on Census, Statistics, and Postal Personnel of the House Committee on Post Office and Civil Service 103-7," June 30, 1993, 162.

CHAPTER 6

1. "Police-Community Reform and the Two Fergusons," Editorial, *St. Louis Post-Dispatch*, December 3, 2014, www.stltoday.com/news/opinion/columns/the-platform/editorial-police-community-reform-and-the-twofergusons/article_c486f098-588a-5951-af85-036d74bd6999.html.

2. Leah Thorsen, "Shooting of Teen by Ferguson Police Officer Spurs Angry Backlash," *St. Louis Post-Dispatch*, August 10, 2014; available from Lexis-Nexis Academic.

3. "Ferguson Timeline," *St. Louis Post-Dispatch*, August 2, 2015; available from Lexis-Nexis Academic.

4. Tim Barker, "Ferguson-Area Businesses Cope with Aftermath of Weekend Riot," *St. Louis Post-Dispatch*, August 12, 2014; available from Lexis-Nexis Academic.

5. Joe Holleman and Kevin Johnson, "Ferguson Notes Ferguson Police Shooting," *St. Louis Post-Dispatch*, November 22, 2014; available from Lexis-Nexis Academic.

6. Amanda Paulson, "In Ferguson's Wake, Outcries Arise about Police Shootings in Other Cities," *Christian Science Monitor*, August 19, 2014; available from Lexis-Nexis Academic.

7. "When Does a Moment Become a Movement?," *Washington Post,* August 24, 2014; available from Lexis-Nexis Academic.

8. Christine Byers, "Darren Wilson Resigns from Ferguson Police Department: 'It Is My Hope That My Resignation Will Allow the Community to Heal,'" *St. Louis Post-Dispatch,* November 30, 2014; available from Lexis-Nexis Academic.

9. Frances Robles and Michael S. Schmidt, "Shooting Accounts Differ as Holder Schedules Visit," *New York Times,* August 20, 2014; available from Lexis-Nexis Academic.

10. Julie Bosman, "Bruised and Weary, Ferguson Struggles to Heal," *New York Times,* October 7, 2014; available from Lexis-Nexis Academic.

11. "Police-Community Reforms and the Two Fergusons."

12. Patrick Jonsson, "How Current Events Might Play into America's Shift in Favor of Gun Rights," *Christian Science Monitor,* December 11, 2014; available from Lexis-Nexis Academic.

13. Pew Research Center, "Across Racial Lines, More Say Nation Needs to Make Changes to Achieve Racial Equality," August 5, 2015, www.people-press.org/2015/08/05/across-racial-lines-more-say-nation-needs-to-make-changes-to-achieve-racial-equality; Scott Clement, "A Year after Ferguson, 6 in 10 Americans Say Changes Are Needed to Give Blacks and Whites Equal Rights," *Washington Post,* August 5, 2015, https://www.washingtonpost.com/news/the-fix/wp/2015/08/05/what-changed-since-ferguson-americans-are-far-more-worried-about-black-rights.

14. See Paul M. Sniderman, Richard A. Brody, and Philip E. Tetlock, *Reasoning and Choice: Explorations in Political Psychology* (New York: Cambridge University Press, 1991).

15. Angus Campbell et al., *The American Voter* (Chicago: University of Chicago Press, 1960), 151.

16. Philip E. Converse, "The Nature of Belief Systems in Mass Publics," in *Ideology and Discontent,* ed. David E Apter (London: The Free Press of Glencoe, 1964), 212.

17. Michael Delli Carpini and Scott Keeter, *What Americans Know about Politics and Why It Matters* (New Haven, CT: Yale University Press, 1996).

18. John Zaller, *The Nature and Origins of Mass Opinion* (New York: Cambridge University Press, 1992).

19. While Zaller also maintains the traditional distinction between elite and mass opinion, his work emphasizes the ability of masses to draw on political elites in the process of constructing opinions.

20. Samuel L. Popkin, *The Reasoning Voter: Communication and Persuasion in Political Campaigns* (Chicago: University of Chicago Press, 1991), 212.

21. Arthur Lupia and Mathew D. McCubbins, *The Democratic Dilemma: Can Citizens Learn What They Need to Know?* (New York: Cambridge University Press, 1998).

22. Wendy M. Rahn, "The Role of Partisan Stereotypes in Information Processing about Political Candidates," *American Journal of Political Science* 37, no. 2 (1993): 472–96.

23. See James Surowiecki, *The Wisdom of Crowds* (New York: Doubleday, 2004).

24. Benjamin I. Page and Robert Y. Shapiro, *The Rational Public: Fifty Years of Trends in Americans' Policy Preferences* (Chicago: University of Chicago Press, 1992), 14.

25. Robert D. Behn, "What Right Do Public Managers Have to Lead?" *Public Administration Review* 58, no. 3 (1998): 209–24.

26. Pew Research Center, "Questionnaire Design," www.pewresearch.org/methodology/u-s-survey-research/questionnaire-design.

27. Darren W. Davis and Brian D. Silver, "Stereotype Threat and Race of Interviewer Effects in a Survey on Political Knowledge," *American Journal of Political Science* 47, no. 1 (2003): 33–45.

28. Bosman, "Bruised and Weary"; Fred I. Greenstein, "The Benevolent Leader: Children's Images of Political Authority," *American Political Science Review* 54, no. 4 (1960): 934–43; David Easton and Robert D. Hess, "The Child's Political World," *Midwest Journal of Political Science* 6, no. 3 (1962): 229–46. For a deeper view of the effectiveness of parent-child transmission of political attitudes and values, see M. Kent Jennings and Richard G. Niemi, "The Transmission of Political Values from Parent to Child," *American Political Science Review* 62, no. 1 (1968): 169–84.

29. Christopher H. Achen, "Parental Socialization and Rational Party Identification," *Political Behavior* 24, no. 2 (2002): 151–70.

30. See Kenneth P. Langton and M. Kent Jennings, "Political Socialization and the High School Civics Curriculum in the United States," *American Political Science Review* 62, no. 3 (1968): 852–67.

31. Lisa Brown, "Hundreds of Protesters March to Ferguson Police Department," *St. Louis Post-Dispatch,* August 21, 2014; available from Lexis-Nexis Academic.

32. Pew Research Center, "Stark Racial Divisions in Reactions to Ferguson Police Shooting," August 18, 2014, www.people-press.org/files/2014/08/8-18-14-Ferguson-Release.pdf.

33. Michael Dawson, *Black Visions: The Roots of Contemporary African American Political Ideologies* (Chicago: University of Chicago Press, 2001).

34. Dennis Chong and Dukhong Kim, "The Experiences and Effects of Economic Status among Racial and Ethnic Minorities," *American Political Science Review* 100, no. 3 (2006): 335–51.

35. Evelyn M. Simien, "Race, Gender, and Linked Fate," *Journal of Black Studies* 35, no. 5 (2005): 529.

36. Pew Research Center, "Stark Racial Divisions."

37. Bosman, "Bruised and Weary."

38. Julie Hirschfeld Davis, "Calling for Calm in Ferguson, Obama Cites Need for Improved Race Relations," *New York Times*, August 19, 2014.

39. "When Does a Moment Become a Movement?"

40. Mitch Smith, "A Year on, Ferguson Killing Is Recalled," *New York Times*, August 8, 2015, http://www.nytimes.com/2015/08/09/us/a-year-on-ferguson-killing-is-recalled.html?_r=0.

41. "1 Person Shot, Crowd Scatters as Gunshots Ring Out Late Sunday in Ferguson," *St. Louis Post-Dispatch*, August 10, 2015; available from Lexis-Nexis Academic.

42. Mitch Smith, "A Year on, Ferguson Killing Is Recalled," *New York Times*, August 8, 2015, www.nytimes.com/2015/08/09/us/a-year-on-ferguson-killing-is-recalled.html?_r=0.

43. Zeeshan Aleem, "The First Democratic Debate Proved That Black Lives Matter Is Making a Difference," Mic, October 14, 2015, http://mic.com/articles/126730/the-first-democratic-debate-proved-that-black-lives-matter-is-making-a-difference.

44. Aleem, "The First Democratic Debate."

45. Aleem.

46. Lilly Fowler, "Members of the Congressional Black Caucus Arrive in Ferguson to Pledge Their Support," *St. Louis Post-Dispatch*, January 19, 2015; available from Lexis-Nexis Academic.

47. Fowler, "Members of the Congressional Black Caucus."

48. Jeremy Kohler, "Prominent Ferguson Protesters Publish Anti-Police Violence Policy Platform," *St. Louis Post-Dispatch*, August 22, 2015; available from Lexis-Nexis Academic.

49. Kohler, "Prominent Ferguson Protesters."

50. It was not until the third week of the preseason, when a photo showed him sitting during the anthem, that his protests garnered significant attention.

51. "Colin Kaepernick Protests Anthem over Treatment of Minorities," ESPN.com News Services, August 27, 2016, http://theundefeated.com/features/colin-kaepernick-protests-anthem-over-treatment-of-minorities/.

52. Adam Stiles, "Everything You Need to Know about NFL Protests during the National Anthem," SBNation.com, October 19, 2017, https://www.sbnation.com/2017/9/29/16380080/donald-trump-nfl-colin-kaepernick-protests-national-anthem.

53. Stiles, "Everything You Need to Know."

54. "Final Report: Independent Review of the 2017 Protest Events in Charlottesville, Virginia," Hunton & Williams LLP, accessed July 31, 2018, https://www.huntonak.com/images/content/3/4/v4/34613/final-report-ada-compliant-ready.pdf,

p. 6; see also Laurel Wamsley, "What Went Wrong in Charlottesville? Almost Everything, Says Report," National Public Radio, December 1, 2017, https://www.npr.org/sections/thetwo-way/2017/12/01/567824446/charlottesville-made-major-mistakes-in-handling-protest-review-finds.

55. Glenn Thrush and Rebecca R. Ruiz, "White House Acts to Stem Fallout from Trump's First Charlottesville Remarks," *New York Times*, August 13, 2017, https://www.nytimes.com/2017/08/13/us/charlottesville-protests-white-nationalists-trump.html.

56. *The New York Times*, "What We Know About the Death of George Floyd in Minneapolis," September 12, 2020, https://www.nytimes.com/article/george-floyd.html, accessed September 20, 2020.

57. Larry Buchanan, Quoctrung Bui and Jugal K. Patel, "Black Lives Matter may be the largest protest movement in U.S. History," *The New York Times*, July 3, 2020, A1.

58. *Ibid.*

59. Deja Thomas and Juliana Menasche Horowitz, "Support for Black Lives Matter has decreased since June but remains strong among Black Americans," *Pew Research Center*, September 16, 2020, https://www.pewresearch.org/fact-tank/2020/09/16/support-for-black-lives-matter-has-decreased-since-june-but-remains-strong-among-black-americans/, accessed September 20, 2020.

60. John W. Kingdon, *Agendas, Alternatives, and Public Policies*, 2nd ed. (New York: Longman, 2003), 1.

61. Mark Trumbull, "How Differently Do Blacks and Whites View Ferguson? Here Are the Numbers," *Christian Science Monitor*, November 21, 2104; available from Lexis-Nexis Academic.

62. Bosman, "Bruised and Weary."

CHAPTER 7

1. Eric Johnson, "Full Transcript: Hillary Clinton at Code 2017," Recode, May 31, 2017, https://www.vox.com/2017/5/31/15722218/hillary-clinton-code-conference-transcript-donald-trump-2016-russia-walt-mossberg-kara-swisher.

2. Johnson, "Full Transcript."

3. Johnson.

4. National Intelligence Council, *Assessing Russian Activities and Intentions in Recent US Elections*, ICA 2017-01D, ii, Washington, DC: Office of the Director of National Intelligence, National Intelligence Council, January 6, 2017.

5. President Donald J. Trump (@realDonald Trump), "Julian Assange said 'a 14 year old could have hacked Podesta' - why was DNC so careless? Also said Russians did not give him the info!," Twitter, January 4, 2017, 6:22 a.m.,

https://twitter.com/realdonaldtrump/status/816620855958601730?lang=en.

6. David French, "A Beginner's Guide to the Trump/Russia Controversy," *National Review,* March 31, 2017, www.nationalreview.com/article/446339/donald-trump-russia-2016-election-controversy-explained.

7. Office of the Inspector General, U.S. Department of Justice, "Review of Four FISA Applications and Other Aspects of the FBI's Crossfire Hurricane Investigation," December 9, 2019, https://www.justice.gov/storage/120919-examination.pdf.

8. Ian Schwartz, "Trump Reacts to Mueller Hearing: 'This Was Treason, This Was High Crimes,'" July 25, 2019, RealClearPolitics, https://www.realclearpolitics.com/video/2019/07/25/trump_reacts_to_mueller_hearing_this_was_treason_this_was_high_crimes.html.

9. Schwartz, "Trump Reacts to Mueller Hearing."

10. Amber Athey, "Study: Broadcast Networks Obsessed with Russia," Daily Caller, June 27, 2017, http://dailycaller.com/2017/06/27/study-broadcast-networks-obsessed-with-russia.

11. Amanda Hess, "This Is the Moment Rachel Maddow Has Been Waiting For," *New York Times*, October 1, 2019.

12. James Carson, "What Is Fake News? Its Origins and How It Grew in 2016," *Telegraph*, March 16, 2017, www.telegraph.co.uk/technology/0/fake-news-origins-grew-2016.

13. Project Veritas, "American Pravda: CNN Producer Says Russia Narrative 'Bullsh★t,'" YouTube, June 26, 2017, https://www.youtube.com/watch?v=jdP8TiKY8dE.

14. Project Veritas, "American Pravda."

15. Project Veritas, "Van Jones: Russia Is 'Nothing Burger'—American Pravda: CNN Part 2," YouTube, June 28, 2017, https://www.youtube.com/watch?v=l2G360HrSAs.

16. Michael M. Grynbaum, "3 CNN Journalists Resign after Retracted Story on Trump Ally," *New York Times*, June 26, 2017, https://www.nytimes.com/2017/06/26/business/3-cnn-journalists-resign-after-retracted-story-on-trump-ally.html.

17. Jake Tapper, "Trump: 'I Think It Was Russia' behind Election Hacks," CNN.com, January 11, 2017, www.cnn.com/videos/politics/2017/01/11/jake-tapper-defends-donald-trump-intelligence-report-fake-news-sot.cnn.

18. Patrick Novotny, *The Press in American Politics, 1787–2012* (Denver, CO: Praeger, 2014), 1.

19. Novotny, *The Press in American Politics*, 2.

20. Max Farrand, ed., *The Records of the Federal Convention of 1787, Volume II* (New Haven, CT: Yale University Press, 1911), 334.

21. Michael Schudson, *Discovering the News: A Social History of American Newspapers* (New York: Basic Books, 1978), 15–16.

22. Schudson, *Discovering the News*, 18.

23. John D. Stevens, *Sensationalism and the New York Press* (New York: Columbia University Press, 1991).

24. David Protess, *The Journalism of Outrage: Investigative Reporting and Agenda Building in America* (New York: Guilford Press, 1991).

25. Melanie Magin and Peter Maurer, "Beat Journalism and Reporting," *Oxford Research Encyclopedia of Communication*, March 2019, 10.1093/acrefore/9780190228613.013.905.

26. Novotny, *The Press in American Politics*, 96.

27. Jeffrey M. Berry and Sarah Sobieraj, *The Outrage Industry: Political Opinion Media and the New Incivility* (New York: Oxford University Press, 2014), 7.

28. Shane Harris et al., "Bernie Sanders Briefed by U.S. Officials That Russia Is Trying to Help His Presidential Campaign," *Washington Post*, February 21, 2020, https://www.washingtonpost.com/national-security/bernie-sanders-briefed-by-us-officials-that-russia-is-trying-to-help-his-presidential-campaign/2020/02/21/5ad396a6-54bd-11ea-929a-64efa7482a77_story.html.

29. Harris et al., "Bernie Sanders Briefed."

30. Aaron Maté, "The Failed Russiagate Playbook Can't Stop Bernie Sanders," *The Nation*, February 20, 2020, https://www.thenation.com/article/politics/bernie-sanders-russiagate/.

31. See, for example, Bernard Goldberg, *Bias: A CBS Insider Exposes How the Media Distort the News* (New York: Perennial, 2002).

32. See, for example, William Schneider and I. A. Lewis, "Views on the News," *Public Opinion* 8, no. 4 (1985): 6–13.

33. D. Domke et al., "The Politics of Conservative Elites and the 'Liberal Media' Argument," *Journal of Communication* 49, no. 4 (1999): 35–58.

34. Gloria Goodale, "Brian Williams Suspended: How Big a Blow Was Dealt to Network News?," *Christian Science Monitor,* February 10, 2015; available from Lexis-Nexis Academic.

35. Matthew A. Baum and Angela S. Jamison, "The Oprah Effect: How Soft News Helps Inattentive Citizens Vote Consistently," *Journal of Politics* 68, no. 4 (2006): 946–59.

36. Matthew A. Baum, "Sex, Lies, and War: How Soft News Brings Foreign Policy to the Inattentive Public," *American Political Science Review* 96, no. 1 (2002): 91–109.

37. Jody Baumgartner and Jonathan S. Morris, "The *Daily Show* Effect: Candidate Evaluations, Efficacy, and American Youth." *American Politics Research* 34, no. 3 (2006): 341–67.

38. Thomas E. Patterson, "Doing Well and Doing Good: How Soft News and Critical Journalism Are Shrinking the News Audience and Weakening Democracy—and What News Outlets Can Do

about It" (Faculty Research Working Paper Series RWP01-001, John F. Kennedy School of Government, Harvard University Cambridge, MA, December 2000).

39. Larry J. Sabato, *Feeding Frenzy: How Attack Journalism Has Transformed American Politics* (New York: Free Press, 1991).

40. *The West Wing,* season 1, episode 13, "Take Out the Trash Day," directed by Ken Olin, written by Aaron Sorkin, featuring Rob Lowe, Moira Kelly, and Dulé Hill, aired January 26, 2000, on NBC.

41. Garrett Hardin, "The Tragedy of the Commons," *Science* 162, no. 3859 (1968): 1243–48; *Annual Report of the Federal Radio Commission to the Congress of the United States for the Fiscal Year Ended June 30, 1927* (Washington, DC: Government Printing Office, 1927), 1.

42. *Annual Report of the Federal Radio Commission.*

43. "Applicability of the Fairness Doctrine in the Handling of Controversial Issues of Public Importance," 29 Fed. Reg. 10426 (1964). Quoted in Kathleen Ann Ruane, *Fairness Doctrine: History and Constitutional Issues* (Washington, DC: Congressional Research Service, July 13, 2011), 2.

44. Doris A. Graber and Johanna Dunaway, *Mass Media and American Politics,* 10th ed. (Washington, DC: CQ Press, 2017), 53.

45. This section also draws heavily on "War of the Worlds," *American Experience,* directed by Cathleen O'Connell, written by Michelle Ferrari and A. Brad Schwartz, aired October 29, 2013, on WGBH.

46. John Gosling, *Waging the War of the Worlds: A History of the 1938 Radio Broadcast and Resulting Panic* (Jefferson, NC: McFarland & Company, 2009), 34.

47. Howard Koch, "'The War of the Worlds' (Original Script for Radio)," reprinted in A. Brad Schwartz, *Broadcast Hysteria: Orson Welles's War of the Worlds and the Art of Fake News* (New York: Hill and Wang, 2015), 202.

48. Koch, "The War of the Worlds," 202–3.

49. Brad Schwartz, *Broadcast Hysteria: Orson Welles's War of the Worlds and the Art of Fake News* (New York: Hill and Wang, 2015), 77.

50. Koch, "The War of the Worlds," 218.

51. Schwartz, *Broadcast Hysteria,* 103.

52. Bernard R. Berelson, Paul F. Lazarsfeld, and William N. McPhee, *Voting: A Study of Opinion Formation in a Presidential Campaign* (Chicago: University of Chicago Press, 1954).

53. James N. Druckman and Kjersten R. Nelson, "Framing and Deliberation: How Citizens' Conversations Limit Elite Influence," *American Journal of Political Science* 47, no. 4 (2003): 730. See also Thomas E. Nelson, Rosalee A. Clawson, and Zoe M. Oxley, "Media Framing of a Civil Liberties Conflict and Its Effect on Tolerance," *American Political Science Review* 91, no. 3 (1997): 567–83.

54. Harold Lasswell, "The Structure and Function of Communication in Society," in *Mass Communications,* ed. Wilbur Schram (Urbana: University of Illinois Press, 1969), 103, as discussed in Graber and Dunaway, *Mass Media and American Politics,* 5.

55. Graber and Dunaway, *Mass Media and American Politics,* 5.

56. Pew Research Center, "What Americans Know: 1989–2007," April 15, 2007, www.people-press. org/files/legacy-pdf/319.pdf.

57. Markus Prior, *Post-Broadcast Democracy: How Media Choice Increases Inequality in Political Involvement and Polarizes Elections* (New York: Cambridge University Press, 2007).

58. Prior, *Post-Broadcast Democracy,* 142.

59. Andrea Caumont, "Who's Not Online? 5 Factors Tied to the Digital Divide," Pew Research Center, November 8, 2013, www.pewresearch.org/fact-tank/2013/11/08/whos-not-online-5-factors-tied-to-the-digital-divide.

CHAPTER 8

1. Mike McMahon, "Democratic Frontrunner Bernie Sanders Plays the Hits to a Packed House at San Antonio Rally," *San Antonio Current,* February 23, 2020, https://www.sacurrent.com/the-daily/archives/2020/02/23/democratic-frontrunner-bernie-sanders-plays-the-hits-to-a-packed-house-at-san-antonio-rally.

2. Nate Silver, "Sanders—and the Media—Learned the Wrong Lessons from Trump in 2016," FiveThirtyEight, April 9, 2020, https://fivethirtyeight.com/features/sanders-and-the-media-learned-the-wrong-lessons-from-trump-in-2016/.

3. Sam Levin, Scott Bixby, and Tom McCarthy, "Sanders and Clinton Hold Final Rallies ahead of Nevada Primary—as It Happened," *The Guardian,* February 20, 2016, https://www.theguardian.com/us-news/live/2016/feb/19/presidential-campaign-2016-south-carolina-republican-primary-nevada-democratic-caucus-trump-clinton-sanders.

4. Perry Bacon Jr., "Why Bernie Sanders Lost," FiveThirtyEight, April 8, 2020, https://fivethirtyeight.com/features/why-bernie-sanders-lost/.

5. Center for Responsive Politics, "Hillary Clinton (D): Top Industries, Federal Election Data," February 22, 2016, http://www.opensecrets.org/pres16/indus.php?id=N00000019&cycle=2016&type=f&src=o.

6. Jonathan Martin, "Alarmed Clinton Supporters Begin Focusing on Sanders's Socialist Edge," *New York Times*, January 19, 2016, http://www.nytimes.com/2016/01/20/us/politics/alarmed-hillary-clinton-supporters-begin-focusing-on-bernie-sanders-socialist-edge.html.

7. D. Stephen Voss, "Will Superdelegates Pick the Democratic Nominee? Here's Everything You Need to Know," *Washington Post*, February 26, 2016, https://www.washingtonpost.com/news/monkey-cage/wp/2016/02/26/will-superdelegates-pick-the-democratic-nominee-heres-everything-you-need-to-know.

8. Amy Chozick, "After Michigan Loss, Hillary Clinton Sharpens Message on Jobs and Trade," *New York Times*, March 9, 2016, http://www.nytimes.com/2016/03/10/us/politics/after-michigan-loss-hillary-clinton-retools-message-on-jobs-and-trade.html?_r=0.

9. Chozick, "After Michigan Loss."

10. Dylan Scott, "Clinton Is Moving Left on Social Security," *National Journal*, August 13, 2015, http://www.govexec.com/management/2015/08/clinton-moving-left-social-security/119093/.

11. Silver, "Sanders—and the Media."

12. "Washington's Farewell Address," Digital History, (1796) 2016, http://www.digitalhistory.uh.edu/disp_textbook.cfm?smtID=3&psid=160.

13. American Political Science Association, "A Report of the Committee on Political Parties: Toward a More Responsible Two-Party System," *American Political Science Review* 44, no. 3 (September 1950): pt. 2, supplement.

14. Austin Ranney, "Toward a More Responsible Two-Party System: A Commentary," *American Political Science Review* 45, no. 2 (1951): 488–99.

15. V. O. Key Jr., *Politics, Parties, and Pressure Groups*, 5th ed. (New York: Cromwell, 1964).

16. Jonathan Rauch, "The Secret to Saner Elections? Stronger State Parties," *Los Angeles Times*, March 22, 2016, http://www.latimes.com/opinion/op-ed/la-oe-0322-rauch-state-parties-20160322-story.html.

17. Drew DeSilver, "So Far, Turnout in This Year's Primaries Rivals 2008 Record," Pew Research Center, March 8, 2016, www.pewresearch.org/fact-tank/2016/03/08/so-far-turnout-in-this-years-primaries-rivals-2008-record.

18. Marty Cohen et al., *The Party Decides: Presidential Nominations before and after Reform* (Chicago: University of Chicago Press, 2008), 3.

19. Steve Inskeep and Shankar Vedantam, "Why Compromise Is a Bad Word in Politics," National Public Radio, March 13, 2012, http://www.npr.org/2012/03/13/148499310/why-compromise-is-terrible-politics.

20. See, for example, Morris P. Fiorina, *Culture War? The Myth of a Polarized America* (New York: Longman/Pearson, 2011).

21. John H. Aldrich, *Why Parties? The Origin and Transformation of Political Parties in America* (Chicago: University of Chicago Press, 1995), 261. See also V. O. Key Jr., "A Theory of Critical Elections," *Journal of Politics* 17, no. 1 (February 1955): 3–18.

22. Amy Kittelstrom, "Ignorance, Racism and Rage: The GOP's transformation to the party of stupid started long before Donald Trump," Salon, April 9, 2016, www.salon.com/2016/04/09/ignorance_racism_and_rage_the_gops_transformation_to_the_party_of_stupid_started_long_before_donald_trump/?utm_source=twitter&utm_medium=socialflow.

23. Kittelstrom, "Ignorance, Racism and Rage," 1002.

24. "2000 Presidential Election Results," U.S.ElectionAtlas.org, accessed July 31, 2018, http://uselectionatlas.org/RESULTS/national.php?year=2000.

25. The size of the House was fixed at 435 members by the Reapportionment Act of 1929. The number rose to 437 for a time after the admission of Alaska and Hawaii as states, but it has stayed at 435 since the apportionment following the 1960 census. Washington, DC, has three nonvoting delegates in the House.

26. Wesberry v. Sanders, 376 U.S. 1 (1964); Reynolds v. Sims, 377 U.S. 533 (1964).

27. Aaron Bycoffe, Ella Koeze, David Wasserman, and Julia Wolfe, "The Atlas of Redistricting," FiveThirtyEight, January 25, 2018, https://projects.fivethirtyeight.com/redistricting-maps/.

28. David Wasserman and Ally Finn, "Introducing the 2017 Cook Political Report Partisan Voter Index," The Cook Political Report, April 7, 2017, https://cookpolitical.com/introducing-2017-cook-political-report-partisan-voter-index.

29. Thornburg v. Gingles, 478 U.S. 30 (1986); Shaw v. Reno, 509 U.S. 630 (1993).

30. David R. Mayhew, *Congress: The Electoral Connection* (New Haven, CT: Yale University Press), 5. See also David R. Mayhew, "Congressional Elections: The Case of the Vanishing Marginals," *Polity* 6, no. 3 (Spring 1974): 295–317.

31. Mayhew, *Congress*, 49–77.

32. Gary C. Jacobson, *The Politics of Congressional Elections*, 8th ed. (New York: Pearson, 2012), 27.

33. Buckley v. Valeo, 424 U.S. 1 (1976).

34. Citizens United v. Federal Election Commission, 558 U.S.___ (2010).

35. Sidney Verba and Norman H. Nie, *Participation in America: Political Democracy and Social Equality* (New York: Harper & Row, 1972), 46–48.

36. Russell J. Dalton, "The Myth of the Disengaged American," Comparative Study of Electoral Systems (CSES), 2005, http://www.cses.org/resources/results/POP_Oct2005_1.htm.

37. Jeffrey M. Jones, "Democratic, Republican Identification Near Historical Lows," Gallup, January 11, 2016, www.gallup.com/poll/188096/democratic-republican-identification-near-historical-lows.aspx?g_source=Politics&g_medium=lead&g_campaign=tiles.

38. Rauch, "The Secret to Saner Elections?"

39. Raymond E. Wolfinger and Steven J. Rosenstone, *Who Votes?* (New Haven, CT: Yale University Press, 1980).

40. See Eric Plutzer, "Becoming a Habitual Voter: Inertia, Resources, and Growth in Young Adulthood," *American Political Science Review* 96, no. 1 (March 2002): 41–56.

41. Center for American Women and Politics, "Fact Sheet: Gender Differences in Voter Turnout," July 2017, http://www.cawp.rutgers.edu/sites/default/files/resources/genderdiff.pdf.

42. Angus Campbell et al., *The American Voter*, Midway Reprint (Chicago: University of Chicago Press, 1960).

43. "Voter Registration Deadlines for the General Election by State," USA.gov, accessed February 17, 2016, https://www.usa.gov/voter-registration-deadlines.

44. Voters without photo identification in those states may cast a provisional ballot but must return with identification in order to have their vote count. Wendy Underhill, "Voter Identification Requirements/Voter ID Laws," National Conference of State Legislatures, February 24, 2020, https://www.ncsl.org/research/elections-and-campaigns/voter-id.aspx.

45. Wendy Underhill, "Online Voter Registration," National Conference of State Legislatures, January 27, 2020, https://www.ncsl.org/research/elections-and-campaigns/electronic-or-online-voter-registration.aspx.

46. Tarana Burke, "The Inception," meetoomvmnt.org, accessed April 5, 2020, https://metoomvmt.org/the-inception/.

47. Sandra E. Garcia, "The Woman Who Created #MeToo Long Before Hashtags," *New York Times*, October 20, 2017, https://www.nytimes.com/2017/10/20/us/me-too-movement-tarana-burke.html.

48. Alyssa Milano (@Alyssa Milano), "If you've been sexually harassed or assaulted write 'me too' as a reply to this tweet," Twitter, October 15, 2017, 3:21 p.m., https://twitter.com/Alyssa_Milano/status/919659438700670976.

49. Monica Anderson and Skye Toor, "How Social Media Users Have Discussed Sexual Harassment Since #MeToo Went Viral," Pew Research Center, October 18, 2018, https://www.pewresearch.org/fact-tank/2018/10/11/how-social-media-users-have-discussed-sexual-harassment-since-metoo-went-viral/.

50. Ashwini Tambe, "Reckoning with the Silences of #MeToo," *Feminist Studies* 44, no. 1 (2018): 197–203.

51. Jessica T. Feezell, "Predicting Online Political Participation: The Importance of Selection Bias and Selective Exposure in the Online Setting," *Political Research Quarterly* 69, no. 3 (2016): 495–509.

52. Peter Dahlgren, "The Internet, Public Spheres, and Political Communication: Dispersion and Deliberation," *Political Communication*, 22, no. 2 (2006): 147–62.

53. K. Mendes, J. Ringrose, and J. Keller, "#MeToo and the Promise and Pitfalls of Challenging Rape Culture through Digital Activism," *European Journal of Women's Studies* 25, no. 2 (2018): 236–46.

54. Mendes et al., "#MeToo and the Promise."

55. Aisha Harris, "She Founded Me Too. Now She Wants to Move Past the Trauma," *New York Times*, October 15, 2018, https://www.nytimes.com/2018/10/15/arts/tarana-burke-metoo-anniversary.html.

56. Carol Hanisch, "The Personal Is Political," carolhanisch.org, accessed April 4, 2020 (repr., February 1969), http://www.carolhanisch.org/CHwritings/PIP.html. Hanisch notes that she did not choose the title for the essay herself but attributes the decision to the editors of the volume in which it first appeared, Shulie Firestone and Anne Koedt.

57. *Hanisch*, "The Personal Is Political."

58. Catharine A. MacKinnon, "Where #MeToo Came From, and Where It's Going," *The Atlantic*, March 24, 2019, https://www.theatlantic.com/ideas/archive/2019/03/catharine-mackinnon-what-metoo-has-changed/585313/.

CHAPTER 9

1. Chairman Ben. S. Bernanke, "The Economic Outlook," testimony before the Joint Economic Committee, United States Congress, March 28, 2007, www.federalreserve.gov/newsevents/testimony/bernanke20070328a.htm.

2. U.S. Department of the Treasury, "The Financial Crisis Response in Charts," April 2012, www.treasury.gov/resource-center/

data-chart-center/Documents/20120413_
FinancialCrisisResponse.pdf.

3. Helen Kennedy, "Economy Is Headin' for Cliff! OK Bailout Soon or Else, Says Treasury Chief," *New York Daily News,* September 22, 2008; available from Lexis-Nexis Academic.

4. Kennedy, "Economy Is Headin' for Cliff!"

5. Jeffrey H. Birnbaum, "Vital Part of Housing Bill Is Brainchild of Banks," *Washington Post,* June 25, 2008, www.washingtonpost.com/wp-dyn/content/article/2008/06/24/AR2008062401389.html.

6. Jenny Anderson, Vikas Bajaj, and Leslie Wayne, "Big Financiers Start to Lobby for Wider Aid," *New York Times,* September 21, 2008, www.nytimes.com/2008/09/22/business/22lobby.html?_r=0.

7. Jerry Zremski, "Bailout Plan Hit by Backlash; Congress Expresses Outrage; Reflects Taxpayers' Mood amid Call for Quick Action," *Buffalo News* (New York), September 24, 2008; available from Lexis-Nexis Academic.

8. Tony Pugh, "Groups Say Bailout Doesn't Do Enough for Struggling Homeowners," Knight Ridder Washington Bureau, September 23, 2008; available from Lexis-Nexis Academic.

9. Helen Kennedy, "Dems Balk at Bailout. Press Help for Homeowners, Exec Pay Cuts as Part of Deal," *New York Daily News,* September 23, 2008; available from Lexis-Nexis Academic.

10. Kennedy, "Dems Balk at Bailout."

11. Juan Gonzalez, "Bailout Dish Has Heaping Side of Pork," *New York Daily News,* October 3, 2008; available from Lexis-Nexis Academic.

12. Kenneth Stier, "Tax Break for Arrows? Why It's Part of the Bailout," CNBC.com, October 2, 2008, https://www.cnbc.com/id/26995651.

13. Stephen Labaton and Jackie Calmes, "Obama Proposes a First Overhaul of Finance Rules," *New York Times,* May 14, 2009; available from Lexis-Nexis Academic.

14. Deniz Igan, Prachi Mishra, and Thierry Tressel, "A Fistful of Dollars: Lobbying and the Financial Crisis," National Bureau of Economic Research Working Paper 17076, May 2001, http://www.nber.org/papers/w17076.

15. Igan et al., "A Fistful of Dollars."

16. Alexis de Tocqueville, *Democracy in America,* trans. George Lawrence, ed. J. P. Mayer (New York: Harper Perennial Modern Classics, 1966), 9.

17. For a historical treatment of these ideas, see Arthur M. Schlesinger, "Biography of a Nation of Joiners," *The American Historical Review* 50, no. 1 (October 1944): 1–25.

18. James Madison, *Federalist* No. 54, in *The Federalist Papers,* ed. George W. Carey and James McClellan (Indianapolis: Liberty Fund, 2001), 44.

19. Robert A. Dahl, *Who Governs? Democracy and Power in an American City* (New Haven, CT: Yale University Press, 1961), 3.

20. C. Wright Mills, *The Power Elite* (New York: Oxford University Press, 1956), 4–5.

21. E. E. Schattschneider, *The Semisovereign People: A Realist's View of Democracy in America* (Hinsdale, IL: The Dryden Press, 1960), 32.

22. David B. Truman, *The Governmental Process: Political Interests and Public Opinion* (New York: Alfred A. Knopf, 1962), 5. Truman used the term *pressure groups* to describe the phenomenon.

23. Mancur Olson, *The Logic of Collective Action: Public Goods and the Theory of Groups* (Cambridge, MA: Harvard University Press, 1965), 2. Italics are the author's.

24. Paul Samuelson, "The Pure Theory of Public Expenditure," *The Review of Economics and Statistics* 36, no. 4 (November 1954): 387–89. Technically, the characteristic is called *nonexcludability.* Public goods also exhibit the characteristic of *nonrivalry,* referring to the fact that the consumption of the good by one individual does not reduce its availability to others.

25. Olson, *The Logic of Collective Action,* 14–15.

26. David C. King and Jack L. Walker, "The Provision of Benefits by Interest Groups in the United States," *Journal of Politics* 54, no. 2 (May 1992): 394–426.

27. Sandy Mackenzie, "The Impact of the Financial Crisis on Older Americans," *Insight on the Issues, AARP Public Policy Institute* 19 (December 2008): 11.

28. Anthony J. Nownes, *Total Lobbying: What Lobbyists Want (and How They Try to Get It)* (New York: Cambridge University Press, 2006), 6.

29. Center for Responsive Politics, "Lobbying Database," OpenSecrets.org, 2014, https://www.opensecrets.org/lobby. Their figures were calculated from data obtained from the Senate Office of Public Records.

30. Kay Lehman Schlozman and John T. Tierney, *Organized Interests and American Democracy* (New York: Harper & Row, 1986), 148–57.

31. Joseph White, "Making Connections to the Appropriations Process," in *The Interest Group Connection: Electioneering, Lobbying, and Policymaking in Washington,* 2nd ed., ed. Paul S. Herrnson, Ronald G. Shaiko, and Clyde Wilcox (Washington, DC: CQ Press, 2005), 164–88.

32. Administrative Procedure Act of 1946.

33. Scott R. Furlong, "Exploring Interest Group Participation in Executive Policymaking," in Herrnson et al., *The Interest Group Connection,* 282–97.

34. Marver Bernstein, *Regulating Business by Independent Commission* (Princeton, NJ: Princeton University Press, 1955).

35. Gregory A. Caldeira and John R. Wright, "Organized Interests and Agenda Setting in the U.S. Supreme Court," *The American Political Science Review* 82, no. 4 (December 1988): 1109–27.

36. Lee Epstein and C. K. Rowland. "Debunking the Myth of Interest Group Invincibility in the Courts," *The American Political Science Review* 85, no. 1 (March 1991): 205–17.

37. Citizens United v. Federal Election Commission, 558 U.S. ___ (2010).

38. Norman J. Ornstein and Shirley Elder, *Interest Groups, Lobbying, and Policymaking* (Washington, DC: CQ Press, 1978), 88.

39. Ken Kollman, *Outside Lobbying: Public Opinion and Interest Group Strategies* (Princeton, NJ: Princeton University Press, 1998), 80.

40. Kenneth M. Goldstein, *Interest Groups, Lobbying, and Participation in America* (New York: Cambridge University Press, 1999), 125.

41. Grant McConnell, *Private Power & American Democracy* (New York: Alfred A. Knopf, 1966), 5.

42. Kay Lehman Schlozman, "What Accent the Heavenly Chorus? Political Equality and the American Pressure System," *The Journal of Politics* 46, no. 4 (November 1984): 1006–32.

43. Dara Z. Strolovitch, *Affirmative Advocacy: Race, Class, and Gender in Interest Group Politics* (Chicago: University of Chicago Press, 2007).

44. Maud Dillingham, "Top 5 Targets of Occupy Wall Street," *The Christian Science Monitor*, October 24, 2011; available from Lexis-Nexis Academic.

45. Dillingham, "Top 5 Targets."

46. John Wellington Ennis, "Three Years Later, What Has Come of Occupy Wall Street?," *Huffington Post*, September 17, 2014, www.huffingtonpost.com/john-wellington-ennis/three-years-later-what-ha_b_5833682.html.

47. Occupy★Posters, Tumblr, accessed July 3, 2016, http://owsposters.tumblr.com/post/11944143747/if-us-land-mass-were-distributed-like-us.

48. James C. McKinley Jr., "At the Protests, the Message Lacks a Melody," *New York Times*, October 19, 2011; available from Lexis-Nexis Academic.

49. Harold Brubaker, "'Occupy Wall Street' Protest Movement Seeks a Philadelphia Foothold," *Philadelphia Inquirer*, October 2, 2011; available from Lexis-Nexis Academic.

50. Brad Knickerbocker, "Occupy Wall Street Protest 'about People Claiming Some Autonomy,'" *Christian Science Monitor*, October 2, 2011; available from Lexis-Nexis Academic.

51. Jonathan Easley, "GOP: Dems Mum on Anti-Semitism from Occupy Wall Street Protestors," The Hill.com, October 20, 2011; available from Lexis-Nexis Academic.

52. Alice Speri, "Struggling to Make 'the 99%' More Representative of Reality," *New York Times*, October 29, 2011; available from Lexis-Nexis Academic.

53. Speri, "Struggling to Make 'the 99%' More Representative."

54. NYC General Assembly, #Occupy Wall Street, "Declaration of the Occupation of New York City," September 29, 2011, accessed December 4, 2014, http://www.nycga.net/resources/documents/declaration/.

55. Cara Buckley and Colin Moynihan, "A Protest Reaches a Crossroads," *New York Times*, November 6, 2011; available from Lexis-Nexis Academic.

56. Michelle Nichols, "Wall Street Demonstrators Evicted by New York Police," Reuters, November 16, 2011; available from Lexis-Nexis Academic.

57. Letter to the Editor, *New York Times,* November 17, 2011; available from Lexis-Nexis Academic.

58. Gloria Goodale, "Occupy Wall Street: Time to Become More Overtly Political?," *The Christian Science Monitor*, November 16, 2011; available from Lexis-Nexis Academic.

59. See, for example, Dennis Chong, *Collective Action and the Civil Rights Movement* (Chicago: University of Chicago Press, 1991).

60. This section draws upon Ken Kollman, *The American Political System* (New York: W. W. Norton, 2012), 378–79.

61. Christian Davenport, "How Social Movements Die—the Blog Entry (Book on the Way)," Mobilizing Ideas, The Center for the Study of Social Movements at the University of Notre Dame, December 2, 2013, https://mobilizingideas.wordpress.com/2013/12/02/how-social-movements-die-the-blog-entry-book-on-the-way.

62. Edwin Amenta, "Failure Is Not an Option," Mobilizing Ideas, The Center for the Study of Social Movements at the University of Notre Dame, December 2, 2013, https://mobilizingideas.wordpress.com/2013/12/02/failure-is-not-an-option.

63. Erik W. Johnson, "Social Movement Size, Organizational Diversity and the Making of Federal Law," *Social Forces* 86, no. 3 (2008): 967–93.

64. John W. Kingdon, *Agendas, Alternatives, and Public Policies*, updated 2nd ed. (Boston: Longman 2011).

65. David S. Meyer and Steven A. Boutcher, "Signals and Spillover: *Brown v. Board of Education* and Other Social Movements," *Perspectives on Politics* 5, no. 1 (2007): 81–93.

CHAPTER 10

1. Hanna Fenichel Pitkin, *The Concept of Representation* (Berkeley: University of California Press, 1972).

2. There had been a total of four women serving in the Senate at some point during the 102nd Congress. Sen. Jocelyn Burdick (D-ND) had served as an interim appointee before retiring in December 1992, and the success of Sen. Dianne Feinstein (D-CA) in the election on November 3, 1992, enabled her to serve out the remainder of the term of interim appointee Sen. John F. Seymour (R-CA). The numbers for the House of Representatives do not include nonvoting delegates.

3. Chris Chrystal, "Democratic Women Battle for 2 California Senate Seats," UPI, May 31, 1992, www.upi.com/Archives/1992/05/31/Democratic-women-battle-for-2-California-Senate-seats/6261707284800.

4. Debra L. Dodson et al., *Voices, Views, Votes: The Impact of Women in the 103rd Congress* (New Brunswick, NJ: Rutgers, Eagleton Institute of Politics, Center for American Women and Politics, 1995), 2.

5. Clara Bingham, "Queens of the Hill: Will the Newly Empowered Women Lawmakers Clean Up Congress?" *Washington Monthly*, January–February 2007, www.washingtonmonthly.com/features/2007/0701.bingham.html.

6. Michael X. Delli Carpini and Ester R. Fuchs, "The Year of the Woman? Candidates, Voters, and the 1992 Election," *Political Science Quarterly* 108, no. 1 (1993): 34–35.

7. Barbara Mikulski et al., *Nine and Counting: The Women of the Senate* (New York: Perennial, 2001), 48–49.

8. "The Year of the Woman. Then and Now: Women in U.S. Politics in 1992 and 2008," International Museum of Women, Global Fund for Women, http://exhibitions.globalfundforwomen.org/exhibitions/women-power-and-politics/elections/year-woman.

9. Mikulski et al., *Nine and Counting*, 47.

10. Linda L. Fowler and Robert D. McClure, *Political Ambition: Who Decides to Run for Congress* (New Haven, CT: Yale University Press, 1989), xii. See also Jennifer L. Lawless, *Becoming a Candidate: Political Ambition and the Decision to Run for Office* (New York: Cambridge University Press, 2012).

11. Mikulski et al., *Nine and Counting*, 44.

12. Julie Kohler and Felicia Wong, "Why 2018 Might Not Be the Year of the Woman, *The Nation*, April 27, 2018, https://www.thenation.com/article/why-2018-might-not-be-the-year-of-the-woman/.

13. Heather Caygle, "Record-Breaking Number of Women Run for Office," Politico, March 8, 2018, https://www.politico.com/story/2018/03/08/women-rule-midterms-443267.

14. Kate Ackley, "Women—and the Power of the Purse—Will Be Key in 2018," *Roll Call*, October 26, 2017, https://www.rollcall.com/news/politics/99810-2.

15. Caygle, "Record-Breaking Number of Women Run for Office."

16. Margaret Talbot, "The Women Running in the Midterms during the Trump Era," *New Yorker*, April 18, 2018, https://www.newyorker.com/news/news-desk/2018-midterm-elections-women-candidates-trump.

17. Kayla Epstein and Eugene Scott, "The Historic Firsts of the 2018 Midterms," *Washington Post*, November 7, 2018, https://www.washingtonpost.com/politics/2018/11/07/historic-firsts-midterms/?noredirect=on.

18. Abby Finkenauer (D-IA) was also twenty-nine when elected to the 116th Congress.

19. Maureen Dowd, "It's Nancy Pelosi's Parade," *New York Times*, July 6, 2019.

20. Dowd, "It's Nancy Pelosi's Parade."

21. "Will 'the Squad' vs. Pelosi Be a Big Problem for Democrats in 2020?" FiveThirtyEight, July 17, 2019, https://fivethirtyeight.com/features/will-the-squad-v-pelosi-be-a-big-problem-for-democrats-in-2020/.

22. Although they are only required by the Constitution to live in the states that they represent, members of the House are, by custom, expected to maintain a residence in their electoral district.

23. James Madison, *Federalist* No. 52, in *The Federalist Papers*, ed. George W. Carey and James McClellan (Indianapolis: Liberty Fund, 2001), 273.

24. Also referred to as The Congressional Budget Control and Impoundment Act of 1974, Pub. L. No. 93-344.

25. Mathew McCubbins and Thomas Schwartz, "Congressional Oversight Overlooked: Police Patrols versus Fire Alarms," *American Journal of Political Science* 28 (1984): 165–79.

26. U.S. Const. art. I, § 8.

27. If the president is being tried for impeachment, the chief justice of the Supreme Court presides (U.S. Const. art. 1, § 3).

28. Richard F. Fenno Jr., *Congressmen in Committees* (Boston: Little, Brown, 1973).

29. Barbara Sinclair, *Unorthodox Lawmaking: New Legislative Processes in the U.S. Congress*, 2nd ed. (Washington, DC: CQ Press, 2000), 33.

30. Sinclair, *Unorthodox Lawmaking*, 3.

31. The term *filibuster* has also been generally used to describe several other delaying tactics in the Senate.

32. Sinclair, *Unorthodox Lawmaking*, 43.

33. Carl Hulse, "Trump Gets a Win He Wasn't Counting On: He Saved the Filibuster," *New York Times*, May 3, 2017, https://www.nytimes.com/2017/05/03/us/politics/trump-filibuster.html?rref=collection%2Ftimestopic%2FFilibusters%20and%20Debate%20Curbs&action=click&contentCollection=timestopics&region=stream&module=streas_unit&version=latest&contentPlacement=2&pgtype=collection&_r=0.

34. Hulse, "Trump Gets a Win."

35. Sinclair, *Unorthodox Lawmaking*, 58.

36. See Charles M. Cameron, *Veto Bargaining: Presidents and the Politics of Negative Power* (New York: Cambridge University Press, 2000).

37. Richard F. Fenno Jr., *Home Style: House Members in Their Districts* (New York: HarperCollins, 1978).

38. John W. Kingdon, *Congressmen's Voting Decisions*, 3rd ed. (Ann Arbor: University of Michigan Press, 1989).

39. Fenno, *Home Style*.

40. Jane Mansbridge calls the former *promissory representation* and the latter *anticipatory representation*. Jane Mansbridge, "Rethinking Representation," *American Political Science Review* 97, no. 4 (November 2003): 515–28.

41. R. Douglas Arnold, *The Logic of Congressional Action* (New Haven, CT: Yale University Press, 1990).

42. Arnold, *The Logic of Congressional Action*.

43. Tracy Sulkin, *Issue Politics in Congress* (New York: Cambridge University Press, 2005).

44. Richard L. Hall, *Participation in Congress* (New Haven, CT: Yale University Press, 1996).

45. "1994 Committee Supplement: Senate Judiciary," *CQ Weekly*, March 5, 1994, http://library.cqpress.com/cqweekly/wr103403788.

46. Dodson et al., *Voices, Views, Votes*, 13.

47. See Morris P. Fiorina, Samuel J. Abrams, and Jeremy C. Pope, *Culture War? The Myth of a Polarized America*, 3rd ed. (New York: Longman, 2011); and Alan I. Abramowitz, *The Disappearing Center: Engaged Citizens, Polarization, and American Democracy* (New Haven, CT: Yale University Press, 2010).

48. Jane Mansbridge, "Should Blacks Represent Blacks and Women Represent Women? A Contingent 'Yes,'" *Journal of Politics* 61, no. 3 (August 1999): 628.

49. Mansbridge, "Should Blacks Represent Blacks?," 632.

50. Carol M. Swain, *Black Faces, Black Interests: The Representation of African Americans in Congress* (Cambridge, MA: Harvard University Press, 1995), 5.

51. Mansbridge, "Should Blacks Represent Blacks?," 637.

52. Pitkin, *The Concept of Representation*, 114.

53. Mansbridge, "Should Blacks Represent Blacks?," 634.

54. John W. Kingdon, *Agendas, Alternatives, and Public Policies*, 2nd ed. (New York: Longman, 2003).

55. Mansbridge, "Rethinking Representation," 522.

56. Mikulski et al., *Nine and Counting*, 197.

CHAPTER 11

1. Hal Lancaster, "Fight over Fights: Donald Trump Vies for Las Vegas's Boxing Crown," *Wall Street Journal*, October 16, 1987.

2. Lancaster, "Fight over Fights."

3. Mark Mazzetti and Katie Benner, "Mueller Finds No Trump-Russia Conspiracy, but Stops Short of Exonerating President on Obstruction," *New York Times*, March 24, 2019, https://www.nytimes.com/2019/03/24/us/politics/mueller-report-summary.html.

4. Ben Hubbard, "Dozens Suffocate in Syria as Government Is Accused of Chemical Attack," *New York Times*, April 8, 2018, https://www.nytimes.com/2018/04/08/world/middleeast/syria-chemical-attack-ghouta.html.

5. Tom Embury-Dennis, "Russia Will Shoot Down US Missiles Fired at Syria and Retaliate against Launch Sites, Says Ambassador," Independent.co.uk, April 11, 2018, https://www.independent.co.uk/news/world/middle-east/russia-us-missiles-syria-launch-sites-lebanon-zasypkin-putin-a8298941.html.

6. President Donald J. Trump (@realDonaldTrump), "Russia vows to shoot down any and all missiles fired at Syria. Get ready Russia, because they will be coming, nice and new and 'smart!' You shouldn't be partners with a Gas Killing Animal who kills his people and enjoys it!" Twitter, April 11, 2018, 3:57 a.m., https://twitter.com/realDonaldTrump/status/984022625440747520.

7. Gregory Krieg, "John Bolton on: Bombing Iran, North Korea, Russia and the Iraq War," CNN, March 23, 2018, https://www.cnn.com/2018/03/23/politics/what-john-bolton-said-iraq-iran-north-korea/index.html.

8. Peter Baker, Gardiner Harris, and Mark Landler, "Trump Fires Rex Tillerson and Will Replace Him with C.I.A. Chief Pompeo," *New York Times*, March 13, 2018, https://www.nytimes.com/2018/03/13/us/politics/trump-tillerson-pompeo.html.

9. Russell Berman, "The Humbling of Mike Pompeo," *The Atlantic*, April 17, 2018, https://www.theatlantic.com/politics/archive/2018/04/

pompeo-trump-secretary-state-cia-senate-confirmation/558242/.

10. Kathryn Dunn Tenpas, "Why Is Trump's Staff Turnover Higher Than the 5 Most Recent Presidents?" Brookings, January 19, 2018, https://www.brookings.edu/research/why-is-trumps-staff-turnover-higher-than-the-5-most-recent-presidents/.

11. Helene Cooper, "Mattis Wanted Congressional Approval before Striking Syria. He Was Overruled," *New York Times*, April 17, 2018, https://www.nytimes.com/2018/04/17/us/politics/jim-mattis-trump-syria-attack.html.

12. Jeffrey Goldberg, "James Mattis Denounces President Trump, Describes Him as a Threat to the Constitution," *The Atlantic*, June 3, 2020, https://www.theatlantic.com/politics/archive/2020/06/james-mattis-denounces-trump-protests-militarization/612640/.

13. Jonathan Martin and Maggie Haberman, "A Key G.O.P. Strategy: Blame China. But Trump Goes Off Message," *New York Times*, April 20, 2020.

14. David J. Lynch and Emily Rauhala, "Trump Lashes Out at China, Orders Action on Hong Kong," *Washington Post*, May 30, 2020.

15. Pew Research Center, "In Their Own Words: Why Voters Support—and Have Concerns About—Clinton and Trump," September 21, 2016, https://www.people-press.org/2016/09/21/in-their-own-words-why-voters-support-and-have-concerns-about-clinton-and-trump/. The percentages of responses in the survey exceed 100 percent due to multiple responses by those surveyed.

16. Maggie Haberman, Glenn Thrush, and Peter Baker, "Inside Trump's Hour-by-Hour Battle for Self-Preservation," *New York Times*, December 9, 2017, https://www.nytimes.com/2017/12/09/us/politics/donald-trump-president.html.

17. Haberman et al., "Inside Trump's Hour-by-Hour Battle."

18. Pew Research Center, "Few Americans Express Positive Views of Trump's Conduct in Office," March 5, 2020, https://www.people-press.org/2020/03/05/few-americans-express-positive-views-of-trumps-conduct-in-office/.

19. See James David Barber, *The Presidential Character: Predicting Performance in the White House*, 4th ed. (Englewood Cliffs, NJ: Prentice Hall, 1992).

20. Richard E. Neustadt, *Presidential Power and the Modern Presidents: The Politics of Leadership from Roosevelt to Reagan* (New York: Free Press, 1990), 163.

21. Neustadt, *Presidential Power*, 30.

22. Ulysses S. Grant unsuccessfully sought a third term in 1880.

23. In some states, widows with property were allowed to participate in public and political life.

24. Max Farrand, *The Framing of the Constitution of the United States* (New Haven, CT: Yale University Press, 1913), 163.

25. Many of these titles are in Clinton Rossiter, *The American Presidency*, 2nd ed. (Baltimore: Johns Hopkins University Press, 1987).

26. U.S. Const. art. II, § 1.

27. U.S. Const. art. II, § 1; art. II, § 3.

28. U.S. Const. art. II, § 2.

29. U.S. Const. art. II, § 2, 3.

30. Rossiter, *The American Presidency*, 12.

31. U.S. Const. art. II, § 2.

32. Edward S. Corwin, *Presidential Power and the Constitution: Essays* (Ithaca, NY: Cornell University Press, 1976), 163.

33. Pub. L. No. 93-148, 87 Stat. 555 (November 7, 1973). Codified in 50 U.S.C. 33, Sections 1541–48 (1973). It is also called the War Powers Act, which was the title of the version of the joint resolution passed in the Senate.

34. Louis Fisher and David Gray Adler, "The War Powers Resolution: Time to Say Goodbye," *Political Science Quarterly* 113, no. 1 (1998): 1.

35. War Powers Resolution, Section 2(a).

36. War Powers Resolution, Section 2(c).

37. War Powers Resolution, Section 4(a). The president must notify both the Speaker of the House and the president of the Senate pro tempore.

38. Congress authorized military operations in Afghanistan in Authorization for Use of Military Force, Pub. L. No. 107-40 (2001), and in Iraq in Authorization for Use of Military Force against Iraq Resolution of 2002, Pub. L. No. 107-243 (2002).

39. See Fisher and Adler, "The War Powers Resolution."

40. U.S. Const. art. II, § 3.

41. Charles M. Cameron, *Veto Bargaining: Presidents and the Politics of Negative Power* (New York: Cambridge University Press, 2000).

42. U.S. Const. art. II, § 2.

43. U.S. Const. art. I, § 3.

44. U.S. Const. art. II, § 2.

45. U.S. Const. art. II, § 4.

46. The chief justice presides only when presidents are impeached. Otherwise, the presiding office of the Senate would chair the proceedings.

47. Farrand, *The Framing of the Constitution*.

48. U.S. Const. art. I, § 3.

49. Rossiter, *The American Presidency*, 123.

50. The *Report of the President's Committee on Administrative Management* (1937), also known as the Brownlow Committee Report. The

Reorganization Act of 1939 provided the legislative authorization for President Roosevelt's reorganization of the executive branch.

51. For a challenge to the argument that divided government necessarily leads to legislative gridlock, see David R. Mayhew, *Divided We Govern: Party Control, Lawmaking, and Investigations, 1946–1990* (New Haven, CT: Yale University Press, 1991).

52. Rossiter, *The American Presidency*, 54, 56.

53. J. D. Richardson, ed., *Messages and Papers of the Presidents* (New York, 1879), 3, quoted in Benjamin I. Page and Mark P. Petracca, *The American Presidency* (New York: McGraw-Hill, 1983), 118.

54. Samuel Kernell, *Going Public: New Strategies of Presidential Leadership* (Washington, DC: CQ Press, 2007), 1–2.

55. James A. Stimson, "Public Support for American Presidents: A Cyclical Model," *The Public Opinion Quarterly* 40, no. 1 (1976): 1–21.

56. Lester G. Seligman, "On Models of the Presidency," *Presidential Studies Quarterly* 10, no. 3 (1980): 356.

57. Alexander Hamilton, *Federalist* No. 74, in *The Federalist Papers*, ed. George W. Carey and James McClellan (Indianapolis, IN: Liberty Fund, 2001), 385.

58. James Bryce, *The American Commonwealth*, vol. 1 (New York: Macmillan, 1888), 83–84.

59. Dina Temple-Rastan, "Kill and Tell: Inside the President's Terrorist Hunt," *Washington Post*, June 17, 2012, B01; available from Lexis-Nexis Academic.

60. Mark Mazzetti, Charlie Savage, and Scott Shane, "A U.S. Citizen in America's Cross Hairs," *New York Times*, March 10, 2013, A1; available from Lexis-Nexis Academic.

61. "Details of Al-Awlaki's Death," *Yemen Times*, October 3, 2011; available from Lexis-Nexis Academic.

62. Scott Shane and Souad Mekhennet, "From Condemning Terror to Preaching Jihad," *New York Times*, May 9, 2010, A1; available from Lexis-Nexis Academic.

63. Scott Shane and Mark Mazzetti, "A Newly Religious Immigrant Is Linked to a Militant Yemeni-American Cleric," *New York Times*, May 7, 2010, A13; available from Lexis-Nexis Academic.

64. Anthony Shadid and David D. Kirkpatrick, "As the West Celebrates a Cleric's Death, the Mideast Shrugs," *New York Times*, October 2, 2011, A14; available from Lexis-Nexis Academic.

65. Shane and Mekhennet, "From Condemning Terror to Preaching Jihad."

66. Shane and Mekhennet.

67. Shane and Mekhennet.

68. Scott Shane, "Judging a Long, Deadly Reach," *New York Times*, October 1, 2011, A1; available from Lexis-Nexis Academic.

69. Charlie Savage, "Top U.S. Security Official Says 'Rigorous Standards' Used for Drone Strikes," *New York Times*, May 1, 2012, A8; available from Lexis-Nexis Academic.

70. Charlie Savage, "Secret U.S. Memo Made Legal Case to Kill a Citizen," *New York Times*, October 9, 2011, A1; available from Lexis-Nexis Academic.

71. Scott Shane, "A Legal Debate as C.I.A. Stalks a U.S. Jihadist," *New York Times*, May 10, 2010, A1; available from Lexis-Nexis Academic.

72. "Startling from Baltimore: The Northern Troops Mobbed and Fired Upon," *New York Times*, April 19, 1861; available from ProQuest Historical Newspapers.

73. "Testimony of William Lynch, September 9, 1861," quoted in Jonathan W. White, *Abraham Lincoln and Treason in the Civil War: The Trials of John Merryman* (Baton Rouge: Louisiana State University Press, 2011), 13.

74. Brian McGinty, *The Body of John Merryman: Abraham Lincoln and the Suspension of Habeas Corpus* (Cambridge, MA: Harvard University Press, 2011), 67.

75. Corwin, *Presidential Power*, 130.

76. Corwin.

77. Ex parte Merryman, 17 Fed. Cases 146 (1861).

78. See McGinty, *The Body of John Merryman*.

79. George William Brown, *Baltimore and the Nineteenth of April 1861: A Study of the War* (Baltimore: Johns Hopkins University Press, 1887), 88.

80. *Ex parte Merryman*. The legal term *ex parte* refers to a decision that affects one party only or a suit that is brought by or on behalf of one individual. Justice Taney, in standard practice at the time, also served as a circuit court judge, with Baltimore included in his circuit. Scholars continue to debate whether Taney was properly acting as chief justice of the Supreme Court (which the *Merryman* opinion so identifies him as) or in his role as circuit judge when he issued the opinion.

81. Brown, *Baltimore and the Nineteenth of April 1861*, 89.

82. U.S. Const. art. I, § 9.

83. *Ex parte Merryman*.

84. Page and Petracca, *The American Presidency*, 51.

85. Habeas Corpus Suspension Act of March 3, 1863, 12 Stat 755 (1863).

86. Corwin, *Presidential Power and the Constitution*, 112, 158.

87. U.S. Const. art. I, § 9.

88. Page and Petracca, *The American Presidency*, 40.

89. See, for example, Mark J. Rozell, "The Law: Executive Privilege: Definition and Standards of Application," *Presidential Studies Quarterly* 29, no. 4 (1999): 918–30.

90. United States v. Nixon, 418 U.S. 683 (1974).

91. Kenneth R. Mayer, *With the Stroke of a Pen: Executive Orders and Presidential Power* (Princeton, NJ: Princeton University Press, 2001).

92. Executive Order 9066, 7 *Federal Register* 1407 (February 19, 1942).

93. Executive Order 9066, 7 *Federal Register* 1407 (February 19, 1942).

94. Thomas E. Cronin and Michael A. Genovese, *The Paradoxes of the American Presidency,* 2nd ed. (New York: Oxford University Press, 2004).

CHAPTER 12

1. "Crushing Weight of Harvey's Floodwaters Pushed Houston Down, GPS Data Reveals," ABC13.com, September 13, 2017, http://abc13.com/science/crushing-weight-of-harvey-flood-pushed-houston-down/2413363/.

2. Mike Tolson and Cindy George, "Harvey's Heartbreaking Losses: Collective Human Damage Tells a Story of Its Own," *Houston Chronicle*, September 15, 2017, http://www.houstonchronicle.com/news/houston-texas/houston/article/Harvey-s-heartbreaking-losses-12201961.php.

3. Eric Levenson, "3 Storms, 3 Responses: Comparing Harvey, Irma, and Maria," CNN, September 27, 2017, http://www.cnn.com/2017/09/26/us/response-harvey-irma-maria/index.html.

4. Cassandra Pollock, "The Brief: Harvey-Flooded Houston Homeowners Left in the Lurch," *Texas Tribune*, October 12, 2017, https://www.texastribune.org/2017/10/12/brief-oct-12/.

5. Levenson, "3 Storms, 3 Responses."

6. Ed Morales, "Puerto Rico in the Dark," *New York Times*, November 4, 2017, https://www.nytimes.com/2017/11/04/opinion/sunday/puerto-rico-hurricane-maria.html.

7. Levenson, "3 Storms, 3 Responses."

8. Jeffrey C. Mays, "Protesters Demand Audit of Hurricane Maria Death Toll in Puerto Rico," *New York Times*, June 2, 2018, https://www.nytimes.com/2018/06/02/nyregion/protesters-puerto-rico-hurricane-maria.html.

9. Mays, "Protesters Demand Audit."

10. Katrina was not the only *K* name to have been retired; Klaus and Keith had been retired since the modern naming system rules were put into place.

11. Tamara Lush, "For Forecasting Chief, No Joy in Being Right," *St. Petersburg Times,* August 30, 2005, 3A; available from Lexis-Nexis Academic.

12. Lush, "For Forecasting Chief."

13. Donald F. Kettl, *The Next Government of the United States: Why Our Institutions Fail Us and How to Fix Them* (New York: W. W. Norton, 2009), 18.

14. Deana Poole and Pat Beall, "New Orleans Emptying: Katrina on Path to Bring Disaster," *Palm Beach Post*, August 28, 2005, 1A.

15. John Ashton, "Thousands Flee as Hurricane Nears U.S. Coast," *Birmingham Post*, August 29, 2005, 9; available from Lexis-Nexis Academic.

16. Tina Hesman, "Most People Killed by Katrina Were Elderly, Researcher Finds," *St. Louis Post-Dispatch,* February 17, 2006, A5; available from Lexis-Nexis Academic.

17. Bryan Dean and Ryan McNeill, "Facing the Future: Hurricane Survivors Express Thanks to State," *The Oklahoman*, September 5, 2005, 1A; available from Lexis-Nexis Academic.

18. Sarah Ladislaw, "Hurricane Sandy: Evaluating the Response One Year Later," Center for Strategic and International Studies, November 4, 2013, https://www.csis.org/analysis/hurricane-sandy-evaluating-response-one-year-later.

19. Jason Samenow, "Forecasts for Harvey Were Excellent but Show Where Predictions Can Improve," *Washington Post*, August 28, 2017, https://www.washingtonpost.com/news/capital-weather-gang/wp/2017/08/28/forecasts-for-harvey-were-excellent-but-show-where-predictions-can-improve/?noredirect=on&utm_term=.250fcf8536c5.

20. Ledyard King, "Mostly Positive FEMA Reports under Obama Removed," *USA Today*, March 10, 2018, https://www.usatoday.com/story/news/politics/2018/03/09/government-watchdog-removes-fem/411369002/.

21. Steven Horwitz, "Recovery Lessons from Katrina, Harvey, Irma, and Maria," *Fort Worth Star Telegram*, October 3, 2017, http://www.star-telegram.com/opinion/opn-columns-blogs/other-voices/article176821186.html.

22. The Uniform Time Act of 1966 (15 U.S.C. §§ 260-64) established the system of uniform daylight saving time. States are allowed to opt out of the national daylight savings program. If they do participate, they must change the time according to a federally set schedule.

23. Max Weber, "The Permanent Character of the Bureaucratic Machine," in *From Max Weber: Essays in Sociology,* ed. H. H. Gerth and C. Wright Mills (New York: Oxford University Press, 1959), 229.

24. Max Weber, *Economy and Society: An Outline of Interpretive Sociology,* trans. and ed. Guenther Roth and Claus Wittich (Berkeley: University of California Press, 1978), 987. The work was first published in Germany, posthumously, in 1922.

25. Weber, *Economy and Society,* 975.

26. Chester I. Barnard, *The Functions of the Executive* (1938; repr., Cambridge, MA: Harvard University Press, 1968), 72.

27. Barnard, *The Functions of the Executive,* 82.

28. James Q. Wilson, *Bureaucracy: What Government Agencies Do and Why They Do It* (New York: Basic Books, 1989), 173.

29. Wilson, *Bureaucracy,* 175. Wilson calls this category of bureaucracies coping organizations.

30. Public education is largely governed by the states, not the federal government; however, the illustration applies to the actions of federal bureaucrats as well.

31. See Scott F. Abernathy, *No Child Left Behind and the Public Schools* (Ann Arbor: University of Michigan Press, 2007), 25–45.

32. James Q. Wilson, "The Rise of the Bureaucratic State," *The Public Interest* 41 (Fall 1975): 77.

33. U.S. Const. art. II, § 2.

34. Roughly 1,350 of 6,500 presidentially nominated officials require Senate confirmation.

35. U.S. Const. art. II, § 2, 4.

36. Leonard D. White, *The Federalists: A Study in Administrative History* (New York: The Macmillan Company, 1948), 20.

37. Myers v. United States, 272 U.S. 52 (1926).

38. White, *The Federalists,* 258. Quoting George Washington to Edward Rutledge, March 21, 1789.

39. White, *The Federalists,* 259.

40. White.

41. David H. Rosenbloom, *Federal Service and the Constitution: The Development of the Public Employment Relationship* (Ithaca, NY: Cornell University Press, 1971), 35. See also Brian J. Cook, *Bureaucracy and Self-Government: Reconsidering the Role of Public Administration in American Politics* (Baltimore: The Johns Hopkins University Press, 1996), 45.

42. The Department of Agriculture was given full cabinet status in 1889.

43. Stephen Skowronek, *Building a New American State: The Expansion of National Administrative Capacities, 1877–1920* (New York: Cambridge University Press, 1982).

44. Theda Skocpol, *Protecting Soldiers and Mothers: The Political Origins of Social Policy in the United States* (Cambridge, MA: Belknap Press of Harvard University Press, 1992). Professor Skocpol also examined the gendered aspects of American social welfare policy and how the degree to which recipients were seen as "deserving" shaped the policies themselves.

45. In *The Jungle* (Urbana: University of Illinois Press, 1988), Upton Sinclair described unhealthy and dangerous working conditions in the meatpacking industry, which helped secure the passage of the Pure Food and Drug Act as well as the Federal Meat Inspection Act of 1906.

46. The National Security Act of 1947 also reorganized the cabinet structure of the departments and agencies involved in defense.

47. Pub. L. No. 88-352, 78 Stat. 241.

48. Thomas Binion, "Here's What Trump Has Done Right in His First 6 Months," *Fortune,* July 20, 2017, https://fortune.com/2017/07/20/donald-trump-twitter-news-drain-swamp-6-months/.

49. The U.S. armed forces, which are part of the executive branch, have a different organizational structure, though the secretary of defense and deputy and assistant secretaries are political appointees.

50. For a foundational study of the challenges of implementation, see Jeffrey L. Pressman and Aaron Wildavsky, *Implementation,* 3rd ed. (Berkeley: University of California Press, 1984).

51. Pressman and Wildavsky, *Implementation,* 4.

52. Michael Lipsky, *Street-Level Bureaucracy: Dilemmas of the Individual in Public Services* (New York: Russell Sage Foundation, 1980).

53. Cornelius M. Kerwin, *Rulemaking: How Government Agencies Write Laws and Make Policy* (Washington, DC: CQ Press, 1994), 4.

54. Kenneth J. Meier, "Representative Bureaucracy: A Theoretical and Empirical Exposition," in *Research in Public Administration,* ed. James Perry (Greenwich, CT: JAI Press, 1993).

55. Sally Coleman Selden, *The Promise of Representative Bureaucracy: Diversity and Responsiveness in a Government Agency* (Armonk, NY: M. E. Sharpe, 1997).

56. Charles T. Goodsell, *The Case For Bureaucracy: A Public Administration Polemic,* 2nd ed. (Chatham, NJ: Chatham House Publishers, 1985), 63.

57. William A. Niskanen, "The Peculiar Economics of Bureaucracy," *The American Economic Review* 58, no. 2 (May 1968): 293–305.

58. John Brehm and Scott Gates, *Working, Shirking, and Sabotage: Bureaucratic Responses to a Democratic Public* (Ann Arbor: University of Michigan Press, 1997).

59. For a classic study of the challenges posed by outside pressures on bureaucrats and how bureaucratic agencies deal with them, see Herbert Kaufman, *The Forest Ranger: A Study*

in Administrative Behavior (Washington, DC: Resources for the Future, 1960).

60. Joel D. Aberbach, *Keeping a Watchful Eye: The Politics of Congressional Oversight* (Washington, DC: Brookings Institution, 1990), 4.

61. The legislative and judicial branches also contain bureaucratic organizations, though these are few in number and small in size compared to the departments, agencies, and bureaus in the executive branch.

62. Coral Davenport, "Trump's Environmental Rollbacks Find Opposition Within: Staff Scientists," *New York Times*, March 27, 2020.

63. Coral Davenport, "Trump Removes Pollution Controls on Streams and Wetlands," *New York Times*, January 22, 2020.

64. U.S. Government Accountability Office, "Preliminary Observations on Hurricane Response," February 1, 2006. GAO-06-365R, www.gao.gov/assets/100/94002.pdf.

65. Mathew D. McCubbins and Thomas Schwartz, "Congressional Oversight Overlooked: Police Patrols versus Fire Alarms," *American Journal of Political Science* 28, no. 1 (February 1984): 165–79.

66. William Douglas and Steven Thomas, "On Katrina Anniversary, Bush Returns to Gulf Coast," Knight Ridder Washington Bureau, August 28, 2006; available from Lexis-Nexis Academic.

67. John J. DiIulio Jr., Gerald Garvey, and Donald F. Kettl, *Improving Government Performance: An Owner's Manual* (Washington, DC: Brookings Institution, 1993), 64.

68. David Osborne and Ted Gaebler, *Reinventing Government: How the Entrepreneurial Spirit Is Transforming the Public Sector* (New York: Plume/Penguin Books, 1993), xix.

69. Wilson, *Bureaucracy*, 134–136. Professor Wilson did not necessarily condemn efforts at privatization, instead pointing out differences in mandates and structure. In the provision of services in which outputs and outcomes are difficult to measure—such as education—he pointed out that parents, and not supervisors, might be more effective at measuring the quality of the product (364).

70. Brad Delong, "Katrina Reveals the Presidential Flaws," *Financial Times*, September 7, 2005, 13; available from Lexis-Nexis Academic.

71. Anthony Lonetree, "From the Wreckage of Katrina to the Walls of Local Art Centers: Artwork That Survived or Was Influenced by the Hurricane Makes Its Way Here from Mississippi in Yet Another Step in the Long Recovery," *Star Tribune*, January 11, 2006, 1B; available from Lexis-Nexis Academic.

72. David Hench, "Katrina Response Brings Out the Best, Worst in People," *Portland Press Herald* (Maine), September 15, 2005; available from Lexis-Nexis Academic.

73. "See Katrina's Trail," *Gold Coast Bulletin*, December 17, 2005, 96; available from Lexis-Nexis Academic.

74. Rhonda Abrams, "6 Sources of Small Business Help after Hurricane Harvey," *USA Today*, September 6, 2017, https://www.usatoday.com/story/money/small-business/2017/09/06/6-sources-small-business-help-after-hurricane-harvey/640142001/.

75. Public Affairs Council, "Private Sector Stepping-Up During Disasters," accessed June 16, 2020, https://pac.org/impact/private-sector-steps-disaster-response.

76. Donna Borak, Martin Savidge, and Greg Wallace, "How Whitefish Landed Puerto Rico's $300 Million Power Contract," CNN.com, October 29, 2017, http://money.cnn.com/2017/10/27/news/economy/puerto-rico-whitefish-montana-deal/index.html.

77. Borak et al., "How Whitefish Landed Puerto Rico's $300 Million Power Contract."

78. Leah Hodges, written testimony, Select Bipartisan Committee to Investigate the Preparation for and Response to Hurricane Katrina, December 6, 2005.

CHAPTER 13

1. The title refers to Alexander Hamilton's characterization in *Federalist* No. 78 of the federal judiciary as "least dangerous to the political rights of the Constitution." Alexander Hamilton, *Federalist* No. 78, in *The Federalist Papers*, ed. George W. Carey and James McClellan (Indianapolis: Liberty Fund, 2001), 402. Alexander M. Bickel also chose the phrase from the title of his critique of judicial power: *The Least Dangerous Branch: The Supreme Court at the Bar of Politics* (Indianapolis: Bobbs-Merrill Educational Publishing, 1962).

2. Robert Barnes and Michael A. Fletcher, "Riskiest Choice on Obama's List Embodies His Criteria; President and Judge Cite Her Life Experience," *Washington Post*, May 27, 2009; available from Lexis-Nexis Academic.

3. Charlie Savage, "Conservatives Map Strategies on Court Fight," *New York Times*, May 17, 2009; available from Lexis-Nexis Academic.

4. Savage, "Conservatives Map Strategies."

5. Sonia Sotomayor, "A Latina Judge's Voice," *Berkeley La Raza Law Journal* 13, no. 1 (Spring 2002): 87–93.

6. Sotomayor, "A Latina Judge's Voice."

7. David S. Broder, "After Bork—and Obama; Confirmation Fights Still Echo," *Washington Post*, June 4, 2009; available from Lexis-Nexis Academic.

8. "GOP Senator Sums Up Sotomayor Issue," *Washington Post*, June 7, 2009; available from Lexis-Nexis Academic.

9. Peter Baker and Neil A. Lewis, "Judge Focuses on Rule of Law at the Hearings," *New York Times*, July 14, 2009; available from Lexis-Nexis Academic.

10. N. C. Aizenman, "For Latinos, Confirmation Is an Emotional Moment," *Washington Post*, August 7, 2009; available from Lexis-Nexis Academic.

11. Martha A. Miles and Caroline Rand Herron, "The Nation: Bork Opponents: N.A.A.C.P., N.E.A., and Biden, Too," *New York Times*, July 12, 1987; available from Lexis-Nexis Academic.

12. David Hoffman, "Confirm Bork, Reagan Urges," *Washington Post*, July 30, 1987; available from Lexis-Nexis Academic.

13. Kevin J. McMahon, "Political Regimes and Contentious Supreme Court Nominations: A Historical Institutional Model," *Law & Social Inquiry*, 32, no. 4 (Fall 2007): 919–54.

14. Edward Walsh and Al Kamen, "Ideological Stakes High in Bork Fight: On Eve of Hearings, Both Sides Seem Eager to Keep Calm," *Washington Post*, September 13, 1987; available from Lexis-Nexis Academic.

15. Roe v. Wade, 410 U.S. 113 (1973).

16. Ruth Marcus, "Bork on 'Judicial Imperialism': Judges Accused of Inventing Constitutional Rights to Fit Their Views," *Washington Post*, July 2, 1987; available from Lexis-Nexis Academic.

17. Robert H. Bork, *The Tempting of America: The Political Seduction of the Law* (New York: Free Press, 1990), 313–14.

18. Edward Walsh and Ruth Marcus, "Bork Rejected for High Court: Senate's 58-to-42 Vote Sets Record for Margin of Defeat," *Washington Post*, October 24, 1987; available from Lexis-Nexis Academic.

19. "There's So Much You Don't Know about Brett Kavanaugh," *New York Times*, July 9, 2019.

20. Forrest McDonald, *Novus Ordo Seclorum: The Intellectual Origins of the Constitution* (Lawrence: University Press of Kansas, 1985), 253.

21. The delegates did debate the need to raise judges' salaries to keep up with changes in the cost of living, but they ultimately left the issue of pay raises out of the document.

22. U.S. Const. art. III, § 1.

23. U.S. Const. art. II, § 2.

24. McDonald, *Novus Ordo Seclorum*, 254–55.

25. U.S. Const. art. III, § 1.

26. U.S. Const. art. II, § 1.

27. U.S. Const. art. VI.

28. The term *jurisdiction* is also applied in other contexts, such as the authority of a specific law enforcement agency to investigate a case. However, we will focus only on the jurisdiction of courts in this chapter.

29. Hamilton, *Federalist* No. 78, 402.

30. Hamilton.

31. "The Judiciary Act of 1789," in *Documents of American History*, 6th ed., ed. Henry Steele Commager (New York: Appleton-Century-Crofts, 1958), 153.

32. "The Judiciary Act of 1789," 155.

33. Kyle Kim, "Trump Appointing Judges at a Rapid Pace," *Los Angeles Times*, January 19, 2019, http://www.latimes.com/projects/la-na-pol-trump-federal-judiciary/.

34. Kim, "Trump Appointing Judges."

35. Trump's percentage of appellate appointments, however, was in line with earlier presidents such as Carter and Nixon. Russell Wheeler, "Judicial Appointments in Trump's First Three Years: Myths and Realities," Brookings, January 28, 2020, https://www.brookings.edu/blog/fixgov/2020/01/28/judicial-appointments-in-trumps-first-three-years-myths-and-realities/.

36. Kevin T. McGuire and James A. Stimson, "The Least Dangerous Branch Revisited: New Evidence on Supreme Court Responsiveness to Public Preferences," *Journal of Politics* 66, no. 4 (November 2004): 1018–35.

37. John Adams and Alexander Hamilton were not always in complete agreement. Adams and other Federalists sometimes expressed misgivings about Hamilton's ardent nationalism.

38. Jefferson's party is often referred to as the Democratic-Republican Party, though it was more commonly called the Republican Party at the time. "Jeffersonian Republicans" is also a commonly used label today.

39. "Thomas Jefferson, First Inaugural Address, 4 March 1801," in *Basic Writings of Thomas Jefferson*, ed. Philip S. Foner (New York: Wiley Book Company, 1944), 333.

40. U.S. Const. art. III, § 1.

41. Kathryn Turner, "Federalist Policy and the Judiciary Act of 1801," *The William and Mary Quarterly* 22, no. 1 (January 1965): 32. Turner noted that as many of the provisions in the Judiciary Act of 1801 had been introduced prior to the election, there were other reasons for these provisions, particularly a desire to strengthen the power of the national government. The electoral results, however, "gave a driving urgency to the fight for its passage" (32).

42. David Loth, *Chief Justice: John Marshall and the Growth of the Republic* (New York: W. W. Norton, 1949), 176.

43. Oliver Ellsworth, the former chief justice, had retired shortly before.

44. The four plaintiffs were William Marbury, Dennis Ramsay, Robert Townsend Hope, and William Harper.

45. Marbury v. Madison, 5 U.S. 137 (1803).

46. For fans of the television and film series *Star Trek,* Marshall's dilemma might be seen as one of America's first political Kobayashi Maru scenarios. In *Star Trek* lore, Captain James T. Kirk only defeated the no-win training scenario by cheating, something that several historians and scholars have accused Marshall of doing in his interpretation and reading of the Constitution and Judiciary Act of 1789.

47. *Marbury v. Madison.*

48. *Marbury v. Madison.*

49. *Marbury v. Madison.*

50. Section 13 of the Judiciary Act of 1789.

51. *Marbury v. Madison.*

52. Dred Scott v. Sandford, 60 U.S. 393 (1857).

53. For cases heard on appeal, the petitioner is the party that lost in the lower court and the respondent is the other party in the case.

54. Another category of law, called procedural law, refers to proceedings and rules through which laws are enforced, such as how law enforcement officials interact with those accused of crimes.

55. Many of the definitions of legal terms in this chapter are informed by Bryan A. Garner, ed., *Black's Law Dictionary,* 8th ed. (St. Paul, MN: Thomson West, 2004).

56. As of September 2016, thirty states had the death penalty. (Death Penalty Information Center, "States with and without the Death Penalty," www.deathpenaltyinfo.org/states-and-without-death-penalty.) The U.S. government also has the authority to impose the death penalty for conviction under certain federal laws. In addition, the military retains the death penalty for conviction of certain offenses under the Uniform Code of Military Justice, though it has not been carried out since 1961.

57. Two states, Texas and Oklahoma, have separate state supreme courts for criminal and civil cases.

58. U.S. Const. art. III, § 2.

59. A small set of cases may bypass the appellate courts in this process, such as those involving voting rights and aspects of the 1964 Civil Rights Act.

60. The Supreme Court automatically hears a small set of cases on appeal—those involving voting rights and congressional redistricting. Unless overturned by the Supreme Court, appellate court decisions are binding but only within the jurisdiction of that specific court of appeals. Such jurisdictions (excepting the DC and federal circuits) are geographically determined.

61. The opposition files a "brief in opposition to a petition for a writ of certiorari." Briefs in opposition are only mandatory in capital cases. U.S. Supreme Court, *Rules of the Supreme Court of the United States,* Rule 15, www.supremecourt.gov/ctrules/2013RulesoftheCourt.pdf.

62. U.S. Supreme Court, Rule 10.

63. Only attorneys admitted to the bar of the Court may file amicus curiae briefs (U.S. Supreme Court, Rule 37).

64. Gregory A. Caldiera and John R. Wright, "Amici Curiae before the Supreme Court: Who Participates, When, and How Much?," *Journal of Politics* 52, no. 3 (August 1990): 782–806.

65. See, for example, Timothy R. Johnson, Paul J. Wahlbeck, and James F. Spriggs Jr., "The Influence of Oral Arguments on the U.S. Supreme Court," *American Political Science Review* 100, no. 1 (February 2006): 99–113.

66. Another option for the Court is to send it back to the lower court under the status of review being improvidently granted. In such a case, the Court has decided that after review, it now chooses not to give a full hearing to the case. If so, the lower ruling stands, but the Court has not officially weighed in on that ruling.

67. Bickel, *The Least Dangerous Branch,* 17.

68. Bickel, 29–33.

69. Jack Knight and Lee Epstein, "The Norm of Stare Decisis," *American Journal of Political Science* 40, no. 4 (November 1996): 1018–35. For an analysis that challenges the use of stare decisis, especially when crafting dissenting opinions, see Jeffrey A. Segal and Harold J. Spaeth, "The Influence of Stare Decisis on the Votes of United States Supreme Court Justices," *American Journal of Political Science* 40, no. 4 (November 1996): 971–1003.

70. Glendon A. Schubert, *The Judicial Mind: The Attitudes and Ideologies of Supreme Court Justices, 1946–1963* (Evanston, IL: Northwestern University Press, 1965).

71. Jeffrey A. Segal and Albert D. Cover, "Ideological Values and the Votes of U.S. Supreme Court Justices," *American Political Science Review* 83, no. 2 (June 1989): 557–65.

72. Walter F. Murphy, *Elements of Judicial Strategy* (Chicago: University of Chicago Press, 1964), 3–4.

73. Murphy, *Elements of Judicial Strategy,* 35–36.

74. Charles M. Cameron et al., "Strategic Auditing in a Political Hierarchy: An Informational Model of the Supreme Court's *Certiorari* Decisions," *American Political Science Review* 94, no. 1 (March 2000): 101–16.

75. James F. Spriggs II, Forrest Maltzman, and Paul J. Wahlbeck, "Bargaining on the U.S. Supreme Court: Justices' Responses to Majority Opinion Drafts," *The Journal of Politics* 61, no. 2 (May 1999): 485–506.

76. The cases listed under the year 1929 were decided in 1930 following Hughes's confirmation as chief justice in February 1930.

CHAPTER 14

1. Editorial Board, "American Dreamers," *New York Times*, accessed June 21, 2020, https://www.nytimes.com/interactive/projects/storywall/american-dreamers.

2. Department of Homeland Security, "Consideration of Deferred Action for Childhood Arrivals (DACA)," accessed June 21, 2010, https://www.uscis.gov/archive/consideration-deferred-action-childhood-arrivals-daca.

3. Editorial Board, "American Dreamers."

4. Bradley Jones, "Americans' Views of Immigration Marked by Widening Partisan, Generational Divides," Pew Research Center, April 15, 2016, https://www.pewresearch.org/fact-tank/2016/04/15/americans-views-of-immigrants-marked-by-widening-partisan-generational-divides&ie=UTF-8&oe=UTF-8/?year=2016&ie=UTF-8&oe=UTF-8&post_type=fact-tank&fact-tank=americans-views-of-immigrants-marked-by-widening-partisan-generational-divides.

5. Audrey Singer, Nicole Prchal Svajlenka, and Jill H. Wilson, "Local Insights from DACA for Implementing Future Programs for Unauthorized Immigrants," Brookings Metropolitan Policy Program, April 2015, 2, https://www.brookings.edu/wp-content/uploads/2016/06/BMPP_Srvy_DACAImmigration_June3b.pdf.

6. In this chapter, we will generally use the term *Latino*, though with occasional references to *Hispanic* when quoting others or referring to census data and other official categorizations.

7. Stephanie Ewert, "U.S. Population Trends: 2000 to 2060," U.S. Census Bureau, October 15, 2015, http://www.ncsl.org/Portals/1/Documents/nalfo/USDemographics.pdf.

8. James Barragán, "Immigration hard-liners try to force Trump's hand on DACA," *Dallas Morning News*, July 3, 2017, https://www.dallasnews.com/news/immigration/2017/07/03/immigration-hard-liners-try-to-force-trump-s-hand-on-daca/.

9. Department of Homeland Security, "Memorandum on Recission of Deferred Action for Childhood Arrivals," September 5, 2017, https://www.dhs.gov/news/2017/09/05/memorandum-rescission-daca.

10. Department of Homeland Security v. Regents of the University of California 591 U.S. ___ (2020).

11. My thanks go to Professor John J. DiIulio Jr. for his thoughts on this topic, learned mostly through an independent study on the bureaucracy at Princeton, to which he was so generous to agree.

12. John W. Kingdon, *Agendas, Alternatives, and Public Policies*, 2nd ed. (New York: Longman, 2003), 1.

13. Jeffrey L. Pressman and Aaron Wildavsky, *Implementation*, 3rd ed. (Berkeley: University of California Press, 1984).

14. "Remarks of President Barack Obama—Address to Joint Session of Congress," White House, Office of the Press Secretary, February 24, 2009, https://www.whitehouse.gov/the-press-office/remarks-president-barack-obama-address-joint-session-congress.

15. In economics, this phenomenon is known as adverse selection.

16. National Federation of Independent Business v. Sebelius, 567 U.S. ___ (2012). The Court also upheld portions of the Medicaid expansion, though with limitations.

17. King v. Burwell, 576 U.S. 988 (2015).

18. Misty Williams, "ObamaCare Stands," *Atlanta Journal-Constitution*, June 26, 2015; available from Lexis-Nexis Academic.

19. H.R. 1628, American Health Care Act of 2017. States had already been allowed to opt out of the Medicaid expansion.

20. Julie Rovner, "What to Watch for as Trump Takes Aim at ACA Protections," National Public Radio, June 8, 2018, https://www.npr.org/sections/health-shots/2018/06/08/618240606/trump-takes-aim-at-aca-protections-in-court-challenge-5-things-to-know.

21. Pub. L. No. 74-271, 49 Stat. 620-648 (1935). The programs were collectively called Old Age Security and Disability Insurance (OASDI) and commonly referred to as Social Security. Aid to Dependent Children was later renamed Aid to Families with Dependent Children (AFDC), which was abolished in 1996 and replaced with Temporary Assistance for Needy Families (TANF).

22. *Federal Register*, "Annual Update of the HHS Poverty Guidelines," accessed June 22, 2020, https://www.federalregister.gov/documents/2020/01/17/2020-00858/annual-update-of-the-hhs-poverty-guidelines.

23. The Republican Party gained fifty-four seats in the House of Representatives and eight seats in the Senate.

24. Clean Air Act, 42 U.S.C. § 7401 (1970).

25. Pedro Brinca and Joao B. Duarte, "Is the COVID-19 Pandemic a Supply or Demand Shock?" Federal Reserve Bank of St. Louis, May 5, 2020, https://research.stlouisfed.org/publications/economic-synopses/2020/05/20/is-the-covid-19-pandemic-a-supply-or-a-demand-shock.

26. Brinca and Duarte, "Is the COVID-19 Pandemic a Supply or Demand Shock?" Supply and demand shocks can be positive, of course, although those do not produce the same level of policy response as negative shocks.

27. Brinca and Duarte.

28. Families First Coronavirus Response Act (FFCRA), Pub. L. No. 116-123.

29. Congressional Budget Office, "The Budgetary Effects of Laws Enacted in Response to the 2020 Coronavirus Pandemic, March and April 2020," June 2020, https://www.cbo.gov/system/files/2020-06/56403-CBO-covid-legislation.pdf.

30. Families First Coronavirus Response Act (FFCRA), Pub. L. No. 116-127.

31. Congressional Budget Office, "The Budgetary Effects of Laws."

32. Coronavirus Aid, Relief, and Economic Security (CARES) Act, Pub. L. No. 116-136.

33. Congressional Budget Office, "The Budgetary Effects of Laws."

34. Paycheck Protection Program and Health Care Enhancement Act (PPPHCEA), Pub. L. No. 116-139.

35. Congressional Budget Office, "The Budgetary Effects of Laws."

36. Federal Reserve Governor Ben S. Bernanke, "Deflation: Making Sure 'It' Doesn't Happen Here," Board of Governors of the Federal Reserve System, November 21, 2002, https://www.federalreserve.gov/boarddocs/Speeches/2002/20021121/default.htm.

37. Milton Friedman, *The Optimum Quantity of Money: And Other Essays* (Chicago: Aldine, 1969), 4–6.

38. Congressional Budget Office, "Monthly Budget Review for May 2020," June 8, 2020, https://www.cbo.gov/system/files/2020-06/56390-CBO-MBR.pdf.

39. "Washington's Farewell Address 1796," Yale Law School, Lillian Goldman Law Library, Avalon Project, accessed January 8, 2016, http://avalon.law.yale.edu/18th_century/washing.asp.

40. The purchase price, about three cents per acre, included a payment of $11.25 million and forgiveness of $3.75 million in debt (Jesse Greenspan, "8 Things You May Not Know about the Louisiana Purchase," History in the Headlines, accessed January 4, 2016, http://www.history.com/news/8-things-you-may-not-know-about-the-louisiana-purchase).

41. "The First Barbary War," Monticello, accessed January 2, 2016, https://www.monticello.org/site/research-and-collections/first-barbary-war.

42. It should be noted that combatants from occupied nations—Poland, for example—also made major contributions to the Allied war effort.

43. Steven W. Hook, *U.S. Foreign Policy: The Paradox of World Power*, 4th ed. (Washington, DC: CQ Press, 2013), 47.

44. American allies France and Great Britain were also clearly victors, but their industries and economies had been devastated by the European fighting.

45. Winston S. Churchill, "Sinews of Peace" (speech delivered at Westminster College, Fulton, MO, March 5, 1946), International Winston Churchill Society, accessed August 10, 2018, https://winstonchurchill.org/resources/speeches/1946-1963-elder-statesman/the-sinews-of-peace/.

46. North Atlantic Treaty Organization, The North Atlantic Treaty, Article I, accessed January 4, 2016, http://www.nato.int/cps/en/natolive/official_texts_17120.htm.

47. White House, "President Bush Delivers Graduation Speech at West Point," June 1, 2002, http://georgewbush-whitehouse.archives.gov/news/releases/2002/06/20020601-3.html.

48. "Full Text of Colin Powell's Speech," *The Guardian*, February 5, 2003, https://www.theguardian.com/world/2003/feb/05/iraq.usa.

49. See, for example, "Former Aide: Powell WMD Speech 'Lowest Point in My Life,'" CNN.com, August 23, 2005, http://www.cnn.com/2005/WORLD/meast/08/19/powell.un/.

50. Mark Thompson, "How Disbanding the Iraqi Army Fueled ISIS," *Time*, May 28, 2015, http://time.com/3900753/isis-iraq-syria-army-united-states-military/.

51. Amanda Bennett, "Daesh? ISIS? Islamic State? Why What We Call the Paris Attackers Matters," *Washington Post*, November 25, 2015, https://www.washingtonpost.com/news/in-theory/wp/2015/11/25/daesh-isis-islamic-state-why-what-we-call-the-paris-attackers-matters/.

52. Andrew Hosken, "Islamic State's Deep, Poisonous Roots," *Wall Street Journal*, January 1, 2016, http://www.wsj.com/articles/islamic-states-deep-poisonous-roots-1451684170.

53. Gary Younge, "Immigration Is Not a Domestic Issue," Global Policy Forum, February 6, 2013, https://www.globalpolicy.org/nations-a-states/citizenship-and-nationality/52243-immigration-is-not-a-domestic-issue.html.

54. Yasmine Ryan, "The Tragic Life of a Street Vendor," Al Jazeera, January 20, 2011, http://www.aljazeera.com/indepth/features/2011/01/201111684242518839.html.

55. Yasmine Ryan, "How Tunisia's Revolution Began," Al Jazeera, January 26, 2011, http://www.aljazeera.com/indepth/features/2011/01/2011126121815985483.html.

56. Mohamed Eishinnawi, "Arab Spring Became Brutal Winter, Analysts Say," VOA News, January 19, 2016, http://www.voanews.com/content/arab-spring-brutal-winter-analysts-say/3153382.html.

57. The Sykes-Picot Agreement of 1916, reached between Britain and France (with Russian involvement), had divided up the former Ottoman Empire into spheres of influence and laid the basis for many of the national boundaries in the region.

58. Max Fisher, "9 Questions about Syria You Were Too Embarrassed to Ask," *Washington Post*, August 29, 2013, https://www.washingtonpost.com/news/worldviews/wp/2013/08/29/9-questions-about-syria-you-were-too-embarrassed-to-ask/.

59. "'They Cut Off Heads': Syrians Speak to RT about ISIS Atrocities," RT.com, December 1, 2015, https://www.rt.com/news/324120-isis-sex-slavery-trafficking/.

60. Seymour M. Hersh, "The Red Line and the Rat Line," *London Review of Books* 36, no. 6 (April 17, 2014), http://www.lrb.co.uk/v36/n08/seymour-m-hersh/the-red-line-and-the-rat-line.

61. U.S. Department of State, "Report to Congress on Proposed Refugee Admissions for FY 2020," accessed June 20, 2020, https://www.state.gov/reports/report-to-congress-on-proposed-refugee-admissions-for-fy-2020/.

62. Central Intelligence Agency, "The World Factbook," accessed June 20, 2020, https://www.cia.gov/library/publications/the-world-factbook/geos/sy.html.

63. UNHCR, "Global Trends: Forced Displacement in 2017," accessed June 19, 2018, http://www.unhcr.org/globaltrends2017/.

64. U.S. Department of State, Bureau of Population, Refugees, and Migration, "Congressional Presentation Document (PRM) FY 2019," accessed June 20, 2020, https://www.state.gov/wp-content/uploads/2018/12/Congressional-Presentation-Document-for-Fiscal-Year-2019.pdf.

65. Avi Asher-Schapiro, "The Young Men Who Started Syria's Revolution Speak about Daraa, Where It All Began," Vice News, March 15, 2016, https://news.vice.com/article/the-young-men-who-started-syrias-revolution-speak-about-daraa-where-it-all-began.

66. Hugh Macleod, "How Schoolboys Began the Syrian Revolution," CBS News, April 26, 2011, http://www.cbsnews.com/news/how-schoolboys-began-the-syrian-revolution/.

67. Joe Sterling, "Daraa: The Spark That Lit the Syrian Flame," CNN.com, March 1, 2012, http://www.cnn.com/2012/03/01/world/meast/syria-crisis-beginnings/.

68. "Paris Attacks: What Happened on the Night," BBC News, December 9, 2015, http://www.bbc.com/news/world-europe-34818994.

69. Ishaan Tharoor, "Were Syrian Refugees Involved in the Paris Attacks? What We Know and Don't Know," *Washington Post*, November 17, 2015, https://www.washingtonpost.com/news/worldviews/wp/2015/11/17/were-syrian-refugees-involved-in-the-paris-attacks-what-we-know-and-dont-know/.

70. Haley Sweetland Edwards, "Why Texas' Attempt to Block a Syrian Refugee Family Probably Won't Work," *Time*, December 3, 2015, http://time.com/4134620/texas-lawsuit-to-block-syrian-refugees/.

71. Ben Russell, "Syrian Family Finds Opportunity in North Texas," 5NBCDFW.com, accessed January 20, 2016, http://www.nbcdfw.com/news/local/Syrian-Family-Finds-Opportunity-in-North-Texas-353149931.html.

72. Alex Altman, "A Syrian Refugee Story: Inside One Family's Two-Year Odyssey from Daraa to Dallas," *Time*, accessed July 7, 2020, http://time.com/a-syrian-refugee-story/.

73. Molly Hennessey Fiske, "Meet Two Syrian Families in Texas Who Had the Welcome Mat Pulled Out from under Them," *Los Angeles Times*, December 3, 2015, http://www.latimes.com/nation/la-na-syrian-texas-20151204-story.html.

74. Jon Kamp, "Texas Sues to Stop Resettlement of Six Syrian Refugees," *Wall Street Journal*, December 3, 2015, http://www.wsj.com/articles/texas-sues-to-stop-resettlement-of-six-syrian-refugees-1449101946. The lawsuit also sought to block resettlement of members of another family.

75. Fiske, "Meet Two Syrian Families in Texas."

76. Rescue.org, "After an Uncertain Welcome, a Syrian Family Finds a Home in Texas," June 1, 2016, https://www.rescue.org/article/after-uncertain-welcome-syrian-family-finds-home-texas.

77. Russell, "Syrian Family Finds Opportunity in North Texas."

78. Walt Whitman, "O Me! O Life!," *Leaves of Grass* (Champaign, IL: Project Gutenberg, 1892).

INDEX

Note: Page Locators with 'f" and 't' denotes figures and tables.

Abington School District v. Schempp, 106
Abolitionist movement, 150–151
Absentee ballots, 249
Adams, John, 16, 40, 109, 332, 389
Adams, Samuel, 15–16, 20, 40
Adversarial system, 393
Affirmative action, 149, 232
Agency capture, 269, 367
Agenda-setting, 214
Aggregating, 210
Aid to Families with Dependent Children (AFDC), 421
Al-Assad, Bashar, 319, 442–443
Al-Awlaki, Anwar, 338–339, 342
Albany Congress, 13
Albany Plan, 13
Alien and Sedition Acts, 109, 111
Ali, Zine El Abidine Ben, 441
Al-Qaeda, 338–339, 439, 443
Al-Qaeda in the Arabian Peninsula (AQAP), 339
ALS. *See* Lou Gehrig's disease
Al Sharaa, Faez, 444–445
Al-Zarqawi, Abu Musab, 440
Amendment, 49
Amendment exchange, 305
Amendments to the Constitution (text), 467–473. *See also* Bill of Rights
American Bar Association, 387
American Citizen Abroad in the Fight against Terrorism, 338
American Civil Liberties Union (ACLU), 99, 133
American Civil War, 79, 136
American dream, 10–11, 224, 411, 445–446
American dreamers, 412
American exceptionalism, 12, 361
American federalism, evolution of, 422

American Health Care Policy, 417–423
environmental policy, 422–423
housing policy, 422
Medicaid program, 418
Medicare, 417–418
need-based public assistance programs, 421–422
Obama's health care reform, 418
old age assistance programs, 420
old age insurance, 420
politics of, 417
social insurance programs, 420
social security, 417
American legal system
adversarial system of justice, 393
appellate courts, 395, 398
brief, 398
civil law, 393
courts of original jurisdiction, 398
criminal law, 393
defendant, 393
federal district courts, 394–395
federal judiciary and, 393–400
modern court system, 395f
movement of cases through court system, 397f
oral argument, 400
plaintiff, 393
plea bargaining, 393–394
precedent, 399
solicitor general, 399
standing, 398
state courts, 394
structure of, 393
Supreme Court, 395–396, 398
writ of certiorari, 399
American political culture, 8–10, 26, 198
economic equality, 9
equality, 9
exceptionalism, 12

inalienable rights, 9
key elements of, 8
liberty, 10
political equality, 9
pursuit of happiness, 10
roots, 10
social equality, 9
American Political Science Association, 227
American Red Cross, 351
American Revolution, 4, 7, 12, 22, 31, 34, 37, 38. *See also* Colonial-era America
Americans with Disabilities Act (ADA), 133–134
Amyotrophic lateral sclerosis (ALS), 123
Anthony, Susan B., 152
Anti-Defamation League, 276
Anti-Federalist Papers, 57
Anti-Federalists, 31, 55–61, 101–102, 121, 123, 199, 384–385
Appellate Courts, 395
Appellate jurisdiction, 384, 394, 396, 398, 400
Apportionment, 234
legislative structure, 45t
Appropriation, 293, 364, 369
Arab Spring, 441–442, 444
Arnold, R. Douglas, 307
Arthur, Chester A., 361
Articles of Confederation, 34–36, 40, 42–43, 46, 53–55, 59–60, 65, 70, 73, 325, 453–458
Articles of Confederation and Perpetual Union, 34–35
Assange, Julian, 195
Associated Press, 200
Astroturf lobbying, 272
Atlantic hurricane season (2018), 350

Bache, Sarah Franklin, 19
Bail, 103, 119, 261, 401
Bailout, 261–262
Bakke, Allan, 149
Balance of power, 51
Barnard, Chester, 355
Barnard's theory, 355
Barron, John, 78
Barron v. Baltimore (1833), 77
Beat system, 201
Bedford, Gunning, 43
Benton v. Maryland (1969), 104
Bernanke, Ben, 259
Bicameral legislature, 44
Biden, Joe, 222, 225–226, 241, 296,
    319, 380
Biggs, Tyrell, 318
Bill, 300
Billings, Henry, 139
Bill of Rights, 50, 60–61, 73, 97,
    101–104, 113, 116, 118–119,
    121, 123, 134, 199
  center stage in the ratification
      debates, 102–105
  civil liberties, 101–105
  civil liberties protections,
      102–104
  constitutional protections, 170
  due process clause, 102
  fundamental freedoms, 103
  incorporation of, 104–105
  overview of protections, 103t
  press freedom and, 199
  ratification debates, 60–61
  relationship between members of
      indigenous nations and, 105
  selective incorporation, 103
  See also Media
Bipartisan Campaign Reform Act
    (BCRA), 242
Bishop, George, 175
Black codes, 136
#BlackLivesMatter, 164, 182–185,
    188, 187, 279
Blackmun, Harry, 122
Black Panthers, 132
Blake, Jacob, 186–187
Block Grant, 87f, 89
Bloomberg, Michael, 277
Bork, Robert H., 380
Boston Massacre in 1770, 16
Boston Tea Party, 16–17
Bouazizi, Mohamed, 441–442
Boxer, Barbara, 287
Brandenburg v. Ohio (1969), 110

Braun, Moseley, 288–289, 308,
    312–313
Brennan, John, 339
Breyer, Stephen, 68, 92
Brief, 398
British tax policies, 15–16
Broadcast media, 201
Brown, Michael, 164–165, 179,
    182–183
Brown, Oliver, 142
Brown v. Board of Education (1964),
    139, 141–142, 144, 146, 402
Buckley v. Valeo (1976), 242
Budget Act, 293
Budget and Accounting Act of
    1921, 424
Budget deficit, 430, 433
Budget resolution, 425
Budget surplus, 430
Bureaucracy
  executive branch, 358f
  Jacksonian era, 359–360
  military bureaucracy, 362
  post–civil war growth, 360–361
  preserve efficiency, 356–357
  role of, 356–359
  tyranny, 356–357
Bureaucratic adjudication, 366
Bureaucratic discretion, 366
Bureaucratic drift, 367
Bureaucratic organization, 353–356
  Barnard's theory, 355
  characteristics of, 353
  incentives, 355
  principal-agent problem, 355
  private bureaucracies, 354
  state and local bureaucracies, 353
  Weber's theory, 354
  Wilson's Theory, 355–356
Bureaucratic reform, 359, 363
Burke, Tarana, 250
Bush, George H. W., 363
Bush, George W., 241, 261, 320,
    339, 350–351, 439

Cabinet departments, 360, 362–363
Cable News Media, 195–196
Cable television news, 202–203
Calhoun, John, 79
Califano Jr., Joseph, 131
Campaigns, 221
Cannabis Regulation and
    Tax Act, 66
Cantwell v. Connecticut (1940),
    104, 108

Capitalist system, 25, 280
Carpenter v. United States (2018),
    99, 117
Carson, André, 183
Carter, Jimmy, 131
Categorical grant, 86–89, 87f
Caucus, 228
Cell phone tracking
  civil liberties, 98–101
  Supreme Court restrictions, 98–99
Center for Independent Living, 131
Center for Responsive Politics, 224,
    267, 289
Centers for Disease Control and
    Prevention (CDC), 372
Central Intelligence Agency (CIA),
    194, 320, 362, 443
Chaplinksy v. New Hampshire
    (1942), 112
Charlottesville tragedy, 186–187
Chávez, César, 132
Christian Science Monitor, 274
Churchill, Winston, 436
Citizen journalists, 203
*Citizens United v. Federal Election
    Commission* (2010), 242
Civic education, 178
Civic engagement, 244
Civil disobedience, 145, 278
Civil law, 393
Civil liberties, 5, 7, 97, 99–102, 106,
    109, 113, 124, 129, 157, 266,
    369, 435
  accused rights to trials and
      representation, 118–119
  assembly, 109–114
  bill of rights, 101–105
  cell phone tracking, 98–101
  challenges to, 99–101
  criminal justice system, 115–119
  defense produced by accused, 118
  fences, 124
  First Amendment protections,
      105–109
  freedom of assembly, 113
  freedoms in the nation, 119
  free exercise clauses, 105–109
  guaranteed by bill of rights,
      115–119
  guards against cruel and unusual
      punishment, 119
  Ninth and Tenth Amendments,
      119–124
  petitioning the government,
      109–114

press, 109–114
privacy, 121–123
protection against unlawful
    search, seizure, warrants,
    and evidence, 116–117
protections for Americans' Civil
    Liberties, 101–105
right of same-sex couples,
    120–121
rights of sexual conduct, 122
rights to privacy involved the use
    of contraceptives, 122
speech, 109–114
state powers protection, 123
symbolic speech, 111–112
woman's decision to terminate a
    pregnancy, 122–123
Civil rights, 129
    affirmative action, 149
    amendments, 134–139
    Americans with Disabilities Act,
        133–134
    for American women, 150–155
    challenges persist for other
        groups, 156–157
    civil disobedience, 145–148
    constitutional amendments
        abolish slavery, 136
    denial of citizenship rights
        to African Americans,
        134–135
    desegregation, 144–145
    diversity of Americans' identities,
        155–157
    enfranchisement, 150–152
    504 protesters, 132
    gender discrimination, 154–155
    inequalities, 152–154
    intersectionality, 156
    Kennedy's efforts, 147
    legal segregation, 139–149
    protections against gender
        discrimination, 153
    protest, 145–148
    rights for Americans with
        disabilities, 130–134
    school segregation, 140–142
    sexual harassment, 154–155
    strengthening by Court, 148
Civil Rights Act of 1866, 137
Civil Rights Act of 1875, 137
Civil Rights Act of 1957, 144
Civil Rights Act of 1964, 147, 152,
    154, 362
Civil War in Syria, 442–443

Clark, Kenneth, 143
Clark, Mamie, 143
Clark, Tom C., 106
Clean Air Act (1963), 423
Clear and present danger test, 110
Clientele agencies, 360, 362
Clinton, Bill, 89, 120, 241, 295, 363,
    418, 421
Clinton, Hillary, 194, 222, 224–225,
    241, 322, 418
Closed primaries, 228
Cloture, 303–304, 418
Cold War, 328, 362, 435–436, 438
Collective action, 264–266
    collective good, 265
    free riders, 265
    material rewards, 265
    purposive benefits, 266
    selective benefits, 265
    social benefits, 265
Collective good, 265
Colonial-era America, 12–22
    colonial settlements, 12–13
    global war, 13–14
    idea of independence, 14
    independence becomes
        institutionalized, 20–22
    indigenous peoples, 19–20
    revolutionaries take action, 15–17
    revolutionary women, 18–19
    slavery, 17–18
    See also American Revolution
Colvin, Claudette, 145
Commerce clause, 72
Commercial bias, 207
Committee chairs, 298
Committee of Detail, 53
Committee system, 298–299
    committee chairs, 298
    party leaders and seniority, 298
    roles, 298–299
    types, 298–299
Communications Act of 1934,
    209–210
Communications Decency Act of
    1996, 113
Communist economy, 25f
Communist system, 24
Compassionate Use Act of 1996, 67
Concurrence, 400
Concurrent powers, 73
Confederal system, 34–39, 70
    articles of confederation, 34–35
    equal representation of states, 35
    fears of unrest, 37

original thirteen colonies, 36f
rebellion, 37–38
Shays' rebellion, 37
slavery and representation, 36–37
sovereignty of states, 35
weak design, 35
Western territories, 36f
Congress, 284, 289, 291, 293,
    295, 297, 299, 303, 305, 307,
    311, 313
    advice and consent and senatorial
        courtesy, 295
    budgeting process, 293
    challenge of inclusive
        representation, 285–291
    committee system, 298–299
    complexity of representation, 313
    congressional bureaucracy, 299
    congressional staff, 299
    descriptive representation,
        308–311
    election of, 1992, 286–289
    essentialism, 311
    formal and informal rules,
        296–300
    House and Senate, 291–292
    impeachment power, 295–296
    informal norms, 299–300
    key aspects of lawmaking,
        307–308
    key powers, 293–295
    legislative authority, 293
    legislative deliberation, 312
    legislative powers of
        congress, 294t
    legislative process, 300–305
    legislators' voting decisions, 306
    partisan polarization, 308
    political party affiliations,
        483–487
    power of oversight, 293
    racial and ethnic
        gerrymandering, 310
    representation of women,
        311–313
    representatives' actions, 307
    structure and powers, 291–296
    substantive representation, 311
    visible and invisible legislative
        work, 306
    "Year of the Woman" (2018),
        289–291
Confederation Congress, 35, 38,
    46, 54, 65
Congressional Black Caucus, 165

Congressional Budget and Impoundment Control Act of 1974, 293, 424
Congressional Budget Office (CBO), 293, 424
Congressional bureaucracy, 299
Congressional incumbents, 239–240
Congressional staff, 299
Congressional testimony, 373
Conservatism, 179
Consideration, 170
Constituencies, 233
Constitution, 31, 40, 42, 60, 62, 66, 91, 379
Constitutional Convention, 31, 39–45, 53–54, 57, 61–62, 78, 101, 134–135, 141, 198–199, 291, 325, 332, 356, 383
  bicameral legislature, 44
  equal votes in legislature, 43–44
  great compromise, 44
  New Jersey plan, 43–44
  powers of the national government, 41–42
  proportional representation for the states, 42–43
  representation debate, 41–42
  representation methods in Chamber, 44
  Virginia plan, 42–43
Constitutional government, 24, 40
Constitutional interpretation, 381, 386, 392, 402
Consumer price index (CPI), 424
Consumer Product Safety Act of 1972, 364
Containment, 437–438
Controlled Substances Act (CSA) 1970, 67
Conyers, John, 165
Cooperative federalism, 80–81, 85–86, 88, 90, 414, 422
Coronavirus Aid, Relief, and Economic Security (CARES) Act, 429
Coronavirus Preparedness and Response Supplemental Appropriations Act, 428
Corporate welfare, 223
Corporation for Public Broadcasting, 210
Countermajoritarian difficulty, 401–403
Counterpressure, 260–261
Court-packing plan, 84–85

COVID-19, 93, 226, 296, 319, 322, 372, 426, 433
  coronavirus relief, 427–430
  demand shock, 426
  depression-fighting policies, 428
  extended unemployment benefits, 429
  fiscal stimulus, 427
  negative GDP, 427, 428f
  paycheck protection program, 429
  response to, 426–433
  stimulus, 428
  student debt relief, 429
  supply shock, 426
  unemployment rates, 427, 427f
  See also Economic policy
Criminal law, 116, 393
Critical elections, 231
Crossfire hurricane, 195
Cruel and unusual punishment, guard against, 119. See also Eighth Amendment
Cues and information shortcuts, 171

Daily Advertiser, 198
The Daily Show with Trevor Noah, 208
Dakota Access Pipeline protests, 74
Dalrymple, Jack, 6
Daughters of Liberty, 19
David, James, 324
Davids, Sharice, 290
Decision of 1789, 357
Declaration of Independence, 4, 7–9, 20–21, 31, 33, 129, 134, 151, 356, 449–452
Declaration of Rights and Grievances, 15
Declaration of Sentiments, 151
De facto segregation, 148–149
Defendant, 393
Defense of Marriage Act (DOMA), 120–121
De Jonge v. Oregon (1937), 104, 113
De jure segregation, 148
Delegates, 228
Demand shock, 426
Democracy, 8
Democracy in America, 263
"Democratic" aristocracy, 60
Democratic National Committee (DNC), 194, 224
"Democratic remedy", 246
Democratic representation, 182–187
  Charlottesville tragedy, 186–187
  national anthem protests, 184–185

Demographics, 232, 412
Demographic changes, 412–413
Deregulation, 363, 369–370
  federal bureaucracy, 370–372
Descriptive representation, 310
Desegregation, 91, 141–142, 144–145, 148, 157
De Tocqueville, Alexis, 263
Devolution, 89
Digital divide, 216–217
Digital participation, 244, 251
Digital political participation, 250–253
  immediacy, 251–253
  interactivity, 251–253
  political discourse in social media outlets, 252f
  vs. traditional political participation, 251
  See also Political participation, 250
Direct democracy, 23, 58
Direction, 176
Discretionary spending, 425
Dissent, 100, 110, 139, 343, 400
District of Columbia v. Heller, 114
Domestic policy, 320, 327, 416, 420, 422–423, 441
Double jeopardy, 103, 118
Douglass, Frederick, 151
Downs, Anthony, 246
Dred Scott v. Sandford (1857), 134–135, 137, 139, 392
Druckman, James, 214
Drug Enforcement Administration (DEA), 67
Dual federalism, 78, 85–86, 88–89, 414, 422
Due process clause, 77, 102–103
Dust Bowl, 81

Earned Income Tax Credit (EITC), 422
Economic equality, 9
Economic interest groups, 266
Economic policy, 411
  budgeting process, 416
  favour for merchants, 55
  response to COVID-19, 426–433
  role of Congress, 293
Economic recession, 424
Economic systems, 25f
Economy, 24
Eighth Amendment, 102–103, 119, 393

Election of, 1992
    departure of congressional
        incumbents, 288
    mobilization in electoral bids,
        288–289
    new field of candidates, 286–288
    opportunity for women, 288
Elections, 221
Electoral college, 47, 48, 241, 389
Electoral politics, foreign
    interference, 194
Elementary and Secondary
    Education Act of 1965
    (ESEA), 88
Elites, 170
Elitist theory, 263
Elk, Linda Black, 6
Emancipation Proclamation,
    133, 136
Emergency Highway Energy
    Conservation Act, 416
Employment Division v. Smith
    (1990), 108
Endangered Species Act, 423
Energy Reorganization Act of
    1974, 364
Enfranchisement, 150–152
Engel v. Vitale (1962), 106
Entitlement programs, 421
Enumerated powers, 72
Environmental Protection Agency
    (EPA), 4, 423
Equal protection clause, 137, 149,
    155. *See also* Fourteenth
    Amendment
Equal Rights Amendment (ERA),
    153–154
Equal time rule, 211
Eshoo, Anna, 289
Espionage Act of 1917, 110
Essentialism, 311
Establishment clause, 106–107
European Union (EU), 437
Evacuation points, 373
Evening Post, 198
Everson v. Board of Education
    (1947), 104, 106–107
Exclusionary rule, 117
Executive agreements, 343
Executive branch, 46–47, 49t
Executive Office of the President
    (EOP), 333
Executive orders, 343, 366,
    368, 414
Executive political appointees, 364

Executive power during the
    American Civil War, 340–342
    defends his emergency
        powers, 341
    defies the federal judiciary, 340
Executive privilege, 342–343
Exit poll, 175, 177
Ex parte Merryman (1861), 341
Exploratory committee, 240
Ex post facto laws, 116
Extended republic, 58, 263

Faction, 57, 58–59, 258, 262–263,
    274, 280, 290, 334, 363, 389
Fairness doctrine, 211
Fake news, 196–198, 211–212,
    217, 318
Families First Coronavirus
    Response Act (FFCRA), 429
Federal bureaucracy
    adjudication, 366
    bureaucratic action, 348–353
    bureaucratic discretion, 366, 368
    bureaucratic drift, 367
    bureaucrats can act as
        representatives, 366–367
    cabinet departments, 363
    deregulation, 370–372
    development and expansion
        of, 360
    executive branch, 358f
    executive political appointees, 364
    focuses on labor, 361
    funding for, 369
    government corporations, 364
    Harvey hurricanes, 348–350
    hierarchical authority, 364–365
    historical development, 356–363
    implementation, 365
    independent regulatory
        agencies, 364
    Irma hurricane, 348–350
    Jacksonian era, 359–360
    judiciary, 369–370
    Katrina hurricane, 350–352
    late twentieth century, 362–363
    media, 369–370
    mid-twentieth century, 362
    military bureaucracy, 362
    patronage elimination, 361
    post-civil war growth, 360–361
    president is at the top of, 368–369
    private contractors, 364
    privatization, 370–372
    progressive era expansion, 361

public opinion, 369–370
    reform and scaling back, 362–363
    reform efforts, 370–372
    role of the bureaucracy, 356–359
    rulemaking, 366, 368
    senior executive service (SES), 365
    separation of powers, 368–370
    shielded from politics, 366–367
    social safety net, 362
    street-level bureaucrats, 365
    structure of, 363–367
    theories of bureaucratic
        organization, 353–356
    tools of, 367–372
    twentieth-century crises, 362
    web of organizations, 363–364
Federal Bureau of Investigation
    (FBI), 194, 318, 382
Federal civil service, 361, 365
Federal Communications
    Commission (FCC), 209
Federal courts of appeals, 395
Federal Deposit Insurance
    Corporation (FDIC), 364
Federal district courts, 394, 398
Federal Election Commission
    (FEC), 242
Federal Emergency Management
    Agency (FEMA), 348–349,
    351–353, 364, 371–372
Federal Employees Political
    Activities Act of 1993, 367
Federal Housing Administration
    (FHA), 422
Federalism, 65
    African Americans' rights, 79
    attempts to roll back national
        power, 88–89
    challenges, 86–93
    challenges to cooperation, 90–93
    civil war and reconstruction,
        78–79
    commerce clause, 72
    confederal systems, 70
    cooperative, 80
    development of, 76
    devolution, 88–89
    division of power, 71
    dual, 78–81
    elastic clause, 71
    elements of the U.S.
        Constitution, 70
    enumerated, concurrent, and
        reserved powers, 74
    enumerated powers, 72

evolution of, 93–94
Great Depression and, 81–86
implied powers, 72
interests of state governments, 89–90
in the modern era, 86–93
national expansion, 80
necessary and proper clause, 71
new deal, 85–86
state and federal laws, 65–70
states' rights, 78–79
supremacy clause, 71
unitary systems, 70
Federalist No. 10, 57, 58, 223, 262, 474–478
Federalist No. 16, 59
Federalist No. 46, 90
Federalist No. 51, 57, 59, 223, 479–481
Federalist No. 74, 337
Federalist No. 78, 385, 403
Federalist No. 84, 101
The Federalist Papers, 56–57, 59–60, 199
Federalists, 55
Federalists and Anti-Federalists, ratification debate, 55–61, 56t
anti-federalists fear losing representation, 60
federalists argue for a strong national government, 59
forms of Tyranny, 58
Federal judiciary, 379–403
American legal system and, 393–400
appellate Courts, 395
appellate jurisdiction, 384
approaches to Constitutional interpretation, 401–402
attitudinal model, 402–403
cases involving federal questions, 396
definition, 377
doctrine of stare decisis, 402
election of 1800, 389–390
federal district courts, 394–395
impactfull cases handled by, 394–396
judicial activism, 403, 405–406
judicial restraint, 403, 405–406
legal model, 402
Marbury v. Madison, 391–392
modern court system, 396f
original jurisdiction, 384
political appointment, 385–387

power of the, 377, 401
principle of Judicial Review, 388–392
relation between judicial review and justices' ideologies, 404
strategic model, 403
structure and powers of, 383–388
supremacy over lower state courts, 384
Supreme Court, 395
theories of judicial decision, 401–406
"trial" of John Marshall, 388–392
Federal reserve system, 431–432
Expansion of the Fed's Balance Sheet, 432f
Federal systems, 70
Federation for American Immigration Reform, 414
Feeding frenzy, 208
Feinstein, Dianne, 286, 288
Felon disenfranchisement, 249
The Feminine Mystique, 153
Ferguson event, 163–168
racial identity, 166f
reflections, 165
Fifteenth Amendment, 79, 137–138, 152
Fifth Amendment, 77, 78, 118–120, 332
Fighting words, 112
Filburn, Roscoe, 68
Filibuster, 303–305, 380, 382, 386, 389, 418
Financial Engineering, 258–259
Fire alarm oversight, 293, 295, 369
Fireside chats, 201
First Amendment, 97, 102–103, 107–109, 111–113, 157, 242, 262, 267
boundaries of the establishment of religion, 107
boundaries of the freedom of religious expression, 107–109
civil liberties, 105–109
funding for religious schools, 106
prayer in schools, 106–107
separation of church and state, 105–109
First Reconstruction Act of 1867, 137
Fiscal policy, 423–424
approaches and goals, 423–433
Congress Acts, 425–426
discretionary spending, 425

government monitors the economic health, 424
mandatory spending, 425
national budget, 424–426
president proposes a budget, 424–425
See also Public policy
Fiscal stimulus, 427
Floyd, George, 187, 296, 319, 322
Focus group, 173
Focusing events, 178
Food and Drug Administration (FDA), 417
Food Stamp Program. *See* Supplemental Nutrition Assistance Program (SNAP)
Ford, Gerald R., 331
Foreign policy, 411, 433–440
American influence in the western hemisphere, 434
cold war, 436
collapse of the Soviet Union, 438
connect with immigration policy, 440–446
Cuban missile crisis, 436
development of, 433
global wars, 434–440
internationalism, 434
isolationist, 433–434
Marshall plan, 437
nuclear proliferation, 438
policy of containment toward Soviet expansion, 437–438
proxy wars, 436
Reagan doctrine, 437
regional conflicts, 436
war against Iraq, 440
war on terror, 438–440
World War I (major global player), 435
World War II (superpower), 435–436
Founders of the American Republic, 40, 62
Fourteenth Amendment, 79, 102–103, 134, 137, 139, 143, 149, 154–155, 157
Fourth Amendment, 99–100, 102, 116–117
Fowler, Linda, 287
Framing, 177, 214, 223, 279
Franklin, Benjamin, 13, 19, 54
Frazier, Bernie, 181
Freedom of Assembly, 113
Freedom of expression, 97, 109

Freedom of the Press, 199
Freedoms in the Nation and across
    the States, 119–124. *See also*
    Ninth and Tenth Amendments
Free exercise clause, 106, 108
Free Expression Was Challenged, 109
Free riders, 265
Free speech, chilling effect on, 113
Free Syrian Army (FSA), 444
Friday Campaign Zero, 183
Friedan, Betty, 153
Front-loading, 229
Full faith and credit clause, 48, 120
Fundamental rights and freedoms,
    4–7, 97, 106, 124, 129, 244.
    See also Standing Rock protests

Gage, Thomas, 20
Garland, Merrick, 382
Garner, Eric, 164, 179
Gazette of the United States, 200
Gender discrimination, 154–155
Gender gap, 180
Generation Z, 93
Gerry, Elbridge, 44
Gerrymandering, 234, 239,
    310–311
Get-out-the-vote (GOTV)
    campaigns, 249, 272
Gibbons, Thomas, 77
Gibbons v. Ogden (1824), 77
Gideon v. Wainwright (1963),
    104, 119
Gitlow v. New York (1925), 103–104
Going public, 336
Goldstein, Kenneth, 272
Gonzales v. Raich (2005), 68–69
Gorsuch, Neil, 382, 389
Government, 3
    authoritarian, 24
    capitalist system, 25
    communist system, 24
    constitutional government, 24
    direct democracy, 23–24
    interest groups, 266
    political institutions, 22–25
    representative democracy, 23–24
    socialist system, 24
    totalitarian, 24
    types of, 24f
Government Accountability Office
    (GAO), 299, 369
The Governmental Process, 264
Government corporations, 364
"Government to government", 74

Graber, Doris, 211, 214
Graham, Lindsey, 322
Grand Convention (Federal
    Convention), 40
Grand jury, 103, 118, 182
Grant-in-aid, 86, 87f, 89
Gray, Mary, 371
Great Compromise, 44, 45t, 61, 291
Great Depression, 65, 81–83, 86,
    202, 212, 231–232, 337, 362,
    364, 422–423, 427
    Democratic party dominance,
        231–232
    federalism and, 81–86
Great Society program, 88, 417
Gridlock, 230–232, 308, 334
Griswold v. Connecticut (1965), 122
Gross domestic product (GDP), 424
Grotesque, 133
Guaranteed the right to vote to
    African American men
    (Fifteenth Amendment), 79
Gun-Free School Zones Act in
    1994, 93
Gun-Free School Zones Act of
    1990, 92
"Gut rationality", 172

Haaland, Deb, 290
Halbritter, Ray, 4
Haley, Nikki, 319–320
Hamilton, Alexander, 40, 46, 56, 101,
    199, 357, 359, 385, 389, 403
Hanisch, Carol, 253
Harlan, John Marshall, 139
Harvard Law Review, 141
Harvey Hurricane, 348–350
Hashtag feminism, 251
Hatch Act, 367
Hate speech, 112
Haynes, Lemuel, 18
Helicopter Ben, 431
Helms, Jesse, 312
Henry, Patrick, 40
Hersh, Seymour, 443
Heumann, Judith, 129–131, 134
Higher Education Act of 1965, 153
Hill, Anita, 286
Hindenburg, 212
Holmes, Oliver Wendell, 110
Honeymoon period, 336
Horchani, Rochdi, 441
Horse race phenomenon, 208
Hostile working environment, 155
House Committee on Rules, 302

House majority leader, 297
House of Representatives, 44,
    46–47, 154, 233–234, 241,
    288–292, 295, 297, 319, 322,
    389, 418, 420
    house majority leader, 297
    role of party leaders, 297–298
    speaker of the house, 297
House of Representatives *vs.*
    Senate, 292t
Housing and Urban Development
    (HUD), 362, 422
Housing bubble, 258–261
    bailout, 261–262
    counterpressure, 260–261
    crash of the housing market, 260f
    financial engineering, 258–259
    lobbyists' pressure, 259–260
Housing, Education, and Welfare
    (HEW), 130
Housing policy, 422
Hundred Days, 82
Hussein, Saddam, 176, 439–440
Hutchinson, Thomas, 17
Hutchison, Kay Bailey, 312

The "I-85 District", 236f
Ima hurricane, 348–350
Immigration policy, 440–446
    connection with foreign policy, 440
    displacement of Syrians, 443
    final authority over, 444
Immigration reform, 412, 414
Impeachment, 295, 378
Implementation, 365
Implied powers, 72
Impoundment Control Act of
    1974, 424
Inalienable rights, 9
Incentives, 355
Income inequality, 275
Incrementalism, 62
Incumbency advantage, 240
Independent executive agency, 362
Independent regulatory agencies,
    360, 364
Indian Country Today, 4
Indigenous peoples, 19–20
Individual and group identities,
    179–182
Inequalities, 152–154
    protections against gender
        discrimination, 153
Inflation, 424
Infotainment, 207

Initiative, 272
In re Oliver, (1948), 104
Inside lobbying, 268
Intensity, 176
Interagency rivalry, 370
Interest group, 257–258
  bailout, 261–262
  challenges associated with,
    262–266
  challenges in representation, 273
  challenges of faction, 263–264
  collective action challenges,
    264–266
  counterpressure, 260–261
  economic interest groups, 266
  exert influence through webs and
    networks, 270
  financial engineering, 258–259
  governmental interest groups, 266
  in election-related activities, 271
  "inside" interest groups lobby,
    267–272
  lobbyists' pressure, 259–260
  public interest groups, 266
  single-issue groups, 266
  theories of, 263–264
  types of, 266–273
Interest rates, 422, 431
Intergovernmental lobbying, 90
Intermediate scrutiny, 155
Internal Revenue Service (IRS), 271
Internationalism, 434
International Swaps and Derivatives
    Association, 261
Intersectionality, 156
Intolerable Acts, 16
Investigative journalism, 200
Iron triangle, 270, 271f
Islamic State of Iraq and Syria
    (ISIS), 440, 442–443
Islamic State of Iraq and the Levant
    (ISIL), 440
Isolationism, 433–434
Issue network, 270

Jackson, Andrew, 231, 336, 359
Jackson, Jesse, 132
Jay, John, 56, 199
Jefferson, Thomas, 4, 8–10, 20–21,
    31, 33, 40, 107, 200, 231, 357,
    359, 389–391, 433–434
Jim Crow laws, 138–139
Johnson, Andrew, 136, 295, 331
Johnson, Lyndon, 88, 144, 328,
    362, 417, 423

Joint Comprehensive Plan of Action
    (JCPOA), 438
Judicial activism, 403
Judicial branch, 47, 49t
Judicial restraint, 401, 403
Judicial review, 392
Judiciary, 47–48
Judiciary Act of 1789, 385, 391, 394
Judiciary Act of 1801, 389–391

Katrina hurricane, 350–352,
    369, 372
Katz v. United States (1967), 116
Kavanaugh, Brett, 382–383
Kennedy, Anthony, 92, 121,
    124, 382
Kennedy, John F., 147, 202
Key Jr., V. O., 227
King, Angus, 296
Kingdon, John, 188, 416
King George III, 14, 16, 22, 37, 356
King Jr., Martin Luther, 130, 133,
    145, 151
King v. Burwell (2015), 419
Kirchmeier, Kyle, 6
Klopfer v. North Carolina, (1967), 104
Kollman, Ken, 272
Korematsu v. United States
    (1944), 343
Ku Klux Klan, 110, 138

Laden, Osama bin, 439
Ladies Association of
    Philadelphia, 19
Laissez-faire capitalist economy, 25f
Lawrence v. Texas (2003), 122
Lee Resolution, 21
Lee, Richard Henry, 21
Legal Defense Fund, 139, 270
Legal segregation, 138–149
  affirmative action, 149
  civil disobedience, 145–148
  de facto segregation, 148
  de jure segregation, 148
  desegregation, 144–145
  Marshall's strategy, 140–142
  protest, 145–148
  racial identity, 139
  racial segregation, 147–148
Legislative branch, 42, 46, 48, 49t,
    102, 295, 329
Legislative deliberation, 312
Legislative process
  bill introduction, 300, 302
  bills go back to the floor, 305

cloture, 303
committee and subcommittee
    action, 302
filibuster, 303
house committee on rules, 302
individual senators' role, 303
legislative process, 301f
markup session, 302
president's action, 305
referral to committee, 302
resolve differences between
    House and Senate, 304–305
roll-call vote, 303
rules and institutions shape
    consideration, 302
Legislative structures, 45t
Legislature, equal votes in, 43–44
Lemon test, 107
Lemon v. Kurtzman (1971), 107
Lesbian, Gay, Bisexual, and
    Transgender (LGBT), 119,
    121, 266, 310
Libel, 112
Liberalism, 179
Libertarianism, 179
Liberty, 10
Liberty Further Extended, 18
Lincoln, Abraham, 133, 136, 328,
    340–341, 435
Linked fate, 181
Lippmann, Walter, 170
Livingston, Robert, 32
Lobbying, 90, 133, 261–262,
    267–270, 272
  Astroturf lobbying, 272
  grassroots Lobbying, 272
  influence executive branch
    implementation, 269
  influence legislation in Congress,
    268–269
  initiative, 272
  inside lobbying, 268
  lobbyists influence judicial
    actions, 269–270
  modern lobbying, 267
  outside (grassroots) lobbying, 272
  professionalism of lobbyists,
    267–268
  referendum, 272
  regulated activities, 270
  revolving door phenomenon, 268
Lobbyists' pressure, 259–260
Logroll, 53
London Review of Books, 443
Lopez Jr., Alfonso, 92

Lou Gehrig's disease, 123
Lowey, Nita, 287
Lyndon Johnson's Great Society, 88, 417

Mac, Freddie, 259
MacKinnon, Catharine A., 253
Maddow, Rachel, 196
Madison, James, 31–34, 39–44, 46, 50, 54, 56–62, 90, 102, 106, 141, 199–200, 223, 231–263, 274, 325, 390–392
Majority, 233
Majority-minority districts, 235, 311
Major League Baseball, 66
Malapportionment, 236
Malloy v. Hogan, (1964), 104
Mandatory spending, 424–425
Mapp v. Ohio (1961), 104, 117
Marbury v. Madison (1803), 390–391
Marbury, William, 390, 392
Marijuana legalization, 75–76
Marijuana policy, 65–70
Markup, 302
#Markus Prior, 217
Marshall Court, 77, 78
Marshall, John, 77, 96, 139, 377, 388, 390
Marshall Plan, 437
Marshall, Thurgood, 129, 133–134, 139–141, 143, 148, 402
Marx, Karl, 57
Masses, 170, 231
Mass media, 197, 200
Material rewards, 265
Mattis, James, 321
Mayfield, Max, 350, 352
Mayhew, David, 239
McCain, John, 419
McClure, Robert, 287
McCulloch v. Maryland (1819), 77
McDonald v. Chicago, 104, 114
McLaurin, George, 142–143
McLaurin v. Oklahoma State Regents for Higher Education, 142
Media, 177, 193–217, 335, 369
  activists, 200–201
  agenda-setting, 214
  aggregating, 210
  beat system, 201
  bias issue, 204–208
  broadcast media, 201
  cable news media, 195–196
  citizen journalists, 203

commercial bias, 207
consolidation of media ownership, 209f
contemporary pressures, 208
debates about the power, 217
decline in confidence in television news, 206f
digital divide, 216–217
early newspapers, 198–199
effects, 213
fairness doctrine, 211
"fake news", 196–198
federal bureaucracy, 369–370
framing, 214
freedom of the press, 199
historical development of, 198–204
horse race phenomenon, 208
infotainment, 207
internet and modern communications, 203
journalists and, 200–201
mass media, 200
media effects, 213
net neutrality, 210
new media, 203–204
news can function as entertainment, 207–208
news media, 193
objectivity of, 204–208
ownership, 193
pamphlets, 198–199
partisan bias, 205
partisan politics, 193
partisan press, 200
penny presses, 199–200
perspectives of ownership and media content, 208–211
political news consumption, 204f
power of, 211–217
priming, 214
problem in media coverage, 205–207
radio and TV news, 201–203
regulation, 209–211
scholars views, 213–214
sensationalism, 200
social media, 203
soft news, 207
technology-driven change, 193
trustworthiness, 193
24/7 news coverage, 203
Yellow journalism, 200
Medicaid, 88, 418–419, 425
Mercury Theatre on the Air, 212

Merit system, 361, 365
Merryman, John, 340
Metaphors of power, 287
#MeToo movement, 250–253, 289
Meyer, Richard, 68
Milano, Alyssa, 250
Miller v. California (1973), 113
Milliken v. Bradley (1974), 148
Mills, C. Wright, 263, 273
Minimalist paradigm, 169–171
Miranda rights, 118. *See also* Fifth Amendment
Miranda v. Arizona (1966), 118
Missouri Compromise, 135, 392
MLK Day, 130
Moderate Syrian rebels, 443
Monetary policy, 431
Monroe doctrine, 434
Monson, Diane, 65, 67–69, 72
Mortgage-backed securities (MBSs), 258–259
Moseley, Carol, 288, 312
Motor voter law, 250
Mott, Lucretia, 151
Mount Vernon plantation, 38
Muckrakers, 200, 361
Mueller III, Robert S., 195, 318
Murray, Patty, 286, 288, 307
Myers v. United States (1926), 357

Nagin, Mayor C. Ray, 351
NASA (National Aeronautics and Space Administration), 348
National Anthem Protests, 184–185
National Association for the Advancement of Colored People (NAACP), 129, 257, 402
National Bureau of Economic Research, 262
National Conference of State Legislatures, 90
National Conservation Commission, 422
National conventions, 229, 240
National debt, 363, 430
National elections, 233–242
  apportionment, 234
  congressional elections, 233
  congressional incumbents, 239–240
  constituencies, 233–234
  decision to vote or not vote, 246
  digital participation, 244

factors shape electoral
    participation, 247–249
gerrymandering project, 237
majority-minority districts, 235
malapportionment, 236
members of the House, 234
partisan gerrymandering, 234–235
party identification, 245
plurality of votes, 233
political ideology, 245
political participation, 242–253
presidential elections, 240–242
racial and ethnic
    gerrymandering, 235
redistricting, 234
rules of the electoral college, 241
runoff election, 233
senators, 234
split-ticket voting, 245
2020, state elections, 239
National Federation of Independent
    Business v. Sebelius (2012), 419
National Football League (NFL),
    184–185
National Gazette, 200
National Governors Association, 90
National Hurricane Center, 350,
    352, 369
National Industrial Recovery Act
    (NIRA), 82–84
National League of Cities, 90
National Oceanic and Atmospheric
    Administration, 352
National Organization for Women
    (NOW), 153–154, 266
National Prohibition Act, 100
National Recovery Administration
    (NRA), 82–84
National Security Act of 1947, 362
National Security Agency (NSA),
    100, 194
National Weather Service, 352
Natural-born rights, 62
Natural rights, 8
Natural Rights of African
    Americans, 17–18
Near v. Minnesota ex rel. Olson,
    (1931), 104
Necessary and proper clause, 71
Need-based assistance
    programs, 421
Negative freedoms, 97
Nelson, Kjersten, 214
Net neutrality, 210
Neustadt, Richard, 323

Neutrality test, 108
New Deal, 82
New Deal programs, 85, 367, 422
New Jersey Plan, 43–47, 45t
News media, 193
New York Stock Exchange, 273
New York Times, 6, 165, 182, 196,
    261, 276–277, 291, 322,
    338–339, 368, 383, 412
New York Times v. United States
    (1971), 111
Nichols, Michelle, 277
Nie, Norman H., 242
Nineteenth Amendment, 152
Ninth Amendment, 102, 119–124
Nixon, Richard, 88–89, 111,
    202, 224, 328, 342, 381, 416,
    418, 423
No Child Left Behind Act of
    2002, 91
#NoDAPL, 5
Nomination, 228
Nonattitudes, 170
North Atlantic Treaty Organization
    (NATO), 436
Norton, Eleanor Holmes, 287
Nuclear proliferation, 438
Nuclear Regulatory
    Commission, 364

O'Brien, David Paul, 111
Obama, Barack, 69, 182, 210, 226,
    261, 274, 320, 338, 352, 379,
    382, 418, 443
Obergefell v. Hodges (2015), 124, 157
Obscenity and pornography, 112
Ocasio-Cortez, Alexandria, 290
Occupy Wall Street (OWS), 257,
    264, 273–280
    early efforts of, 275
    origins of, 274
    quickly went national, even
        international, 276
    reasons for joining, 274
    strategic use of social media, 276
Office of Management and Budget
    (OMB), 333, 424
Old Age Assistance programs, 420
Old Age Insurance, 420
Old-Age, Survivors, and Disability
    Insurance (OASDI) trust
    fund, 421
Olmstead v. United States (1928), 100
Olson, Mancur, 264
Omar, Ilhan, 284, 289

Open primaries, 228
Oral argument, 100, 400
Original jurisdiction, 384
Outside (grassroots) lobbying, 272
Oversight, 293

Packers, Green Bay, 184
Page, Benjamin, 172
Pamphleteers, 14, 18, 20
Paris attacks, 444–445
Parker v. Gladden, (1966), 104
Partisan bias, 205
Partisan identification, 179–182
Partisan polarization, 308, 309f
Partisan press, 200
Partisanship Gridlock, 232
"Partisan voter index", 237
The Party Decides, 229
Party elites, 224
Party establishment, 222, 224, 230
Party identification, 172, 178, 245
Party platform, 230
Party systems, 231
Path dependence, 361
Patient Protection and Affordable
    Care Act (ACA), 418–419
    efforts to repeal and replace, 419
    key provisions of, 419t
Paul, Alice, 153
Paul, Rand, 320
Paycheck Protection Program and
    Health Care Enhancement Act
    (PPPHCEA), 429
Pelosi, Nancy, 261, 290, 319
Pendleton Act, 361
Pendleton Civil Service Reform Act
    of 1883, 361
Pennsylvania's state constitution, 40
Pennsylvania Evening Post, 198
Penny presses, 199–200.
    See also Media
Personal Responsibility and Work
    Opportunity Reconciliation
    Act of 1996 (PRWORA), 89,
    421–422
Petitioning the government, 109–114
Pew Research Center, 165–166, 176,
    187, 322
Philadelphia Convention, 37, 39, 50
Pinckney, Charles, 199
Ping-ponging strategy. *See*
    Amendment exchange
Pitkin, Hanna, 311
Plaintiff, 393
"Plan of Union", 13

Plea bargaining, 393
Plessy, Homer, 79, 139
Plessy v. Ferguson (1896), 79–80, 138, 142. *See also* Racial segregation
Pletz, Rachel, 275
Pluralism, 263
Plurality, 187, 233, 241, 322, 400
Pocket veto, 305
Podesta, John, 194
Pointer v. Texas, (1965), 104
Police patrol oversight, 293, 295, 369
Police powers, 73, 88, 414
Policy agenda, 264, 280, 403, 416
Policy entrepreneurs, 416–417
Political action committees (PACs), 242, 271
Political ambition, 287–288
Political efficacy, 247
Political equality, 9
Political ideology, 178–179, 245
    Conservatism, 179
    Liberalism, 179
    Libertarianism, 179
    Socialism, 179
Political institutions, 22–25
    core features of, 22
    direct democracy, 23
    representative democracy, 23
Political mobilization, 249
Political participation, 222, 242–253
    age, 247
    categories of, 243f
    challenges of digital political participation, 250–253
    civic engagement, 244
    decision to vote or not vote, 246
    educational attainment, 247
    factors shape electoral participation, 247–249
    Gender, 248–249
    legal and institutional factors, 249
    parties strive to get voters, 244–245
    partisan attachment, 249
    patterns of voter turnout by age, 248f
    racial and ethnic identities, 247–248
    socioeconomic status (SES), 247
    split-ticket voting, 245
    traditional and nontraditional forms, 242
    voter turnout in midterm elections by racial and ethnic identity, 248f

Political parties
    "baneful effects", 226
    civil war, 231, 231
    closed primaries, 228
    critical elections, 231
    decentralization of, 227
    delegates, 228
    front-loading, 229
    gridlock, 230–232
    minor parties, 233
    national campaigns, 231
    national conventions, 229
    nomination, 228
    open primaries, 228
    partisanship, 232
    party platform, 230
    party systems, 231
    political polarization, 230–233
    power to choose the nominees, 229–230
    presidential primary elections, 228
    proportional representation systems, 232
    realignment, 231
    responsible party model, 227
    roles of, 226–233
    select candidates through the nomination process, 228–229
    shape elections by recruiting and supporting candidates, 228
    single-member plurality system, 232
    slavery, 231, 231
    superdelegates, 229
    two-party dominance, 231–232
    unite people as organizations, 227–228
Political party, 221
Political patronage, 359, 361, 367
    rise of, 359–360
Political polarization, 230
Political powers, distribution of, 45–55
    distribution of, slavery, 48–55
    executive branch, 46–47
    judicial branch, 47–48
    legislative branch, 46
    separation of powers, 48
Political propaganda, 14, 170, 435
Political socialization, 178
    civic education, 178
    focusing events, 178–179
    individual attitudes, 178–179
    party identification, 178
    personal experience, 178

Politics, 3
Positive freedoms, 129
Poverty line, 421
Powell v. Alabama, (1932), 104
Power elite, 263–264
Powers, 72–74
    concurrent powers, 73
    enumerated, concurrent, and reserved, 74f
    explicit powers, 72
    implied powers, 72
    legislative structure, 45t
    members of indigenous nations, 73–74
    powers of state governments, 73
Precedent, 399
Preemptive war, 439
Presidency, 319, 325, 327, 329, 333, 335, 339, 341, 343
    cabinet's role, 333
    executive branch bureaucracy role, 333
    executive branch turnover, 321f
    executive office of the president, 333–335
    first spouse, 334
    foreign policy, 338
    importance of, 318
    influence on public opinion, 335–336
    political parties and, 334–335
    political party affiliations, 483–487
    power during wartime, 337
    presidency, presidential approval ratings, 337f
    presidential powers, 325–331
    top of the Federal bureaucracy, 368
    turnover in the president's administration, 320–321
The Presidential Character: Predicting Performance in the White, 324
Presidential elections
    exploratory committee, 240
    foundations by candidates, 240
    nominees in general election, 240–241
    party's nomination, 240
    rules of the electoral college, 241
    summary of, 488–492
Presidential pardon, 330
Presidential powers
    considerable powers, 326–330
    constitutionally limited powers, 330–331
    constitutional provisions, 326

constitutional war-making power, 328
diplomatic power, 327
executive agreements, 343
executive orders, 343
executive privilege, 342
foreign policy, 327–329
institutional and informal sources, 331
legislative process powers, 330
length of terms, 325–326
pardoning, 330
powers and limits, 331t
proposes a budget, 424–425
qualifications for office, 325–326
questions of selection, 325–326
recess appointment, 327
responsible for the nation's security, 328–329
role in the legislative process, 343
signing statements, 343
state of the union address, 329
Supreme Court nominations, 386–387
vice presidency role, 332–333
war powers resolution, 329
Presidential primary elections, 228, 240
Press, civil liberties, 109–114
Pressley, Ayanna, 284
Priming, 214
Principal-agent problem, 355
Printing press, 14, 55, 198, 200
Prior restraint, 111
Pritzker, J. B., 66
Privacy, 121–123
  sexual conduct between consenting adults, 122
  use of contraceptives, 122
  woman's decision to terminate a pregnancy, 121–123
  See also Ninth Amendment
Private bureaucracies, 354, 371
Private contractors, 364, 371
Privatization, 370
  opponents of, 371
Procedural justice, 116
Progressive era, 200, 361
Project Veritas, 197
Proportional representation for the states, 42–43
Proportional representation systems, 232
Protest, 278
Proxy wars, 436–437

Public Affairs Act of 1975, 175
Public interest groups, 266, 273
Public opinion, 163
  academic use, 177
  attitudes, 169–172
  central challenge of, 163
  Charlottesville tragedy, 186–187
  civic education, 178
  commercial use, 177
  construction of, 175
  direct and indirect channels, 172–173
  direction of the opinion, 176
  dynamic and contested, 163
  effect on Democratic Representation, 182–187
  ethnic identity, 181
  exit poll, 175
  federal bureaucracy, 369–370
  Ferguson event, 163–168
  focus group, 173
  gender, 180
  government and media influence, 181–182
  individual and group identities, 179–182
  individual beliefs, 169–172
  intensity of opinion, 176
  meaning of, 169–172
  minimalist paradigm, 169–171
  national anthem protests, 184–185
  nonattitudes, 170
  overcome information gaps, 171–172
  partisan identification, 179–182
  party identification, 178
  political ideology, 177–182
  political socialization and, 177–182
  political use, 177
  push poll, 177
  question order, 176
  question wording, 176
  race of interviewer effects, 176
  racial identity, 165, 166f, 181
  random digit dialing, 175
  random selection, 174
  reflections, 165
  respondents, 174
  salience of, 177
  sample, 174
  sampling error, 174
  scientific poll, 173–174
  self-selected listener opinion poll (SLOP), 175

  stability of opinion, 176
  stereotype, 170
  straw poll, 174
  theories, 169–172
  transmitting and measuring of, 172–177
  unrest after the killing of George Floyd, 187
  validity, 173
  validity by type, 174–175
  weighting, 174
Public opinion survey, 165
Public policy, 411
  agenda-setting, 416
  American health care policy, 417–423
  budgeting process, 416–417
  changes in demographics, 412–413
  domestic policy process, 414–415
  evaluation, 417
  implementation, 417
  policy entrepreneurs, 416
  policy formation and adoption, 416
  policymaking process, 415f
  problem definition, 416
  social welfare policies, 414
  stages of, 415
  steps in the policymaking, 412–417
  termination, 417
Publius, 56, 199
Purposive benefits, 266
Push poll, 177
Putin, Vladimir, 194

Question order, 176
Question wording, 176–177
Quid pro quo harassment, 155
Quincy Railroad v. City of Chicago, (1897), 104

Race of interviewer effects, 176
Racial and ethnic gerrymandering, 310–311
Racial segregation, 24, 79, 138, 147–148
  history of, 134
Radio Act of 1927, 209
Radio and TV News, 201–203
Raich, Angel, 65, 67–68
Randolph, William, 200
Random digit dialing, 175
Random selection, 174

Ratification debates, 31, 55–61, 93, 123, 199, 384
  anti-federalists views, 55
  bill of rights, 102–105
  extended republic, 58
  federalist papers, 56
  federalists views, 55
  judicial abuse of power, 384–385
Rational-legal authority, 354
Rauch, Jonathan, 227, 245
R.A.V. v. St. Paul (1992), 112
Reagan Doctrine, 437
Reagan, Ronald, 89, 362–363, 370, 380–383, 437
Realignment, 231–232
Reasonableness standard, 154–155
Recess appointment, 327
Reconstruction, 136
Reconstruction amendments, 79, 137
Reconstruction process, 79
Recruitment, 228
Redistricting, 234, 239
Red tape, 367. *See also* Federal bureaucracy
Reed, Esther de Berdt, 19
Referendum, 272
Reform efforts, 370–372
Regents of the University of California v. Bakke (1978), 149
Registration requirements, 247, 249
Regulated capitalist economy, 25f
Regulatory capture, 269
Rehabilitation Act of 1973, 130
Rehnquist, William, 92
Religious expression, boundaries of, 107–109
Religious schools, funding for, 106
Removal curious, 353
Represent, 285
Representative democracy, 23
Republican Party, 89, 138, 174, 179, 231–232, 245, 297, 322, 389, 421
Republics, 31–33, 58–59, 62
Reserved powers, 73, 123
Respondents, 165, 174–176
Responsible party model, 227
Revolutionary war veterans, 38
Revolutionary women, 18–19
Revolving door phenomenon, 268
Rights for Americans with Disabilities, 130–134
Rights of same-sex couples, 120–121

Rights to trials and representation, 118–119. *See also* Sixth Amendment
Riot Act, 38
Robinson v. California, (1962), 105
Roe v. Wade (1973), 122–123, 154, 222, 381
Roll-call vote, 303
Romney, Mitt, 296
Roosevelt, Franklin, 65, 81–93, 201–202, 231, 326, 334–336, 343, 362, 367, 414, 422, 434
  court-packing plan, 84–85
  depression-fighting policies, 202
  expands the role of the national government, 82–83
  new deal economic reconstruction programs, 422
  new deal expansions, 83–84
  response to Great Depression, 81–86
Roosevelt, Theodore, 361, 422, 434
Rosenberg, Gerald, 144
Rosenstein, Rod, 195
Roth v. United States (1957), 113
Rulemaking, 366
Runoff election, 233
The Rush Limbaugh Show, 202

St. Louis Post-Dispatch, 179, 183
Salience, 177
Same-sex couples, rights of, 120–121
Sample, 174
Sampling error, 174
Sanders, Bernie, 183, 194, 205, 222–226, 230, 241, 279, 296, 418
  built a passionate bloc of supporters, 223
  change the party's ideological focus, 223
  criticizing so-called corporate welfare, 223
  implementation of a wealth tax, 225
  as an "independent socialist,", 223
  proposed a tax on wall street, 224
  runs against the establishment, 225–226
  Super Tuesday, 226
Sandy Hurricane, 352–353
Scalia, Antonin, 68, 382, 389
Schattschneider, E. E., 264, 273
Schechter, 83–84

Schechter Poultry Corp. v. United States (1935), 83–84
Schenck, Charles, 109
Schenck v. United States (1919), 110
School segregation, 140–142
Schools, prayers in, 106–107
Schroeder, Pat, 287
Scientific poll, 173
Scientific polling, 173–174
  random selection, 174
  respondents, 174
  sample, 174
  sampling error, 174
  validity, 173
  weighting, 174
  See also Public opinion
Second amendment, 114–115
Second Continental Congress, 20–21, 31, 34, 42
Second New Deal, 84
"Section 504 protesters", 131
Securities Act of 1933, 364
Securities Industry and Financial Markets Association, 260
Selective benefits, 265
Selective incorporation, 103
Self-selected listener opinion poll (SLOP), 175
Senate, 292
  majority leader, 298, 303, 418
  role of party leaders, 298
Senatorial courtesy, 295, 386
Seneca Falls Convention, 151
Senior Executive Service (SES), 365
Separate but equal, 80, 139, 142
Separation of Church and State, 105–109
  boundaries of the establishment of religion, 107
  boundaries of the freedom of religious expression, 107–109
  clause over prayer in school, 106–107
  funding for religious schools, 106
Separation of powers, 48, 230, 368–370
Seventh Amendment, 395
Seven Years' War, 13, 15
Sexual harassment, 154–155
Shapiro, Robert, 172
Shaw v. Reno, 238
Shays, Daniel, 37–38
Shays' Rebellion, 37–39, 56, 58
Shepard, William, 38

Signing statements, 343
Single-issue groups, 266
Single-member plurality system, 232
Sixth Amendment, 118, 249, 395
Skocpol, Theda, 360
Slander, 112
The Slaughter-House Cases
    (1873), 103
Slavery, 17–18, 36, 48–55, 50, 54,
    59, 134, 136, 231
  abolished, 79
  fateful compromise on, 50, 53–54
  James Madison's contradictory
      views, 54
  representation and, 36–37
  slave population by state, 51f
  three-fifths compromise, 53
  See also Thirteenth Amendment
Social benefits, 8, 265
Social contract, 8, 23
Social equality, 9
Social insurance programs, 420
Socialism, 179, 245
Socialist economy, 25f
Socialist system, 24
Social media, 203
Social movement, 257, 273,
    278–280.
    See also Occupy Wall Street
      (OWS)
Social Safety Net, 362
Social Security Act of 1935, 85,
    417, 420
Social welfare policies, 414
Socioeconomic status (SES), 247
Soft news, 207
Soil conservation service, 422
Solicitor general, 399
Sons of Liberty, 15
Sotomayor, Sonia, 100,
    379–380, 382
Souter, David H., 379
Southern plantation owners, 50
Sovereignty resolutions, 91
Speaker of the House, 290,
    297, 304
Speech, 109–114
Spicer, Sean, 197
Split-ticket voting, 245
Spoils system, 359
Spyer, Thea, 119–120
Stability, 176
Stamp Act, 15
Standard operating procedures,
    354, 360, 367

Standing, 398
Standing Rock protests, 6–7, 423
Standing Rock Sioux Nation, 4–5,
    7–8, 74, 157
Stare decisis, 402
State and local bureaucracies, 353
State of the Union address, 329
State powers protection, 123.
    See also Tenth Amendment
State sovereignty resolutions, 91
States' rights, 78–79
Statutes, 138, 293
Steamboat monopoly case, 77
Stereotype, 170
Stewart, Maria W., 155
Stock market, crash of (1929), 81.
    See also Great Depression
Stored Communications Act
    (1986), 99
Stratton, Juliana, 66
Straw poll, 174
Street-level bureaucrats, 365–366
Strict scrutiny, 154
Student Nonviolent Coordinating
    Committee (SNCC), 147
Substantive representation, 311, 313
Suffrage, 249
Superdelegates, 229
Super PACs, 242, 271
Superpower, 436
Supplemental Nutrition Assistance
    Program (SNAP), 422
Supply shock, 426
Supremacy clause, 71
Supreme Court, 377
  Brett Kavanaugh's confirmation,
      382–383
  effect social change, 146
  on gender discrimination, 154–155
  John Marshall confronts politics
      and power of, 390–391
  limitations on the power of,
      387–388
  oral argument, 400
  politics of, 378–383
  power of agenda-setting, 388
  power of judicial review, 392
  presidential nominees, 378
  proper role of, 378
  Robert Bork's unsuccessful
      nomination, 380–381
  role in national policymaking,
      387–388
  role of politics in, 378–383
  on sexual harassment, 154–155

Sotomayor's appointment,
    379–380
  trial of federal judiciary, 377
  whether to take cases on appeal,
      398–399
  See also Federal judiciary
*Swann v. Charlotte-Mecklenburg
    Board of Education* (1971), 148
Swaps and derivatives, 261
Sweatt, Heman, 141
Sweatt v. Painter, 142
Symbolic speech, 111–112
  fighting words, 112
  hate speech, 112
  libel, 112
  obscenity and pornography, 112
  slander, 112
System of checks and balances, 48

Taney, Roger, 134, 392
Taylor, Breonna, 187
Tea Act, 16
Telecommunications Act of
    1996, 209
Temporary Assistance for Needy
    Families (TANF), 89, 422
Tenth Amendment, 73, 91, 97, 102,
    119–124
Tenure of Office Act (1867), 357
Term limits, 292
Terrorism, 138, 439
Texas v. Johnson (1989), 111
Third party (minor party), 233
"Third rail" of American politics, 421
Thirteenth Amendment, 137
Three-Fifths Compromise, 53
Timbs v. Indiana, (2019), 105
Time magazine, 164
Title VII of the Civil Rights Act of
    1964, 154–155, 157
Tlaib, Rashida, 284, 289
Tradable discharge permits
    (TDPs), 423
Trade and navigation disputes, 33
Treaty of Paris in 1763, 13, 22
Treaty on the Non-Proliferation of
    Nuclear Weapons, 438
Truman, David, 264
Truman, Harry S., 362
Trump, Donald, 6, 69, 112, 187,
    194–197, 207, 210–211, 217,
    222, 225–226, 239, 241, 289,
    295, 304, 318–320, 322, 325,
    328, 335–336, 339, 349, 353,
    363–364, 368–369, 382–383,

387, 389, 414, 419–420, 438, 443
bureaucratic agenda, 368
challenges China during the global pandemic, 322
conflict at the center, 318–319
conflict on the world stage, 319–332
conflict with defense department over Syria, 321–322
federal judicial appointments, 387
impeachment of, 290
presidential style, 318
rescission of DACA, 414
style of leadership, 323f
supporters and his opponents, 322
Truth, Sojourner, 156
Turf wars, 359
Twenty-Fifth Amendment (1967), 332
Twenty-Second Amendment (1951), 326
Two-party Dominance, 230, 232
Tyranny, 56
Tyranny of the majority, 58–59, 401
Tyson, Mike, 318

Unemployment rate, 424
Unfunded mandates, 90
Unitary systems, 70
United farm workers of America, 132
United Nations, 322, 350, 437–438, 440, 444
United Nations Refugee Agency, 444
United Nations Security Council (UNSC), 319
United States v. Lopez (1995), 91
United States v. Miller, 114
United States v. Nixon (1974), 342
United States v. O'Brien (1968), 111
United States v. Windsor (2013), 121, 123
Unlawful search, seizure, warrants, and evidence, 116–117. *See also* Fourth Amendment
Unorthodox lawmaking, 300
Unsoel, Jolene, 287
U.S. Army Corps of Engineers (USACE), 348, 351–352, 369

USA Today, 124
U.S. Constitution
    arguments of federalists and anti-federalists, 55–61
    bicameral legislature, 44
    compromise over states' interests, 39–44
    confederal system, 34–39
    distribution of political power, 45–55
    equal votes in legislature, 43–44
    great compromise, 44
    James Madison's efforts, 32–33
    Madison's efforts, 31
    New Jersey plan, 43–44
    proportional representation for the states, 42–43
    Virginia plan, 42–43

Validity, 173
Verba, Sidney, 242
Verzbickis, Julia, 412
Veto, 305
Vice Presidency role, 332–333
Virginia Plan, 42–46, 45t
Voluntary associations, 257
Voter Registration Act of 1993, 250
Voter turnout, 246–247, 249–250
"Vote watch" party, 380
Voting and citizenship rights for African Americans, 136
Voting Rights Act of 1965, 147, 157

Wall Street Journal, 318, 440
The War of the Worlds, 212–213, 217
War on terror, 116, 339, 435, 438–439
War Powers Resolution of 1973, 328
Warrant, 116
Warren, Earl, 143
Warren, Elizabeth, 225, 241, 279
Warren, Mercy Otis, 61
Warsaw Pact, 436
Washington, George, 22, 33, 38, 41, 226, 231, 326, 342, 357, 389, 433
Washington Post, 111, 182, 204–205, 379
Washington v. Texas, (1967), 104

Watergate scandal, 331, 418
Water Quality Act, 423
Weberian bureaucracy, 354
Weber's theory, 354
Weighting, 174
Weinstein, Harvey, 250, 253
Welles, Orson, 211, 213
Whig Party, 231
Whip, 297–298
Whitman, Walt, 446
Wickard v. Filburn, 68
WikiLeaks, 195
William Frantz Elementary School, 80
Wilson, Darren, 163–164
Wilson, Edith Bolling Galt, 334
Wilson, James, 40, 43, 355, 371
Wilson's theory, 355–356
Windsor, Edith, 119–120, 123
Wire service, 200
Wolf v. Colorado, 104
Women
    abolitionist movement, 150–151
    civil rights, 150–155
    enfranchisement, 150–152
    gender discrimination, 154–155
    inequalities, 152–154
    protections against gender discrimination, 153
    revolutionary women, 18–19
    sexual harassment, 154–155
World Health Organization (WHO), 322
World Meteorological Organization, 350
Writ of certiorari, 399
Writ of habeas corpus, 116, 340–341

"Year of the Woman" (2018), 289–291
    women's voices, 289–290
Yellow journalism, 200

Zaller, John, 171
Zelensky, Volodymyr, 295
Zimmerman, George, 164
Zuccotti Park protest, 274–277, 279